Toyota Automotive Repair Manual

by J H Haynes
Member of the Guild of Motoring Writers
and P Ward

Models covered:

UK: Toyota 2000 Saloon & Estate. 1968 cc

USA: Toyota Corona Sedan, Hardtop* & Wagon,
120 cu in (1968 cc)
134 cu in (2189 cc)
144.4 cu in (2366 cc)
Coverage includes SR and SR5 versions.

ISBN 0 85696 769 6

ABCDE
FG

Printed in the USA   (8W4 – 360)

629.287

Haynes Publishing Group
Sparkford Nr Yeovil
Somerset BA22 7JJ England

Haynes North America, Inc
861 Lawrence Drive
Newbury Park
California 91320 USA

1185393 X

Acknowledgements

Thanks are due to Toyota Motor Co. (GB) Limited who kindly gave us permission to reproduce certain of their illustrations and also provided technical information. Castrol Limited who supplied lubrication details and the Champion Sparking Plug Company for the illustrations showing the various spark plug conditions. The bodywork repair photographs used in this manual were supplied by Lloyds Industries Limited who supply 'Turtle Wax', 'Dupli-Color Holts', and other Holts range products.

The Section in Chapter 10 dealing with suppression of radio interference, was originated by Mr I. P. Davey, and was first published in *Motor* magazine.

Last but not least, thanks are due to all of those people at Sparkford who helped with the production of this manual, especially Ian Robson for planning the layout of each page and John Rose for editing the text.

About this manual

Its aims

The aim of this book is to help you get the best value from your car. It can do so in two ways. First it can help you decide what work must be done (even should you choose to get it done by a garage): the routine maintenance, and the diagnosis and course of action when random faults occur. However, it is hoped that you will also use the second and fuller purpose by tackling the work yourself. On the simpler jobs it may even be quicker than booking the car into a garage and going there twice, to leave and collect it. Perhaps most important, much money can be saved by avoiding the costs a garage must charge to cover their labour and overheads.

The book has drawings and descriptions to show the function of the various components so that their layout can be understood. Then the tasks are described and photographed in a step-by-step sequence so that even a novice can cope with complicated work. Such a person is the very one to buy a car needing repair yet be unable to afford garage costs.

The jobs are described assuming only normal tools are available, and not special tools, and a reasonable outfit of tools will be a worthwhile investment. Many special workshop tools produced by the makers merely speed the work, and in these cases guidance is given on how to do the job without them, the oft quoted example being the use of a large hose clip to compress the piston rings for insertion in the cylinder. On a very few occasions the special tool is essential to prevent damage to components and then its use is described. Though it might be possible to borrow the tool, such work may have to be entrusted to the official agent.

The manufacturer's official workshop manuals are written for their trained staff, and so assume special knowledge; detail is left out. This book is written for the owner, and so goes into detail.

Using the manual

The book is divided into twelve Chapters. Each Chapter is divided into numbered Sections which are headed in **bold type** between horizontal lines. Each Section consists of serially numbered paragraphs.

There are two types of illustration: (1) Figures which are numbered according to Chapter and sequence of occurrence in that Chapter (2) Photographs which have a reference number on their caption. All photographs apply to the Chapter in which they occur so that the reference figure pinpoints the pertinent Section and paragraph number.

Procedures, once described in the text, are not normally repeated. If it is necessary to refer to another Chapter the reference will be given.

When the left or right side of the car is mentioned it is as if looking forward from the rear.

Great effort has been made to ensure that this book is complete and up-to-date. However, it should be noted that manufacturers continually modify their cars even in retrospect.

Whilst every care is taken to ensure that the information in this manual is correct, no liability can be accepted by the authors or publishers for loss, damage or injury caused by any errors in, or omissions from, the information given.

Contents

The Toyota 2000 Saloon (UK Specification)

The Toyota 2000 Estate (UK Specification)

Safety first!

Regardless of how enthusiastic you may be about getting on with the job at hand, take the time to ensure that your safety is not jeopardized. A moment's lack of attention can result in an accident, as can failure to observe certain simple safety precautions. The possibility of an accident will always exist, and the following points should not be considered a comprehensive list of all dangers. Rather, they are intended to make you aware of the risks and to encourage a safety conscious approach to all work you carry out on your vehicle.

Essential DOs and DON'Ts

DON'T rely on a jack when working under the vehicle. Always use approved jackstands to support the weight of the vehicle and place them under the recommended lift or support points.

DON'T attempt to loosen extremely tight fasteners (i.e. wheel lug nuts) while the vehicle is on a jack — it may fall.

DON'T start the engine without first making sure that the transmission is in Neutral (or Park where applicable) and the parking brake is set.

DON'T remove the radiator cap from a hot cooling system — let it cool or cover it with a cloth and release the pressure gradually.

DON'T attempt to drain the engine oil until you are sure it has cooled to the point that it will not burn you.

DON'T touch any part of the engine or exhaust system until it has cooled sufficiently to avoid burns.

DON'T siphon toxic liquids such as gasoline, antifreeze and brake fluid by mouth, or allow them to remain on your skin.

DON'T inhale brake lining dust — it is potentially hazardous (see *Asbestos* below)

DON'T allow spilled oil or grease to remain on the floor — wipe it up before someone slips on it.

DON'T use loose fitting wrenches or other tools which may slip and cause injury.

DON'T push on wrenches when loosening or tightening nuts or bolts. Always try to pull the wrench toward you. If the situation calls for pushing the wrench away, push with an open hand to avoid scraped knuckles if the wrench should slip.

DON'T attempt to lift a heavy component alone — get someone to help you.

DON'T rush or take unsafe shortcuts to finish a job.

DON'T allow children or animals in or around the vehicle while you are working on it.

DO wear eye protection when using power tools such as a drill, sander, bench grinder, etc. and when working under a vehicle.

DO keep loose clothing and long hair well out of the way of moving parts.

DO make sure that any hoist used has a safe working load rating adequate for the job.

DO get someone to check on you periodically when working alone on a vehicle.

DO carry out work in a logical sequence and make sure that everything is correctly assembled and tightened.

DO keep chemicals and fluids tightly capped and out of the reach of children and pets.

DO remember that your vehicle's safety affects that of yourself and others. If in doubt on any point, get professional advice.

Asbestos

Certain friction, insulating, sealing, and other products — such as brake linings, brake bands, clutch linings, torque converters, gaskets, etc. — contain asbestos. *Extreme care must be taken to avoid inhalation of dust from such products since it is hazardous to health.* If in doubt, assume that they *do* contain asbestos.

Fire

Remember at all times that gasoline is highly flammable. Never smoke or have any kind of open flame around when working on a vehicle. But the risk does not end there. A spark caused by an electrical short circuit, by two metal surfaces contacting each other, or even by static electricity built up in your body under certain conditions, can ignite gasoline vapors, which in a confined space are highly explosive. Do not, under any circumstances, use gasoline for cleaning parts. Use an approved safety solvent.

Always disconnect the battery ground (−) cable *at the battery* before working on any part of the fuel system or electrical system. Never risk spilling fuel on a hot engine or exhaust component.

It is strongly recommended that a fire extinguisher suitable for use on fuel and electrical fires be kept handy in the garage or workshop at all times. Never try to extinguish a fuel or electrical fire with water.

Fumes

Certain fumes are highly toxic and can quickly cause unconsciousness and even death if inhaled to any extent. Gasoline vapor falls into this category, as do the vapors from some cleaning solvents. Any draining or pouring of such volatile fluids should be done in a well ventilated area.

When using cleaning fluids and solvents, read the instructions on the container carefully. Never use materials from unmarked containers.

Never run the engine in an enclosed space, such as a garage. Exhaust fumes contain carbon monoxide, which is extremely poisonous. If you need to run the engine, always do so in the open air, or at least have the rear of the vehicle outside the work area.

If you are fortunate enough to have the use of an inspection pit, never drain or pour gasoline and never run the engine while the vehicle is over the pit. The fumes, being heavier than air, will concentrate in the pit with possibly lethal results.

The battery

Never create a spark or allow a bare light bulb near the battery. The battery normally gives off a certain amount of hydrogen gas, which is highly explosive.

Always disconnect the battery ground (−) cable *at the battery* before working on the fuel or electrical systems.

If possible, loosen the filler caps or cover when charging the battery from an external source. Do not charge at an excessive rate or the battery may burst.

Take care when adding water and when carrying a battery. The electrolyte, even when diluted, is very corrosive and should not be allowed to contact clothing or skin.

Always wear eye protection when cleaning the battery to prevent the caustic deposits from entering your eyes.

Household current

When using an electric power tool, inspection light, etc., which operates on household current, always make sure that the tool is correctly connected to its plug and that, where necessary, it is properly grounded. Do not use such items in damp conditions and, again, do not create a spark or apply excessive heat in the vicinity of fuel or fuel vapor.

Secondary ignition system voltage

A severe electric shock can result from touching certain parts of the ignition system (such as the spark plug wires) when the engine is running or being cranked, particularly if components are damp or the insulation is defective. In the case of an electronic ignition system, the secondary system voltage is much higher and could prove fatal.

Introduction to the Toyota Corona

This Manual covers the Toyota Corona models introduced in the USA for 1974 and in the UK for 1976, although both models were made available towards the end of the previous year.

The UK models, and 1974 models, use a 1968 cc (120 cu in) overhead camshaft engine. For 1975 onwards, the USA models use either a 2189 cc (134 cu in) or a 2366 cc (144.4 cu in) overhead camshaft engine with a cylinder head of cross-flow design. According to the model and marketing territory, a 3, 4, or 5-speed manual gearbox is used, or the Aisin-Warner A40 automatic transmission.

The car is conventional in design with a unitized body/chassis structure, and is of the usual high standard of manufacturing quality associated with Toyota.

Buying spare parts and vehicle identification numbers

Buying spare parts

Replacement parts are available from many sources, which generally fall into one of two categories – authorized dealer parts departments and independent retail auto parts stores. Our advice concerning these parts is as follows:

Retail auto parts stores: Good auto parts stores will stock frequently needed components which wear out relatively fast, such as clutch components, exhaust systems, brake parts, tune-up parts, etc. These stores often supply new or reconditioned parts on an exchange basis, which can save a considerable amount of money. Discount auto parts stores are often very good places to buy materials and parts needed for general vehicle maintenance such as oil, grease, filters, spark plugs, belts, touch-up paint, bulbs, etc. They also usually sell tools and general accessories, have convenient hours, charge lower prices and can often be found not far from home.

Authorized dealer parts department: This is the best source for parts which are unique to the vehicle and not generally available else-where (such as major engine parts, transmission parts, trim pieces, etc.).

Warranty information: If the vehicle is still covered under warranty, be sure that any replacement parts purchased – regardless of the source – do not invalidate the warranty!

To be sure of obtaining the correct parts, have engine and chassis numbers available and, if possible, take the old parts along for positive identification.

Vehicle identification plates

Vehicle serial numbers are stamped on the rear firewall of the engine compartment and repeated (on North American vehicles) on the top surface of the facia panel just inside the windshield.

The *engine number* is stamped in the top right face of the cylinder block, adjacent to the fuel pump. (18R) or on the left side of the cylinder block behind the alternator (20R).

Location of Vehicle Identification Number

Engine Serial Number – 18R

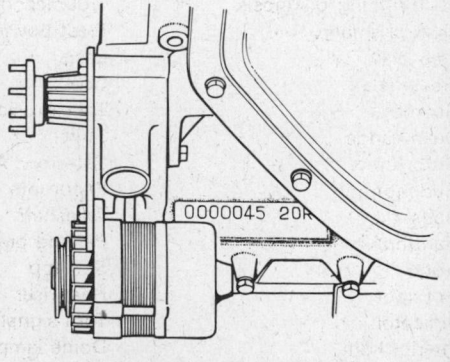

Engine Serial Number – 20R

Use of English

As this book has been written in England, it uses the appropriate English component names, phrases, and spelling. Some of these differ from those used in America. Normally, these cause no difficulty, but to make sure, a glossary is printed below. In ordering spare parts remember the parts list may use some of these words:

English	American	English	American
Accelerator	Gas pedal	Locks	Latches
Aerial	Antenna	Methylated spirit	Denatured alcohol
Anti-roll bar	Stabiliser or sway bar	Motorway	Freeway, turnpike etc
Big-end bearing	Rod bearing	Number plate	License plate
Bonnet (engine cover)	Hood	Paraffin	Kerosene
Boot (luggage compartment)	Trunk	Petrol	Gasoline (gas)
Bulkhead	Firewall	Petrol tank	Gas tank
Bush	Bushing	'Pinking'	'Pinging'
Cam follower or tappet	Valve lifter or tappet	Prise (force apart)	Pry
Carburettor	Carburetor	Propeller shaft	Driveshaft
Catch	Latch	Quarterlight	Quarter window
Choke/venturi	Barrel	Retread	Recap
Circlip	Snap-ring	Reverse	Back-up
Clearance	Lash	Rocker cover	Valve cover
Crownwheel	Ring gear (of differential)	Saloon	Sedan
Damper	Shock absorber, shock	Seized	Frozen
Disc (brake)	Rotor/disk	Sidelight	Parking light
Distance piece	Spacer	Silencer	Muffler
Drop arm	Pitman arm	Sill panel (beneath doors)	Rocker panel
Drop head coupe	Convertible	Small end, little end	Piston pin or wrist pin
Dynamo	Generator (DC)	Spanner	Wrench
Earth (electrical)	Ground	Split cotter (for valve spring cap)	Lock (for valve spring retainer)
Engineer's blue	Prussian blue	Split pin	Cotter pin
Estate car	Station wagon	Steering arm	Spindle arm
Exhaust manifold	Header	Sump	Oil pan
Fault finding/diagnosis	Troubleshooting	Swarf	Metal chips or debris
Float chamber	Float bowl	Tab washer	Tang or lock
Free-play	Lash	Tappet	Valve lifter
Freewheel	Coast	Thrust bearing	Throw-out bearing
Gearbox	Transmission	Top gear	High
Gearchange	Shift	Torch	Flashlight
Grub screw	Setscrew, Allen screw	Trackrod (of steering)	Tie-rod (or connecting rod)
Gudgeon pin	Piston pin or wrist pin	Trailing shoe (of brake)	Secondary shoe
Halfshaft	Axleshaft	Transmission	Whole drive line
Handbrake	Parking brake	Tyre	Tire
Hood	Soft top	Van	Panel wagon/van
Hot spot	Heat riser	Vice	Vise
Indicator	Turn signal	Wheel nut	Lug nut
Interior light	Dome lamp	Windscreen	Windshield
Layshaft (of gearbox)	Countershaft	Wing/mudguard	Fender
Leading shoe (of brake)	Primary shoe		

Routine maintenance

Maintenance is essential for ensuring safety, and desirable for the purpose of getting the best in terms of performance and economy from the car. Over the years the need for periodic lubrication - oiling, greasing and so on - has been drastically reduced if not totally eliminated. This has unfortunately tended to lead some owners to think that because no such action is required, the items either no longer exist or will last for ever. This is a serious delusion. It follows therefore that the largest initial element of maintenance is visual examination. This may lead to repairs or renewals.

In the summary given here the essential for safety items are shown in **bold type**. These **must** be attended to at the regular frequencies shown in order to avoid the possibility of accidents and loss of life. Other neglect results in unreliability, increased running costs, more rapid wear and more depreciation of the vehicle in general.

The items listed which are not applicable to your particular car should be ignored.

Every 250 miles (400 km) travelled or weekly - whichever comes first

Steering
Check tyre pressures (when cold).
Examine tyres for wear or damage.
Is steering smooth and accurate?

Brakes
Check reservoir fluid level.
Is there any fall off in braking efficiency?
Try an emergency stop. Is adjustment necessary?

Lights, wipers and horns
Do all bulbs work at front and rear?
Are headlamp beams aligned properly?
Do wipers and horns work?
Check windscreen washer fluid level.

Engine
Check sump oil level and top-up if required.
Check radiator coolant level and top-up if required.
Check battery electrolyte level and top-up with distilled water as necessary.

Every 6000 miles (10000 km) or six monthly - whichever comes first

Engine
Change oil. Renew oil filter.
Check distributor points gap/dwell angle/damping spring gap.
Check and clean spark plugs.
Check engine drive belt tension and adjust if necessary.
Check valve clearances and adjust if necessary.
Lubricate distributor.
Clean air cleaner element and set intake to seasonal position.

Transmission
Check oil level and top-up if necessary.
Check rear axle oil level and top-up if necessary.

Clutch
Check pedal free movement and for oil leakage at cylinders.
Check fluid reservoir level and top-up if necessary.

Body
Lubricate all locks and hinges.
Check that water drain holes at bottom of doors are clear.
Ensure seat belts, locking system and starter interlock systems are operating correctly.

Steering
Examine all steering linkage rods, joints and bushes for signs of wear or damage.

Check front wheel hub bearings and adjust if necessary.
Check tightness of steering gear mounting bolts.
Check oil level in steering box and top-up if necessary.

Brakes
Examine disc pads and drum shoes to determine amount of friction material left. Renew if necessary.
Examine all hydraulic pipes, cylinders and unions for signs of chafing, corrosion, dents or any other form of deterioration or leaks.
Check pedal free movement and for oil leakage at cylinders.

Suspension
Examine all nuts, bolts and shackles securing the suspension units, front and rear. Tighten if necessary.
Examine rubber bushes for signs of wear and play.

Every 12000 miles (20000 km) or annually - whichever comes first

Engine
Check crankcase ventilation valve.
Check fuel storage evaporative emission control system.
Check exhaust emission control system.
Fit new spark plugs.
Fit new distributor contact breaker points (except semi-transistorized ignition system).
Check ignition HT leads for deterioration.
Check ignition timing.
Clean carburettor float chamber and jets.

Steering
Check wheel alignment.

Suspension
Check efficiency of shock absorbers.

Transmission
Check security of propeller shaft bolts.

Every 24000 miles (40000 km) or two yearly - whichever comes first

Engine
Flush cooling system and refill with new anti-freeze mixture.
Renew air cleaner element.
Renew PCV valve.
Renew fuel line filter.
Fit new distributor contact breaker points (Semi-transistorized ignition system).
Fit new distributor cap, rotor, HT leads and condenser.

Suspension
Dismantle front hubs, clean out old lubricant and repack with fresh grease. Assemble and adjust.

Brakes
Lubricate handbrake linkage.

Transmission
Drain manual gearbox and refill with fresh oil.
Drain rear axle and refill with fresh oil.
Check propeller shaft universal joints for wear, and recondition if necessary.

Steering
Lubricate ball joints (remove plug and fit grease nipple, where applicable)
Lubricate front suspension upper arm bushes.

Headlights
Check beam alignment.

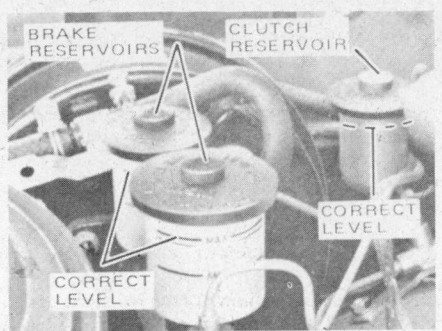

Brake and clutch fluid reservoirs

18R engine oil filler cap

20R engine oil filler cap

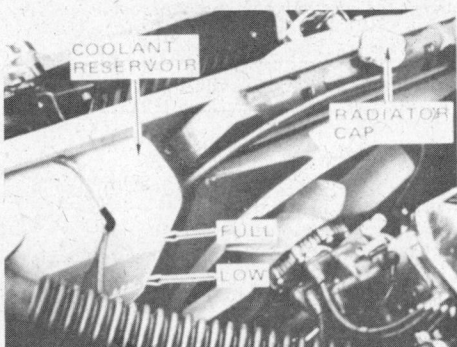

Radiator and coolant reservoir

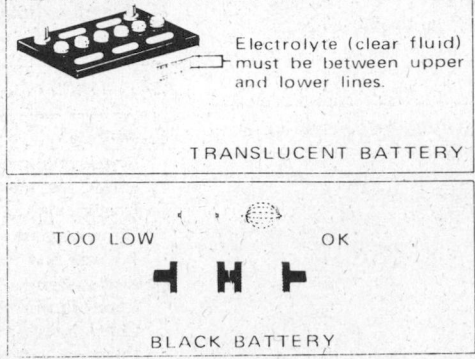

Electrolyte level checks

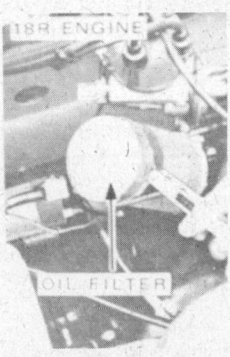

Removing oil filter (18R engine shown)

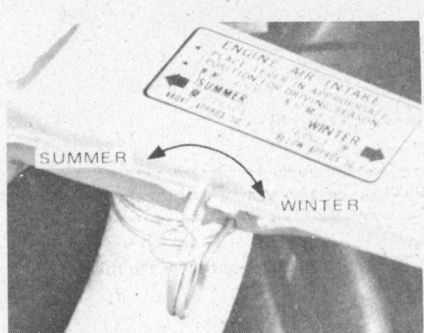

Summer/winter air cleaner settings

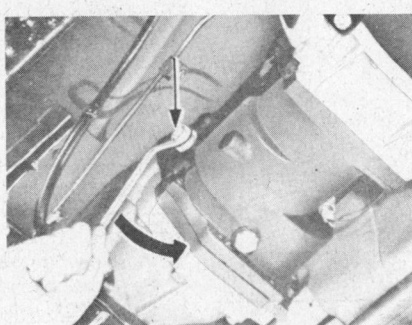

Gearbox filler/level plug

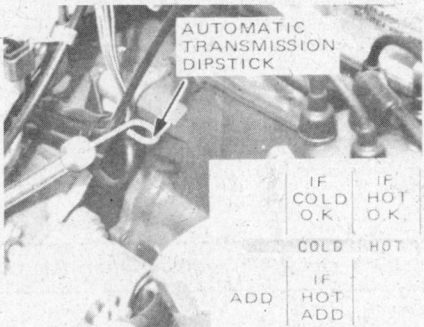

Automatic transmission filler/dipstick (Note: position is different on some cars)

Rear axle filler and drain plugs

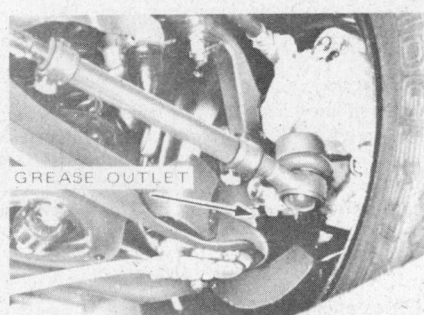

Grease fitting and grease outlet on suspension lower balljoint

Every 48000 miles (80000 km) or four yearly - whichever comes first

Brakes

Drain hydraulic system, renew all cylinder seals and refill with fresh fluid. Bleed system.

Clutch

Drain hydraulic system, renew master and slave cylinder seals, refill with fresh fluid. Bleed system.

The following should be carried out at regular intervals

Cleaning

Examination of components requires that they be cleaned. The same applies to the body of the car, inside and out, in order that deterioration due to rust or unknown damage may be detected. Certain parts of the body frame, if rusted badly, can result in the vehicle being declared unsafe and it will not pass the annual test for roadworthiness.

Exhaust system

An exhaust system must be leakproof, and the noise level below a certain maximum. Excessive leaks may cause carbon monoxide fumes to enter the passenger compartment. Excessive noise constitutes a public nuisance. Both these faults may cause the vehicle to be kept off the road. Repair or renew defective sections when symptoms are apparent.

Jacking and towing

The jacking points on the saloon and hardtop models are located beneath the side body sills. On the estate wagon, the rear should be jacked under the road springs. These jacking points should be used for changing roadwheels only. Where work is being carried out under the vehicle then axle stands or blocks should be positioned under the body-frame members. To raise the complete front end for servicing or repair work, place the jack under the front crossmember; **on no account position it under the rear one.** The rear end may be jacked-up under the axle casing.

A towing eye is positioned at the front of all vehicles but attachment of a towline at the rear should be made at the rear spring shackle. When a vehicle fitted with automatic transmission is being towed, read the information given in Section 25 of Chapter 6.

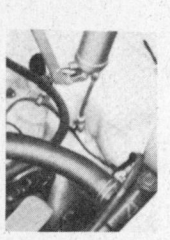

Front suspension upper bush grease points (not applicable to all models)

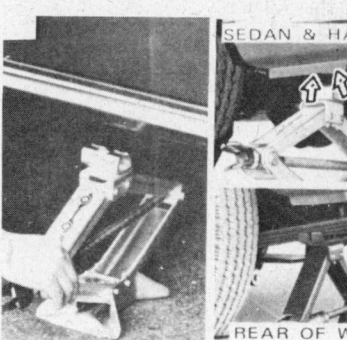

Use of the car jack

Front towing hook

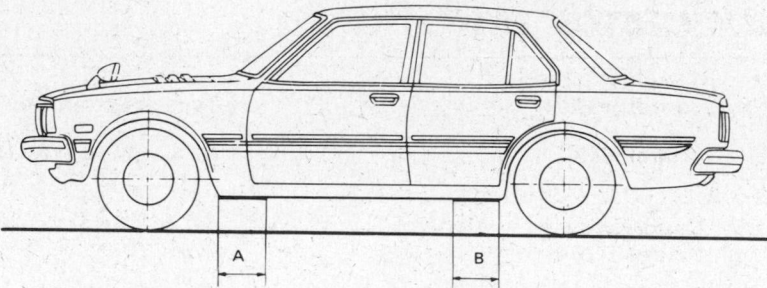

A = B = 10 in (250 mm)

Body supporting points

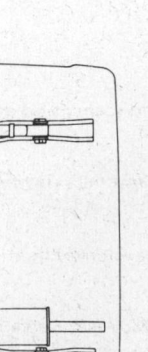

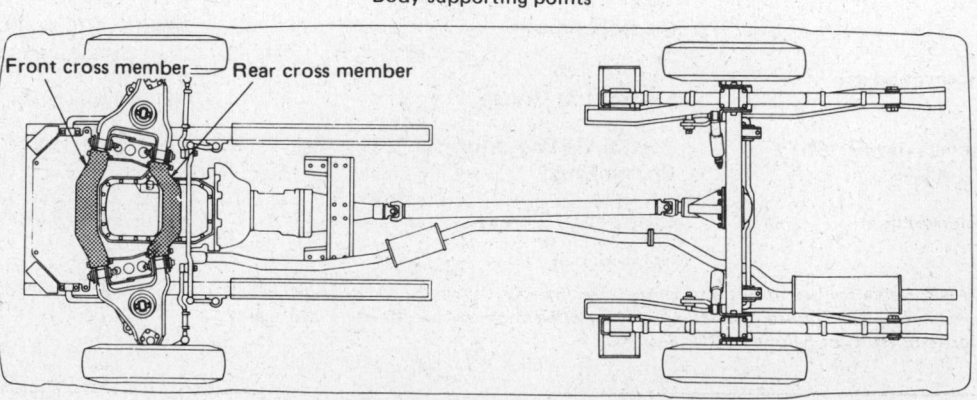

Front end lifting point - under front crossmember only

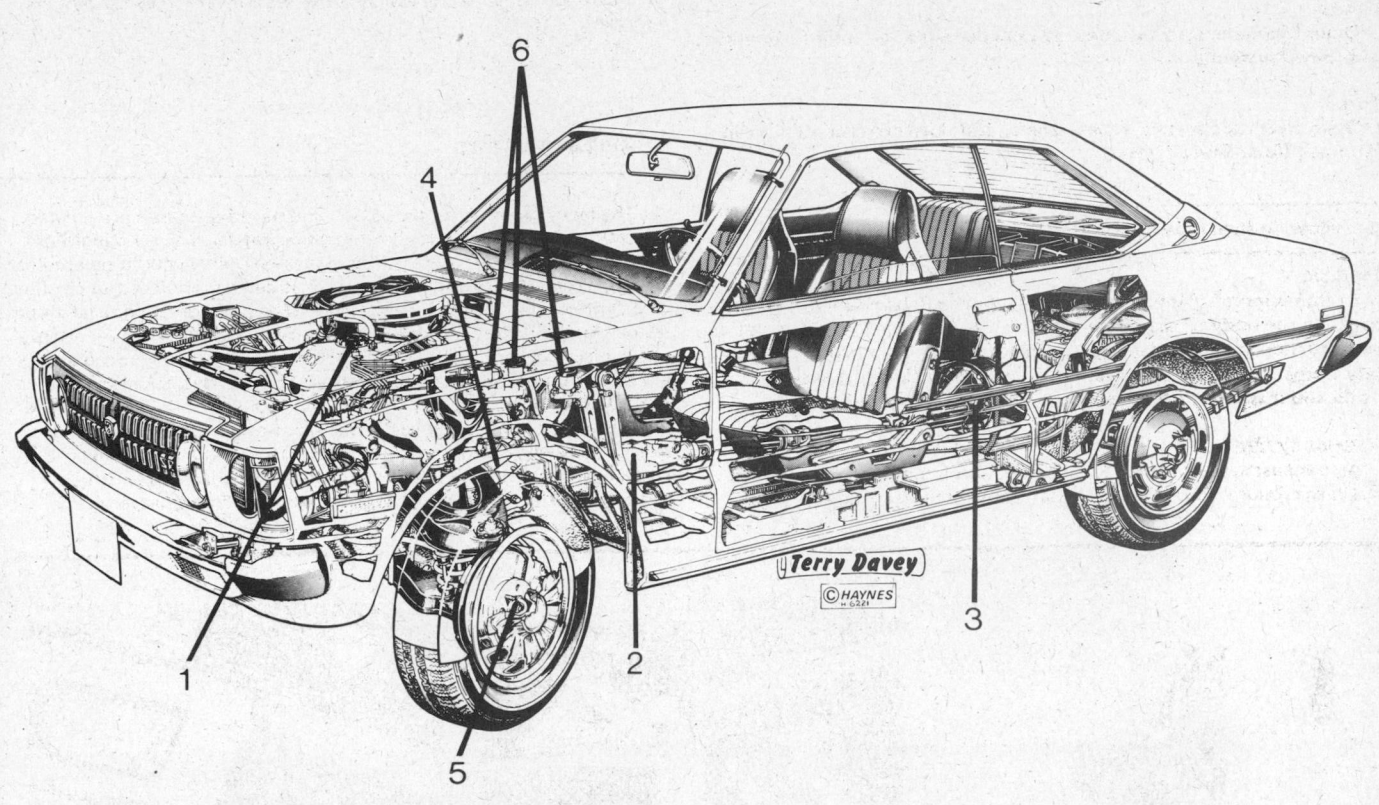

Recommended lubricants and fluids

Component	Castrol grade	Type or Specification
Engine (1)	Castrol GTX	Multigrade, type SE or better*
Transmission (2) Manual Automatic	Castrol Hypoy Castrol TQF	API GL - 4 (SAE 90 EP) Type F
Rear axle (3)	Castrol Hypoy B	API GL - 5/MIL-L-2105B (SAE 90 EP)**
Steering box (4)	Castrol Hypoy	API GL - 4 (SAE 90 EP)
Wheel bearings and suspension arm upper bearings (5)	Castrol LM Grease	Multipurpose grease
Brake and clutch master cylinders (6)	Castrol Girling Universal Brake and Clutch Fluid	DOT 3 SAE J1703C
Steering and suspension balljoints	Castrol MS 3 grease	Multipurpose grease with molybdenum disulphide

*20W/50 Multigrade is suitable for use in hot and temperate climates. When the car is to be used at temperatures below 14°F (−10°C) consult your Toyota dealer or the Toyota owners manual supplied with the car for other lubricants.
** Use SAE 80 EP for temperatures below −10°F (−23°C).

Tools and working facilities

Introduction

A selection of good tools is a fundamental requirement for anyone contemplating the maintenance and repair of a motor vehicle. For the owner who does not possess any, their purchase will prove a considerable expense, offsetting some of the savings made by doing-it-yourself. However, provided that the tools purchased are of good quality, they will last for many years and prove an extremely worthwhile investment.

To help the average owner to decide which tools are needed to carry out the various tasks detailed in this manual, we have compiled three lists of tools under the following headings: Maintenance and minor repair, Repair and overhaul and Special. The newcomer to practical mechanics should start off with the 'Maintenance and minor repair' tool kit and confine himself to the simpler jobs around the vehicle. Then, as his confidence and experience grows, he can undertake more difficult tasks, buying extra tools as, and when, they are needed. In this way, a 'Maintenance and minor repair' tool kit can be built up into a 'Repair and overhaul' tool kit over a considerable period of time without any major cash outlays. The experienced do-it-yourselfer will have a tool kit good enough for most repair and overhaul procedures and will add tools from the 'Special' category when he feels the expense is justified by the amount of use these tools will be put to.

It is obviously not possible to cover the subject of tools fully here. For those who wish to learn more about tools and their use there is a book entitled 'How to Choose and Use Car Tools' available from the publishers of this manual.

Maintenance and minor repair tool kit

The tools given in this list should be considered as a minimum requirement if routine maintenance, servicing and minor repair operations are to be undertaken. We recommend the purchase of combination spanners (ring one end, open-ended the other); although more expensive than open-ended ones, they do give the advantages of both types of spanner.

Combination spanners - 10, 11, 12, 13, 14, 17 mm
Adjustable spanner - 9 inch
Engine sump/gearbox/rear axle drain plug key (where applicable)
Spark plug spanner (with rubber insert)
Spark plug gap adjustment tool
Set of feeler gauges
Brake adjuster spanner (where applicable)
Brake bleed nipple spanner
Screwdriver - 4 in. long x ¼ in. dia. (plain)
Screwdriver - 4 in. long x ¼ in. dia (crosshead)
Combination pliers - 6 inch
Hacksaw, junior
Tyre pump
Tyre pressure gauge
Grease gun (where applicable)
Oil can
Fine emery cloth (1 sheet)
Wire brush (small)
Funnel (medium size)

Repair and overhaul tool kit

These tools are virtually essential for anyone undertaking any major repairs to a motor vehicle, and are additional to those given in the Basic list. Included in this list is a comprehensive set of sockets. Although these are expensive they will be found invaluable as they are so versatile-particularly if various drives are included in the set. We recommend the ½ in square-drive type, as this can be used with most proprietary torque wrenches. If you cannot afford a socket set, even bought piecemeal, then inexpensive tubular box spanners are a useful alternative.

The tools in this list will occasionally need to be supplemented by tools from the Special list.

Sockets (or box spanners) to cover range 6 to 30 mm
Reversible ratchet drive (for use with sockets)
Extension piece, 10 inch (for use with sockets)
Universal joint (for use with sockets)

Torque wrench (for use with sockets)
'Mole' wrench - 8 inch
Ball pein hammer
Soft-faced hammer, plastic or rubber
Screwdriver - 6 in. long x 5/16 in. dia. (plain)
Screwdriver - 2 in. long x 5/16 in. square (plain)
Screwdriver - 1½ in. long x ¼ in. (crosshead)
Screwdriver - 3 in. long x 1/8 in. dia. (electricians)
Pliers - electricians side cutters
Pliers - needle nosed
Pliers- circlip (internal and external)
Cold chisel - ½ inch
Scriber (this can be made by grinding the end of a broken hacksaw blade)
Scraper (this can be made by flattening and sharpening one end of a piece of copper pipe)
Centre punch
Pin punch
Hacksaw
Valve grinding tool
Steel rule/straight edge
Allen keys
Selection of files
Wire brush (large)
Axle stands
Jack (strong scissor or hydraulic type)

Special tools

The tools in this list are those which are not used regularly, are expensive to buy, or which need to be used in accordance with their manufacturers instructions. Unless relatively difficult mechanical jobs are undertaken frequently, it will not be economic to buy many of these tools. Where this is the case, you could consider clubbing together with friends (or motorists club) to make a joint purchase or borrowing the tools against a deposit from a local garage or tool hire specialist.

The following list contains only those tools and instruments freely available to the public, and not those special tools produced by the vehicle manufacturer specifically for its dealer network. You will find occasional references to these manufacturers special tools in the text of this manual. Generally, an alternative method of doing the job without the vehicle manufacturers special tool is given. However, sometimes, there is no alternative to using them. Where this is the case and the relevant tool cannot be bought or borrowed you will have to entrust the work to a franchised garage.

Valve spring compressor
Piston ring compressor
Ball joint separator
Universal hub/bearing puller
Impact screwdriver
Micrometer and/or vernier gauge
Carburettor flow balancing device (where applicable)
Dial gauge
Stroboscopic timing light
Dwell angle meter/tachometer
Universal electrical multi-meter
Cylinder compression gauge
Lifting tackle
Trolley jack
Light with extension lead

Buying tools

For practically all tools, a tool factor is the best source since he will have a very comprehensive range compared with the average garage or accessory shop. Having said that, accessory shops often offer excellent quality tools at discount prices, so it pays to shop around.

Remember, you don't have to buy the most expensive items on the shelf, but it is always advisable to steer clear of the very cheap tools. There are plenty of good tools around, at reasonable prices, so ask the proprietor or manager of the shop for advice before making a purchase.

Care and maintenance of tools

Having purchased a reasonable tool kit, it is necessary to keep the tools in a clean and serviceable condition. After use, always wipe off any dirt, grease and metal particles using a clean, dry cloth, before putting the tools away. Never leave them lying around after they have been used. A simple tool rack on the garage or workshop wall, for items such as screwdrivers and pliers is a good idea. Store all normal spanners and sockets in a metal box. Any measuring instruments, gauges, meters, etc., must be carefully stored where they cannot be damaged or become rusty.

Take a little care when the tools are used. Hammer heads inevitably become marked and screwdrivers lose the keen edge on their blades from time-to-time. A little timely attention with emery cloth or a file will soon restore items like this to a good serviceable finish.

Working facilities

Not to be forgotten when discussing tools, is the workshop itself. If anything more than routine maintenance is to be carried out, some form of suitable working area becomes essential.

It is appreciated that many an owner mechanic is forced by circumstance to remove an engine or similar item, without the benefit of a garage or workshop. Having done this, any repairs should always be done under the cover of a roof.

Wherever possible, any dismantling should be done on a clean flat workbench or table at a suitable working height.

Any workbench needs a vice: one with a jaw opening 4 in (100 mm) is suitable for most jobs. As mentioned previously, some clean dry storage space is also required for tools, as well as the lubricants, cleaning fluids, touch-up paints and so on which soon become necessary.

Another item which may be required, and which has a much more general usage, is an electric drill with a chuck capacity of a least 5/16 in, (8 mm). This together with a good range of twist drills, is virtually essential for fitting accessories such as wing mirrors and reversing lights.

Last, but not least, always keep a supply of old newspapers and clean, lint-free rags available, and try to keep any working area as clean as possible.

Spanner jaw gap comparison table

Jaw gap (in.)	Spanner size
0.250	1/4 in. AF
0.275	7 mm AF
0.312	5/16 in. AF
0.315	8 mm AF
0.340	11/32 in. AF/1/8 in. Whitworth
0.354	9 mm AF
0.375	3/8 in. AF
0.393	10 mm AF
0.433	11 mm AF
0.437	7/16 in. AF
0.445	3/16 in. Whitworth/1/4 in. BSF
0.472	12 mm AF
0.500	1/2 in. AF
0.512	13 mm AF
0.525	1/4 in. Whitworth/5/16 in. BSF
0.551	14 mm AF
0.562	9/16 in. AF
0.590	15 mm AF
0.600	5/16 in. Whitworth/3/8 in. BSF
0.625	5/8 in. AF
0.629	16 mm AF
0.669	17 mm AF
0.687	11/16 in. AF
0.708	18 mm AF
0.710	3/8 in. Whitworth/7/16 in. BSF
0.748	19 mm AF
0.750	3/4 in. AF
0.812	13/16 in. AF
0.820	7/16 in. Whitworth/1/2 in. BSF
0.866	22 mm AF
0.875	7/8 in. AF
0.920	1/2 in. Whitworth/9/16 in. AF
0.937	15/16 in. AF
0.944	24 mm AF
1.000	1 in. AF
1.010	9/16 in. Whitworth/5/8 in. BSF
1.023	26 mm AF
1.062	1 1/16 in. AF/27 mm AF
1.100	5/8 in. Whitworth/11/16 in. BSF
1.125	1 1/8 in. AF
1.181	30 mm AF
1.200	11/16 in. Whitworth/3/4 in. BSF
1.250	1 1/4 in. AF
1.259	32 mm AF
1.300	3/4 in. Whitworth/7/8 in. BSF
1.312	1 5/16 in. AF
1.390	13/16 in. Whitworth/15/16 in. BSF
1.417	36 mm AF
1.437	1 7/16 in. AF
1.480	7/8 in. Whitworth/1 in. BSF
1.500	1 1/2 in. AF
1.574	40 mm AF/15/16 in. Whitworth
1.614	41 mm AF
1.625	1 5/8 in. AF
1.670	1 in. Whitworth/1 1/8 in. BSF
1.687	1 11/16 in. AF
1.811	46 mm AF
1.812	1 13/16 in. AF
1.860	1 1/8 in. Whitworth/1 1/4 in. BSF
1.875	1 7/8 in. AF
1.968	50 mm AF
2.000	2 in. AF
2.050	1 1/4 in. Whitworth/1 3/8 in. BSF
2.165	55 mm AF
2.362	60 mm AF

Chapter 1 Engine

For modifications and information applicable to later USA models, refer to Supplement at end of manual

Contents

Specifications

Engine type
UK model and 1974 USA models ...	4-cylinder in-line, overhead camshaft
USA models, 1975 onwards	4-cylinder in-line, overhead camshaft, cross-flow type

Engine type designation
UK models	18R
1974 USA models	18R-C
1975 onwards USA models	20R

Engine general

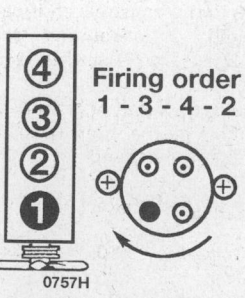

	18R	18R-C	20R
Bore and stroke	3.48 x 3.15 in (88.5 x 80.0 mm)	3.48 x 3.15 in (88.5 x 80.0 mm)	3.48 x 3.50 in (88.5 x 89.0 mm)
Piston displacement	1968 cc (120 cu in)	1968 cc (120 cu in)	2189 cc (133.6 cu in)
Compression ratio	8.5 : 1	8.5 : 1	8.4 : 1
Maximum bhp	86 at 5000 rpm	97 at 5500 rpm*	96 at 4800 rpm* (90 at 4800 rpm for later California models)
Torque	129 lbf ft at 3600 rpm	106 lbf ft at 3600 rpm	120 lbf ft at 2800 rpm
Firing order (No. 1 cylinder nearest radiator) Compression ... pressure at 250 rpm	1 - 3 - 4 - 2 128 to 170 lbf/in^2 (9 to 12 kgf/cm^2)	128 to 170 lbf/in^2 (9 to 12 kgf/cm^2)	1 - 3 - 4 - 2 128 to 156 lbf/in^2 (9 to 11 kgf/cm^2)

Firing order 1 - 3 - 4 - 2

Cylinder location and distributor rotation

* Net value

Note: *In the following table, X indicates that the relevant information will be found in the column to the left*

Cylinder head
	18R and 18R-C	20R
Material	Cast-iron	Aluminium
Maximum permissible warpage ...	0.002 in (0.05 mm)	0.006 in (0.15 mm)

	18R and 18R-C	20R
Cylinder block		
Material	Cast-iron	X
Maximum permissible warpage	0.002 in (0.05 mm)	X
Bore	3.484 to 3.486 in (88.5 to 88.55 mm)	3.4842 to 3.4854 in (88.5 to 88.53 mm)
Maximum permissible cylinder bore wear	0.008 in (0.2 mm)	X
Maximum permissible bore difference between cylinders	0.002 in (0.05 mm)	X
Maximum permissible taper or out of round	0.0008 in (0.02 mm)	X
Pistons and rings		
Standard diameter	3.481 to 3.484 in (88.44 to 88.49 mm)	3.4827 to 3.4839 in (88.46 to 88.49 mm)
Oversize - 0.25	3.492 to 3.494 in (88.69 to 88.74 mm)	N/A N/A
Oversize - 0.50	3.502 to 3.504 in (88.94 to 88.99 mm)	3.5024 to 3.5035 in (88.96 to 88.99 mm)
Oversize - 0.75	3.521 to 3.523 in (88.19 to 89.24 mm)	N/A N/A
Oversize - 1.00	3.512 to 3.523 in (89.44 to 89.49 mm)	3.5220 to 3.5232 in (89.46 to 89.49 mm)
Gudgeon pin diameter	0.8663 to 0.8669 in (22.004 to 22.019 mm)	X X
Gudgeon pin bore in piston	0.8661 to 0.8667 in (22.00 to 22.015 mm)	X X
Piston ring end-gap	0.004 to 0.012 in (0.1 to 0.3 mm)	0.004 to 0.012 in (0.1 to 0.3 mm)
Piston ring to groove clearance:		
Compression rings	0.0012 to 0.0028 in (0.03 to 0.07 mm)	0.008 in (0.2 mm)
Oil control ring	Zero (spring type)	X
Piston to cylinder wall clearance	0.0020 to 0.0028 in (0.05 to 0.07 mm)	0.0012 to 0.0020 in (0.03 to 0.05 mm)
Connecting rods		
Length (between centres)	5.441 to 5.445 in (138.20 to 138.30 mm)	X X
Big-end bore	2.2047 to 2.2057 in (56.0 to 56.024 mm)	X X
Standard endfloat	0.006 to 0.010 in (0.16 to 0.26 mm)	X X
Maximum endfloat	0.012 in (0.3 mm)	X
Small end bush internal diameter (after reaming)	0.8666 to 0.8672 in (22.012 to 22.027 mm)	X X
Gudgeon pin to small end bush running clearance	0.0002 to 0.0004 in (0.005 to 0.011 mm)	X
Maximum permissible gudgeon pin to small end bush clearance	0.0008 in (0.02 mm)	0.0006 in (0.015 mm)
Big-end bearing running clearance:		
Standard	0.0010 to 0.0021 in (0.025 to 0.055 mm)	X X
Maximum permissible big-end bearing running clearance	0.003 in (0.08 mm)	X
Crankshaft		
Number of main bearings	5	X
Endfloat	0.0008 to 0.008 in (0.02 to 0.20 mm)	X X
Maximum permissible endfloat	0.12 in (0.3 mm)	X
Maximum out-of-round or taper for journals and crankpins	0.0004 in (0.01 mm)	X
Crankshaft journal and crankpin running clearance	0.0008 to 0.0020 in (0.02 to 0.05 mm)	0.0010 to 0.0022 in (0.025 to 0.055 mm)
Maximum journal or crankpin running clearance	0.003 in (0.08 mm)	X
Crankpin journal finished diameter:		
Standard bearing	2.3613 to 2.3622 in (59.976 to 60.000 mm)	X X
Undersize - 0.25	2.3504 to 2.3508 in (59.701 to 59.711 mm)	X X
Undersize - 0.50	2.3406 to 2.3410 in (59.451 to 59.461 mm)	N/A N/A
Undersize - 0.75	2.3307 to 2.3311 in (59.201 to 59.211 mm)	N/A N/A
Undersize - 1.00	2.3209 to 2.3213 in (58.951 to 58.961 mm)	N/A N/A
Flywheel		
Maximum permissible run-out	0.008 in (0.2 mm)	X
Maximum regrind	0.04 in (1.0 mm)	Not recommended

Camshaft

	18R and 18R-C	20R
Standard endfloat	0.0017 to 0.0066 in (0.042 to 0.168 mm)	0.0031 to 0.0071 in (0.08 to 0.18 mm)
Maximum permissible endfloat	0.010 in (0.25 mm)	
Bearing running clearance	0.001 to 0.002 in (0.03 to 0.05 mm)	0.0004 to 0.0020 in (0.01 to 0.05 mm)
Maximum bearing running clearance	0.004 in (0.1 mm)	X
Cam lift:		
Inlet	0.317 in (8.04 mm)	1.6783 to 1.6819 in (42.63 to 42.72mm)
Exhaust	0.319 in (8.10 mm)	1.6806 to 1.6841 in (42.69 to 42.78 mm)
Camshaft journal finished diameter:		
Standard bearing	1.3768 to 1.3778 in (34.972 to 34.996 mm)	1.2984 to 1.2990 in (32.98 to 33.00 mm)
Undersize - 0.125	1.3718 to 1.3722 in (34.843 to 34.853 mm)	N/A N/A
Maximum journal out-of-round or taper	0.0004 in (0.01 mm)	0.008 in (0.2 mm)

Oil pump driveshaft

	18R and 18R-C	20R
Standard enfloat	0.002 to 0.005 in (0.06 to 0.13 mm)	N/A N/A
Maximum permissible endfloat	0.012 in (0.3 mm)	N/A
Driveshaft bearing running clearance	0.0010 to 0.0026 in (0.025 to 0.066 mm)	N/A N/A
Maximum permissible driveshaft running clearance	0.003 in (0.08 mm)	N/A

Valves

	18R and 18R-C	20R
Head diameter:		
Inlet	1.608 to 1.620 in (40.85 to 41.15 mm)	X X
Exhaust	1.411 to 1.423 in (35.85 to 36.15 mm)	X X
Overall length	4.457 in (113.2 mm)	In. 4.52 in (115 mm) Ex. 4.46 in (113.4 mm)
Valve stem diameter:		
Inlet	0.3140 to 0.3144 in (7.975 to 7.985 mm)	0.3138 to 0.3144 in (7.97 to 7.99 mm)
Exhaust	0.3132 to 0.3140 in (7.955 to 7.975 mm)	0.3136 to 0.3142 in (7.87 to 7.98 mm)
Standard stem to guide clearance:		
Inlet	0.0010 to 0.0022 in (0.025 to 0.055 mm)	0.0006 to 0.0024 in 0.02 to 0.06 mm)
Exhaust	0.0014 to 0.0030 in (0.035 to 0.075 mm)	0.0012 to 0.0026 in (0.03 to 0.07 mm)
Maximum stem to guide clearance:		
Inlet	0.003 in (0.08 mm)	X
Exhaust	0.004 in (0.10 mm)	X
Valve head contact angle	45°	X
Valve clearance (cold):		
Inlet	0.007 in (0.18 mm)	N/A
Exhaust	0.013 in (0.33 mm)	N/A
Valve clearance (hot):		
Inlet	0.008 in (0.20 mm)	0.008 in (0.2 mm)
Exhaust	0.014 in (0.36 mm)	0.012 in (0.3 mm)
Valve guide overall length:		
Inlet	1.949 to 2.185 in (49.5 to 55.5 mm)	X X
Exhaust	2.303 to 2.343 in (58.5 to 59.5 mm)	X X
Valve guide inner diameter (after reaming)	0.315 to 0.316 in (8.01 to 8.03 mm)	X
Valve guide outer diameter:		
Standard	0.5521 to 0.5528 in (14.023 to 14.041 mm)	X X
Oversize - 0.05	0.5541 to 0.5548 in (14.073 to 14.091 mm)	X X
Valve guide projection	0.63 in (16.0 mm)	X
Valve spring free length:		
Inner	1.74 in (44.1 mm)	N/A
Outer	1.83 in (46.5 mm)	1.787 in (45.4 mm)
Valve rocker shaft outside diameter	0.7269 to 0.7277 in (18.464 to 18.483 mm)	1.6287 to 1.6295 in (15.97 to 15.99 mm)
Rocker arm bush running clearance	0.0007 to 0.0020 in (0.017 to 0.051 mm)	0.0004 to 0.0020 in (0.01 to 0.05 mm)
Maximum permissible running clearance	0.003 in (0.08 mm)	0.003 in (0.08 mm)

Timing chain tensioners

Lower tensioner spring free length	2.70 in (67.4 mm)	N/A
Upper tensioner spring free length	3.08 in (77.0 mm)	N/A

Engine oil capacity (including filter)

All models	8.8 Imp pt/10.6 US pt (5 litres)

Engine oil type

... ...	Multigrade, grade SE or better (see lubrication chart)

Torque wrench settings

18R and 18R-C engines

	lb f ft	kg f m
Crankshaft main bearing cap bolts	75	10.35
Big-end bearing cap bolts	45	6.2
Camshaft bearing cap bolts	15	2.1
Crankshaft rear oil seal retainer bolts	15	2.1
Oil pump driveshaft thrust plate bolts	15	2.1
Camshaft sprocket to driveshaft bolt	70	9.7
Crankshaft pulley bolt	50	6.9
Cylinder head bolts	87	12
Camshaft sprocket bolts	12	1.6
Rocker shaft pillar bolts	15	2.1
Rocker shaft oil pipe unions	15	2.1
Drive plate to torque converter bolts	32	4.4
Clutch bellhousing to cylinder block bolts	50	6.9
Timing cover bolts ... ...;	15	2.1
Manifold bolts	35	4.8
Flywheel to crankshaft bolts	48	6.6

20R engine

	lb f ft	kg f m
Camshaft bearing cap	15	2.1
Thermostatic valve bolts	15	2.1
Inlet manifold bolts	15	2.1
EGR valve	11	1.5
Exhaust manifold bolts	35	4.8
Cylinder head/rocker bolts ...		
Stage 1	25	3.4
Stage 2	40	5.5
Stage 3	64	8.8
Front chain cover bolt	11	1.5
Distributor drivegear retaining bolt	65	9.0
Rocker cover bolts	11	1.5
Exhaust pipe flange nuts	32	4.4
Timing cover bolts	11	1.5
Crankshaft pulley bolt	94	13
Big-end bearing bolts	45	6.2
Main bearing bolts	80	11
Flywheel bolts	68	9.4
Bellhousing to cylinder block	50	6.9
Driveplate to torque converter bolts	32	4.4

1 General description

Two different engines are used in the models covered by this manual, but both are an in-line overhead camshaft type.

UK models use the 18R engine which, designated as 18R-C, was used in the 1974 USA models. Mechanically these engines are identical, the only differences being in the associated carburation, emission control and ignition equipment.

USA models for 1975 onwards use the 20R engine which has a cylinder head of crossflow design.

2 Major operations possible with engine in position

1 The following operations can be carried out with the engine installed in the bodyframe:

   a) *Removal and refitting of the camshaft.*
   b) *Removal and refitting of the cylinder head.*
   c) *Removal and refitting of the engine front mountings and the transmission rear mounting.*

2 If a hoist is attached to the engine lifting hooks and its weight is taken by the hoist, the engine mountings can be removed and the engine raised a little. Disconnect the steering relay rod, drop arm and idler arm rods, (Chapter 11) to permit the following operations to be carried out:

   a) *Removal and refitting of the sump.*
   b) *Removal and refitting of the oil pump.*
   c) *Removal and refitting of the piston/connecting rod assemblies (through the top of the cylinder block).*
   d) *Removal and refitting of the timing chain and gears.*

3 Major operations only possible with the engine removed

1 The following operations are only possible with the engine removed:

   a) *Removal and refitting of the flywheel or driveplate.*
   b) *Removal and installation of the crankshaft and main bearings.*

4 Method of engine removal

The engine may be removed with, or without, the gearbox or automatic transmission. The procedure given in this Chapter is for the engine and gearbox or automatic transmission together. Where the gearbox or automatic transmission is to be left in the car it must first be detached from the engine - see Chapter 6.

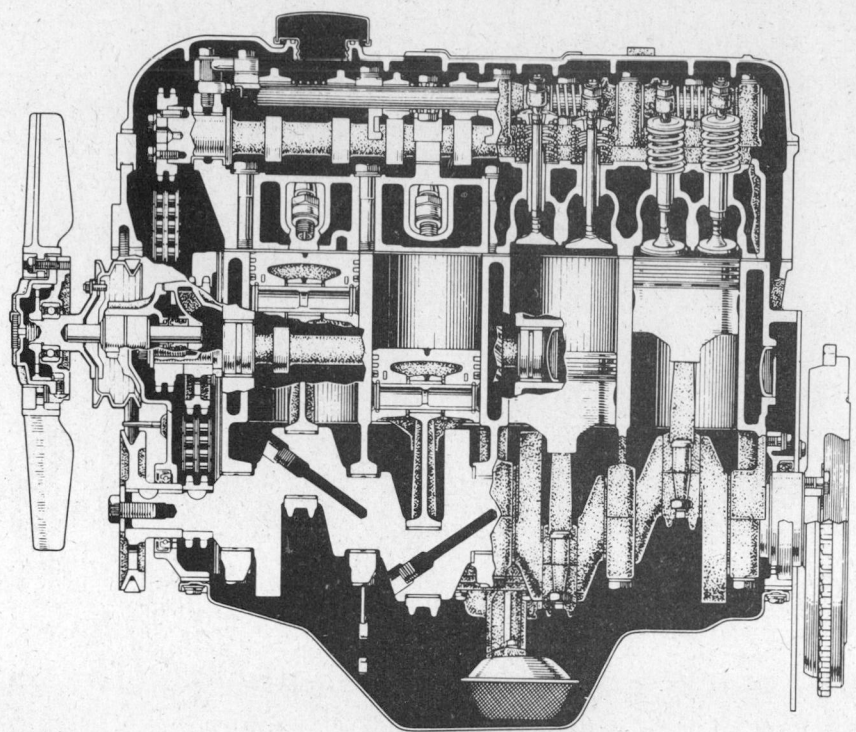

Fig. 1.1a. 18R engine - longitudinal section

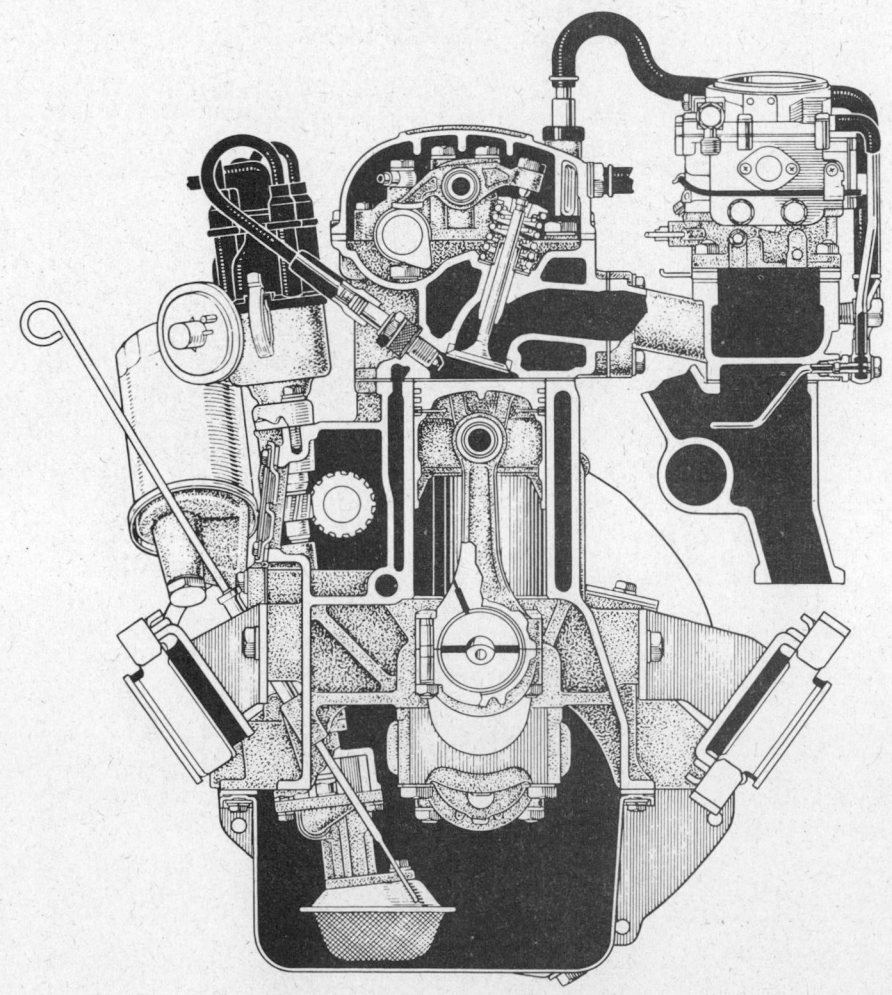

Fig. 1.1b. 18R engine - transverse section

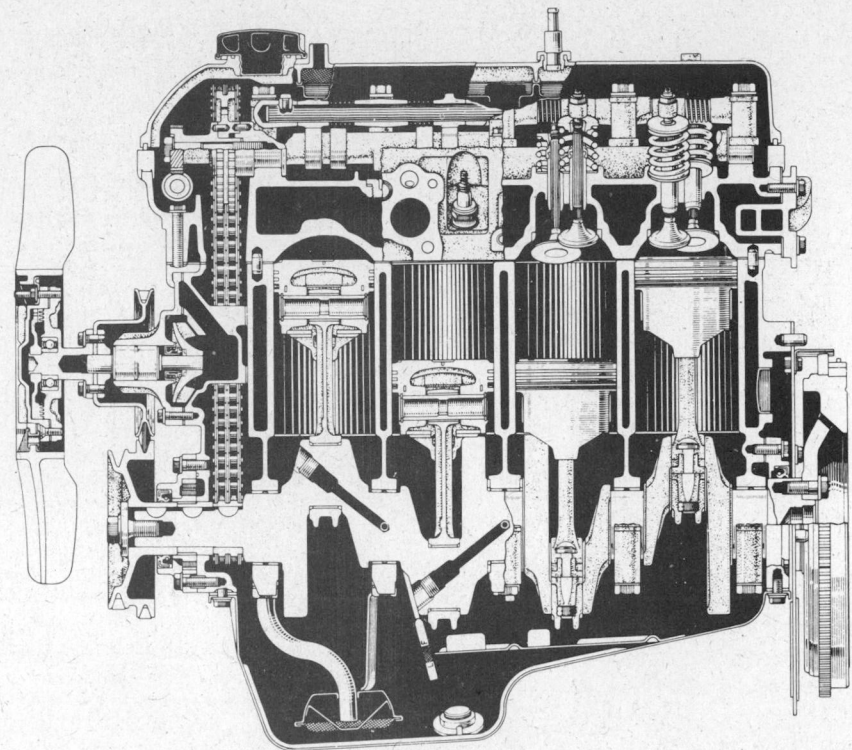

Fig. 1.2a 20R engine - longitudinal section

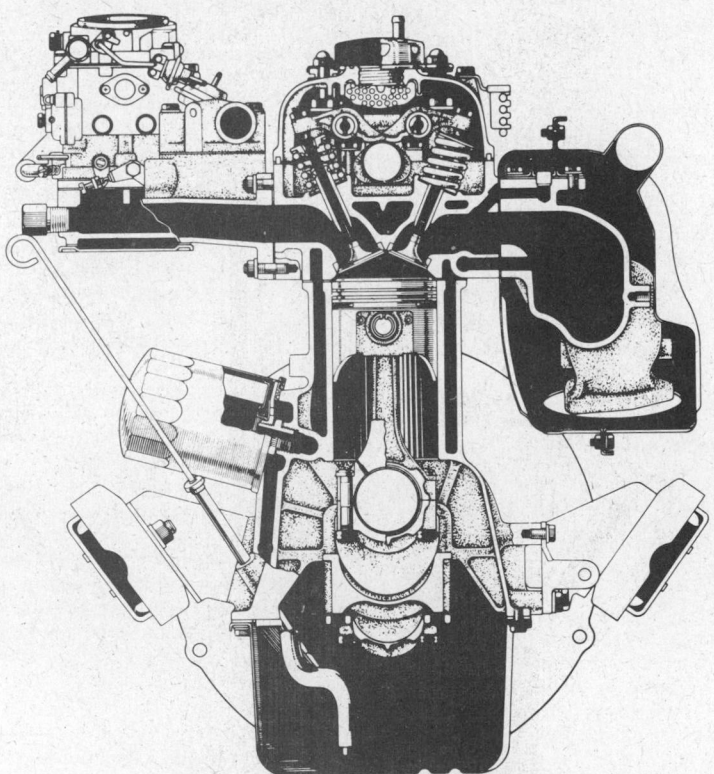

Fig. 1.2b 20R engine - transverse section

5 Engine/transmission - removal

Note: Slight deviation from the procedure given may be required in some instances due to the different vehicle specifications and consequent different ancillary equipment. *On vehicles equipped with air conditioning:* the system must be discharged of refrigerant gas so that the compressor connecting pipes can be disconnected. This and the later recharging of the system are jobs for the service engineer.
1   Disconnect the lead from the battery negative terminal.
2   Drain the cooling system (see Chapter 3).
3   Drain the engine oil.
4   Drain the gearbox oil or automatic transmission fluid, as applicable.
5   Mark the position of the bonnet hinge plates, remove the securing bolts and, with the help of an assistant, lift the bonnet from the vehicle.
6   Remove the radiator grille and the fan shroud(s).
7   Disconnect the upper and lower radiator hoses, unbolt the radiator and remove it from the engine compartment. On vehicles equipped with air conditioning, the condenser is located in front of the radiator and this too will have to be disconnected (system first discharged) and removed. On some models the headlight units may have to be removed to gain access to the condenser mountings. Where an oil cooler is fitted in conjunction with automatic transmission, then the cooler hoses will also have to be removed from the radiator before it can be withdrawn. Also remove the radiator supporting crossmember.
8   Remove the air cleaner from the carburettor.
9   Disconnect the fuel inlet pipe from the fuel pump.
10 Disconnect the heater hoses.
11 Disconnect the controls from the carburettor.
12 Disconnect the brake servo unit vacuum hose from the inlet manifold.
13 Unbolt the clutch operating cylinder from the clutch bellhousing, also the hose support bracket and tie the cylinder up out of the way. There is no need to disconnect the hydraulic line.
14 Disconnect the leads from the following components: Starter solenoid, alternator, oil pressure switch, water temperature transmitter, and coil (HT and LT leads).
15 Disconnect the vacuum hoses and electrical leads from the emission control system. **It is important that these are carefully identified to ensure exact refitting in their original positions.**
16 Working beneath the vehicle, disconnect the exhaust downpipe from the exhaust manifold.
17 Disconnect the exhaust pipe support bracket from the transmission housing.
18 Disconnect the speedometer cable from the transmission housing and disconnect the reverse lamp switch wires.
19 *On vehicles with a three-speed gearbox:* disconnect the high and low speed connecting rods and the cross-shaft from the lower end of the steering column type gearchange mechanism.
20 *On vehicles with a four or five-speed manually operated gearbox:* remove the gear lever retainer plate and pull out the lever (see Chapter 6).
21 *On vehicles equipped with automatic transmission:* disconnect the speed selector rod from the selector lever on the transmission housing, and remove the fluid filler tube and dipstick.
22 Mark the edges of the propeller shaft. Remove the propeller shaft (see Chapter 7).
23 At this point, check that all the appropriate hoses, cables and connections have been detached.
24 Using a suitable hoist and slings positioned securely round the engine, raise the hoist so that it just takes the weight of the engine. Unbolt the engine mountings from the crossmember.
25 Place a jack under the transmission housing, then unbolt and remove the rear mounting support crossmember and the mounting.
26 Lower the jack from below the transmission which will allow it to drop a few inches. Hoist the combined engine/transmission up and out of the engine compartment at a steeply inclined angle.

6 Engine - separation from manual gearbox

1   Remove the starter motor.
2   Unscrew and remove the bolts which connect the clutch bellhousing to the cylinder block.

3   Pull the gearbox from the engine in a straight line, supporting the gearbox so that its weight does not hang on the gearbox input shaft, even momentarily, whilst it is still engaged with the clutch mechanism.

7 Engine - separation from automatic transmission

1   Unscrew and remove the oil cooler pipes.
2   Remove the starter motor.
3   Disconnect the 'kick-down' cable.
4   Remove the two brackets which connect the sides of the transmission casing to the cylinder block.
5   Remove the two rubber plugs from the torque converter housing, and then remove the torque converter to drive plate securing bolts. The drive plate will have to be rotated to reach each of the bolts in turn. Mark the relative position of the drive plate to the torque converter using a spirit pen or dab of quick drying paint so that they can be fitted in their original relative positions.
6   Unscrew and remove the bolts which secure the automatic transmission torque converter housing to the engine. Pull the automatic transmission unit from its connection with the engine, keeping it in a straight line and supporting its weight during the operation. There will probably be some loss of fluid from the torque converter during the separation procedure so be prepared to catch it in a suitable container.

8 Dismantling the engine - general

1   It is best to mount the engine on a dismantling stand but if one is not available, stand the engine on a strong bench so as to be at a comfortable working height. Failing this, the engine will have to be stripped down on the floor.
2   During the dismantling process the greatest care should be taken to keep the exposed parts free from dirt. As an aid to achieving this, it is a sound scheme to thoroughly clean down the outside of the engine, removing all traces of oil and congealed dirt.
3   Use paraffin or a good water-soluble grease solvent. The latter compound will make the job much easier, as, after the solvent has been applied and allowed to stand for a time, a vigorous jet of water will wash off the solvent, and all the grease and filth. If the dirt is thick and deeply embedded, work the solvent into it with a wire brush.
4   Finally wipe down the exterior of the engine with a rag and only then, when it is quite clean, should the dismantling process begin. As the engine is stripped, clean each part in a bath of paraffin or petrol.
5   Never immerse parts with oilways in paraffin (eg, the crankshaft), but to clean, wipe down carefully with a petrol dampened rag. Oilways can be cleaned out with wire. If an air line is present all parts can be blown dry and the oilways blown through as an added precaution.
6   Re-use of old engine gaskets is false economy and can give rise to oil and water leaks, if nothing worse. To avoid the possibility of trouble after the engine has been reassembled **always** use new gaskets throughout.
7   Do not throw the old gaskets away as it sometimes happens that an immediate replacement cannot be found and the old gasket is then very useful as a template for making a new one. Hang up the old gaskets as they are removed on a suitable hook or nail.
8   To strip the engine it is best to work from the top down. The sump provides a firm base on which the engine can be supported in an upright position. When the stage where the sump must be removed is reached, the engine can be turned on its side and all other work carried out with it in this position.
9   Wherever possible, refit nuts, bolts and washers fingertight from wherever they were removed. This helps avoid later loss and muddle. If they cannot be refitted, lay them out in such a fashion that it is clear where they came from.

9 Engine ancillary components - removal

1   With the engine removed from the vehicle and separated from the gearbox, the ancillary components should now be removed before dismantling proper begins.
2   Unbolt the clutch pressure plate assembly from the flywheel and remove the clutch mechanism complete with driven plate (manual

9.5a Remove the oil pressure switch (18R)

9.5b Remove the rear lifting hook ...

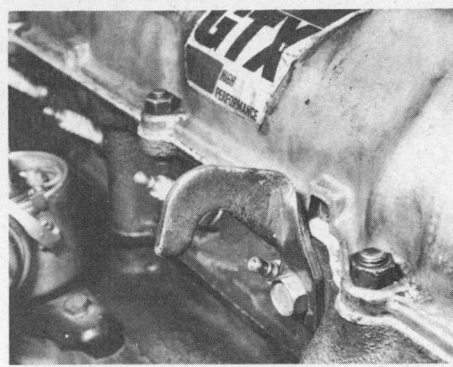
9.5c ... and the front one (18R)

9.6 Remove the water pump bypass hose (18R)

9.7 Remove the water pump and fan assembly (18R)

9.8 Remove the thermostat housing (18R)

gearbox).

3   Bend back the tabs of the locking plates which are located under the bolts which secure the flywheel (or drive plate - automatic transmission) to the crankshaft rear flange. Remove the bolts, and lift off the flywheel or drive plate as the case may be.

4   Where the vehicle is equipped with air conditioning, remove the air compressor and idler pulley. Where applicable, also remove the air pump and associated items.

5   Remove the dipstick, the fuel pipes, and loosen the distributor clamp. Withdraw the distributor complete with cap and HT leads. Remove the spark plugs followed by the fuel pump (not 20R) and the oil filter/mounting assembly. If desired, the side cover, oil pressure switch and engine mounting brackets may also be removed (photos).

6   Remove the heater pipes, the crankcase ventilation hose, and then unbolt and remove the carburettor complete with heat insulator from the inlet manifold. Remove the manifold assembly (manifolds - 20R), water pump bypass hose, drivebelt adjustment strap, alternator, and fan belt. The alternator mounting bracket may be removed if desired (photos).

7   From the front of the engine, remove the water pump and fan assembly.

8   Remove the thermostat housing and the thermostat; also the rocker cover.

9   Finally check that any other removable items, particularly associated with your model, have been, or can be, removed.

10 Engine dismantling (18R)

Rocker gear

1   Unscrew and remove the union bolts and withdraw the oil feed pipe. Also remove the No. 2 chain tensioner bolt and spring.

2   Unscrew the rocker shaft pillar bolts in the sequence shown in Fig. 1.5 to ensure that the pressure of the valve springs is relieved gently to prevent distortion of the shaft.

3   Remove the rocker shaft assembly from the cylinder head.

4   The rocker shaft does not normally require dismantling unless the heels of the rocker arms are scored or badly worn, or one of the coil springs is broken.

5   If dismantling is essential, first remove the retaining screw which secures the rocker shaft front support pillar to the shaft. The rear pillar is retained to the shaft by means of the two securing bolts which engage in cut-outs in the shaft.

6   As each rocker arm, spring and pillar is withdrawn, keep them in strict sequence for refitting.

Camshaft

7   Unbolt the sprocket from the end of the camshaft. A semi-circular plastic plug is provided for access to the bolts.

8   Use a hooked piece of wire to support the chain while the gearwheel is removed and to prevent the chain becoming disconnected from the drive sprocket. This is particularly important when the camshaft is being removed with the engine in position in the car and further dismantling is not anticipated.

9   Remove the four camshaft bearing caps together with their respective bearing shells, keeping them in strict sequence for correct refitting (they are usually numbered 1 to 4). Remove the camshaft.

Cylinder head

10 *If the engine is still in the car,* drain the cooling system and disconnect all leads and hoses from the cylinder head; remove the carburettor, and the spark plugs.

11 Unscrew the cylinder head bolts half a turn at a time in the sequence shown in Fig. 1.7.

12 Unscrew and remove the two bolts which secure the top end of the timing chain cover to the cylinder head.

13 Lift the cylinder head straight up to clear the locating dowels. If the cylinder head is stuck, it is permissible to insert a screwdriver at the point shown in Fig. 1.8 to break the seal. Use a piece of wire to support the chain and camshaft sprocket whilst lifting off the head.

14 Each valve should be removed from the cylinder head using the

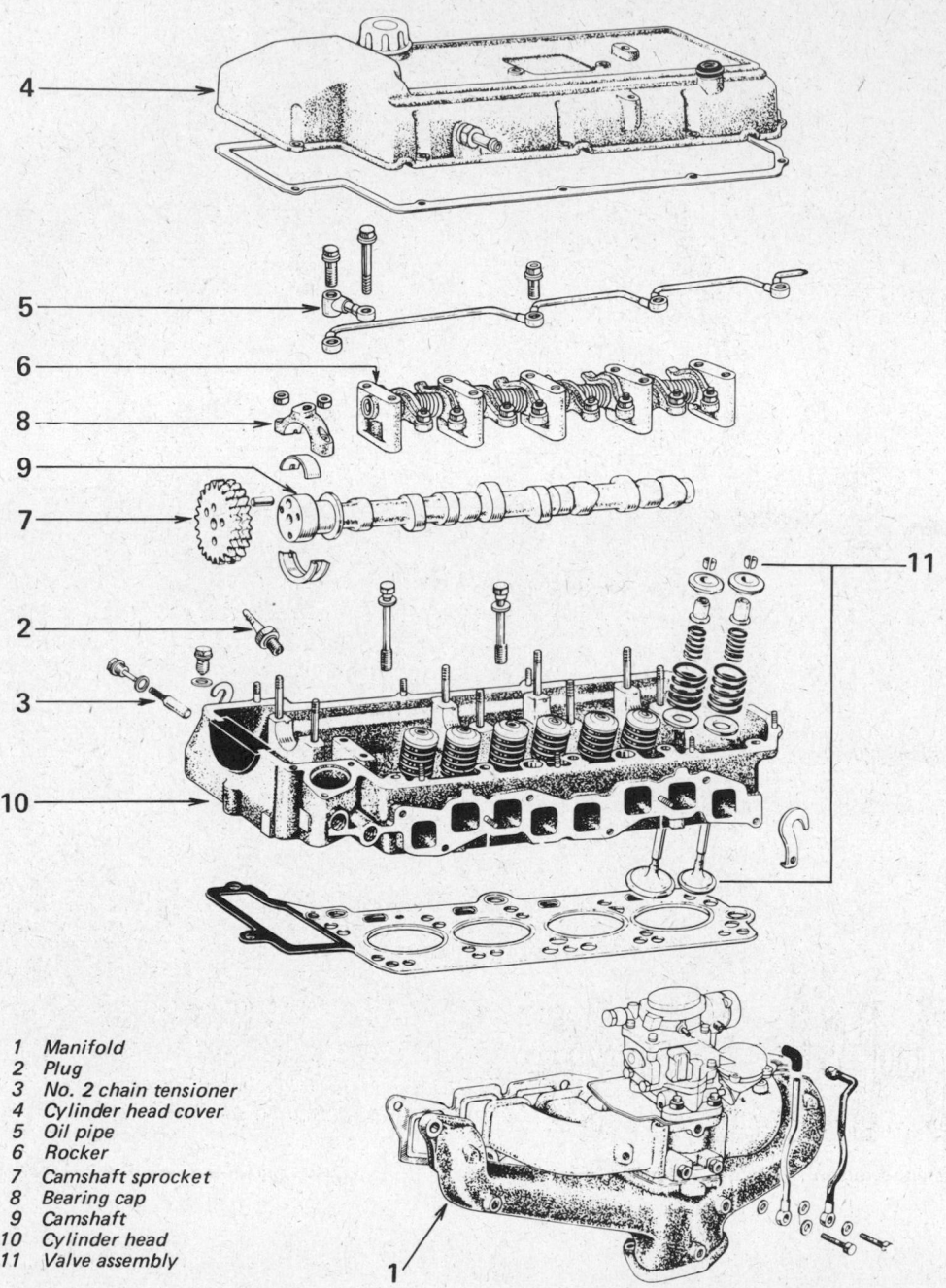

4

5

6

8

9

7

2

3

10

11

1 Manifold
2 Plug
3 No. 2 chain tensioner
4 Cylinder head cover
5 Oil pipe
6 Rocker
7 Camshaft sprocket
8 Bearing cap
9 Camshaft
10 Cylinder head
11 Valve assembly

1

Fig. 1.3. Layout of cylinder head components (18R)

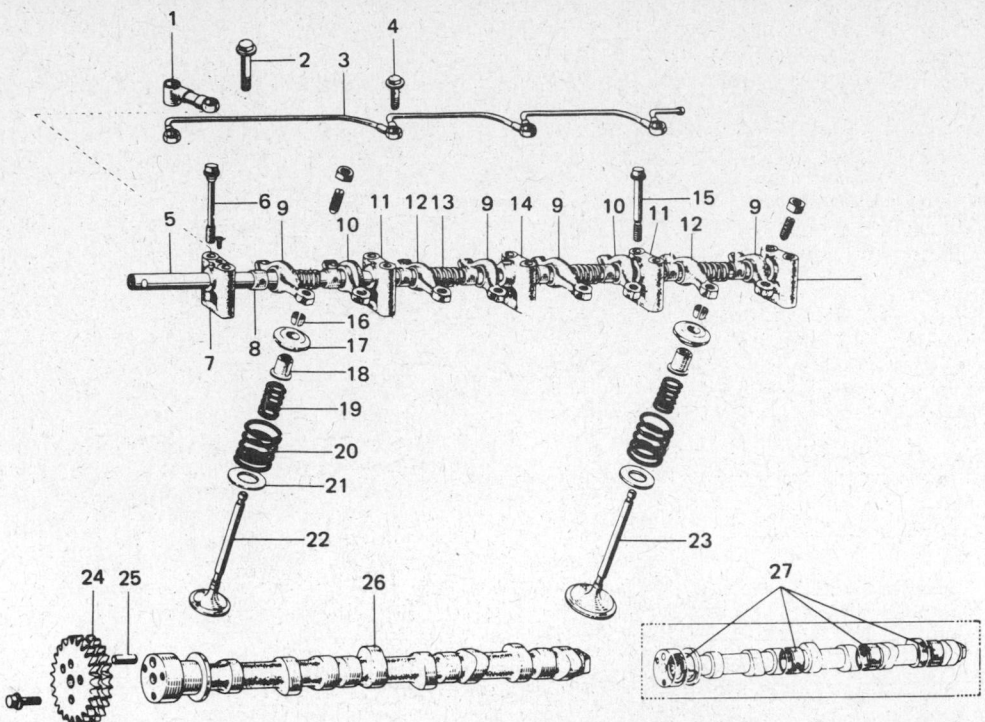

Fig. 1.4. Rocker gear and associated parts (18R)

1 Oil pipe union	8 Bearing	15 Bolt	22 Exhaust valve
2 Union bolt	9 Rocker arm	16 Split collets	23 Inlet valve
3 Oil pipe assembly	10 Rocker arm	17 Valve spring retainer	24 Camshaft sprocket
4 Union bolt	11 Rocker shaft support pillar	18 Valve stem oil seal	25 Dowel pin
5 Rocker shaft	12 Rocker arm	19 Valve (inner) spring	26 Camshaft
6 Bolt	13 Spring	20 Valve (outer) spring	27 Camshaft shell bearings
7 Rocker shaft support pillar	14 Rocker shaft support pillar	21 Plate	

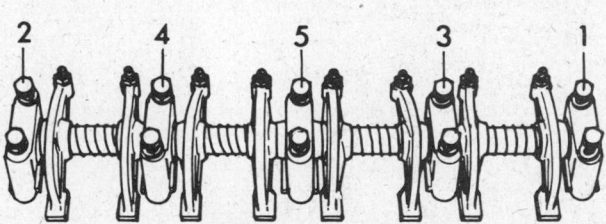

Fig. 1.5. Loosening sequence for rocker assembly (18R)

Fig. 1.6. Measuring camshaft thrust clearance (18R)

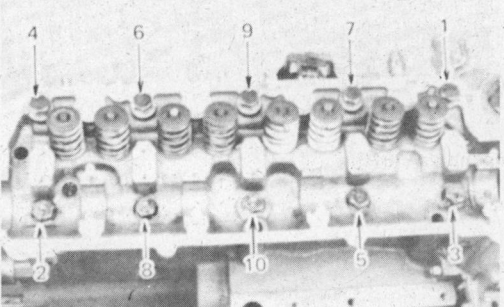

Fig. 1.7. Cylinder head bolt loosening sequence (18R)

Fig. 1.8. Breaking the head seal with a screwdriver (18R)

following method:

15 Compress each spring, using a valve spring compressor, until the collets can be removed. Release the compressor slowly, remove it, then remove the retainer, double springs, oil seal and the washer from the valve stem. Finally withdraw the valve from its guide (photos).

16 If, when the valve spring compressor is screwed down, the valve spring retaining cap refuses to free to expose the collets, do not continue to screw down on the compressor as there is a likelihood of bending the valve stem.

17 Gently tap the top of the tool directly over the cap with a light hammer. This will free the cap. To avoid the compressor jumping off the valve spring retaining cap when it is tapped, hold the compressor firmly in position with one hand.

18 It is essential that the valves are kept in their correct sequences unless they are so badly worn that they are to be renewed. If they are going to be kept and used again, place them in a sheet of card having holes numbered 1 to 8 corresponding to the relative positions the valves were in when fitted. Also keep the valve springs, washers, etc, in the correct order.

Sump and timing gear

Note: The owner may wish to remove the timing cover with the engine in the car, in which case the cylinder head must first be removed followed by the sump. If the sump is not removed, the sump-to-timing cover gasket will be damaged along the front edge (where the sump-to-

timing cover bolts are fitted) when the timing cover is taken off. However, provided that extreme care is taken, it should be possible to cut the appropriate length from a new gasket to use when reassembling, provided that the abutting edges are squarely cut. The use of a silicone/RTV-type gasket sealant should be made at these points to minimize the risk of oil leakage, as well as the use of a normal non-setting sealant on the joint faces.

19 *If the engine is in the car,* drain the engine oil and disconnect the battery negative lead. Remove the cylinder head as described previously in this Section. Remove the radiator.

20 Unbolt and remove the re-inforcement brackets from the rear of the sump.

21 Unscrew and remove the sump securing bolts and detach the sump from the crankcase.

22 Unscrew the crankshaft pulley bolt, with the sump removed, by jamming the crankshaft with a piece of wood to prevent the engine turning as the bolt is loosened. If the pulley is being removed with the sump still fitted, and the car has *a manual gearbox,* engage a gear and apply the handbrake fully to prevent the crankshaft rotating. *With automatic transmission,* remove the starter and jam the ring gear with a large screwdriver or cold chisel.

23 Remove the crankshaft pulley. It will usually pull straight out but if necessary, remove it by placing two tyre levers behind it or use a puller (there are two holes tapped in the pulley for this purpose).

24 Unbolt and remove the timing cover. Note that the upper bolt is

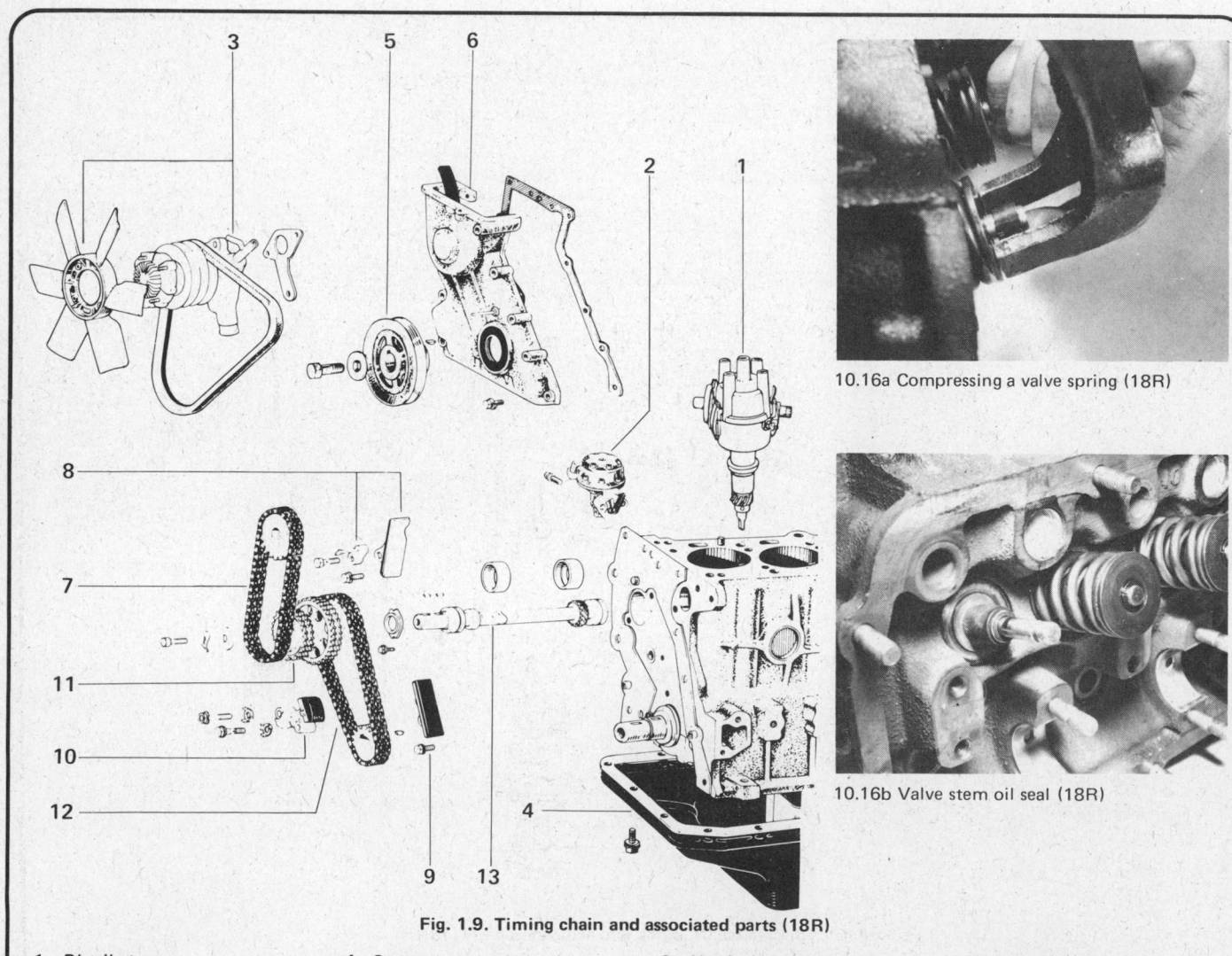

10.16a Compressing a valve spring (18R)

10.16b Valve stem oil seal (18R)

Fig. 1.9. Timing chain and associated parts (18R)

1 Distributor	4 Sump	8 No. 2 chain damper and oil jet	11 Camshaft sprocket
2 Fuel pump	5 Crankshaft pulley	9 No. 1 chain damper	12 No. 1 timing chain and sprocket
3 Fan and water pump	6 Timing cover	10 No. 1 chain tensioner	13 Pump driveshaft
	7 No. 2 timing chain		

entered from the rear.

25 Remove the camshaft drive chain. The oil pump driveshaft sprocket and the chain tensioner should now be withdrawn.

26 Remove the crankshaft sprockets, and the second oil pump driveshaft sprocket, complete with chain as one assembly. Remove the chain damper.

27 Remove the oil pump driveshaft thrust plate, and withdraw the driveshaft and engine front plate. Unbolt and remove the oil pump assembly from within the crankcase.

Piston/connecting rod assemblies

28 *If the engine is still in the vehicle,* first remove the cylinder head and sump as previously described, then turn the crankshaft so that the pistons are all part way down their bores. Using a bearing scraper, carefully remove as much as possible of the 'wear' ridge at the top of each cylinder bore. This operation is essential to prevent the piston rings breaking as the pistons are extracted through the top of the block.

29 With quick drying paint, mark each piston, connecting rod and big-end bearing cap. Number the components of each assembly 1 to 4 (from the front of the engine) and also the relative positions of the components to each other and to the crankcase, so that if the original assembly is to be refitted, it will be refitted in its exact, previously located position.

30 Unbolt the big-end caps from the connecting rods, then push each piston/connecting rod assembly out through the top of the block. Take great care that the threads of the big-end studs do not score the cylinder bores during this operation. If the bearing shells are to be used again, identify them in respect of exact original location.

Piston rings and gudgeon pins

31 With the piston assemblies removed, the piston rings may be removed by opening each of them in turn, just enough to enable them to ride over the lands of the piston body.

32 In order to prevent the lower rings dropping into an empty groove higher up the piston as they are removed, it is helpful to use two or three narrow strips of tin or old feeler blades inserted behind the ring at equidistant points, and then to employ a twisting motion to slide the ring from the piston.

33 To remove a gudgeon pin, first extract the circlips (one at each end) and then immerse the piston in hot water at a temperature of approximately 140°F (60°C). After a few minutes, the gudgeon pin will be able to be pushed out of the piston and connecting rod with finger pressure.

34 Mark each gudgeon pin as it is removed with the piston sequence number (use masking tape) so that it can be refitted in its original location.

Crankshaft and main bearings

35 Unbolt and remove the crankshaft rear oil seal retainer.

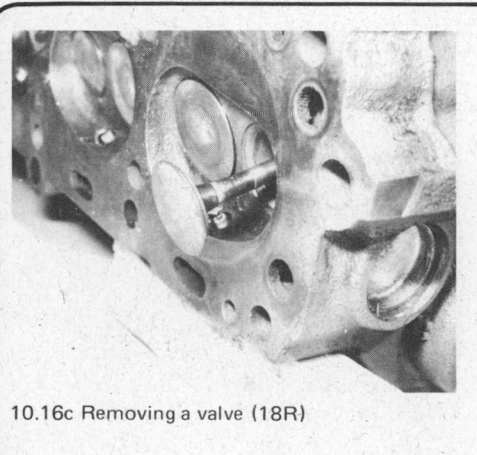

10.16c Removing a valve (18R)

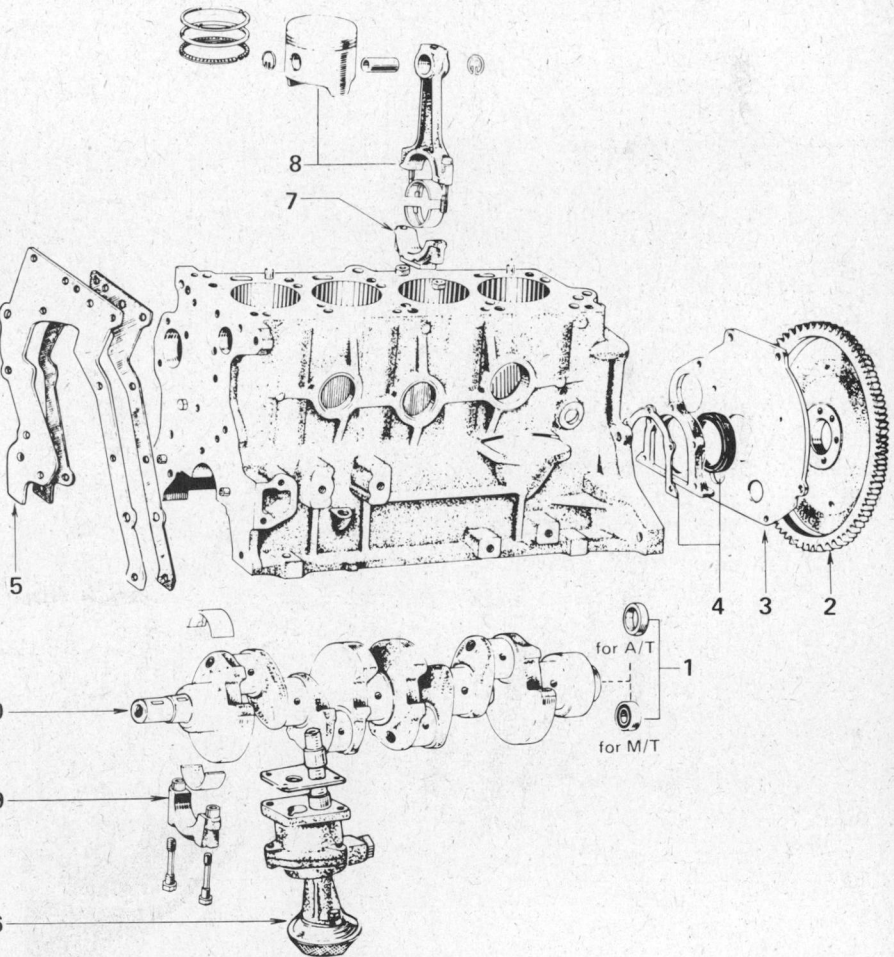

Fig. 1.10. Crankshaft, block and associated parts (18R)

1	Input shaft bearing (alternative for manual and automatic transmission shown)	2	Flywheel
		3	Rear end plate
		4	Rear oil seal
5	Front end plate	8	Piston and connecting rod
6	Oil pump	9	Main bearing cap
7	Connecting rod cap	10	Crankshaft

36 Mark each of the main bearing caps with quick-drying paint
(numbered 1 to 5 from the front of the engine), making sure that the
caps are also marked as to which way round they are to be refitted.
Some caps are marked with a triangle, the apex of which points to the
front of the engine, and they are already numbered, but check before
removing them.

37 Unscrew the main bearing cap bolts and remove the caps complete
with shell bearings. The centre main bearing shells incorporate thrust
flanges.

38 Lift the crankshaft from the crankcase. If the bearing shells are to
be used again, identify them in respect of exact original location.

39 If not already removed, the input shaft bearing (clutch pilot
bearing) can be extracted from the rear end of the crankshaft.

11 Lubrication system, oil pump and filter (18R engine)

1   Pressure for the engine lubrication system is generated by a trochoid
type oil pump located within the crankcase. The pump is driven by an
extension of the distributor driveshaft which in turn is meshed with a
short driveshaft driven by chain from the crankshaft sprocket. The
pressurised oil is first passed through an externally mounted cartridge
type disposable oil filter, then to all the bearings and friction surfaces
of the engine. Oil pressure also actuates the timing chain tensioners.
Excess oil pressure is controlled by an integral relief valve within the oil
pump.

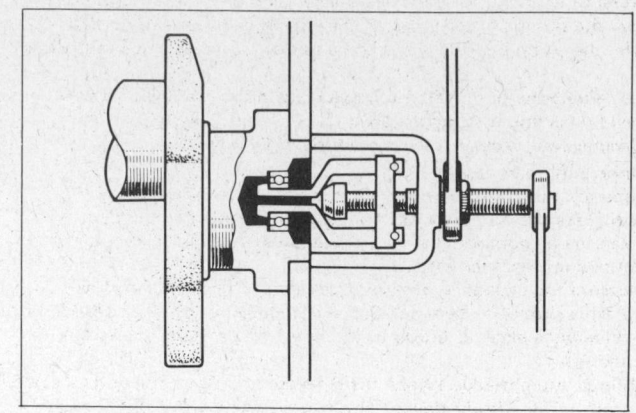

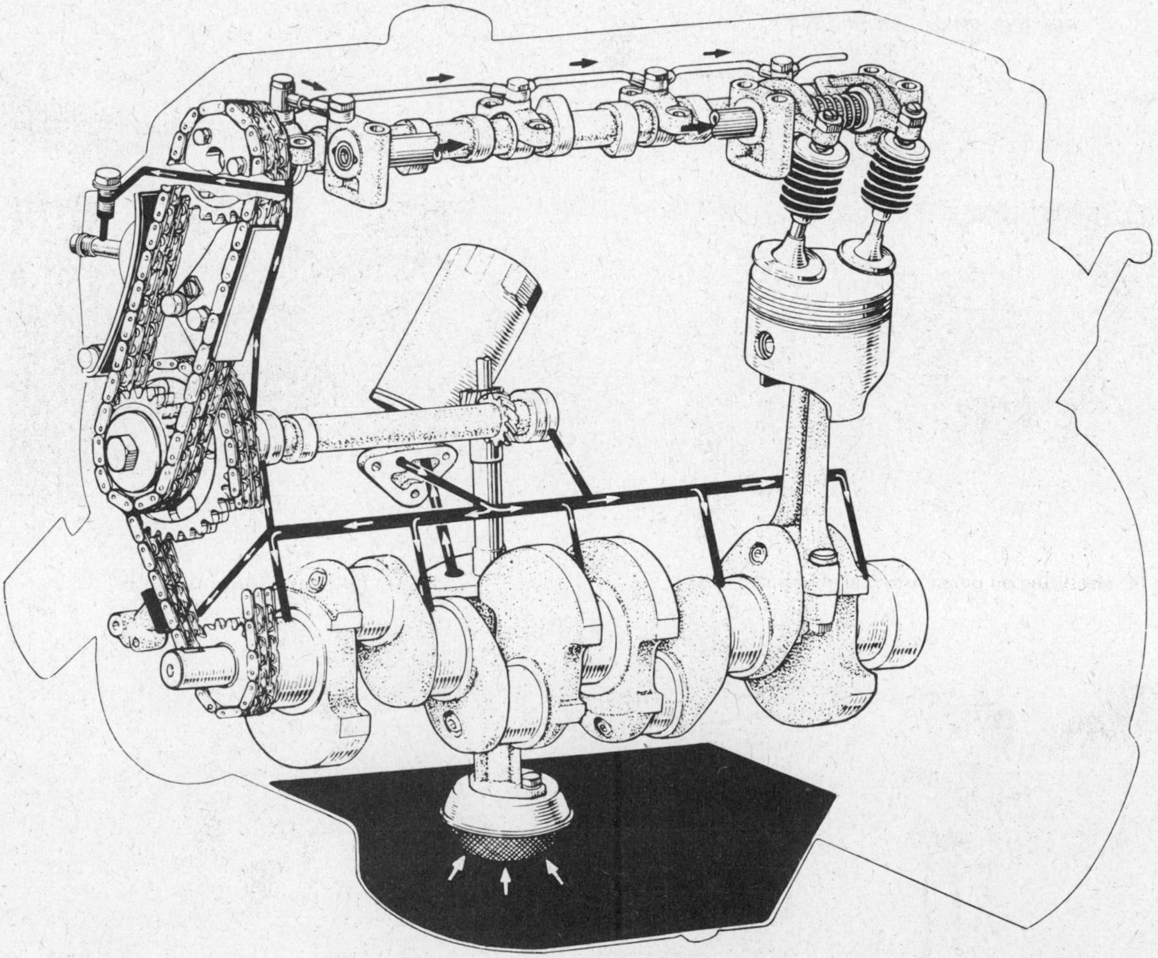

Fig. 1.11. Extracting input shaft bearing (18R)

Fig. 1.12. Engine lubrication system (18R)

2 The oil pump normally has a very long life but in the event of low oil pressure (not due to worn bearings or lack of oil) being observed, remove the pump for servicing. If the engine is in position in the vehicle, the sump will first have to be removed as described in Section 10.

3 To service the pump, first remove it from the crankcase (three screws) by pulling it straight down.

4 Unscrew and remove the pressure relief valve.

5 Unbolt the oil strainer.

6 Separate the cover from the pump body (three screws).

7 Withdraw the oil pump shaft and driven rotor from the body.

8 Examine all components for wear and using feeler blades, carry out the following clearance tests.

9 Measure the clearance between the tips of the drive and driven rotors. This should be between 0.004 and 0.006 in (0.10 and 0.15 mm). If the clearance exceeds 0.008 in (0.2 mm) renew both rotors as a matched set.

10 Using a straight-edge, check the clearance between the end faces of the rotors and the body flange. This should be between 0.001 and 0.003 in (0.03 and 0.07 mm). If the clearance exceeds 0.006 in (0.15 mm) the rotors should be renewed and possibly the pump body as well to achieve the correct tolerance.

11 Finally, measure the clearance between the outer rotor and the inside of the pump body. The clearance should be between 0.004 and 0.006 in (0.10 and 0.16 mm). If the clearance exceeds 0.008 in (0.2 mm), renew the pump body.

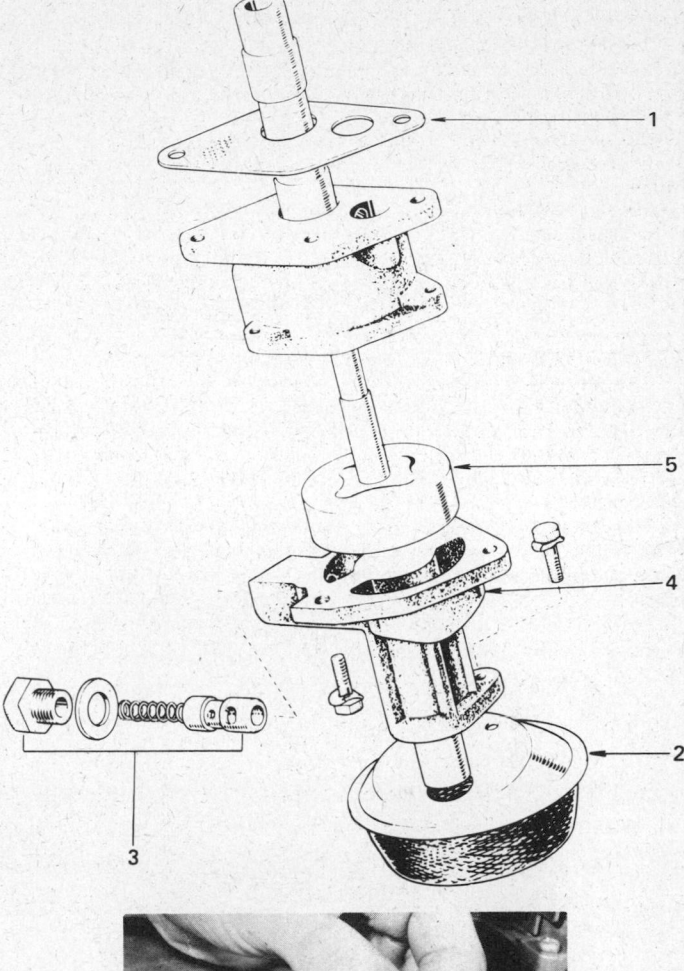

Fig. 1.13. Oil pump (18R)

1 *Gasket*
2 *Strainer*
3 *Relief valve*
4 *Pump cover*
5 *Drive rotor and driven rotor*

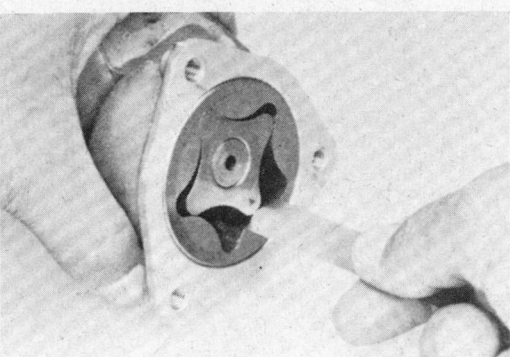

Fig. 1.14. Measuring oil pump rotor tip clearance (18R)

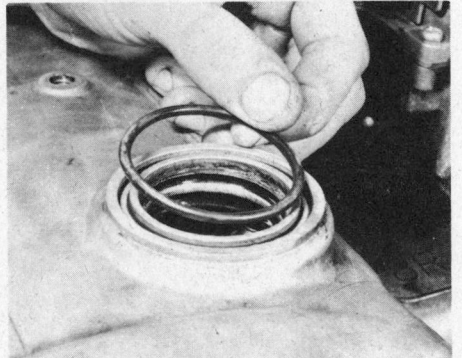

12.3 Oil filler cap O-ring seal (18R)

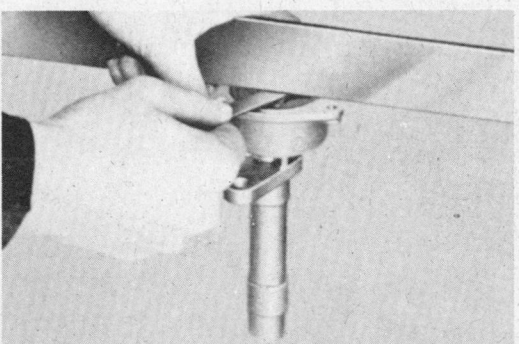

Fig. 1.15. Measuring oil pump and clearance (18R)

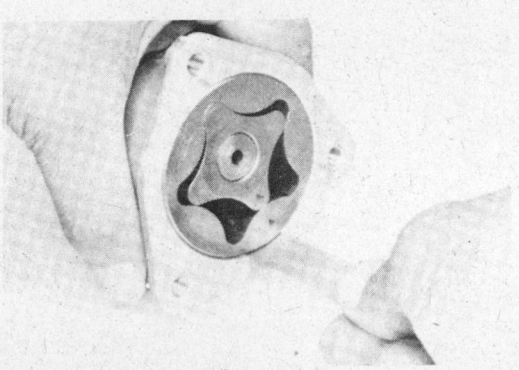

Fig. 1.16. Measuring oil pump body clearance (18R)

12 Check the condition of the relief valve spring and the valve head.
It is a good policy to renew the spring if the engine is undergoing a
major overhaul.
13 Reassembly and refitting are the reverse of the dismantling and
removal procedures, but ensure that the rotor punch marks will face
downwards when the pump is refitted. Always use a new gasket when
fitting the pump to the crankcase.
14 The cartridge type oil filter incorporates a non-return valve to
prevent oil draining from the filter when the engine is switched off. A
bypass valve is built into the filter base which opens in the event of the
filter clogging to ensure normal (though unfiltered) oil circulation.
15 The filter cartridge can be removed using a chain wrench or special
filter strap. Fit the filter using hand pressure only. Always use the new
gasket supplied and smear its sealing face with grease before tightening.

12 Crankcase ventilation system (18R engine)

1   As part of the emission control system (described in Chapter 3), a
positive crankcase ventilation system is fitted.
2   Every 12000 miles (20000 km) check the operation of the PCV
valve. To do this, let the engine run at idling speed and first pinch and
then release the hose just above the valve, at the same time, listening
for the sound of the valve seating. If it does not close, or is sluggish in
operation, remove it and wash it thoroughly in fuel. Other indications
of a faulty PCV valve are evidence of oil in the air cleaner and rough
idling.

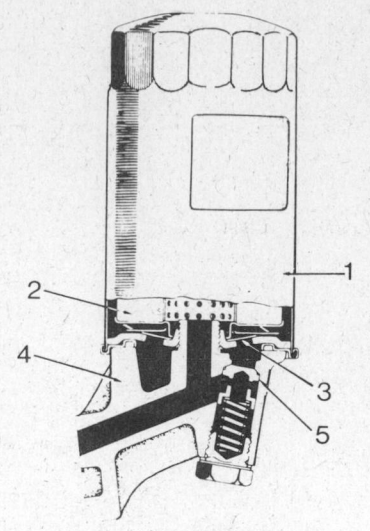
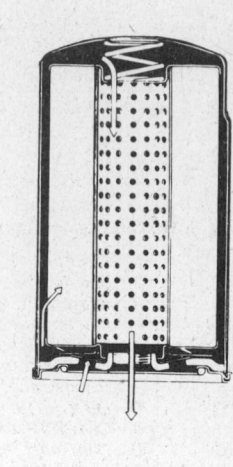

Fig. 1.17. Oil filter (18R)

1 Filter casing	4 Oil filter base
2 Element	5 Bypass valve
3 Non-return valve	

Fig. 1.18. Positive crankcase ventilation system (18R)

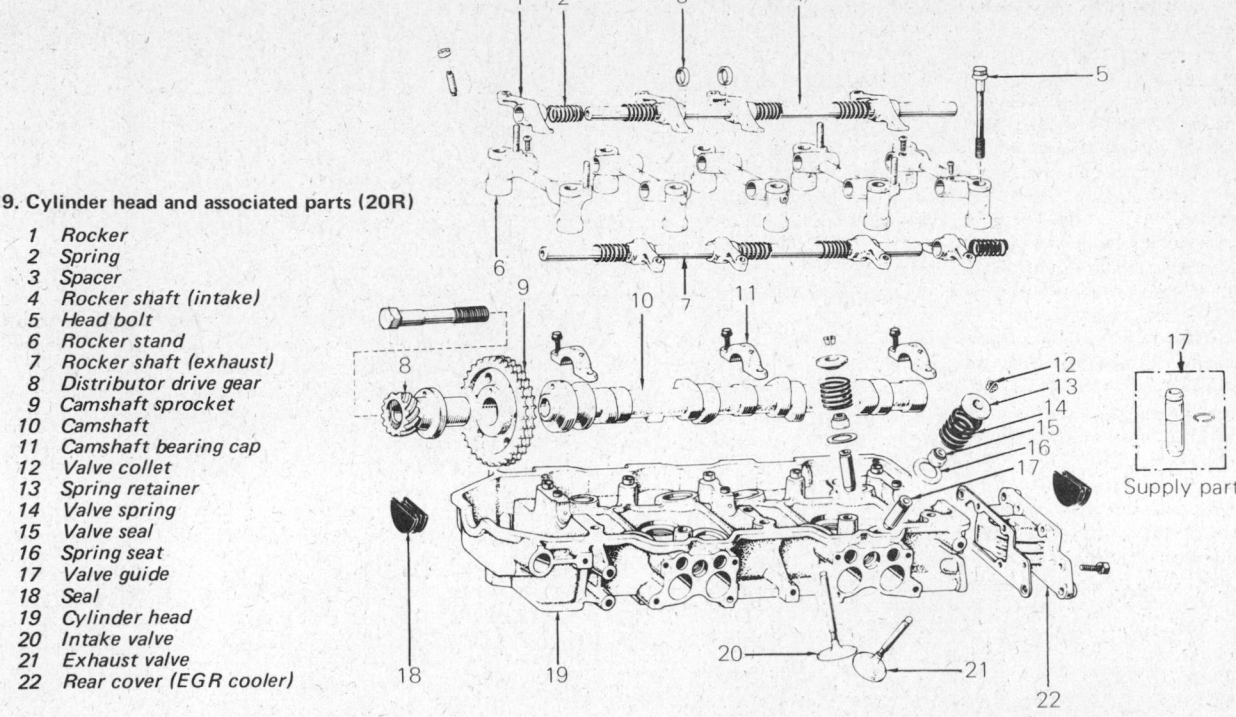

Fig. 1.19. Cylinder head and associated parts (20R)

1 *Rocker*
2 *Spring*
3 *Spacer*
4 *Rocker shaft (intake)*
5 *Head bolt*
6 *Rocker stand*
7 *Rocker shaft (exhaust)*
8 *Distributor drive gear*
9 *Camshaft sprocket*
10 *Camshaft*
11 *Camshaft bearing cap*
12 *Valve collet*
13 *Spring retainer*
14 *Valve spring*
15 *Valve seal*
16 *Spring seat*
17 *Valve guide*
18 *Seal*
19 *Cylinder head*
20 *Intake valve*
21 *Exhaust valve*
22 *Rear cover (EGR cooler)*

Supply part

Fig. 1.20. Removing distributor drive (20R)

3 Every 24000 miles (38000 km) renew the PCV valve and at all times make sure that the connecting hoses and clips are secure and in good condition, also the O-ring seal of the oil filler cap (photo).

Fig. 1.21. Removing chain cover bolt (20R)

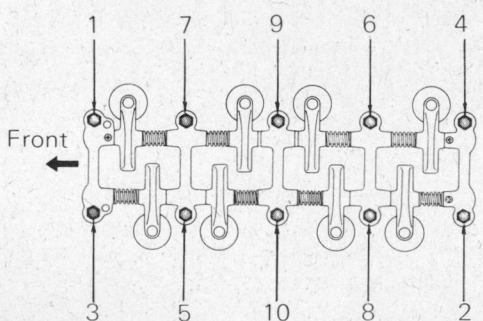

Front ←

Fig. 1.22. Rocker/cylinder head bolt loosening sequence (20R)

13 Engine dismantling (20R engine)

Cylinder head, rocker shafts and camshaft
1 *If the engine is in the vehicle,* disconnect the battery negative lead, all hoses, controls and leads from the rocker cover, cylinder head and carburettor. Disconnect the exhaust downpipe, drain the cooling system and remove the air cleaner and the distributor.
2 Unbolt and remove the rocker cover. Remove the rubber semicircular plug from the front edge of the cylinder head and remove the bolt which is exposed.
3 Using a quick drying paint, put alignment marks on the timing chain and camshaft sprocket.
4 Withdraw the distributor drive gear but leave the cam sprocket and chain undisturbed.
5 Remove the chain cover bolt from directly in front of the cam sprocket. **This must be done before attempting to remove the cylinder head bolts.**
6 Unscrew the cylinder head bolts in the sequence shown in Fig. 1.22 to prevent warpage of the cylinder head.

7   Withdraw the rocker assembly which is secured by the cylinder head bolts (now removed). The rocker pillars are located on dowels and both ends of the assembly must be turned upwards simultaneously to prevent distortion.

8   Push the cam sprocket forward off its mounting flange and allow it to rest on the ends of the chain dampers. Remove the cylinder head by lifting both ends simultaneously as this too is located on dowels.

9   If this work is being carried out while the engine is still in the vehicle, once the cylinder head is removed, it is recommended that the engine oil is drained and discarded as it will have become contaminated with coolant. Failure to observe this recommendation may result in corroded crankcase components.

10   Remove the EGR valve from the cylinder head.

11   Unbolt and remove the inlet manifold complete with carburettor.

12   Remove the thermostatic valve.

13   Unbolt and remove the exhaust manifold heat insulator.

14   With the heat insulator removed, unbolt and withdraw the exhaust manifold.

15   Unscrew and remove the spark plugs.

16   At this stage, measure the camshaft endfloat, using a feeler blade. If it exceeds 0.0098 in (0.25 mm), the complete cylinder head assembly will have to be renewed.

17   Remove the camshaft bearing caps and lift out the camshaft.

18   Remove the valve from the cylinder head using a valve spring compressor. Extract the split collets and withdraw the valve spring retainers, the springs, valves, seals and seats.

19   Keep the valves in their original fitted sequence. A piece of card with holes numbered 1 to 8 punched in it is useful for this purpose.

Sump and timing gear

Note: The owner may wish to remove the timing cover with the engine in the car, in which case the cylinder head must first be removed followed by the sump. If the sump is not removed, the sump-to-timing cover gasket will be damaged along the front edge (where the sump-to-timing cover bolts are fitted) when the timing cover is taken off. However, provided that extreme care is taken, it should be possible

to cut the appropriate length from a new gasket when reassembling, provided that the abutting edges are squarely cut. The use of a silicone/RTV-type gasket sealant should be made at these points to minimise the risk of oil leakage, as well as the use of a normal non-setting sealant on the joint faces.

20   *If the engine is in the car,* drain the engine oil and disconnect the battery negative lead. Remove the cylinder head as described previously in this Section. Remove the radiator.

21   Remove the drive belts. Detach the air pump and the alternator link from the timing cover.

22   Unscrew and remove the sump securing bolts and detach the sump from the crankcase.

23   Remove the crankshaft pulley bolt and draw off the pulley using a suitable extractor.

24   Remove the two bolts which secure the water bypass tube.

25   Remove the single bolt which is located at the rear of the timing cover on the left-hand side of the crankcase.

26   Unscrew and remove the timing cover bolts as indicated in Fig. 1.28. The bolts which are not arrowed secure the oil pump in position.

27   Remove the timing cover by tapping it off with a plastic faced mallet.

28   Remove the timing chain together with the camshaft sprocket.

29   If necessary, the crankshaft sprocket and oil pump drive can be withdrawn using a two-legged extractor.

30   Unbolt and remove the chain tensioner and guides.

Pistons and connecting rods

31   *If the engine is still in position in the vehicle,* remove the cylinder head and sump as previously described.

32   Carefully scrape away any wear ridge from around the tops of the cylinder bores. If this is not done, the piston rings or piston itself could be damaged during removal from the top of the cylinder block.

33   Unbolt and remove the oil pick-up tube/filter screen.

34   Repeat the operations described in Section 10, paragraphs 31 and 32.

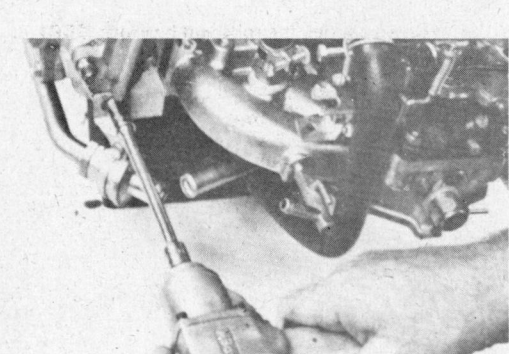

Fig. 1.23. Removing EGR valve (20R)

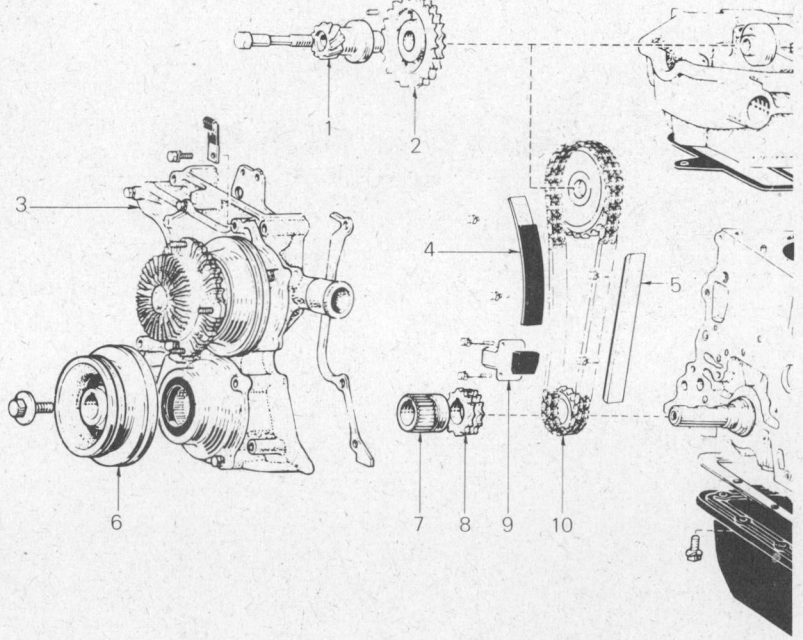

Fig. 1.25. Timing gear and associated parts (20R)

1	Distributor drive gear	6	Crankshaft pulley
2	Cam sprocket	7	Pump drive spline
3	Chain cover assembly	8	Crankshaft sprocket
4	Damper No. 2	9	Chain tensioner
5	Damper No. 1	10	Chain

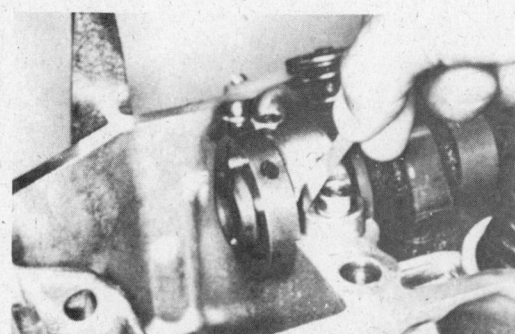

Fig. 1.24. Measuring camshaft sprocket (20R)

Fig. 1.26. Removing water pump bypass tube bolts (20R)

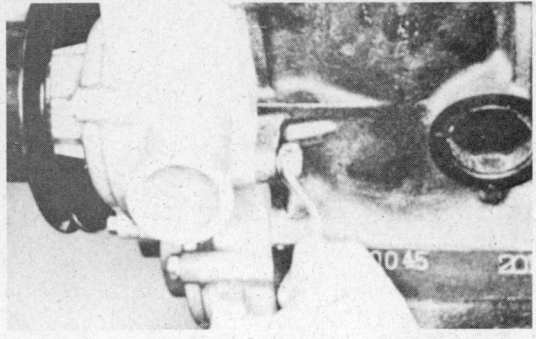

Fig. 1.27. Removing single bolt from timing cover (20R)

Fig. 1.28. Removing the cover bolt (arrowed) - (20R)

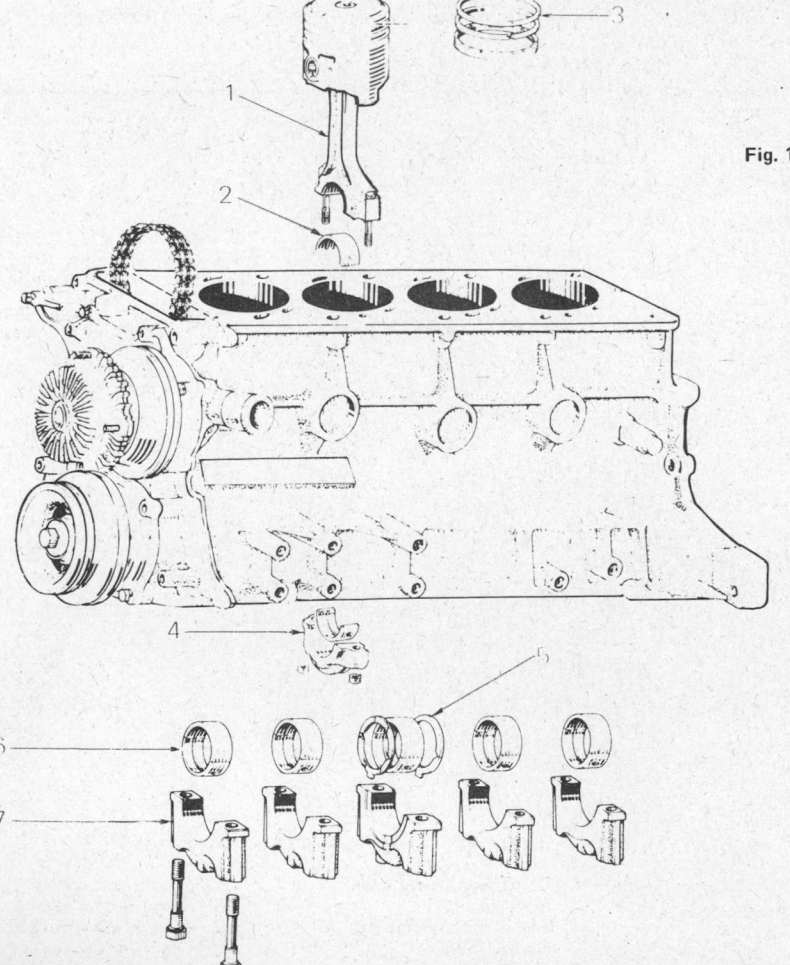

Fig. 1.29. Pistons, connecting rods and bearings (20R)

1   Connecting rod and piston
2   Rod bearing
3   Piston rings
4   Rod cap
5   Thrust bearing
6   Main bearing
7   Main bearing cap

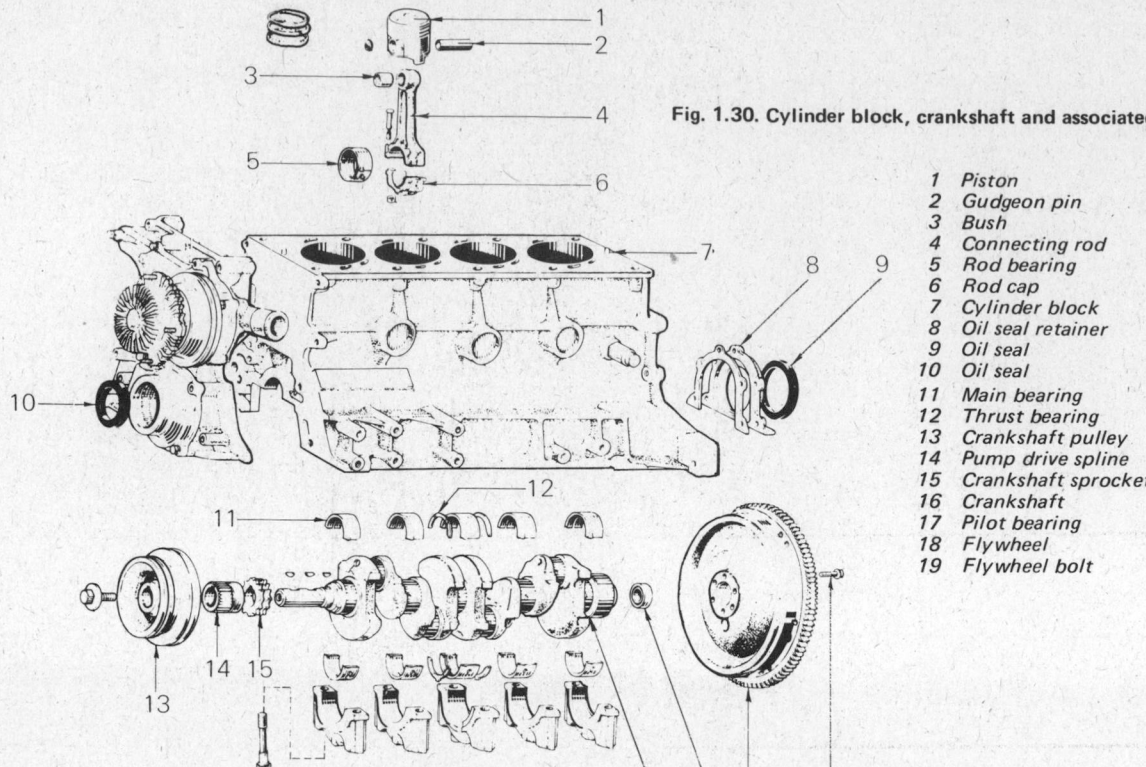

Fig. 1.30. Cylinder block, crankshaft and associated parts (20R)

1 Piston
2 Gudgeon pin
3 Bush
4 Connecting rod
5 Rod bearing
6 Rod cap
7 Cylinder block
8 Oil seal retainer
9 Oil seal
10 Oil seal
11 Main bearing
12 Thrust bearing
13 Crankshaft pulley
14 Pump drive spline
15 Crankshaft sprocket
16 Crankshaft
17 Pilot bearing
18 Flywheel
19 Flywheel bolt

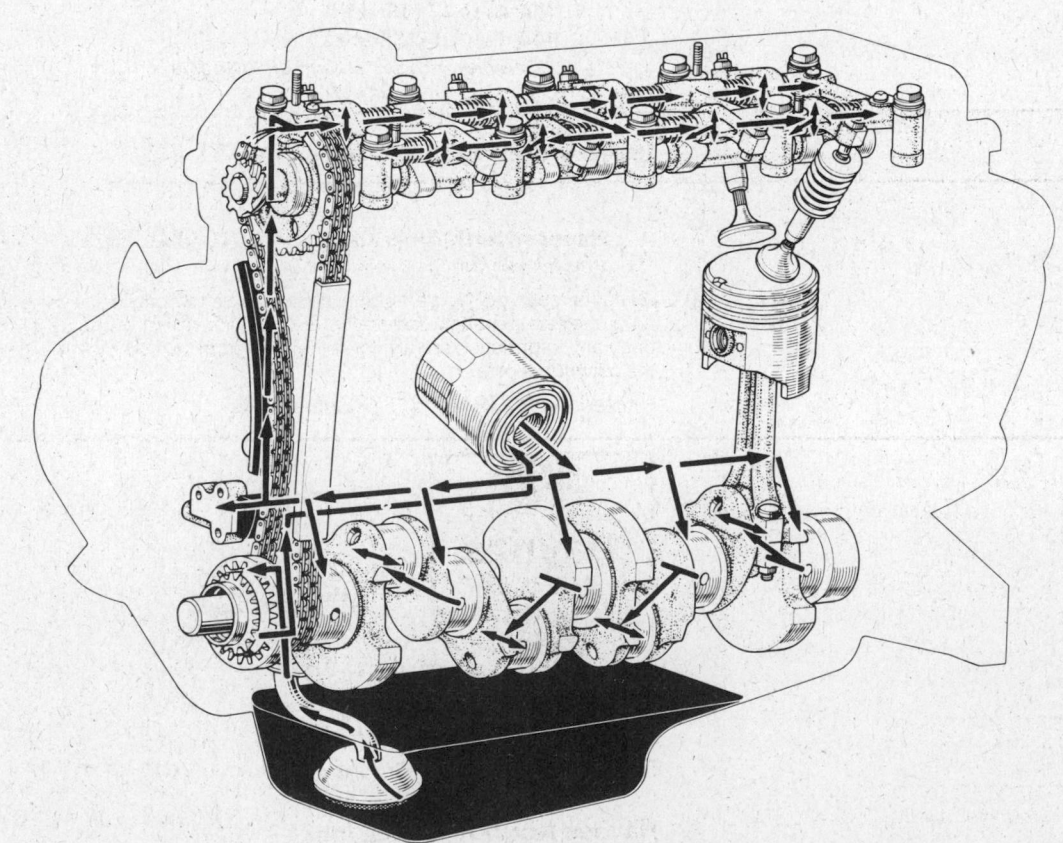

Fig. 1.31. Engine lubrication system (20R)

Piston rings and gudgeon pins

35 Repeat the dismantling operations described in Section 10, paragraphs 33 to 36 inclusive.

Crankshaft and main bearings

36 Repeat the dismantling operations described in Section 10, paragraphs 37 to 40.

---

14 Lubrication system, oil pump and filter (20R engine)

1 Pressure for the engine lubrication system is generated by a gear type oil pump located on the front end of the crankshaft just behind the crankshaft pulley.

2 The pressurised oil is first passed through an externally mounted, cartridge type disposable oil filter, then to all the bearings and friction surfaces of the engine. Excess oil pressure is controlled by an integral relief valve within the pump. Oil pressure also actuates the timing chain tensioner.

3 The oil pump normally has a very long life but in the event of low oil pressure being observed (not due to worn bearings or low oil level), remove the oil pump for servicing.

4 Remove the sump and oil pick-up tube/strainer.

5 Remove the drivebelts from the crankshaft pulley and withdraw the pulley.

6 Unbolt and remove the oil pump. Pick out the sealing O-ring.

7 Withdraw the pump drive gear from the front end of the crankshaft.

8 Unscrew and remove the relief valve components and then withdraw the inner and outer gears from the pump body.

9 Clean and inspect all components for damage.

10 Using a feeler blade, check the clearance between the outer gear and the pump body. This should not exceed 0.008 in (0.2 mm) otherwise renew one or both components.

11 Now measure the tip to crescent clearance between the gears which should not exceed 0.012 in (0.3 mm), when all gears are in position within the pump body.

12 Using a straight-edge and a feeler blade, measure the gear endfloat within the pump body. This should not exceed 0.0059 in (0.15 mm).

13 Renew the oil seal if there have been signs of oil seepage from this part of the engine. Drive out the defective seal with a piece of tubing and refit the new one in the same way.

14 Reassembly is a reversal of dismantling but make sure that the punch marks are visible when the gears are refitted.

15 When refitting the oil pump, renew the O-ring and apply jointing compound to the threads of the uppermost securing bolt.

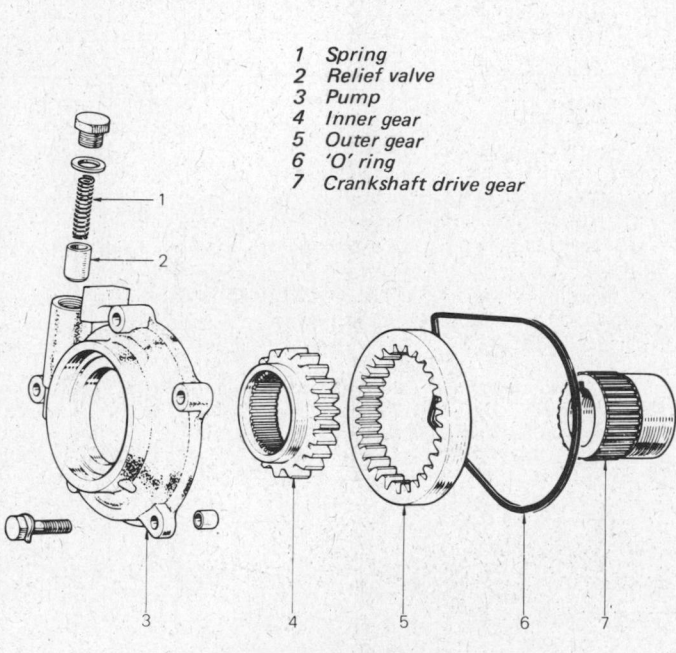

1 Spring
2 Relief valve
3 Pump
4 Inner gear
5 Outer gear
6 'O' ring
7 Crankshaft drive gear

Fig. 1.32. Oil pump parts (20R)

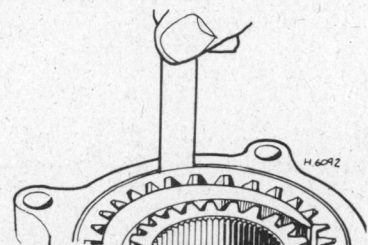

Fig. 1.33. Checking oil pump outer gear clearance (20R)

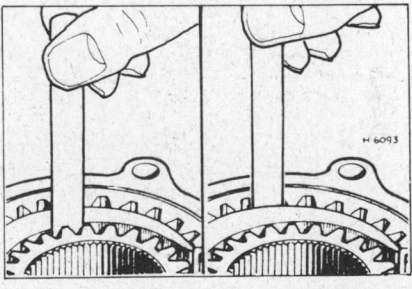

Fig. 1.34. Checking tip to crescent clearances (20R)

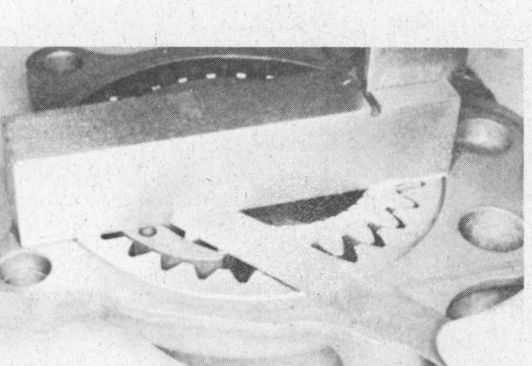

Fig. 1.35. Checking oil pump gear endfloat (20R)

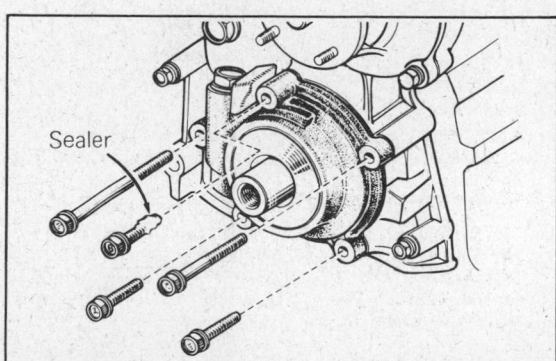

Sealer

Fig. 1.36. Oil pump securing bolts (20R)

15 Crankcase ventilation system (20R engine)

1   Refer to Section 12 but note the difference in layout of the system on this engine.

16 Examination and renovation - general

With the engine stripped down and all parts thoroughly cleaned, it is now time to examine everything for wear. The following items should be checked and where necessary renewed or renovated as described in the following Sections. The information applies to all engine types except where specifically annotated.

17 Crankshaft and main bearings - examination and renovation

1   Examine the crankpin and journal surfaces for signs of scoring or scratches. Check the ovality of the crankpins at several different positions using a micrometer. If more than 0.001 in (0.0254 mm) out of round, the crankshaft will have to be reground. Check the journals in the same manner.
2   If it is necessary to regrind the crankshaft and to fit new bearings, your Toyota dealer will decide how much to grind off and he will supply new oversize shell bearings to suit. Details of regrinding tolerances and bearings are given in the Specifications.
3   If the crankshaft is in good condition and requires no attention, it is always worthwhile renewing the bearing shells at the time of a major overhaul. Renew them with ones of the same size as the originals.
4   It is possible (although difficult, and not really recommended), to renew the main bearing shells while the engine is still in the car. To do this, remove the sump and then detach one of the main bearing caps.
5   Renew the bearing shell in the cap.
6   Insert a flat-headed screw in the crankshaft journal oil hole and carefully turn the crankshaft. The head of the screw will push the second bearing shell from its seat. Install the new shell in a similar way, having first oiled it liberally.
7   The crankshaft endfloat should be checked now by temporarily installing all the main bearing caps and shells and tightening to the specified torque.
8   Push and pull the crankshaft in both longitudinal directions and measure the total endfloat with feeler blades or a dial gauge. The endfloat should be as stated in the Specifications according to engine type.
9   Where the endfloat is incorrect, renew the centre main bearing shells which incorporate the thrust washers (18R engine). On 20R engine, semi-circular thrust washers are used (photo).
10 When carrying out the operations just described, make sure that the arrows on the main bearing caps point towards the front of the engine and that the caps and shells are located in their original sequence.
11 The clutch input shaft spigot bearing is located in the centre of the rear mounting flange of the crankshaft. Renew if worn, greasing its reverse side before fitting.

18 Connecting rods and bearings - examination and renovation

1   Big-end bearing failure is indicated by a knocking from within the crankcase and a slight drop in oil pressure.
2   Examine the big-end bearing surfaces for pitting and scoring. Renew the shells in accordance with the sizes specified in the Specifications. Where the crankshaft has been reground, the correct oversize big-end shell bearings will be supplied by the engineer (photo).
3   Fit each connecting rod to its respective crankpin and, using a feeler blade, check the side-float. If this exceeds the tolerance specified in the Specifications, the connecting rod will have to be renewed.
4   Check each small-end bush for wear or scoring. Each gudgeon pin should be a push fit in its bush using thumb pressure only. If the bush is worn it will have to be pressed out and a new one fitted, ensuring that the oil holes of the bush and the connecting rod coincide. As the bush will have to be reamed after fitting, this is probably a job best left to your Toyota dealer.

19 Cylinder bores - examination and renovation

1   The cylinder bores must be examined for taper, ovality, scoring and scratches. Start by carefully examining the top of the cylinder bores. If they are at all worn, a very slight ridge will be found on the thrust side. This marks the top of the piston ring travel. The owner will have a good indication of the bore wear prior to dismantling the engine, or removing the cylinder head. Excessive oil consumption accompanied by blue smoke from the exhaust is a sure sign of worn cylinder bores and piston rings.
2   Measure the bore diameter just under the ridge with a micrometer and compare it with the diameter at the bottom of the bore, which is not subject to wear. If the difference between the two measurements is more than 0.008 in (0.2 mm) then it will be necessary to fit special pistons and rings or to have the cylinder rebored and fit oversize pistons. If no micrometer is available remove the rings from a piston and place the piston in each bore in turn about halfway down the bore. If a 0.0012 in (0.03 mm) feeler gauge, slid between the piston and cylinder wall, requires less than a pull of between 2.2 and 5.5 lbs (1.0 and 2.5 kg) to withdraw it, using a spring balance, then remedial action must be taken. Oversize pistons are available as listed in the Specifications.
3   These are accurately machined to just below the indicated measurements so as to provide correct running clearances, in bores taken out to the exact oversize dimensions.
4   If the bores are slightly worn, but not so badly worn as to justify reboring them, then special oil control rings and pistons can be fitted which will restore compression and stop the engine burning oil. Several different types are available and the manufacturer's instructions concerning their fitting must be followed closely.
5   If new pistons or rings are being fitted and the bores have not been reground, it is essential to slightly roughen the hard glaze on the sides of the bores with fine glass paper so the new piston rings will have a chance to bed in properly.
6   If the cylinder bores have been bored out beyond the limit so that the maximum oversize pistons available cannot be fitted, then sleeves can be supplied which after fitting and boring will accept standard sized pistons. This again is a job for your Toyota dealer or motor engineering works.

20 Pistons and piston rings - examination and renovation

1   If the original pistons are to be refitted, carefully remove the piston rings as described in Section 10, paragraph 30 onwards.
2   Clean the grooves and rings free from carbon, taking care not to scratch the aluminium surfaces of the pistons.
3   If new rings are to be fitted, then order the top compression ring to be stepped to prevent it impinging on the 'wear ring' which will almost certainly have been formed at the top of the cylinder bore.
4   Before fitting the rings to the pistons, push each ring in turn down to the bottom of its respective cylinder bore (use an inverted piston to do this so that the ring is kept square in its bore) and then measure the piston ring end gap. This should be as shown in the Specifications. If the gap is incorrect, carefully grind the ends of the ring.
5   Now test each ring in its groove in the piston for side clearance using a feeler blade. If the clearance exceeds that specified, renew the piston as it will be the groove that is worn.
6   Where necessary a piston ring which is slightly tight in its groove may be rubbed down holding it perfectly squarely on an oilstone or a sheet of fine emery cloth laid on a piece of plate glass. Excessive tightness can only be rectified by having the grooves machined out.
7   The gudgeon pin should be a push fit into the piston when heated in water to a temperature of 140°F (60°C). If it appears slack, then both the piston and gudgeon pin should be renewed.

21 Camshaft and camshaft bearings - examination and renovation

18R engines
1   Check the camshaft journals for scoring or grooves and then measure each journal at several different points to detect any taper or out of round. If the difference between the measurements exceeds 0.0004 in (0.01 mm) the camshaft must be reground and oversize shell bearings

fitted. This is a job for your Toyota dealer.

2   With the camshaft on the cylinder head complete with shell bearings and caps and the cap bolts tightened as specified, check the camshaft endfloat. This should be as shown in the Specifications, otherwise renew the bearing shell which incorporates the thrust flanges.

3   Firstly examine the camshaft lobes for scoring or wear. Using a micrometer, check the overall lengths of the inlet and exhaust valve cam lobes and compare them with those specified. If they are worn, renew the camshaft complete.

20R engines

4   Check the camshaft for wear, as described in the preceding paragraphs but where bearing running clearance or camshaft endfloat is found to be excessive, then the cylinder head will have to be renewed

as the camshaft runs directly in bearings and caps which are in-line machined, no detachable bearing shells are fitted.

22 Timing components - examination and renovation

1   Examine all the sprocket teeth for wear or 'hooked' appearance and renew if necessary.

2   Wash the timing chains thoroughly in paraffin and examine for wear or stretch. If the chain is supported at both ends so that the rollers are vertical then a worn chain will take on a deeply bowed appearance while an unworn one will dip slightly at its centre point.

3   Check the chain tensioners and guides for wear, and renew the slippers if they are cut or grooved.

17.9 Centre main bearing shell incorporating thrust washer (18R)

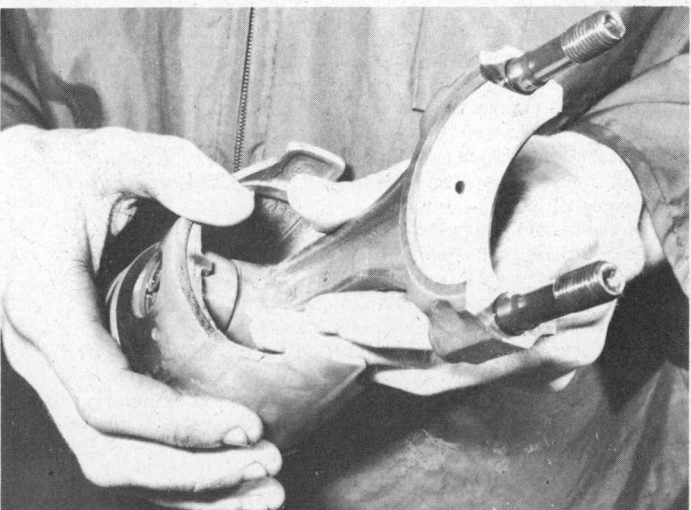

18.2 Big end bearing shell and oil hole (18R)

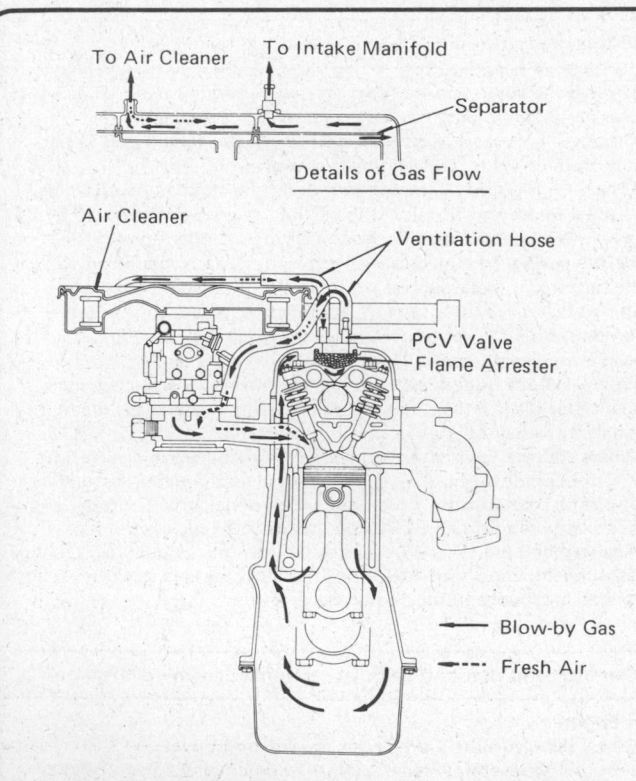

Fig. 1.37. Positive crankcase ventilation system (20R)

To Air Cleaner
To Intake Manifold
Separator
Details of Gas Flow
Air Cleaner
Ventilation Hose
PCV Valve
Flame Arrester
Blow-by Gas
Fresh Air

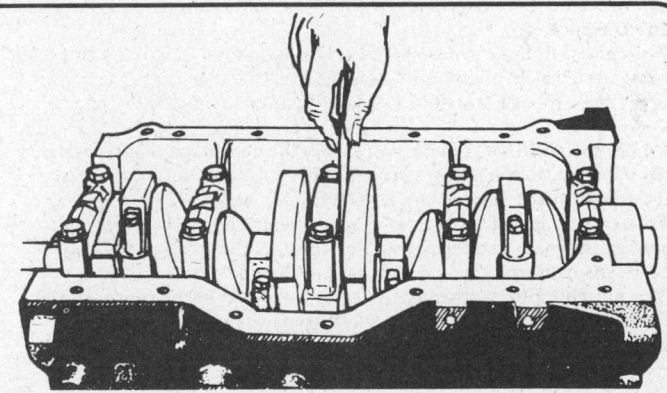

Fig. 1.38. Measuring crankshaft endfloat - typical

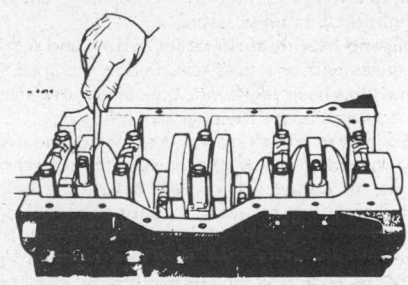

Fig. 1.39. Measuring connecting rod sidefloat - typical

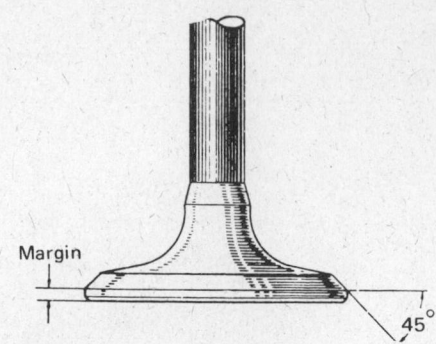

Fig. 1.40. Valve margin measurement

Margin

45°

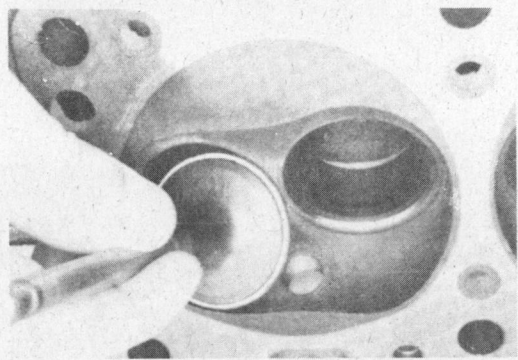

Fig. 1.41. Valve seating contact area

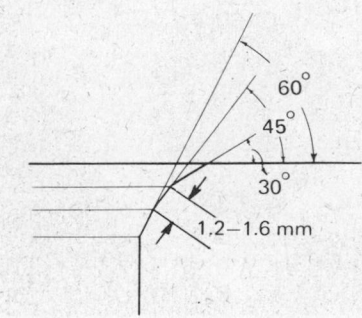

60°
45°
30°
1.2 – 1.6 mm

Fig. 1.42. Valve seat correction angles (18R)

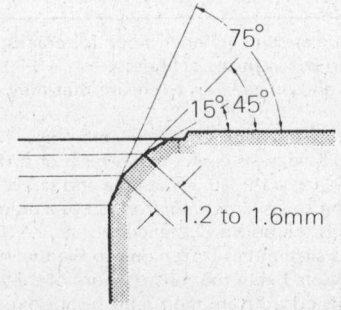

75°
15° 45°
1.2 to 1.6mm

Fig. 1.43. Valve seat correction angles (20R)

23 Cylinder head and valves - examination, renovation and decarbonising

1   Examine the heads of the valves for pitting and burning, especially the heads of the exhaust valves. The valve seatings should be examined at the same time. If the pitting on valve and seat is very slight the marks can be removed by grinding the seats and valves together with coarse, and then fine, valve grinding paste.

2   Where bad pitting has occurred to the valve seats, it will be necessary to recut them and fit new valves. In practice, it is very seldom that the seats are so badly worn that they require renewal. Normally, it is the valve that is too badly worn to use again, and the owner can easily purchase a new set of valves and match them to the seats by grinding. Where the seat has to be recut, a 45° cutter should be used, and only the minimum amount of metal removed to provide a satisfactory finish. Ensure that the valve margin (see Fig. 1.40) is not less than 0.024 in (0.6 mm), then apply a little prussian blue to the valve seating surfaces and check the contact area. The seat contact should be in the middle of the valve face with a width of 0.047 to 0.063 in (1.2 to 1.6 mm). If the seating is too high, a 15° or 30° and 45° cutter should be used to correct it; if the seating is too low, a 75° or 60° and 45° cutter should be used to correct it (see Figs. 1.42 and 1.43).

3   Valve grinding where the seats do not have to be recut, is carried out as follows: Smear a trace of coarse carborundum paste on the seat face and apply a suction grinder tool to the valve head. With a semi-rotary motion, grind the valve head to its seat, lifting the valve occasionally to redistribute the grinding paste. When a dull matt, even surface finish is produced on both the valve seat and the valve, wipe off the paste and repeat the process with fine carborundum paste, lifting and turning the valve to distribute the paste as before. A light spring placed under the valve head will greatly ease this operation. When a smooth unbroken ring of light grey matt finish is produced, on both valve and valve seat faces, the grinding operation is complete.

4   Scrape away all carbon from the valve head and the valve stem. Carefully clean away every trace of grinding compound, taking care to leave none in the ports or in the valve guides. Clean the valves and valve seats with a paraffin soaked rag then with a dry rag, and finally, if an air line is available, blow the valves, valve guides and valve ports clean.

5   Wear in the valve guides can best be checked by inserting a new valve and testing for rocking movement in all directions. The clearance between the guide and valve stem must not exceed that shown in the Specifications.

6   To renew a valve guide, first check whether the existing one has a snap-ring retaining it. Where this is so, use a hammer and a brass drift to snap the valve guide off, then drive out the remaining part.

7   Where there is no snap-ring, drive out the valve guide with a suitable drift.

8   All new valve guides have snap-rings, and the guide is simply driven in until the snap-ring locates in the groove. The guide must now be reamed to obtain the specified clearance.

9   The valve springs should be compared with their specified free lengths. Renew the springs as a set if they differ from their specified new length or have been in operation for more than 24000 miles (38000 km). Always renew the valve stem oil seals.

10 With the cylinder head removed, use a blunt scraper to remove all trace of carbon and deposits from the combustion spaces and ports. Scrape the cylinder head free from scale or old pieces of gasket or jointing compound. Clean the cylinder head by washing it in paraffin, and take particular care to pull a piece of rag through the ports and cylinder head bolt holes. Any grit remaining in these recesses may well drop onto the gasket or cylinder block mating surface as the cylinder head is lowered in position and could lead to a gasket leak after reassembly is complete.

11 With the cylinder head clean, test for distortion if a history of coolant leakage has been apparent. Carry out this test using a straight edge and feeler gauges or a piece of plate glass. If the surface shows any warping in excess of 0.002 in (0.05 mm), then the cylinder head will have to be resurfaced which is a job for a specialist engineering company.

12 Clean the piston and top of the cylinder bores. If the pistons are still in the block, then it is essential that great care is taken to ensure that no carbon gets into the cylinder bores, as this could scratch the cylinder walls or cause damage to the piston and rings. To ensure this does not happen, first turn the crankshaft so that two of the pistons

are at the top of their bores. Stuff a rag into the other two bores or seal them off with paper and masking tape. The waterways should also be covered with small pieces of masking tape to prevent particles of carbon entering the cooling system and damaging the water pump.

13 Press a little grease into the gap between the cylinder walls and the two pistons which are to be worked on. With a blunt scraper carefully scrape away the carbon from the piston crown, taking great care not to scratch the aluminium. Also scrape away the carbon from the surrounding lip of the cylinder wall. When all carbon has been removed, scrape away the grease which will now be contaminated with carbon particles, taking care not to press any into the bores. To assist prevention of carbon build-up the piston crown can be polished with a metal polish. Remove the rags or masking tape from the other two cylinders and turn the crankshaft so that the two pistons which were at the bottom are now at the top. Place a rag or masking tape in the cylinders which have been decarbonised and proceed as just described.

24 Oil pump driveshaft (18R engine) - servicing

1 The oil pump driveshaft bearings should be inspected for scoring or scratches.
2 The correct running clearances between the shaft and bearings is between 0.0010 and 0.0026 in (0.025 and 0.066 mm). Where the clearance exceeds 0.003 in (0.08 mm) the bearings must be renewed.
3 To do this, remove the plug at the back of the rear shaft bearing and using a suitably stepped mandrel, drive out the old and insert the new bearings.
4 Check the endfloat of the driveshaft; this must not exceed 0.012 in (0.03 mm). If it does, renew the thrust plate to provide the standard endfloat of between 0.002 and 0.005 in (0.06 and 0.13 mm).

25 Flywheel - servicing

1 Examine the clutch driven plate contact surface of the flywheel for scoring or grooves. If they are deep or tiny cracks are visible, it is recommended that the flywheel is renewed.
2 Check the starter ring gear for cracks or chipped teeth.
3 If the ring gear is damaged on a 20R engine, the flywheel must be renewed.
4 If the ring gear is damaged on an 18R engine, either obtain a replacement flywheel complete with ring gear, or proceed as follows:
5 Either split the ring with a cold chisel after making a cut with a hacksaw blade between two teeth, or use a soft headed hammer (not steel) to knock the ring off, striking it evenly and alternately at equally spaced points. Take great care not to damage the flywheel during this process.
6 Heat the new ring in either an electric oven to about 200°C (392°F) or immerse in a pan of boiling oil.
7 Hold the ring at this temperature for five minutes and then quickly fit it to the flywheel so the chamfered portion of the teeth faces the gearbox side of the flywheel.
8 The ring should be tapped gently down onto its register and left to cool naturally when the contraction of the metal on cooling will ensure that it is a secure and permanent fit. Great care must be taken not to overheat the ring (indicated by the ring turning light metallic blue) as if this happens the temper of the ring will be lost.

26 Driveplate (automatic transmission) - servicing

1 Examine the starter ring gear for worn or broken teeth; where these are evident, renew the driveplate complete.
2 Check the torque converter securing bolt holes for elongation and if apparent, renew the driveplate.

27 Oil seals - renewal

1 During a major overhaul, always discard the old oil seals and fit new ones during reassembly.
2 Renew the timing cover and crankshaft rear oil seals on 18R engines. Renew the oil pump oil seal and crankshaft rear oil seal on 20R engines (photo).

Fig. 1.44. Removing a valve guide - typical

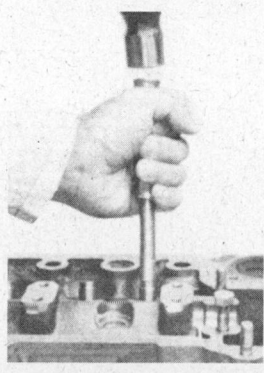

Fig. 1.45. Fitting a valve guide - typical

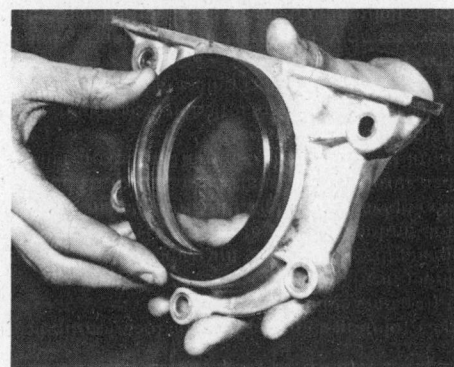

27.2 Installing the crankshaft rear oil seal retainer (18R)

28 Cylinder block - examination and renovation

1 Examine the crankcase and cylinder block for cracks, especially around bolt holes and between the cylinders.
2 Probe waterways and oil galleries to ensure that they are not blocked.
3 Check the security and condition of the core plugs. To renew a core plug, first drill a hole in its centre and lever it out. If it is particularly stubborn, tap a thread in the hole and screw in a bolt, using a piece of tubing and a large washer to act as a point of leverage and extract the plug as the bolt is tightened.
4 Where the cooling system has frozen due to the use of a weak anti-freeze mixture, it is quite likely that one or more of the core plugs will have been partially dislodged from their seats by the expansion of the ice. In such an event, drive the plug fully home or better still, renew it. The engine side cover can be removed to gain access to the threaded type core plug located behind the oil pump driveshaft on 18R engines.

Fig. 1.46. Tightening order for main bearing caps (20R)

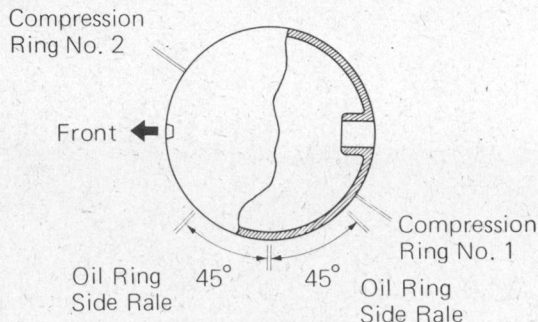

Fig. 1.47. Correct position of piston rings (18R)

Fig. 1.48. Timing marks aligned in chain (18R)

Fig. 1.49. Installing the lower chain (18R)

29 Engine reassembly - general

1   To ensure maximum life with minimum trouble from a rebuilt engine, not only must everything be correctly assembled but everything must be spotlessly clean, all the oilways must be clear, locking washers and spring washers must always be fitted where indicated and all bearing and other working surfaces must be thoroughly lubricated during assembly.

2   Before assembly begins renew any bolts or studs, the threads of which are in any way damaged and whenever possible use new spring washers.

3   Apart from your normal tools, a supply of clean rags, an oil can filled with engine oil, a new supply of assorted spring washers, a set of new gaskets and a torque spanner, should be collected together.

30 Engine reassembly (18R engine)

Crankshaft and main bearings

1   Locate the main bearing shells in their crankcase recesses and lubricate them with engine oil (photo).

2   Carefully lower the crankshaft into position.

3   Fit the main bearing caps complete with shell bearings, noting that the caps (previously numbered 1 to 5) should have their arrows pointing towards the front of the engine (photo).

4   Note that the centre bearing incorporates the thrust washers (photos).

5   Tighten the main bearing cap bolts to the specified torque in two stages in the order shown in Fig. 1.46 (photo).

6   Bolt on the crankshaft rear oil seal retainer complete with new seal and gasket (photos). Tighten the securing bolts to the specified torque. Check that the crankshaft turns freely.

Pistons, rings and connecting rods

7   Assemble the piston to the connecting rod so that the marks on the connecting rod and the piston crown are in alignment. These marks face the front of the engine when fitted.

8   Connect the two components by pushing in the gudgeon pin by thumb pressure only (immerse the piston in hot water if necessary). Fit new circlips, one at each end of the gudgeon pin.

9   Fit the rings to the pistons, using the same method as for removal. It is vital that the rings are fitted in the correct order with their tapers running the correct way. This will be achieved if the ring markings face upwards. Stagger the piston ring gaps as indicated in Fig. 1.47.

10 Lubricate the piston rings liberally and the piston bore, fit a piston ring compressor to the piston and place the assembly into a cylinder bore until the ring compressor meets the block surface. Using the handle of a hammer, tap the piston/connecting rod assembly into the cylinder bore **so that the directional mark on the piston crown is towards the front of the engine** (photo).

11 Rotate the crankshaft so that the crankpin is at the lowest point, engage the connecting rod big-end with the crankpin and then fit the big-end bearing cap so that the marks made prior to dismantling on the rod and cap are adjacent and on the same side (photo).

12 Tighten the big-end cap nuts to the specified torque.

13 Repeat the procedure with the other three piston/connecting rod assemblies, then check that the crankshaft turns smoothly.

Oil pump and timing gear

14 Fit the oil pump to the crankcase using a new joint gasket (photo).

15 Fit the front plate complete with new gasket, and secure it with the single bolt which is adjacent to the oil pump driveshaft hole (photo).

16 Insert the oil pump driveshaft and the thrust plate, tightening to the specified torque.

17 Fit the lower chain tensioner, so that the projection on the slipper is visible when fitted. Also fit the lower chain damper (photo).

18 Rotate the crankshaft and oil pump driveshaft so that their keyways are both pointing towards the top (cylinder head) face of the block. Check that the keys are in position.

19 Locate the crankshaft and oil pump driveshaft sprockets inside the run of the chain so that the timing marks are aligned as shown in Fig. 1.48, then carefully fit the assembly. Don't use too much force tapping on the oil pump driveshaft sprocket or the rear plug in the block may be forced out.

20 Fit the timing cover gasket, sticking it in position with jointing

30.1 Lubricating main bearing shells (18R)

30.3 Main bearing cap directional mark and arrow (18R)

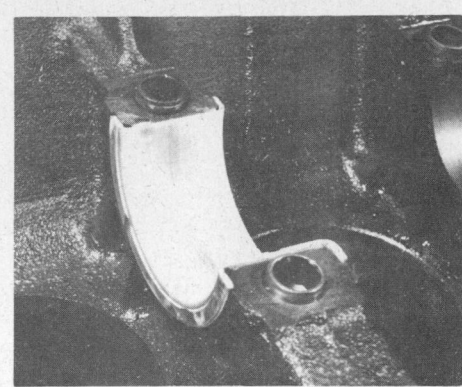
30.4 Centre main bearing shell (18R)

30.5 Tightening main bearing bolt (18R)

30.6a Crankshaft rear oil seal retainer gasket (18R)

30.6b Installing rear oil seal retainer (18R)

30.10. Installing piston (18R)

30.11 Installing a big end cap (18R)

30.14 Installing oil pump (18R)

30.15 Installing front plate and gasket (18R)

30.17 Timing chain lower tensioner (18R)

30.22 Tightening camshaft drive sprocket (18R)

30.27 Fitting rear plate to engine (18R)

30.28 Tightening flywheel bolts (18R)

30.31 Installing sump (18R)

30.33 Installing valve springs (18R)

30.34 Valve assembly correctly installed (18R)

30.39 Cylinder head gasket in position (18R)

30.45 Camshaft bearing cap in position (18R)

30.51 Installing the rocker shaft assembly (18R)

Fig. 1.50. No. 2 chain aligned on sprocket (18R)

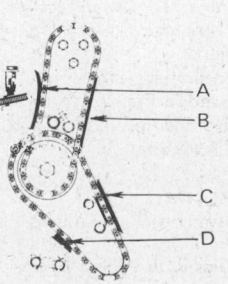

Fig. 1.51. Timing chains correctly installed (18R)

A Upper (No. 2) tensioner slipper   C Lower (No. 1) damper
B Upper (No. 2) damper   D Lower (No. 1) tensioner

compound.

21 Fit the upper chain damper and oil jet bolt ensuring it is correctly located, and the slipper.

22 Fit the camshaft drive sprocket to the oil pump driveshaft and tighten the retaining bolt to the specified torque. Use a wooden bar to wedge the crankshaft against the crankcase to prevent it from rotating (photo).

23 Position the camshaft drive chain on the oil pump driveshaft sprocket so that the two bright links are as shown in Fig. 1.50, then fit the sprocket to the shaft. If the engine is in the car, or the correct way up, use a hooked piece of wire to keep the chain engaged with the sprocket teeth pending fitting the timing cover and cylinder head.

24 Fit the timing cover, using gasket cement on its mating faces and on the right-hand upper securing bolt. Tighten the timing cover bolts to the specified torque.

25 Fit the crankshaft pulley (a piece of tubing may be used to drive it into position). Tighten the pulley securing bolt, with its washer, to the specified torque.

26 Fit a new input shaft bearing at the rear end of the crankshaft.

Flywheel (or driveplate - automatic tranmission)

27 Bolt on the engine rear plate (photo).

28 Refitting either the flywheel or driveplate is the reverse of the removal procedure, but tighten the securing bolts to the specified torque, and bend up the tabs of the locking plates (photo).

Sump

29 Ensure that the mating faces of the sump and crankcase are quite clean and free from old pieces of gasket.

30 Smear the crankcase flange with jointing compound and stick a new gasket into position.

31 Smear the sump flange with jointing compound and bolt it into position. Do not overtighten the sump securing bolts (photo).

Cylinder head and valves

32 Install the first valve into its respective guide, having first lubricated its stem with engine oil.

33 Fit the valve stem washer, oil seal, double valve springs and cap. Note that the closer coils of the spring are fitted nearer the cylinder head (photo).

34 Fit the valve spring retainer, and then compress the valve springs with a compressor and fit the split collets. Gently release the compressor and check that the collets are correctly seated (photo).

35 Repeat the operations on the remaining valves making sure that each valve is returned to its original guide or, if a new valve has been fitted, into the seat into which it has been ground.

36 When all the valves have been reassembled into the cylinder head, tap the end of each valve stem using a block of hardwood and a hammer in order to settle the valve components.

37 Check that the surfaces of the cylinder head and block are scrupulously clean.

38 Smear the top of the block with a thin film of non-setting gasket cement, making sure that none runs down into the oil or water passages or the bolt holes.

39 Lay a new gasket carefully into position on the block (photo).

40 Smear the face of the cylinder head with a film of non-setting gasket cement and then lower the head straight down onto the block so that the positioning dowels engage first time. Do not slide the head about to position it as this will damage the gasket.

41 Make sure that the threads of the cylinder head bolts are clean and screw them in finger tight.

42 Tighten the bolts progressively (½ turn at a time) and in the reverse sequence to that indicated in Fig. 1.7 to the specified torque. The timing chain should have been pulled through the aperture in the cylinder head with the hooked wire.

Camshaft and rocker gear

43 Fit the camshaft lower bearing shells into their recesses on the top of the cylinder head.

44 Lubricate the bearings with engine oil and lower the camshaft into position.

45 Fit the bearing caps, complete with shell bearings. The caps should be numbered 1 to 4 (counting from the front of the engine) and the flat portion of their upper bosses must face the front (photo).

46 Tighten the camshaft bearing cap bolts to the specified torque.

47 Rotate the crankshaft by means of the pulley bolt until No. 1

piston is at tdc. This is indicated by the timing mark on the pulley and timing chain cover (refer to Chapter 3 if necessary).

48 Turn the camshaft so that the dowel pin and punch marks are uppermost. Pull the timing chain upwards with the hooked piece of wire previously used to retain it on its drive sprocket.

49 Engage the camshaft sprocket within the upper loop of the chain so that the timing marks are aligned as shown in Fig. 1.53, then fit the sprocket ensuring that the dowel engages in the sprocket hole.

50 Tighten the camshaft sprocket bolts to the specified torque.

51 Fit the rocker shaft assembly but make sure that each of the adjusting screws is backed off or damage may occur. If the rocker gear has been dismantled, refit the components in their original order and make sure that the rocker shaft support pillars have their front facing markings correctly set (photo).

52 Tighten the pillar bolts progressively and evenly to the specified torque in the order shown.

53 Ensure that the oilways in the oil feed pipe assembly are unobstructed, then locate the assembly correctly and tighten the bolts to the specified torque.

Fig. 1.52. Setting the crankshaft and camshaft to No. 1 TDC (18R)

Fig. 1.53. Upper chain correctly installed (18R)

Fig. 1.54. Tightening order for camshaft pillar bolts (18R)

31.3 Adjusting valve clearances (18R)

31.4 Installing the rocker cover

Fig. 1.55. Checking valves, 1, 2, 3 and 5 (18R)

Fig. 1.56. Checking valves, 4, 6, 7 and 8 (18R)

31 Valve clearances (18R engine) - adjustment

Note: Valve clearances should be adjusted when the engine is hot. Where the adjustment is made with a cold engine (eg, during rebuild), it must be checked again, after running up to normal operating temperature.

1   If the engine is in the car, it will be necessary to first remove the rocker cover. Take careful note of where any hoses and electrical connections are fitted. For information on removal of the air cleaner, refer to Chapter 3.

2   Rotate the crankshaft until the camshaft sprocket dowel hole and timing mark are uppermost. This sets No. 1 piston at tdc on its compression stroke, and allows valves Nos. 1, 2, 3 and 5 to be adjusted.

3   Select the appropriate size of feeler gauge (see Specifications) for the inlet valves (2, 3, 6 and 7) and the exhaust valves (1, 4, 5 and 8), and insert it between the end of the valve stem and the rocker arm. The feeler should be a firm sliding fit if the clearance is correct. To adjust, loosen the nut on the adjusting screw, then tighten or loosen the screw to obtain the correct clearance. Tighten the nut and recheck the clearance. Having adjusted the first four valves, the crankshaft can be rotated 360° and valves 4, 6, 7 and 8 adjusted (photo).

4   Refit the rocker cover using a new gasket, don't forget the semi-circular plugs at the front and rear of the block, if removed (photo).

5   If the engine is in the car, refit the ancillaries which had to be removed.

6   Where adjustment has been made with a cold engine, don't forget to check the settings after the engine has warmed up.

32 Engine reassembly (20R engine)

Crankshaft and main bearings

1   Carry out the operations described in Section 30, paragraphs 1 to 6.

Pistons, rings, connecting rods, sump and flywheel

2   Carry out the operations described in Section 30, paragraphs 7 to 13.

3   Fit the oil pick-up tube and screen, and the sump, using a new gasket and applying jointing compound to the covers as shown in Fig. 1.58.

4   Fit the flywheel (or driveplate - automatic transmission) and tighten the bolts to the specified torque.

Timing gear, chain and cover

5   Fit the chain guides and the chain tensioner.

6   Rotate the crankshaft until the Woodruff key at its front end is pointing upwards (ie, towards the cylinder head).

7   Engage the timing chain so that its single bright link is opposite the mark on the crankshaft sprocket (Fig. 1.59).

8   Engage the camshaft sprocket within the loop of the timing chain so that the mark on the sprocket is between the two bright links on the chain (Fig. 1.60).

9   Fit the oil pump drive gear onto the front end of the crankshaft.

10 Fit the timing cover gasket, and then gently turn the camshaft sprocket in an anticlockwise direction to remove any slack from the chain.

11 Fit the timing cover complete with oil pump onto the locating dowels; refit the bolts and tighten to the specified torque.

12 Fit the crankshaft pulley. When tightening the retaining bolt, do not turn the crankshaft but either jam one of the crankshaft webs with a block of wood or refit the flywheel and jam the starter ring gear.

Cylinder head

13 Refer to Section 30, paragraphs 32 to 36, but note that single valve springs are used on this engine.

14 Fit the camshaft and the bearing caps, in their correct sequence with arrows pointing to the front of the engine. Make sure that all the bearing surfaces are oiled before reassembly. Tighten the cap bolts to the specified torque wrench settings.

15 Fit the thermostatic valve, the inlet manifold, the EGR valve, the exhaust manifold, the heat insulator to the cylinder head.

16 Make sure that the surfaces of the cylinder head and block are

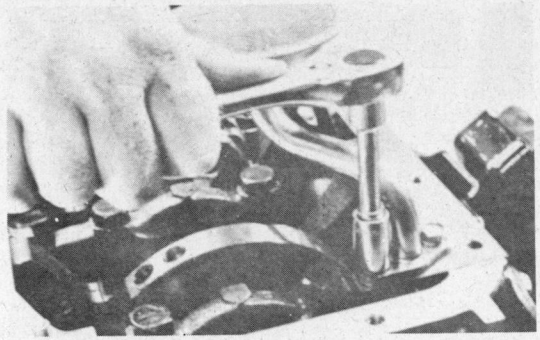

Fig. 1.57. Fitting oil pick-up tube and screen (20R)

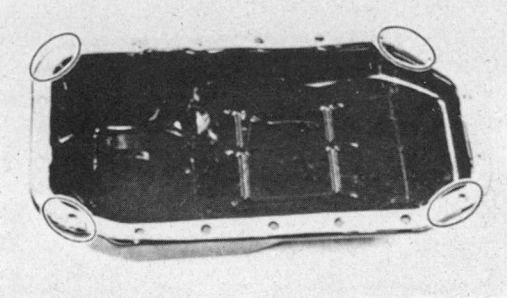

Fig. 1.58. Jointing compound application points (20R)

Fig. 1.59. Correct position of bright link on camshaft sprocket (20R)

Fig. 1.60. Correct position of bright links on camshaft sprocket (18R)

Fig. 1.61. Installing the oil pump drive gear (20R)

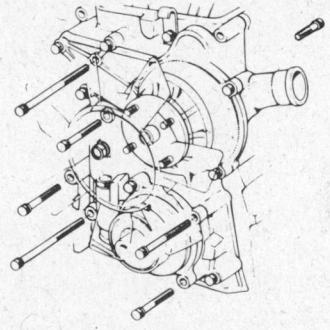

Fig. 1.62. Installing the timing cover (20R)

Fig. 1.63. Tightening a camshaft bearing cap

quite clean; smear jointing compound at the locations indicated in Fig. 1.64, then fit a new cylinder head gasket.

17 Fit the cylinder head onto its locating dowels.

18 Without moving the head, rotate the camshaft so that the dowel on its flange and the timing mark are at the top. This is No. 1 tdc.

19 Apply tension upwards to retain the timing chain and sprocket in engagement, then turn the crankshaft by means of its pulley retaining bolt until the hole in the camshaft sprocket is in alignment with the flange dowel on the camshaft.

20 If the rocker gear has been dismantled, reassemble it, making sure that the arrows on the shaft support pillars face towards the front of the engine when fitted.

21 Fit the rocker assembly, and insert the combined cylinder head/rocker pillar bolts, tightening them to the specified torque in the reverse sequence to that shown in Fig. 1.22.

22 Screw in the chain cover bolt (Fig. 1.21).

23 Fit the camshaft sprocket/chain assembly to the dowel on the camshaft flange, and then push on the distributor drive gear and tighten the securing bolt to the specified torque.

33 Valve clearances (20R engine) - adjustment

The procedure for valve clearance adjustment on the 20R engine is similar to that given for the 18R engine in Section 31. Fig. 1.67 shows the first four valves to be adjusted; Fig. 1.68 shows the second four valves to be adjusted. Note that no separate figures are given for a cold engine so the hot adjustment figures must be used.

34 Engine ancillary components - refitting

This is largely a reverse of the removal procedure, and will depend upon the particular engine model and market. Take your time over this to ensure that nothing is forgotten or incorrectly fitted.

Fig. 1.64. Jointing compound application points (20R)

Fig. 1.65. Camshaft set at No. 1 TDC (20R)

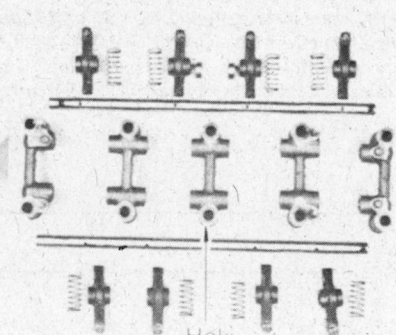

Fig. 1.66. Rocker assembly (20R)

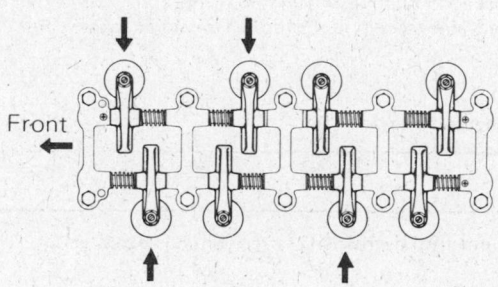

Fig. 1.67. First four valves to be adjusted (arrowed) - (20R)

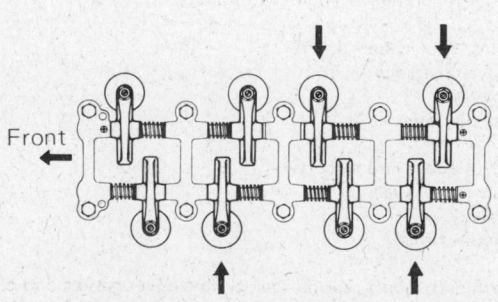

Fig. 1.68. Second four valves to be adjusted (arrowed) - (20R)

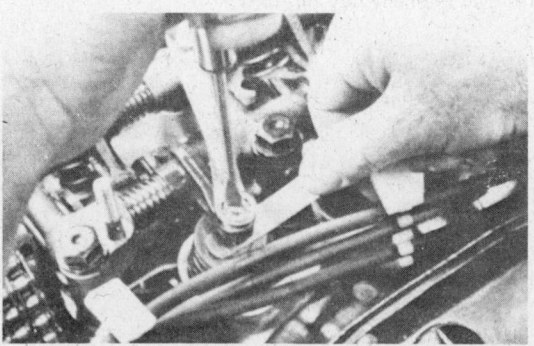

Fig. 1.69. Valve clearance adjustment (20R)

35 Engine to manual gearbox - reconnection

This is the reverse of the separation procedure - see Section 6.

36 Engine to automatic transmission - reconnection

1 This is the reverse of the separation procedure given in Section 7, but observe the following points:
2 Check that the two projections on the torque converter key with the slots in the transmission fluid pump impeller, particularly if the torque converter has been partially withdrawn during dismantling operations.
3 Make sure that the driveplate is bolted to the torque converter with the marks made prior to dismantling in alignment.
4 Tighten all bolts to the specified torque, and check the security of the transmission drain plug.

37 Engine/transmission - refitting

1 Locate slings or chains round the engine and support the weight of the combined unit on suitable lifting tackle. Where a fixed hoist is being used, raise the power unit and roll the car under it.
2 Lower the unit into the engine compartment ensuring that nothing fouls during the operation.
3 With the front engine mountings roughly aligned, jack-up the transmission so that the rear crossmember and mounting can be installed. Remove the jack.
4 With the hoist still supporting the weight of the engine, the engine/transmission can be moved fractionally so that the front mountings can be aligned and bolted up.
5 Refit the propeller shaft making sure that the rear driving flanges have their marks (made before dismantling) in alignment.
6 Reconnect the gearchange or selector mechanism according to transmission type.
7 Reconnect the speedometer cable to the transmission housing.
8 Reconnect the reverse light switch leads.
9 Reconnect the exhaust downpipe to the manifold and secure the support bracket to the transmission housing.
10 Reconnect the vacuum hoses to the emission control unit.

11 Reconnect the emission control electrical leads.
12 Reconnect the choke and throttle controls.
13 Reconnect all electrical leads.
14 Bolt the clutch slave cylinder to the bellhousing (manual gearbox).
15 Reconnect the brake servo pipe to the inlet manifold.
16 Reconnect the heater hoses.
17 Reconnect the fuel inlet pipe to the fuel pump.
18 Refit the air cleaner.
19 Refit the radiator and connect the top and bottom hoses.
20 On vehicles equipped with air conditioning, install the condenser in front of the radiator and reconnect the pipes and hoses both to the condenser and the compressor pump.
21 Check that any other item of equipment on your particular car have been, or can now be, refitted.
22 Refit the radiator grille, upper and lower shields and the fan shrouds.
23 Refit the bonnet.
24 Refill the cooling system.
25 Refill the engine with oil.
26 Refill the gearbox or automatic transmission unit.
27 Connect the lead to the battery negative terminal.

38 Initial start-up after major repair or overhaul

1 Start the engine and check for oil or water leaks. None should be apparent if new gaskets have been used throughout and the specified torque wrench settings adhered to.
2 Where an air conditioning system is installed, have the system professionally recharged with refrigerant gas.
3 Run the vehicle until normal operating temperature is reached and check the following:

   a) *Carburettor and emission control settings (Chapter 3).*
   b) *Ignition timing (Chapter 4).*
   c) *Check the torque of the cylinder head bolts (unscrew each bolt a quarter-turn and retighten to specified figure and in correct sequence). Check them again after 500 miles (800 km).*
   d) *Check the valve clearances (Section 31 or 33) but this time with the engine hot (refer to the Specifications for the limits).*
   e) *Recheck all oil levels and top-up the engine oil to make up for the amount absorbed by the new filter element.*

39 Fault diagnosis - engine

Symptom	Cause
Engine will not turn over when starter switch is operated	Flat battery. Bad battery connections. Bad connections at solenoid switch and/or starter motor. Starter motor jammed. Defective solenoid. Starter motor defective.
Engine turns over normally but fails to start	No spark at plugs. No fuel reaching engine. Too much fuel reaching the engine (flooding).
Engine starts but runs unevenly and misfires	Ignition and/or fuel system faults. Incorrect valve clearances. Burnt out valves. Worn out piston rings.
Lack of power	Ignition and/or fuel system faults. Incorrect valve clearances. Burnt out valves. Worn out piston rings.
Excessive oil consumption	Oil leaks from crankshaft rear oil seal, timing cover gasket and oil seal, rocker cover gasket, sump gasket, sump plug washer. Worn piston rings or cylinder bores resulting in oil being burnt by engine. Worn valve guides and/or defective valve stem seals.

Excessive mechanical noise from engine

Wrong valve to rocker clearances.
Worn crankshaft bearings.
Worn cylinders (piston slap).
Slack or worn timing chain and sprockets.

Poor idling.

Leak in inlet manifold gasket.
Perforated or leaking PCV connecting pipe.
Perforated or leaking brake servo pipe.

Note: *When investigating starting and uneven running faults, do not be tempted into snap diagnosis. Start from the beginning of the check procedure and follow it through. It will take less time in the long run. Poor performance from an engine in terms of power and economy is not normally diagnosed quickly. In any event, the ignition and fuel systems must be checked first before assuming any further investigation needs to be made.*

In addition to the foregoing, reference should also be made to the fault finding chart for emission control equipment which is to be found at the end of Chapter 3. Such a fault can have an immediate effect upon engine performance.

Chapter 2 Cooling System

Contents

Specifications

System type	Pressurized with radiator, water pump, thermostat and viscous-coupled fan
Coolant capacity	
18R and 20R engines	15 Imp pt/17 US pt (8 litres)
Radiator pressure cap setting	12.8 lbf/in^2 (0.9 kgf/cm^2)

Thermostat opening temperature	Starts to open	Fully open
18R engine, except USA	177/182ºF (80.5/83.5ºC)	203ºF (95ºC)
18RC engine, USA	188/193ºF (86.5/89.5ºC)	212ºF (100ºC)
20R engine	179.6ºF (82ºC)	203ºF (95ºC)

Thermostat travel	0.31 in 8.0 mm
Antifreeze type	Ethylene-glycol

1 General description

The cooling system comprises the radiator, top and bottom water hoses, water pump, cylinder head and block water jackets, radiator cap with pressure relief valve, and flow and return heater hoses. The thermostat is located in a recess at the front of the cylinder head. The principle of the system is, that cold water in the bottom of the radiator circulates upwards through the lower radiator hose to the water pump, where the pump impeller pushes the water round the cylinder block and head, through the various cast-in passages, to cool the cylinder bores, combustion surfaces and valve seats. When sufficient heat has been absorbed by the cooling water, and the engine has reached an efficient working temperature, the water moves from the cylinder head past the now open thermostat into the top radiator hose and into the radiator header tank.

The water then travels down the radiator tubes where it is rapidly cooled by the in-rush of air when the vehicle is in forward motion. A four bladed fan, mounted on the water pump pulley, assists this cooling action. The water, now cooled, reaches the bottom of the radiator and the cycle is repeated.

When the engine is cold the thermostat remains closed until the coolant reaches a pre-determined temperature (see Specifications).

This assists rapid warming-up.

On all models the fan is a variable speed type having a fluid coupling incorporated in the central hub. This allows the fan to run at a lower speed at high engine speeds, and thus reduces fan noise and power dissipation from the engine. Certain models have a 'tempered' cooling fan which additionally incorporates a bi-metal. This bi-metal opens and closes a valve in the fluid coupling according to the engine compartment temperature, and provides varying amounts of fan 'slip' to maintain optimum cooling efficiency.

The heater is supplied with hot water from the engine cooling system, and a water temperature transmitter unit and gauge or warning light are fitted.

2 Cooling system - draining

1 If the engine is cold remove the filler cap from the radiator by turning the cap anti-clockwise. If the engine is hot having just been run, then turn the filler cap very slightly until the pressure in the system has had time to disperse. Use a rag over the cap to protect your hand from escaping steam. If, with the engine very hot, the cap is released suddenly, the drop in pressure can result in the water boiling. With the pressure released the cap can be removed.

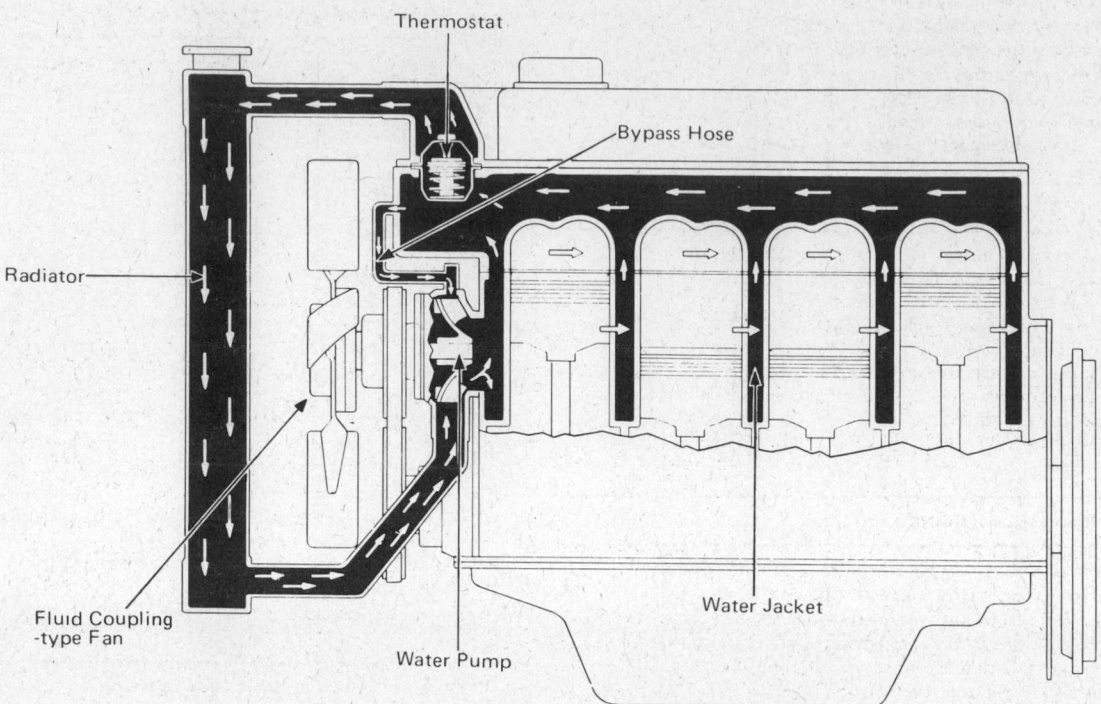

Fig 2.1. Cooling system schematic diagram - 18R engine

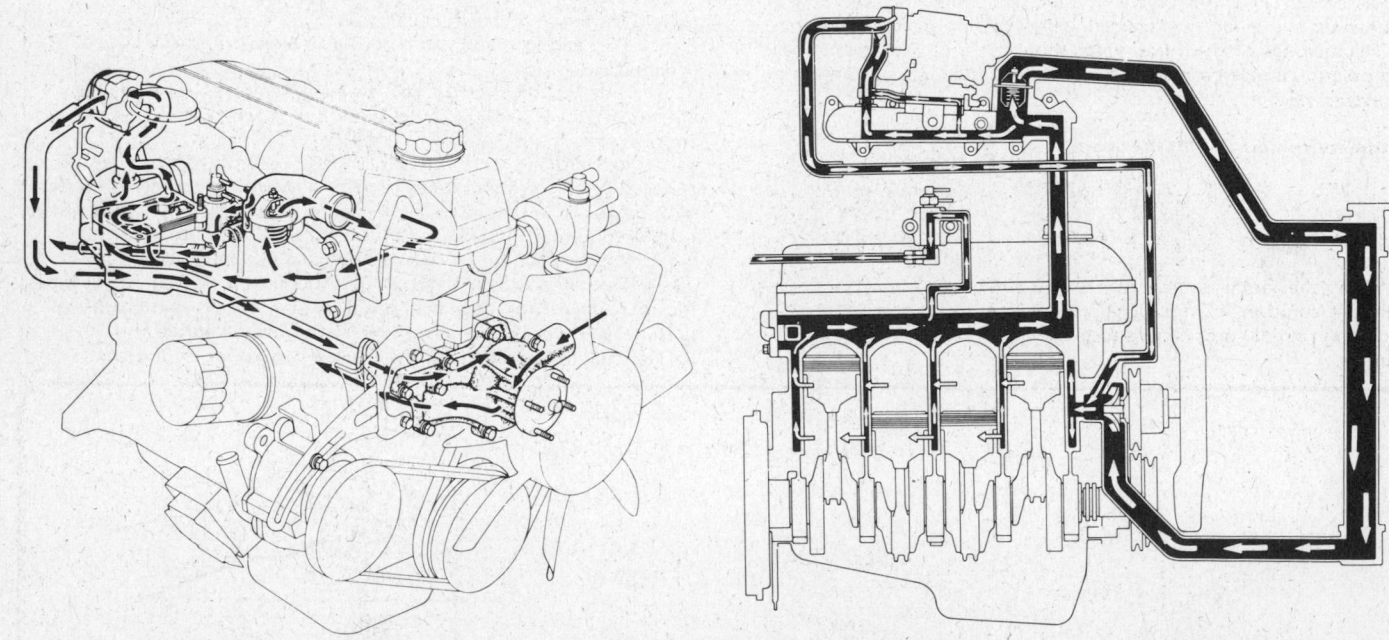

Fig. 2.2. Cooling system diagrams - 20R engine

2   Place the heater control in the 'HOT' position, and unscrew the radiator drain plug and the one on the left-hand side of the cylinder block. (If there is no radiator drain plug, remove the radiator bottom hose.)

3   Cooling system - flushing

1   The radiator and waterways in the engine after some time may become restricted or even blocked with scale or sediment which

reduces the efficiency of the cooling system. When this condition occurs or the coolant appears rusty or dark in colour the system should be flushed. In severe cases reverse flushing may be required as described later.

2   Place the heater controls to the 'HOT' position and unscrew fully the radiator and cylinder block drain taps.

3   Remove the radiator filler cap and place a hose in the filler neck. Allow water to run through the system until it emerges from both drain taps quite clear in colour. **Do not flush a hot engine with cold water.**

4 In severe cases of contamination of the coolant in the system, reverse flush by first removing the radiator cap and disconnecting the lower radiator hose at the radiator outlet pipe.

5 Remove the top hose at the radiator connection end and remove the radiator as described in Section 6.

6 Invert the radiator and place a hose in the bottom outlet pipe. Continue flushing until clear water comes from the radiator top tank.

4 Cooling system - filling

1 Place the heater control in the 'HOT' position and check that the radiator and cylinder block taps are closed. Pour coolant slowly into the radiator filler neck until it is full to the brim.

2 Run the engine at idling speed and watch the level of coolant at the filler neck drop, continuing to top up until the level no longer falls. Switch off the engine and refit the radiator pressure cap.

3 Remove the cap from the radiator reservoir tank and fill to the 'FULL' level with similar coolant.

4 Refit the reservoir cap.

5 Antifreeze and corrosion inhibiting mixtures

1 It is recommended that the system is filled with an antifreeze mixture. The system should be drained, flushed and refilled every alternate Autumn. The use of antifreeze solutions for periods of longer than two years is likely to cause damage and encourage the formation of rust and scale due to the corrosion inhibitors gradually losing their efficiency. If the use of antifreeze mixture is not necessary because of favourable climatic conditions, never use ordinary water but always fill the system with a corrosion inhibiting mixture of the recommended brand.

2 Before adding antifreeze to the system, check all hose connections and check the tightness of the cylinder head bolts as such solutions are searching. The cooling system should be drained and refilled with clean water as previously explained, before adding antifreeze.

3 The quantity of antifreeze which should be used for various levels of protection is given in the table below, expressed as a percentage of the system capacity.

Antifreeze volume	Protection to	Safe pump circulation
25%	−26°C (−15°F)	−12°C (10°F)
30%	−33°C (−28°F)	−16°C (3°F)
35%	−39°C (−38°F)	−20°C (−4°F)

4 Where the cooling system contains an antifreeze or corrosion inhibiting solution, any topping-up should be done with a solution made up in similar proportions to the original in order to avoid dilution.

6 Radiator - removal, inspection and refitting

Note: The procedure given may vary on some models according to the year of manufacture and operating territory.

1 Drain the engine coolant.

2 Remove the lower shield to gain access to the bottom hose clamps. Remove the fan shroud.

3 Disconnect the top and bottom radiator hoses.

4 Remove the reservoir (three bolts).

5 Unbolt the radiator and lift it from the engine compartment.

Note:

On vehicles equipped with automatic transmission, before the radiator can be removed, the oil cooler hoses will first have to be disconnected from the bottom of the unit.

On vehicles equipped with an air conditioning system, the condenser is mounted in front of the radiator; this must not be disconnected or damaged during the radiator removal operations.

6 Radiator repair is best left to a specialist (minor leaks may be temporarily rectified with a proprietary sealant, but this has to be done with the radiator fitted).

7 With the radiator removed, brush accumulations of flies and leaves from the fins, and examine and renew, if necessary, any hoses or clips which have deteriorated.

8 The radiator can be flushed as described in Section 3.

9 Check the pressure rating of the radiator cap and have its operation tested by a service station.

7 Thermostat - removal, testing and refitting

1 A faulty thermostat can cause overheating or slow engine warm-up. It will also affect the performance of the heater.

2 Drain enough coolant from the radiator so that the level is below the thermostat housing joint face. A good indication that the correct level has been reached is when the cooling tubes are exposed when viewed through the radiator filler cap.

3 On 20R engine models, remove the air cleaner (refer to Chapter 3 if necessary).

4 Unscrew and remove the two retaining bolts, and withdraw the thermostat cover sufficiently to permit the thermostat to be removed from its seat.

5 To test whether the unit is serviceable, suspend the thermostat by a piece of string in a pan of water being heated. Using a thermometer, with reference to the opening and closing temperature in Specifications, its operation may be checked. The thermostat should be renewed if it is stuck open or closed, or fails to operate at the specified temperature. The operation of a thermostat is not instantaneous and sufficient time must be allowed for movement during testing. Never refit a faulty unit - leave it out if no replacement is available immediately.

6 Refitting is the reverse of the removal procedure. Ensure the

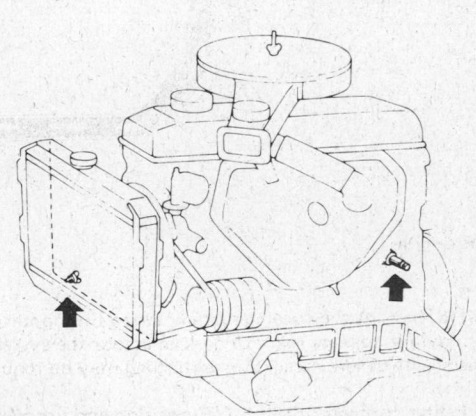

Fig. 2.3. Engine and radiator drain plugs (arrowed) - typical

Fig. 2.4. Checking the thermostat

Fig. 2.5. Removing the water pump bolts (20R engine)
Note: *On the 18R engine there are three bolts*

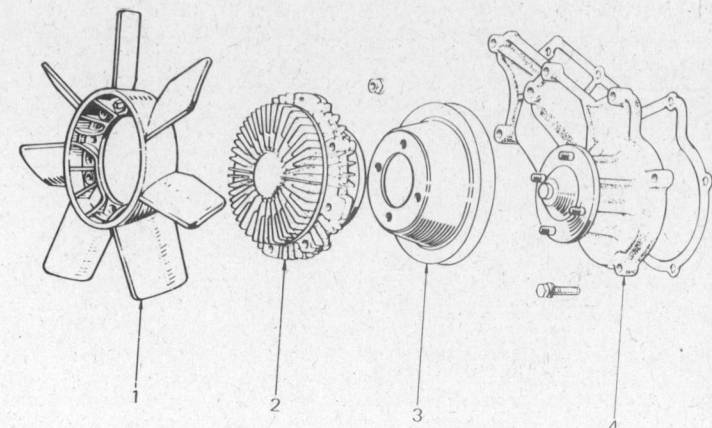

Fig. 2.6. Water pump fan and coupling - 20R engine

1 Fan	3 Pulley
2 Fluid coupling	4 Water pump

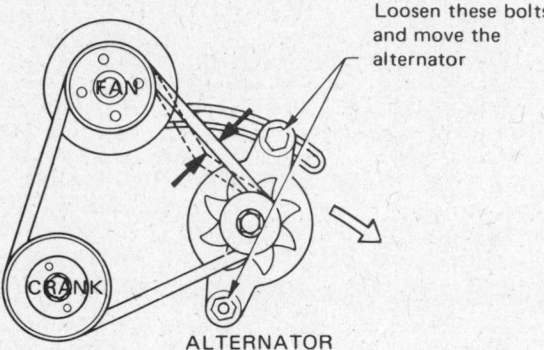

Fig. 2.7. Drive belt tension check - 18R engine

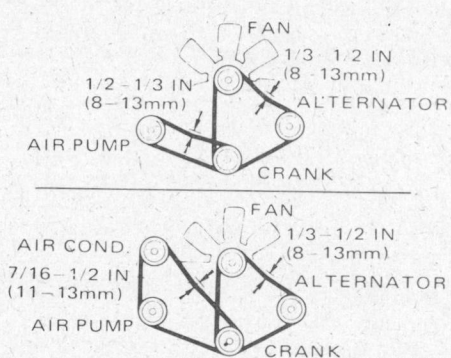

Fig. 2.8. Drive belt tension check - 20R engine

mating faces of the housing are clean. Use a new gasket with jointing compound. The word 'TOP' which appears on the thermostat face must be visible from above. Do not forget to top up the coolant on completion.

8 Water pump - removal and refitting

1 Drain the cooling system.
2 Remove the radiator.
3 Slacken the alternator mountings and remove the adjustment strap. Push the alternator in towards the engine and remove the drivebelt. On models equipped with air conditioning compressor or an air pump, it may also be necessary to remove these drivebelts.
4 On 18R engine models, disconnect the water pump by-pass hose and heater hose.
5 Remove the fan and fluid coupling from the water pump.
6 Unscrew and remove the water pump securing bolts and lift the pump and fan assembly from the front face of the cylinder block.
7 Refitting is the reverse of the removal procedure, but always use a new gasket and check that pieces of old gasket are not adhering to the mating faces of either the pump or the cylinder block.
8 Adjust the drivebelt tension as described in Section 10. Do not forget to refill the cooling system on completion.

9 Water pump and fluid coupling - overhaul

It is not recommended that any attempt is made to repair a faulty

water pump or fluid coupling, due to the special tools required. Where a fault has occurred, the fluid coupling can be removed (and the pulley on 20R engines or 18R engines with a tempered cooling fan) and a new unit obtained.

10 Drivebelts - tensioning and renewal

1 Depending upon the equipment fitted, the drivebelt arrangement will differ - see Figs. 2.7 and 2.8.
2 . The drivebelt tension should be checked by pressing down on the longest belt run with the thumb and checking for a deflection of 0.3 to 0.5 in (8 to 13 mm). If an air conditioning compressor is fitted, its drivebelt deflection should be 0.43 to 0.5 in (11 to 13 mm).
3 Adjustment of the alternator/fan drivebelt tension is by loosening the mounting and adjustment link bolts, and repositioning the alternator as necessary. A little leverage is permitted but take care not to overdo it or permanent damage may occur.
4 Tighten the bolts, then recheck the adjustment.
5 The air pump or air pump/air conditioning compressor drivebelt is adjusted in a similar way, but do not use leverage against the air pump body.
6 Where the belts are to be removed completely, loosen the mounting and adjustment bolts as previously described, and push the component in towards the engine so that the belt can be 'peeled' off the pulley. Refitting is a reversal of the removal procedure.

11 Fault diagnosis - cooling system

Symptom	Reason/s
Overheating	Insufficient water in cooling system.
	Fan belt slipping (accompanied by a shrieking noise on rapid engine acceleration).
	Radiator core blocked or radiator grille restricted.
	Bottom water hose collapsed, impeding flow.
	Thermostat not opening properly.
	Ignition advance and retard incorrectly set (accompanied by loss of power, and perhaps, misfiring).
	Carburettor incorrectly adjusted (mixture too weak).
	Exhaust system partially blocked.
	Oil level in sump too low.
	Blown cylinder head gasket.
	Engine not yet run-in.
	Brakes binding.
	Fan fluid coupling faulty.
Cool running	Thermostat jammed open.
	Incorrect thermostat fitted allowing premature opening of valve.
	Thermostat missing.
	Fan fluid coupling faulty.
Loss of cooling water	Loose clips on water hoses.
	Hoses perished and leaking.
	Radiator core leaking.
	Thermostat gasket leaking.
	Radiator pressure cap spring worn or seal ineffective.
	Blown cylinder head gasket.
	Cylinder wall or head cracked.

Chapter 3 Carburation; fuel, exhaust and emission control systems

For modifications and information applicable to later USA models, refer to Supplement at end of manual

Contents

Specifications

Fuel pump type
18R, 18R-C engine	Mechanical
20R engine	Electrical

Fuel pump discharge pressure
Mechanical	2.8 to 4.3 lbf/in^2 (0.2 to 0.3 kgf/cm^2)
Electrical	2.1 to 4.3 lbf/in^2 (0.15 to 0.3 kgf/cm^2)

Fuel tank capacity
Saloon, UK	13.2 Imp gall (60 litres)
Estate, UK	12.7 Imp gall (58 litres)
Saloon and Coupe, USA	1.5 US gal (59 litres)
Estate, USA	14.3 US gal (54 litres)

Fuel octane rating
1974 USA models	90 octane (regular) or unleaded
UK models	90 octane (regular) - 2 star
1975 USA models onwards:	
With catalytic converter	Unleaded fuel only
Without catalytic converter	90 octane (regular) or unleaded

Carburettor type
... ...	Aisia, dual barrel downdraught

Carburettor specifications
	18R	18R-C without EGR	18R-C with EGR
Main jet (primary)	0.0457 in (1.16 mm)	0.0457 in (1.16 mm)	0.0465 in (1.18 mm)
Main jet (secondary)	0.065 in (1.65 mm)	0.0638 in (1.62 mm)	0.0661 in (1.68 mm)
Slow jet (primary)	0.0213 in (0.54 mm)	0.0207 in (0.525 mm)	0.0213 in (0.54 mm)
Slow jet (secondary)	0.0335 in (0.85 mm)	0.0335 in (0.85 mm)	0.0335 in (0.85 mm)
Power jet	0.0197 in (0.50 mm)	0.0236 in (0.60 mm)	0.050 in (0.0197 mm)
Pump jet	0.0197 in (0.50 mm)	0.0197 in (0.50 mm)	0.0197 in (0.50 mm)
Thermostatic valve opening temperature	140°F (60°C)	140°F (60°C)	140°F (60°C)

									20R
Main jet (primary)	...	...	...	...	...	...	...	...	0.0476 in (1.21 mm) or 0.0469 in (1.19 mm)
Main jet (secondary)	...	...	...	...	...	...	...	...	0.0697 in (1.77 mm)
Slow jet (primary)	...	...	...	...	...	...	...	...	0.0201 in (0.51 mm)
Power jet ...	...	...	...	...	...	...	...	...	0.020 in (0.5 mm)
Pump jet ...	...	...	...	...	...	...	...	...	0.020 in (0.5 mm)

Tune up specifications

		20R
Float adjustment:		
Raised (from air horn lower face)		0.20 in (5 mm)
Lowered (float lip gap)		0.04 in (1 mm)
Kick up clearance between body and secondary throttle		0.008 in (0.2 mm)
Fast idle clearance between body and primary valve:		
18R and 18R-C		0.04 in (1.0 mm)
20R		0.047 in (1.2 mm)
Idle mixture screw initial setting:		
18R and 18R-C		2½ turns
20R		1¾ turns
Engine idle speed:		
18R and 18R-C, manual gearbox		650 ± 50 rpm
18R and 18R-C automatic transmission		800 ± 50 rpm in 'N'
20R, manual gearbox		850 rpm (800 rpm for 1977)
20R, automatic transmission		850 rpm in 'N'
Fast idle speed:		
18R and 18R-C		2600 ± 200 rpm
20R		2400 rpm (EGR disconnected)
CO_2 content at idle speed:		
USA models		Refer to tune-up decal
ECE models		2 ± 1%

1 General description

All models have a rear-mounted fuel tank, a dual barrel down-draught carburettor, a mechanical or electrical fuel pump, and an in-line fuel filter.

Details of the exhaust and fuel vapour emission control system, primarily applicable to models for the USA market, are given later in the Chapter.

2 Air cleaners - description and servicing

1 Two different types of air cleaner are used on the models covered by this manual. Both types use a paper element, and they are similar in appearance.

2 Models supplied for the UK market, and possibly some earlier USA models, have a flap valve on the air cleaner intake which allows air to be drawn either from the engine compartment (where it is relatively cool) or from a heat store around the exhaust manifold (where it is relatively hot). With this type of air cleaner it is left to the owner to select which setting he requires according to the seasonal temperature.

3 Other models use an automatic temperature controlled (hot air intake) air cleaner which incorporates a sensor and valve device which 'mixes' the air being drawn into the carburettor to maintain the air temperature at the pre-determined level, thus preventing icing of the carburettor, reduction of toxic exhaust emissions and reduced condensation within the rocker cover. Hot air is drawn from the interior of a deflector plate attached to the exhaust manifold and cool air is drawn in from the engine compartment. When the engine is operating under full load, a vacuum diaphragm connected to the inlet manifold opens the control valve fully to exclude hot air and override the sensor 'mixing' device.

4 Correct operation of the temperature controlled air cleaner is best checked by observing the position of the intake spout deflector valve under (i) cold engine operational temperature and (ii) normal engine operating temperature. The deflector should be open to warm air immediately after the engine has been started, and closed when the engine is thoroughly hot.

5 At the intervals specified in the Routine Maintenance section, remove the central wing nut on the lid of the air cleaner, release the rim clamps and remove the lid. Extract the filter element and tap it on a block of hardwood to remove any adhering dirt or dust. If an air line is available, remove the dust by applying the air nozzle to the **internal**

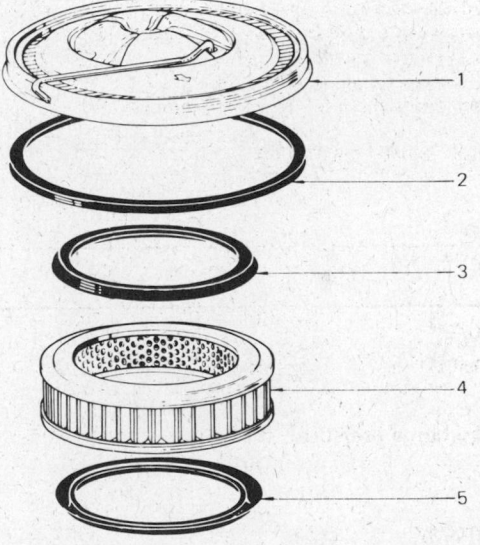

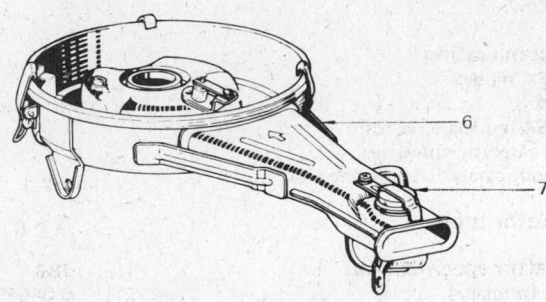

Fig. 3.1. Exploded view of air cleaner - typical

1	Cover	5	Seal
2	Seal	6	Case
3	Seal	7	Diaphragm (temperature
4	Element		controlled air cleaner only)

surface of the element. Refit the element, so that a fresh surface is presented to the intake spout. Renew the element at the specified intervals, and, when doing so, clean the interior of the air cleaner casing, and check that the rubber seals are in good condition. When refitting the air cleaner cover, make sure that any arrows on the cover and air inlet duct are in alignment.

6   The air cleaner casing is secured by brackets attached to the rocker cover. If it is to be removed, carefully detach the hoses (noting where they are attached) and any electrical leads; detach the air inlet duct, and remove the mounting bracket bolts.

7   Refitting is a reversal of the removal procedure.

3   Mechanical fuel pump - testing and overhaul

1   On 18R and 18R-C engines the fuel pump is actuated by an eccentric cam on the oil pump driveshaft.

2   Presuming that the fuel lines and unions are in good condition, and that there are no leaks anywhere, check the performance of the fuel pump in the following manner: Disconnect the fuel pipe at the carburettor inlet union, and the high tension lead to the coil, and with a suitable container or a large rag in position to catch the ejected fuel, turn the engine over on the starter motor. A good spurt of fuel should emerge from the end of the pipe every second revolution.

3   If the pump does not operate correctly, disconnect the inlet and outlet pipes from the pump by unscrewing the two unions.

4   Unscrew and remove the two bolts which secure the pump to the cylinder block. Withdraw the pump, together with insulator and gaskets.

5   Remove the securing screws and lift off the cover (a) (Fig. 3.2).

6   Remove the gasket (2).

7   Scratch an alignment mark on the flange edges of the upper and lower halves of the pump body, and then remove the flange securing screws and separate the two halves.

8   From the lower body, unhook the diaphragm operating rod from the rocker arm by depressing the rod and twisting it sideways. With-

draw the diaphragm/rod assembly.

9   Remove the oil seal, retainer and spring.

10 If essential, due to a worn rocker arm, the pin (13) may be removed, and then the arm and spring.

11 Examine all components for wear. If this is severe, it will probably be more economical to renew the pump complete, on an exchange basis.

12 Check the operation of the valves in the upper body, by alternatively sucking and blowing with the mouth at the inlet and outlet ports. When blowing (through the inlet port), the valve should open and close positively when sucked. When blowing (through the outlet port), the valve should close and open when sucked. The valves are staked in position and in the event of a fault occurring, it is recommended that a new upper body complete with valves is obtained.

13 If the pump components are in good order, obtain a repair kit which will contain all the necessary renewable items. The diaphragm/rod assembly cannot be dismantled and is renewed complete.

14 Reassembly and refitting are the reverse of the dismantling and removal procedures. Ensure that the flange markings are correctly aligned; tighten the flange screws diagonally and evenly with the rocker arm fully depressed. Use a rear gasket on each side of the insulating block when refitting to the engine.

4   Electrically operated fuel pump - checking, removal and refitting

1   This type of fuel pump is located in the fuel tank.

2   In the event of lack of fuel at the carburettor, first check that there is fuel in the tank, and that the filter is not clogged.

3   Check the electrical supply lead to the pump terminal, also the earth lead from the pump to the bodyframe for security and good contact.

4   It is possible for a faulty oil pressure switch to cause a fault in the fuel pump as they operate on a common circuit.

5   Assuming that the oil pressure was normal when the engine was last operating, pull off the lead from the oil pressure switch so that the

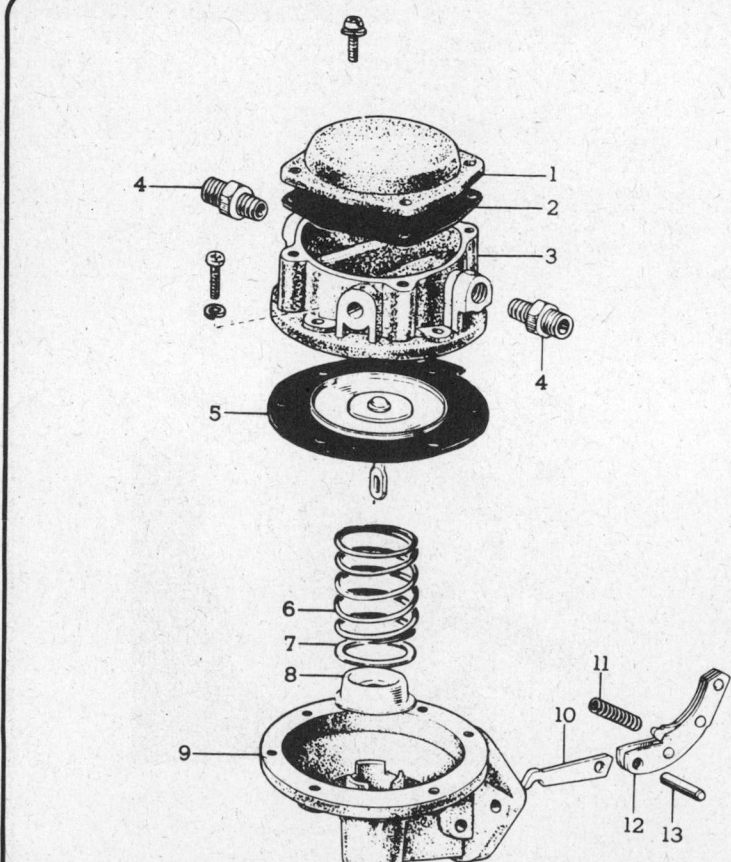

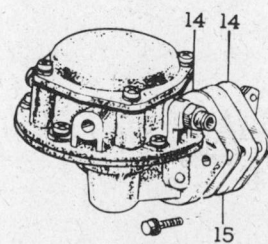

Fig. 3.2. Typical mechanical fuel pump - exploded view

1 Cover	9 Lower body
2 Gasket	10 Rocker arm link
3 Upper body	11 Spring
4 Unions	12 Rocker arm
5 Diaphragm/rod assembly	13 Pivot pin
6 Spring	14 Gaskets
7 Oil seal retainer	15 Insulator
8 Oil seal	

fuel pump relay will actuate when the ignition is switched on.
6 Switch on the ignition and the pump should operate smoothly and quietly. If the pump does not run, the pump relay, resistor or pump itself may be faulty, and should be renewed after the individual components have first been tested by your dealer.
7 To remove the pump, first detach the battery earth lead, then detach the fuel and electrical connections from the pump. Remove the screws securing the pump assembly to the fuel tank, then withdraw it.
8 When refitting the pump, always use a new gasket.

5 In-line fuel filter - renewal

1 The fuel filter used on most models is of the disposable type and it should be renewed as specified in the Routine Maintenance section.
2 It is located within the engine compartment. Renewal is carried out by disconnecting the inlet and outlet pipes from it, and pulling the filter from its retaining clip (photo).
3 When fitting the new filter, make sure that the flow directional arrow is pointing towards the carburettor.

6 Carburettor - general description

The carburettors used on the two engines are basically very similar, being dual barrel, downdraught types. Both types use an automatic choke mechanism; the 18R/18R-C carburettor senses the carburettor/ ambient temperature for control of the choke mechanism, whereas the 20R carburettor senses the engine coolant temperature.

7 Carburettor (18R/18R-C) - adjustments on the car

Note: Carburettor adjustments should only be made with the aid of a tachometer and vacuum gauge as detailed in this Section. On some models a plastic cap is fitted on the idle mixture screw; this must be removed for any adjustment, but note that it may be necessary to use the Toyota tool No. 09243-00010 to turn the screw.
1 Initially check that the fuel level is up to the centre of the window in the float chamber.
2 Ensure that the valve clearances are correctly set, that the air

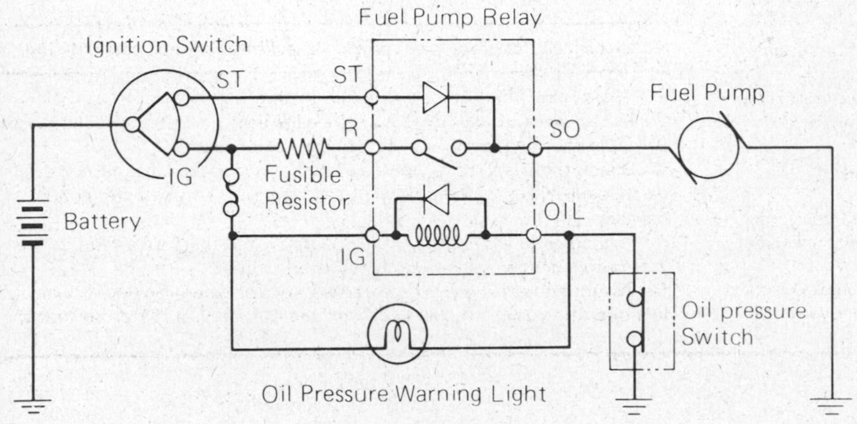

Fig. 3.3. Electric fuel pump circuit diagram

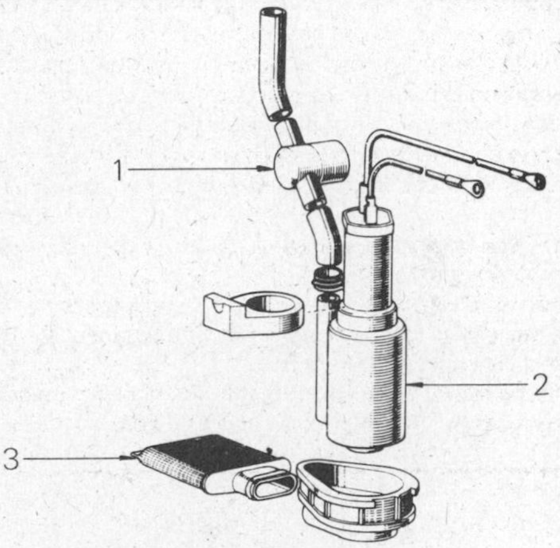

Fig. 3.4. Electric fuel pump
1 Relief valve
2 Pump
3 Filter

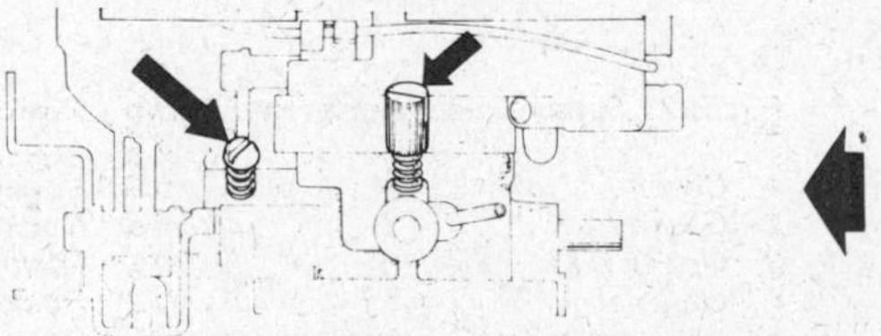

Fig. 3.6. Carburettor adjustment points (arrowed)
Left   Idle speed screw
Right Idle mixture screw

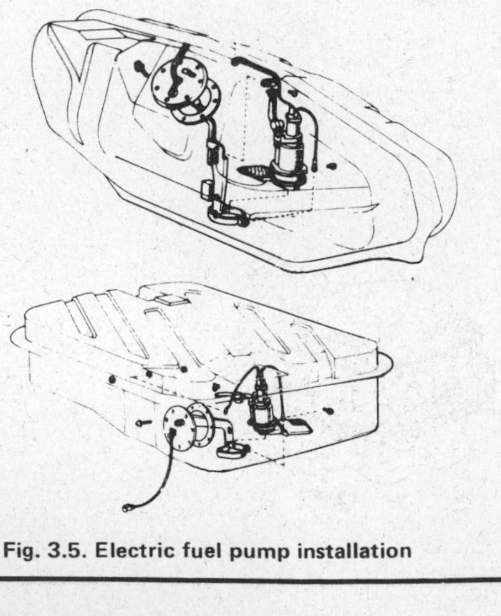

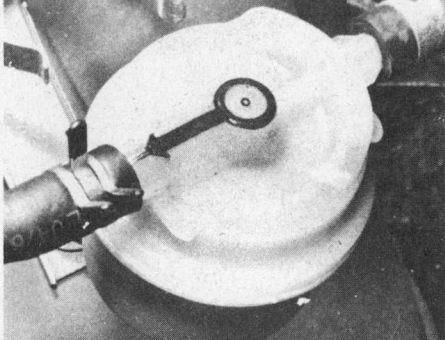
5.2 Typical inline fuel filter

Fig. 3.5. Electric fuel pump installation

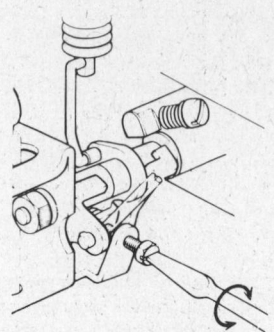

Fig. 3.7. Fast idle adjustment

Fig. 3.8. Removing hose from EGR valve

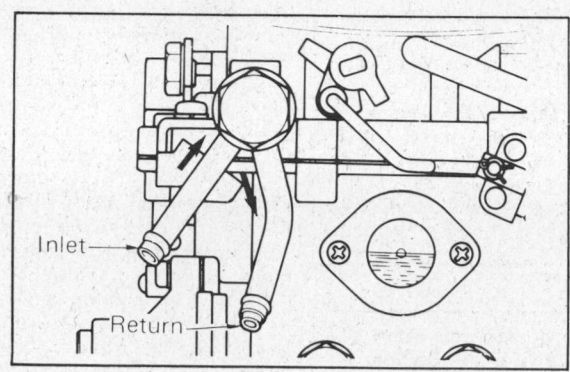

Fig. 3.9. Inlet and return pipes of 20R carburettor

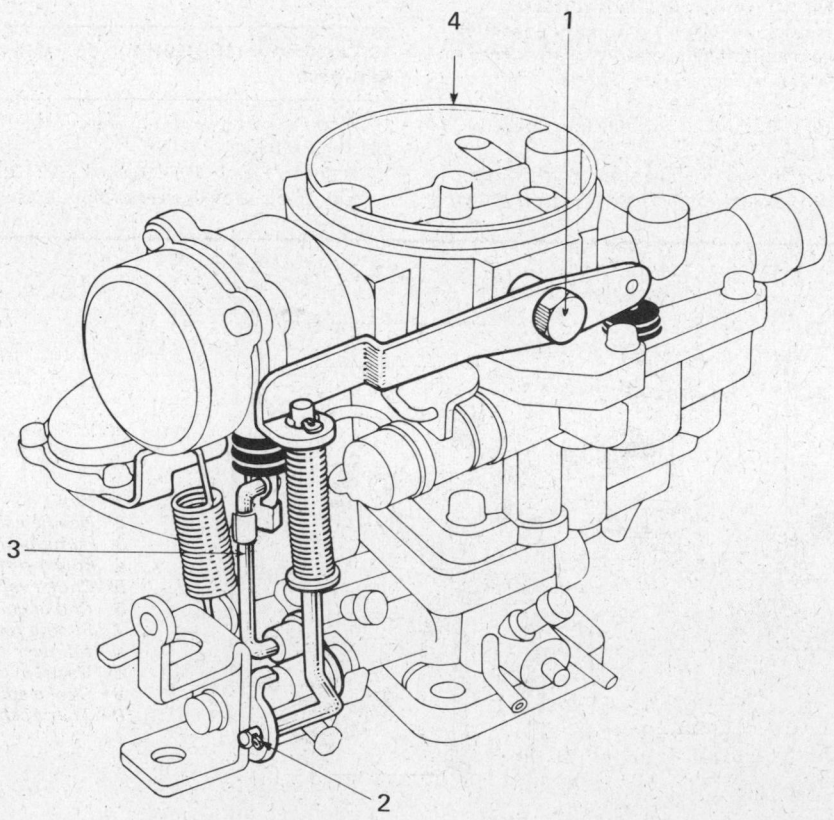

Fig. 3.10. Air horn removal (18R/18R-C carburettor)

1 Pump lever   2 Pump connecting link   3 Fast idle connecting link   4 Air horn

cleaner element is clean and that the ignition system is correctly adjusted (eg, spark plugs, points gap/dwell angle, ignition timing, etc.).

3   Run the engine up to the normal operating temperature, then connect a tachometer and vacuum gauge in accordance with the manufacturer's instructions. The vacuum gauge is connected into the distributor/carburettor vacuum line.

4   With the engine running, turn the idle speed adjusting screw to obtain the specified idle speed, then turn the idle mixture adjusting screw to obtain the highest possible vacuum reading. This should be about 16.3 in Hg (415 mm Hg). Adjust the idle speed again as necessary until both settings can be achieved.

5   Now turn the mixture adjusting screw clockwise until the engine is running very unevenly, and is just about to stall. This is the lean roll point and the mixture is now very weak. Turn the screw back 1½ turns anti-clockwise, then readjust the idle speed if necessary. The check may be repeated as necessary.

6   To set the fast idle, switch off the engine and remove the air cleaner. Open the throttle valve slightly, then close the choke valve with a finger and release the throttle valve. Start the engine without touching the accelerator pedal and check the fast idle speed. If necessary, adjust it by means of the fast idle adjusting screw. Refit the air cleaner on completion.

7   Slight adjustment of the automatic choke is permissible by loosening the three clamp screws and turning the housing clockwise to weaken or anti-clockwise to richen the mixture. One graduation of the scale corresponds to 9°F (5°C) of change in the choke opening temperature.

8 Carburettor (20R) - adjustments on the car

Note: Carburettor adjustments should only be made with the aid of a tachometer and CO_2 exhaust gas analyser as detailed in this Section.

1   Initially check that the fuel level is up to the centre of the window in the float chamber.

2   Ensure that the valve clearances are correctly set, that the air cleaner element is clean, and that the ignition system is correctly adjusted (eg, spark plugs, points gap/dwell angle, ignition timing, etc).

3   Run the engine up to normal operating temperature, then connect a tachometer and exhaust gas analyser in accordance with the manufacturer's instructions.

4   With the engine running, turn the idle mixture adjusting screw to obtain the highest possible idle speed.

5   Turn the idle speed adjusting screw to obtain a setting of 900 rpm; this is the idle mixture speed. If necessary, these steps may be repeated

to achieve this setting.

6   Now turn the idle speed screw to obtain the specified idle speed. At this point, check that the exhaust gas CO_2 content is in accordance with the emission control decal on the particular vehicle. Slight adjustment of the idle mixture screw is permitted if necessary.

7   To set the fast idle, switch off the engine then detach the vacuum hose from the EGR valve and remove the air cleaner. Open the throttle valve slightly, then close the choke valve with a finger and release the throttle valve. Start the engine without touching the accelerator pedal and check the fast idle speed. If necessary, adjust it by means of the fast idle adjusting screw. Refit the air cleaner and EGR valve hose on completion.

8   Slight adjustment of the automatic choke is permissible by loosening the three clamping plate screws, and turning the housing clockwise to weaken, or anti-clockwise to richen, the mixture. One graduation of the scale corresponds to 9°F (5°C) of change in the choke opening temperature.

9 Carburettor - removal and refitting

1   Initially remove the air cleaner - refer to Section 2 if necessary.

2   Disconnect the fuel pipe(s) from the carburettor float chamber.

3   Disconnect the throttle linkage at the carburettor.

4   On 20R engine, have a suitable container ready then detach one of the choke heater hoses. Allow the coolant to drain as necessary, then detach the other hose.

5   Remove the electrical connection from the anti-run-on valve.

6   Detach the vacuum connections from the carburettor, noting the points to which they are fitted.

7   Remove the mounting flange nuts and lift off the carburettor.

8   Refitting is the reverse of the removal procedure, but make sure that the flange surfaces are clean, and that a new gasket is used. After refitting, where original settings may have been altered, set the idle mixture screw to the specified initial setting, then carry out all the idle adjustments.

10 Carburettor (18R/18R-C) - dismantling, reassembly and adjustment

1   With the carburettor removed from the engine, clean away all the external dirt and oil.

2   Refer to Figs. 3.10, 3.11 and 3.12 which indicate clearly the components and their relationship to each other. Remove only those

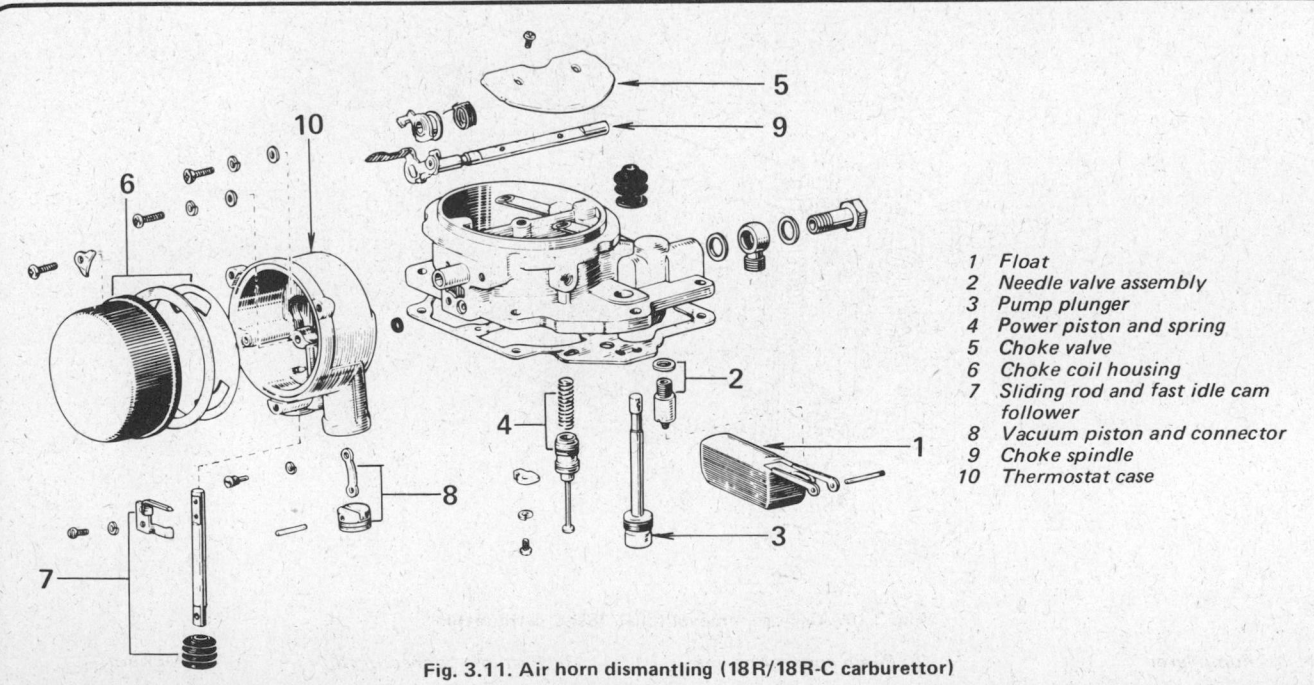

1   Float
2   Needle valve assembly
3   Pump plunger
4   Power piston and spring
5   Choke valve
6   Choke coil housing
7   Sliding rod and fast idle cam follower
8   Vacuum piston and connector
9   Choke spindle
10   Thermostat case

Fig. 3.11. Air horn dismantling (18R/18R-C carburettor)

1   Primary small venturi
2   Secondary small venturi
3   Power valve
4   Pump damping spring and small
    steel ball
5   Pump discharge weight and
    large steel ball
6   Slow jet
7   Thermostatic valve
8   Primary main jet
9   Secondary main jet
10 Level glass
11 Diaphragm assembly
12 Anti run-on solenoid valve
13 Throttle positioner
    lever

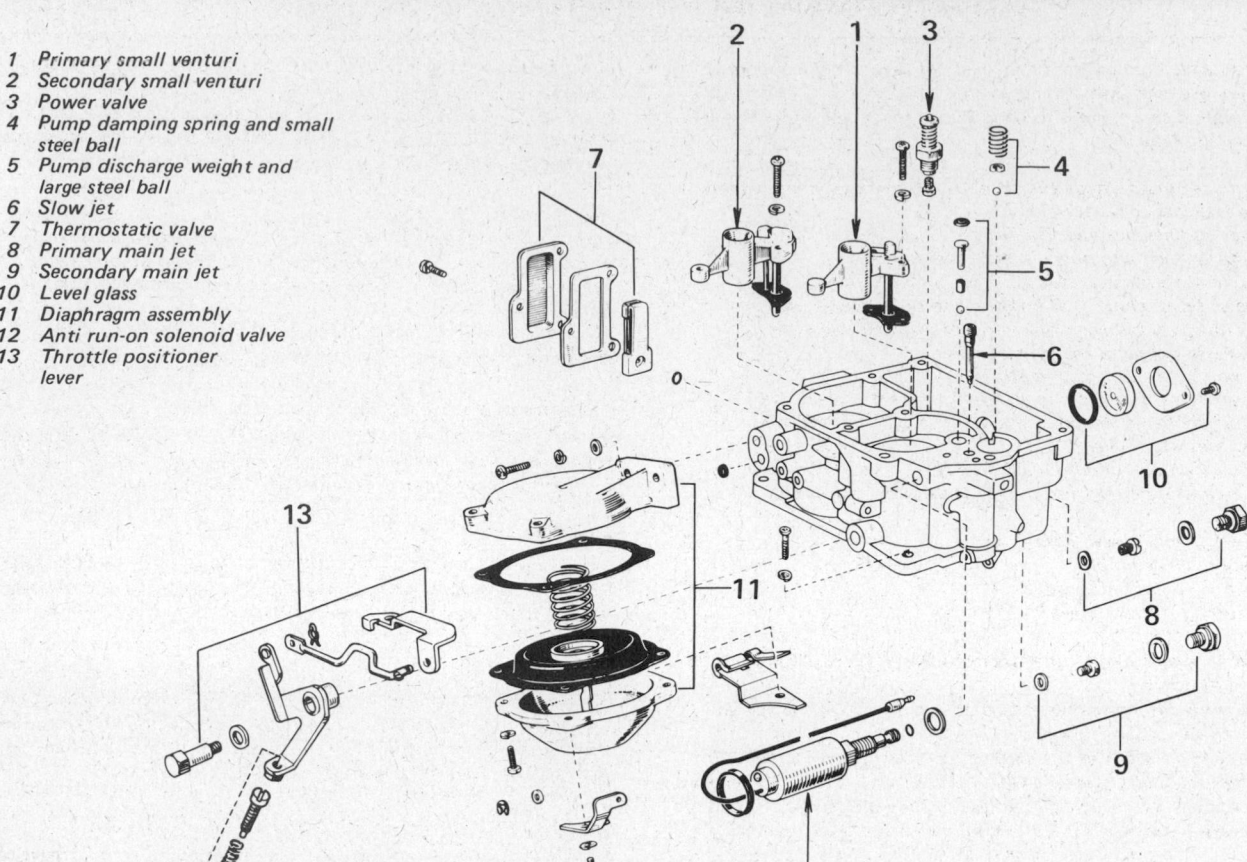

Fig. 3.12. Body dismantling (18R/18R-C carburettor)

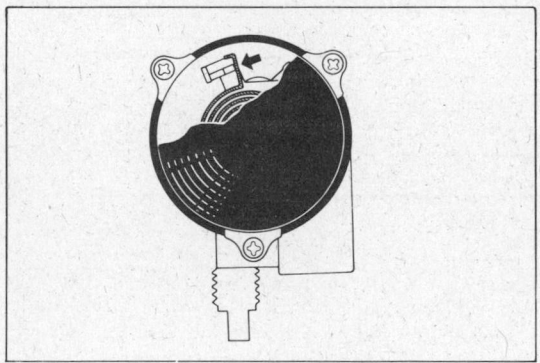

Fig. 3.13. Aligning the choke bimetal (18R/18R-C)

Fig. 3.14. Aligning the choke case lines (18R/18R-C)

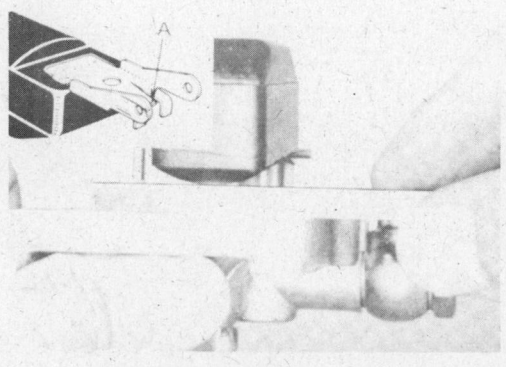

Fig. 3.15. Adjusting float travel

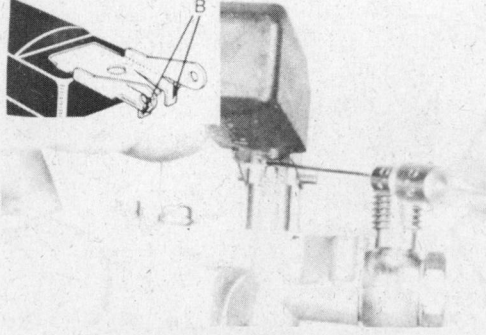

Fig. 3.16. Adjusting float lowered position

components which are worn or damaged. Note that the parts are numbered in order of dismantling.

3 If complete dismantling is to be undertaken, then remove the parts in the following sequence:

  a) *Air horn: first remove the pump lever, pump connecting link and fast idle connecting link.*
  b) *Float and needle valve assembly.*
  c) *Pump plunger and power piston spring.*
  d) *Choke butterfly (carefully file off the peened ends of the screws first), choke coil housing and plate, sliding rod and fast idle cam follower, and vacuum piston and connector.*
  e) *Choke spindle and thermostat case.*
  f) *Primary and secondary venturis.*
  g) *Power valve, pump damping spring and small steel bolt, pump discharge weight and large steel ball, and slow jet.*
  h) *Thermostatic valve.*
  j) *Primary and secondary main jets. Note that the primary jet is brass coloured and the secondary jet is chrome coloured.*
  k) *Float chamber level glass.*
  l) *Diaphragm assembly.*
  m) *Anti-run-on solenoid valve.*
  n) *Throttle positioner lever.*

No further dismantling, other than shown in the exploded view, should be attempted.

4 Renew any worn components and obtain a repair kit which will contain all the necessary gaskets.

5 While the jets are out of the carburettor, take the opportunity of checking their calibration marks with those listed in the Specifications.

6 Reassembly is the reverse of the dismantling procedure. As the work proceeds, carry out the following checks and adjustments.

Choke initial setting

7 Having fitted the butterfly to the spindle and peened the screws,

align the bi-metal spring with the choke spindle when fitting the housing.

8 Align the case scale centre line with the housing scale centre line, then check that the choke plate closes fully when released from the open position (ambient temperature above 77°F/25°C).

Float level

9 With the air horn inverted and the float hanging under its own weight, bend tab A of the float lip (Fig. 3.15) to obtain the specified 'raised' dimensions between the tip of the float and the air horn.

10 Lift up the float and check the clearance between the needle valve plunger and float lip. Adjust by bending tabs B (Fig. 3.16).

Throttle openings

11 Fully open both throttle valves separately, and check that they are at right angles to the mounting flange. If necessary, adjust by bending the primary or secondary throttle stops.

Kick-up

12 With the primary throttle open at an angle of 64 to 90°, adjust the kick-up clearance between the secondary throttle valve and body to obtain that specified, by bending the secondary throttle lever.

Fast idle

13 To obtain the preliminary fast idle setting, close the choke valve, then rotate the fast idle screw to obtain the specified clearance between the primary throttle valve and the body. The unmarked shank of a No. 60 twist drill may be used for this check.

Unloaded

14 With the primary throttle fully open, adjust the choke valve angle to 47° (from the closed position) by bending the fast idle cam follower or choke spindle lip.

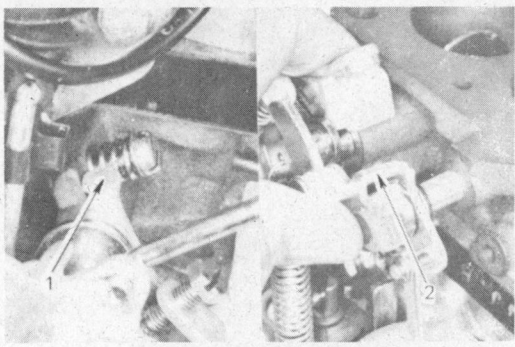

Fig. 3.17. Throttle valve setting (18R/18R-C)
1 Primary stop   2 Secondary stop

Fig. 3.18. Kick-up adjustment (18R/18R-C)
1 Secondary throttle lever

Fig. 3.19. Fast idle setting (18R/18R-C)
1 Fast idle screw

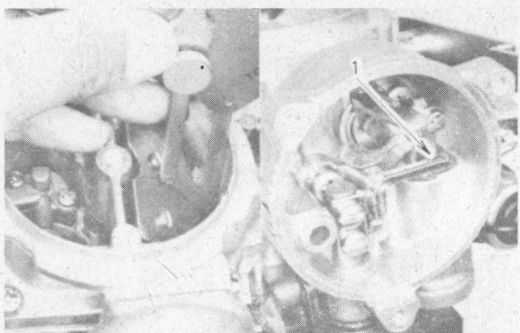

Fig. 3.20. Setting unloader angle (18R/18R-C)
1 Fast idle cam follower

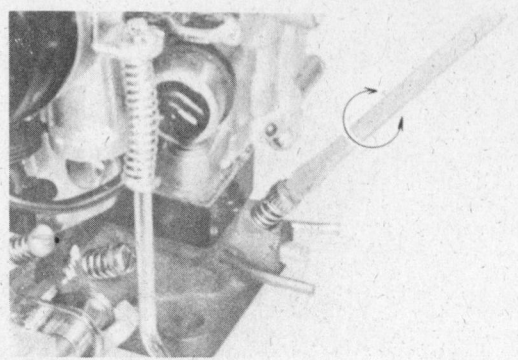

Fig. 3.21. Idle mixture setting (18R/18R-C)

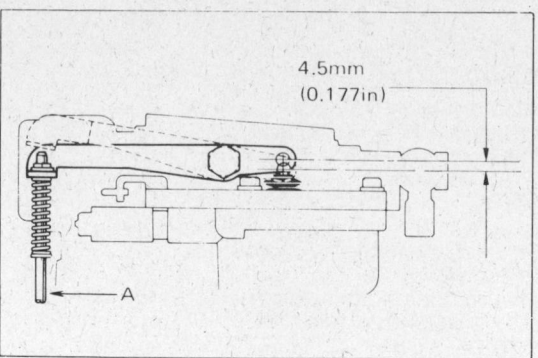

Fig. 3.22. Accelerator pump setting (18R/18R-C)
A   Adjustment point

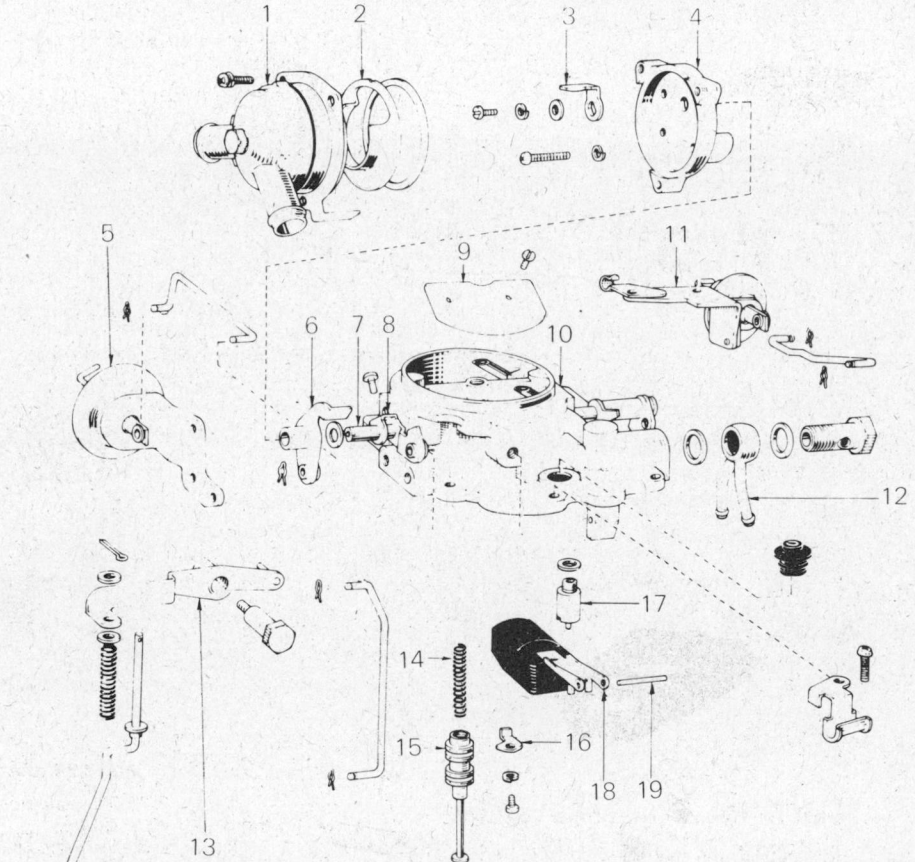

1   Water and coil housing
2   Coil housing plate
3   Choke lever
4   Coil housing body
5   Choke breaker
6   Relief lever
7   Choke spindle
8   Connecting lever
9   Choke valve
10 Air horn
11 Choke opener
12 Fuel union
13 Pump arm
14 Spring
15 Power piston
16 Piston retainer
17 Needle valve assembly
18 Float
19 Float pivot pin

Fig. 3.23. Air horn - exploded view (20R carburettor)

Idle mixture

15 To obtain a provisional setting for the idle mixture, screw in the mixture screw until it just contacts its seat, then screw it out the specified number of turns.

Accelerator pump

16 Bend the accelerator pump rod A (Fig. 3.22) as necessary to obtain a pump stroke of 0.177 in (4.5 mm). After any bending, ensure that the linkage operates smoothly.

11 Carburettor (20R) - dismantling, reassembly, and adjustments

1   With the carburettor removed from the engine, clean away all the external dirt and oil.

2   Refer to the illustrations and commence dismantling by disconnecting the accelerator pump arm and connecting rod. (See Figs. 3.23, 3.24 and 3.25.)

3   Remove the connecting links and choke opener, and lift the air horn assembly from the carburettor body after having extracted the seven securing screws.

4   Remove the float assembly and the fuel inlet valve.

5   Remove the accelerator pump plunger and power piston assembly.

6   Remove the automatic choke housing (three screws).

7   Remove the choke lever now exposed, and coil housing body.

8   Remove the choke breaker and relief lever.

9   The choke valve plate and spindle should only be dismantled if essential, in which case, file off the peened ends of the valve plate

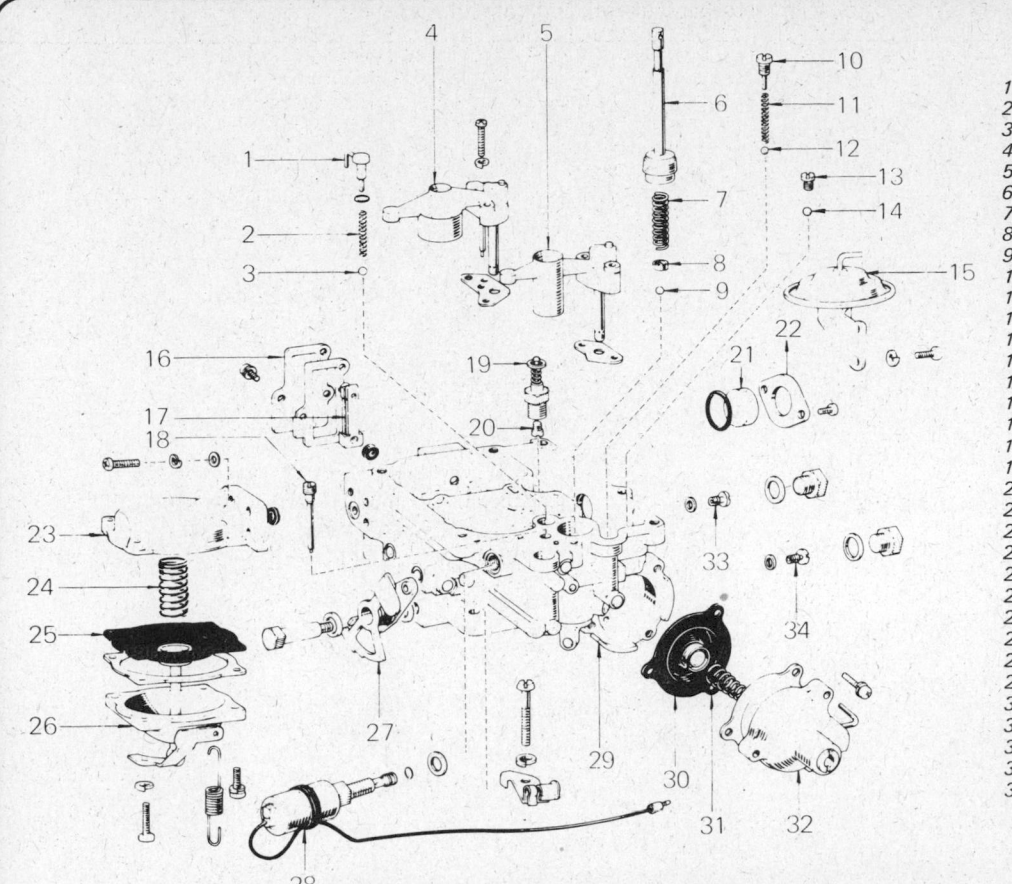

1 Pump jet
2 Spring
3 Outlet check ball
4 Secondary venturi
5 Primary venturi
6 Pump plunger
7 Spring
8 Ball retainer
9 Inlet check ball
10 Plug
11 Spring
12 AAP outlet check ball
13 Plug
14 AAP inlet check ball
15 Throttle positioner
16 Thermostatic valve cover
17 Thermostatic valve
18 Primary slow jet
19 Power valve
20 Power jet
21 Sight glass
22 Retainer
23 Diaphragm cap
24 Spring
25 Diaphragm
26 Housing
27 Fast idle cam
28 Anti run-on solenoid valve
29 Carburettor body
30 Diaphragm
31 Spring
32 AAP housing
33 Secondary main jet
34 Primary main jet

Fig. 3.24. Body parts - exploded view (20R carburettor)

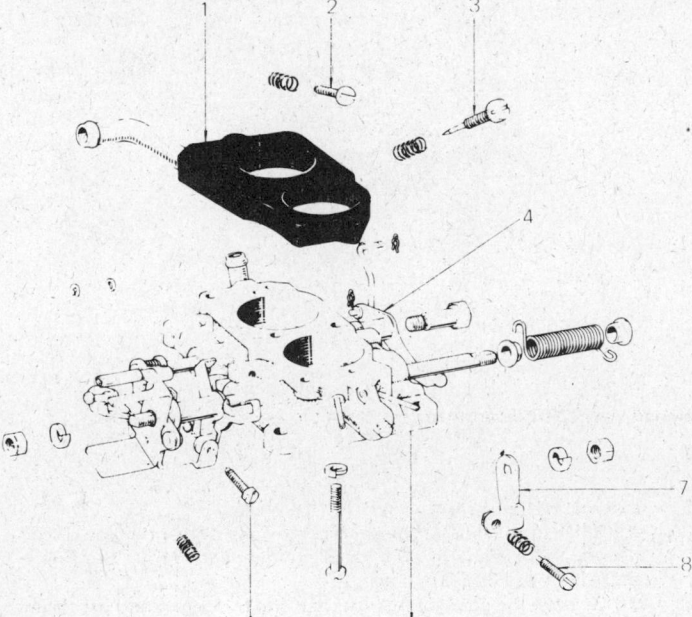

Fig. 3.25. Flange parts - exploded view (20R carburettor)

1 Insulator
2 Idle speed screw
3 Idle mixture screw
4 Positioner lever
5 Fast idle screw
6 Flange
7 Throttle lever
8 Throttle positioner adjusting screw

Fig. 3.26. Correct assembly of levers (20R)

1 Throttle positioner lever
2 Collar
3 Spring
4 Collar
5 Throttle lever

Fig. 3.27. Installing choke connecting lever (20R)

Fig. 3.28. Installing choke breaker (20R)

Fig. 3.29. Installing choke housing plate (20R)
Arrow shows alignment pin

Fig. 3.30. Aligning choke housing (20R)

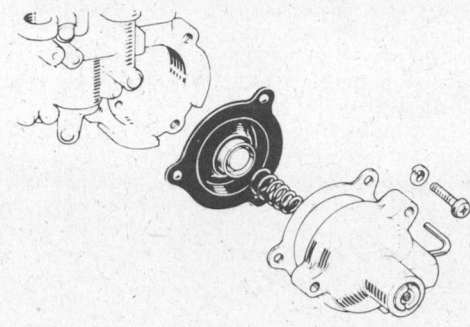

Fig. 3.31. Assembling auxiliary accelerator pump (AAP) - 20R

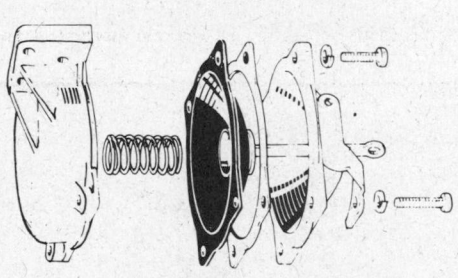

Fig. 3.32. Assembling diaphragm (20R)

Fig. 3.33. Installing fast idle cam

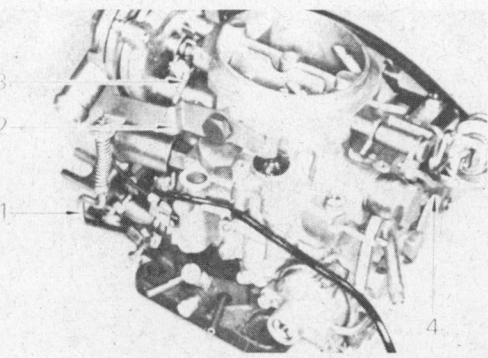

Fig. 3.34. Connecting linkates (20R)

1 Pump linkages   3 Fast idle link
2 Pump arm   4 Choke opener

Fig. 3.35. Setting throttle openings (20R)

1 Primary stop   2 Secondary stop

screws before unscrewing them.

10 From the carburettor body, remove the venturis, the pump jet assembly, including the 'O' ring, spring and ball, then extract the slow jet and the power valve.

11 Remove the plugs and the main jets.

12 Unscrew the cover and extract the thermostatic valve and the 'O' ring. Do not dismantle the thermostatic valve.

13 Remove the sight glass from the float chamber, then remove the throttle positioner and link.

14 Remove the auxillary accelerator pump components.

15 Remove the diaphragm assembly; unscrew the fuel cut off solenoid valve and remove the fast idle cam.

16 Disconnect the carburettor body from the flange (three screws). The flange should be dismantled only if necessary.

17 Clean and inspect all components for wear, particularly the diaphragm. Suck the nozzle on the choke breaker; if the connecting rod does not move, renew the choke breaker complete. Check jet calibrations with those given in the Specifications in case a previous owner has substituted any for ones of a different size.

18 Reassembly is the reverse of the dismantling procedure, but the following detailed instructions are given where any confusion might arise.

19 Install the choke breaker and relief lever as shown (Fig. 3.28).

20 Fit the choke housing plate and gasket so that the hole in the plate is in alignment with the pin.

21 As the choke housing is offered up, make sure that the bi-metal spring engages with the choke lever. Tighten the three securing screws after the Vee notch in the choke housing plate is in alignment with the centre line on the body scale and the line on the coil housing.

22 Once the float has been fitted, turn the air horn upside down and measure the distance between the lowest point of the float and the surface of the air horn (no gasket) while the float is hanging under its own weight. Bend tab A of the float lip (Fig. 3.15) to obtain the specified 'raised' dimension.

23 Lift up the float and check the clearance between the needle valve plunger and float lip. Adjust by bending tab B (Fig. 3.16).

24 When reassembly is complete, carry out the following checks.

Throttle opening

25 Fully open both throttle valves separately, and check that they are at right angles to the mounting flange. If necessary, adjust by bending the primary or secondary throttle stops.

Kick-up

26 With the primary throttle fully open, adjust the kick-up clearance between the secondary throttle valve and body, to obtain the specified clearance by bending the secondary throttle lever.

Fast idle

27 To obtain the preliminary fast idle setting, close the choke valve, then rotate the fast idle screw to obtain the specified clearance between the primary throttle valve and the body. The unmarked shank of a No. 56 twist drill may be used for this check.

Unloader

28 With the primary throttle fully open, adjust the choke valve angle to 50° (from the closed position) by bending the fast idle lever.

Choke opener

29 Push the connecting rod on the choke opener vacuum capsule so that the choke valve plate opens as far as possible. The valve plate angle should be 55° (from the closed position); adjust if necessary by bending the choke opener link.

Choke breaker

30 Push the connecting rod into the choke breaker vacuum capsule as far as possible. The choke valve plate angle should be 40° (from the closed position); adjust if necessary by bending the relief lever.

Throttle positioner

31 With the throttle released, the clearance between the edge of the primary throttle valve plate and the venturi bore should be:

Manual gearbox   0.024 in (0.6 mm) — No. 73 twist drill shank
Automatic transmission   0.020 in (0.5 mm) — No. 76 twist drill shank

Adjust by turning the throttle positioner adjusting screw.

Idle mixture

32 To obtain a provisional setting for the idle mixture, screw in the

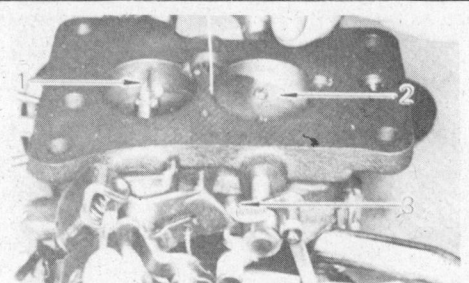

Fig. 3.36. Checking kick-up (20R)
1   Primary throttle   3   Secondary throttle lever
2   Secondary throttle

Fig. 3.38. Adjusting choke opener (20R)
1   Choke opener rod   2   Link

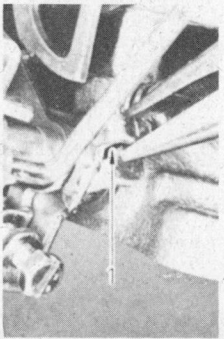

Fig. 3.37. Adjusting unloader (20R)
1   Fast idle lever

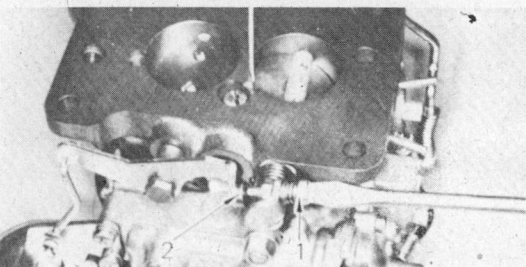

Fig. 3.39. Adjusting throttle positioner (20R)
1   Throttle positioner adjusting   2   Throttle lever tab
screw

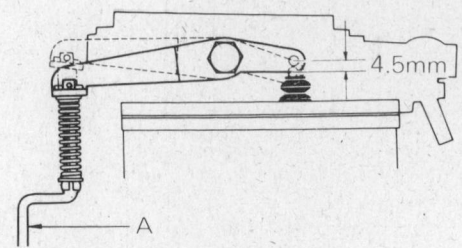

Fig. 3.40. Accelerator pump setting (20R)

A   Adjustment point

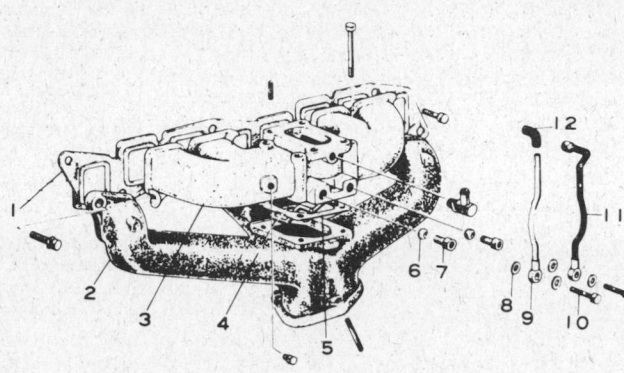

Fig. 3.41. Manifolds - (18R/18R-C)

1   *Gasket*
2   *Exhaust manifold*
3   *Intake manifold*
4   *Automatic choke heater pipe*
5   *Gasket*
6   *Olive*
7   *Union*
8   *Gasket*
9   *Automatic choke inlet heater pipe*
10 *Bolt*
11 *Automatic choke outlet heater pipe*
12 *Connector*

mixture screw until it **just** contacts its seat, then screw it out the specified number of turns.

Accelerator pump

33 Bend the accelerator pump rod A (Fig. 3.40) as necessary to obtain a pump stroke of 0.177 in (4.5 mm). After any bending, ensure that the linkage operates smoothly.

12 Inlet and exhaust manifolds

1   On the 18R/18R-C engines, the inlet and exhaust manifolds are bolted together on the left-hand side of the cylinder head. They are shown in Fig. 3.41.
2   On the 20R engine, the inlet manifold is on the right-hand side of the head, and the exhaust manifold is on the left-hand side. They are shown in Figs. 3.42 and 3.43.
3   There are no special points to note when removing manifolds except that the cooling system must be partially drained on 20R engines. On the 18R/R-C engines, the manifolds are best removed as an assembly, then separated afterwards if required.
4   When manifolds are removed, it is worthwhile checking them for cracking and warping on the attachment faces. An overall warpage on the cylinder head attachment face of up to 0.008 in (0.2 mm) is acceptable for the inlet manifold; on the exhaust manifold up to 0.012 in (0.3 mm) is acceptable.
5   When refitting, always use new gaskets at the joint faces.

13 Emission control - general description

1   To prevent pollution of the atmosphere, a number of emission control systems are fitted to all vehicles. Their complexity depends upon the operating territory, but, vehicles destined for North America have the most comprehensive and sophisticated systems.
2   All vehicles have a *Crankcase Ventilation System*, as described in Chapter 1.
3   USA vehicles will have all or some of the following systems:

a) *Auxiliary acceleration pump (incorporated in carburettor) - 1974, 1975, 1976 models.*
b) *Automatic choke (incorporated in carburettor) - all models.*
c) *Automatic hot air intake air cleaner (see Section 2) - all except 1974 non-California models*

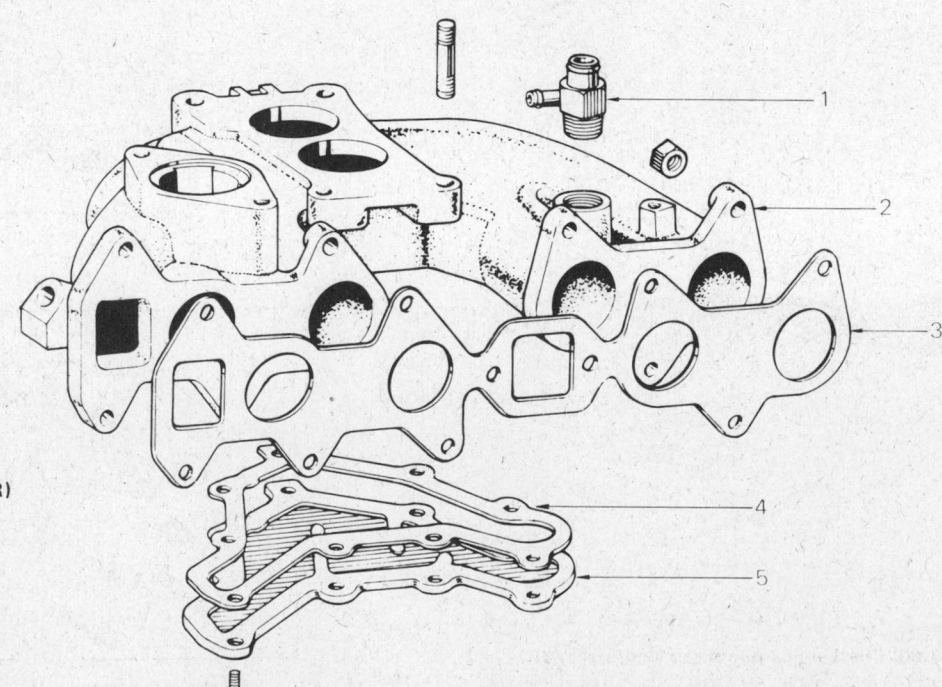

Fig. 3.42. Inlet manifold (20R)

1   *Hose union*
2   *Manifold*
3   *Gasket*
4   *Gasket*
5   *Cover plate*

d) Semi-transistorized ignition (see Chapter 4) - 1974, 1975, 1976
    models.
e) Throttle positioner - all models
f) Transmission controlled spark - 1975, 1976 models.
g) Spark control system - 1977 models.
h) Exhaust gas recirculation - 1975, 1976, 1977 models.
j) Air injection system - 1975, 1976, 1977 models.
k) Catalytic converter - 1975, 1976, 1977 California models: 1977
    high altitude models.
l) Choke opener - 1975 models.
m) Choke breaker - 1977 models.
n) High altitude compensation - 1977 California models.
p) Evaporative emission control system - all models.

4   It must be emphasised that correct tuning and adjustment of the
vehicles' fuel system and ignition system are extremely important in
the maintenance of low levels of exhaust fume emission.

14 Throttle positioner system (TPS) - description and testing

1   This system controls the emission of hydrocarbons and carbon
monoxide exhaust gases during deceleration.
2   This circuit is designed to open the throttle valve plate very slightly
when the accelerator pedal is released, in order to increase the fuel/air
supply to ensure complete combustion.
3   When the vehicle is operating at medium and high speeds, the speed
sensor causes the vacuum switching valve to be energised. The valve
operates and allows air at atmospheric pressure to be introduced into
the throttle positioner diaphragm. This overrides the intake manifold
vacuum on the same side of the diaphragm and the throttle positioner
is in position to prevent the throttle valve from closing fully should

the accelerator pedal be released.
4   When the vehicle enters the low speed range (11 to 19 mph for
18R-C engine: 14 to 20 mph for 1975/76 20R engines: 7 to 11 mph
for 1977 20R engines), the speed sensor causes the vacuum switching
valve to be de-energised, shutting off the atmospheric air to the
diaphragm. With the manifold vacuum acting on the diaphragm, the
throttle positioner is released from the throttle valve, which then
returns to the normal idle position.
5   The TPS system can be tested as follows; Have the engine running
at idle speed then disconnect the vacuum hose from the throttle
positioner diaphragm capsule. Increase the engine speed, then release
the accelerator pedal.
6   The throttle positioner adjusting screw should be hard against the
throttle valve lever giving the engine a rather higher speed than the
normal idle speed.
7   Immediately connect the diaphragm capsule directly to the intake
manifold, which should have the effect of releasing the throttle
positioner screw and to permit the engine to return to normal idle. If
this does not happen, check for faulty linkage; if the linkage is
satisfactory, renew the diaphragm capsule unit.
8   With the engine ar normal operating temperature, and the vacuum
hose disconnected from the throttle positioner diaphragm capsule,
accelerate the engine and then release the accelerator. The engine
speed (checked on a tachometer) should be as follows:

18R-C, manual and automatic transmission   1400 ± 100 rpm
20R, manual transmission   1400 ± 100 rpm
20R, automatic transmission   1050 ± 100 rpm

    Turn the throttle positioner adjusting screw as necessary, then
reconnect the vacuum hose.

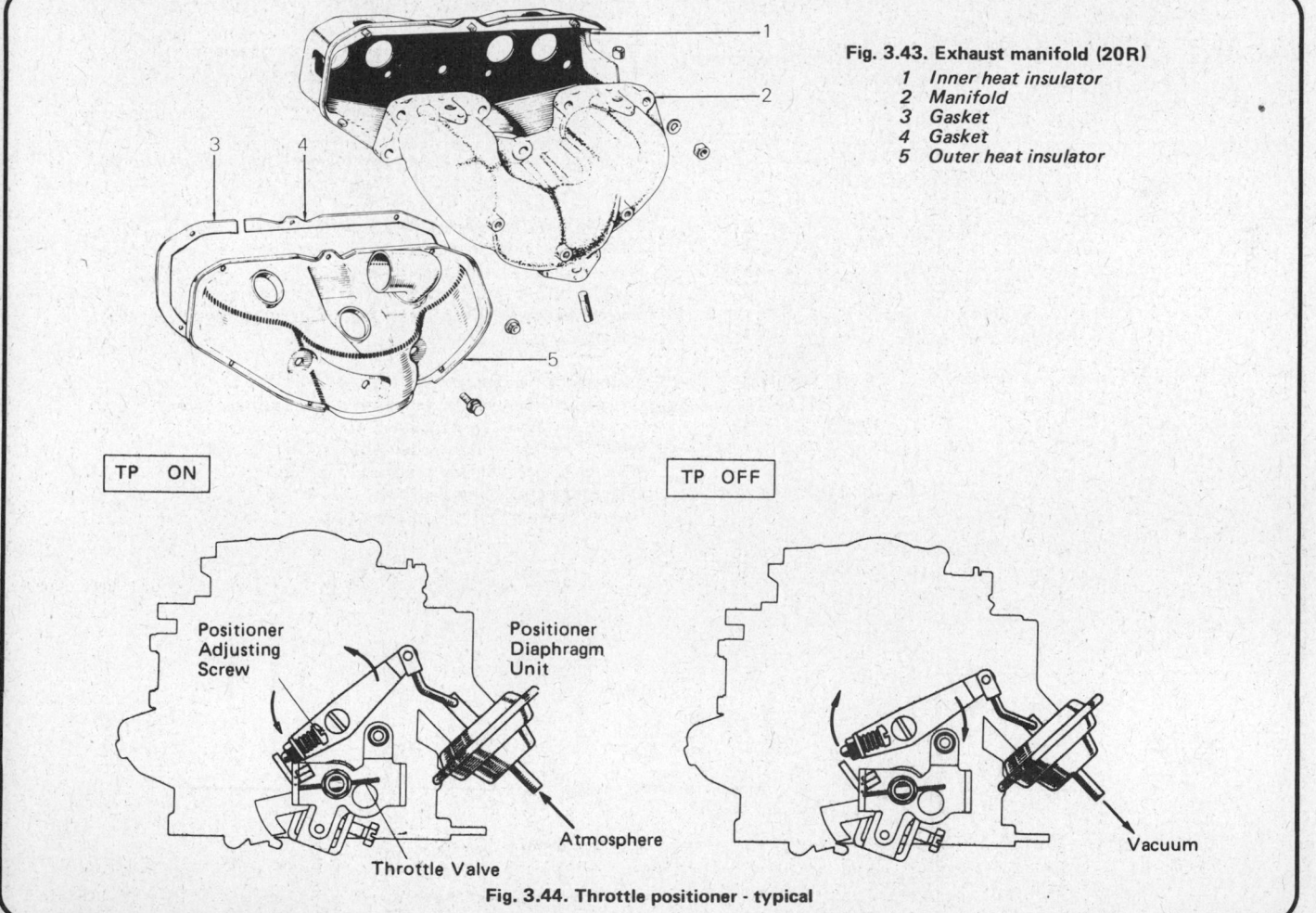

Fig. 3.43. Exhaust manifold (20R)
    1   Inner heat insulator
    2   Manifold
    3   Gasket
    4   Gasket
    5   Outer heat insulator

TP ON

TP OFF

Positioner
Adjusting
Screw

Positioner
Diaphragm
Unit

Atmosphere

Throttle Valve

Vacuum

Fig. 3.44. Throttle positioner - typical

15 Transmission controlled spark (TCS) system - description and testing

1   The TSC system is designed to reduce the emission of nitrogen oxides, by reducing the amount of spark advance under certain running conditions. The system comprises a speed sensor, computer, vacuum switching valve (VSV), thermostatic vacuum switch valve (TVSV) and the associated connections. On later models a thermoswitch is also used, together with a modified TVSV.

2   At coolant temperature below 122°F (50°C) the TVSV will be closed so that vacuum from the intake manifold operates the distributor advance unit in the normal way regardless of engine speed. Even when the coolant temperature is above 122°F (50°C), if the vehicle speed is above 41 mph when accelerating or above 20 mph when decelerating, the same normal advance unit operation occurs because the VSV cannot energise.

3   When the engine speed is below these values, provided that the coolant temperature is above 122°F (50°C), the VSV energizes and allows the distributor vacuum line to bleed to the atmosphere, reducing the spark advance.

4   Apart from checking the hose and electrical connections, little testing of the system can be carried out. The solenoid can be checked by earthing the lead to the computer, when it should energize.

16 Spark control (SC) system - description and testing

1   The SC system is designed to reduce the emission of nitrogen oxides, by reducing the amount of spark advance under certain running conditions. The system comprises a thermostatic vacuum switching valve (TVSV), a vacuum transmitting valve (VTV) and the associated connections.

2   At coolant temperatures below 122°F (50°F) the TSV is closed under spring tension and the normal vacuum signal is transmitted from the advance port to the distributor diaphragm unit.

3   At temperatures above 122°F (50°C) with small throttle openings, the thermowave capsule expands and opens the TVSV, allowing atmospheric pressure from the SC port to mix with the advance port vacuum. This reduces the vacuum signal to the distributor and produces a smaller amount of spark advance.

4   At higher throttle openings a full vacuum signal is applied to the diaphragm through the SC and advance ports, but there is a delay in the signal reaching the distributor due to the restricting orifice in the VTV. Thus the spark is only advanced gradually.

5   At wide throttle openings or when decelerating, there is a low vacuum signal from the TVSV to the VTV and there is no advance. If the throttle is opened suddenly, the increase of pressure (ie, loss of vacuum) causes the VTV check valve to open, as there is a greater vacuum between it and the distributor. This allows the vacuum to decrease and a faster response is obtained at the distributor.

6   It is possible to carry out simple checks of the system by checking whether the octane selector on the distributor moves when the engine speed is increased and decreased with a cold engine. With the engine warm and running at about 2000 rpm, the spark should advance; with the hose to the SC port pinched there should be a delay in the spark advance occurring. With the hose still pinched, the spark should retard immediately when the engine returns to idle speed.

17 Exhaust gas recirculation (EGR) system - description and maintenance

1   This system recirculates a proportion of the exhaust gases into the intake manifold in order to reduce the combustion temperature and so helps to decrease the volume of nitrogen oxide produced.

2   The main component of the system is the EGR valve which either receives signals from a speed sensor, thermoswitch and computer, or from a thermostatic vacuum switching valve.

3   Periodically, check the operation of the EGR valve. To do this, warm up the engine and then remove the cover from the air cleaner.

4   Let the engine idle and connect the EGR valve directly to the intake manifold with a length of vacuum hose. A bubbling noise should be heard coming from the carburettor. Disconnect the hose from the EGR valve and the bubbling noise should immediately cease.

5   Maintenance consists of periodically checking the security of all electrical leads and hose connections. A faulty EGR valve should be renewed complete.

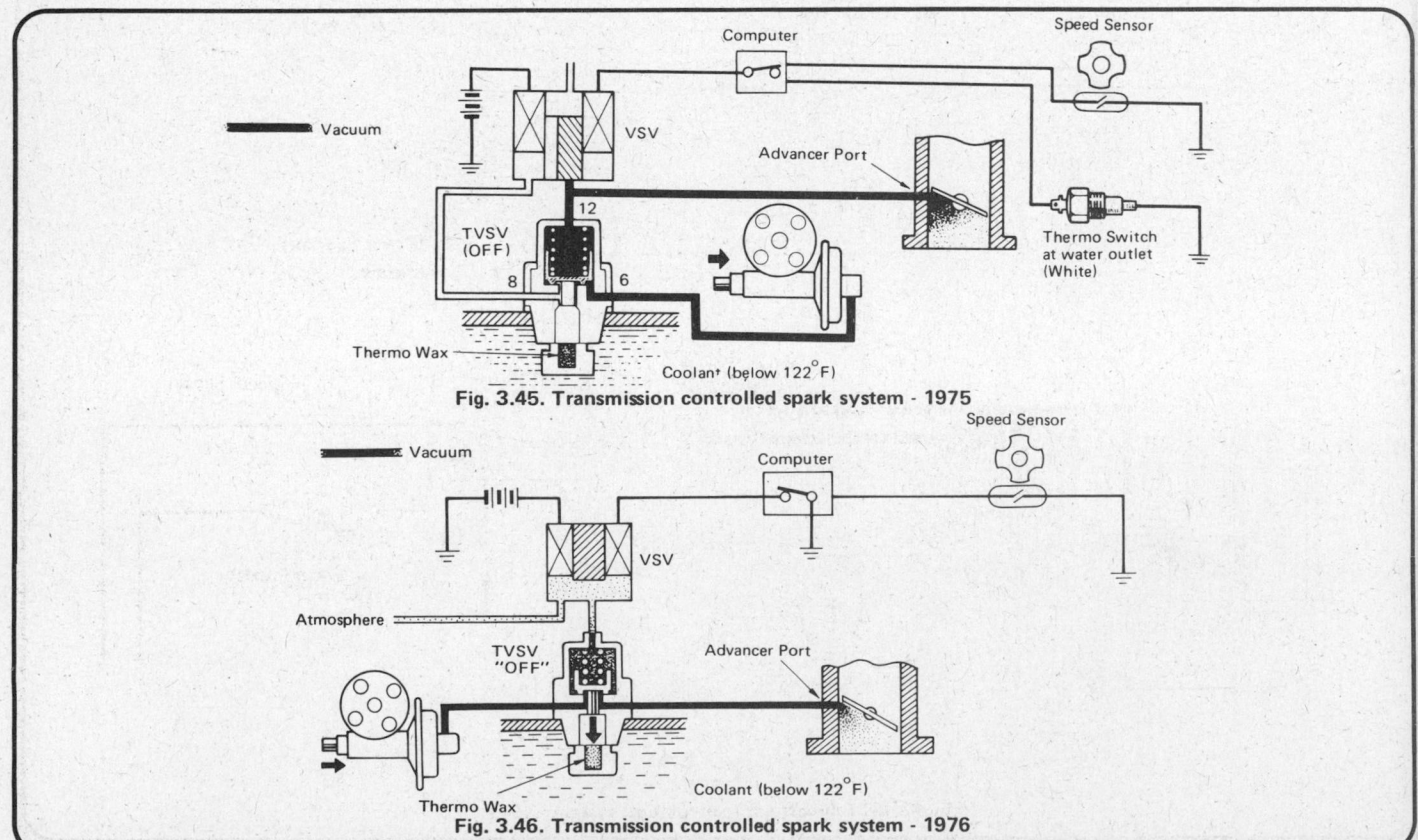

Fig. 3.45. Transmission controlled spark system - 1975

Fig. 3.46. Transmission controlled spark system - 1976

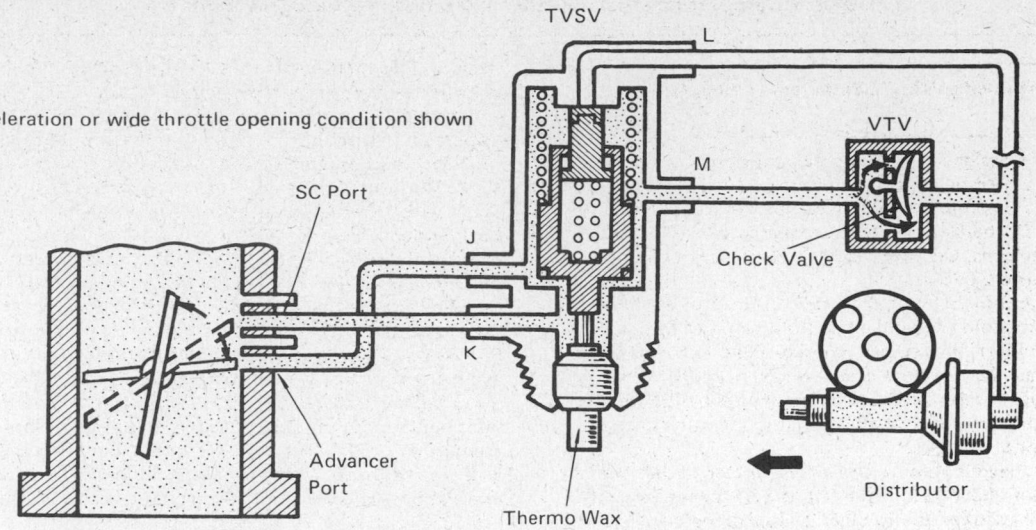

Deceleration or wide throttle opening condition shown

Fig. 3.47. Spark control system - 1977

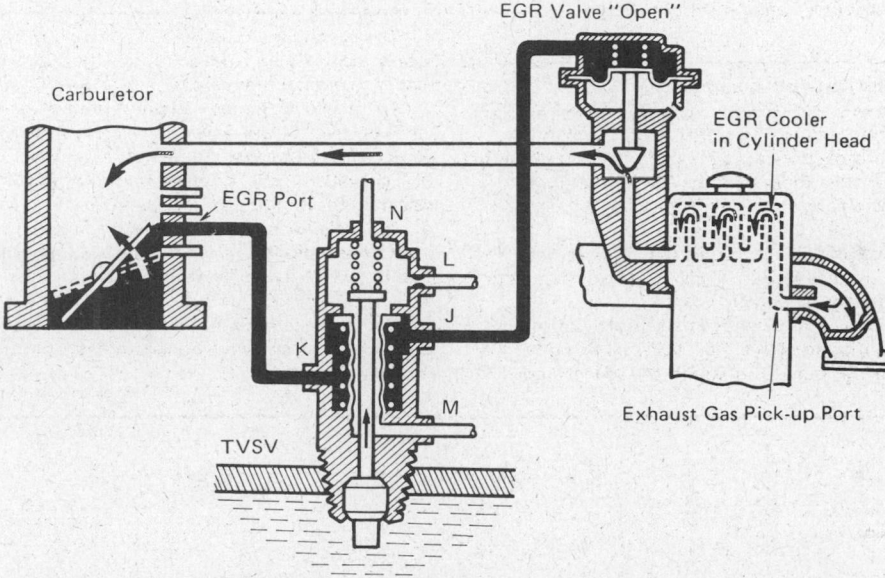

Fig. 3.48. Exhaust gas recirculation system - 1975/76

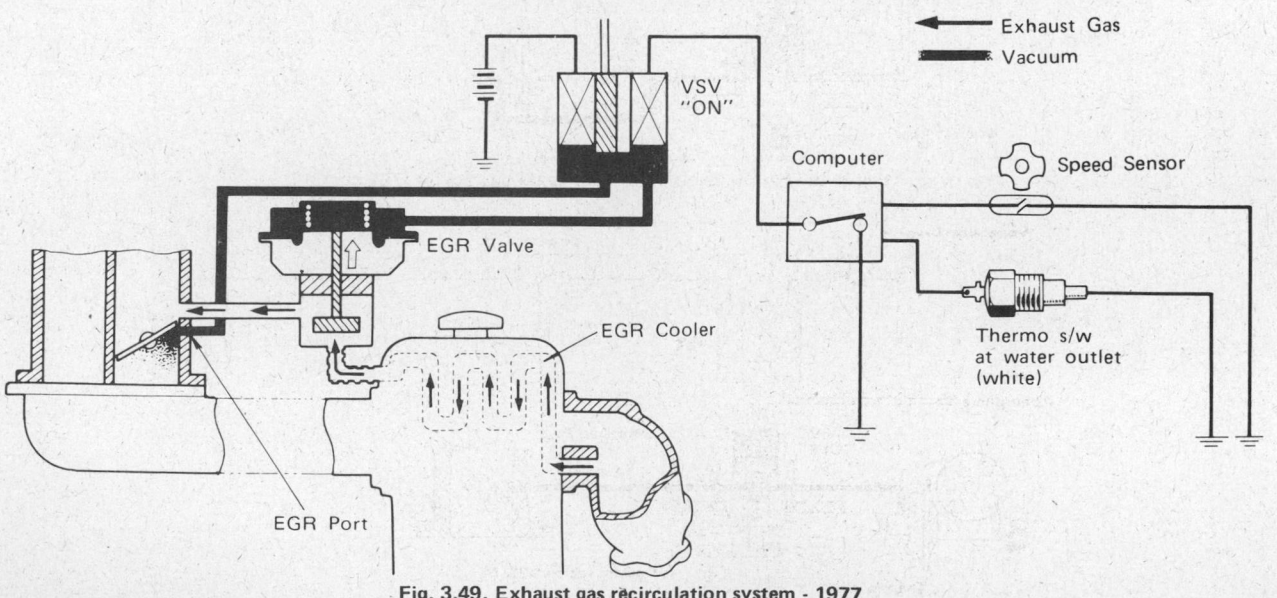

Fig. 3.49. Exhaust gas recirculation system - 1977

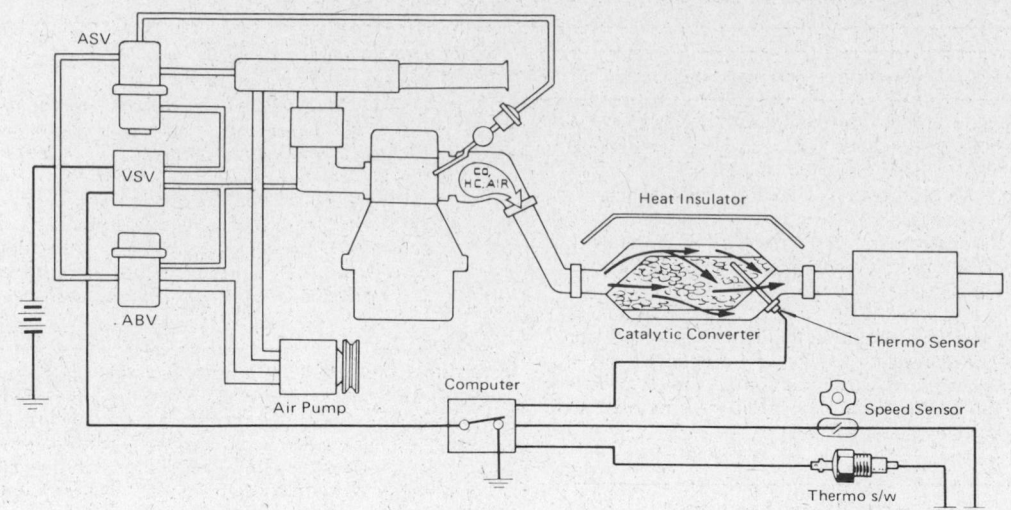

Fig. 3.50. Typical catalytic converter system

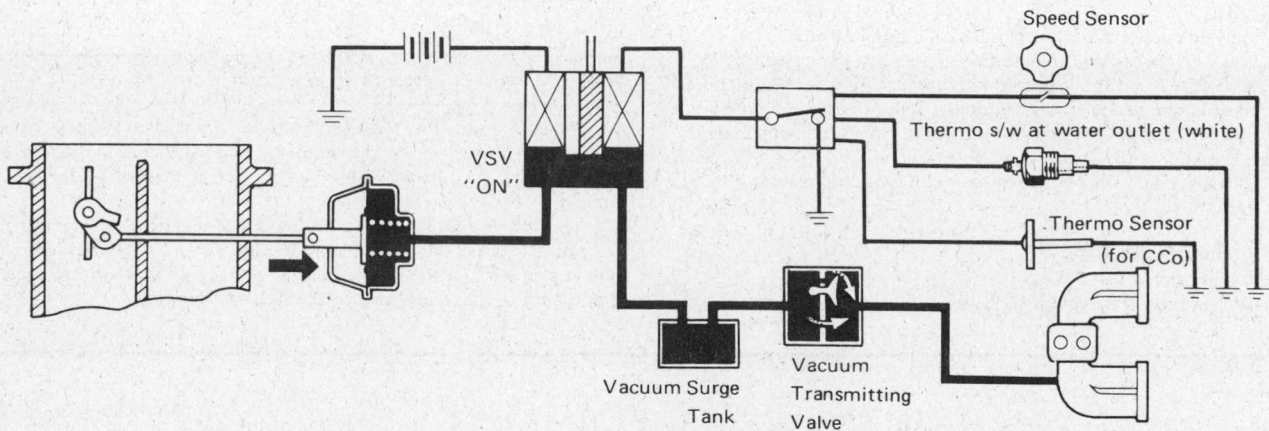

Fig. 3.51. Choke opener system

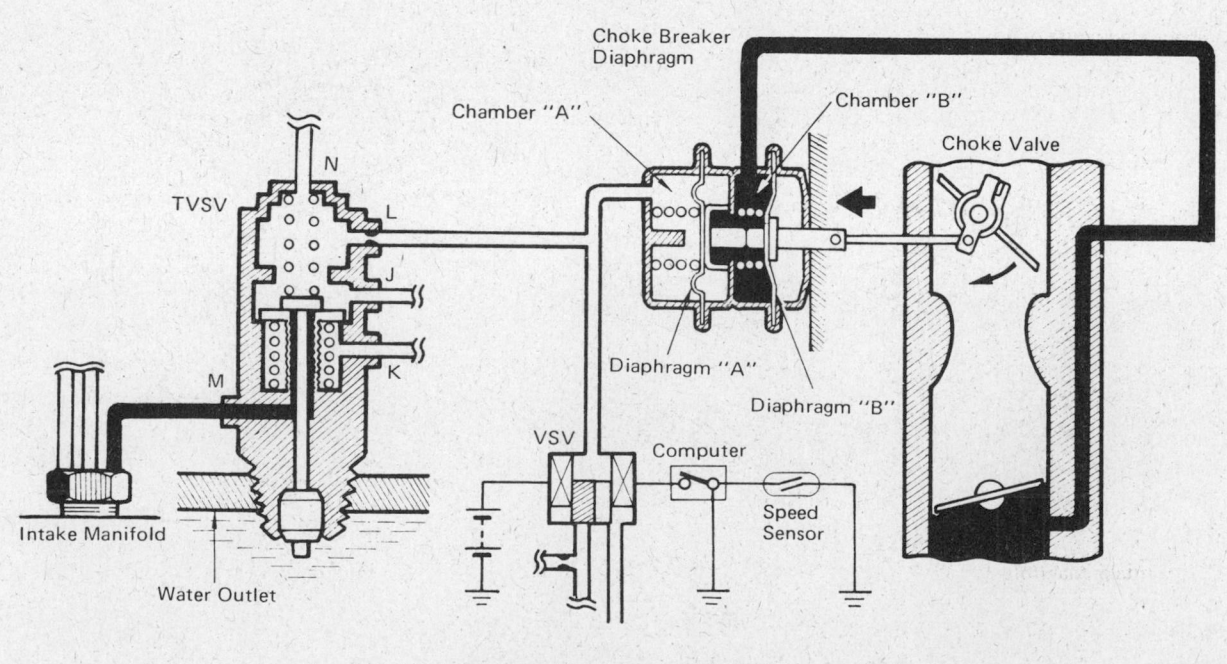

Fig. 3.52. Choke breaker system

18 Air injection system (AIS) - description and maintenance

1   This system is designed to reduce the emission of toxic exhaust gases by mixing pressurised air, (injected near each exhaust valve) with the gases as they leave the engine combustion chambers.
2   The required air pressure is generated by an air pump which is driven by a belt from the crankshaft pulley.
3   Normal maintenance consists of checking the tension of the belt and keeping the connecting hoses tight and in good order. Adjust the tension of the drivebelt as described in Chapter 2.
4   Occasionally test the operation of the air bypass valve. To do this, run the engine at idling speed and listen for a hiss of escaping air from the valve. If evident, renew the valve. Run the engine at about half throttle, then suddenly release the accelerator control rod. A single ejection of air should be heard from the valve. If no air is released, or air keeps on escaping, the valve must be renewed.

19 Catalytic converter (CCo) - description and precautions

1   The catalytic converter is a container of platinum or palladium coated granular alumina. When the exhaust gases pass through it, the hydrocarbons and carbon monoxides are converted to water and carbon dioxide.
2   The catalytic converter only operates efficiently at high temperatures, but, because the temperature will rise excessively if a large volume of unburnt gas is passed through it, a sensor and warning light circuit are provided. If the warning light illuminates during normal running, (it should always illuminate during the engine start sequence), investigate the cause immediately.
3   The following precautions should be taken on systems with catalytic converters:

a) *Use only unleaded fuel.*
b) *Avoid excessive fast idling.*
c) *Avoid running the engine with a defective spark plug, or a plug lead disconnected.*
d) *Avoid severe engine braking.*
e) *Avoid engine overrunning with the ignition off or when the fuel tank is empty.*
f) *Where a tachometer is connected for testing purposes, connect the tachometer '+' terminal to the ignition coil '−' terminal, **NOT** to the distributor '+' terminal.*
g) *When working beneath the car do not touch the catalytic converter if the engine has recently been running or you may be burnt. The internal temperature is typically in the order of 1600°F (870°C) during normal running.*

20 Choke opener - description and testing

1   To prevent the automatic choke from remaining closed too long when the engine speed is too high, when the coolant temperature is too high, or (California only) when the catalytic converter temperature is too high, a vacuum signal from the intake manifold is transmitted to the carburettor choke opener diaphragm which opens the choke.
2   Apart from checking the pneumatic and electrical connections, the only other check that can readily be done is to remove the diaphragm unit hose, and to suck at the diaphragm connection to check that the linkage operates.

21 Choke breaker - description and testing

1   The choke breaker is used to hold the choke slightly open when a cold engine is started and driven immediately, to reduce the resultant heavy discharge of hydrocarbon and carbon monoxide in the exhaust gas.
2   Apart from checking the pneumatic and electrical connections, the only other checks that can readily be done are to remove the hoses one at a time from the choke breaker diaphragm unit, and to suck at the diaphragm connection to see if the linkage operates.

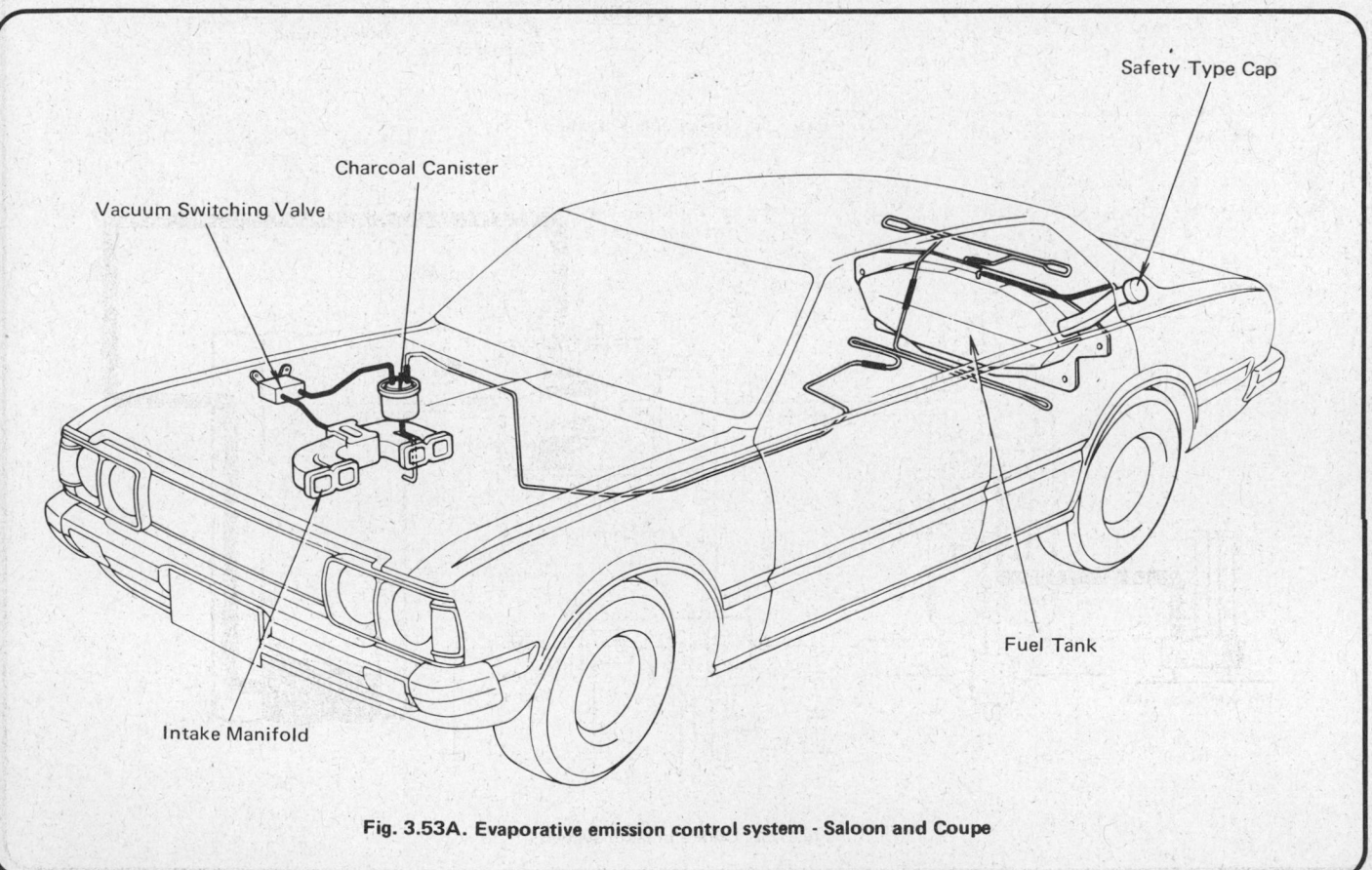

Fig. 3.53A. Evaporative emission control system - Saloon and Coupe

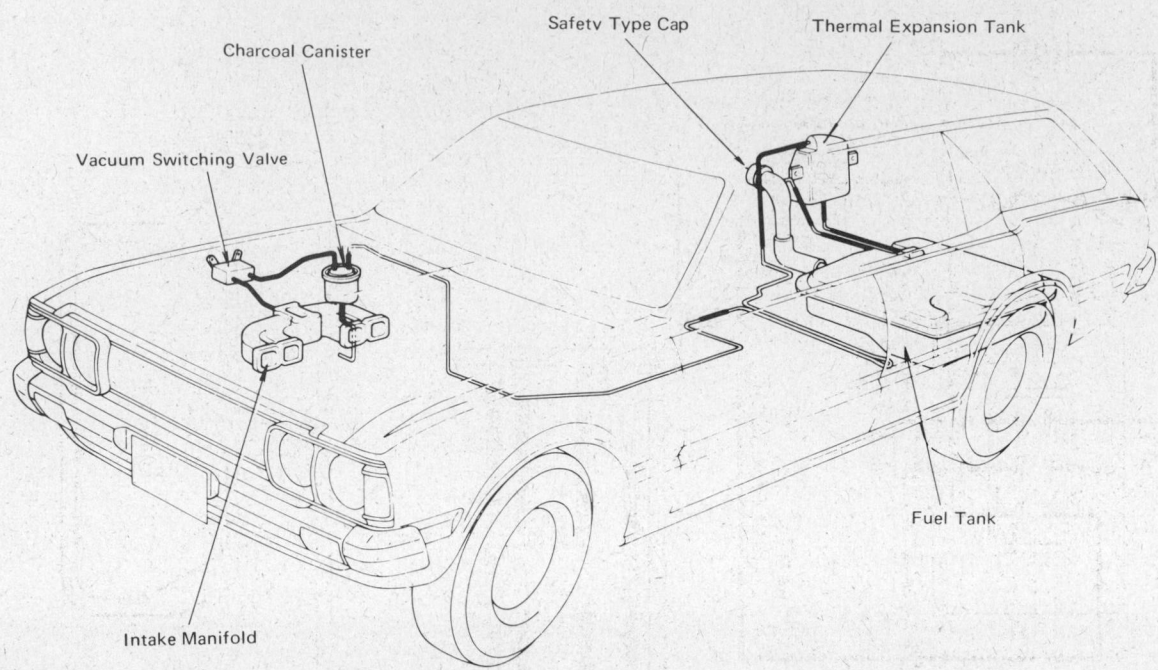

Fig. 3.53B. Evaporative emission control system - Estate car

22 High altitude compensation (HAC) system - description

1   To prevent an over-rich mixture occurring at high altitudes (because the air density is lower), the HAC system supplies additional air to the carburettor and advances the ignition timing to improve engine performance.
2   The only maintenance that is required is to periodically check the condition of the hoses.

23 Fuel evaporative emission control system - description and maintenance

1   The system is designed to reduce the emission of fuel vapour to the atmosphere by directing the vapour from the fuel tank through a non-return valve into an absorbent charcoal canister. At vehicle speeds above 11 mph the vacuum switching valve operates and the vapour stored in the canister is drawn into the inlet manifold where it is then burned as a controlled fuel/air mixture within the engine combustion chambers.
2   The fuel tank filler cap incorporates a valve which opens to admit air should a partial vacuum be created within the tank due to vapour removal.
3   Regularly inspect the condition and security of the system connecting hoses and the filler cap seal, and renew as necessary.
4   Renew the charcoal canister every 5 years or at 50000 miles (80000 km) intervals, whichever occurs sooner.

See page 81 for fault diagnosis

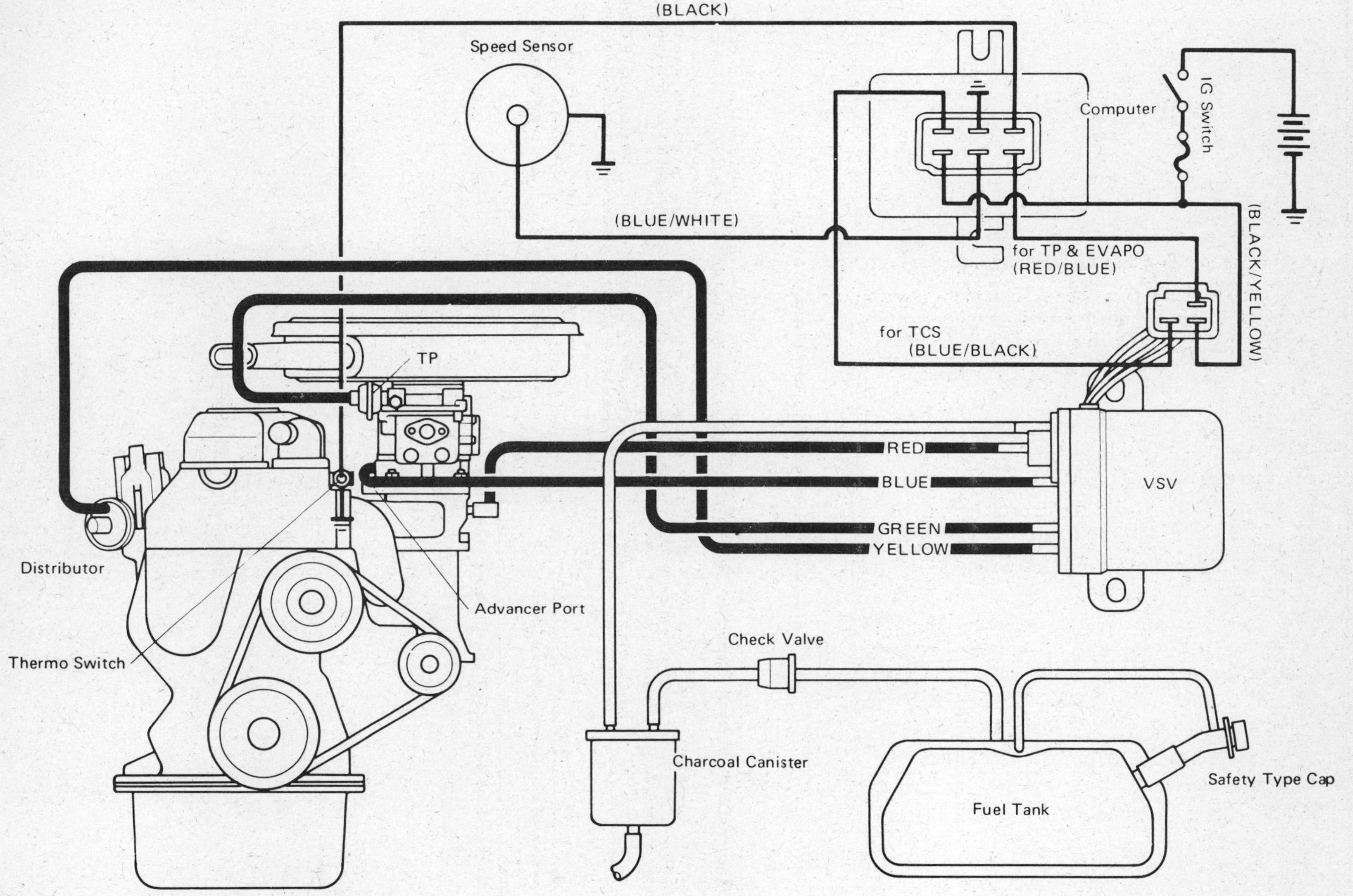

IG Switch

(BLACK/YELLOW)

Computer

for TP & EVAPO
(RED/BLUE)

for TCS
(BLUE/BLACK)

VSV

Safety Type Cap

Fuel Tank

(BLACK)

(BLUE/WHITE)

RED

BLUE

GREEN

YELLOW

Speed Sensor

Check Valve

Charcoal Canister

TP

Advancer Port

Distributor

Thermo Switch

Fig. 3.54. Emission control schematic diagram - 1974 USA models

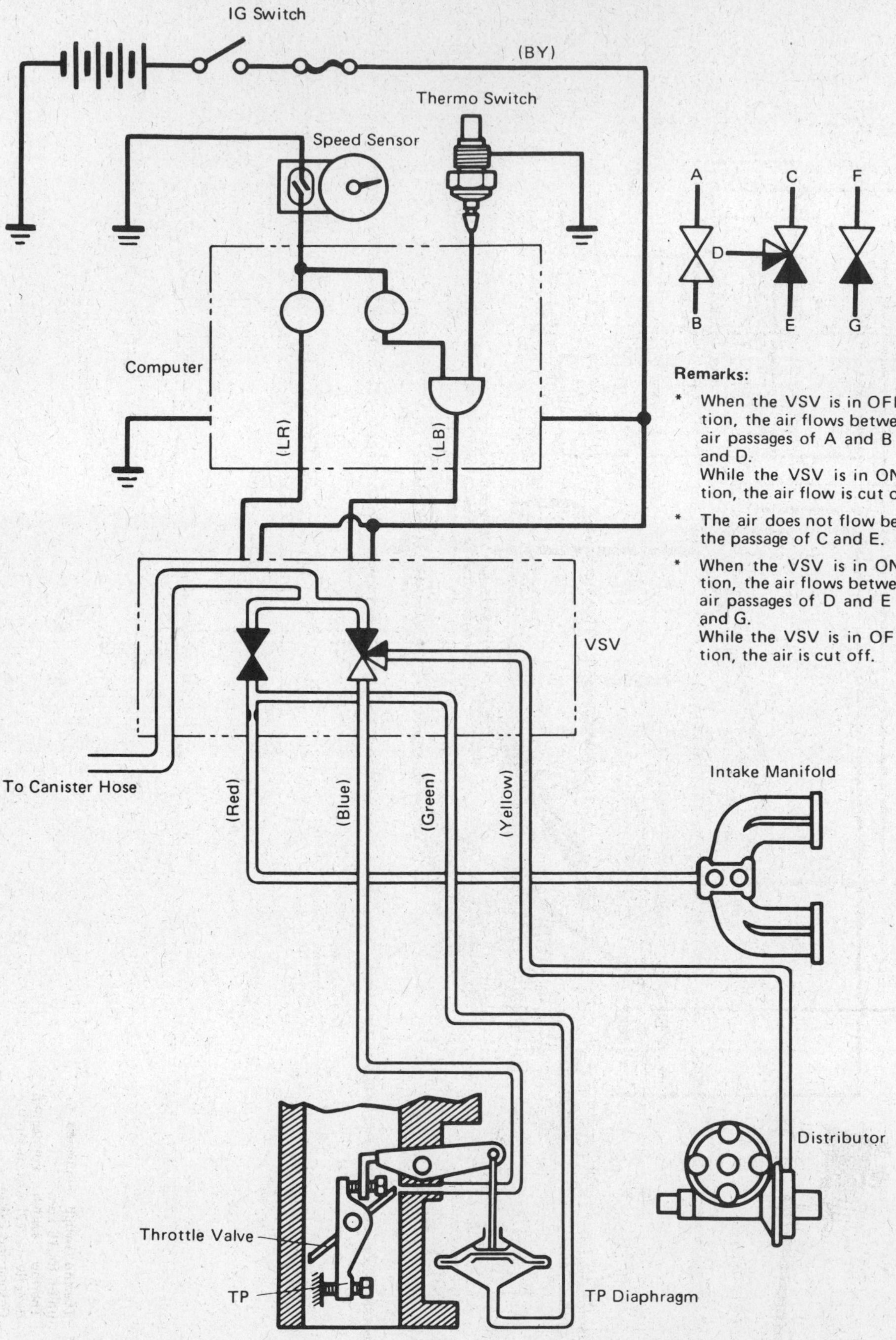

IG Switch

(BY)

Thermo Switch

Speed Sensor

Computer

(LR)

(LB)

A

C

F

D

E

G

Remarks:

* When the VSV is in OFF position, the air flows between the air passages of A and B also C and D.
  While the VSV is in ON position, the air flow is cut off.

* The air does not flow between the passage of C and E.

* When the VSV is in ON position, the air flows between the air passages of D and E also F and G.
  While the VSV is in OFF position, the air is cut off.

VSV

To Canister Hose

(Red)

(Blue)

(Green)

(Yellow)

Intake Manifold

Distributor

Throttle Valve

TP

TP Diaphragm

Fig. 3.55. Emission control schematic diagram - 1974 USA models

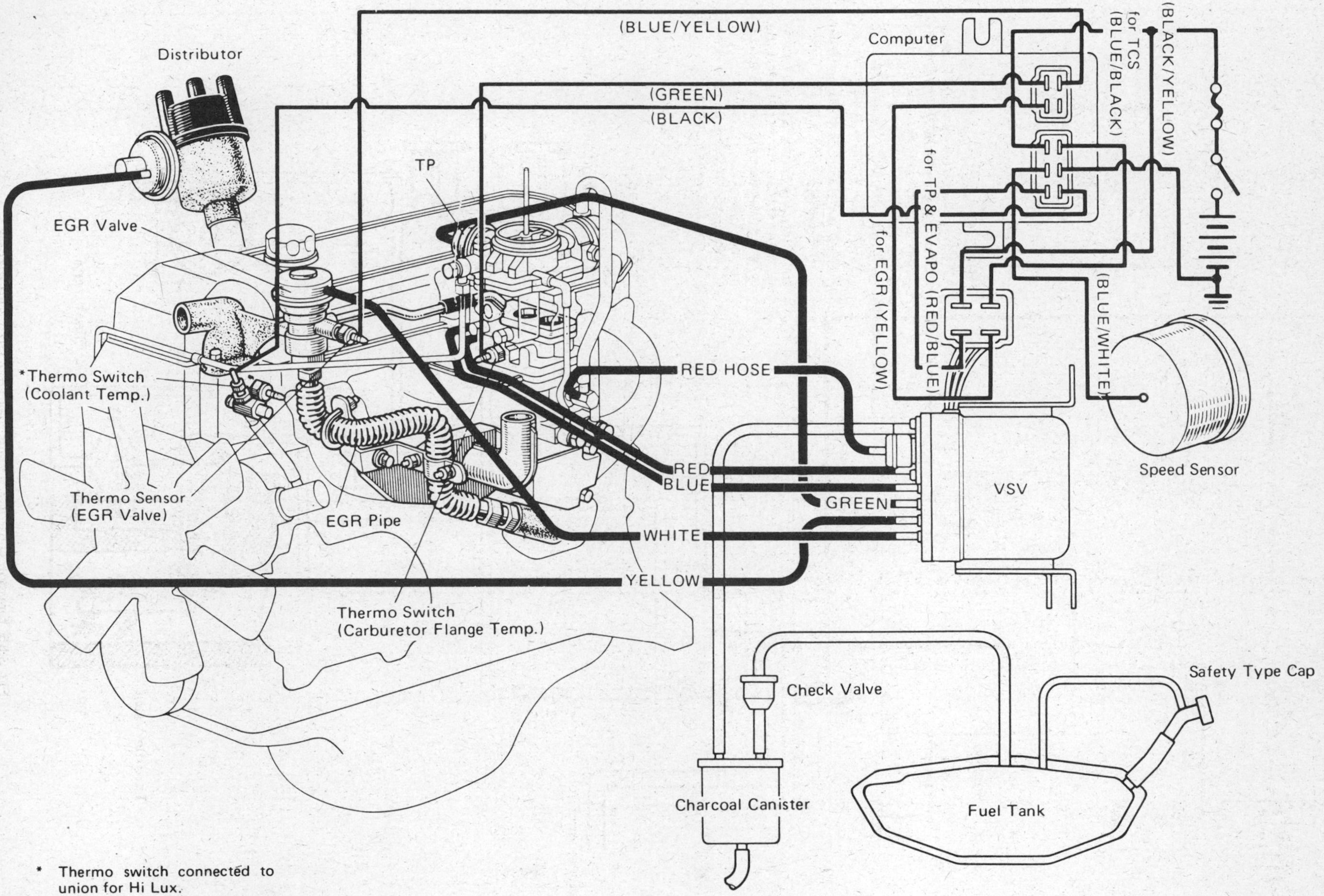

(BLACK/YELLOW)

for TCS
(BLUE/BLACK)

(BLUE/WHITE)

Speed Sensor

Safety Type Cap

for TP & EVAPO (RED/BLUE)

for EGR (YELLOW)

Computer

VSV

Fuel Tank

Check Valve

(BLUE/YELLOW)

(GREEN)

(BLACK)

RED HOSE

RED
BLUE

GREEN

WHITE

YELLOW

Charcoal Canister

TP

Thermo Switch
(Carburetor Flange Temp.)

EGR Pipe

Distributor

EGR Valve

*Thermo Switch
(Coolant Temp.)

Thermo Sensor
(EGR Valve)

Fig. 3.56. Emission control connections diagram - 1974 California models

* Thermo switch connected to
union for Hi Lux.
Thermo switch connected
directly to cylinder head for
Corona and Celica.

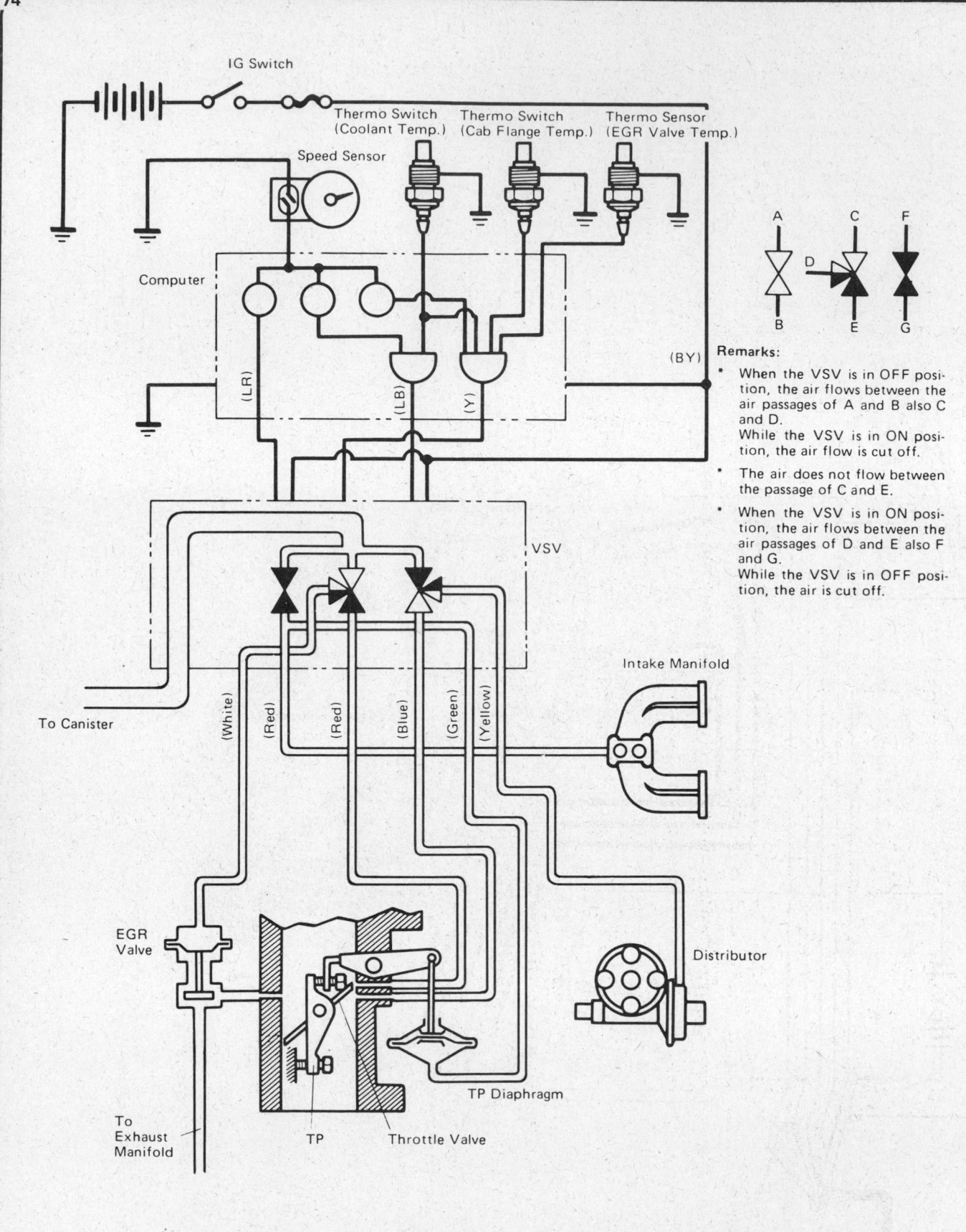

IG Switch

Thermo Switch (Coolant Temp.) **Thermo Switch** (Cab Flange Temp.) **Thermo Sensor** (EGR Valve Temp.)

Speed Sensor

Computer

(LR)   (LB)   (Y)   (BY)

VSV

To Canister

(White) (Red) (Red) (Blue) (Green) (Yellow)

Intake Manifold

EGR Valve

Distributor

TP Diaphragm

To Exhaust Manifold

TP   **Throttle Valve**

Remarks:

* When the VSV is in OFF position, the air flows between the air passages of A and B also C and D.
  While the VSV is in ON position, the air flow is cut off.

* The air does not flow between the passage of C and E.

* When the VSV is in ON position, the air flows between the air passages of D and E also F and G.
  While the VSV is in OFF position, the air is cut off.

A   C   F
D
B   E   G

Fig. 3.57. Emission control schematic diagram - 1974 California models

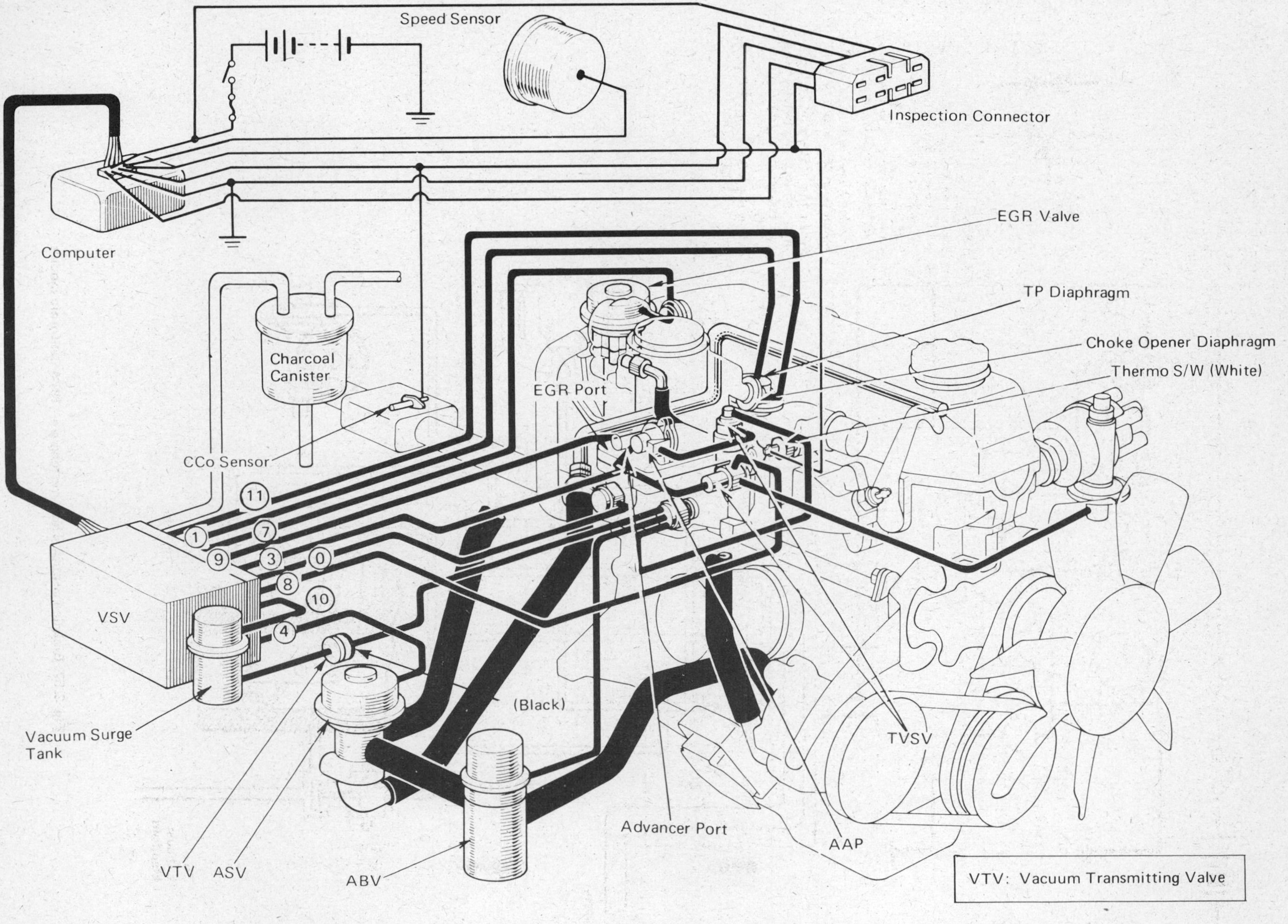

Inspection Connector

EGR Valve

TP Diaphragm

Choke Opener Diaphragm
Thermo S/W (White)

VTV: Vacuum Transmitting Valve

TVSV

AAP

Advancer Port

Speed Sensor

EGR Port

(Black)

ABV

Charcoal Canister

VTV ASV

CCo Sensor

11
7
3
8
10
4

9
1
0

Computer

VSV

Vacuum Surge Tank

Fig. 3.58. Emission control connections diagram - 1975 models

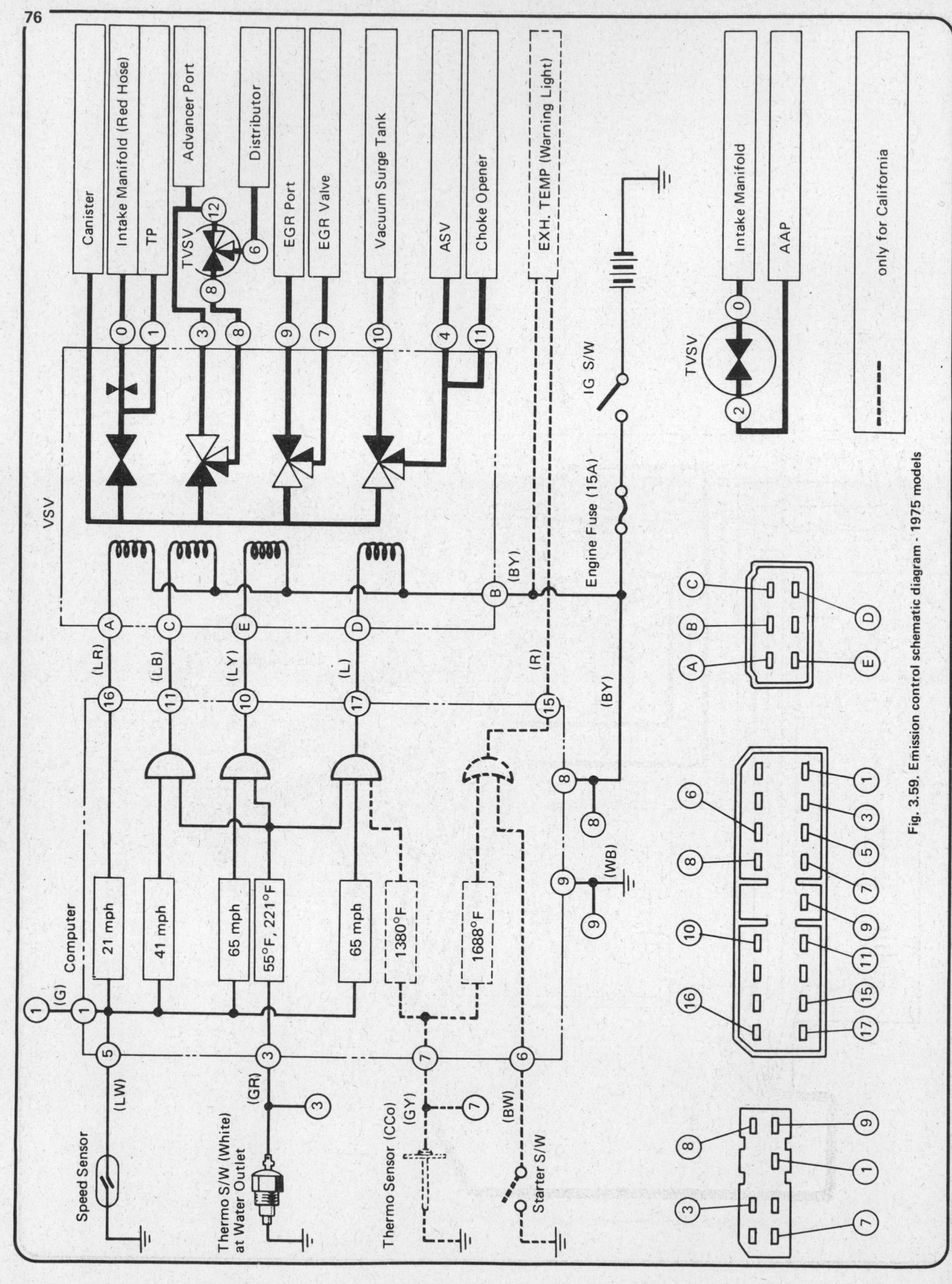

Fig. 3.59. Emission control schematic diagram - 1975 models

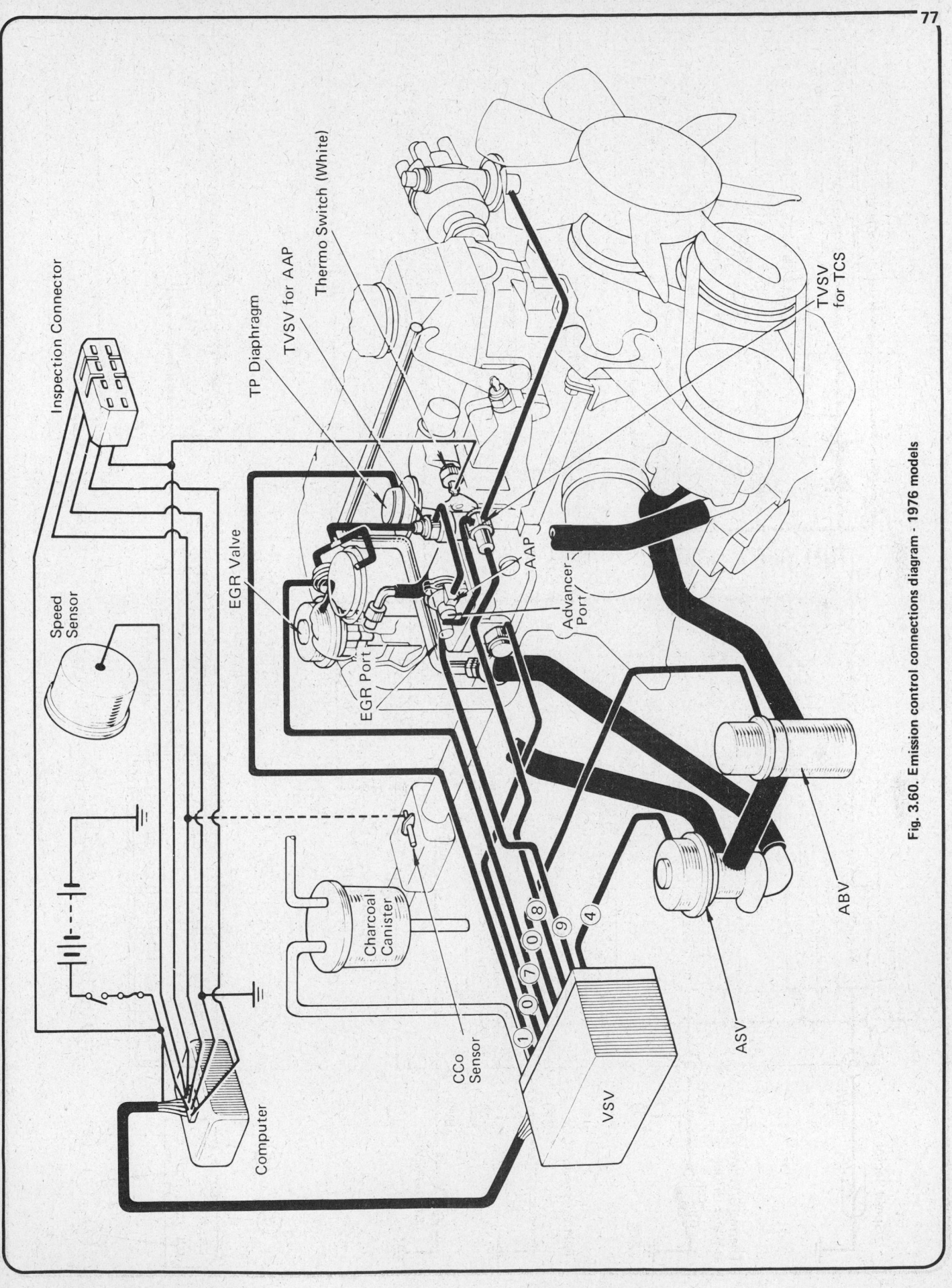

Inspection Connector

Thermo Switch (White)

TVSV for AAP

TP Diaphragm

TVSV for TCS

Speed Sensor

EGR Valve

EGR Port

AAP

Advancer Port

Charcoal Canister

ABV

ASV

CCo Sensor

VSV

Computer

Fig. 3.60. Emission control connections diagram - 1976 models

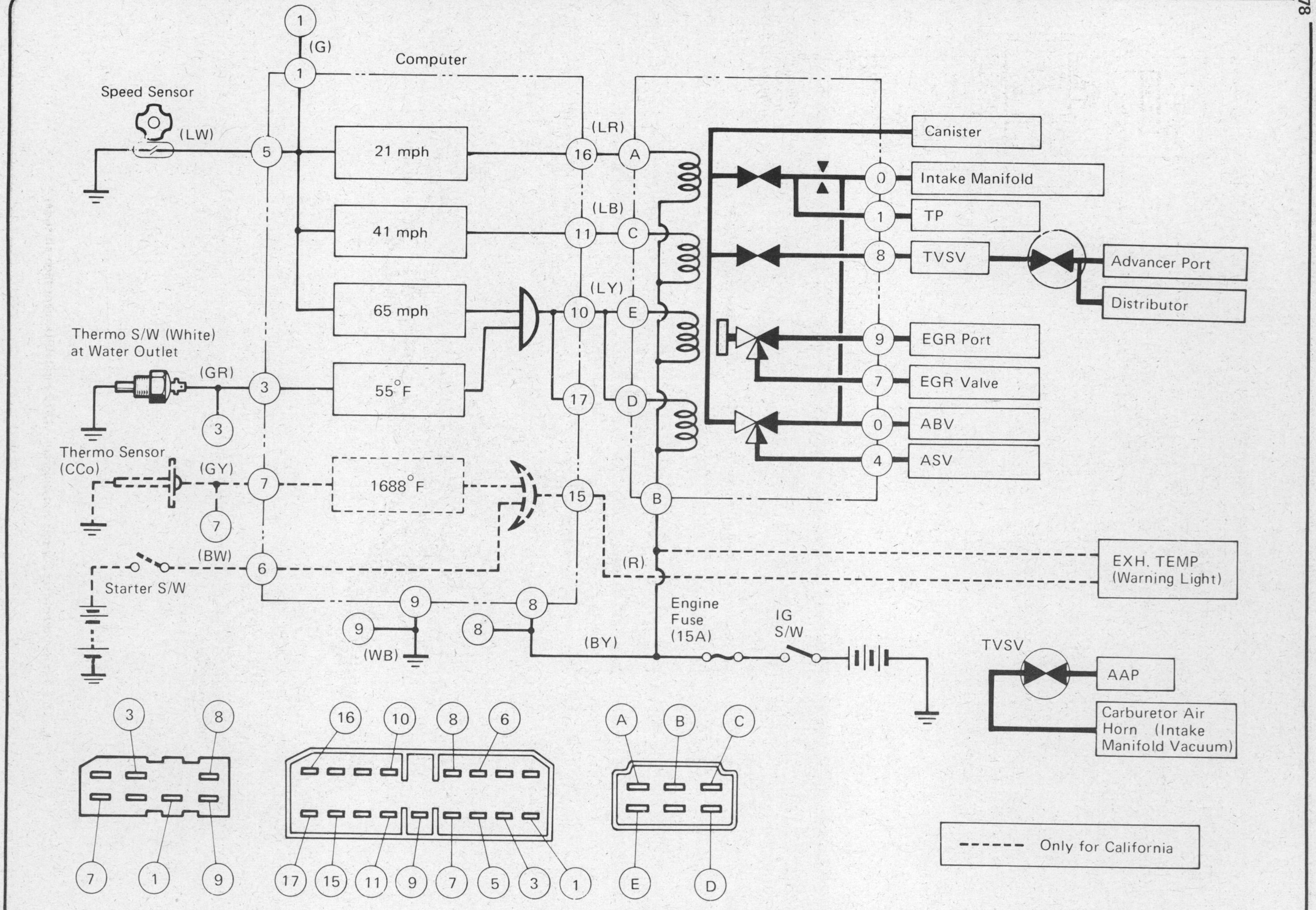

Fig. 3.61. Emission control schematic diagram - 1976 models

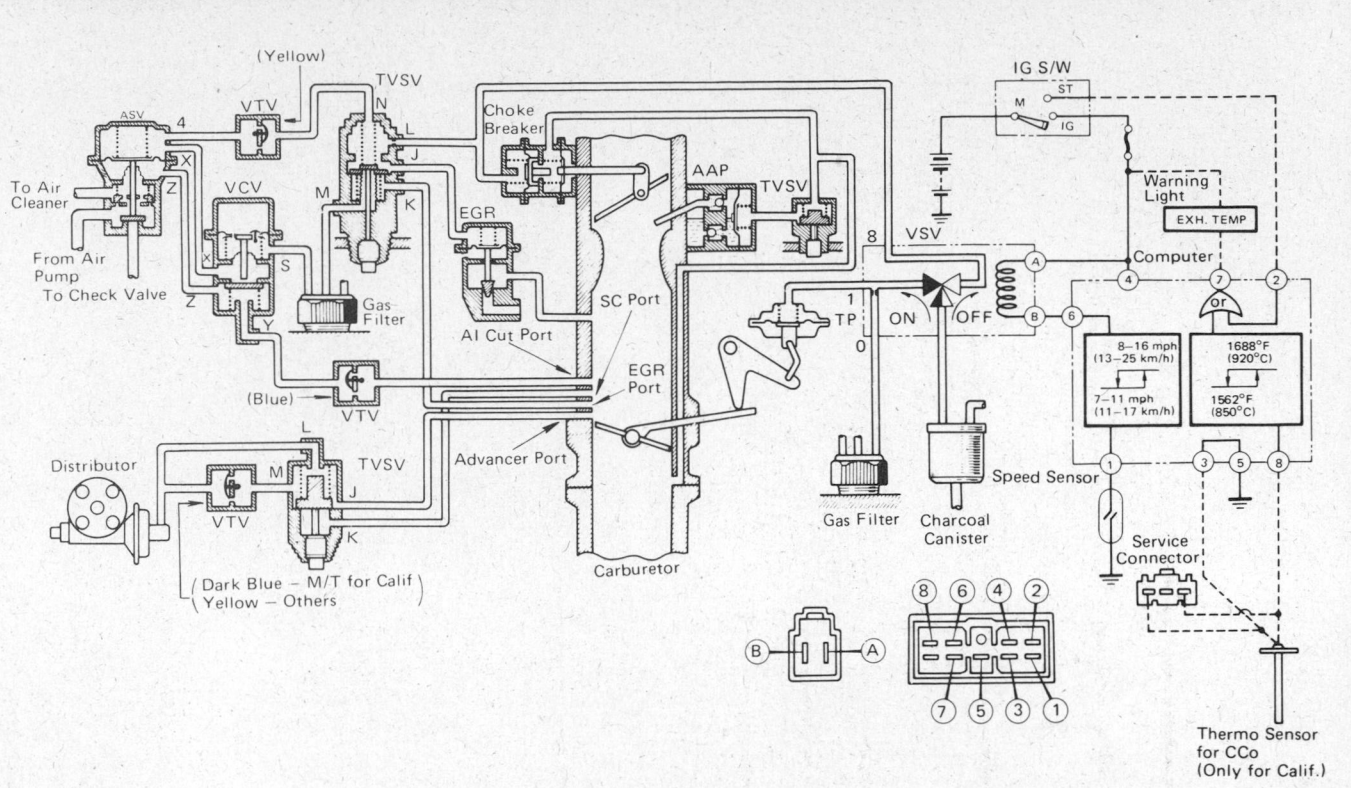

Fig. 3.62. Emission control schematic diagram - 1977 models (except high altitude)

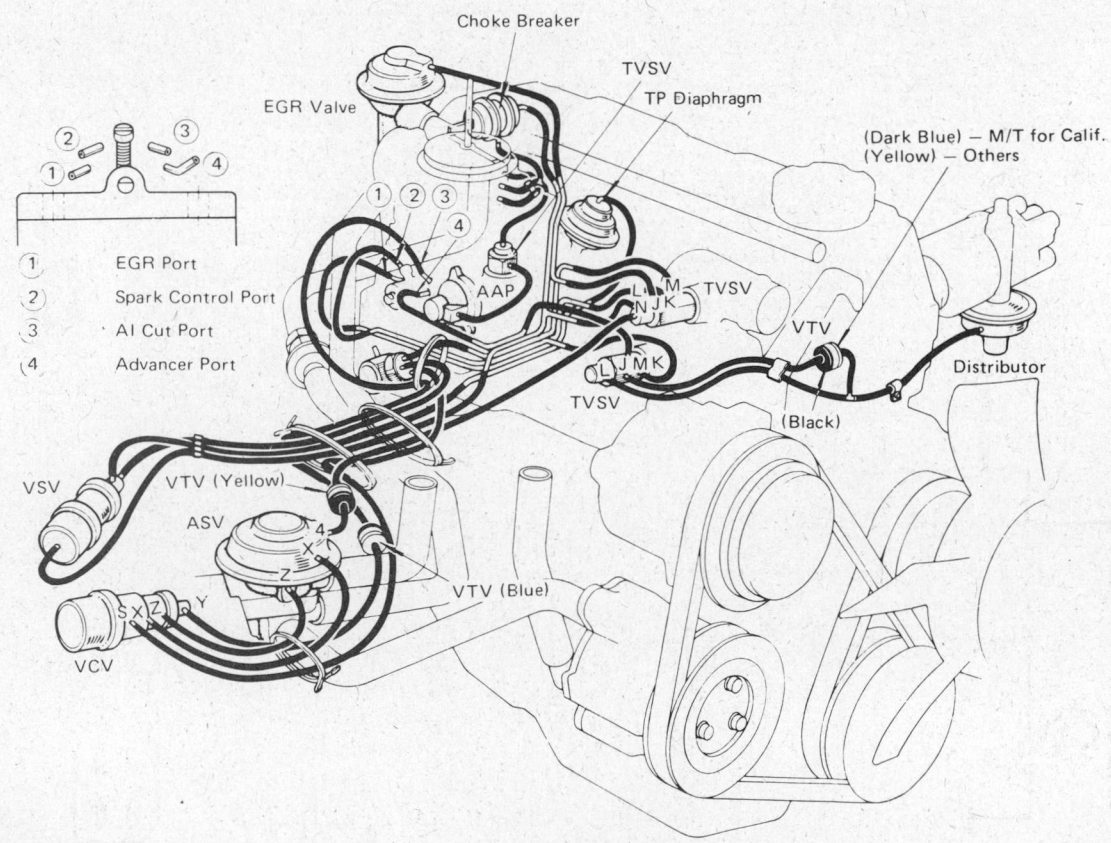

Fig. 3.63. Emission control connection diagram - 1977 models (except high altitude)

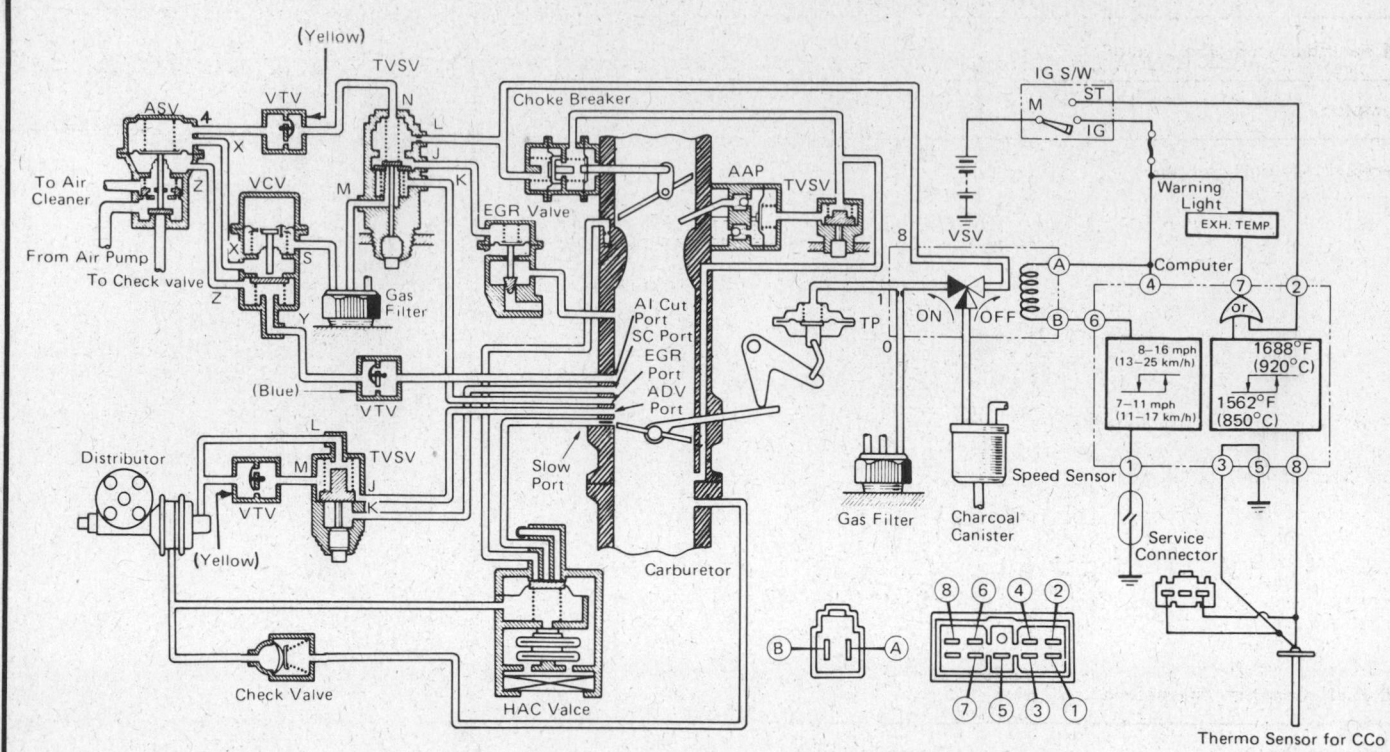

Fig. 3.64. Emission control schematic diagram 1977 (high altitude models)

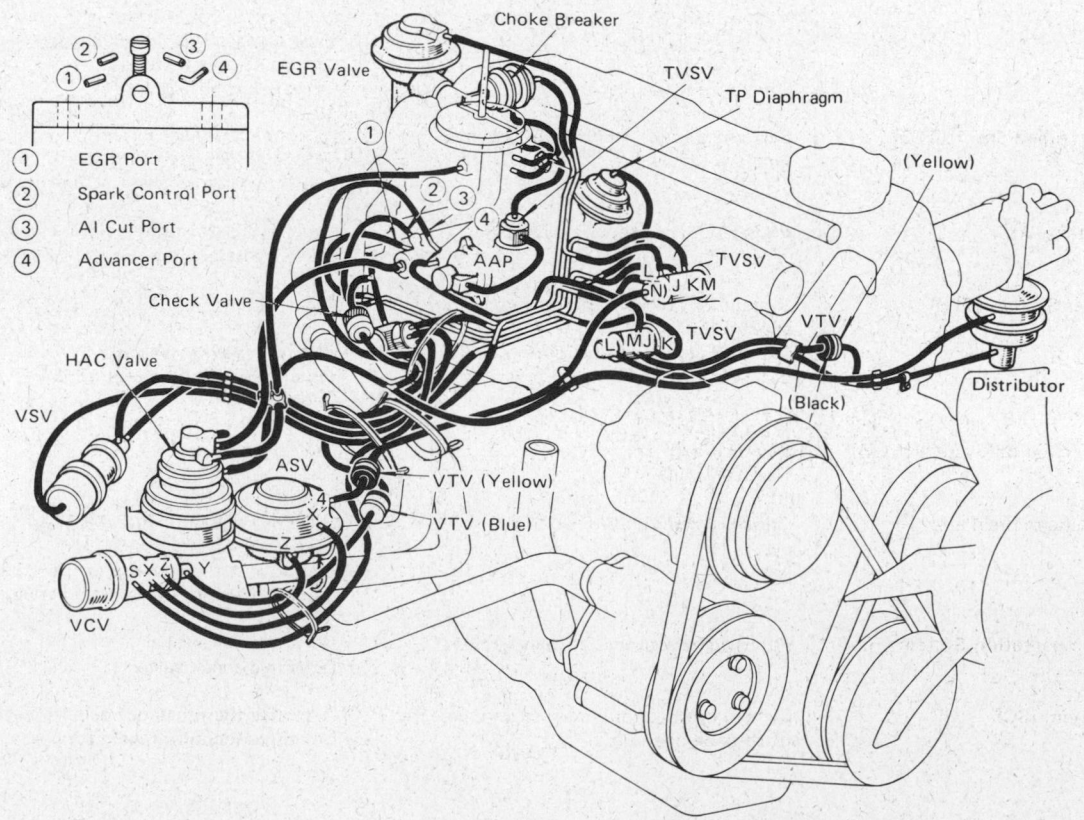

Fig. 3.65. Emission control connection diagram 1977 (high altitude models)

24 Fault diagnosis - fuel system

Symptom	Cause
Excessive fuel consumption	Air filter choked. Leakage from pump, carburettor or fuel lines or fuel tank. Float chamber flooding. Distributor condenser faulty. Distributor weights or vacuum capsule faulty. Mixture too rich. Contact breaker gap too wide. Incorrect valve clearances. Incorrect spark plug gaps. Tyres under inflated. Dragging brakes. Choke sticking closed.
Fuel starvation or mixture weakness	Clogged fuel line filter. Float chamber needle valve clogged. Faulty fuel pump valves. Fuel pump diaphragm split. Fuel pipe unions loose. Fuel pump cover leaking. Inlet manifold gasket or carburettor flange gasket leaking. Incorrect adjustment of carburettor.

25 Fault diagnosis - emission control system

System or circuit	Symptom	Cause
Crankcase ventilation	Oil fume seepage from engine	Stuck or clogged PCV valve. Split or collapsed hoses.
Fuel Evaporative Emission Control	Fuel odour Vapour will not be drawn into manifold Rough running engine	Stuck filler cap valve. Choked canister. Collapsed or split hoses. Vacuum switching valve defective. Speed sensor defective. Defective non-return valve.
Transmission Controlled Spark (TCS)	System operates at incorrect speed or temperature	Defective speed sensor. Defective vacuum switch valve. Defective thermostatic vacuum switching valve.
Air Injection System (AIS)	Fume emission from exhaust pipe	Slack or broken air pump drive belt. Split or broken hoses. Clogged air filter. Defective air pump.
Throttle Positioner System (TPS)	System fails to operate during acceleration System fails to turn off during deceleration	Adjust linkage, check vacuum hose to diaphragm unit. Defective diaphragm. Defective vacuum switching valve. Defective sensor.
Exhaust Gas Recirculation System (EGR)	Erratic idling Reduced power	Faulty valve. Faulty valve.
Choke opener or choke breaker	Choke remains closed too long	Defective choke opener diaphragm. Defective vacuum switch valve. Defective thermosensors or speed sensor. Blocked vacuum transmitting valve.
High Altitude Compensation System (HAC)	Poor engine response at high altitude	Defective HAC valve. Defective check valve.
Spark control system (SC)	System operates at incorrect temperature of throttle opening	Defective thermostatic vacuum switch valve. Defective vacuum transmitting valve.

Chapter 4 Ignition system

For modifications and information applicable to later USA models, refer to Supplement at end of manual

Contents

Specifications

System type ... ... Battery, coil and contact breaker. Electronic ignition system used on USA models with 20R engine

Engine firing order ... ... 1 - 3 - 4 - 2 (No 1 cylinder nearest radiator)

Ignition timing
18R engine:
    1974 models on, automatic transmission ... ... 7⁰ btdc at 800 rpm in 'N'
    1974 models on, manual transmission ... ... 7⁰ btdc at 650 rpm
20R engine:
    Pre-1977 models ... ... 8⁰ btdc at 850 rpm
    1977 models, automatic transmission ... ... 8⁰ btdc at 850 rpm in 'N'
    1977 models, manual transmission ... ... 8⁰ btdc at 800 rpm
    1977 models, high altitude (up to 4000 ft/1220 m) ... ... 8⁰ btdc at 700/900 rpm
    1977 models, high altitude (over 4000 ft/1220 m) ... ... 13⁰ btdc at 700/900 rpm

Distributor
Contact breaker points gap ... ... 0.018 in (0.45 mm)
Dwell angle ... ... 50 to 54⁰
Damping spring gap ... ... 0.004 to 0.016 in (0.1 to 0.4 mm)
Condenser capacity (not applicable to electronic ignition) ... ... 0.22 mfd
Direction of rotor rotation ... ... Clockwise

Spark plugs
Type:
    18R engine, Europe ... ... Nippondenso W20EPR
                                              NGK   BPR6ES
    18R engine, other markets ... ... Nippondenso W20EP
                                              NGK   BP6ES
    20R engine ... ... Nippondenso W16EP or W16EX-U
                                              NGK   BP5ES-L or BP5EA-L
Electrode gap ... ... 0.031 in (0.8 mm)

Ignition coil

	18R engine	20R engine
Primary resistance	1.3 to 1.6 ohms	1.3 to 1.5 ohms
Secondary resistance	9500 to 14500 ohms	6500 to 10500 ohms
External series resistance	1.3 to 1.7 ohms	1.3 to 1.7 ohms

Torque wrench setting

	lb f ft	kg f m
Spark plugs	15	2.1

1 General description

Two different types of ignition system are used on models covered by this Manual. These are the conventional contact breaker type and a semi-transistorized ignition system, introduced for 1975 USA models (20R engine).

Conventional type

The ignition system comprises the following components:

The battery which provides a current to the coil.

The ignition/starter switch.

The coil which acts as a transformer to step up the 12 volt battery voltage to many thousands of volts, sufficient to jump the spark plug gaps.

The distributor which comprises, contact breaker, condenser, rotor arm, distributor cap with brush, and centrifugal and vacuum advance and retard mechanism, and is driven by the oil pump driveshaft or camshaft at half crankshaft speed.

The spark plugs which are the medium to ignite the compressed mixture in the combustion chambers.

Low and high tension wires connecting the various components.

When the ignition is switched on, a current flows from the battery to the ignition switch, through the coil primary winding to the moving contact breaker inside the distributor cap and to earth when the contact breaker points are in the closed position. During this period of points closure, the current flows through the primary winding of the coil and magnetises the laminated iron core which in turn creates a magnetic field through the coil primary and secondary windings.

Each time the points open due to the rotation of the distributor cam, the current flow through the primary winding of the coil is interrupted. This causes the induction of a very high voltage (25,000 volts) in the coil secondary winding. This HT (high tension) current is distributed to the spark plugs in correct firing order sequence by the rotor arm and by means of the cap brush and HT leads.

A condenser is fitted to the distributor, and is connected between the moving contact breaker and earth. It prevents excessive arcing and pitting of the contact breaker points, and also assists in the rapid breakdown of the coil magnetic field.

The actual point of ignition of the fuel/air mixture which occurs a few degrees before tdc is determined by correct static setting of the ignition timing as described in Section 6. The ignition is advanced to meet varying operating conditions by the centrifugal counterweights fitted in the base of the distributor body and by vacuum from the inlet manifold operating through a capsule linked to the movable distributor baseplate.

Slight variations of the static ignition setting may be made by means of the vernier adjuster to compensate for different fuel qualities.

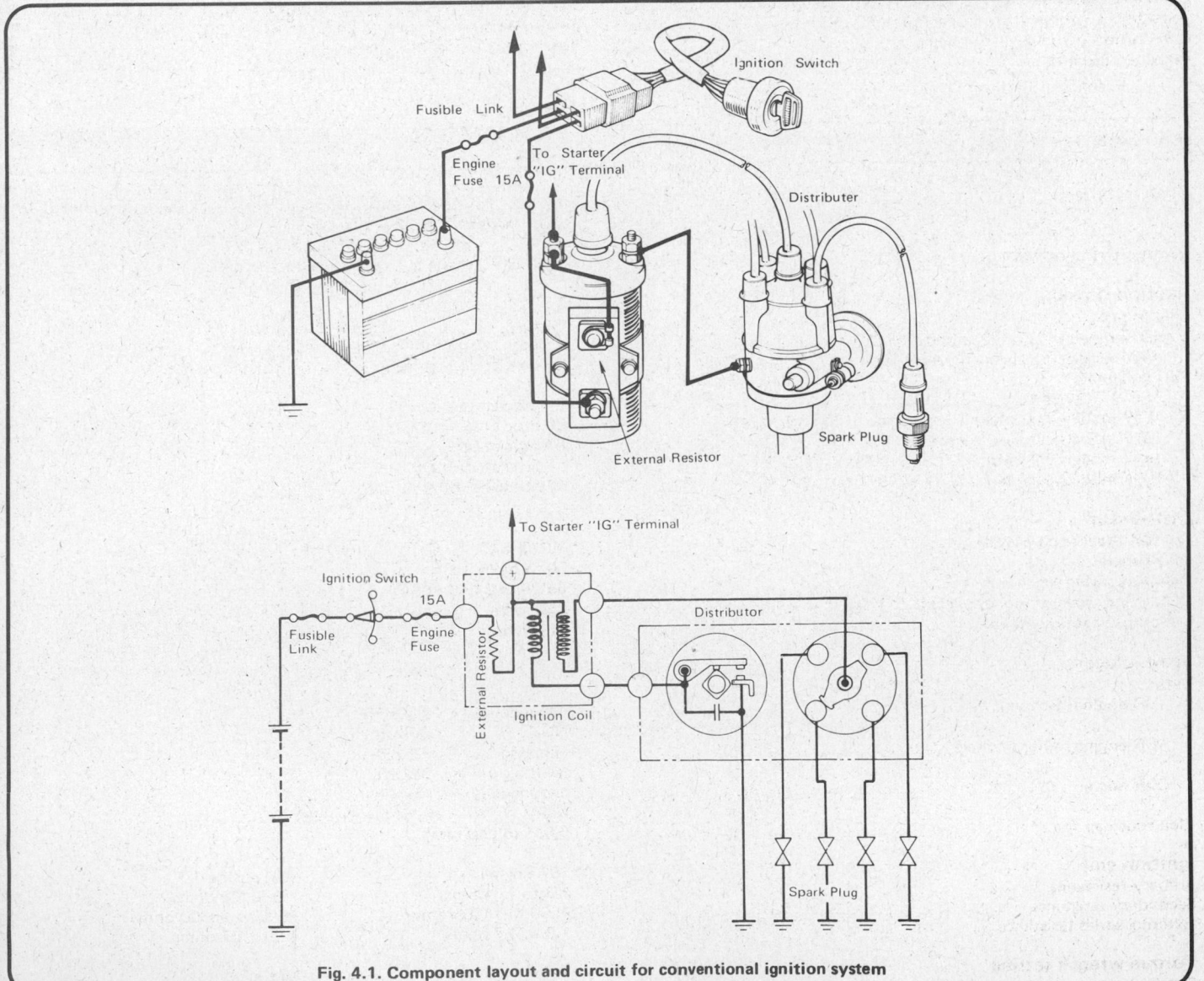

Fig. 4.1. Component layout and circuit for conventional ignition system

Semi-transistorized type

In the semi-transistorized ignition circuit, the contact breaker part of the circuit is modified by the deletion of the condenser which is normally connected in parallel with the contact breaker points. Instead, an electronic switching circuit (igniter) is incorporated, which helps to prolong the life of the points and produces an improved spark during starting and slow running conditions. The distributors used for the conventional and semi-transistorized systems are almost identical; high altitude distributors have a dual diaphragm unit - see High Altitude Compensation in Chapter 3.

When the contact breaker points are closed current flows in the path shown in heavy lines in Fig. 4.2; this flows through the ignition coil primary winding in the same way as with the 'conventional' system.

When the contact breaker points open, no current flows through the igniter and the coil primary current is switched off. This induces a high coil secondary voltage in a similar manner to that in the 'conventional' system.

In the event of failure of the semi-transistorized system an emergency measure can be taken to prevent the vehicle from being immobilized. This requires a 0.22 mfd condenser being connected to the distributor body terminal and earth, the distributor body terminal being connected to the ignition coil '—' terminal, and the original igniter terminations being disconnected completely.

Note: Where a semi-transistorized ignition system is fitted it is essential that any tachometer connection is made to the ignition coil - terminal instead of the distributor body terminal, if this is not done, the engine may misfire.

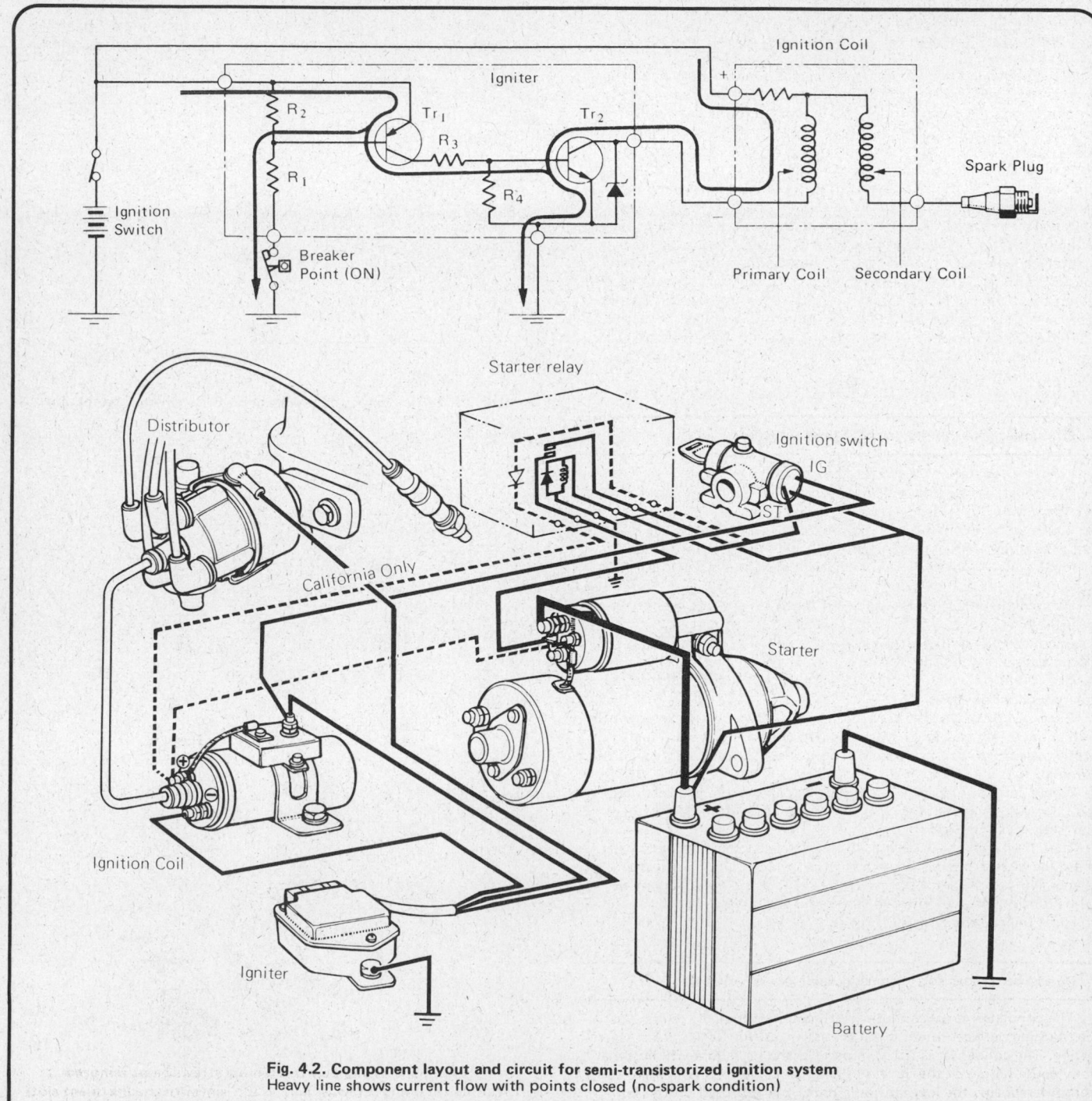

Fig. 4.2. Component layout and circuit for semi-transistorized ignition system
Heavy line shows current flow with points closed (no-spark condition)

2 Contact breaker points and damping spring - adjustment

Note: Wherever possible, adjustment of the contact breaker points should be by the Dwell Angle method to obtain the most accurate setting. For this, a proprietary Dwell Angle meter should be used in accordance with the manufacturer's instructions. Adjustment of the dwell angle is the same procedure as adjustment of the points gap.

1   Pull off the HT leads from the spark plugs and mark them 1 to 4 for easy identification.
2   Spring back the distributor cover securing clips and lift the cover to one side. Withdraw the rotor and the dustproof cover.
3   Using a spanner on the crankshaft pulley securing bolt, rotate the engine in its normal direction of rotation until the heel of the movable contact breaker arm is on one of the 4 high points of the cam. Removal of the spark plugs will make turning the engine easier.
4   Examine the contact faces of the (now open) points and, if they are pitted or burnt, they must be removed and dressed as described in the next Section.
5   If the points are in good order, check the gap by inserting a feeler gauge of the specified thickness. Insert the feeler blade in a vertical position and if the gap is correct, it will just fall by its own weight. If the gap is incorrect, adjust the fixed contact arm by loosening the retaining screw and moving it, as necessary, by means of a screwdriver blade inserted in the cut-out in the contact arm.
6   When the gap is correct, tighten the contact arm screw and remove the feeler gauge.
7   Now rotate the crankshaft, if necessary, so that the rubbing block of the damping spring is towards one of the lowest points of the cam.
8   Using a feeler gauge, check the gap between the cam and the rubbing block. If adjustment is necessary to obtain the gap specified, loosen the damping spring retaining screw and reposition the spring as necessary. Recheck the gap after tightening the screw.
9   Refit the dust cover, rotor arm and distributor cap, and reconnect the HT leads. Ensure that the ring spanner has been removed from the crankshaft pulley bolt.

3 Contact breaker points - removal and refitting

1   Carry out operations 1 and 2 of the preceding Section.
2   Detach the spring retaining clip from the top of the contact breaker arm pivot post.
3   Unscrew the nuts on the LT terminal on the outside of the distributor body just enough to enable the contact arm lead and spade terminal to be withdrawn, then lift the movable arm from the baseplate.
4   Remove the securing screw and lift the fixed contact breaker arm from the baseplate.
5   Examine the points. After a period of operation, one contact face should have a pip and the other a crater caused by arcing. This is a normal condition which should be removed by dressing the faces squarely on an oilstone.
6   Excessive pitting of the contact points may be caused by operation with an incorrect gap, the voltage regulator setting too high, faulty or wrong type of condenser, loose distributor baseplate or battery terminals.
7   Where contact breaker points are so badly worn or the pitting so deep that excessive rubbing would be required to eliminate it, then they should be renewed.
8   Wipe the faces of the points with methylated spirit before fitting, smear the high points of the cam with petroleum jelly. Apply a drop of engine oil to the pivot points of the contacts and mechanism and to the lubrication pad on top of the cam.
9   Refit the rotor, cap and HT leads.

4 Condenser (capacitor) - removal, testing and refitting

1   The condenser ensures that with the contact breaker points open, the sparking between them is not excessive, as this would cause severe pitting. The condenser is fitted in parallel and its failure will automatically cause failure of the ignition system as the points will be prevented from interrupting the low tension circuit. It is not used on the semi-transistorized ignition system.
2   Testing for an unserviceable condenser may be effected by switch-

ing on the ignition and separating the contact points by hand. If this action is accompanied by a blue flash then condenser failure is indicated. Difficult starting, missing of the engine after several miles running or badly pitted points are other indications of a faulty condenser.
3   The surest test is by substitution of a new unit.
4   To remove the condenser, unscrew its retaining screw and detach its lead from the LT terminal on the distributor body.
5   Refitting is the reverse of the removal procedure.

5 Distributor - removal and refitting

1   Remove No 1 spark plug and place a finger over the hole to feel the compression being generated as the engine is rotated by means of the crankshaft pulley bolt.
2   As soon as compression is felt this will indicate that No 1 piston is rising on its compression stroke. Continue turning the engine until the

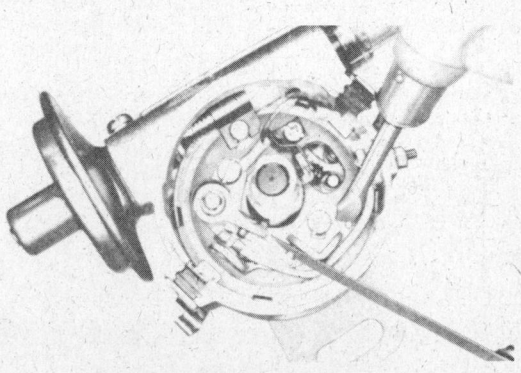

Fig. 4.3. Setting points gap - note screwdriver in adjustment slot

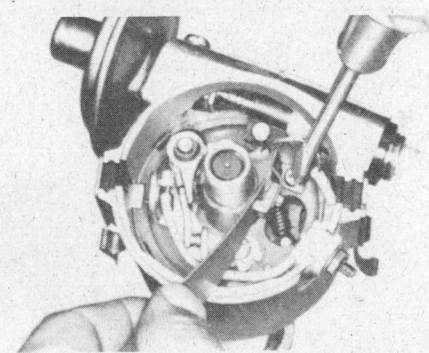

Fig. 4.4. Setting damping spring gap

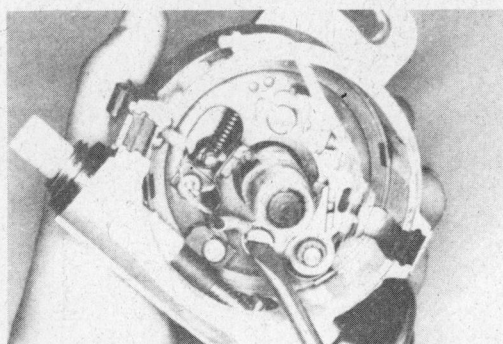

Fig. 4.5. One of the points retaining screws being removed (the other retaining screw is next to the screwdriver adjustment slot)

timing mark (not tdc mark) on the crankshaft pulley is in line with the pointer on the timing cover.

3   Remove the distributor cap, and mark the rim of the distributor body at a point opposite to the centre line of the contact end of the rotor arm. This is equivalent to alignment with No 1 contact in the distributor cap. Also mark the installed position of the distributor body for reference.

4   Disconnect the LT wire from the terminal on the distributor body.

5   Disconnect the vacuum tube from the distributor advance diaphragm unit.

6   Unbolt the distributor clamp plate and withdraw the distributor.

7   The distributor cap may be withdrawn if the HT leads are first disconnected from the spark plugs and coil centre socket.

8   If the engine is turned while the distributor is removed, reset the crankshaft pulley timing mark opposite the timing cover pointer (No 1 piston on compression stroke) as described in paragraph 1, before fitting the distributor.

9   On 18R engines, align the distributor as shown in Fig. 4.8 and insert it into the crankcase. As it is pressed down, the rotor will turn clockwise and should finally be as shown in Fig. 4.9. Now rotate the distributor body anticlockwise until the points **just** open and tighten the clamp plate bolt. The marks made before removal should now align.

10   On 20R engines, fit the distributor body with the octane selector pointing upwards and the rotor pointing towards the cap upper hold-down spring. As the distributor is pushed fully home, the rotor will turn anticlockwise and should then be in the position shown in Fig. 4.10. Turn the distributor clockwise to close the points then slowly anticlockwise until the points **just** open; tighten the clamp plate bolt in this position.

11   Refit the distributor cap, leads and vacuum pipe, then check the timing as described in Section 6.

---

6   Ignition timing - checking and adjustment

---

1   If the ignition timing point has been lost completely, it will be necessary to check that the distributor is fitted in the correct position with regard to the crankshaft. This is dealt with in Section 5.

2   To check the static ignition timing, first check the distributor points gap and/or dwell angle as described previously (Section 2).

3   Rotate the crankshaft to get No 1 piston at the correct timing point (see Specifications) as described in Paragraphs 1 and 2 of Section 5. Remove the distributor cap.

4   Connect a 12V bulb of 5 watts maximum rating between an earth point on the engine and the terminal on the distributor body.

5   Switch on the ignition. If the timing is correctly set, the bulb should have just illuminated at this point, but it will be necessary to rotate the crankshaft anticlockwise slightly until the bulb extinguishes, then rotate it clockwise again until it illuminates.

6   Check the point at which the bulb **just** illuminates; this should be as the timing mark aligns with the pointer. If the bulb illuminates before the mark on the flywheel is reached, the ignition is too far advanced and the distributor must be turned clockwise a little to correct it. If the bulb illuminates after the mark on the flywheel reaches the pointer, the ignition is too far retarded and the distributor must be turned anticlockwise a little. **Note:** This adjustment can be done using the octane selector to advance or retard the ignition, but if this method is used the datum point will be altered. For most practical purposes this does not matter.

7   After any adjustment, tighten the distributor clamp bolt and recheck the setting. Refit the distributor cap.

8   Having checked the static setting, the timing should now be checked dynamically with the engine running at idle speed using a stroboscopic lamp in accordance with the manufacturer's instructions. It may be necessary to reposition the distributor slightly now, or to alter the position of the octane selector. No variation in timing should be obtained whether the distributor vacuum line is connected or not at idle speed.

9   With the engine idling and the vacuum line disconnected, check that the timing point varies with throttle opening. This checks that the centrifugal advance is operating.

10   With the engine idling, detach the distributor vacuum hose at the carburettor and apply suction (by mouth) to the distributor diaphragm;

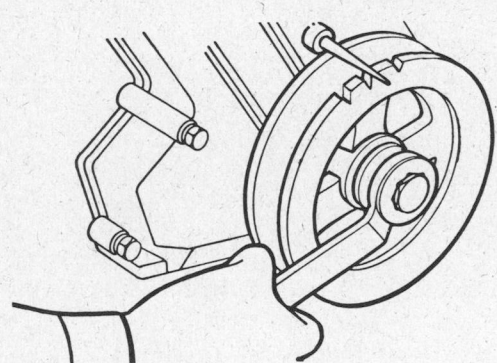

Fig. 4.6. **Ignition timing marks on 18R engine** The centre mark (red) is 7° BTDC; the one on the left is TDC

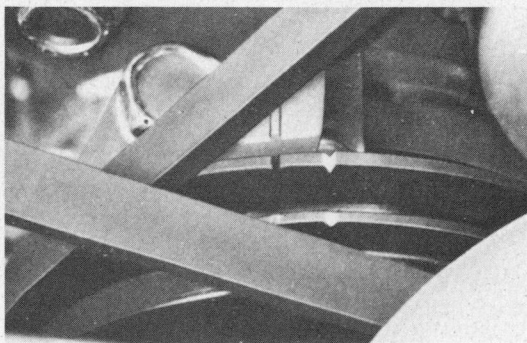

Fig. 4.7. **Ignition timing marks on 20R engine** The mark on the right (white) is the static timing mark; the one on the left is TDC

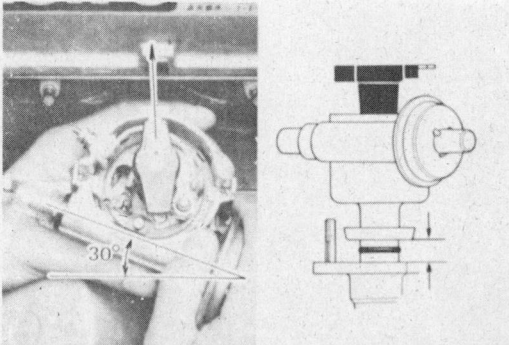

Fig. 4.8. **Distributor installation showing rotor position before gear engages (18R)**

Fig. 4.9. **Distributor installation showing rotor position after gear engages (18R)**

Fig. 4.10. Distributor installation (20R) The line shows the rotor position before the gear has engaged

the timing should now advance.

11 It may be necessary to make a minor adjustment to prevent 'pinking' from the engine when labouring or when a low octane fuel is being used. In this event, retard the ignition slightly by means of the octane selector.

7 Distributor - dismantling, inspection and reassembly

1 Remove the distributor cap, rotor and dustproof cover.
2 Remove the vacuum advance adjuster (octane selector) cap.
3 Pull off the point cover, where applicable.
4 Detach the points wire from the terminal on the distributor body; also detach the condenser wire, where applicable. Lift out the terminal insulator.
5 Remove the contact breaker points assembly and the damping spring.
6 Where applicable, remove the condensor from its attachment point.
7 Remove the screw (models without a condenser) and detach the vacuum advance unit.
8 Pull out the two rubber plates, and unscrew the hold-down clips and earth wire screws.
9 Lift out the breaker plate, and detach the mechanical advance springs. The springs are not identical, so check which way round they are fitted.
10 Remove the E-ring, and take out the governor weights and bearings.
11 Remove the grease stopper and screw from the top of the spindle, and remove the cam.
12 Carefully drill out the pin retaining the gear; detach the gear from the spindle.
13 Remove the screws from the base of the distributor body and pull out the spindle (and bearing, where applicable).
14 Remove the remaining parts from the spindle.
15 Check for wear between the spindle and body on the 18R distributor. If evident, it is recommended that a new distributor body is obtained. Examine all the other parts for wear and damage (including the bearing on 20R distributors), renewing parts as necessary. Suck on

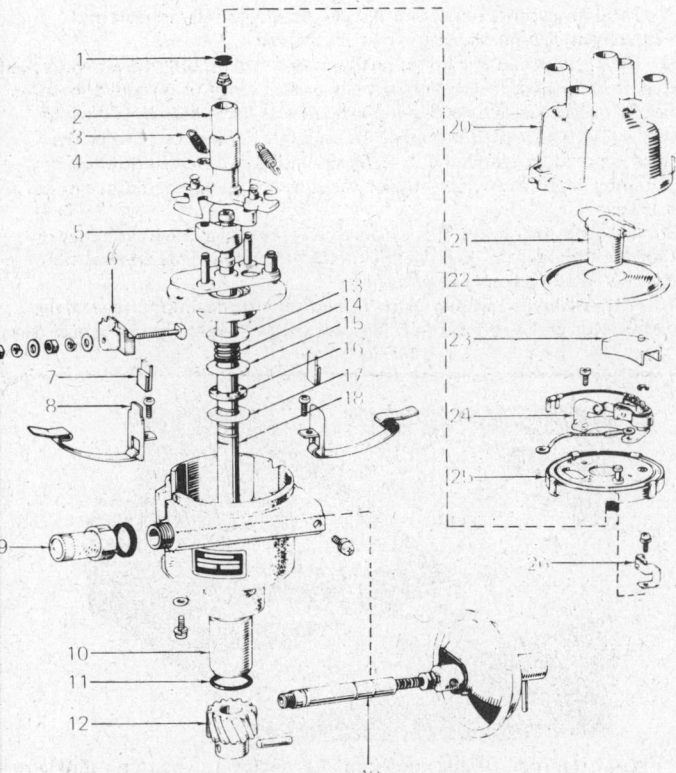

Fig. 4.11. Distributor - exploded view

The 20R distributor is shown.
The 18R distributor is similar except for the washers, bearing and associated parts on the spindle; also a condenser is fitted

1	Grease stopper	14	Spring
2	Cam	15	Washer
3	Spring	16	Bearing
4	E-ring	17	Washer
5	Weight	18	Spindle
6	Terminal insulator	19	Vacuum advance unit
7	Rubber plate	20	Cap
8	Hold-down clip	21	Rotor
9	Cap	22	Dustproof cover
10	Distributor body	23	Points cover
11	O-ring	24	Breaker points
12	Gear	25	Breaker plate
13	Washer	26	Damping spring

Fig. 4.12. Removing vacuum advance unit (20R distributor)
This screw also holds the condenser on 18R distributors

Fig. 4.13. Removing a hold-down clip

the diaphragm unit connection and check that the spindle moves. Examine the cap for cracks or tracking; if evident renew the cap.

16 Assembly of the distributor is basically the reverse of the dismantling procedure, but note the following:

a) *Lightly lubricate the rubbing surfaces of the spindle and body or bearing with a general purpose grease.*

b) *Ensure that the spindle and washer (18R) or spindle, bearings and washers (20R) are assembled as shown in Figs. 4.14 and 4.15.*

c) *When fitting the weights, align the 13.5 mark with the stopper - see Figs. 4.16 and 4.17.*

d) *Set the damping spring gap to that given in the Specifications. The gap is measured between the end of the rubbing block and one of the flats of the cam, and is adjusted by means of the spring attachment screw.*

e) *After setting the points gap, set the octane selector to the standard (datum) line.*

f) *Do not forget to peen over the ends of the gear pin if this was renewed.*

8 Semi-transistorized ignition unit (igniter)

1   This unit requires no maintenance apart from being kept clean and dry externally. In the event of malfunction, it can be bypassed as described in Section 1. If an internal fault occurs, the unit should be repaired by a Toyota dealer or an exchange unit obtained.

9 Spark plugs and leads

1   The correct functioning of the spark plugs is vital for the correct running and efficiency of the engine. The plugs fitted as standard are listed in the specification page.

2   At the intervals stated in Routine Maintenance the plugs should be

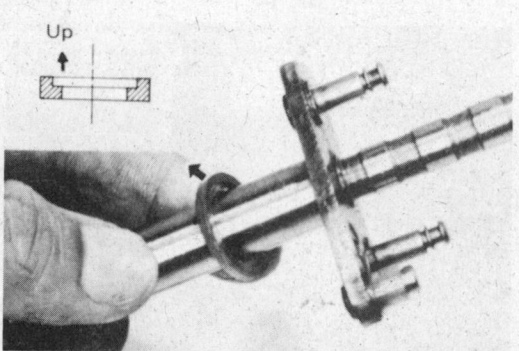

Fig. 4.14. Spindle and washer - 18R distributor

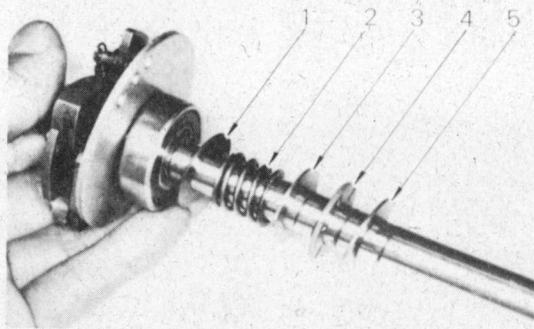

Fig. 4.15. Spindle and associated parts - 20R distributor
1 *Blue washer*   3 *Thin washer*   5 *Thick washer*
2 *Spring*   4 *Bearing*

Fig. 4.16. 13.5 mark alignment - 18R distributor

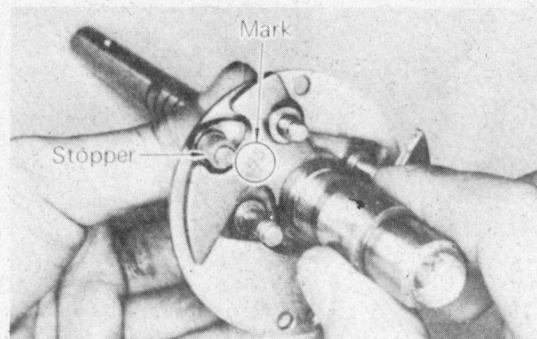

Fig. 4.17. 13.5 mark alignment - 20R distributor

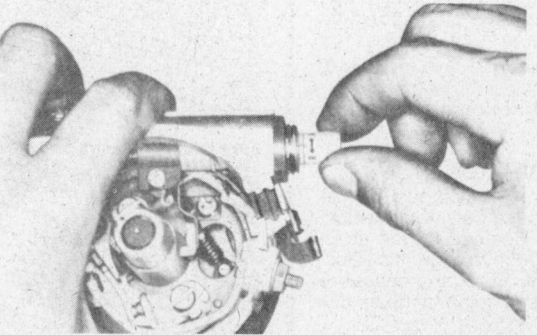

Fig. 4.18. Octane selector on standard (datum) line

CARBON DEPOSITS

Symptoms: Dry sooty deposits indicate a rich mixture or weak ignition. Causes misfiring, hard starting and hesitation.

Recommendation: Check for a clogged air cleaner, high float level, sticky choke and worn ignition points. Use a spark plug with a longer core nose for greater anti-fouling protection.

OIL DEPOSITS

Symptoms: Oily coating caused by poor oil control. Oil is leaking past worn valve guides or piston rings into the combustion chamber. Causes hard starting, misfiring and hesition.

Recommendation: Correct the mechanical condition with necessary repairs and install new plugs.

TOO HOT

Symptoms: Blistered, white insulator, eroded electrode and absence of deposits. Results in shortened plug life.

Recommendation: Check for the correct plug heat range, over-advanced ignition timing, lean fuel mixture, intake manifold vacuum leaks and sticking valves. Check the coolant level and make sure the radiator is not clogged.

PREIGNITION

Symptoms: Melted electrodes. Insulators are white, but may be dirty due to misfiring or flying debris in the combustion chamber. Can lead to engine damage.

Recommendation: Check for the correct plug heat range, over-advanced ignition timing, lean fuel mixture, clogged cooling system and lack of lubrication.

HIGH SPEED GLAZING

Symptoms: Insulator has yellowish, glazed appearance. Indicates that combustion chamber temperatures have risen suddenly during hard acceleration. Normal deposits melt to form a conductive coating. Causes misfiring at high speeds.

Recommendation: Install new plugs. Consider using a colder plug if driving habits warrant.

GAP BRIDGING

Symptoms: Combustion deposits lodge between the electrodes. Heavy deposits accumulate and bridge the electrode gap. The plug ceases to fire, resulting in a dead cylinder.

Recommendation: Locate the faulty plug and remove the deposits from between the electrodes.

NORMAL

Symptoms: Brown to grayish-tan color and slight electrode wear. Correct heat range for engine and operating conditions.

Recommendation: When new spark plugs are installed, replace with plugs of the same heat range.

ASH DEPOSITS

Symptoms: Light brown deposits encrusted on the side or center electrodes or both. Derived from oil and/or fuel additives. Excessive amounts may mask the spark, causing misfiring and hesitation during acceleration.

Recommendation: If excessive deposits accumulate over a short time or low mileage, install new valve guide seals to prevent seepage of oil into the combustion chambers. Also try changing gasoline brands.

WORN

Symptoms: Rounded electrodes with a small amount of deposits on the firing end. Normal color. Causes hard starting in damp or cold weather and poor fuel economy.

Recommendation: Replace with new plugs of the same heat range.

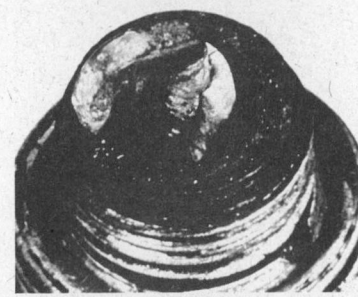

DETONATION

Symptoms: Insulators may be cracked or chipped. Improper gap setting techniques can also result in a fractured insulator tip. Can lead to piston damage.

Recommendation: Make sure the fuel anti-knock values meet engine requirements. Use care when setting the gaps on new plugs. Avoid lugging the engine.

SPLASHED DEPOSITS

Symptoms: After long periods of misfiring, deposits can loosen when normal combustion temperature is restored by an overdue tune-up. At high speeds, deposits flake off the piston and are thrown against the hot insulator, causing misfiring.

Recommendation: Replace the plugs with new ones or clean and reinstall the originals.

MECHANICAL DAMAGE

Symptoms: May be caused by a foreign object in the combustion chamber or the piston striking an incorrect reach (too long) plug. Causes a dead cylinder and could result in piston damage.

Recommendation: Remove the foreign object from the engine and/or install the correct reach plug.

removed, examined, cleaned and, if worn excessively, renewed. The condition of the spark plug will also tell much about the overall condition of the engine.

3   If the insulator nose of the spark plug is clean and white, with no deposits, this is indicative of a weak mixture, or too hot a plug. (A hot plug transfers heat away from the electrode slowly - a cold plug transfers it away quickly).

4   If the top and insulator nose is covered with hard black looking deposits, then this is indicative that the mixture is too rich. Should the plug be black and oily, then it is likely that the engine is fairly worn, as well as the mixture being too rich.

5   If the insulator nose is covered with light tan to greyish brown deposits, then the mixture is correct and it is likely that the engine is in good condition.

6   If there are any traces of long brown tapering stains on the outside of the white portion of the plug, then the plug will have to be renewed, as this shows that there is a faulty joint between the plug body and the insulator, and compression is being allowed to leak away.

7   Plugs should be cleaned by a sand blasting machine, which will free them from carbon more thoroughly than cleaning by hand. The machine will also test the condition of the plugs under compression. Any plug that fails to spark at the recommended pressure should be renewed.

8   The spark plug gap is of considerable importance, as, if it is too large or too small the size of the spark and its efficiency will be seriously impaired. The spark plug gap should be set to the gap given in the Specifications.

9   To set it, measure the gap with a feeler gauge, and then bend open, or close the outer plug electrode until the correct gap is achieved. The centre electrode should never be bent as this may crack the insulation and cause plug failure.

10 The HT leads to the coil and sparking plugs are of internal resistance, carbon core type. They are used in the interest of eliminating interference caused by the ignition system and have a resistance not exceeding 25 kohms. They are much more easily damaged than copper cored cable and they should be pulled from the spark plug terminals by gripping the metal end fitting at the end of the cable. Occasionally wipe the external surfaces of the leads free from oil and dirt using a fuel moistened cloth.

11 Always check the connection of the HT leads to the spark plugs is in the correct firing order sequence 1 - 3 - 4 - 2.

10 Ignition system - fault finding

Failures of the ignition system will either be due to faults in the HT or LT circuits. Initial checks should be made by observing the security of spark plug terminals, switch terminals, coil and battery connection. More detailed investigation and the explanation and remedial action in respect of symptoms of ignition malfunction in a 'conventional' system are described in the next Section.

If a fault develops in a semi-transistorized ignition system, the procedure in the following Section can be followed as far as is practicable, but the easiest way of eliminating the igniter unit is to disconnect it and connect a 0.22 mfd condenser across the distributor breaker points - see Section 1.

11 Ignition system - fault symptoms

Engine fails to start

1   If the engine fails to start and the car was running normally when it was last used, first check there is fuel in the tank. If the engine turns over normally on the starter motor and the battery is evidently well charged, then the fault may be in either the high or low tension circuits. First check the HT circuit. **Note**: If the battery is known to be fully charged; the ignition light comes on, and the starter motor fails to turn the engine **check the tightness of the leads on the battery terminals** and also the secureness of the earth lead to its **connection to the body**. It is quite common for the leads to have worked loose, even if they look and feel secure. If one of the battery terminal posts gets very hot when trying to work the starter motor this is a sure indication of a faulty connection to that terminal.

2   One of the commonest reasons for bad starting is wet or damp spark plug leads and distributor. Remove the distributor cap. If condensation is visible internally, dry the cap with a rag and also wipe over the leads. Refit the cap.

3   If the engine still fails to start, check that current is reaching the plugs, by disconnecting each plug lead in turn at the spark plug end, and hold the end of the cable about 3/16th inch (4 mm) away from the cylinder block. Spin the engine on the starter motor.

4   Sparking between the end of the cable and the block should be fairly strong with a regular blue spark. (Hold the lead with rubber gloves to avoid electric shocks.) If current is reaching the plugs, then remove them, and clean and regap them. The engine should now start.

5   If there is no spark at the plug leads take off the HT lead from the centre of the distributor cap and hold it to the block as before. Spin the engine on the starter once more. A rapid succession of blue sparks between the end of the lead and the block indicate that the coil is in order and that the distributor cap is cracked, the rotor arm faulty, or the carbon brush in the top of the distributor cap is not making good contact with the spring on the rotor arm. Possibly the points are in bad condition. Clean and reset them as described in Section 2.

6   If there are no sparks from the end of the lead from the coil, check the connections at the coil end of the lead. If it is in order start checking the low tension circuit.

7   Use a 12V voltmeter or a 12V bulb and two lengths of wire. With the ignition switch on and the points open test between the low tension wire to the coil (it is marked +) and earth. No reading indicates a break in the supply from the ignition switch. Check the connections at the switch to see if any are loose. Refit them and the engine should run. A reading shows a faulty coil or condenser, or broken lead between the coil and the distributor.

8   Take the condenser wire off the points assembly and with the points open, test between the moving point and earth. If there now is a reading, then the fault is in the condenser. Fit a new one and the fault is cleared.

9   With no reading from the moving point to earth, take a reading between earth and the '—' terminal of the coil. A reading here shows a broken wire which will need to be renewed between the coil and distributor. No reading confirms that the coil has failed and must be renewed, after which the engine will run once more. Remember to refit the condenser wire to the points assembly. For these tests it is sufficient to separate the points with a piece of dry paper while testing with the points open.

Engine misfires

10 If the engine misfires regularly run it at a fast idling speed. Pull off each of the plug caps in turn and listen to the note of the engine. Hold the plug cap in a dry cloth or with a rubber glove as additional protection against a shock from the HT supply.

11 No difference in engine running will be noticed when the lead from the defective circuit is removed. Removing the lead from one of the good cylinders will accentuate the misfire.

12 Remove the plug lead from the end of the defective plug and hold it about 3/16 in (4 mm) away from the block. Restart the engine. If the sparking is fairly strong and regular the fault must lie in the spark plug.

13 The plug may be loose, the insulation may be cracked, or the points may have burnt away giving too wide a gap for the spark to jump. Worse still, one of the points may have broken off. Either renew the plug, or clean it, reset the gap, and then test it.

14 If there is no spark at the end of the plug lead, or if it is weak and intermittent, check the ignition lead from the distributor to the plug. If the insulation is cracked or perished, renew the lead. Check the connections at the distributor cap.

15 If there is still no spark, examine the distributor cap carefully for tracking. This can be recognised by a very thin black line running between two or more contacts, or between a contact and some other part of the distributor. These lines are paths which now conduct electricity across the cap thus letting it run to earth. The only answer is a new distributor cap.

16 Apart from the ignition timing being incorrect, other causes of misfiring have already been dealt with under the section dealing with the failure of the engine to start. To recap - these are that:

a) *The coil may be faulty giving an intermittent misfire.*
b) *There may be a damaged wire or loose connection in the low tension circuit.*
c) *The condenser may be faulty.*

d) *There may be a mechanical fault in the distributor (broken driving spindle or contact breaker spring).*

17 If the ignition timing is too far retarded, it should be noted that the engine will tend to overheat, and there will be a quite noticeable drop in power. If the engine is overheating and the power is down, and the ignition timing is correct, then the carburettor should be checked, as it is likely that this is where the fault lies.

Chapter 5 Clutch

Contents

Specifications

Type	Single dry plate, diaphragm spring, hydraulically operated.
Clutch pedal height	
Right-hand drive	6.22 to 6.61 in (158 to 168 mm)
Left-hand drive	6.34 to 6.73 in (161 to 171 mm)
Clutch pedal play	0.04 to 0.28 in (1 to 7 mm)
Release fork tip play	0.079 to 0.118 in (2 to 3 mm)
Minimum friction plate lining thickness above rivet heads	0.012 in (0.3 mm)
Maximum friction plate run-out	0.020 in (0.5 mm)
Clutch fluid type	DOT 3 or SAE J1703C

Torque wrench settings	lb f ft	kg f m
Clutch housing to engine bolts	50	7
Reservoir retaining bolts	18	2.6

1 General description

1 All vehicles fitted with a manual gearbox, are equipped with a single dry plate diaphragm spring type clutch. Operation is by means of a pendant foot pedal and hydraulic circuit.

2 The clutch comprises a pressure plate assembly which contains the pressure plate, diaphragm spring and fulcrum rings. The assembly is bolted by means of its cover to the rear face of the flywheel.

3 The driven plate (friction disc) is free to slide along the gearbox input shaft and it is held in place between the flywheel and pressure plate faces by the pressure exerted by the diaphragm spring. The friction lining material is riveted to the driven plate which incorporates a rubber cushioned hub designed to absorb transmission rotational shocks and to assist in ensuring smooth take offs.

4 The circular diaphragm spring assembly is mounted on shouldered pins and held in place in the cover by two fulcrum rings. The spring itself is held in place by three spring steel clips.

5 Depressing the clutch pedal pushes the release bearing mounted on its hub retainer, forward to bear against the fingers of the diaphragm

spring. This action causes the diaphragm spring outer edge to deflect and so move the pressure plate rearwards to disengage the pressure plate from the driven plate.

6 When the clutch pedal is released, the diaphragm spring forces the pressure plate into contact with the friction linings of the driven plate and at the same time pushes the driven plate fractionally forward on its splines to ensure full engagement with the flywheel. The driven plate is now firmly sandwiched between the pressure plate and the flywheel and so the drive is taken up.

2 Clutch - adjustment

1 For correct clutch operation, adjustment must be carried out to the pedal and to the hydraulic operating cylinder. Free-play at the clutch pedal is essential to ensure that the clutch engages and disengages fully, otherwise difficult gear changing or clutch slip can occur.

2 Adjust the pedal return stop bolt until the distance between the centre of the upper surface of the pedal pad and the floor (surface of anti-drumming sheet - carpet removed) is as given in the Specifications

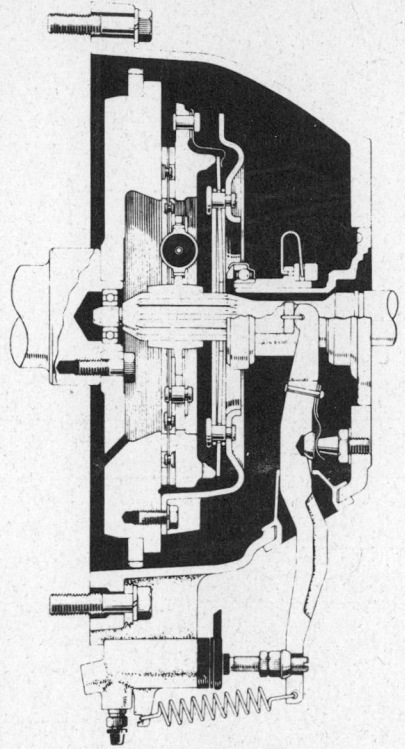

Fig. 5.1. Sectional view of clutch

for pedal height.

3   Working underneath the vehicle, check that the free movement between the end of the clutch operating cylinder pushrod and the release fork arm is as specified. Establish this movement by detaching the release fork arm return spring and gently moving the arm back and forth. If necessary, adjust the clearance by loosening the locknut on the pushrod and rotating the pushrod.

4   Now measure the clutch pedal free-movement which should also be as specified. If it is not, loosen the locknut on the master cylinder pushrod and rotate the pushrod until the free-movement is correct.

5   Tighten all locknuts without altering the adjustment, and reconnect the return springs.

3   Master cylinder - removal and refitting

1   Disconnect the master cylinder pushrod from the clutch pedal.
2   Disconnect the flexible hydraulic hose at its junction with the rigid line. Plug or cap the open hoses to prevent dirt entering the system.
3   Unbolt the master cylinder from the engine rear bulkhead taking care not to spill any hydraulic fluid onto the paintwork.
4   Refitting is the reverse of the removal procedure, but on completion, check the pedal free-movement as described in the preceding Section, and bleed the hydraulic system (Section 7).

4   Master cylinder - dismantling and reassembly

1   Remove the reservoir cap and float and tip out the fluid.
2   Operate the pushrod two or three times to eject any fluid from the cylinder.
3   Unscrew the reservoir securing bolt (accessible within the reservoir) and remove the reservoir.
4   Unscrew and remove the flexible hose from the master cylinder.
5   Peel back the rubber boot from the end of the cylinder and remove the circlip.
6   Extract the piston/seal assembly from the cylinder.
7   Wash all components in clean hydraulic fluid and discard all rubber seals. If there are any 'bright' wear areas on the piston or cylinder bore surfaces, renew the complete unit.
8   If the components are in good condition, obtain a repair kit which will contain all the necessary seals and other items requiring renewal.
9   Reassembly is the reverse of the dismantling procedure, but locate the rubber seals using the fingers only, to avoid damaging them, and noting that their lips face the cap end of the master cylinder. Dip each component in clean hydraulic fluid before fitting it into the cylinder. Tighten the reservoir securing bolt to the specified torque.

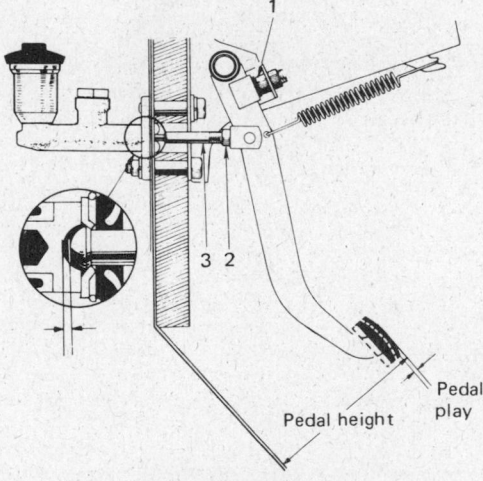

Fig. 5.2. Clutch pedal adjustment
1 Locknut 2 Pushrod nut 3 Pushrod

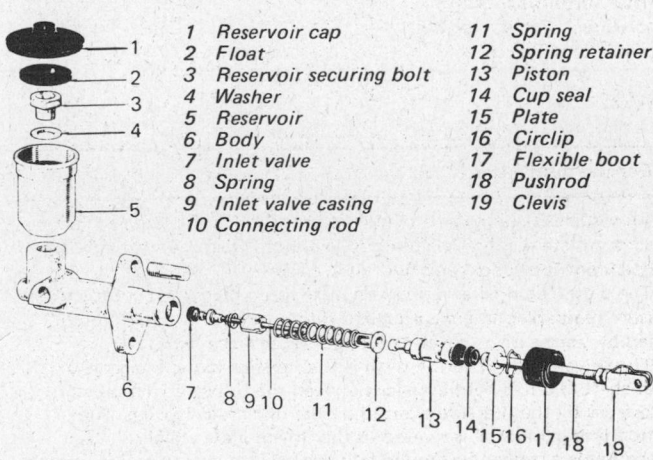

1	Reservoir cap	11	Spring
2	Float	12	Spring retainer
3	Reservoir securing bolt	13	Piston
4	Washer	14	Cup seal
5	Reservoir	15	Plate
6	Body	16	Circlip
7	Inlet valve	17	Flexible boot
8	Spring	18	Pushrod
9	Inlet valve casing	19	Clevis
10	Connecting rod		

Fig. 5.4. Exploded view of master cylinder

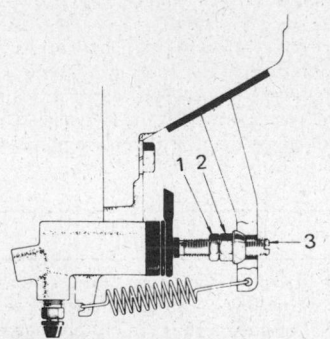

Fig. 5.3. Release fork adjustment
1 Stop bolt 2 Locknut 3 Pushrod

5 Operating cylinder - removal and refitting

1   Disconnect the hydraulic pipe at its union on the operating cylinder body.
2   Disconnect the return spring.
3   Unscrew and remove the securing bolts and withdraw the cylinder.
4   Refitting is the reverse of the removal procedure, but check the pushrod to release arm free-movement after the hydraulic system has been bled (Sections 2 and 7).

6 Operating cylinder - dismantling and reassembly

1   Depress the pushrod two or three times to eject any hydraulic fluid and then pull out the pushrod assembly complete with rubber boot.
2   Eject the piston assembly by applying air pressure at the fluid inlet or by tapping the end of the cylinder on a block of wood.
3   Wash components in clean hydraulic fluid and discard all rubber seals. If there are any 'bright' wear areas on the piston or cylinder bore surfaces, renew the complete unit.
4   If the components are in good condition, obtain a repair kit which will contain all the necessary seals and other items requiring renewal.
5   Reassembly is the reverse of the dismantling procedure, but manipulate the seals into position using the fingers only to avoid damaging them. Dip each component in clean hydraulic fluid before inserting it into the cylinder.

7 Hydraulic system - bleeding

1   Gather together a clean glass jar, a length of rubber or plastic tubing which fits tightly over the bleed nipple on the operating cylinder, a tin of hydraulic brake fluid and someone to help.
2   Check that the master cylinder is full. If it is not, fill it and cover the bottom two inches of the jar with hydraulic fluid.
3   Remove the rubber dust cap from the bleed nipple on the operating cylinder and, with a suitable spanner, open the bleed nipple approximately three quarters of a turn.
4   Place one end of the tube securely over the nipple and insert the other end into the jar so that its open end will remain submerged in the fluid.
5   Have your assistant depress the clutch pedal to the limit of its travel and then remove his foot, so that the pedal can return to its normal position without being obstructed.
6   Repeat this operation until no more air can be seen being expelled from the end of the tube submerged in the jar. Keep the reservoir well topped-up with fluid to prevent air being drawn into the system again.
7   With the pedal fully depressed, tighten the bleed nipple.
8   Refit the dust cap. Always use new hydraulic fluid for topping-up the reservoir, which has been stored in an air tight tin and has not been

shaken during the preceding 24 hours. Always discard fluid which has been bled from the system or retain it for bleed jar purposes only.

8 Clutch - removal

1   Access to the clutch assembly and to the clutch release mechanism (Section 10) may be gained in one of two ways; (i) by removing the gearbox leaving the engine in position in the vehicle as described in Chapter 6 or (ii) by removing the engine/gearbox as one unit (at the time of major overhaul) and then separating the gearbox from the engine (Chapter 1).
2   Scribe a mating line from the clutch cover to the flywheel to ensure identical positioning on refitting and then remove the cover to the rear face of the flywheel. Unscrew the bolts diagonally half a turn at a time to prevent distortion to the cover flange.
3   With all the bolts and spring washers removed lift the clutch assembly off the locating dowels. The driven plate or clutch disc may fall out at this stage as it is not attached to either the clutch cover assembly or the flywheel.

9 Clutch - inspection and renovation

1   Examine the clutch disc friction linings for wear and loose rivets and the disc for rim distortion, cracks, perished torsion rubbers and worn splines. The surface of the friction linings may be highly glazed, but as long as the clutch material pattern can be clearly seen this is satisfactory. If the amount of friction lining remaining is less than the minimum given in the Specifications, a new clutch plate should be obtained.
2   Check the machined surfaces of the flywheel and the pressure plate. If either are grooved they should be machined until smooth, or renewed.
3   If the pressure plate is cracked or split it is essential that an exchange unit is fitted, also if the pressure of the diaphragm (or coil springs) is suspect. It is not practical to dismantle the pressure plate assembly as it will have been accurately set up and balanced to very fine limits.
4   If a new clutch disc is being fitted it is a false economy not to renew the release bearing at the same time. This will preclude having to renew it at a later date when wear on the clutch linings is still very small.
5   Check the release bearing for smoothness of operation. There should be no harshness and no slackness in it. It should spin reasonably freely bearing in mind it has been pre-packed with grease.

10 Clutch release bearing - renewal

1   From the open front of the clutch bellhousing, unscrew and remove the release fork pivot bolt or alternatively, if so designed, slide the release fork sideways off its pivot ball stud.
2   Detach the clips which secure the bearing/hub assembly to the release fork.
3   Using a distance piece of suitable diameter, press the hub from the

Fig. 5.5. Removing operating cylinder

1	Union	3 Securing bolts
2	Return spring	

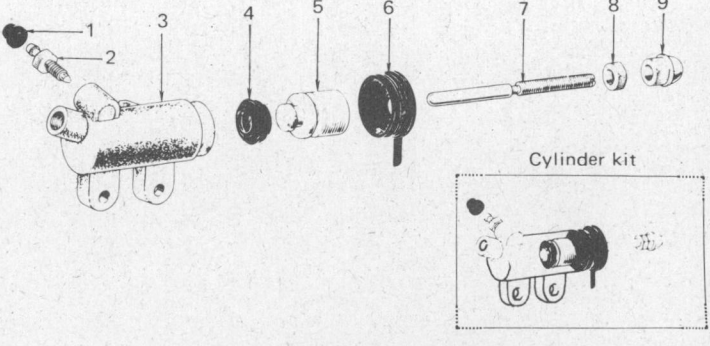

Fig. 5.6. Exploded view of operating cylinder

1	Dust cap	6	Boot
2	Bleed nipple	7	Pushrod
3	Cylinder body	8	Nut
4	Seal	9	Nut
5	Piston		

bearing inner track and press on the new one ensuring that it seats fully on the hub and that it is fitted with the contact plate facing the clutch release fingers.

4 Refitting is the reverse of the removal procedure, but use new clips to retain the bearing/hub to the release fork, and check the condition of the release fork arm rubber dust excluder at the clutch bell-housing aperture.

5 Finally check the condition of the input shaft spigot bearing which is located in the centre of the flywheel. If it is worn, remove it and fit a new one.

11 Clutch - refitting

1 Before the driven plate and pressure plate assembly can be refitted to the flywheel, a centralising guide tool must be obtained or made up. This may be either an old input shaft from a dismantled gearbox or a stepped mandrel.

2 Locate the driven plate against the face of the flywheel ensuring that its flatter side is against the flywheel (photo).

3 Offer up the pressure plate assembly to the flywheel, aligning the

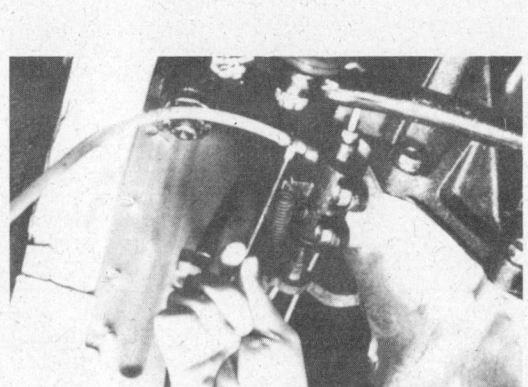

Fig. 5.7. Loosening the bleed nipple

11.2 Fitting clutch to flywheel

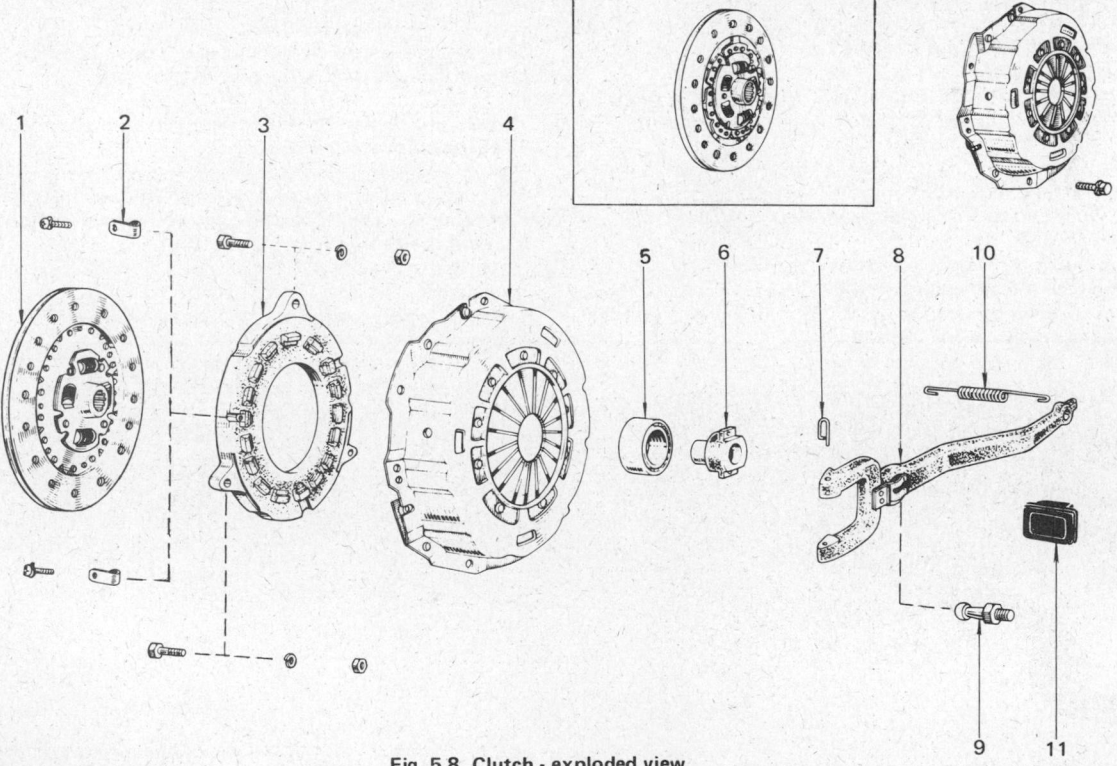

Fig. 5.8. Clutch - exploded view

1 Driven plate	4 Cover	7 Release bearing clip	10 Return spring
2 Spring	5 Release bearing	8 Release fork	11 Flexible boot
3 Pressure plate	6 Release bearing hub	9 Ball pivot stud	

11.4 Centralizing the clutch

marks made prior to dismantling, and insert the retaining bolt finger-tight only. Where a new pressure plate assembly is being fitted, locate it to the flywheel in a similar relative position to the original by reference to the index marking and dowel positions.

4   Insert the guide tool through the splined hub to the driven plate so that the end of the tool locates in the flywheel spigot bush. This action of the guide tool will centralise the driven plate by causing it to move in a sideways direction (photo).

5   Insert and remove the guide tool two or three times to ensure that the driven plate is fully centralised, then tighten the pressure plate securing bolts a turn at a time and in a diametrically opposite sequence.

6   Fit the gearbox (Chapter 6), or connect it to the engine and fit the engine/gearbox (Chapter 1).

7   When refitting is complete, check the pedal and release arm free-movement, and adjust to Specification (see Section 2).

12 Fault diagnosis - clutch

Symptom	Reason/s
Judder when taking up drive	Loose engine or gearbox mountings. Badly worn friction surfaces or contaminated with oil. Worn splines on gearbox input shaft or driven plate hub. Worn input shaft spigot in flywheel.
Clutch spin (failure to disengage) so that gears cannot be meshed	Incorrect release bearing to diaphragm spring due to rust. May occur after vehicle standing idle for long period. Damaged or misaligned pressure plate assembly. Fault in hydraulic system.
Clutch slip (increase in engine speed does not result in increase in vehicle road speed - particularly on gradients)	Incorrect release bearing to diaphragm spring finger clearance. Friction surfaces worn out or oil contaminated.
Noise evident on depressing clutch pedal	Dry, worn or damaged release bearing. Insufficient pedal free-travel. Weak or broken pedal return spring. Weak or broken clutch release lever return spring. Excessive play between driven plate hub splines and input shaft splines.
Noise evident as clutch pedal released	Distorted driven plate. Broken or weak driven plate cushion coil springs. Insufficient pedal free travel. Weak or broken clutch pedal return spring. Weak or broken release lever return spring. Distorted or worn input shaft. Release bearing loose on retainer hub.

Chapter 6 Manual and automatic transmission

For modifications and information applicable to later USA models, refer to Supplement at end of manual

Contents

Specifications

Gearbox types ... ... 3, 4 or 5 forward speeds (all with synchromesh), and one reverse gear

Gearbox identification

Three-speed, saloon	N30
Three-speed, estate car	N31
Four-speed	W40
Five-speed	W50

Gearbox ratios

	N30	N31	W40	W50
Reverse	4.449 : 1	4.863 : 1	4.399 : 1	4.039 : 1
First	3.337 : 1	3.647 : 1	3.579 : 1	3.287 : 1
Second	1.653 : 1	1.807 : 1	2.081 : 1	2.043 : 1
Third	1.000 : 1	1.000 : 1	1.397 : 1	1.394 : 1
Fourth	—	—	1.000 : 1	1.000 : 1
Fifth	—	—	—	0.853 : 1

Gearbox lubricant type ... ... SAE 90 gear oil (API-GL-4)

Lubricant capacity

Three-speed	3 Imp pt/3.6 US pt (1.7 litres)
Four-speed	4.8 Imp pt/5.6 US pt (2.7 litres)
Five-speed	4.6 Imp pt/5.4 US pt (2.6 litres)

Tolerances

N30/31 gearbox (three-speed)

Countershaft gear endfloat	0.0047 to 0.0114 in (0.12 to 0.29 mm)
Circlip thickness availability for countershaft	0.0882 to 0.0902 in (2.24 to 2.29 mm)
	0.0906 to 0.0925 in (2.30 to 2.35 mm)

	0.0929 to 0.0949 in (2.36 to 2.41 mm)
	0.0953 to 0.0972 in (2.42 to 2.47 mm)
	0.0976 to 0.0996 in (2.48 to 2.53 mm)
	0.1000 to 0.1020 in (2.54 to 2.59 mm)

1st, 2nd and reverse gear endfloat:
    Standard   ...   .   0.0039 to 0.0098 in (0.10 to 0.25 mm)
    Limit ...   .   0.0118 in (0.30 mm)
Circlip thickness available for input shaft   ...   .   0.0807 to 0.0827 in (2.05 to 2.10 mm)

	0.0827 to 0.0846 in (2.10 to 2.15 mm)
	0.0846 to 0.0866 in (2.15 to 2.20 mm)
	0.0866 to 0.0886 in (2.20 to 2.25 mm)
	0.0886 to 0.0906 in (2.25 to 2.30 mm)
	0.0906 to 0.0925 in (2.30 to 2.35 mm)

Circlip thickness availability for mainshaft   ...   .   0.0531 to 0.0571 in (1.35 to 1.45 mm)

	0.0571 to 0.0610 in (1.45 to 1.55 mm)
	0.0610 to 0.0650 in (1.55 to 1.65 mm)
	0.0650 to 0.0689 in (1.65 to 1.75 mm)
	0.0689 to 0.0728 in (1.75 to 1.85 mm)

Reverse idler gear thrust collar length availability   ...   .   1.1197 to 1.1220 in (28.44 to 28.50 mm)

	1.1276 to 1.1299 in (28.64 to 28.70 mm)
	1.1354 to 1.1378 in (28.84 to 28.90 mm)
	1.1433 to 1.1457 in (29.04 to 29.10 mm)

W40 gearbox (four-speed)

1st, 2nd and 3rd gear endfloat:
    Standard   ...   .   0.0059 to 0.0098 in (0.15 to 0.25 mm)
    Limit ...   .   0.0118 in (0.30 mm)
Circlip thickness availability for input shaft ...   .   as for three-speed gearbox
Circlip thickness availability for mainshaft (front): ...   .   0.0787 to 0.0807 in (2.00 to 2.05 mm)

	0.0807 to 0.0827 in (2.05 to 2.10 mm)
	0.0827 to 0.0846 in (2.10 to 2.15 mm)
	0.0846 to 0.0866 in (2.15 to 2.20 mm)
	0.0866 to 0.0886 in (2.20 to 2.25 mm)
	0.0886 to 0.0906 in (2.25 to 2.30 mm)

Circlip thickness availability for mainshaft (rear):   ...   .   0.0807 to 0.0827 in (2.05 to 2.10 mm)

	0.0827 to 0.0846 in (2.10 to 2.15 mm)
	0.0846 to 0.0866 in (2.15 to 2.20 mm)
	0.0866 to 0.0886 in (2.20 to 2.25 mm)
	0.0886 to 0.0906 in (2.25 to 2.30 mm)
	0.0906 to 0.0925 in (2.30 to 2.35 mm)
	0.0925 to 0.0945 in (2.35 to 2.40 mm)
	0.0945 to 0.0965 in (2.40 to 2.45 mm)
	0.0965 to 0.0984 in (2.45 to 2.50 mm)
	0.0984 to 0.1004 in (2.50 to 2.55 mm)
	0.1004 to 0.1024 in (2.55 to 2.60 mm)

Countershaft gear spacer thickness availability: ...   .   0.0807 to 0.0846 in (2.05 to 2.15 mm)

	0.0874 to 0.0906 in (2.22 to 2.30 mm)
	0.0925 to 0.0965 in (2.35 to 2.45 mm)
	0.0984 to 0.1024 in (2.50 to 2.60 mm)

W50 gearbox (five-speed)

1st, 2nd, 3rd and reverse idler gear endfloat ...   .   0.0059 to 0.0098 in (0.15 to 0.25 mm)
5th gear endfloat   ...   .   0.0039 to 0.0098 in (0.10 to 0.25 mm)
    Limit ...   .   0.0118 in (0.30 mm)
Circlip thickness availability for input shaft ...   .   as for three-speed gearbox
Circlip thickness availability for mainshaft (front) ...   .   as for four-speed gearbox
Circlip thickness availability for mainshaft (fifth gear)   ...   .   0.0744 to 0.0764 in (1.89 to 1.94 mm)

	0.0768 to 0.0787 in (1.95 to 2.00 mm)
	0.0791 to 0.0811 in (2.01 to 2.06 mm)
	0.0815 to 0.0835 in (2.07 to 2.12 mm)
	0.0839 to 0.0858 in (2.13 to 2.18 mm)
	0.0862 to 0.0882 in (2.19 to 2.24 mm)
	0.0886 to 0.0906 in (2.25 to 2.30 mm)
	0.0909 to 0.0929 in (2.31 to 2.36 mm)
	0.0933 to 0.0953 in (2.37 to 2.42 mm)
	0.0957 to 0.0976 in (2.43 to 2.48 mm)
	0.0980 to 0.1000 in (2.49 to 2.54 mm)
	0.1004 to 0.1024 in (2.55 to 2.60 mm)
	0.1028 to 0.1047 in (2.61 to 2.66 mm)

Circlip thickness availability for countershaft (rear)   ...   .   0.0551 to 0.0571 in (1.40 to 1.45 mm)

	0.0630 to 0.0650 in (1.60 to 1.65 mm)
	0.0709 to 0.0728 in (1.80 to 1.85 mm)
	0.0787 to 0.0807 in (2.00 to 2.05 mm)
Countershaft gear spacer thickness availability:	0.0807 to 0.0846 in (2.05 to 2.15 mm)
	0.0874 to 0.0906 in (2.22 to 2.30 mm)
	0.0925 to 0.0965 in (2.35 to 2.45 mm)
	0.0984 to 0.1024 in (2.50 to 2.60 mm)

Automatic transmission type ... ...   Three element, single stage, two phase converter with planetary gear train

Transmission identification ... ...   Aisin-Warner A40

Transmission ratios

Reverse	2.22 : 1
First	2.45 : 1
Second	1.45 : 1
Third	1.00 : 1

Transmission fluid type ... ...   F-type
Fluid capacity (drain and refill) ... ...   4.2 Imp pt/5 US pt (2.4 litres)

Torque wrench settings

	lb f ft	kg f m
Manual gearbox (all types)		
Clutch bellhousing to engine bolts	33	4.5
Clutch bellhousing to gearbox bolts	50	6.9
Extension housing bolts	30	4.1
3-speed - type N30/31		
Detent plug	35	4.8
Mainshaft rear nut	72	10.0
Mainshaft front nut	58	8.5
4- and 5-speed - types W40 and W50		
Detent plug	22	3.0
Mainshaft rear bearing retainer bolts	15	2.1
Reverse gear shift arm pivot nut	11	1.5
Restrictor pin	30	4.1
Automatic transmission		
Drive plate bolts to crankshaft	43	5.9
Drive plate to torque converter bolts	15	2.1
Torque converter housing to engine bolts	55	7.6
Oil pan (sump) bolts	8.0	1.1
Extension housing bolts	30	4.1
Oil pan (sump) drain plug	13	1.8

Part A: Manual gearbox

1 General description

The gearbox may be of three-, four- or five-speed forward type, according to model and date of manufacture. Synchromesh is fitted on all forwards gears. A floor mounted gearchange is used on the four- and five-speed gearboxes, but the three-speed gearbox only uses a column gearchange.

The different units are referred to separately in this Chapter to avoid confusion.

2 Gearbox (3-speed) - removal and refitting

1 Disconnect the leads from the battery terminals.
2 Drain the cooling system and disconnect the radiator upper hose.
3 Disconnect the accelerator linkage at the carburettor.
4 Disconnect the starter leads and remove the starter from the clutch bellhousing.
5 Either place the vehicle over a pit or jack-up the front and rear sufficiently high so that the gearbox can be withdrawn from below.
6 Disconnect the speedometer cable from the gearbox.
7 Unbolt the clutch operating cylinder from the clutch bellhousing. If the fluid line is detached from its support clip, the complete flexible/rigid line together with operating cylinder can be tied up out of the way without disconnecting the pipes.
8 Unbolt the exhaust downpipes from the manifold.

9 Remove the stiffener plates from the lower half of the front of the clutch bellhousing.
10 Disconnect the gearchange control at the points shown (Fig. 6.2).
11 Drain the gearbox, then remove the propeller shaft as described in Chapter 7.
12 Support the gearbox on a jack (preferably trolley type) and remove the gearbox rear mounting.
13 Unscrew and remove the clutch bellhousing to engine securing bolts, lower the jack until the gearbox is inclined at the right attitude to be removed rearwards.
14 Withdraw the gearbox in a straight line so that its weight will at no time hang upon the input shaft while the shaft is still engaged with the clutch mechanism. During this operation, the engine will be supported on a second jack placed under the engine sump.
15 Refitting is the reverse of the removal procedure, but lightly grease the splines of the input shaft before offering up the unit to the clutch mechanism.
16 If the clutch has been dismantled, centralise the driven plate as described in Chapter 5. Tighten the clutch bellhousing to engine bolts to the specified torque.
17 Check and adjust the clutch pedal free-movement (Chapter 5), and refill the gearbox with the correct quantity and type of oil.

3 Gearbox (3-speed) - dismantling into major assemblies

1 Clean the outside of the gearbox using paraffin or a water soluble

100

Fig. 6.1. Sectional views of gearboxes used on Corona models

3-Speed
(N30 & N31)

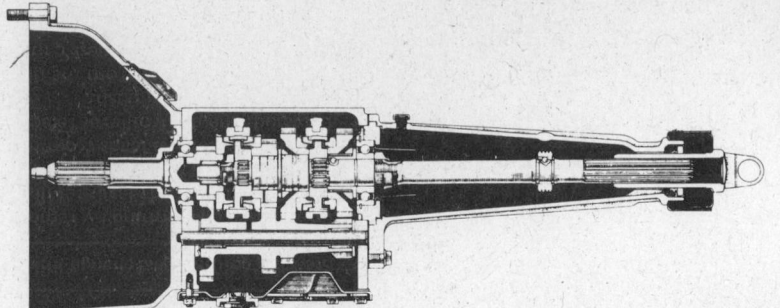

4-Speed (W40)

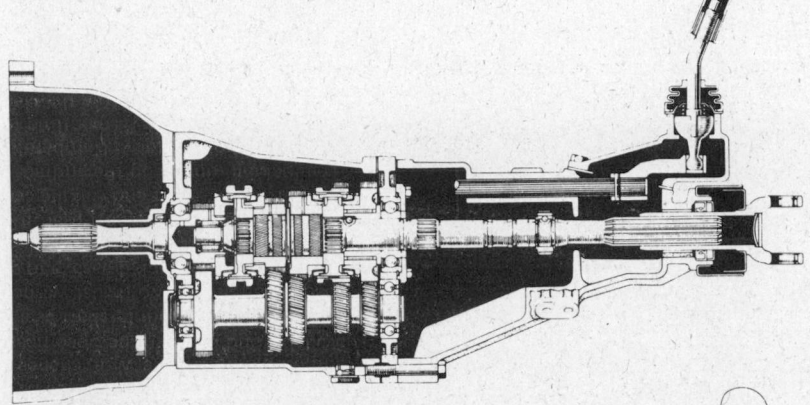

5-Speed (W50)

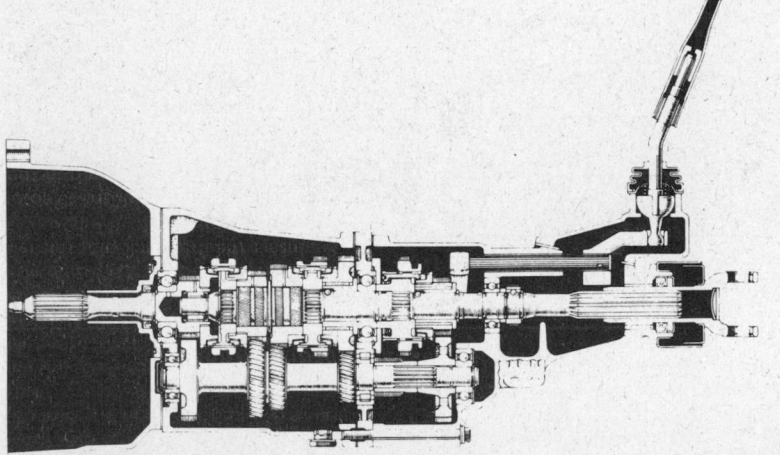

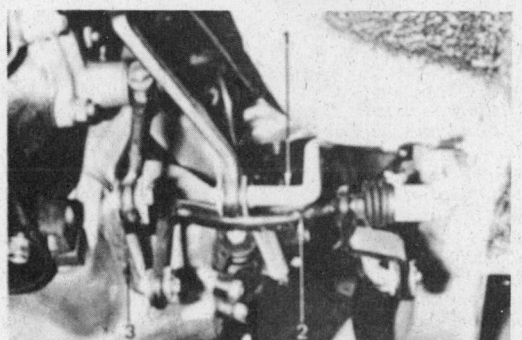

Fig. 6.2. Detaching gearshift linkage

1　Low gear connecting rod　　　3　Gearshift rod
2　Cross shaft

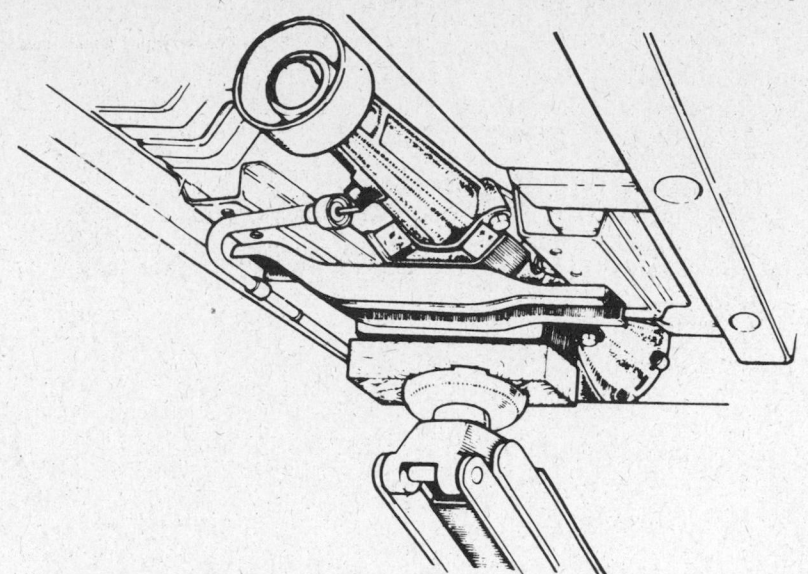

Fig. 6.3. Gearbox supported on trolley jack

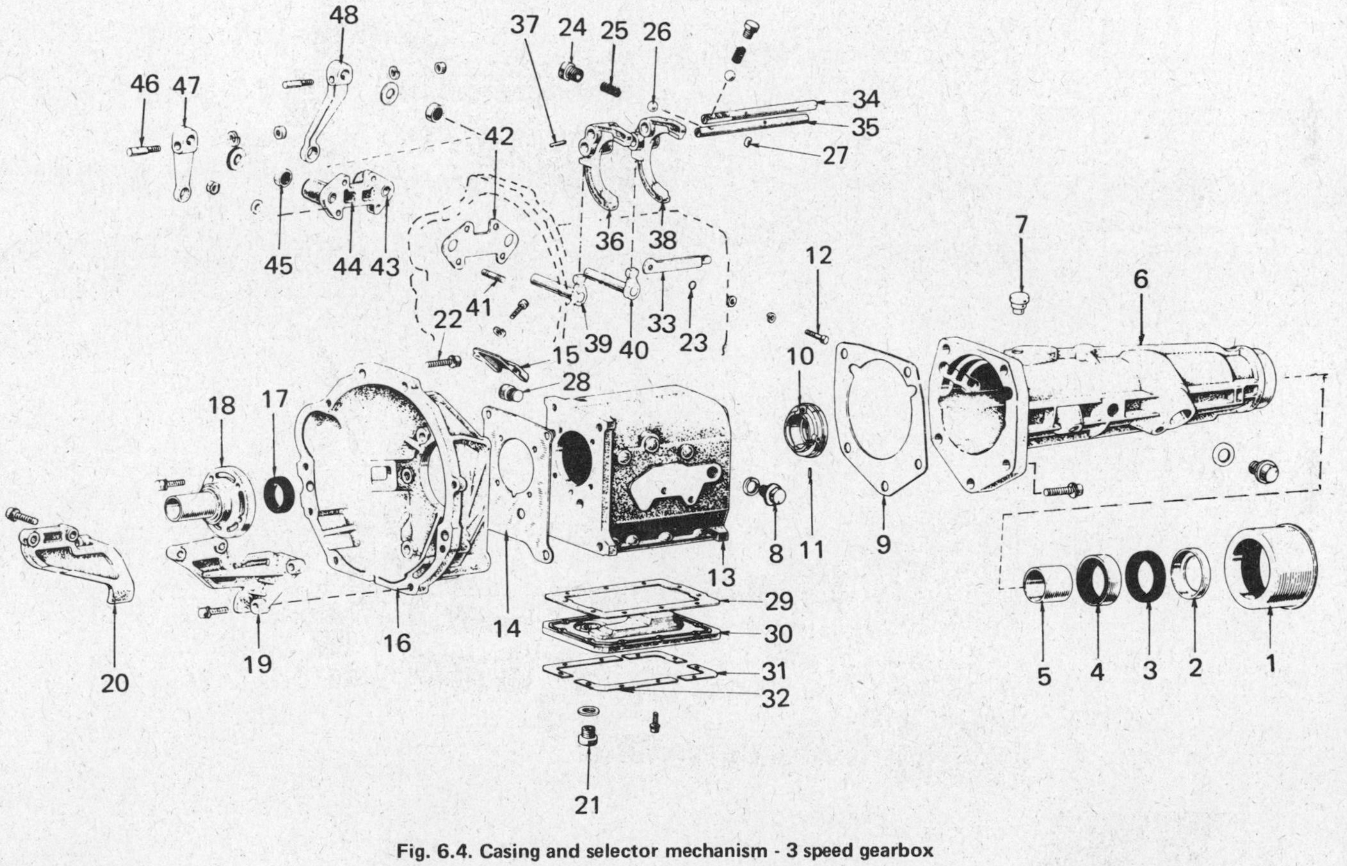

Fig. 6.4. Casing and selector mechanism - 3 speed gearbox

1	Dust deflector	13	Casing	25	Spring	37	Spring pin
2	Dust seal retainer	14	Gasket	26	Shift fork lock ball	38	Shift fork No. 2
3	Dust seal	15	Clutch housing cover No. 1	27	Shift interlock pin No. 2	39	Shift lever shaft No. 2
4	Oil seal	16	Clutch housing	28	Plug	40	Shift lever shaft No. 1
5	Bimetal bushing	17	Oil seal	29	Gasket	41	Stud
6	Extension housing	18	Front bearing retainer	30	Bottom cover	42	Gasket
7	Breather plug	19	Stiffener plate (LH)	31	Plate	43	Bimetal bushing
8	Filler plug	20	Stiffener plate (RH)	32	Plate	44	Shift lever shaft housing
9	Gasket	21	Drain plug	33	Oil catcher	45	Shift lever oil seal
10	Output shaft rear bearing retainer	22	Bolt	34	Shift fork shaft No. 2	46	Lever lock pin
11	Spring pin	23	'O' ring	35	Shift fork shaft No. 1	47	Shift outer lever No. 2
12	Plug	24	Plug	36	Shift fork No. 2	48	Shift outer lever No. 1

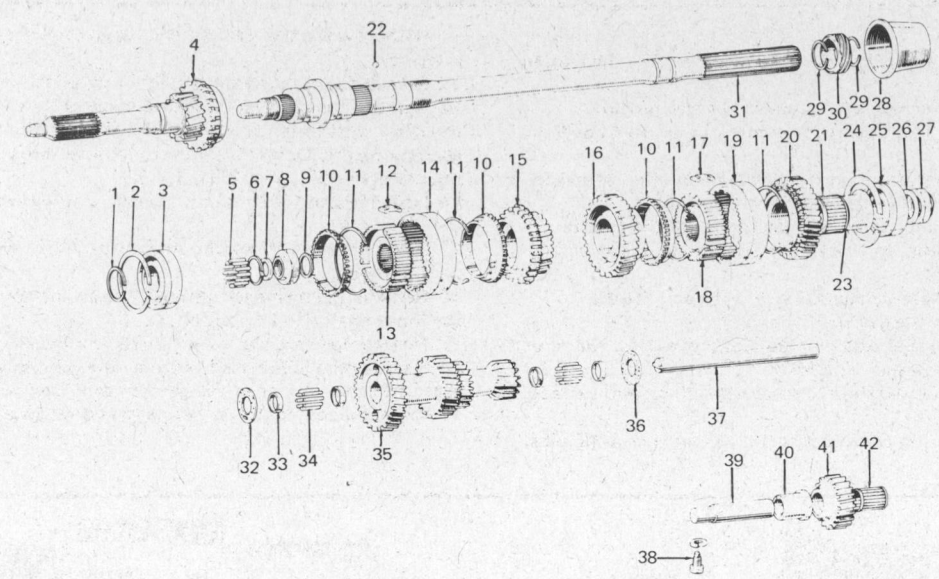

Fig. 6.5. Gear assemblies - 3-speed gearbox

1 Circlip	12 Shift key	23 Bearing inner race	33 Spacer
2 Circlip	13 Clutch hub No. 2	24 Circlip	34 Roller
3 Bearing	14 Hub sleeve No. 2	25 Bearing	35 Counter gear
4 Input shaft	15 Second gear	26 Shim	36 Thrust washer
5 Roller	16 First gear	27 Nut	37 Countershaft
6 Circlip	17 Shift key	28 Oil deflector	38 Shaft retainer bolt
7 Spacer	18 Clutch hub No. 1	29 Circlip	39 Reverse idler gear shaft
8 Nut	19 Hub sleeve No. 1	30 Speedometer drive gear	40 Thrust washer
9 Shim	20 Reverse gear	31 Mainshaft	41 Reverse idler gear
10 Synchronizer ring No. 2	21 Bearing	32 Counter gear case side	42 Bearing
11 Shift key spring	22 Reverse shift restrict ball	thrust washer	

Fig. 6.6. Checking reverse idler gear endfloat - 3-speed gearbox

Fig. 6.7. Removing countershaft - 3-speed gearbox

Fig. 6.8. Removing reverse idler gear - 3-speed gearbox

Fig. 6.9. Removing plugs, springs and bolts - 3-speed gearbox

1 Plug
2 Spring pin
3 Ball

cleaner.

2 Remove the clutch release fork and bearing from within the clutch bellhousing.

3 Unbolt and remove the clutch bellhousing from the gearbox.

4 Unbolt and remove the front bearing retainer, the bottom cover and its gasket.

5 Remove the speedometer driven gear assembly from the extension housing, then unbolt and remove the extension housing.

6 Before further dismantling, measure the endfloat of the countergear and the reverse idler gear, and make a note of it for reference on reassembly (Fig. 6.6).

7 Drive out the countershaft using a suitable drift, and lift the countergear assembly from the gearbox (Fig. 6.7).

8 Remove the reverse idle gear retaining bolt, and withdraw the reverse idler shaft, gear and thrust washer (Fig. 6.8).

9 Unscrew and remove the two shift fork screwed plugs, and extract the springs and balls.

10 Now remove the remaining two plugs and drive out the spring pins.

11 Withdraw the gear selector shafts one at a time, and remove the interlock pin.

12 Detach the cranked and straight shift external levers.

13 Remove the nuts which secure the shaft housing (1) and then push the inner shift levers until they are horizontal and in contact with the gearbox casing. Do not attempt to remove the shaft housing or inner shift levers at this stage (Fig. 6.11).

14 Push 1st/2nd synchro unit towards the reverse gear and withdraw the shift fork.

15 The second shift fork should be withdrawn with the gears in the neutral mode.

16 Remove the mainshaft assembly from the gearbox which will leave the input shaft still in position.

17 Now remove the shift lever shafts and housing (see paragraph 13).

18 Remove the input shaft bearing outer circlip and push the input shaft into the interior of the gearbox and then withdraw it.

19 Inspect all components for wear, and renew as necessary.

Fig. 6.10. Removing plug and spring pin - 3-speed gearbox

1 Plug   2 Spring pin

Fig. 6.11. Removing shift fork - 3-speed gearbox

1 Shift lever shaft housing   3 Shift outer lever No. 1
2 Inner lever   4 Shift outer lever No. 2

Fig. 6.12. Removing shift fork No. 2 - 3-speed gearbox

1 Clutch hub No. 1   2 Shift fork No. 2

Fig. 6.13. Removing mainshaft assembly - 3-speed gearbox

Fig. 6.14. Removing input shaft bearing circlip - 3-speed gearbox

4 Mainshaft (3-speed gearbox) - servicing

1 Before commencing to dismantle, measure the endfloats of the 1st, 2nd, and reverse gears. Make a note of them pending reassembly.
2 Hold the mainshaft assembly very securely in the jaws of a vice (fitted with soft metal jaw protectors of adequate thickness) and remove the spacer from the front (input) end of the shaft. Relieve the staking on the nut; unscrew and remove it, together with the shim.
3 Withdraw the 2nd/3rd synchro unit, the ring and 2nd gear. Mark the synchro unit with a piece of masking tape to prevent confusion with 1st/2nd synchro which is identical.
4 From the rear end of the mainshaft, remove the circlips, speedometer drive gear and ball, and the oil deflector.

5 Relieve the staking, and unscrew the nut. Remove the shim.
6 The rear bearing will have to be removed on a press.
7 Withdraw reverse gear and the needle roller bearings, inner race and ball. Then remove the 1st/2nd synchro ring and first gear.
8 Wash all components in paraffin and dry thoroughly. Inspect the gears for chipped or worn teeth and the shaft for scoring, grooves or distortion.
9 The running clearances between the first and second gears and the mainshaft should not exceed 0.0051 in (0.13 mm)
10 Inspect the condition of the synchroniser units. If there has been a history of noisy gear-changing or the synchromesh could easily be 'beaten', renew the unit complete. In any event, fit the synchro ring onto the gear and measure the clearance. This should not be less than 0.031 in (0.8 mm).

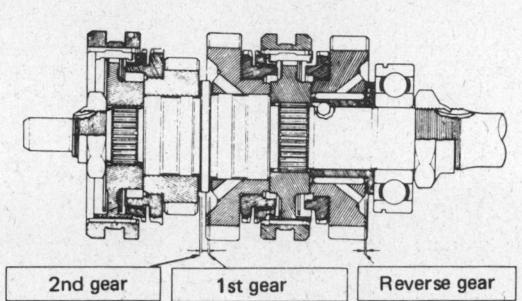

Fig. 6.15. Endfloat measuring points - 3-speed gearbox

2nd gear | 1st gear | Reverse gear

Fig. 6.16. Removing 2nd/3rd synchro unit

1 Synchro ring   *3 3-speed gearbox*
2 2nd gear

Fig. 6.17. Reverse gear

1 Reverse gear   *4 Locking ball*
2 Inner race   *5 Synchro unit*
3 Inner track   *6 Sleeve*

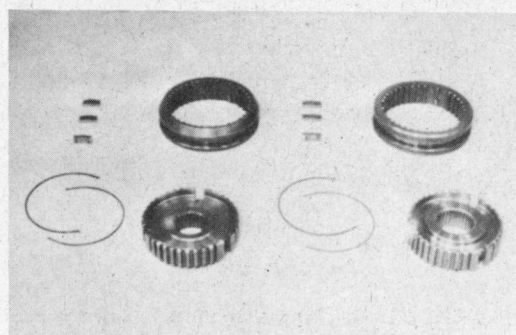

Fig. 6.18. Exploded view of synchro units - 3-speed gearbox

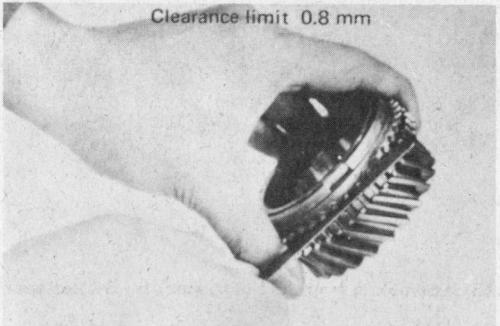

Clearance limit 0.8 mm

Fig. 6.19. Measuring synchro ring-to-gear clearance - 3-speed gearbox

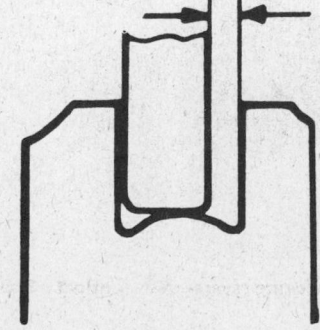

Fig. 6.20. Shift fork-to-sleeve clearance - 3-speed gearbox

11 Fit the shift forks to the synchro sleeves and check for side clearance. If this exceeds 0.039 in (1 mm), renew one or both components as necessary.

12 Correct assembly of the two synchro units must be carried out before installing them to the mainshaft. Ensure that the spring ends do not engage in the same gaps on opposite sides of the unit.

13 To the rear end of the mainshaft, fit the first gear, 1st/2nd synchro ring and sleeve. Press the synchro unit towards the first gearwheel and measure the clearance. This should be between 0.0039 and 0.0098 in (0.10 and 0.25 mm) with a maximum of 0.0118 in (0.30 mm).

14 Locate the ball and install reverse gear, the bearing and inner race. Make sure that the ball aligns with the slot in the inner race, and that the synchro ring slots align with the shift keys.

15 Press a new bearing onto the rear end of the mainshaft so that its outer circlip groove is nearer the front.

16 Fit the shim and tighten the nut to the specified torque.

17 Check that the reverse gear endfloat is between 0.0039 and 0.0098 in (0.10 and 0.25 mm) with a maximum of 0.0118 in (0.30 mm). Recheck the first gear endfloat (see paragraph 13). Stake the nut to the mainshaft.

18 Locate the circlips, ball and speedometer drive gear to the rear end of the mainshaft.

19 To the front end of the mainshaft, assembly the 2nd gear, and synchro ring. Fit the 2nd/3rd synchro unit followed by the shim and nut. Make sure that the synchro ring slots are in alignment with the shift keys, and tighten the nut to the specified torque.

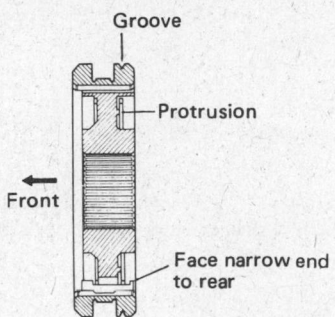

Fig. 6.21. 1st/2nd synchro unit - 3-speed gearbox

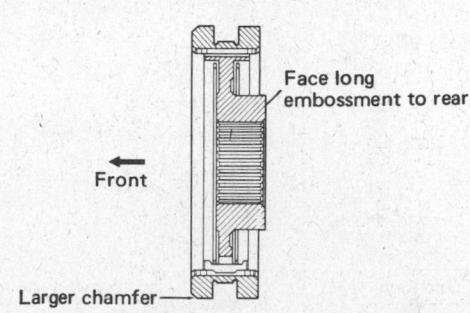

Fig. 6.22. 2nd/3rd synchro unit - 3-speed gearbox

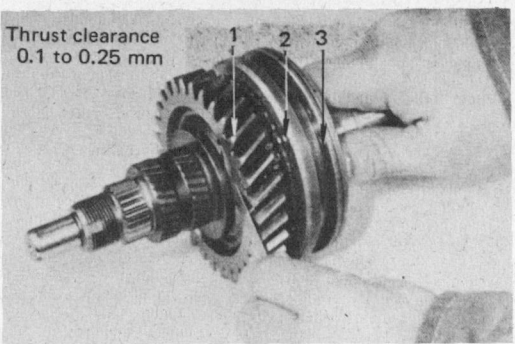

Fig. 6.23. Checking 1st gear endfloat - 3-speed gearbox

1 1st gear
2 Synchro ring
3 1st/2nd synchro unit

Fig. 6.24. Installing 1st gear - 3-speed gearbox

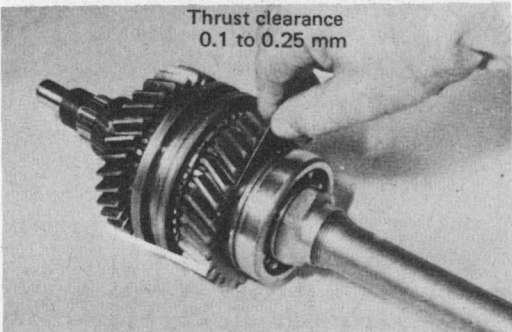

Fig. 6.25. Checking reverse gear endfloat - 3-speed gearbox

Fig. 6.26. Assembling front end of mainshaft - 3-speed gearbox

1 2nd gear
2 Synchro ring
3 2nd/3rd synchro unit
4 Shims
5 Nut

Fig. 6.27. Checking 2nd gear endfloat - 3-speed gearbox

Fig. 6.28. Selecting a rear bearing groove circlip - 3-speed gearbox

1   Oil deflector

Fig. 6.29. Countershaft gear assembly - 3-speed gearbox

Fig. 6.30. Reverse idler gear assembly - 3-speed gearbox

20 Measure the second gear endfloat, this should be as for reverse gear (paragraph 17). If the clearance is correct, stake the nut to the mainshaft.

21 To the mainshaft rear bearing, fit the outer circlip and oil deflector. A circlip should be selected from those available to provide the minimum side clearance in the groove. Circlips are available in thicknesses as listed in the Specifications Section.

5   Input shaft (3-speed gearbox) - servicing

1   Inspect the gear teeth for chipping, and the splines and shaft surfaces for wear.

2   Locate the synchro ring to the rear end of the input shaft and check the clearance between the two components. It should be between 0.039 and 0.079 in (1 and 2 mm) with a maximum of 0.031 in (0.8 mm) ; if otherwise, renew the ring.

3   Check the internal bore of the needle bearing recess and the condition of the bearing itself.

4   If the main bearing requires renewal, it will have to be removed on a press. When pressing on the new one, make sure that the outer circlip groove is nearer the front of the shaft. Select a shaft circlip to give the minimum side clearance in the shaft groove from those listed in the Specifications Section.

6   Countershaft and reverse gear assemblies (3-speed gearbox) - servicing

1   The countershaft assembly cannot be dismantled and must be renewed if the gears are worn or chipped. The thrust washers and bearings can be renewed if worn.

2   The reverse idler gear, shaft and bearing should be renewed if worn or scored.

7   Oil seals (3-speed gearbox) - renewal

1   When carrying out a major overhaul of the gearbox, it is recommended that all oil seals and 'O' rings are renewed as a matter of routine.

2   Renew the 'O' rings in the shift lever housing, and at the same time make sure that the housing and levers are in good condition.

3   Renew the speedometer driven gear, 'O' rings, and renew any worn components of the drive or driven gear.

4   Renew the oil seal in the front bearing retainer, using a tubular drift.

5   Renew the oil seal at the end of the rear extension housing in a similar manner to that described in the preceding paragraph. Should the metal bush be worn it can be renewed after heating the rear end of the extension housing in boiling water. When installing the new bush, make sure that the oil feed grooves are in alignment.

8   Gearbox (3-speed) - reassembly

1   Fit the speedometer driven gear assembly to the extension housing.

2   Fit the input shaft by inserting it first into the interior of the gearbox and, when positioned correctly, fit the bearing outer circlip. If working single-handed, the bearing retainer can be temporarily bolted up to hold the input shaft in position.

3   Locate the shift lever shaft housing onto the gearbox casing using a new gasket.

4   Insert the shift lever shafts from the gearbox interior, pushing them until the levers are horizontal and touching the inside of the gearbox casing.

5   Fit the 2nd/3rd synchro ring to the rear end of the input shaft, and the spacer onto the front end of the mainshaft; install the mainshaft assembly from the rear end of the gearbox.

6   Insert the two shift forks so that they engage correctly in the synchro sleeve grooves.

7   Insert the selector shafts so that they and their forks are assembled as shown complete with detent balls and springs. The installation sequence is to position 1st/2nd selector shaft in neutral and align the spring hole. Insert the ball, spring and plug. Drive in the spring pin (4) and screw in the plug (5). This plug should have gasket sealing

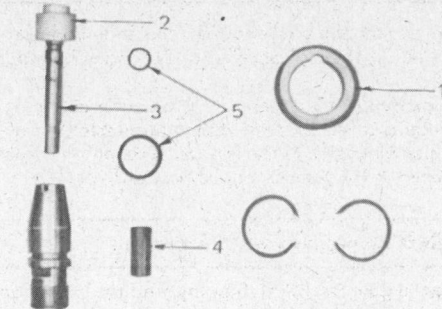

Fig. 6.31. Gear components - 3-speed gearbox

1 Drive gear   4 Bush
2 Driven gear   5 O-rings
3 Shift

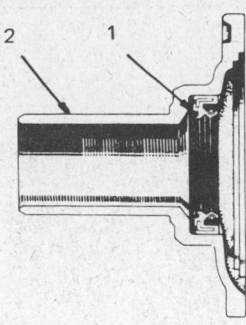

Fig. 6.32. Front bearing retainer oil seal (1) and retainer (2) — 3-speed gearbox

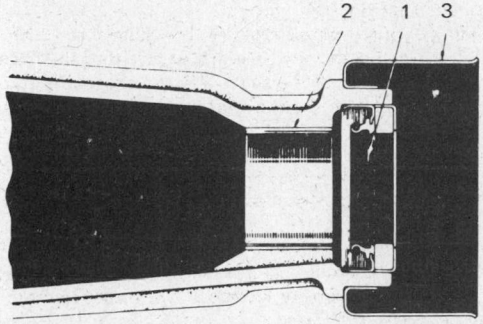

Fig. 6.33. Rear extension oil seal (1) bush (2) and dust deflector (3) - 3-speed gearbox

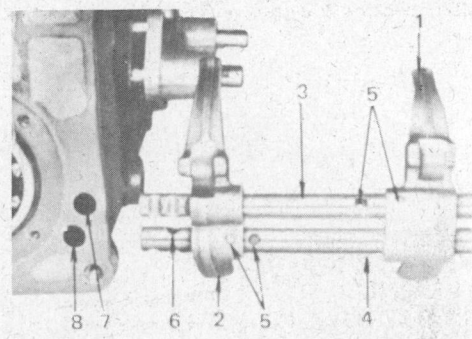

Fig. 6.34. Correct assembly of shift forks and shafts - 3-speed gearbox

1 1st/2nd fork   5 Spring pin holes
2 2nd/3rd fork   6 Interlock pin location
3 1st/2nd selector shaft   7 1st/2nd selector shaft hole
4 2nd/3rd selector shaft   8 2nd/3rd selector shaft hole

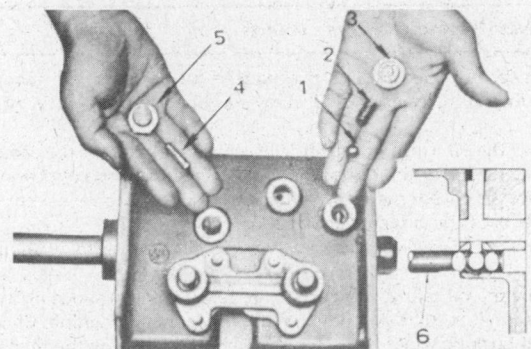

Fig. 6.35. Installing 1st/2nd selector shaft - 3-speed gearbox

1 Ball   4 Spring pin
2 Spring   5 Plug
3 Plug   6 Shaft

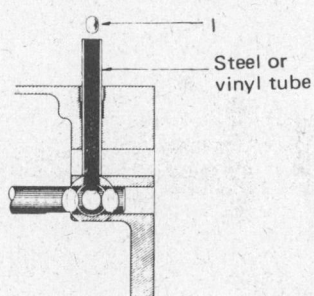

Steel or vinyl tube

Fig. 6.36. Inserting interlock pin (1) - 3-speed gearbox

Fig. 6.37. Installing 2nd/3rd selector shaft - 3-speed gearbox

1 Plug   4 Spring
2 Spring pin 5 Plug
3 Ball   6 Shaft

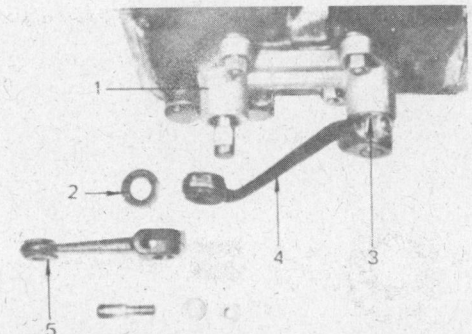

Fig. 6.38. Installing external levers - 3-speed gearbox

1 Shift lever housing   4 Outer lever No. 1
2 Washer   5 Outer lever No. 2
3 Washer

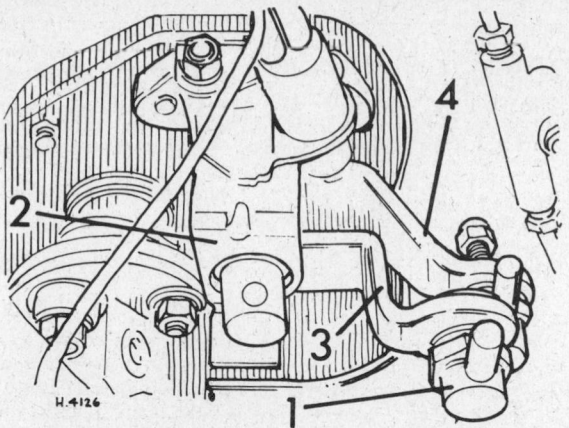

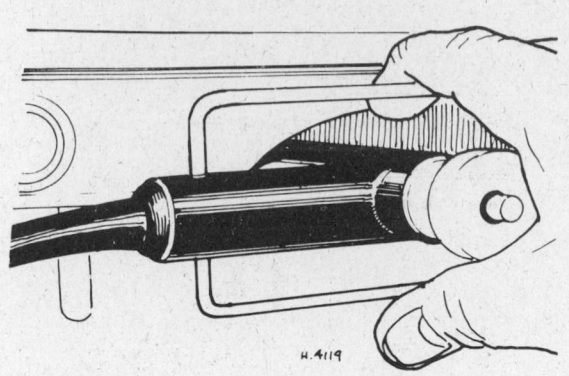

Fig. 6.39. Location of column shift levers - 3-speed gearbox

1 Swivel   3 High gear lever
2 Retainer   4 Low gear lever

Fig. 6.40. Depressing shift lever retaining pins - 3-speed gearbox

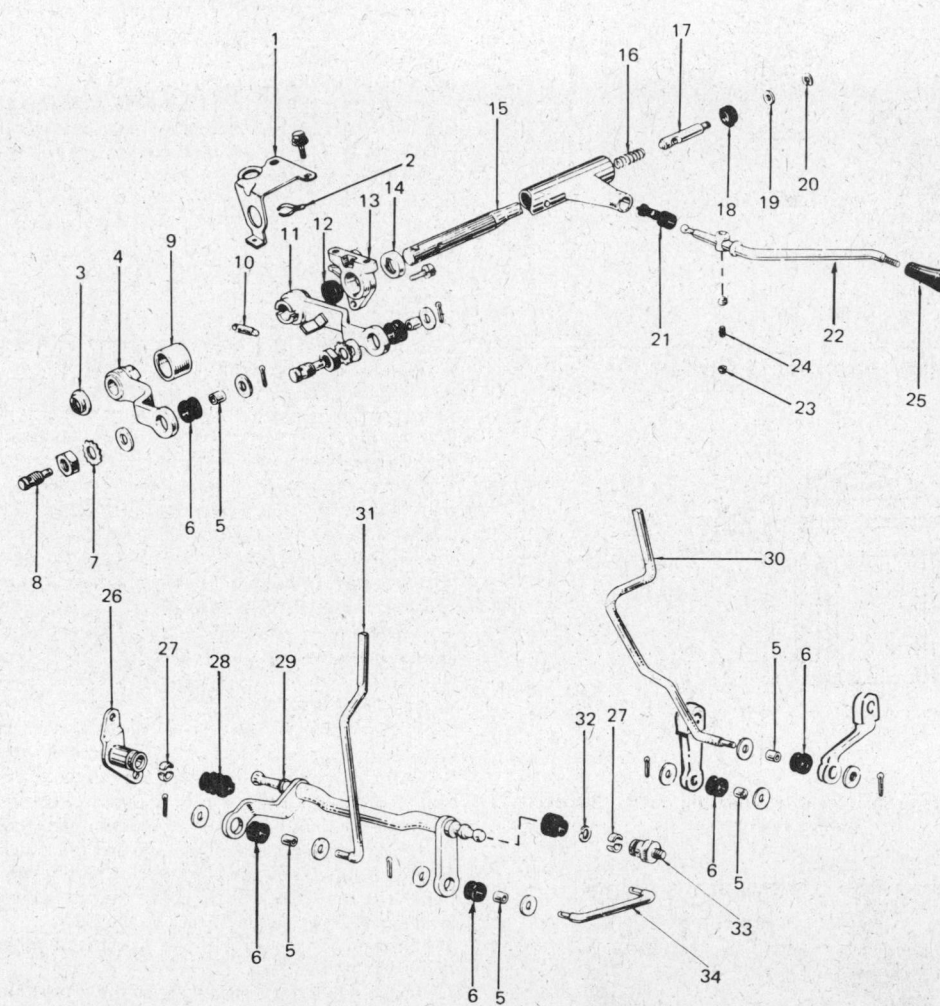

Fig. 6.41. Column shift linkage - 3-speed gearbox

1 Retainer	9 Spacer	17 Upper shaft	26 Crosshaft support
2 Spring	10 Key	18 Bush	27 Bush
3 Dust excluder	11 Low speed lever	19 Washer	28 Dust cover
4 High speed lever	12 Bush	20 Circlip	29 Cross shaft
5 Bush	13 Lower bracket	21 Cover	30 Low speed connecting rod
6 Grommet	14 Dust seal	22 Shift lever	31 High speed rod
7 Star washer	15 Control shaft	23 Shift lever pin	32 Circlip
8 Swivel pin	16 Spring	24 Spring	33 Cross shaft support No. 1
		25 Knob	34 Gear shift rod

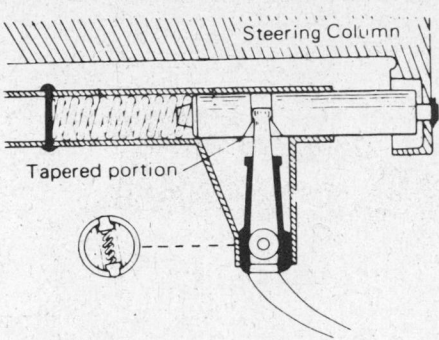

Fig. 6.42. Shift lever installation diagram - 3-speed gearbox

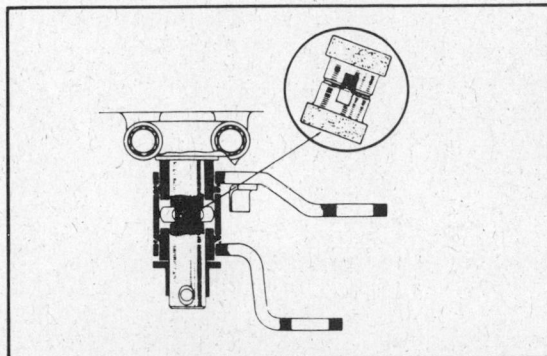

Fig. 6.43. Installing selector key - 3-speed gearbox

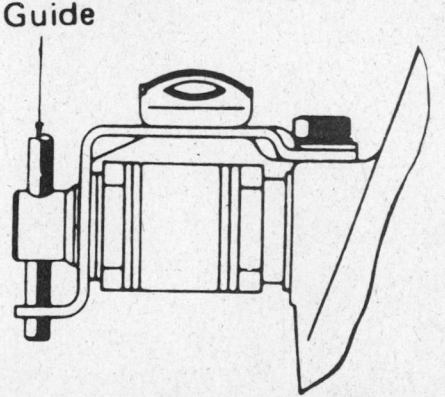

Fig. 6.44. Control shaft-to-shift lever retainer alignment - 3-speed gearbox

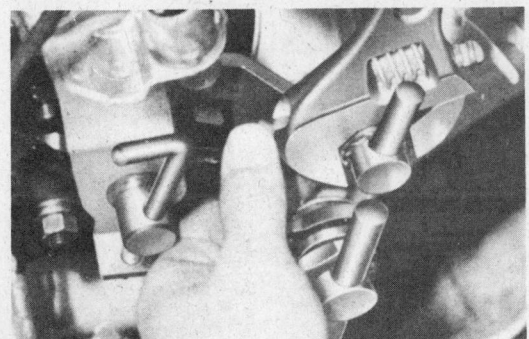

Fig. 6.45. Tightening control rod swivel nut - 3-speed gearbox

compound applied to it and it should be tightened to the specified torque (Fig. 6.35).

8 Insert the interlock pin; this is most easily done by using a piece of tubing as a guide.

9 Now insert the 2nd/3rd selector shaft, passing it through the shift forks and then positioning it in the neutral mode. Fit the pin (2) and plug (1). Insert the ball (3) spring (4) and plug (5). The plugs should be tightened to the specified torque and have gasket sealing compound applied to them (Fig. 6.37).

10 Tighten the shift lever housing nuts, then fit the external shift levers complete with washers and cotters.

11 Install the reverse idler gear by inserting the idler shaft from the rear of the gearbox casing, fitting the gear and thrust washer, and screwing in the locking bolt. The endfloat of the reverse idler gear should compare with the clearance measured before dismantling (see Section 3) which should be between 0.0039 and 0.0098 in (0.10 and 0.25 mm) if otherwise, change the thrust collar from those available and listed in the Specifications.

12 Assemble the countershaft gear complete with bearings and spacers. Stick the two thrust washers to the internal faces of the gearbox casing using thick grease, and ensuring that the projections on the washers locate in the casing grooves.

13 Lower the countershaft gear into the casing and insert the countershaft from the front end, taking care not to displace the thrust washers. The locking tongue on the endface of the countershaft should be positioned horizontally. Compare the endfloat of the countershaft with that measured during dismantling (see Section 3) and change the rear washer if necessary to bring the clearance in line with that which applied originally, this should be between 0.0047 and 0.0114 in (0.12 and 0.29 mm). Rear thrust washers are available in thicknesses as listed in the Specifications.

14 Bolt on the extension housing using a new gasket and tightening the bolts to the specified torque.

15 Fit the bottom cover using a new gasket.

16 Fit the front bearing retainer with a new gasket, making sure that the oil holes are in alignment.

17 Bolt on the clutch bellhousing and fit the speedometer driven gear and release bearing and fork.

9 Steering column gearchange linkage - servicing and adjustment

1 Commence dismantling by removing the two connecting rod swivels (1) and the shift lever retainer (2) (see Fig. 6.39).

2 Remove the dust covers and the high speed lever (3) together with spacer. Disconnect the leads from the reversing lamp switch.

3 Drive out the control lever selecting key and remove the control low speed lever (4) and bush.

4 Remove the shrouds from the upper end of the steering column and unscrew the wiring harness clips.

5 Depress the shift lever spring pins simultaneously with a suitable tool and withdraw the lever.

6 Prise off the circlip and remove the washer, upper shaft and spring. Withdraw the control shaft into the vehicle interior.

7 Remove the low and high speed connecting rods and the cross-shaft from the gearbox end of the control system.

8 Inspect all components for wear and renew as necessary.

9 Commence reassembly by inserting the control shaft into the column followed by the compression spring and upper shaft. The upper shaft must be positioned so that the tapered end of the shift lever hole will be ready to receive the lever.

10 Fit the washer and circlip so that the upper bracket is located between them.

11 Insert the springs and pins into the recesses in the shift lever and depressing both pins at the same time, connect the shift lever to the control shaft.

12 Refit the wiring harness clip and upper steering column shrouds.

13 Install the lower bush, low speed lever and selecting key to the shaft, driving in the key until it projects equally both sides.

14 Grease all moving parts and then fit the spacer, high speed lever, dust cover and shaft lever retainer. Connect the reversing lamp switch leads.

15 Fit the cross-shaft, the low speed connecting rod, the high speed connecting rod and the shift rod.

16 With refitting complete, position the hand shift lever in neutral. Loosen the low and high speed connecting rod swivel nuts. Align the

control shaft adjusting hole with the one in the shift lever retainer and insert a piece of ¼ in (6 mm) diameter rod as a guide pin while the swivel nuts are moved on their rods to the points where no stress is applied to the rod in either direction. Tighten the swivel nuts. Check the operation of the gearchange mechanism by moving the hand shift lever to all gear positions.

10 Gearbox (4-speed) - removal and refitting

The procedure is almost identical to that given for the 3-speed gearbox in Section 2. However, the following points should be noted:

a) *It is also necessary to detach the reverse light switch leads. This can be done when disconnecting the speedometer cable.*
b) *The column shift linkage is not used on the 4-speed transmission.*
c) *From beneath the car, remove the four bolts securing the shift lever ball retainer plate, and lift the lever out.*

d) *Remove the starter motor - refer to Chapter 10 if necessary.*

11 Gearbox (4-speed) - dismantling into major assemblies

1 Remove the clutch release fork and bearing from within the clutch bellhousing. Unbolt the clutch bellhousing from the gearbox.
2 Remove the speedometer driven gear from the extension housing.
3 Unscrew and remove the reverse gear restrict pin, then unbolt and remove the exhaust housing making sure that the swing arm is moved in an anticlockwise direction (when viewed from the rear) to disengage the remote control rod from the selector rods.
4 With the extension housing removed, drive out the tension pin, and remove the remote control rod and swing arm.
5 Remove the reversing lamp switch.
6 From the front face of the gearbox, remove the front bearing retainer, the countershaft cover and spacer.
7 Remove the circlips from the outer tracks of the input shaft and

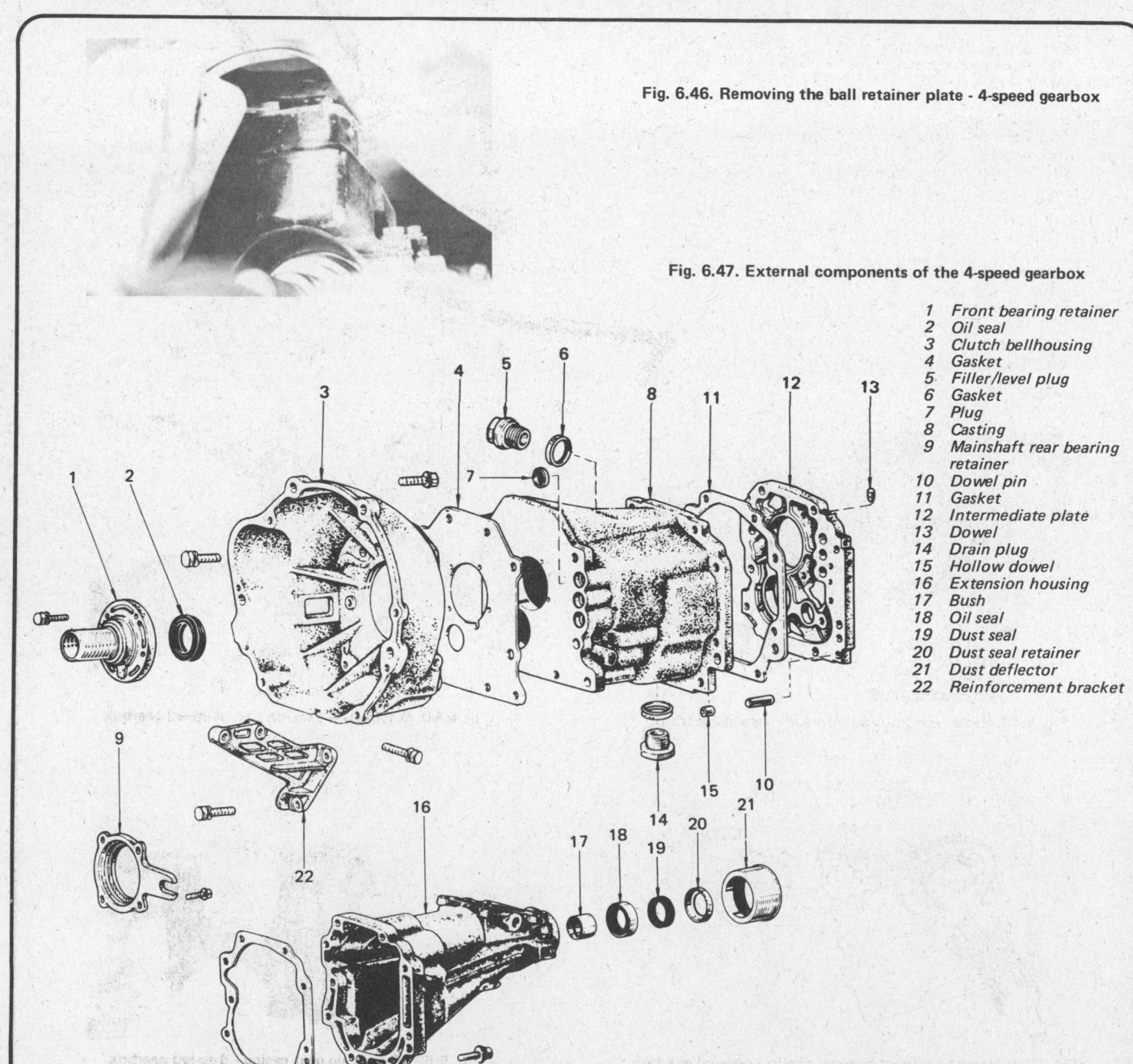

Fig. 6.46. Removing the ball retainer plate - 4-speed gearbox

Fig. 6.47. External components of the 4-speed gearbox

1   Front bearing retainer
2   Oil seal
3   Clutch bellhousing
4   Gasket
5   Filler/level plug
6   Gasket
7   Plug
8   Casting
9   Mainshaft rear bearing retainer
10 Dowel pin
11 Gasket
12 Intermediate plate
13 Dowel
14 Drain plug
15 Hollow dowel
16 Extension housing
17 Bush
18 Oil seal
19 Dust seal
20 Dust seal retainer
21 Dust deflector
22 Reinforcement bracket

Fig. 6.48. Shift and selector components - 4-speed gearbox

1 1st/2nd selector shaft
2 3rd/4th selector shaft
3 Remover selector shaft
4 Interlock pin
5 Interlock pin
6 Detent balls
7 Detent springs
8 Socket screw
9 Socket screw
10 1st/2nd shift fork
11 3rd/4th shift fork
12 Tension pin
13 Reverse shift arm pivot
14 Reverse shift arm
15 Reverse shift arm bracket
16 Gearchange knob
17 Gearchange lever
18 Boot
19 Seat
20 Spring
21 Ball retaining flange
22 Remove control housing
23 Oil deflector
24 Bush
25 Swing arm
26 Remote control rod
27 Washer
28 Reverse restrictor pin

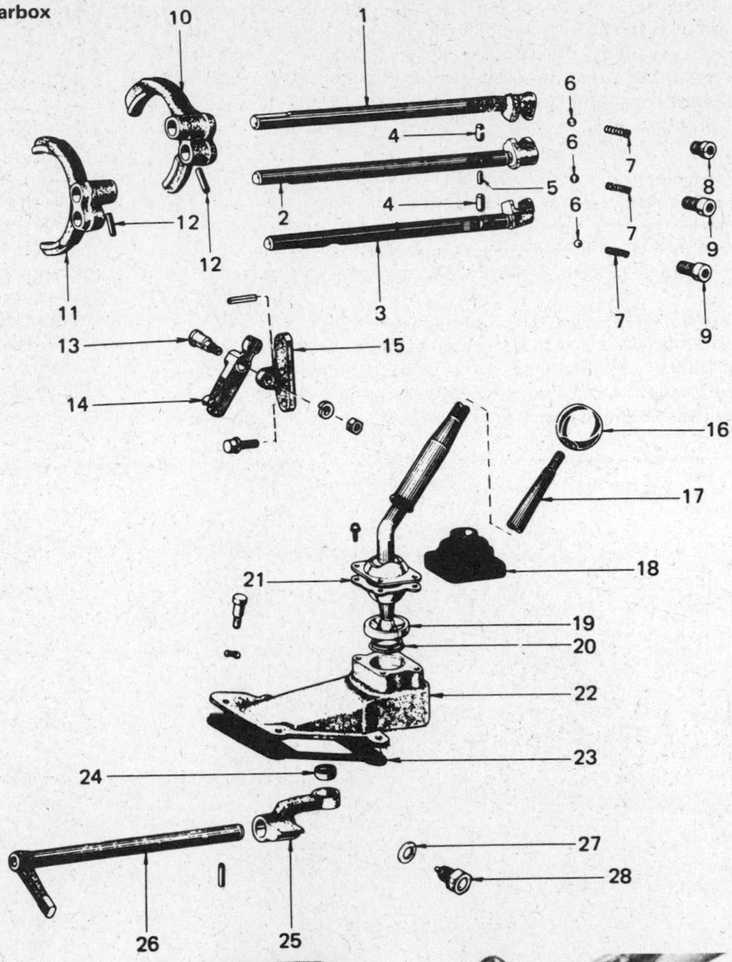

Fig. 6.49. Extension housing removal - 4-speed gearbox

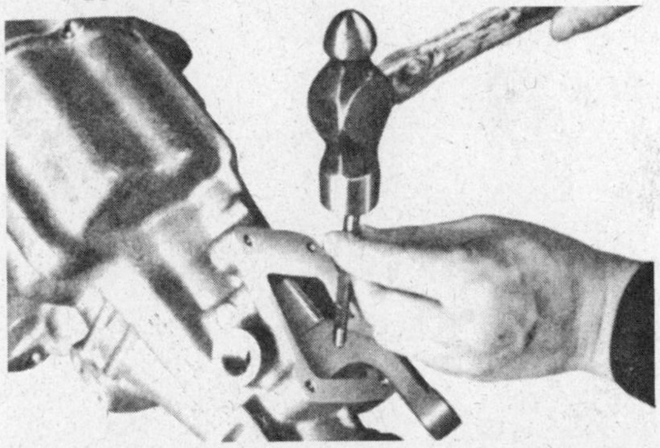

Fig. 6.50. Driving out tension pin - 4-speed gearbox

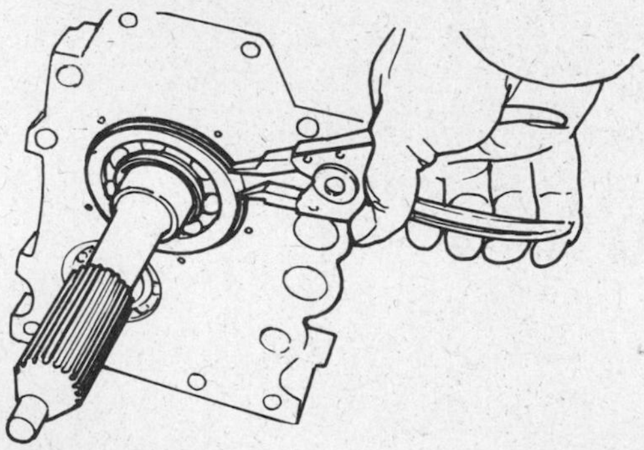

Fig. 6.51. Removing front bearing circlip - 4-speed gearbox

Fig. 6.52. Removing gear casing - 4-speed gearbox

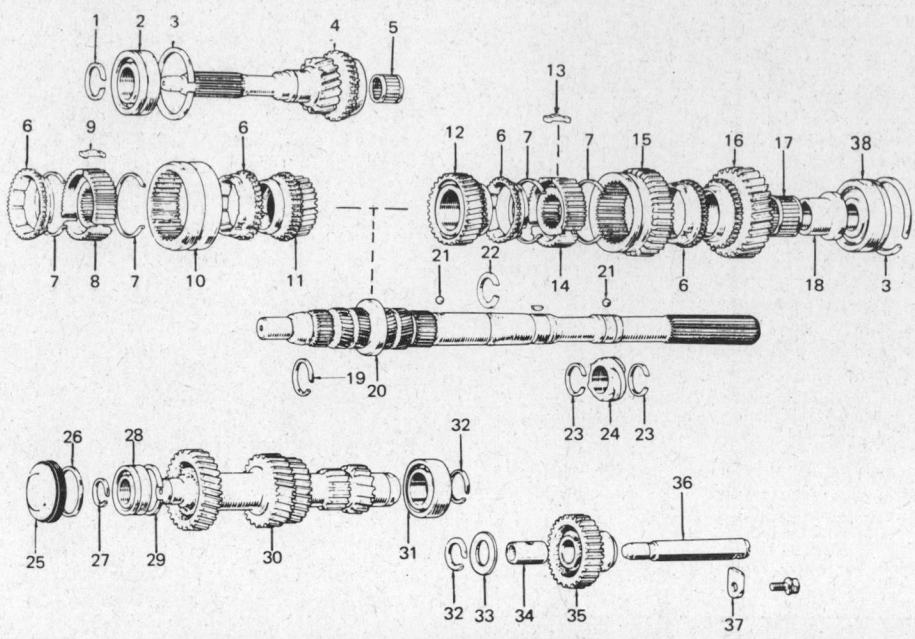

Fig. 6.53. Gears and shafts of 4-speed gearbox

1	Circlip	11	3rd gear
2	Input shaft bearing	12	2nd gear
3	Bearing outer track circlip	13	Blocker bar
4	Input shaft	14	1st/2nd synchro hub
5	Needle roller bearing	15	Reverse gear
6	3rd/4th synchro ring	16	1st gear
7	Spring	17	Needle roller bearing
8	3rd/4th synchro hub	18	1st gear bearing inner track
9	Blocker bar	19	Circlip
10	3rd/4th synchro sleeve		

20	Mainshaft	29	Bearing outer track circlip
21	Lock ball	30	Countergear
22	Circlip	31	Countershaft rear bearing
23	Circlip	32	Circlip
24	Speedometer drive gear	33	Spacer
25	Countershaft cover	34	Bush
26	Spacer	35	Reverse idler gear
27	Circlip	36	Reverse idler shaft
28	Countershaft front bearing	37	Reverse idler shaft stop
		38	Mainshaft rear bearing

Fig. 6.54. Removing reverse idler gear - 4-speed gearbox

Fig. 6.55. Removing a detent plug - 4-speed gearbox

Fig. 6.56. Driving out a spring tension pin - 4-speed gearbox

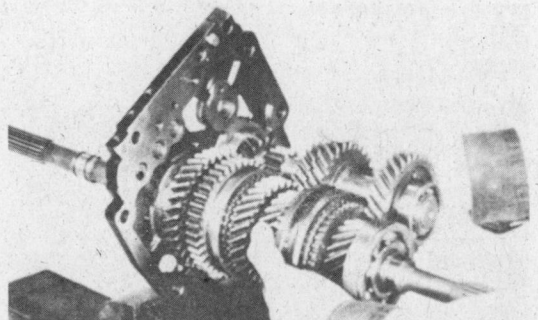

Fig. 6.57. Removing mainshaft and countershaft assemblies - 4-speed gearbox

countershaft front bearings.

8   Separate the casing from the intermediate plate and pull off the casing, leaving all the gear assemblies attached to the intermediate plate.

9   Secure the intermediate plate in the jaws of a vice using jaw protectors to prevent damaging the plate.

10 Remove the speedometer drive gear and extract the locking ball.

11 Drive out the tension pin, slacken the reverse gear shift arm bracket bolt and withdraw the bracket with the shift arm attached.

12 Unbolt the reverse idler gear shaft stop and withdraw the idler gear and shaft towards the front of the gearbox (Fig. 6.54).

13 Unbolt and remove the mainshaft rear bearing retainer.

14 Using an Allen key, unscrew the plugs from the edge of the intermediate plate and extract the springs and detent balls.

15 Drive out the tension pin from each of the shift forks.

16 Withdraw each of the selector shafts in the sequence - reverse, 3rd/4th, 1st/2nd. Remove each of the shift forks as the selector shafts are withdrawn, and retrieve the interlock pins.

17 Remove the circlip from the mainshaft rear bearing outer track, then push the mainshaft and countershaft assemblies simultaneously (meshed together) from the rear face of the intermediate plate (Fig. 6.57).

18 Inspect all the components for wear and renew as necessary.

---

12 Mainshaft (4-speed gearbox) - servicing

1   Pull off the input shaft and synchroniser ring from the front of the mainshaft.

2   Extract the shaft circlip and withdraw the 3rd/4th synchro unit followed by 3rd gear.

3   If the rear bearing is to be removed, extract the shaft circlip and press it from the shaft using a press.

4   With the rear bearing removed, 1st gear, the needle roller bearing and the synchro ring can be drawn off the rear end of the mainshaft. Do not lose the locking balls from the needle bearing inner race.

5   A press must again be used to remove the reverse gear, 1st/2nd synchro unit, second gear and synchro ring.

6   Clean all components thoroughly and examine for worn or chipped teeth, and grooving or scoring of the shaft. The gears should have a running clearance between their internal bores and the shaft of between 0.0014 and 0.0039 in (0.06 and 0.10 mm) with a maximum of 0.0059 in (0.15 mm).

7   Inspect the condition of the synchroniser units. If there has been a history of noisy gearchanging, or the synchromesh could easily be 'beaten', renew the unit complete. In any event, fit the synchro ring onto the gear and measure the clearance. This should not be less than 0.031 in (0.8 mm); if otherwise, renew the ring.

8   Fit the shift forks to the synchro sleeves and check for side clearance. If this exceeds 0.039 in (1.0 mm), renew one or both components as necessary.

9   Correct assembly of the two synchro units must be carried out before fitting them to the mainshaft. Ensure that the spring ends do not engage in the same gaps on opposite sides of the unit.

10 Commence reassembly by installing 3rd gear complete with synchro ring onto the mainshaft. Apply oil liberally to all components.

Fig. 6.58. Removing 3rd/4th synchro and 3rd gear - 4-speed gearbox

Fig. 6.59. Removing output shaft bearing - 4-speed gearbox

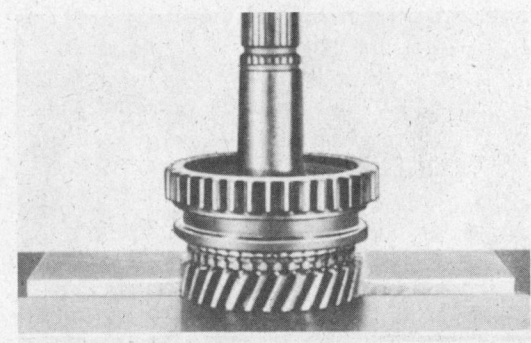

Fig. 6.60. Removing reverse and 2nd gear - 4-speed gearbox

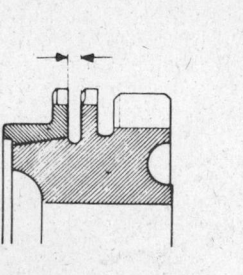
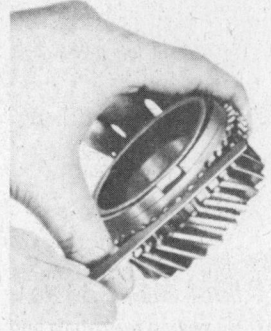

Fig. 6.61. Checking synchro ring-to-gear clearance - 4-speed gearbox

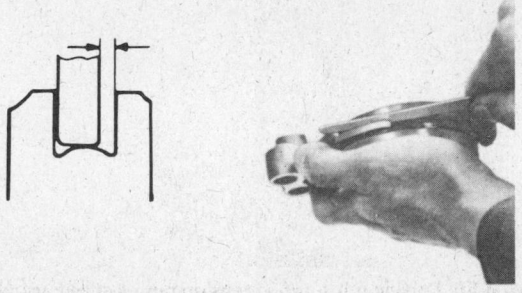

Fig. 6.62. Checking shift-to-synchro groove clearance - 4-speed gearbox

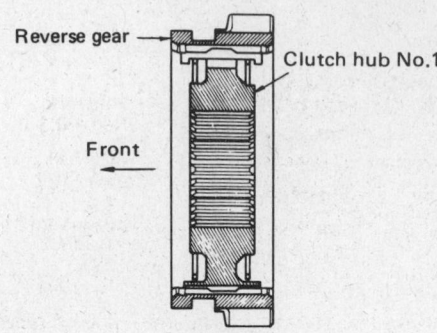

Fig. 6 63. Correct assembly of 1st/2nd synchro - 4-speed gearbox

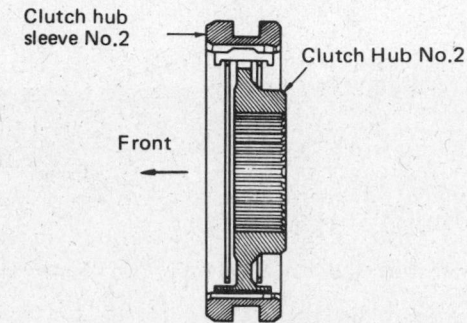

Fig. 6.64. Correct assembly of 3rd/4th synchro - 4-speed gearbox

Thrust clearance
0.15 to 0.25 mm

Fig. 6.65. Checking 3rd gear thrust clearance - 4-speed gearbox

11 Slide the 3rd/4th synchro unit onto the mainshaft until it rests against the shoulder on the shaft. Tap it into position if necessary using a plastic faced hammer and secure it with a circlip that will give a groove clearance of not more than 0.002 in (0.05 mm). Select a circlip from those listed in the Specification Section.

12 Using feeler blades, measure the third gear endfloat, which should be between 0.0059 and 0.0098 in (0.15 and 0.25 mm) with a maximum of 0.0118 in (0.30 mm).

13 Install 2nd gear complete with synchro ring onto the mainshaft.

14 Using a press, install the 1st/2nd synchro unit and reverse gear assembly onto the mainshaft.

15 Measure 2nd gear endfloat which should be within the tolerances specified for 3rd gear in paragraph 12.

16 Using a dab of thick grease, stick the needle bearing inner track locking ball into its shaft recess.

17 Slide 1st gear, 3rd/4th synchro ring, needle bearing and inner track, (held as an assembly) onto the shaft, check that the inner track slot aligns with the locking ball, and that the synchro ring slots are aligned with the shift keys.

18 Press the mainshaft rear bearing onto the shaft end, making sure that the outer track circlip groove is nearer the rear end of the mainshaft.

19 Measure first gear endfloat which again should be as specified for third gear in paragraph 12.

20 Select a circlip for securing the mainshaft rear bearing to the shaft to give the minimum clearance (see Specifications).

---

13 Input shaft (4-speed gearbox) - servicing

The procedure is identical to that described in Section 5.

---

14 Countershaft and reverse gear assemblies (4-speed gearbox) - servicing

1 The countershaft assembly cannot be dismantled and must be renewed if the gears are chipped or worn. The bearings can be renewed using an extractor and press.

2 The reverse idler gear, should be renewed if the teeth are worn or chipped; also the shaft if scored or grooved.

3 If the reverse gear bush is worn, it must be pressed out and the new one fitted so that the oil holes are in alignment, then the bush reamed if necessary to achieve a finished internal diameter of between 0.7890 and 0.7898 in (20.04 and 20.06 mm).

---

15 Oil seals (4-speed gearbox) - renewal

1 The recommendations and procedure are as described in Section 7, excluding paragraph 2.

---

16 Gearbox (4-speed) - reassembly

1 Check that the dowel pin projects between ¼ in and 5/16 in (6.00

Thrust clearance
0.15 to 0.25 mm

Fig. 6.66. Checking 2nd gear endfloat - 4-speed gearbox

Thrust clearance
0.15 to 0.25 mm

Fig. 6.67. Checking 1st gear endfloat - 4-speed gearbox

and 8.0 mm) from the front face of the intermediate plate, then secure the plate in a vice fitted with jaw protectors.

2 Insert the needle roller bearing into the input shaft recess, sticking it in position with grease.

3 Liberally oil all components as they are assembled, commencing by fitting the 3rd/4th synchro ring to the rear end of the input shaft.

4 Fit the input shaft to the front end of the mainshaft.

5 Mesh the mainshaft and countershaft assemblies, and insert them together into the intermediate plate.

6 Fit the circlip to the groove in the mainshaft rear bearing outer track.

7 Connect the reverse idler shaft to the reverse idler gear and fit them to the intermediate plate. Fit the spacer over the shaft and secure with a circlip.

8 Fit the stop to retain the reverse idler shaft in position.

9 Locate 1st/2nd and 3rd/4th shift forks into their respective synchro sleeve grooves. When correctly positioned, the longer bosses of these two shift forks will face each other.

10 Install 1st/2nd selector shaft and interlock pin, followed by 3rd/4th selector shaft and its interlock pin then the third interlock pin and reverse selector shaft. Each selector shaft should be in the neutral position when inserting its interlock pin.

11 Secure the shift forks to their respective selector shafts by driving in the tension pins.

12 Into the holes in the edge of the intermediate plate, insert the detent balls and springs. Apply gasket sealing compound to the plugs and screw them into the specified torque.

13 Bolt the mainshaft rear bearing retainer to the intermediate plate, tightening the bolts to the specified torque.

14 Assemble the reverse shift arm to its bracket, tightening the bolt only finger tight. Locate them on the intermediate plate and drive in the tension pin so that it projects as shown in Fig. 6.69.

15 Select the reverse gear by moving the shift fork, and check the mesh between the reverse gear and reverse idler gear. When correctly meshed, the front faces of the reverse idler gear and reverse gear on the mainshaft should be in alignment. In this situation, the slot in the shift arm pivot bolt will be at right angles to the intermediate plate. Adjust as necessary to achieve this setting, then tighten the pivot nut to the specified torque.

16 Position a new gasket to the front face of the intermediate plate and locate the gearbox casing on the plate.

17 Fit the circlips to the input shaft and countershaft front bearings.

18 Assemble the remote control rod and swing arm into the extension housing by driving in the connecting tension pin.

19 Locate a new gasket on the rear face of the intermediate plate and offer up the extension housing until it is within an inch (25 mm) of its installed position. Move the swing arm clockwise to engage the remote control rod with the shift forks, and push the extension housing fully home.

20 Bolt the extension housing to the gearbox casing, sandwiching the intermediate plate and two gaskets between them. Tighten the bolts to the specified torque.

21 Push the countershaft fully to the rear and measure the distance between the front face of the countershaft front bearing and the front face of the gearbox, using a dial gauge or feeler blades. Select a spacer to correspond with the dimension established from thicknesses available as listed in the Specifications.

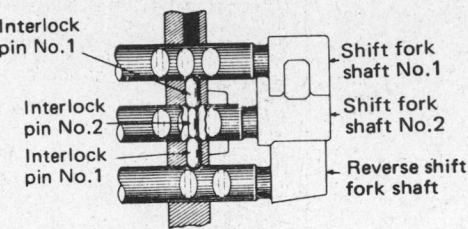

Fig. 6.68. Location of selector shaft interlock pins - 4-speed gearbox

Fig. 6.69. Installing shift arm and tension pin - 4-speed gearbox

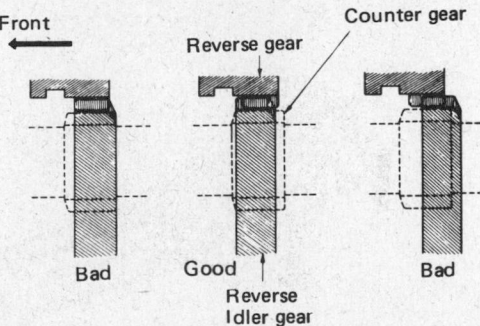

Fig. 6.70. Reverse idler gear adjustment - 4-speed gearbox

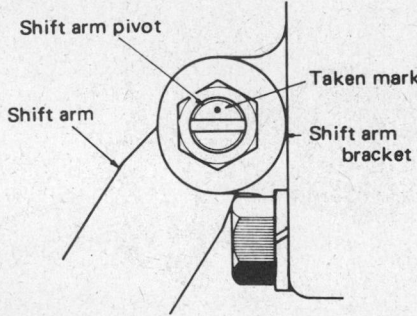

Fig. 6.71. Reverse idler gear pivot position when correctly adjusted - 4-speed gearbox

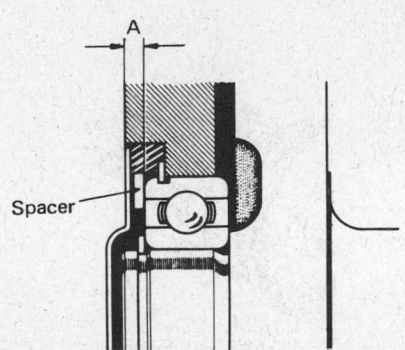

Fig. 6.72. Countershaft front bearing spacer adjustment diagram - 4-speed gearbox

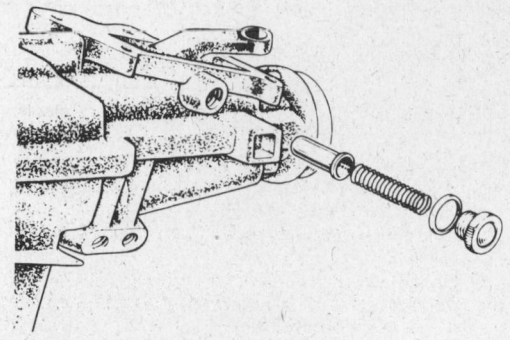

Fig. 6.73. Removing extension housing restrictor pin assembly - 5-speed gearbox

Fig. 6.74. Removing a detent socket screw - 5-speed gearbox

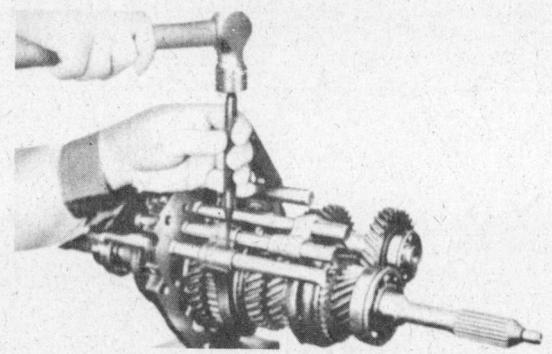

Fig. 6.75 Removing a shift fork tension pin - 5-speed gearbox

Fig. 6.76. Removing mainshaft 5th gear - 5-speed gearbox

Fig. 6.77. External components of the 5-speed gearbox

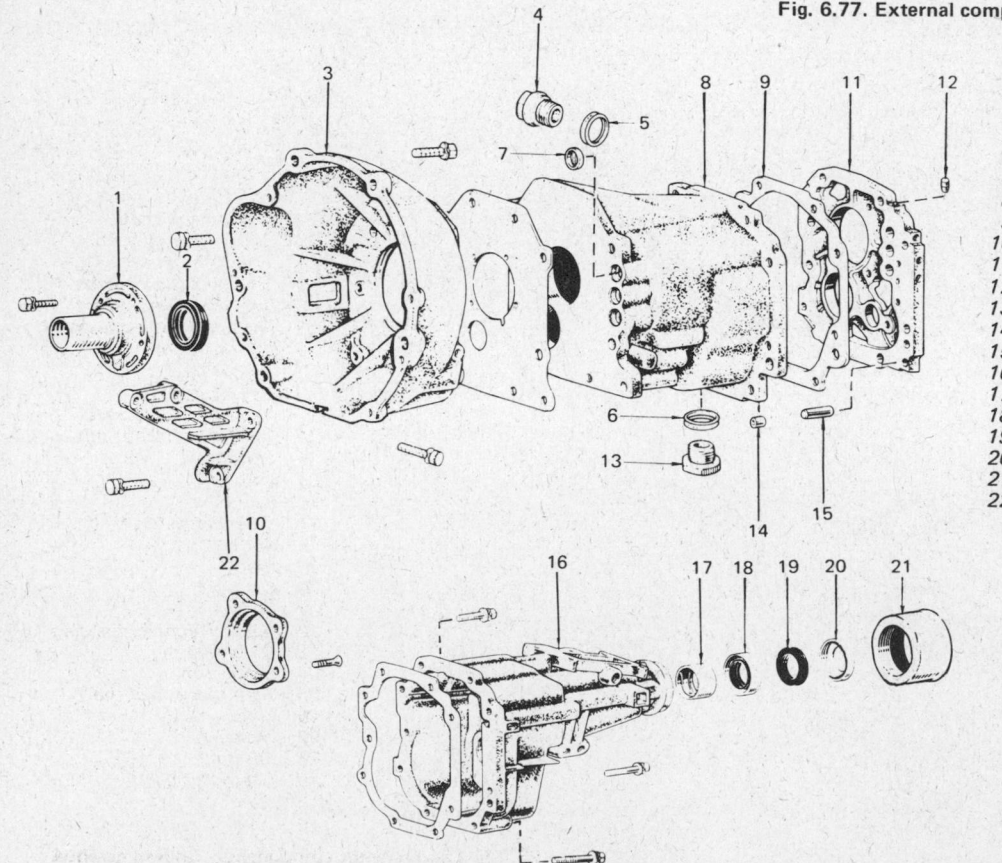

1 Front bearing retainer
2 Oil seal
3 Clutch bellhousing
4 Filler/lever plug
5 Washer
6 Washer
7 Plug
8 Casing
9 Gasket
10 Mainshaft rear bearing retainer
11 Intermediate plate
12 Dowel
13 Drain plug
14 Hollow dowel
15 Dowel
16 Extension housing
17 Bush
18 Oil seal
19 Dust seal
20 Dust seal retainer
21 Dust deflector
22 Reinforcement bracket

22 Fit the selected spacer to the front of the countershaft bearing, followed by the cover.
23 Use a new gasket and bolt on the input shaft bearing retainer, making sure that the oil return holes are in alignment.
24 Use a new gasket and bolt the clutch bellhousing to the front face of the gearbox. Tighten the bolts to the specified torque.
25 Screw in the reverse restrict pin, with its sealing washer, to the specified torque.
26 Fit the speedometer driven gear into the extension housing; also fit the reversing lamp switch.
27 The gearchange lever can be inserted and the retaining flanges bolted up as the gearbox is being installed in the vehicle. Note that the gearchange lever ball spring is installed with its larger diameter end downward.

17 Gearbox (5-speed) - removal and refitting

This is identical to the procedure for the four-speed type gearbox

(see Section 10).

18 Gearbox (5-speed) - dismantling into major assemblies

1 Unbolt the clutch bellhousing from the gearbox casing.
2 Remove the speedometer driven gear and two restrictor pin assemblies from the extension housing.
3 Carry out the operations described in paragraphs 3 to 9 of Section 11.
4 Using a socket wrench, unscrew and remove the plugs from the edge of the intermediate plate, and extract the springs and detent balls.
5 Drive out the tension pins from the shift forks and withdraw the selector shafts taking care not to lose the two interlock pins.
6 Remove the speedometer drive gear and its spacer from the mainshaft after the shaft circlips have been removed. Take care not to lose the locking ball.
7 Using a two legged puller, draw off the bearing from the rear end of the mainshaft.

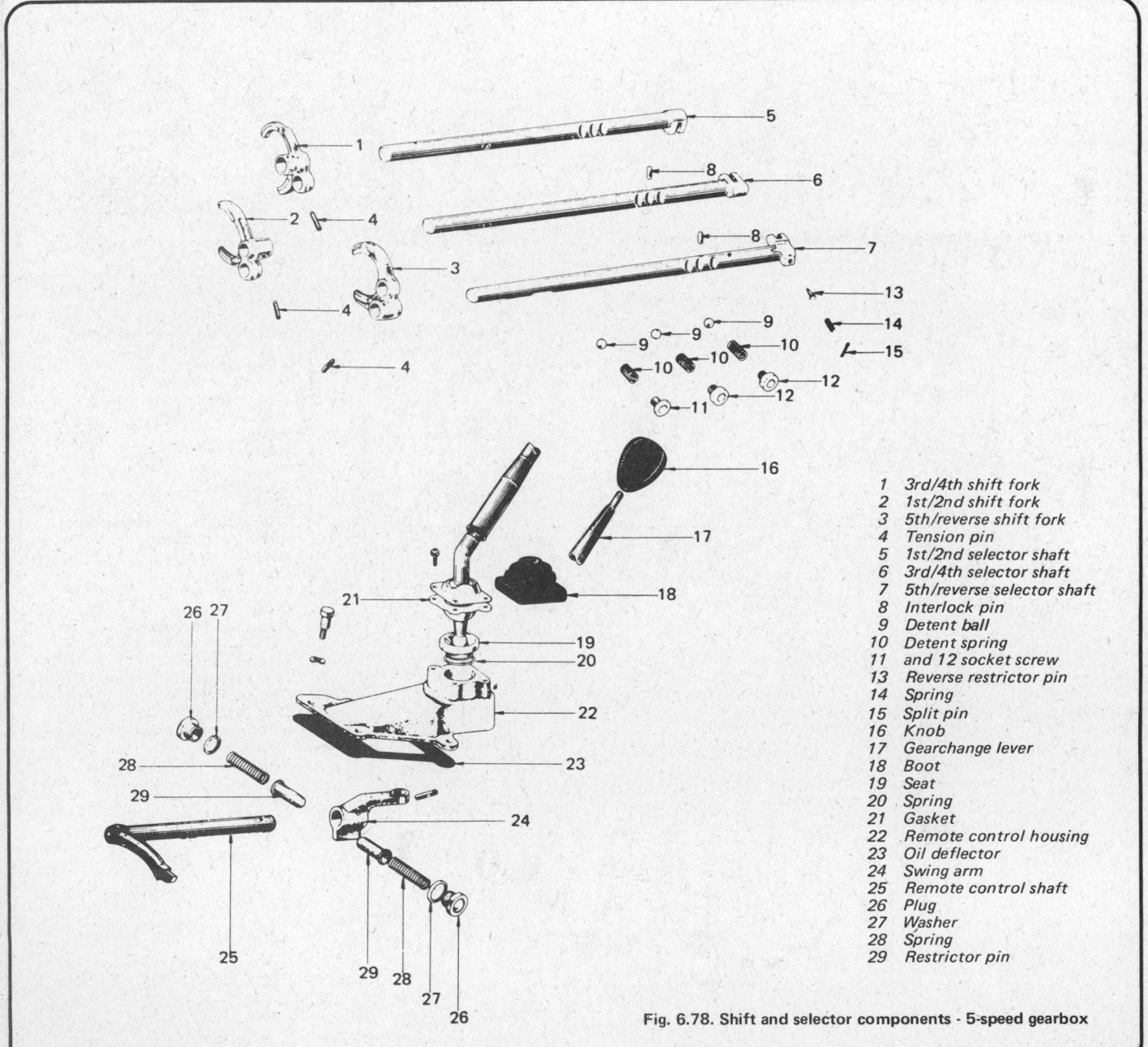

1   3rd/4th shift fork
2   1st/2nd shift fork
3   5th/reverse shift fork
4   Tension pin
5   1st/2nd selector shaft
6   3rd/4th selector shaft
7   5th/reverse selector shaft
8   Interlock pin
9   Detent ball
10 Detent spring
11 and 12 socket screw
13 Reverse restrictor pin
14 Spring
15 Split pin
16 Knob
17 Gearchange lever
18 Boot
19 Seat
20 Spring
21 Gasket
22 Remote control housing
23 Oil deflector
24 Swing arm
25 Remote control shaft
26 Plug
27 Washer
28 Spring
29 Restrictor pin

Fig. 6.78. Shift and selector components - 5-speed gearbox

Fig. 6.79. Removing countershaft bearing outer track - 5-speed gearbox

Fig. 6.80. Removing input shaft and mainshaft assembly - 5-speed gearbox

Fig. 6.81. Removing mainshaft 3rd gear - 5-speed gearbox

Fig. 6.82. Internal components of the 5-speed gearbox

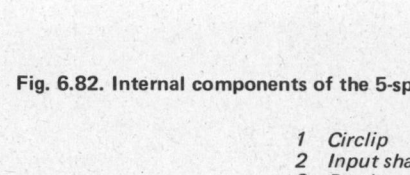

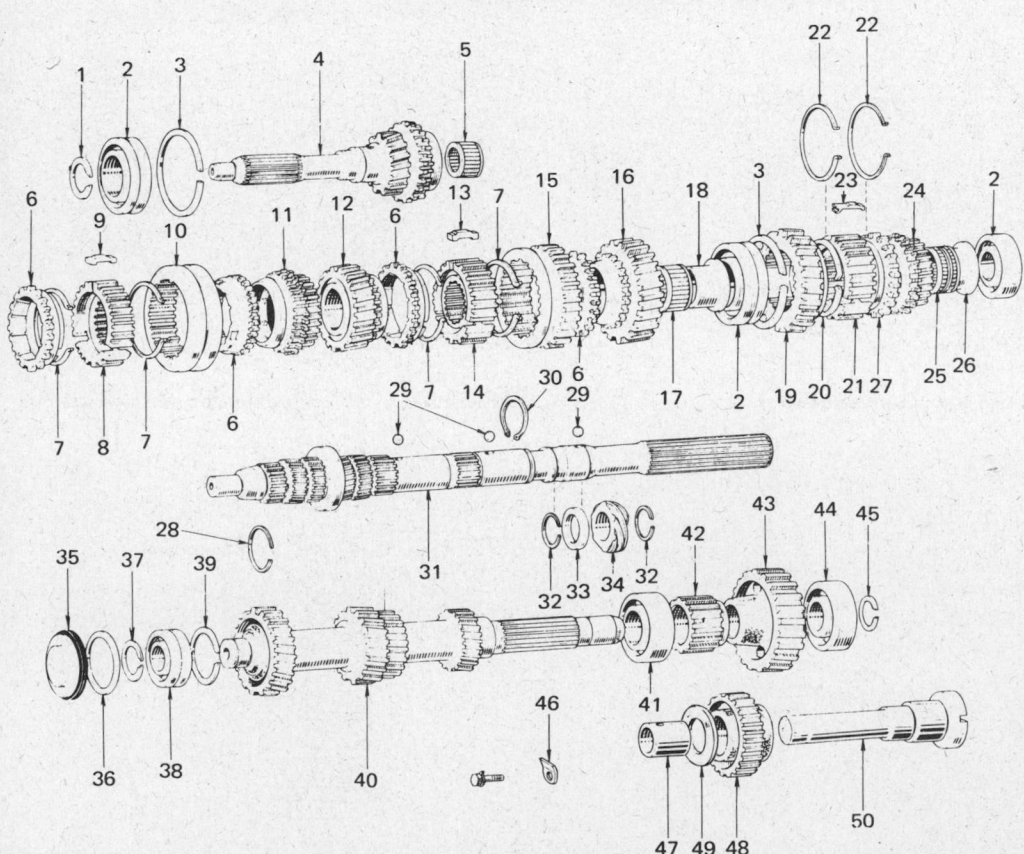

1 Circlip
2 Input shaft bearing
3 Bearing outer track circlip
4 Input shaft
5 Needle roller bearing
6 Synchro ring
7 Spring
8 3rd/4th synchro hub
9 Blocker bar
10 3rd/4th synchro sleeve
11 3rd gear
12 2nd gear
13 Blocker bar
14 1st/2nd synchro hub
15 Reverse gear
16 1st gear
17 Needle bearing
18 Needle bearing inner track
19 Reverse gear
20 Circlip
21 5th gear synchro hub
22 Spring
23 Blocker bar
24 5th gear
25 Needle roller bearing
26 Needle bearing inner track
27 Synchro ring
28 Circlip
29 Lock balls
30 Mainshaft rear bearing circlips
31 Mainshaft
32 Circlip
33 Spacer
34 Speedometer drive gear
35 Countershaft cover
36 Spacer
37 Circlip
38 Countershaft front bearing
39 Bearing outer track circlip
40 Countergear
41 Bearing
42 Reverse gear
43 Fifth gear
44 Bearing
45 Circlip
46 Stop
47 Bush
48 Reverse idler gear
49 Spacer
50 Reverse idler gear shaft

8   Remove the circlip from the mainshaft.
9   From the rear end of the countershaft, remove the circlip and draw off the bearing.
10 Withdraw the countershaft fifth gear and reverse gear.
11 From the mainshaft, remove the circlip and withdraw fifth gear, the synchro ring, needle roller bearing and fifth gear inner bearing track, taking care not to lose the track locking ball.
12 Remove the reverse gear and fifth gear synchro unit.
13 Slacken the bolt which secures the reverse idler shaft stop to the intermediate plate; withdraw the shaft to the rear and remove the reverse idler gear and spacer.
14 Unbolt the mainshaft rear bearing retainer and remove the circlip from the bearing.
15 From the rear end of the countershaft, push the bearing outer track to the rear and withdraw the bearing components. The counter-shaft assembly may now be removed from the intermediate plate.
16 Remove the input shaft and synchro ring from the mainshaft, then withdraw the mainshaft assembly from the intermediate plate.

19 Mainshaft (5-speed gearbox) - servicing

1   Extract the circlip and remove the 3rd/4th synchro unit, the synchro ring and third gear from the front end of the mainshaft.
2   From the rear end of the mainshaft draw off the bearing. A press will be required for this operation (Fig. 6.83).
3   Remove the first gear, the needle roller bearing, bearing inner track and synchro ring. Take care not to lose the inner track locking ball (Fig. 6.84).
4   Press off the second gear complete with synchro ring, and reverse speed gear.
5   Clean all components thoroughly and examine for worn or chipped teeth and grooving or scoring of the shaft. The gears should have a running clearance between their internal bores and the shaft of between 0.0008 and 0.0020 in (0.02 and 0.05 mm) for 1st and 5th gears and 0.0014 and 0.0039 in (0.06 and 0.10 mm) for 2nd and 3rd gears.
6   Check the synchro units as described in Section 12, paragraphs 7, 8

Fig. 6.83. Pressing off mainshaft rear bearing - 5-speed gearbox

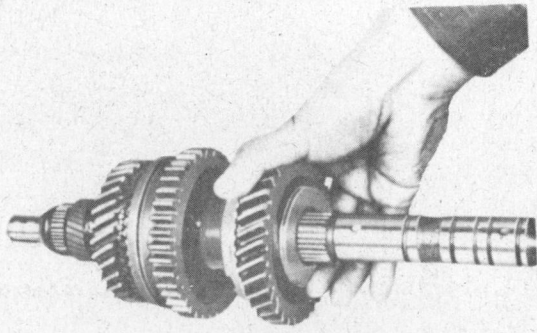

Fig. 6.84. Removing mainshaft 1st gear - 5-speed gearbox

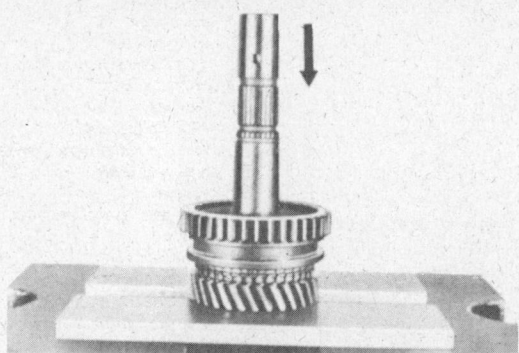

Fig. 6.85. Pressing off reverse and 2nd gears - 5-speed gearbox

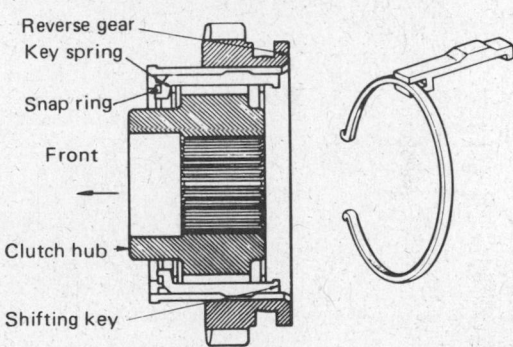

Fig. 6.86. Correct assembly of 1st/2nd synchro - 5-speed gearbox

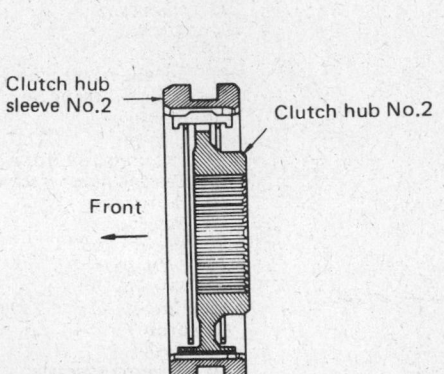

Fig. 6.87. Correct assembly of 3rd/4th synchro - 5-speed gearbox

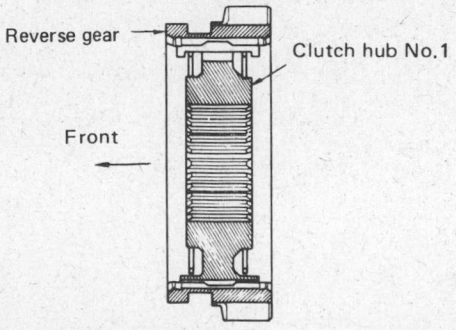

Fig. 6.88. Correct assembly of 5th gear synchro - 5-speed gearbox

and 9 but there are of course three units in the five speed gearbox and they must be assembled as shown (Figs. 6.86, 6.87 and 6.88).
7　Commence reassembly of the mainshaft by installing the 3rd/4th synchro ring to third gear and then fitting them to the shaft.
8　Fit the 3rd/4th synchro unit, positioning it tight against the mainshaft shoulder. Secure it with a circlip to give a groove clearance of between 0 and 0.002 in (0 and 0.05 mm) from those available which are as listed in the Specifications Section.
9　Carry out the operates described in Section 12, paragraph 12 onwards.

20　Input shaft (5-speed gearbox) - servicing

The procedure is identical to that described in Section 5, for the 3-speed gearbox.

21　Countershaft and reverse gear assemblies (5-speed gearbox) - servicing

1　The procedure is similar to that described in Section 18 for four-speed type gearboxes but, when fitting the countershaft cylindrical roller bearing inner track, position it so that its flanged side is towards the front.
2　The bush of the reverse idler gear must be reamed to a finished diameter of between 0.9858 and 1.0260 in (25.04 and 26.06 mm).

22　Oil seals (5-speed gearbox) - renewal

1　The procedure is identical to the operations described in Section 7 excluding paragraph 2.

23　Gearbox (5-speed) - reassembly

1　Check that the intermediate plate dowel pins project by between ¼ in and 5/16 in (6 and 8 mm) from the front face of the intermediate plate, then secure the plate in a vice fitted with jaw protectors.
2　Install the needle roller bearing assembly to the input shaft, then fit the 3rd/4th synchro ring to the cone on the end of the input shaft.
3　Fit the mainshaft assembly to the intermediate plate, then fit the input shaft to the mainshaft.
4　Install the countershaft assembly onto the intermediate plate, then fit the roller bearing onto the shaft from the rear side of the plate; then fit the spacer.
5　Fit the circlip to the outer track of the mainshaft rear bearing.
6　Install the mainshaft rear bearing retainer onto the intermediate plate.

7　Assemble the reverse idler gear and spacer onto the reverse idler shaft, then insert the assembly into the intermediate plate from the rear side. The oil holes in the reverse idler gear must face to the rear.
8　Lock the reverse idler shaft with the stop plate and bolt then check the reverse idler gear endfloat. This should be between 0.0059 and 0.0098 in (0.15 and 0.25 mm) with a maximum of 0.0118 in (0.30 mm).
9　Locate the 5th gear synchro unit (assembled with the reverse gear) onto the mainshaft until it is tight against the inner track of the bearing in the intermediate plate.
10　Fit the locking ball into the mainshaft recess. Use a dab of thick grease to retain it.
11　To the mainshaft, fit the fifth gear, synchro ring, needle roller bearing and inner track, (all assembled together) until the assembly rests against the face of the synchro unit.
12　Secure the assembly to the mainshaft by selecting a circlip to give the minimum clearance.
13　Check fifth gear endfloat; this should be between 0.0039 and 0.0098 in (0.10 and 0.25 mm) with a maximum clearance of 0.0118 in (0.30 mm)
14　Fit the countershaft reverse gear and fifth gear, and drive on the bearing using a piece of tubing as a drift.
15　Fit a circlip to the countershaft and another to the mainshaft. Select the circlips from the thicknesses as listed in the Specifications.
16　Drive the rear bearing onto the mainshaft again using a piece of tubing as a drift and making sure that it rests against the inner track of the bearing.
17　To the mainshaft, fit the spacer, locking ball and speedometer drive gear, and secure them with a circlip.
18　Locate the shift forks in their respective synchro hub grooves, ensuring that the bosses of the forks face the correct way as shown in Fig. 6.95.
19　Insert the 1st/2nd selector shaft and the 5th/reverse selector shaft. The gears should be in neutral when assembling each shaft and the interlock pins correctly inserted.
20　Insert the 3rd/4th selector shaft.
21　Insert the detent balls and springs into their holes in the edge of the intermediate plate. Tighten the socket screws to the specified torque and, in order to prevent leaks, ensure that their threads are coated with jointing compound.
22　Secure the shift forks to the selector shafts by driving in the tension pins.
23　Carry out the operations described in paragraphs 16 to 24 inclusive of Section 16.
24　Insert the restrictor pins and springs, one on each side of the extension housing, and tighten the plugs to the specified torque.
25　Refit the speedometer driven gear to the extension housing, and the reversing lamp switch to the gearbox casing.
26　The gearshift lever will normally be bolted to the extension housing as the gearbox is offered up during refitting.

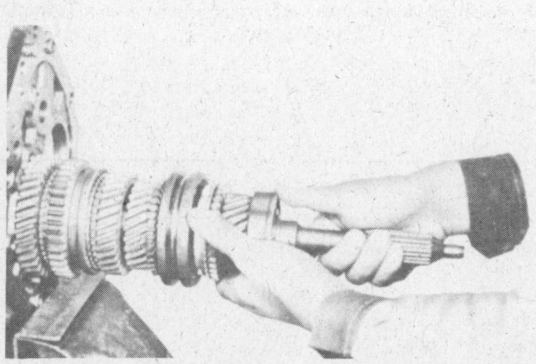

Fig. 6.89. Installing input shaft to mainshaft - 5-speed gearbox

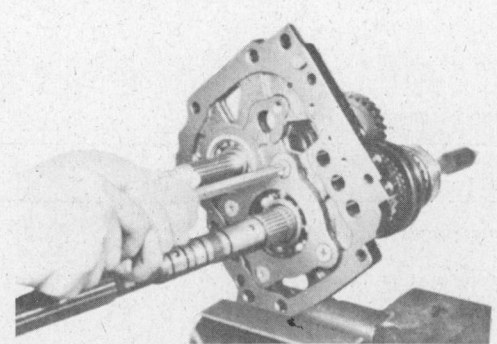

Fig. 6.90. Fitting mainshaft rear bearing retainer - 5-speed gearbox

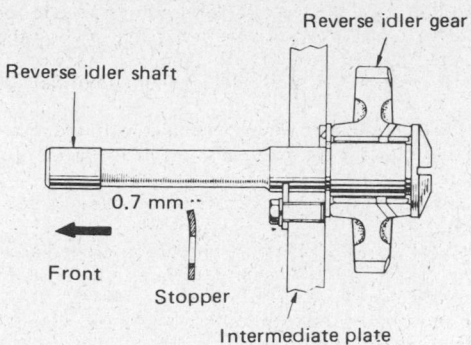

Fig. 6.91. Assembly of reverse idler gear - 5-speed gearbox

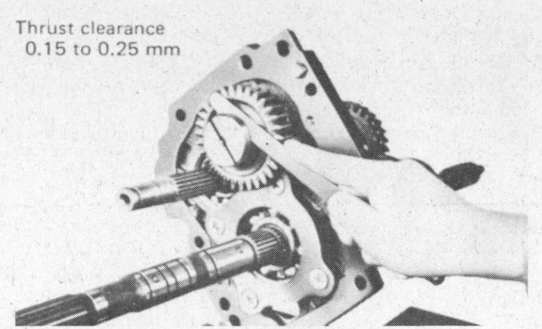

Fig. 6.92. Measuring reverse idle endfloat - 5-speed gearbox

Fig. 6.93. Fitting 5th gear - 5-speed gearbox

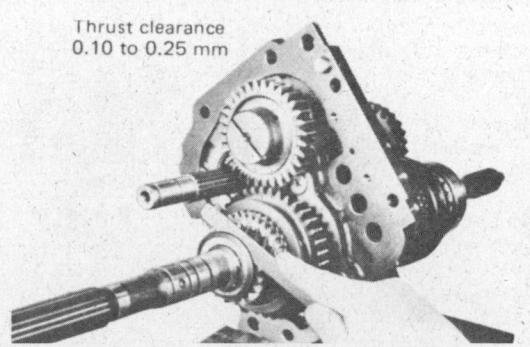

Fig. 6.94. Measuring 5th gear endfloat - 5-speed gearbox

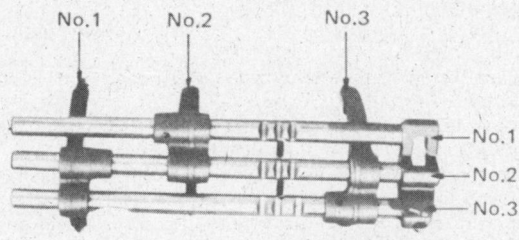

Fig. 6.95. Correct arrangement of selector shafts and shift forks - 5-speed gearbox

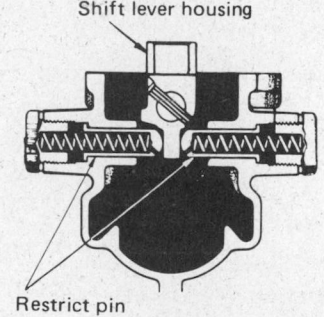

Fig. 6.96. Installation of restrictor pin assemblies in extension housing - 5-speed gearbox

24 Fault diagnosis - gearbox

Symptom	Cause
Ineffective synchromesh on one or more gears	Worn baulk rings. Worn blocker bars.
Jumps out of one or more gears	Weak detent springs. Worn shift forks. Worn engagement dogs. Worn synchro hubs.
Whining, roughness, vibration allied to other faults	Bearing failure and/or overall wear.
Noisy and difficult gear engagement	Clutch not operating correctly.
Sloppy and impositive gear selection	Overall wear throughout the selector mechanism.

Part B: Automatic transmission

25 Automatic transmission - general description and precautions

The Aisin-Warner A40 automatic transmission is a bandless type, and therefore has no internal adjustments. The only external adjustments are to the throttle cable and shift linkage.

Internally, the transmission has a three-element torque converter, two clutches and three multi-disc brakes which actuate the planetary gears, and an oil pump which supplies pressure for actuation of the clutches and brakes.

In the event of breakdown, the vehicle must not be towed in excess of 30 mph (48 km/h), or further than 50 miles (80 km), unless the propeller shaft is disconnected. Failure to observe this requirement may cause damage to the transmission due to lack of lubrication.

Due to the complexities of dismantling and reassembly of automatic transmission units, the operations described in this Chapter are limited to maintenance, adjustment, and removal and refitting.

26 Maintenance

Fluid level checking

1   With the engine running at idle speed and the handbrake (or parking brake) applied, briefly select each gear in turn and finally select PARK.
2   If the transmission fluid is cold, withdraw the dipstick, wipe it, reinsert it and withdraw it again. The fluid level should be within the cold range. If the vehicle has travelled at least 5 miles (8 km) the fluid level should be within the hot range of the dipstick when the same checking procedure is followed. Top-up with fluid of the specified type.

Other maintenance

3   Keep the external surfaces of the transmission unit clean and free from mud and grease to prevent overheating. Check the fluid cooler (where applicable) and make sure that the connecting pipes are secure and in good condition.
4   Periodically, check the condition of the transmission fluid. If it looks black or smells as though it is burnt, it requires renewal, although this may be indicative of an internal fault if the fluid has been changed regularly.
5   At the time interval given in the Routine Maintenance Section, the transmission sump plug should be removed and the contents drained. If necessary, use a new washer when refitting, then top-up the transmission with the appropriate type and quantity of fluid. Check the level as described in Paragraph 1.

27 Selector linkage - adjustment

1   The adjustments described in this and the following Sections are not to be considered as routine, and should only be carried out when wear in the components or incorrect operation of the automatic transmission requires them.
2   The selector lever operates in a six position gate, through a control rod and a cross-shaft to the hydraulic manual valve lever.
3   Loosen the adjustment nut on the linkage, and check that the linkage moves freely.
4   Push the manual valve lever fully forward then back three notches; this is the Neutral position. Now, with the selector held in Neutral by an assistant, tighten the linkage adjustment nut. Check the operation of the lever throughout the full range of travel.

Column shift position indicator

5   Remove the steering column upper bracket and bush as described in Chapter 11.
6   Select neutral, then loosen the nut on the control rod swivel.
7   Move the shift lever to neutral, then insert a feeler gauge of 0.039 in (1 mm) thickness between the shift lever retainer and the stopper pin.
8   Check that the shift position indicator is at neutral; if necessary, adjustment can be made by rotating the stopper pin. After any adjustment, check that the stopper pin length is 0.126 to 0.165 in (3.2 to 4.2 mm) - see Fig. 6.100. If the shift position cannot be set accurately to the 'N' position by rotating the stopper pin, loosen the drive cord retainer at the steering column upper bracket, and move the position indicator (Fig. 6.101).
9   Tighten the control rod swivel nut, then check the shift position indicator throughout the full range of shift lever travel.
10 Refit the steering column upper bracket and bush.

28 Throttle cable - adjustment

1   Remove the air cleaner (refer to Chapter 3 if necessary), then fully depress the throttle pedal and check that the carburettor throttle is fully open.
2   Pull back the rubber boot on the end of the cable, then measure the distance between the end of the accelerator outer cable and the stop collar on the inner cable; this should be 2.05 in (52.0 mm). If necessary, adjust the outer cable by slackening the two locknuts on the support bracket. Where there is no stop collar on the inner cable, close

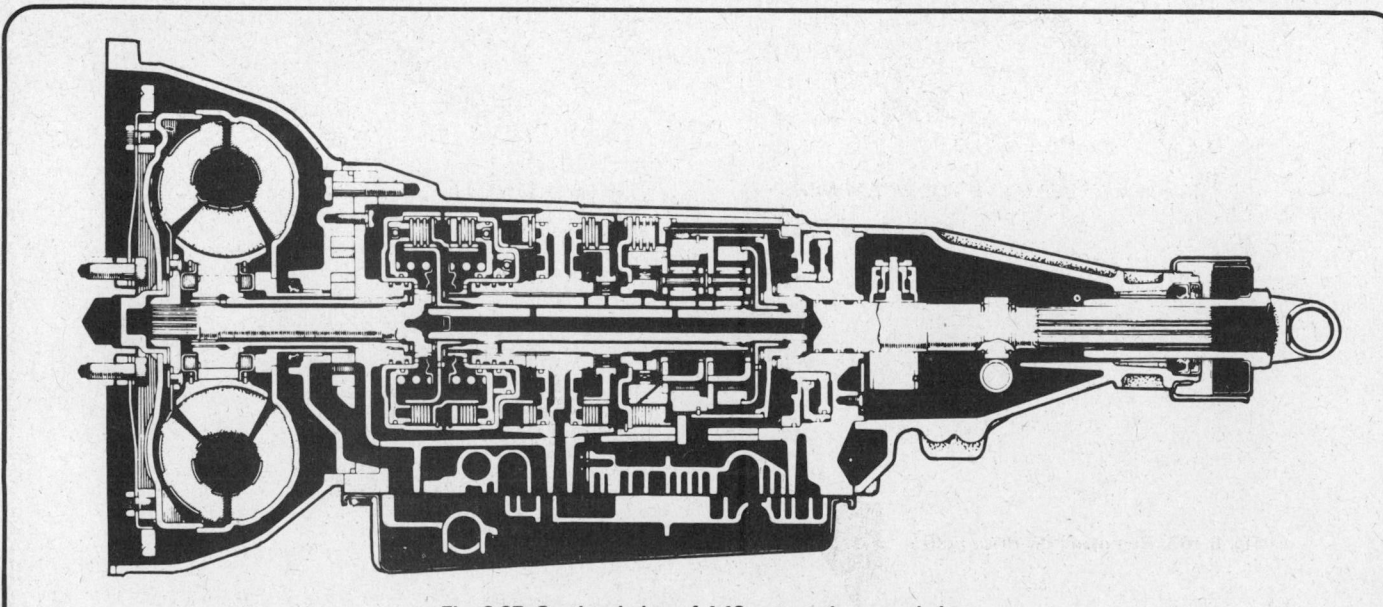

Fig. 6.97. Sectional view of A40 automatic transmission

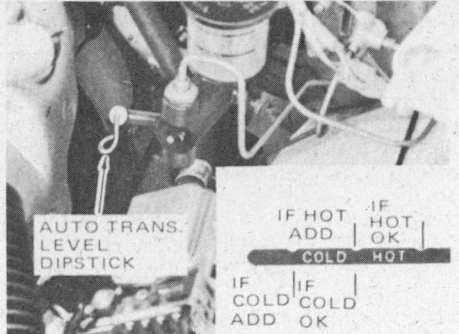

Fig. 6.98. Fluid level dipstick - automatic transmission

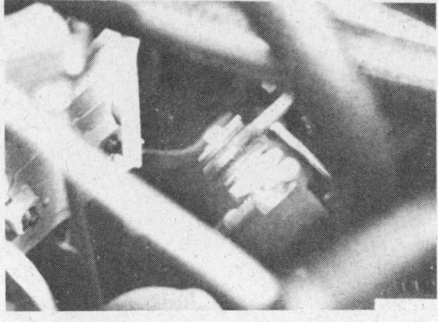

Fig. 6.99. Shift linkage adjustment nut

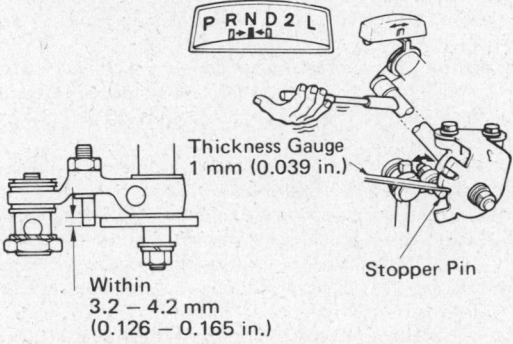

Fig. 6.100. Shift position indicator adjustment

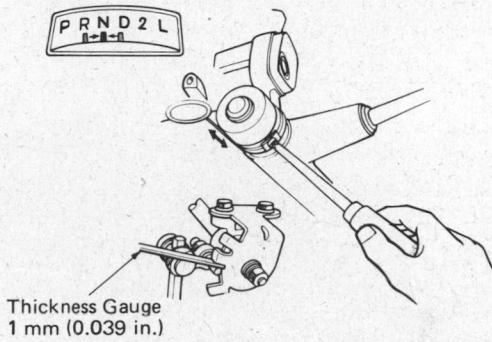

Fig. 6.101. Loosening the drive cord retainer

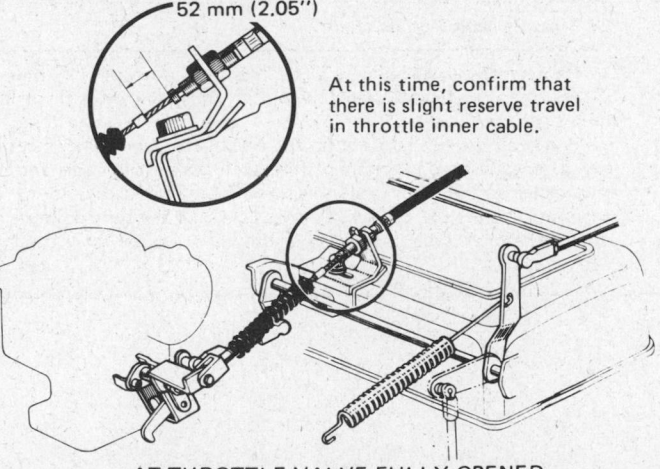

Fig. 6.102. Throttle cable adjustment

Fig. 6.103. Removing the drive pulley

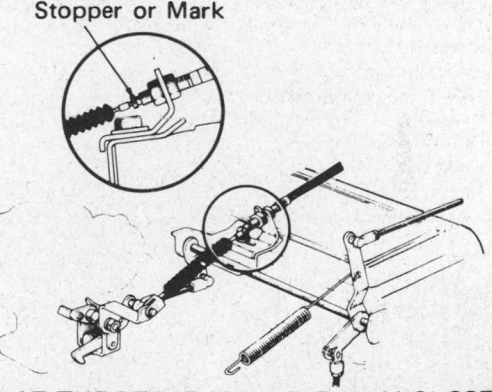

Fig. 6.104. Removing the control position indicator

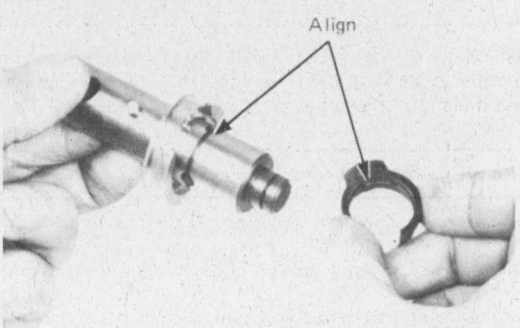

Fig. 6.105. Assembling drive cord pulley and retainer

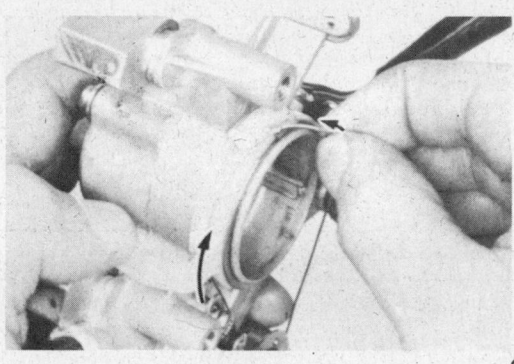

Fig. 6.106. Threading on the drive cord

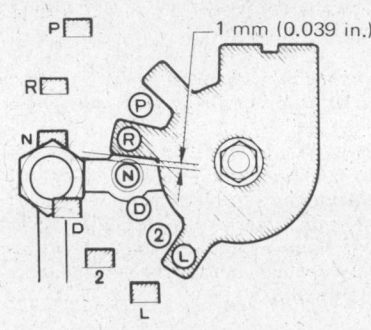

Fig. 6.107. Position indicator adjustment

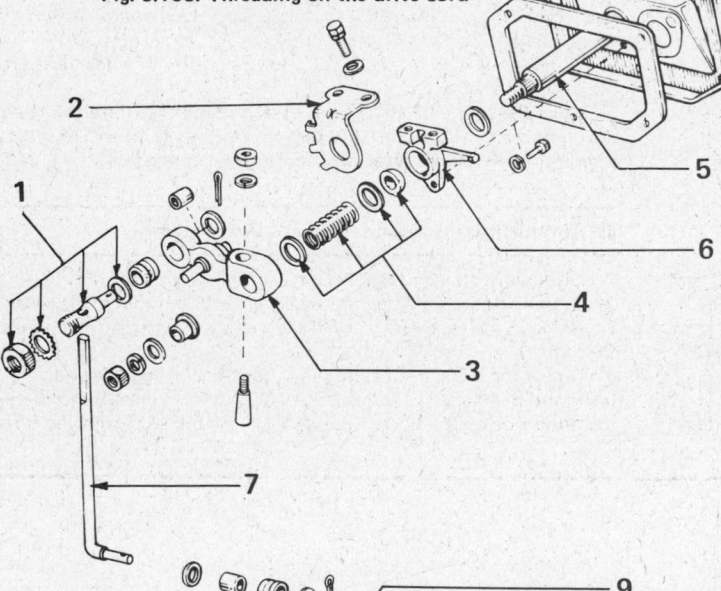

Fig. 6.108. Control shaft and cross shaft parts

1   Control rod swivel
2   Control shaft lever retainer
3   Control shaft lever
4   Washer, spring and bush
5   Control shaft
6   Lower bracket
7   Control rod
8   Support for cross shaft
9   Cross shaft
10 Transmission control shaft lever

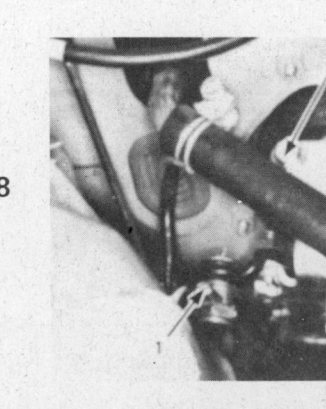

Fig. 6.109. Removing the retainer

1 Control rod   3 Bolts
2 Nut   4 Retainer

the throttle and make a mark on the inner cable relative to the end face of the outer cable. With the throttle valve fully open, adjust the cable so that there is a small amount of reserve travel.

29 Column shift position indicator - removal and refitting

1   Remove the steering column upper bracket and bush as described in Chapter 11.
2   Loosen the drive cord adjuster and retainer, and remove the drive cord.
3   Remove the E-ring and detach the control shaft bracket upper shaft.
4   Remove the position indicator drive pulley and retainer from the bracket upper shaft.
5   Remove the circlip and take off the control position indicator.
6   Check all the parts for wear and damage, and renew as necessary.
7   Reassembly is basically the reverse of the dismantling procedure, but the following should be noted:

> a)   When reassembling the cord drive pulley and retainer to the bracket upper shaft, make sure that the parts are correctly aligned (Fig. 6.105).
> b)   Thread the drive cord onto the position indicator and drive pulley as shown in Fig. 6.106. Fit the drive cord to the pulley groove, and temporarily fit the retainer but do not tighten it until the position indicator is adjusted (paragraph 8). The drive cord should be lightly tensioned only at this point.
> c)   Fit the steering lock cylinder, shift lever and upper bracket as described in Chapter 11.

8   Before refitting the steering column covers and steering wheel, adjust the position indicator as follows:

> a)   Set the shift lever to 'N'. This is set when there is a clearance of 0.039 in (1 mm) between the shift lever retainer and the stopper.
> b)   Lightly secure the indicator housing, then align the indicator to 'N' in the housing.
> c)   Tighten the drive cord retainer, then check that all selected positions are indicated correctly. Now tighten the indicator housing screws.

30 Column shift control shaft and cross shaft - removal and refitting

1   Remove the steering column upper bracket and bush as described in Chapter 11.
2   Remove the split cotter pin and detach the control rod. Now remove the nut and bolts, and take off the control shaft lever retainer.

3   Remove the nut and washer, then drive out the lever lock pin. Remove the control shaft lever.
4   Remove the washer, spring, washer, and bush, and pull out the control shaft.
5   Arrange for an assistant to hold the control shaft lower bracket, then, working from inside the car, remove the bracket retaining bolts.
6   Remove the control rod, cross shaft support and the cross shaft itself.
7   Check all parts for wear and damage, and obtain new parts as necessary.
8   Refitting is basically the reverse of the removal procedure, but the following should be noted:

> a)   Apply a general purpose grease to all pivoting and sliding surfaces at the lower end of the linkage.
> b)   Ensure that the control shaft lower bracket dowel is correctly aligned with the slot in the steering column tube.
> c)   When fitting the control shaft bush, ensure that the protrusion aligns with the slot in the lower bracket.
> d)   When connecting the control rod to the control shaft lever, set the shift lever at 'N' then tighten the control rod swivel nut. Now adjust the selector linkage as described in Section 27.
> e)   Refit the upper bracket and bush.

31 Extension housing oil seal - renewal

1   Renewal of the oil seal may be carried out with the transmission unit in position in the vehicle.
2   Remove the propeller shaft as described in Chapter 7.
3   Knock off the dust deflector towards the rear and prise out the dust seal. Using a suitable extractor, and levering against the end face of the mainshaft, extract the oil seal.
4   Drive in the new oil seal with a tubular drift, fit a new dust seal and refit the dust deflector.
5   Refit the propeller shaft after first greasing the front sliding sleeve both internally and externally. Make sure that the propeller shaft and pinion driving flanges have their mating marks aligned.

32 Automatic transmission - removal and refitting

1   Disconnect the lead from the battery negative terminal.
2   Drain the cooling system and disconnect the radiator top hose.
3   Remove the air cleaner and disconnect the throttle control at the carburettor.
4   Unless the vehicle is over a pit or raised on a hoist, jack-up the front and rear so that there is an adequate working clearance between the underside of the body floor and the ground to permit the torque

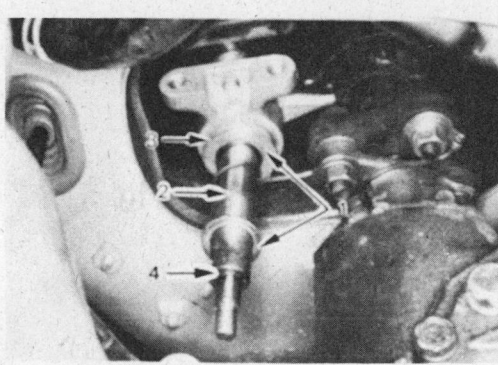

Fig. 6.110. Removing the control shaft

1   Washer   3   Bush
2   Spring   4   Control shaft

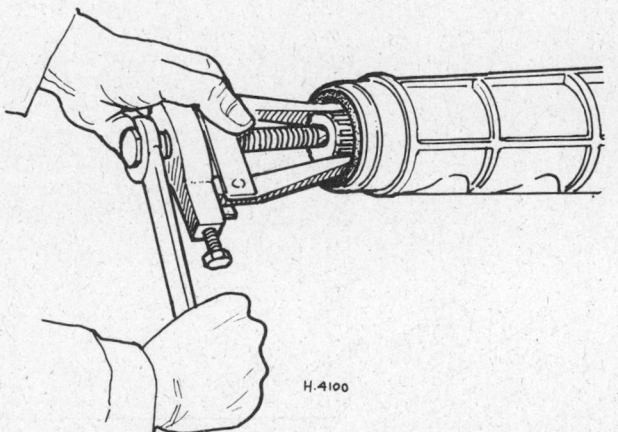

Fig. 6.111. Removing rear extension oil seal

converter housing to be withdrawn.

5 Drain the fluid from the transmission unit.

6 Remove the starter motor.

7 Disconnect the propeller shaft from the rear axle (see Chapter 7) and withdraw it from the transmission rear extension housing.

8 Disconnect the speed selector linkage at the transmission unit.

9 Disconnect the exhaust downpipe from the manifold and remove the support bracket from the transmission unit.

10 Disconnect the fluid cooler pipes from the transmission and plug them. Remove the pipe supports from the transmission.

11 Disconnect the speedometer drive cable.

12 Unbolt the two reinforcement brackets from the torque converter housing. Pull the fluid filler tube from the transmission and retain the 'O' ring seals.

13 Remove the splash shield from below the radiator.

14 Remove the support plate for the handbrake equaliser.

15 Remove the two rubber plugs from the lower half of the front of the torque converter housing.

16 Support the automatic transmission with a jack, then remove the rear crossmember and mounting. Through the open lower half of the torque converter housing, remove the six bolts which secure the drive plate and converter together. These can only be removed in turn by rotating the drive plate. To do this, apply a ring spanner to the crank-shaft pulley securing bolt. Now screw in two guide pins (easily made from two old bolts) into diametrically opposite bolt holes in the front of the drive plate, then rotate the engine until they are horizontal. These pins will act as pivot points during removal of the transmission unit.

17 Place a jack under the engine sump (use a block of wood to protect it), and remove the bolts which secure the torque converter housing to the engine.

18 Lower both jacks progressively until the transmission unit will clear the lower edge of the engine rear bulkhead. Insert two levers between the engine rear plate and the temporary pivot pins, and prise the transmission unit from the engine. Catch the fluid which will run from the torque converter during this operation. **On no account should levers be placed between the drive plate and the torque converter as damage or distortion will result.**

19 The torque converter can now be pulled forward to remove it from the housing. The drive plate can be unbolted from the crankshaft flange if the plate has to be renewed because of worn starter ring gear.

20 Refitting is the reverse of the removal procedure, but tighten all bolts to the specified torque; carry out the adjustments described earlier in this Chapter, after first having refilled the unit with the correct type and quantity of fluid.

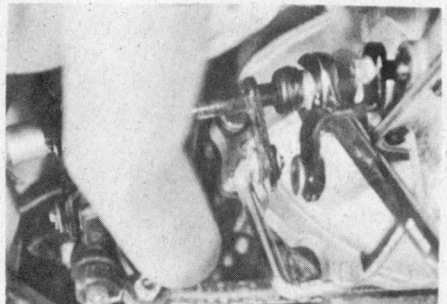

Fig. 6.112. Disconnecting the speed selector linkage

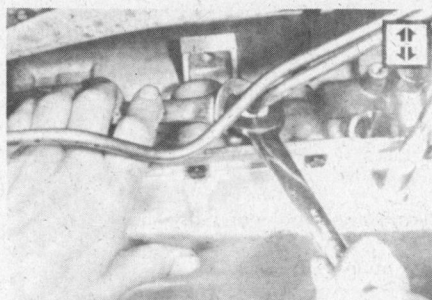

Fig. 6.113. Disconnecting the oil cooler lines

Fig. 6.114. Removing the stiffener brackets

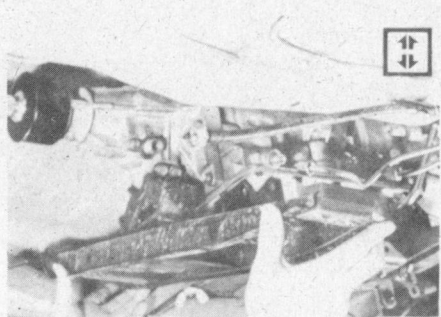

Fig. 6.115. Removing rear crossmember

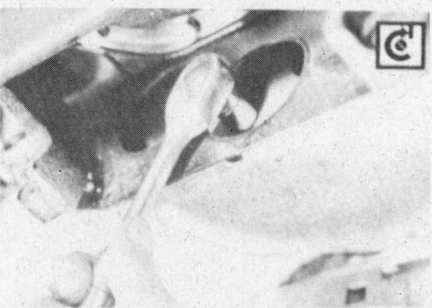

Fig. 6.116. Removing a drive plate securing bolt

Fig. 6.117. Withdrawing the torque converter

33 Fault diagnosis - automatic transmission

Symptom	Cause
Delayed upshifts	Throttle cable adjustment incorrect. Internal transmission fault.
Downshifts from 3rd to 2nd, then back to 3rd	Throttle cable adjustment incorrect. Internal transmission fault.
Slip on upshifts	Shift linkage incorrectly adjusted. Throttle cable incorrect adjusted. Internal transmission fault.
Slow upshifts or failure to upshift	Shift linkage incorrectly adjusted. Internal transmission fault.
Slip, squawk or shudder on take-off	Shift linkage incorrectly adjusted. Internal transmission fault.
Transmission noise (possibly increasing with engine speed)	Broken connector driveplate. (The driveplate can be checked by removing the inspection cones from the converter housing and the engine being slowly turned). Internal transmission fault.
Harsh engagement or shifting	Throttle cable adjustment incorrect. Internal transmission fault.
No waiting after downshift	Throttle cable adjustment incorrect. Internal transmission fault.
No kickdown	Throttle cable adjustment incorrect.
No downshift, or downshift at incorrect speed	Internal transmission fault.
No engine braking in 2nd	Internal transmission fault.
Automatic 2nd to 3rd shift in 2nd range	Internal transmission fault.
Coast downshift occurs at incorrect speed	Throttle cable adjustment incorrect. Internal transmission fault.
Vehicle does not hold in 'P'	Shift linkage incorrectly adjusted. Internal transmission fault.

Chapter 7 Propeller shaft

For modifications and information applicable to later USA models, refer to Supplement at end of manual

Contents

Specifications

Type
... ... Tubular with two or three universal joints according to model. Centre bearing with 3 joint type. Front sliding sleeve

Universal joints
Type ... ... Greased, sealed for life, needle roller bearing
Bearing cup circlip thickness availability ... ... 0.0945 in (2.40 mm)
0.0965 in (2.45 mm)
0.0984 in (2.50 mm)
0.1004 in (2.55 mm)

Torque wrench settings

	lb f ft	kg f m
Propeller shaft drive flange bolts	18	2.5
Centre bearing attachment bolts	28	3.8
Centre flange nut to splined end of shaft		
First tightening	134	18.5
Second tightening	22.5	3.0

1 General description

A two- or three-joint propeller shaft may be fitted according to the particular model.

The universal joints and the sliding sleeve, which fits over the rear end of the gearbox mainshaft, absorb the varying angles and length of the propeller shaft which is caused by the up and down motion of the rear axle due to the deflection of the rear road springs.

The universal joints each comprise a four way trunnion, or 'spider' each leg of which runs in a needle roller bearing race, prepacked with grease and fitted into the bearing journal yokes of the sliding sleeve and propeller shaft and flange. The universal joints are renewable, and the components are supplied in kit form.

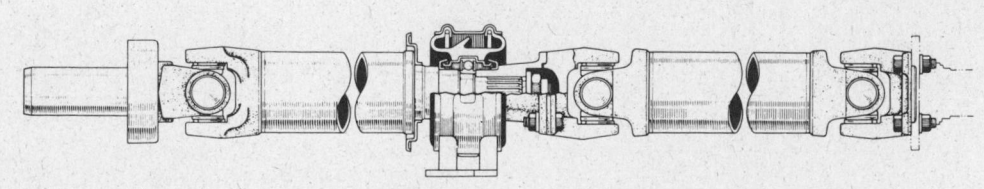

Fig. 7.1. Part-sectioned view of three-joint propeller shaft

2 Maintenance

No lubrication of the universal joints is required as they are pre-packed with grease on assembly. The sliding sleeve of the forward end of the propeller shaft is lubricated from the gearbox. It is recommended that periodic inspection is carried out, however, whenever the car may be undergoing service, to check for any slackness in the universal joints, centre bearing (where applicable), or at the flange bolts.

3 Propeller shaft - removal and refitting

1 Unless the vehicle is over a pit or supported on a hoist, jack up the rear to provide adequate working clearance.
2 Mark the edges of the propeller shaft companion flanges to ensure that they can be refitted in the same positions.

3 On three-joint type propeller shafts, remove the attachment bolts from the centre bearing, retaining the washers and noting their location.
4 Unscrew and remove the four bolts from the rear driving flange. Separate the rear flanges by pulling the propeller shaft forward slightly and then withdraw the propeller shaft from the extension housing of the gearbox or automatic transmission. As the sliding joint is withdrawn from a manual type gearbox, be ready to catch a small quantity of oil.
5 Refitting is the reverse of the removal procedure, but remember to align the companion flange mating marks. On three-joint propeller shafts, align the centre line of the bearing with the centre line of the centre bearing housing. Ensure that the centre line of the bearing housing is at right angles to the centre line of the intermediate shaft.

4 Centre bearing - removal and refitting

1 Mark the edges of the centre bearing companion flanges then remove the bolts and separate the flanges.

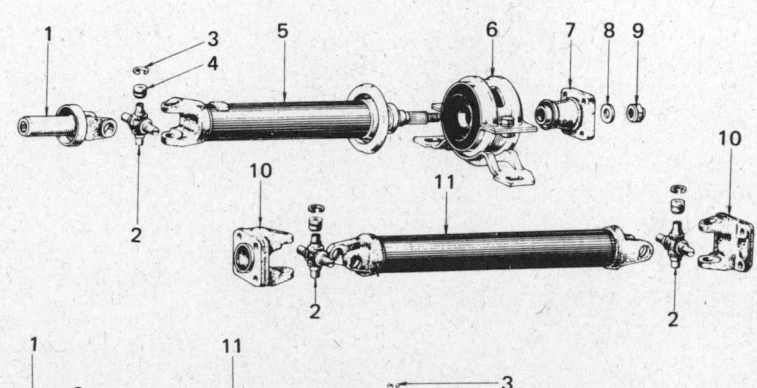

Fig. 7.2. Component parts of propeller shafts

1 Sliding joint yoke
2 Spider
3 Circlip
4 Bearing
5 Intermediate shaft
6 Centre support bearing
7 Universal joint flange
8 Washer
9 Nut
10 Flange yoke
11 Propeller shaft

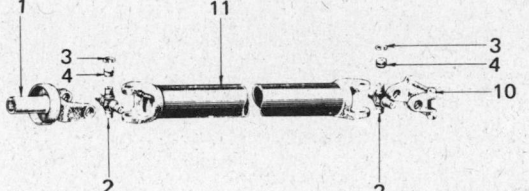

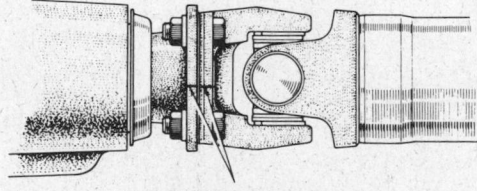

Mating marks

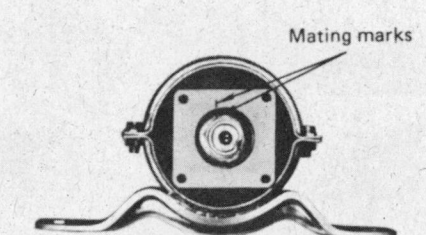

Mating marks

Fig. 7.4. Mating marks on flange and splined end of shaft

Mating marks

Fig. 7.3. Mating marks on the joint flanges

Fig. 7.5. Centre bearing removal

1 Self-locking nut   2 Washer   3 Joint flange

2 Mark the position of the flange to the splined end of the shaft, and remove the nut; withdraw the washer, flange and centre bearing.
3 The centre bearing cannot be dismantled but must be renewed complete if it is worn.
4 Refitting is the reverse of the removal procedure but remember to align the companion flange mating marks, and align the bearing housing as described in the previous Section. A new nut should always be used for the splined end of the shaft. This is initially tightened (see specified first tightening torque)), loosened, then retightened (see specified second tightening torque).

---

5 Universal joints - inspection, dismantling and reassembly

1 Preliminary inspection of the universal joints can be carried out with the propeller shaft on the car.
2 Grasp each side of the universal joint, and with a twisting action, determine whether there is any play or slackness in the joint. Also try an up and down rocking motion for the same purpose. If there is any sign whatsoever of play, the joints need renewing.
3 Remove the propeller shaft as described in Section 3.
4 Dot punch adjacent edges of the yokes so that they will be refitted in their original positions. Remove the circlips.
5 The bearing cups may be removed by one of two methods. Either hit the yoke (supported in the hand) adjacent to the bearing cup hole

with a wooden or plastic mallet until the cup begins to emerge, or press the cup out in a vice using an old bearing cup on one side and tubular spacer on the other to receive the ejected cup. With both methods, screw the cups out of their seats once they have emerged far enough to be able to grip them with a self-locking wrench.
6 Inspect the holes in the yokes for elongation. Evidence of this is only likely in the event of previous neglect or abuse in which case the yokes must be renewed.
7 Obtain the appropriate repair kit for each joint. This will comprise spider, bearing cups, needle bearings and seals.
8 Locate the spider within the yoke, and check that the O-ring seals are in position, and that the dot punch marks mate.
9 Fill the bearing cup 1/3rd full with grease and check that the needle bearings are correctly held in position (with grease) around the inside of the cup.
10 Using a vice and an old bearing cup, press the new bearing cup into the yoke at the same time holding the spider in alignment so that the cup will slide onto the trunnion.
11 Repeat the operations for the remaining three bearings of each universal joint.
12 Insert new circlips **which must be of the same thickness for each opposite pair of bearing cups,** and must be selected from the sizes listed in the Specifications to ensure an axial endfloat of not more than 0.002 in (0.05 mm).

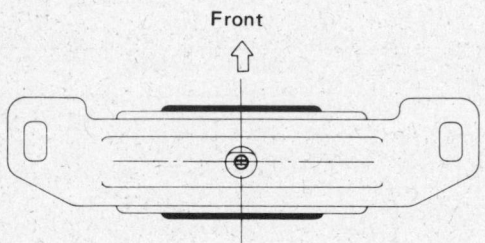

Fig. 7.6. Correct attitude for centre bearing

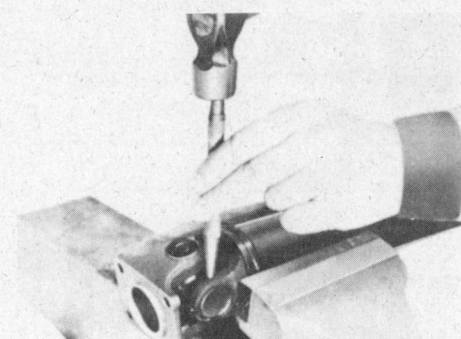

Fig. 7.7. Dot punching the yokes

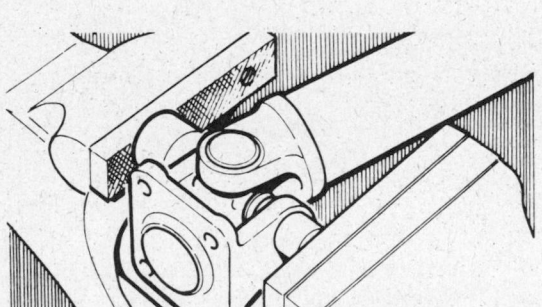

Fig. 7.8. Pressing in a universal joint cup

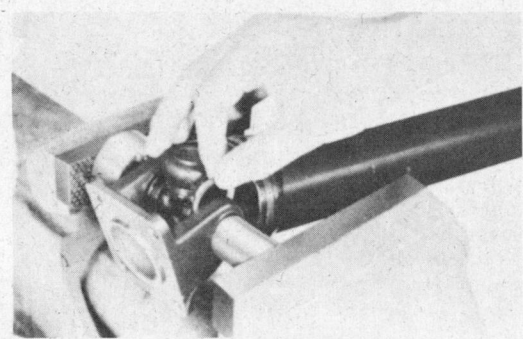

Fig. 7.9. Selecting a circlip

6 Fault diagnosis - propeller shaft and universal joints

Symptom	Cause
Vibration	Worn universal joints. Worn or loose centre bearing. Propeller shaft bent. Extension housing bush worn. Loose drive flange bolts. Propeller shaft out of balance.
Knocking during starting, deceleration, gear-changing, or at the moment of deceleration	Worn universal joints. Worn splines on shafts. Loose drive flange bolts.

Chapter 8 Rear axle

For modifications and information applicable to later USA models, refer to Supplement at end of manual

Contents

Specifications

Axle type ... ... Hypoid, semi-floating

Final drive ratio
Saloon and coupe ... ... 3.909 : 1 or 4.100 : 1
Estate car ... ... 3.900 : 1 or 4.111 : 1

Pinion preload
Saloon and coupe ... ... 5.2 to 9.5 lb f in (6 to 11 kg f cm)
Estate car ... ... 6.9 to 9.5 lb f in (8 to 11 kg f cm)

Lubricant type
Above −23ºC (−10ºF) ... ... SAE 90EP gear oil (API-GL-5)
Below −23ºC (−10ºF) ... ... SAE 80EP gear oil (API-GL-5)

Lubricant capacity ... ... 2.2 Imp pt/2.6 US pt (1.2 litre)

Torque wrench settings	lb f ft	kg f m
Brake backplate bolts	48	6.7
Axle casing breather	20	2.8
Differential carrier bolts	58	8
Compression flange nut (minimum)	80	11

1 General description

The rear axle is of the hypoid semi-floating type with four pinion gears. The final drive ratio differs between the various models and reference should be made to the Specifications for further information.

The crownwheel and pinion, and differential, are mounted as an assembly in the differential carrier and this is bolted to the front of the banjo type axle casing. The advantage of this type of differential carrier is that the differential carrier may be removed complete with crownwheel and pinion, after disconnection of the propeller shaft and partial withdrawal of the halfshafts (axle-shafts).

Operations on the rear axle should be limited to those described in this Chapter. Dismantling and reassembly of the differential is not considered to be within the scope of the home mechanic due to the need for special tools and gauges. When a fault develops through wear or damage, exchange the differential carrier complete for a factory reconditioned unit.

2 Halfshafts, bearings and oil seals - removal and refitting

1   The halfshafts may be withdrawn without disturbing the differential gear. They are removed in order to renew the bearings or oil seals, or if the differential is to be removed. **Read the whole of this Section before starting work.**

2   Jack up the car at the rear and support it firmly on proper stands. Remove the rear wheels, release the handbrake (parking brake), and remove the brake drums. (Details in Chapter 9).

3   Remove the nuts and bolts securing the bearing retainer plate and brake backplate to the axle casing flange. The halfshaft hub, bearing and backplate are now held in position as an assembly by the fit of the outer race of the bearing into the axle casing. Ideally the use of a proper slide hammer removal tool is needed to draw the assembly out. This consists of a flange which bolts to the wheel studs and to which is fitted a long shaft extension with a sliding weight on it. The sliding weight is hit against a flange at the extremity of the shaft and this

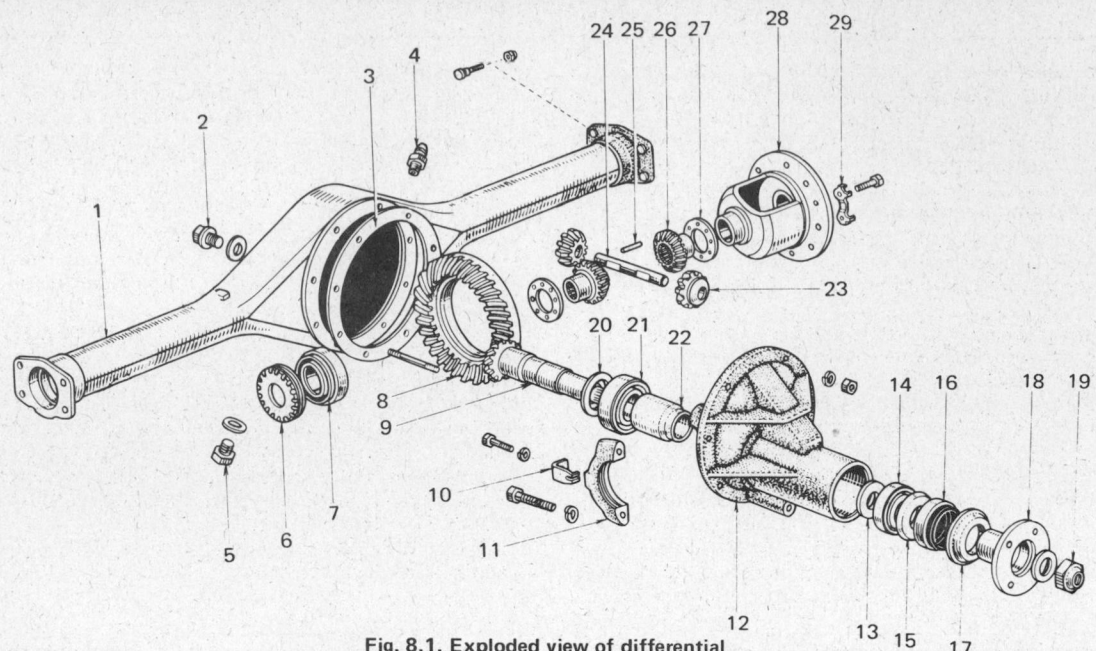

Fig. 8.1. Exploded view of differential

1	Rear axle housing	9	Drive pinion	16	Oil seal	23	Differential pinion
2	Filler plug	10	Adjusting nut lock plate	17	Dust deflector	24	Pinion shaft
3	Gasket	11	Differential carrier cap	18	Companion flange	25	Pin
4	Breather	12	Differential carrier	19	Nut	26	Side gear
5	Drain plug	13	Shim	20	Flat washer	27	Thrust washer
6	Bearing adjusting nut	14	Bearing	21	Bearing	28	Differential case
7	Side bearing	15	Oil slinger	22	Spacer	29	Lock plate
8	Ring gear						

Fig. 8.2. Rear axle shaft and bearing

1	Rear axle shaft	4	Bearing	7	Gasket	10	Brake drum
2	Oil seal	5	Spacer	8	Bearing outer retainer	11	Wheel
3	Bearing inner retainer	6	Gasket	9	Hub bolt		

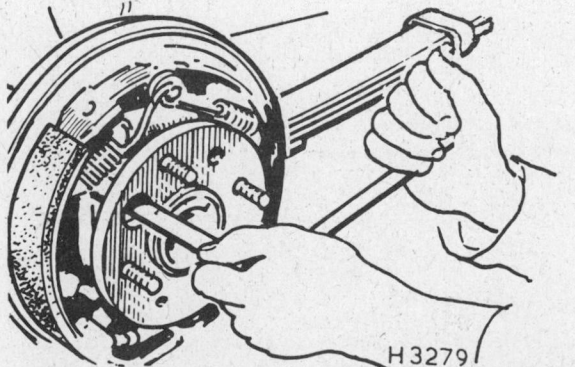

Fig. 8.3. Removing a bearing retainer plate/backing plate nut

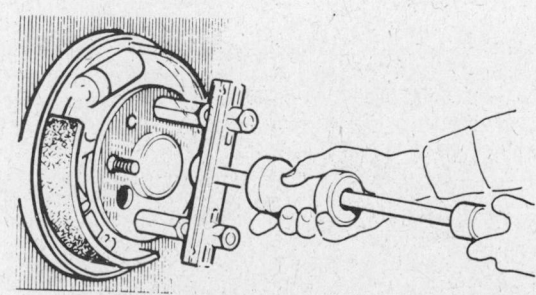

Fig. 8.4. Using a slide hammer to withdraw an axle shaft

draws the axle out. Whatever you do, this principle - of attaching a suitable bracket and striking point to the wheel studs - must be followed. No part of the axle assembly itself must be struck. A sustained pull is also quite ineffective and will probably only result in heaving the car off the stands. So get something suitable organised in advance or you will be wasting your time. One possibility is to use an old wheel rim bolted to the studs and then strike it from the inside with something suitably heavy. The success or otherwise of this method depends on access and the ability to get a good swing at it. Whatever method is used the car should be firmly supported (Figs. 8.3 and 8.4).

4   If both axle shafts are being removed and dismantled for axle bearing renewal, mark all the components 'left' or 'right' as they are not interchangeable from side to side.

5   Grind a groove across the bearing inner retaining collar, then cut it from the axle shaft using a sharp chisel. Do not damage the shaft in any way.

6   Press the bearing from the shaft using a suitable press.

7   It is false economy not to renew the oil seals once the halfshafts have been withdrawn. Remove the seals with a suitable two legged extractor and drive in the new ones with a tubular drift.

8   Having examined the halfshaft for cracks, spline wear and distortion, fit the oil retaining plate and spacer, then press on the bearing. Pressure

must be exerted on the hub end of the halfshaft while the centre track of the bearing is supported on a suitable distance piece.

9   Take a new bearing retaining collar and heat it in an oil bath to 320ºF (160ºC). It will then have to be quickly dropped onto the axle shaft and using a method similar to that used for fitting the bearing, press it onto the shaft until it contacts the inner track of the bearing.

10 The brake backing plate has not been removed during this operation, but should there be signs of oil seepage from the gasket located between the backplate and the axle casing end flange, the old gasket must be removed and a new one fitted.

11 Smear gasket cement to both sides of a new bearing retainer plate gasket and locate it on the outside face of the brake backplate.

12 When refitting the halfshaft, the splines at the inner end should first pick up the splines in the differential side gears. Then enter the bearing into the axle casing recess until the outer edge of the race is nearly flush with the casing; bolt up the backplate evenly, which will draw the bearing completely into position. It is recommended that new self-locking nuts are used to secure the backplate, and are tightened to the specified torque.

13 Refit the brake drum and the roadwheel, and lower the jacks. When assembly is completed, check the oil level in the rear axle.

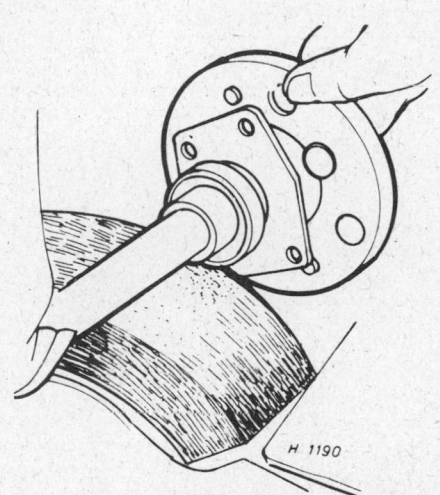

Fig. 8.5. Grinding off an axle bearing collar

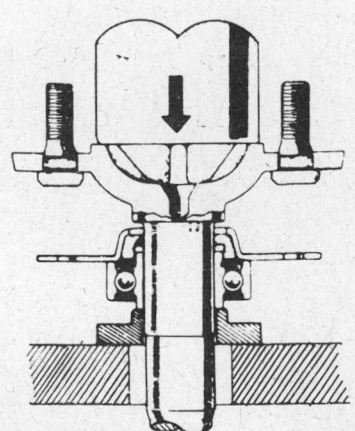

Fig. 8.7. Pressing a bearing onto an axle shaft

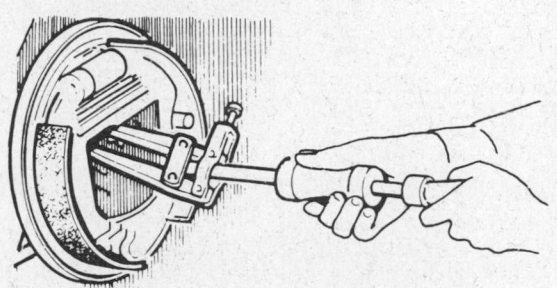

Fig. 8.6. Removing an oil seal from the axle casing

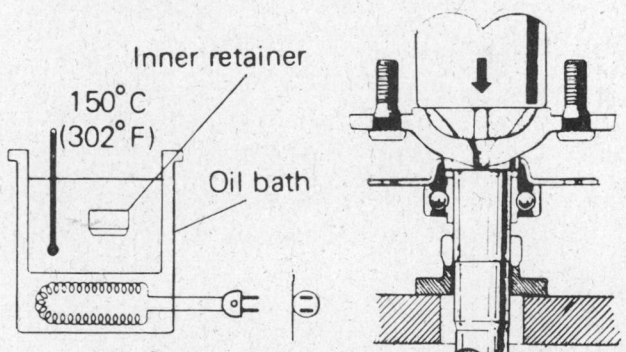

Fig. 8.8. Fitting an axle bearing retaining collar

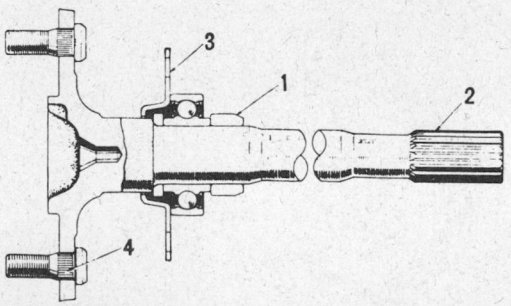

Fig. 8.9. Sectional view of rear axle hub components

1 Bearing retaining collar	3 Bearing retainer plate
2 Half shaft	4 Roadwheel stud

3   Roadwheel studs - renewal

1   Renewal of a sheared stud or one with a damaged thread is simply carried out by first removing the halfshaft as described in the preceding Section.
2   Adequately support the rear face of the hub plate and press or drive the old stud from its splined hole.
3   Press the new stud into position, using a vice and a piece of tubing as a distance piece.

4   Pinion oil seal - renewal

1   The pinion oil seal may be renewed with the differential carrier still in position on the rear axle casing and the casing still attached to the rear suspension.
2   Jack up the rear of the vehicle and mark the edges of the propeller shaft rear flange and the pinion driving flange. Then disconnect the flanges and tie the propeller shaft up out of the way.
3   Ensure that the handbrake (or parking brake) is firmly applied, then drain the axle oil into a suitable container.
4   Mark the pinion coupling in relation to the pinion splines, and knock back the staking on the pinion nut with a drift or narrow chisel.
5   Hold the pinion coupling quite still by bolting a length of flat steel to two of the coupling flange holes and then unscrew the pinion nut. A ring spanner of good length will be required for this.
6   Remove the lever from the coupling flange and withdraw the coupling. If it is tight, use a two or three legged puller but on no account attempt to knock it from the splined pinion. Withdraw the dust deflector.
7   Remove the defective oil seal using a two legged extractor.
8   Refit the new oil seal first having greased the mating surfaces of the seal and the axle housing. The lips of the oil seal must face inwards. Using a piece of brass or copper tubing of suitable diameter, carefully drive the new oil seal into the axle housing recess until the face of the seal is flush with the housing. Make sure that the end of the pinion is not knocked during this operation.
9   Refit the coupling to its original position on the pinion splines after first having located the dust cover.
10   Fit a new pinion nut and, holding the coupling still with the lever, tighten the nut to the minimum specified torque.
11   Rotate the pinion to settle the bearings, then check the preload using a torque wrench on the coupling nut. By slight adjustment of the nut, and rotation of the pinion, obtain a preload figure to match that given in the Specifications. Do not overtighten the nut as it cannot be backed off without having to renew the internal compressible spacer.
12   Stake the nut and refit the propeller shaft, making sure to align the mating marks.

13   Top up the oil level in the axle and lower the car to the ground.

5   Differential carrier - removal and refitting

1   Jack-up the car and support it on stands as for halfshaft removal. Drain the oil from the back axle by removing the drain plug. The half-shafts should then be removed sufficiently far for the inner ends to disengage from the differential side pinions. The propeller shaft should then be detached from the rear axle pinion flange. It is not necessary to draw it out from the gearbox provided it can be conveniently rested out of the way on one side.
2   Undo the ten nuts and washers holding the differential carrier to the casing. The whole unit can be drawn forward off the studs and taken out.
3   When refitting the assembly, ensure that the mating faces are perfectly clean and free from burrs. A new gasket coated with sealing compound should also be used. Otherwise refitting is the reverse of the removal procedure. Tighten the nuts to the specified torque.
4   Refill the unit with the correct grade and quantity of oil.

6   Rear axle - removal and refitting

1   Jack-up the rear of the vehicle, place axle stands under the rear body frame side members and securely chock the front wheels. Place the jack under the differential and take its weight.
2   Remove the roadwheels and disconnect the propeller shaft at the rear axle pinion coupling flange. Remember to mark the edges of the flange before disconnecting them so that they will be refitted in their original positions. Move the rear end of the propeller shaft to one side and support it to avoid strain on the centre universal joint or bearing.
3   Remove the brake drums; disconnect the brake cables from the actuating levers, then detach them from the brake backplate. Refit the drums to protect the brake shoe assemblies.
4   Disconnect the brake hydraulic line at the union on top of the axle casing. Plug both ends of the line to prevent loss of fluid or ingress of dirt.
5   Disconnect the rear shock absorber lower mountings from the road spring support plates.
6   Unscrew and remove the four road spring 'U' bolts.
7   Remove each of the lower rear spring shackle bolts and lower the rear ends of the road springs to the ground.
8   Lower the jack previously placed under the differential until the rear axle assembly can be drawn out sideways from under the vehicle.
9   Refitting is the reverse of the removal procedure but refer to Chapter 11 for details of loading/tightening conditions for the suspension components, and to Chapter 9, for a description of bleeding the hydraulic system.

Fig. 8.10. Pressing in a wheel stud

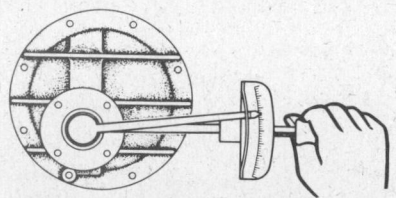

Fig. 8.11. Using a torque wrench to measure pinion bearing preload

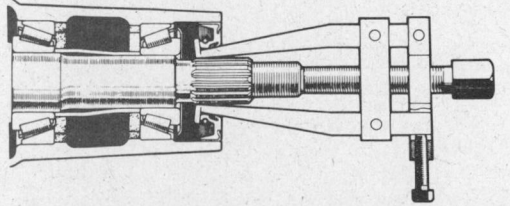

Fig. 8.12. Removing the pinion oil seal

7   Fault diagnosis - rear axle

Symptom	Cause
Noisy differential	
a) During normal running	Lack of oil, damaged or worn gears, incorrect adjustment.
b) During deceleration	Incorrect adjustment or damage to drive pinion bearings.
c) During turning of vehicle	Worn or damaged axle-shaft bearing, worn differential gears.
Noisy rear hub	Worn axle-shaft bearings, buckled roadwheel, defective tyre, bent axle-shaft.
Oil leakage at hub and pinion oil seals	May be caused by blocked breather plug on axle casing or overfilled unit.

Chapter 9 Braking system

For modifications and information applicable to later USA models, refer to Supplement at end of manual

Contents

Specifications

System type ... ...   Four wheel drum or front disc/rear drum, according to model. Vacuum servo assistance on most models; single on dual hydraulic circuits with pressure valve. Hand or foot operated parking brake

Front brakes ... ...   Regulating

Drums
Inner diameter ... ...   9.0 in (228.6 mm)
Maximum wear or regrinding diameter ... ...   9.079 in (230.6 mm)
Friction lining thickness (minimum) ... ...   0.04 in (1 mm)

Disc brake (F-type - single cylinder caliper)
Disc thickness (minimum) ... ...   0.453 in (11.5 mm)
Disc runout (maximum) ... ...   0.0059 in (0.15 mm)
Pad thickness (minimum) ... ...   0.04 in (1 mm)

Disc brake (Girling type - twin cylinder caliper)
Disc thickness (minimum) ... ...   0.453 in (11.5 mm)
Disc runout (maximum) ... ...   0.0059 in (0.15 mm)
Pad thickness (minimum) ... ...   0.04 in (1 mm)

Rear drum brakes
Inner diameter ... ...   9.0 in (228.6 mm)
Maximum wear or regrinding diameter ... ...   9.079 in (230.6 mm)
Friction lining thickness (minimum) ... ...   0.04 in (1 mm)

Adjustments
Servo pushrod/master cylinder piston clearance ... ...   0.004 to 0.02 in (0.1 to 0.5 mm)

Parking brake lever travel
Centre floor type ... ...   3 to 6 notches
Under dash type ... ...   8 to 15 notches

Foot operated parking brake

Lock release rod free play	0.2 to 0.4 in (5 to 10 mm)
Pedal travel	2 to 4 clicks

Foot brake (service brake)

Pedal height	
rhd	6.22 to 6.61 in (158 to 168 mm)
lhd	6.34 to 6.73 in (161 to 171 mm)
Pedal free play	
With servo	0.12 to 0.24 in (3 to 6 mm)
Without servo	0.08 to 0.21 in (2 to 7 mm)
Pedal reserve distance (minimum)	
Cars with handbrake	2.36 in (60 mm)
Cars with foot operated parking brake	3.35 in (85 mm)

Brake fluid type ... ...   DOT 3 or SAE J1703C

Torque wrench settings

	lb f ft	kg fm
Caliper body to stub axle carrier		
Girling type	77	10.7
F-type	57	8
Master cylinder body check valves	48	6.5
Disc brake dust cover to stub axle carrier	57	8

1 General description

The braking system is of the four wheel hydraulic type with servo assistance on most models. The front brakes may be of drum or disc type, according to model, operating territory or date of manufacture. The rear brakes are of drum type on all models. The types of brakes fitted vary and are of differing makes. The handbrake operates on the rear wheels only, through mechanical linkage and the lever itself may be of floor mounted or pull out facia mounted design.

On some later models a foot operated parking brake is used; this has a pull-type brake release lever.

The hydraulic circuit may be of a single or dual design dependent upon the regulations in force where the vehicle is intended to operate.

2 Drum brakes - adjustment

1 The rear drum brakes on all models are self-adjusting. The action of applying the handbrake actuates the adjustment mechanism.

2 Front brakes of the two leading shoe type are not self-adjusting and the following operations must be carried out at regular intervals:
3 Jack-up the front of the vehicle and remove the two plugs from the adjusting holes.
4 Insert a small screwdriver until it engages with the teeth of the adjuster wheel. Turn the adjuster wheel until the brake shoe locks the drum. Now turn the adjuster wheel in the reverse direction until the roadwheel can be rotated without any binding or dragging of the shoe lining.
5 Repeat the adjustment procedure on the second shoe and then on the opposing brake drum.
6 The front drum brakes of the duo servo type are self-adjusting.

3 Disc pad (F-type) - inspection and renewal

1 Jack up the front of the vehicle and remove the roadwheels.
2 Extract the spring clips and withdraw the cylinder guides.
3 Pull the cylinder assembly from the caliper unit and tie it up with a piece of wire so that the flexible hydraulic hose will not be strained.

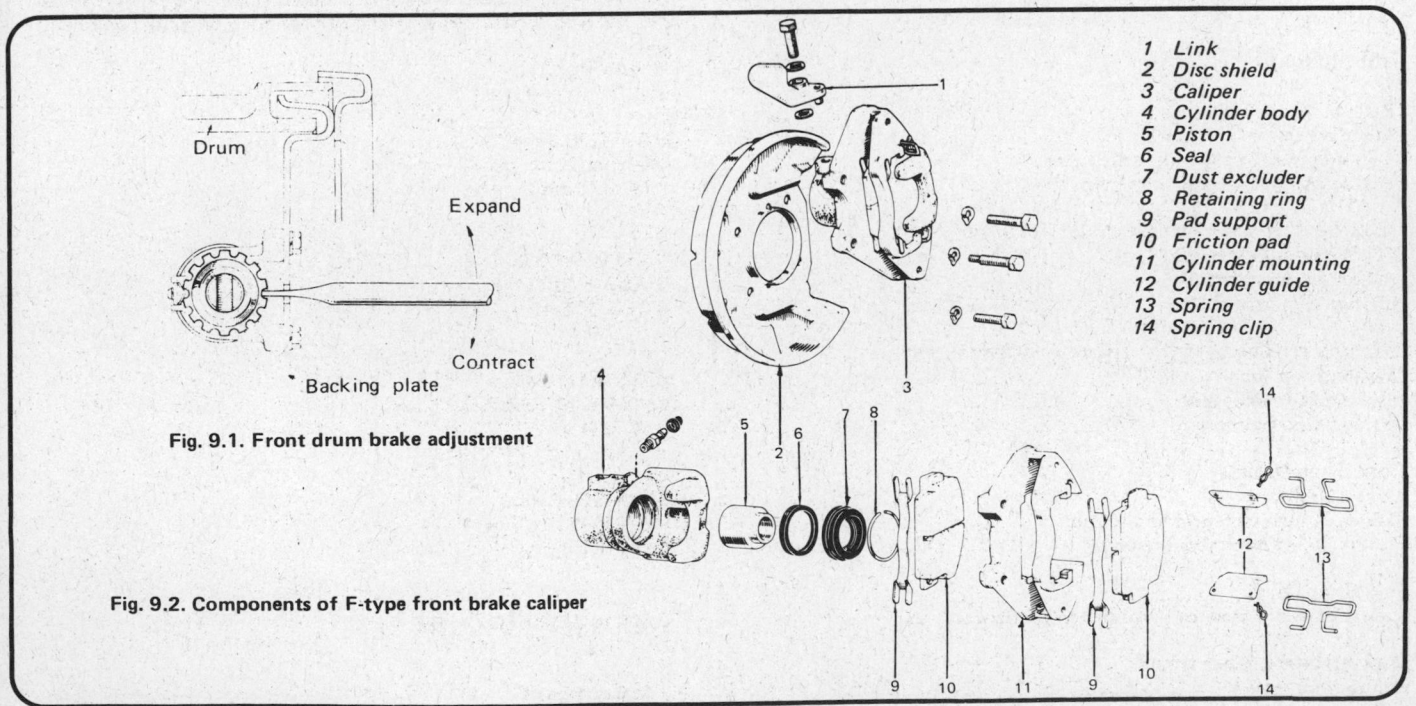

Fig. 9.1. Front drum brake adjustment

Fig. 9.2. Components of F-type front brake caliper

1 Link
2 Disc shield
3 Caliper
4 Cylinder body
5 Piston
6 Seal
7 Dust excluder
8 Retaining ring
9 Pad support
10 Friction pad
11 Cylinder mounting
12 Cylinder guide
13 Spring
14 Spring clip

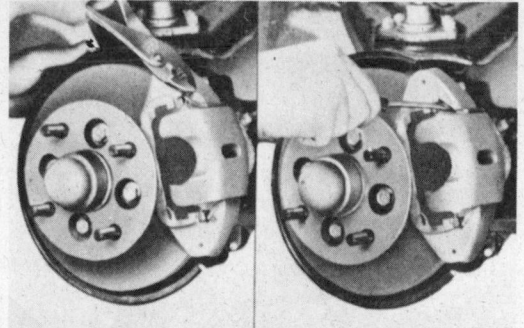

Fig. 9.3. Removing spring clips and cylinder guides (F-type)

Fig. 9.4. Removing a brake pad (F-type)

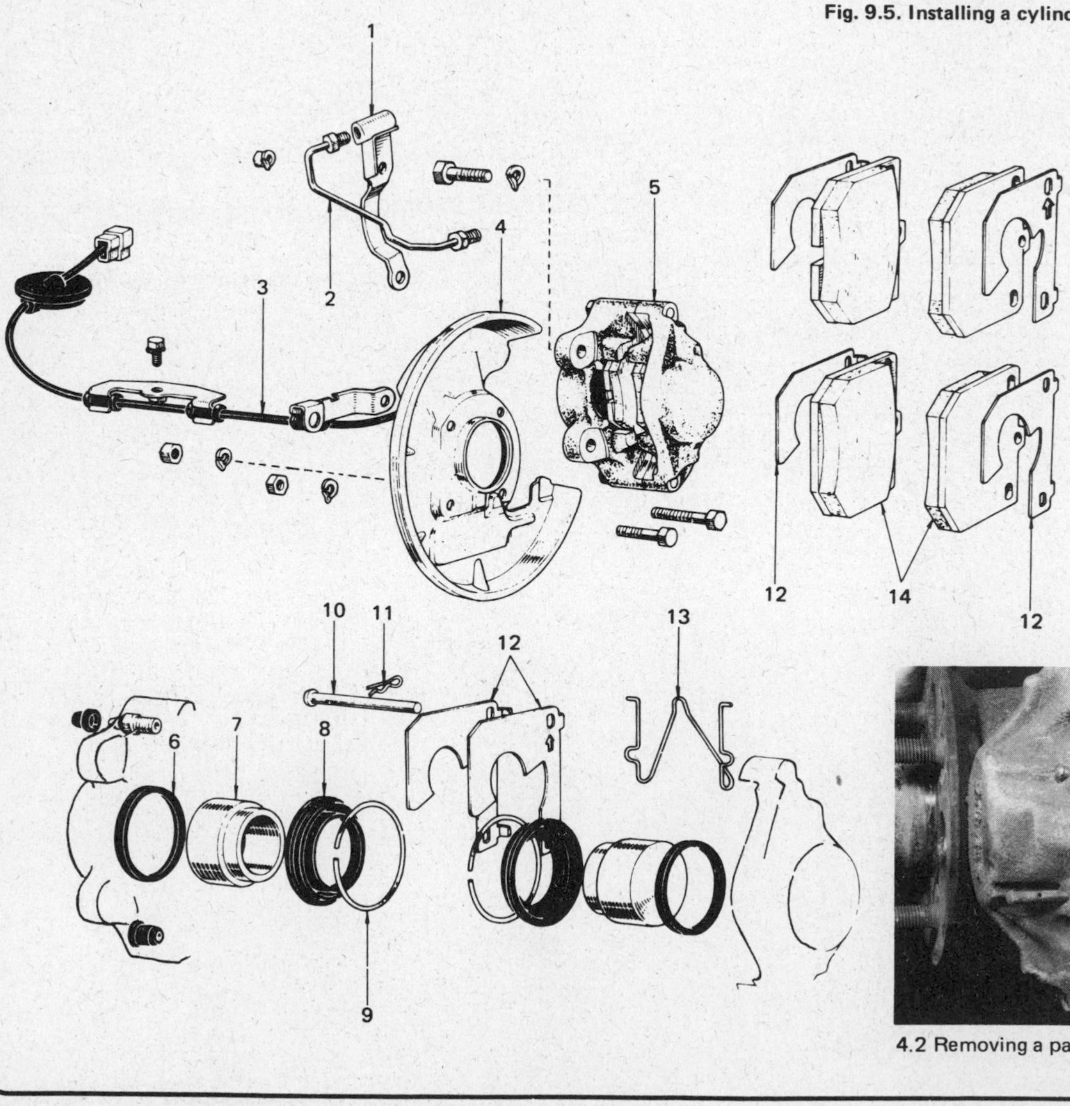

Fig. 9.6. Components of Girling type front brake caliper

1	Connector	8	Dust excluder
2	Bridge pipe	9	Retaining ring
3	Lead for pad wear indicator	10	Pad retaining pin
4	Disc shield	11	Spring clip
5	Caliper	12	Anti-squeal shim
6	Seal	13	Anti-rattle spring
7	Piston	14	Pads

Fig. 9.5. Installing a cylinder guide (F-type)

4.2 Removing a pad retaining pin

4   Inspect the thickness of the friction material of the pads. If they are worn to the minimum specified thickness, they must be renewed as a complete front axle set of four.

5   Pull out the pad on one side of the caliper only, then, using a flat bar or piece of wood, depress the piston into the cylinder, keeping it quite square. This operation is to provide enough room to insert the new, thicker pad and will cause the fluid level to rise in the reservoir unless the caliper bleed plug is opened during the time that the piston is being depressed. Insert the new pad.

6   Remove the other pad and insert the new one as described in paragraph 5.

7   Fit the cylinder assembly, the cylinder guides and the spring clips.

8   Depress the foot brake two or three times in order to bring the pads into contact with the disc.

9   Repeat the foregoing operations on the opposite front brake.

10 Refit the roadwheels, lower the jack, then check the level of the fluid in the hydraulic reservoir.

4   Disc pad (Girling type) - inspection and renewal

1   Jack up the front end of the vehicle and remove the roadwheels. Inspect the pad friction material thickness; if it is less than the minimum specified the pads must be renewed as an axle set of four.

2   Remove the spring clips and withdraw the pad retaining pins (photo).

3   Extract the anti-squeal shims, then withdraw the disc pads, gripping their projections with a pair of pliers (photo). If an ESP disc pad wear indicator is fitted, disconnect the leads which run to the sensor from the pads as they are withdrawn.

4   Wipe out any dust from the interior of the caliper unit and using a flat bar depress each of the pistons into its cylinder squarely. This action will cause the level of the fluid in the hydraulic reservoir to rise unless the bleed nipple on the caliper unit is released.

5   Insert the new pads with their anti-squeal shims correctly located at the rear of the pad backing plates and with the arrows pointing upwards.

6   Fit the anti-rattle springs, retaining pins and spring clips.

7   Apply the footbrake two or three times to bring the pads against the disc, then repeat all the foregoing operations on the opposite front brake.

5   Front drum brake shoes - inspection and renewal

1   Jack up the front of the vehicle and remove the roadwheels.

2   From one hub tap off the grease cap and withdraw the split pin from the castellated nut. **Note:** It is preferable to commence with the left-hand side brake, as this assembly is shown in the illustrations.

3   Unscrew the nut, extract the thrust washer and then withdraw the combined hub drum assembly from the stub axle. Take care that the outer hub bearing does not drop out or it may be damaged. Prevent

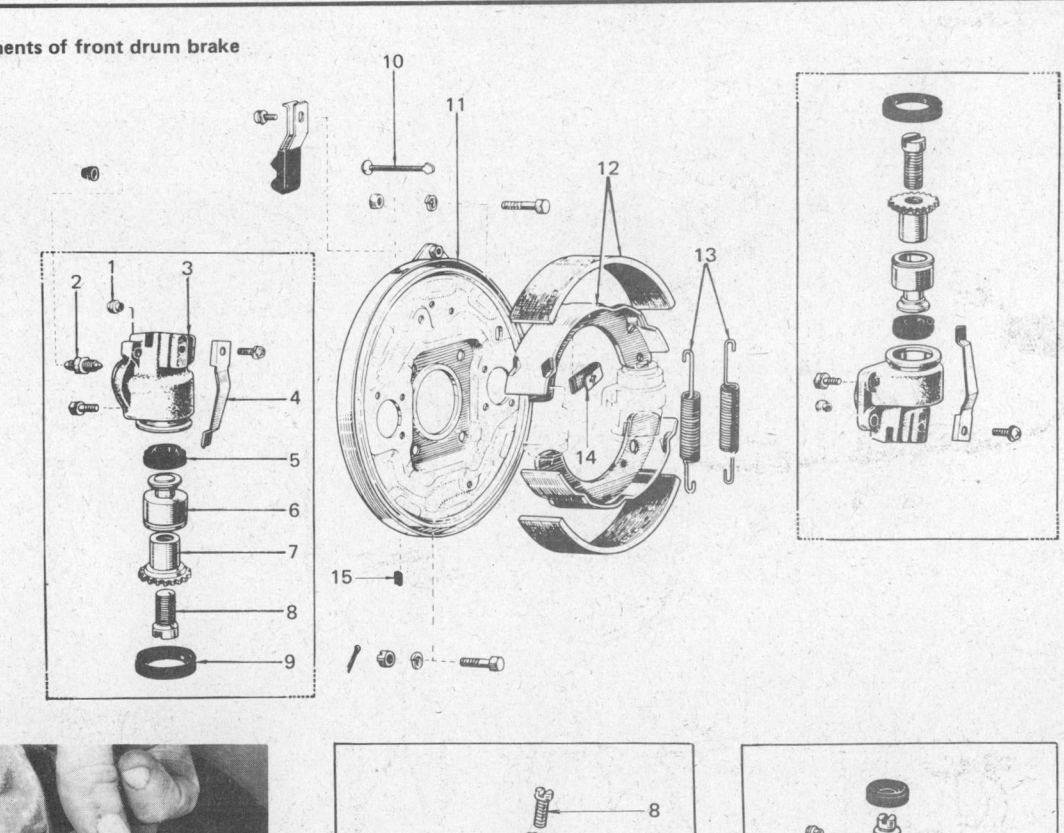

Fig. 9.7. Components of front drum brake

 1   Union seat
 2   Bleed valve
 3   Wheel cylinder body
 4   Adjuster lock spring
 5   Cylinder cup
 6   Piston
 7   Adjusting nut
 8   Adjust bolt
 9   Boot
10   Hold-down spring pin
11   Back plate
12   Brake shoe assembly
13   Tension spring
14   Hold-down spring
15   Adjusting hole plug

Lower insets show
alternative cylinders

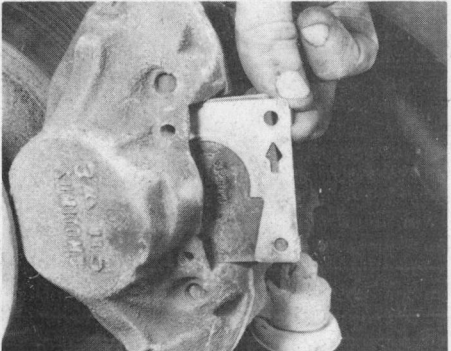

4.3 Disc pad anti-squeal shim

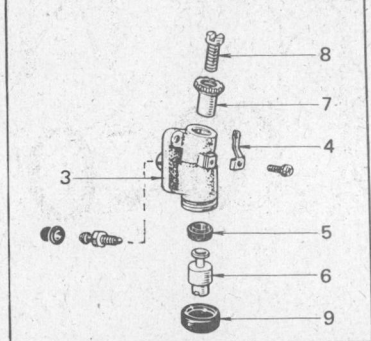

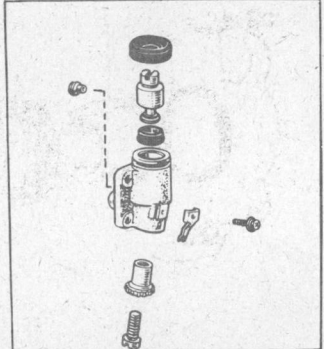

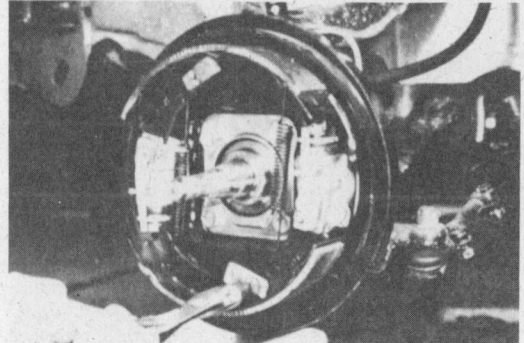

Fig. 9.8. Removing a hold-down spring

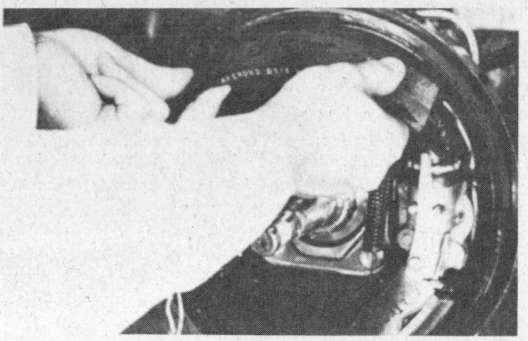

Fig. 9.9. Removing a brake shoe

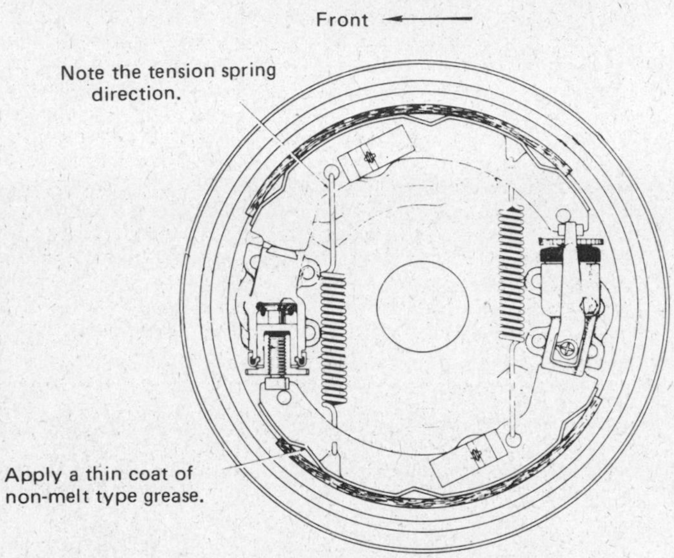
Front
Note the tension spring direction.
Apply a thin coat of non-melt type grease.

Fig. 9.10. Correct layout of front brake assembly

Fig. 9.11. Components of rear brake

1 *Dust cover*
2 *Hold-down spring pin*
3 *Backplate*
4 *Wheel cylinder*
5 *Leading brake shoe*
6 *Anchor tensioner spring*
7 *Trailing brake shoe*
8 *Hold-down spring*
9 *Adjuster*
10 *Automatic adjuster lever*
11 *Tension spring*
12 *Parking brake shoe lever*
13 *Boot*
14 *Piston*
15 *Cylinder cup*
16 *Compression spring*
17 *Bleed valve*
18 *Wheel cylinder body*
19 *Union seat*

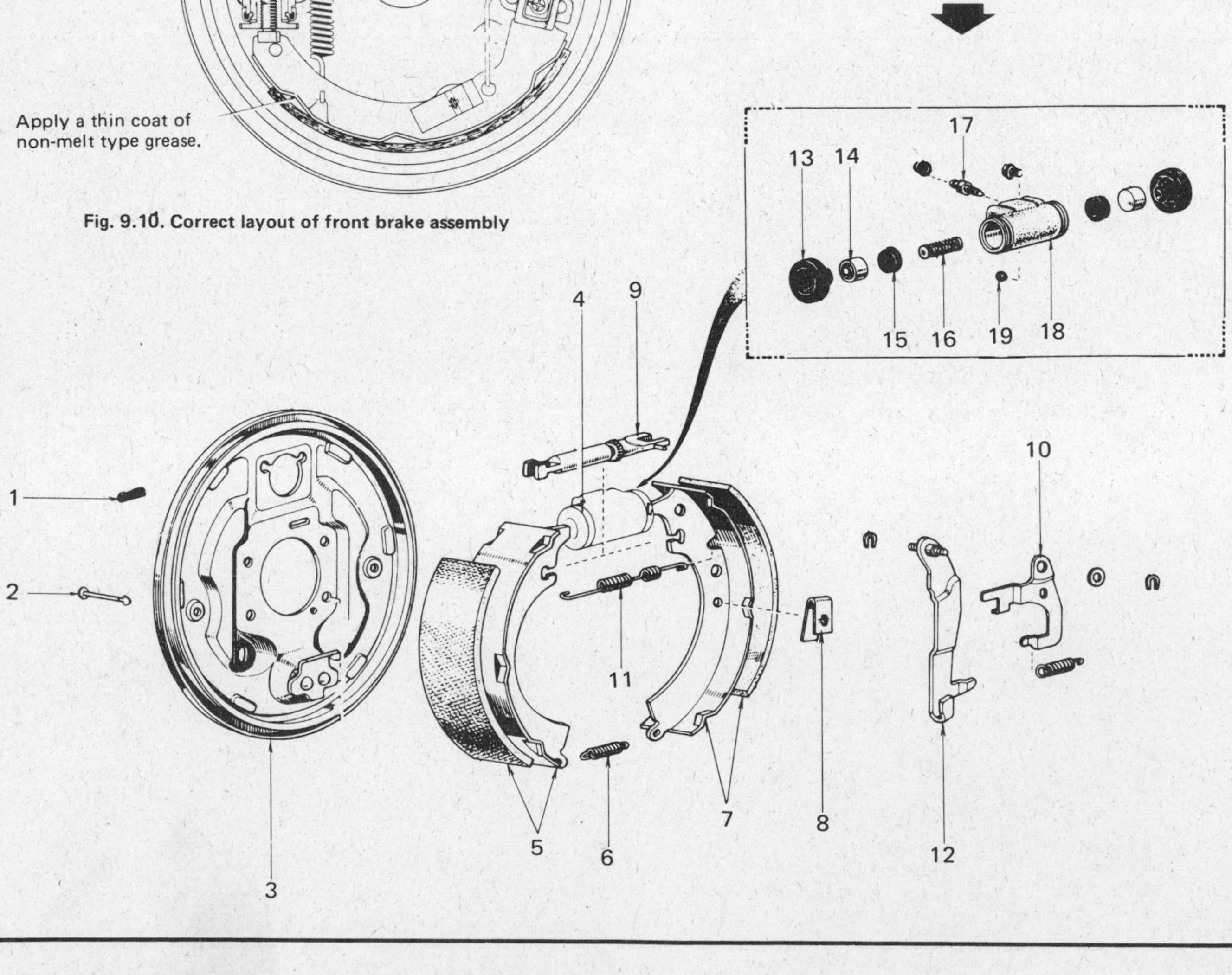
17
13
14
15
16
19
18
4
9
10
1
2
11
3
5
6
7
8
12

any dirt or grit from entering the bearings.

4   Inspect the condition of the friction linings. If they are in good condition, brush any dust from them and from the drum interior, and reassemble the hub/drum.

5   If the linings are worn down to the minimum specified thickness or are grease stained, they must be renewed. If grease contamination is evident, then the oil seal in its retainer must be renewed as described in Chapter 11.

6   It is not recommended that new linings are fitted to the original shoes but rather the old shoes are exchanged for factory relined ones. This will prove much more satisfactory as the linings will be securely riveted or bonded, and ground to contour, to minimise the bedding-in process.

7   Remove the shoe hold-down springs from their posts and slacken the shoe adjusters right off. Prise one shoe from its location, pull it slightly forward and allow it to move towards the hub centre so that the second shoe can be removed and lift away both shoes with return springs still attached.

8   Refitting the shoes is the reverse of the removal procedure, but apply a light smear of high melting point brake grease to the shoe contact points on the backplate, and to the shoe ends where they contact the wheel cylinders and adjusters.

9   Refit the hub/drum assembly, and adjust it as described in Chapter 11.

10 Repeat the operation for the other front brake, then refit the roadwheels and lower the car to the ground.

6   Rear drum brake shoes - inspection and renewal

1   Jack up the rear of the vehicle, remove the roadwheel and the brake drum (two screws).

2   Inspect the condition of the friction linings. If they are in good condition, brush any dust from them and from the drum interior and refit the drum and roadwheel.

3   If the linings are worn down to the minimum specified thickness, or the linings are oil stained, then they must be renewed. If oil contamination is evident, then the rear axle oil seal must be renewed as described in Chapter 8. **Note:** It is preferable to renew the left-hand side brake linings first, as this assembly is shown in the illustrations.

4   It is not recommended that new linings are fitted to the original shoes but rather the old shoes are exchanged for factory relined ones. This will prove much more satisfactory as the linings will be securely riveted or bonded, and ground to contour, to minimise the bedding-in process.

5   Using a suitable tool, unhook the tension spring from the brake shoes.

6   Using pliers, remove the shoe hold-down springs and draw out the shoes. This will allow the front shoe to be removed.

7   Remove the adjuster lever tension spring so that the adjustment lever can be removed.

8   Disconnect the parking brake cable from the shoe lever. The rear shoe and shoe lever can now be removed together.

9   Carefully prise off the E-ring, and detach the lever from the shoe.

10 Refitting the shoes is basically the reverse of the removal procedure. When the E-rings are fitted, use pliers to bend their ends inwards to ensure that they are secure. Apply a light smear of high melting point brake grease to the shoe contact points on the backplate, and to the shoe ends where they contact the wheel cylinder adjuster, and backplate abutments. Note the way in which the springs are fitted; attach the spring to the trailing shoe before it is placed in position, then attach the forward end of the spring to the leading shoe.

11 Refit the drum and roadwheel, then repeat the procedure for the other rear wheel.

12 On completion, with the car on the ground, operate the handbrake (or foot-operated parking brake) several times to adjust the shoes.

Fig. 9.12. Removing the tension spring

Fig. 9.13. Removing the adjuster tension spring

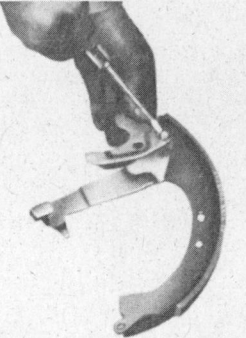

Fig. 9.14. Removing the shoe lever

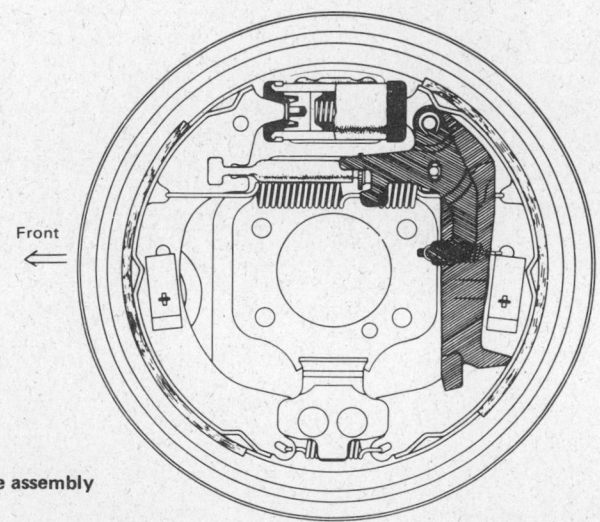

Front

Fig. 9.15. Correct layout of rear brake assembly

7 Front disc caliper (F-type) - removal and refitting

1 Jack up the front of the vehicle and support it securely. Remove the roadwheel.
2 Disconnect the flexible hydraulic hose from the caliper and plug the hose to prevent loss of fluid. An alternative method of preventing loss of fluid is to remove the brake fluid reservoir cap and place a sheet of polythene film over the neck of the reservoir and then screw on the cap. This causes a partial vacuum and prevents the fluid leaking from the master cylinder.
3 Remove the cylinder assembly and disc pads, as described in Section 3.
4 Remove the two bolts which secure the caliper unit to the stub axle carrier, and remove the unit complete with cylinder support springs and pad support plates.
5 Refitting is the reverse of the removal procedure; tighten the caliper bolts to the specified torque and bleed the hydraulic system (Section 17).

8 Front disc caliper (F-type) - servicing

1 Carefully prise out the dust excluder retaining ring and remove the dust excluder.
2 Apply air from a tyre pump at the hydraulic hose connection on the caliper body and eject the piston.
3 Inspect the mating surfaces of the piston and cylinder. If any scoring is evident or 'bright' wear areas, renew the caliper cylinder assembly complete.
4 If these components are in good condition, extract the seal from the cylinder recess and discard it.
5 Wash all components in clean hydraulic fluid or methylated spirit and obtain a repair kit which will contain all the necessary seals and other renewable items.
6 Locate the new seal in its cylinder recess, manipulating it into position using the fingers only to avoid damage.
7 Dip the piston in clean hydraulic fluid and enter it squarely into the cylinder.
8 Fit the new rubber dust excluder and retaining ring.
9 Examine all other components of the caliper unit and renew any that are worn or damaged.

9 Front disc caliper (Girling type) - removal and refitting

1 Remove the pads and ESP wear indicator leads (if fitted), as described in Section 4.
2 Disconnect the hydraulic pipe from the caliper unit, either plugging the line or sealing the reservoir, as described in Section 7.
3 Unscrew and remove the two caliper mounting bolts, and remove the caliper from the stub axle carrier, retaining any mounting shims which may be fitted.
4 Refitting is the reverse of the removal procedure; tighten the caliper securing bolts to the specified torque and bleed the hydraulic system (Section 17).

10 Front disc caliper (Girling type) - servicing

1 Servicing of this type of caliper is very similar to that described for the single cylinder type in Section 8, except that there are of course two cylinders.
2 Place a thin piece of wood between the opposing pistons before ejecting them to prevent damaging their end faces.
3 **On no account loosen or remove the bolts which secure the two halves of the caliper unit together.**
4 Reassembly is similar to that described for the single cylinder type in Section 8.

11 Brake disc - examination, removal and refitting

1 Jack up the front of the vehicle, remove the roadwheel and caliper.
2 Inspect the disc surfaces for deep scoring or grooves. Light scoring is normal.

3 Using a dial gauge or similar instrument, check for run-out (buckle). This should not exceed that given in the Specifications; if it does the disc should be renewed.
4 The disc thickness should not be reduced below the minimum specified, either by normal wear or by grinding to remove scoring.
5 To remove the disc/hub assembly, refer to the procedure given in Chapter 11.
6 Unscrew the disc-to-hub bolts, and separate the two parts.
7 Refitting is the reverse of the removal procedure. Adjust the disc/hub as described in Chapter 11.

12 Front drum wheel cylinders - removal, servicing and refitting

1 Remove the brake shoes, as described in Section 5.
2 Although it is possible to dismantle a wheel cylinder while it is still attached to the backplate, it is recommended that it is removed. To do this, disconnect the fluid line from the cylinder and either plug the line or seal the reservoir filler neck with a sheet of polythene to prevent loss of fluid.
3 Remove the wheel cylinder from the brake backplate.
4 Remove the adjuster wheel and screw, and the dust excluder, then eject the piston by tapping the cylinder on a piece of wood or by applying air from a tyre pump to the fluid inlet.
5 Examine the mating surfaces of the piston and cylinder. If they are scored or any 'bright' wear areas are evident, renew the cylinder complete.
6 Where the components are in good order, discard the seals and wash all items in clean hydraulic fluid or methylated spirit.
7 Obtain a repair kit and manipulate the new seal into position using the fingers. Note that the seal lip is towards the inside of the cylinder.
8 Apply a little high melting point brake grease to the screw threads and sliding surfaces of the adjusters and piston. Smear the piston and seal with clean hydraulic fluid, and insert it into the cylinder. Fit the adjuster wheel, screw and dust excluder.
9 Refit the wheel cylinder to the backplate, and refit the brake shoes and drums.
10 Reconnect the fluid line then bleed the hydraulic system (Section 17).

13 Rear drum wheel cylinders - removal, servicing and refitting

1 The procedure is similar to that described for the front wheel cylinders in Section 12, except that the cylinder has two pistons, seals and dust excluders, and an internal spring (see Fig. 9.23).
2 When servicing the shoe adjuster, apply a little high melting point grease to the screw threads and sliding surfaces.

14 Brake drums - inspection and renovation

1 Whenever the front or rear brake drums are removed, they should be examined for cracks and for internal scoring or grooves.
2 After a considerable mileage, the drums may also become out of round.
3 To remove scoring or to correct out of round, the drums must either be ground or renewed. If the drums are ground then their internal diameter must not exceed the maximum specified.

Fig. 9.16. Removing the caliper cylinder mounting (F-type)

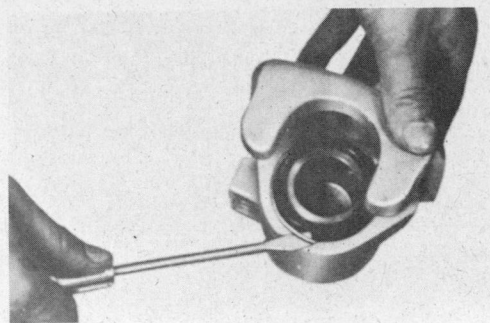

Fig. 9.17. Removing the retainer ring (F-type)

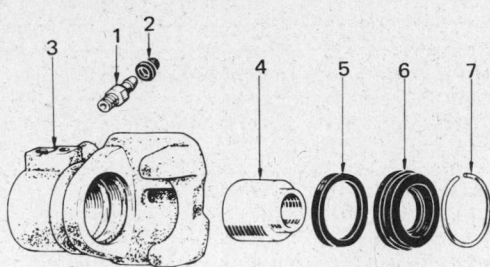

Fig. 9.18. Brake cylinder parts (F-type)

1	Bleed valve	5	Seal ring
2	Cap	6	Cylinder boot
3	Brake cylinder	7	Ring
4	Piston		

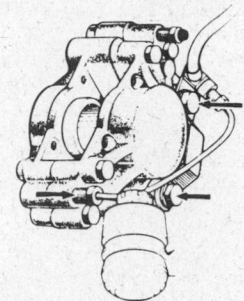

Fig. 9.19. Caliper removal bolts (arrowed) - Girling type

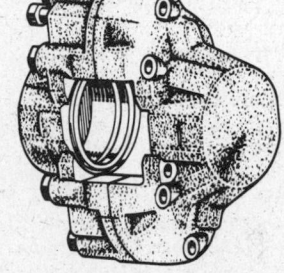

Fig. 9.20. Caliper and piston parts (Girling type)

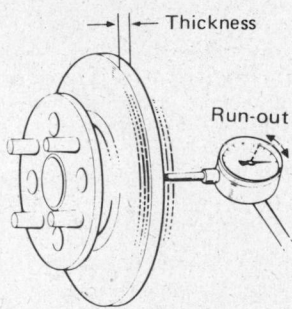

Fig. 9.21. Checking brake disc

Thickness

Run-out

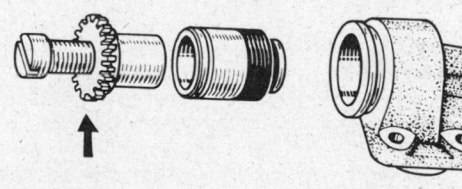

Fig. 9.22. Alternative types of front wheel cylinder have left or right-hand threads

Top	
Wheel	Nut/bolt
RH	RH
LH	LH
Bottom	
Wheel	Nut/bolt
RH	LH
LH	RH

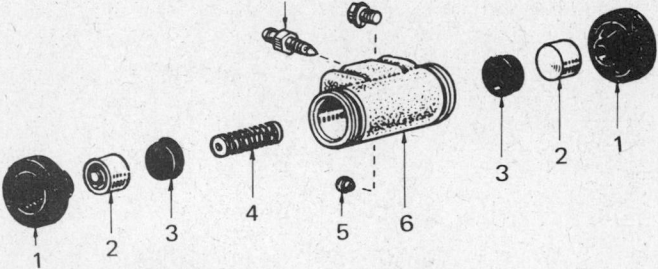

Fig. 9.23. Rear wheel cylinder parts

1	Boot	5	Union seat
2	Piston	6	Cylinder body
3	Cup	7	Bleed valve
4	Compression spring		

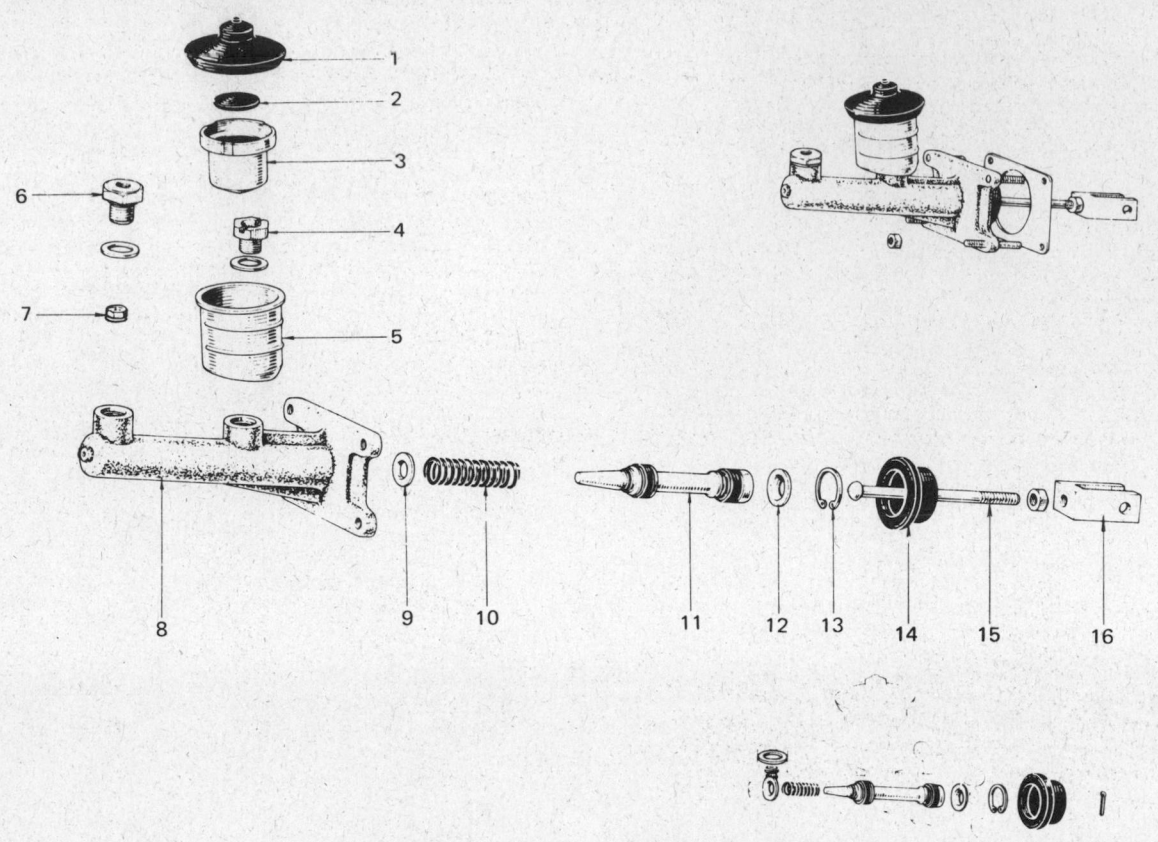

Fig. 9.24. Single master cylinder components

1	Reservoir cap	5	Reservoir	9	Washer	13	Circlip
2	Float	6	Outlet plug	10	Spring	14	Boot
3	Strainer	7	Outlet check valve	11	Piston	15	Push rod
4	Reservoir set bolt	8	Cylinder body	12	Washer	16	Push rod clevis

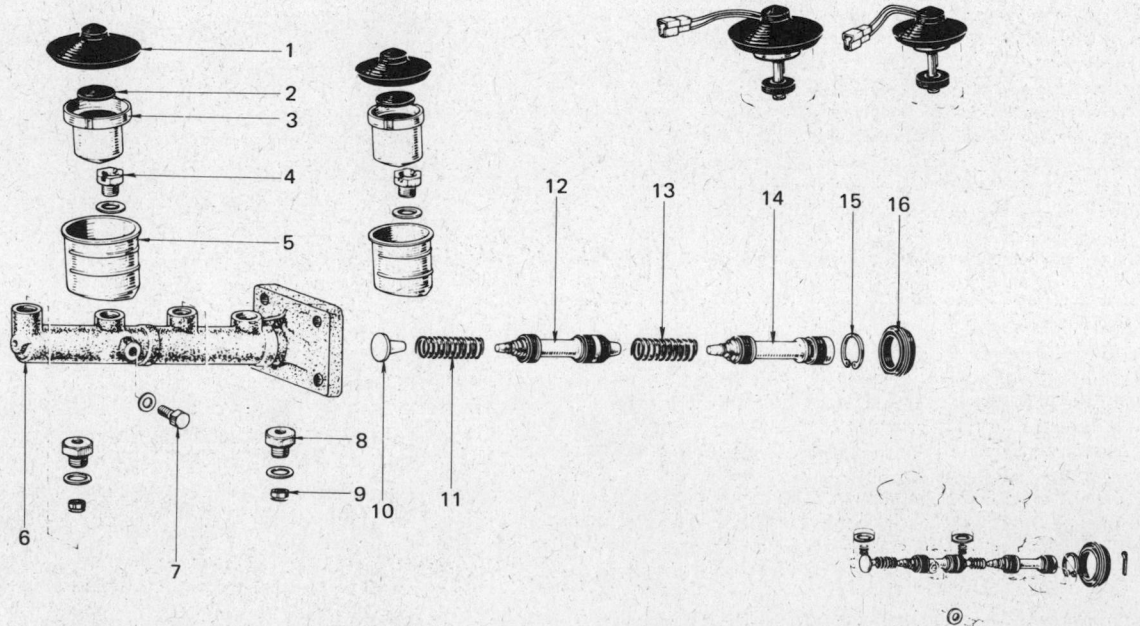

Fig. 9.25. Dual master cylinder components

1	Reservoir cap	5	Reservoir	9	Outlet check valve	13	Spring
2	Float	6	Cylinder body	10	Piston stop	14	Piston No. 1
3	Strainer	7	Stop bolt	11	Spring	15	Circlip
4	Set bolt	8	Outlet plug	12	Piston No. 2	16	Boot

15 Master cylinder (single type) - removal, servicing and refitting

1 *On vehicles without a servo unit,* disconnect the master cylinder pushrod from the brake pedal. Disconnect the fluid pipe from the union on the master cylinder body. Unbolt the master cylinder from the engine compartment rear bulkhead and remove it.
2 *On vehicles with a vacuum servo unit,* disconnect the fluid pipe from the master cylinder body. Remove the nuts from the studs on the front face of the vacuum servo unit and withdraw the master cylinder.
3 Extract the circlip from the end of the cylinder and eject the piston assembly and spring. Remove the reservoir by unscrewing the internal bolt.
4 Wash all the components in clean hydraulic fluid or methylated spirit.
5 Inspect the sliding surfaces of the piston and cylinder for scoring or 'bright' wear areas. If evident, renew the master cylinder complete.
6 Where the components are in good order, discard all rubber seals and obtain a repair kit.
7 Lubricate the new seals with rubber grease or brake fluid, then fit them using the fingers only to manipulate them into position.
8 Dip the internal components in clean hydraulic fluid before reassembling them.
9 Refitting of the master cylinder is the reverse of the removal procedure, but check and adjust the brake pedal height (see Section 24), and bleed the hydraulic system (Section 17).

16 Master cylinder (dual type) - removal, servicing and refitting

1 Disconnect the fluid pipes from the master cylinder body, then remove the nuts and detach the master cylinder from the servo unit.
2 Drain out the fluid from the reservoirs, then remove the bolt and washer from the base of each reservoir; remove the reservoirs.
3 Remove the stop bolt from the side of the master cylinder body.
4 Unscrew the outlet plugs; remove the washers and outlet check valves.
5 Remove the circlip and take out piston No. 1, the spring, piston No. 2, the second spring and the piston stop.
6 Wash all the components in clean hydraulic fluid or methylated spirit.
7 Inspect the sliding surfaces of the pistons and cylinder for scoring or 'bright' wear areas. If evident, renew the master cylinder complete.
8 Where the components are in good order, discard all rubber seals and obtain a repair kit.
9 Lubricate the new seals with rubber grease or brake fluid, then fit them using the fingers only to manipulate them into position.
10 Reassemble the master cylinder, dipping each item in hydraulic fluid. Ensure that the end of the stop bolt is between the seals of piston No. 2, and does not contact them or the lands.
11 Refitting of the master cylinder is the reverse of the removal procedure, but check and adjust the brake pedal height (see Section 24) and bleed the hydraulic system (Section 17).

17 Hydraulic system - bleeding

1 Removal of all the air from the hydraulic system is essential to the correct working of the braking system, but before undertaking this examine the fluid reservoir cap to ensure that both vent holes, one on top and the second underneath (but not in line) are clear; check the level of fluid and top up if required.
2 Check all brake line unions and connections for possible seepage, and at the same time check the condition of the rubber hoses, which may be perished.
3 If the condition of the wheel cylinders is in doubt, check for possible signs of fluid leakage.
4 If there is any possibility of incorrect fluid having been put into the system, drain all the fluid out and flush through with methylated spirit. Renew all piston seals and cups since these will be affected and could possibly fail under pressure.
5 Gather together a clean glass jar, a length of tubing which fits tightly over the bleed nipples, and a tin of the correct brake fluid.
6 To bleed the system clean the areas around the bleed valves, and start on the rear brakes by removing the rubber cup over the bleed valve on the brake furthest from the master cylinder, and fitting the

tube in position.
7 Place the end of the tube in a clean glass jar containing sufficient fluid to keep the end of the tube submerged during the operation.
8 Open the bleed valve with a spanner and quickly press down the brake pedal. After slowly releasing the pedal, pause for a moment to allow the fluid to recoup in the master cylinder and then depress again. This will force air from the system. Continue until no more air bubbles can be seen coming from the tube. At intervals make certain that the reservoir is kept topped-up, otherwise air will enter at this point again. Repeat the procedure for the other brake.
9 Once the rear brakes have been bled, bleed the front brake furthest from the master cylinder followed by the remaining front brake.
10 Tighten the bleed valves when the pedal is in the fully depressed position. Use only clean fluid for topping up purposes and discard fluid from the bleed jar. Fluid used for topping up should have been kept in an air tight container and remained unshaken for the previous 24 hours.

18 Flexible hoses - inspection and renewal

1 Inspect the condition of the flexible hoses leading from under the front wings to the brackets on the front suspension units, and also the single hose on the rear axle casing. If they are swollen, damaged or chafed, they must be renewed.
2 Undo the locknuts at both ends of the flexible hoses, then holding the hexagon nut on the flexible hose steady, undo the other union nut and remove the flexible hose and washer.
3 Refitting is a reversal of the removal procedure, but carefully check all the securing brackets are in a sound condition and that the locknuts are tight. Bleed the hydraulic system (Section 17).

19 Rigid brake lines - inspection and renewal

1 At regular intervals wipe the steel pipes clean and examine them for signs of rust or denting caused by flying stones.
2 Examine the securing clips. Bend the tongues of the clips if necessary to ensure that they hold the brake pipes securely without letting them rattle or vibrate.
3 Check that the pipes are not touching any adjacent components or rubbing against any part of the vehicle. Where this is observed, bend the pipe gently away to clear.
4 Any section of pipe which is rusty or chafed should be renewed. Brake pipes are available to the correct length and fitted with end unions from most Toyota dealers and can be made to pattern by many accessory suppliers. When fitting the new pipes use the old pipes as a guide to bending, and do not make any bends sharper than is necessary.
5 The system will of course have to be bled when the circuit has been reconnected (Section 17).

20 Handbrake - adjustment

1 The handbrake is normally adjusted automatically by the action of the automatic adjuster mechanism located within the rear brake drums. However, in the event of cable stretch, additional adjustment may be required as described in the following paragraphs:
2 Underneath the car, release the locknut from the turn-buckle or the

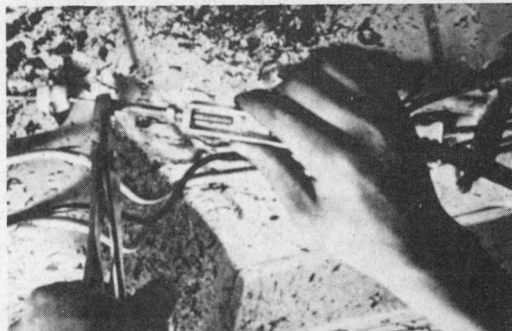

Fig. 9.26. Handbrake cable turnbuckle

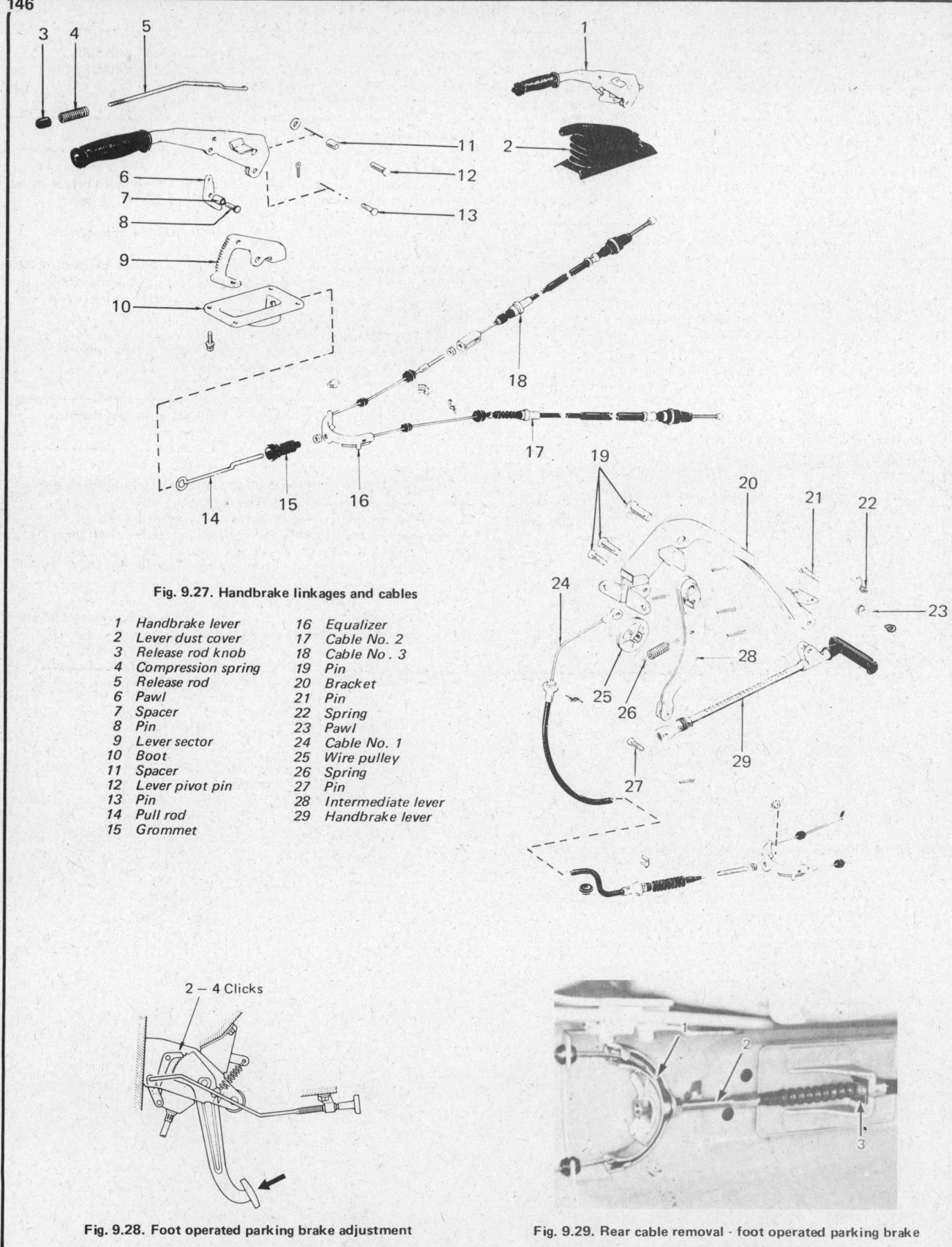

Fig. 9.27. Handbrake linkages and cables

1	Handbrake lever	16	Equalizer
2	Lever dust cover	17	Cable No. 2
3	Release rod knob	18	Cable No . 3
4	Compression spring	19	Pin
5	Release rod	20	Bracket
6	Pawl	21	Pin
7	Spacer	22	Spring
8	Pin	23	Pawl
9	Lever sector	24	Cable No. 1
10	Boot	25	Wire pulley
11	Spacer	26	Spring
12	Lever pivot pin	27	Pin
13	Pin	28	Intermediate lever
14	Pull rod	29	Handbrake lever
15	Grommet		

Fig. 9.28. Foot operated parking brake adjustment

Fig. 9.29. Rear cable removal - foot operated parking brake

1	Equalizer	3	Clip at reaction bracket
2	Cable		

equaliser.

3   Turn the turn-buckle or equaliser adjuster nut until, with floor-mounted type handbrake levers, the handbrake is fully on after the lever is pulled through three to six notches of the ratchet. On facia-mounted pull-out type handbrake controls, the handbrake should be fully applied after being pulled through eight to fifteen notches.

4   When adjustment is completed, jack up the rear wheels and check that they will turn freely when the handbrake control is fully released.

5   Tighten the turn-buckle or equaliser locknuts.

21 Handbrake lever and cable - removal and refitting

Centre floor type

1   Jack up the car and support it on suitable axle stands.

2   Remove the propeller shaft as described in Chapter 7.

3   Remove the nut and detach the parking brake pullrod from the equaliser.

4   Remove the rear brake shoes as described in Section 6.

5   Push back the cable attachment claw, and detach the cable from the backplate.

6   Disconnect the wiring for the handbrake switch, then remove the four bolts and lift out the lever assembly.

7   Refitting is the reverse of the removal procedure; adjust the handbrake as described in the previous Section.

Under dash type

8   Initially proceed as described in paragraphs 1, 2 and 3. Additionally remove the cable clip from the reaction bracket.

9   Remove the return spring, then remove the wire pulley pin and detach the pulley.

10 Remove the clip and lever pin, and detach the front cable.

11 To remove the rear cable, refer to the procedure in paragraphs 4 and 5.

12 Disconnect the wiring for the handbrake switch, then remove the

three mounting bolts to release the handbrake lever assembly.

13 Refitting is the reverse of the removal procedure; adjust the handbrake as described in the previous Section.

22 Foot operated parking brake - adjustment

1   Initially check that the brake pedal reserve travel is not less than that specified. If it is, this is an indication of mal-adjusted brakes or air in the hydraulic system. These faults should be corrected before attempting to adjust the parking brake.

2   Underneath the car, release the locknut from the turn-buckle or equaliser.

3   Turn the turn-buckle or equaliser adjuster nut until the pedal lock release rod free play and pedal travel are as specified. **Note:** Before checking the pedal travel, depress it firmly at least five times and release it.

4   When the adjustment is completed, jack up the rear wheels and check that they will turn freely with the parking brake released.

5   Tighten the turn-buckle or equaliser locknuts.

23 Foot operated parking brake pedal and cable - removal and refitting

1   Remove the rear cable as described in Section 21.

2   Remove the door outside scuff plate, cowl side trim lower board, and the driver's seat. Pull back the carpet.

3   Remove the heater rear air duct.

4   Remove the cable clamps, and the cable grommet from the transmission tunnel wall.

5   Remove the retaining screws and detach the bonnet release and parking brake release rod.

6   Disconnect the parking brake switch wiring.

7   From the engine compartment side, remove the two retaining nuts and washers, and detach the pedal and front cable.

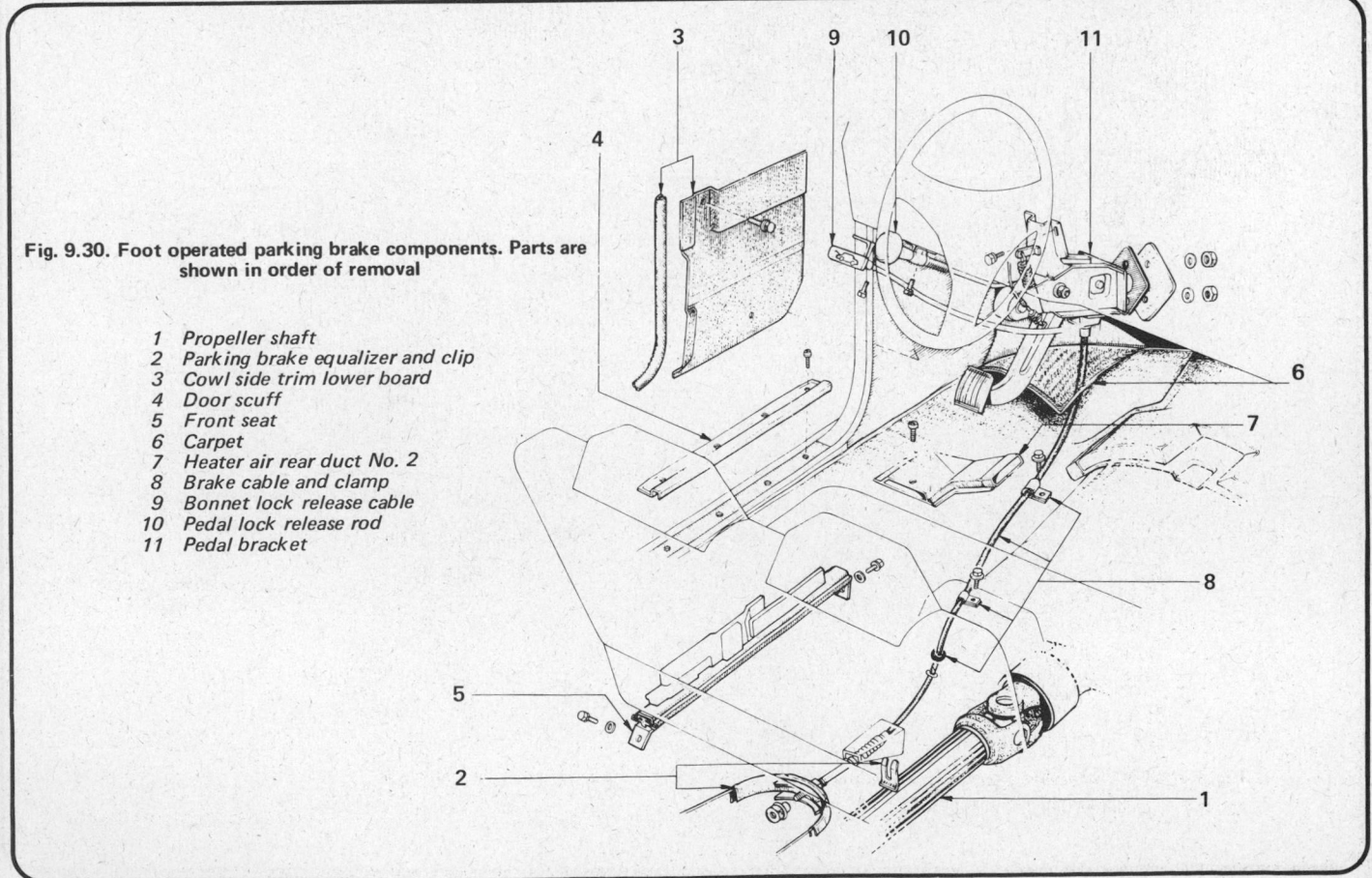

Fig. 9.30. Foot operated parking brake components. Parts are shown in order of removal

1   Propeller shaft
2   Parking brake equalizer and clip
3   Cowl side trim lower board
4   Door scuff
5   Front seat
6   Carpet
7   Heater air rear duct No. 2
8   Brake cable and clamp
9   Bonnet lock release cable
10 Pedal lock release rod
11 Pedal bracket

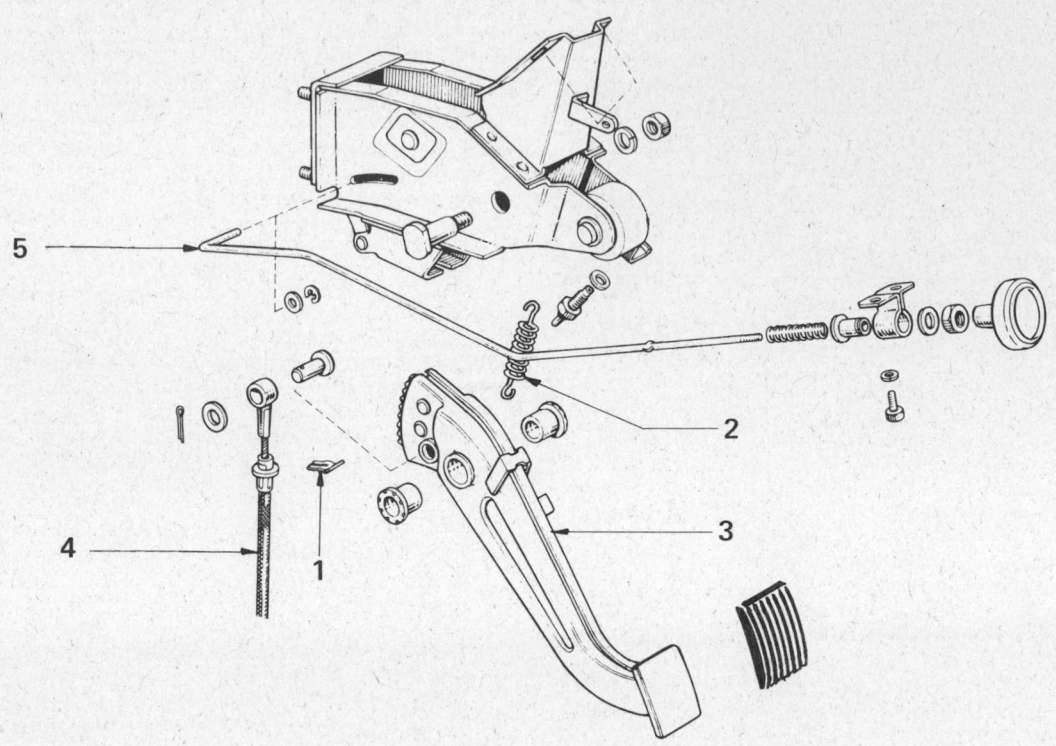

Fig. 9.31. Parking brake pedal assembly

1 Clip
2 Brake pedal
3 Brake pedal
4 Brake cable
5 Brake release rod

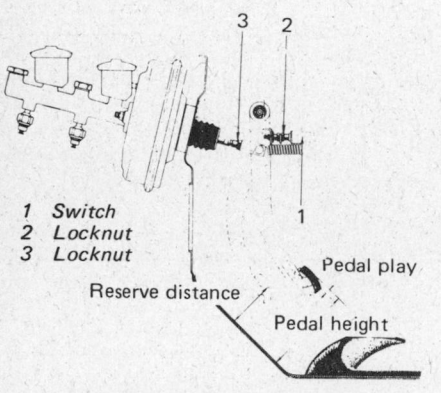

1 Switch
2 Locknut
3 Locknut

Reserve distance
Pedal play
Pedal height

Fig. 9.32. Brake pedal adjustment

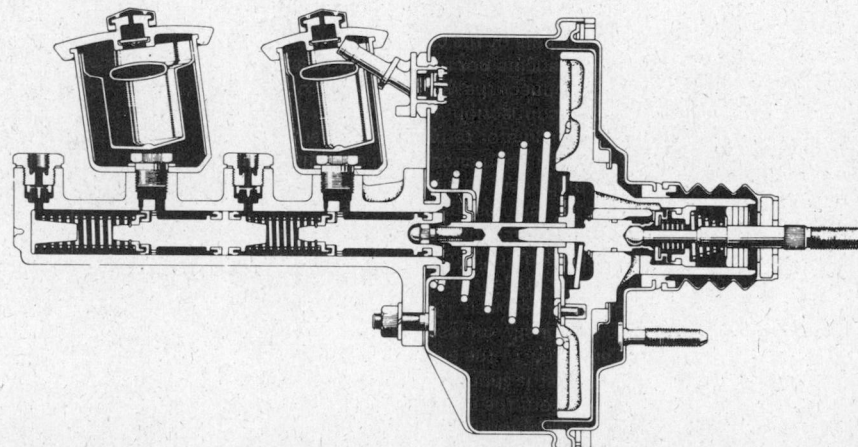

Fig. 9.33. Brake booster and master cylinder - sectional view

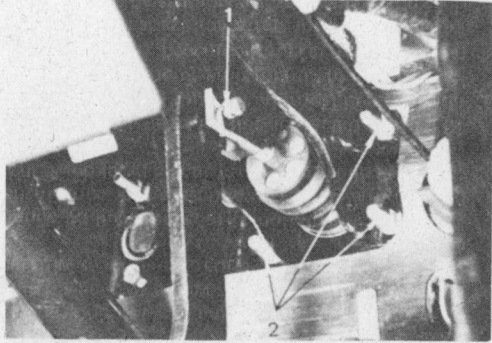

Fig. 9.34. Removing the servo

1 Clevis pin
2 Securing nuts

8 If necessary, the pedal assembly can be dismantled by reference to Fig. 9.32. The parts are numbered in order of dismantling; when reassembling, lubricate all pivoting and rubbing surfaces with multi-purpose grease.

9 Refitting is the reverse of the removal procedure; adjust the parking brake as described in the previous Section.

24 Brake pedal - adjustment

1 The brake pedal should only need adjusting if the pedal assembly, servo unit or master cylinder has been removed.

2 Release the locknut on the stoplamp switch and unscrew the switch so that it no longer contacts the brake pedal arm. On vehicles with a vacuum servo unit, depress the brake pedal several times to destroy the vacuum.

3 Release the locknut on the master cylinder or servo unit pushrod and turn the rod until the distance between the surface of the floor panel (carpet peeled back) and the upper surface of the pedal pad is as given in the Specifications.

4 When the pedal height is correctly set, a certain amount of free-movement should be apparent when the pedal is depressed gently with the fingers. On vehicles without a vacuum servo, this can be adjusted if necessary as described in paragraphs 2 and 3 to obtain the best compromise of pedal height and pedal play.

5 If the pedal reserve travel (the distance from the pedal pad to the floor when fully depressed) is less than the specified limit, the brakes require adjustment (adjustable drum type), the automatic adjusting mechanism is seized or faulty, or the disc pads or shoe linings are worn out.

6 When adjustment is completed, tighten the pushrod locknut and then screw in the stoplamp switch until its plunger is in a partially depressed state and then check (with the ignition switched on) that when the pedal is depressed through 1/8 in (3 mm) the stoplamps illuminate. When the correct setting of the switch has been established, tighten the switch locknut.

25 Vacuum servo (brake booster) unit - description

The vacuum servo unit is designed to supplement the effort applied by the driver's foot to the brake pedal.

The unit is an independent mechanism so that in the event of its failure the normal braking effort of the master cylinder is retained. A vacuum is created in the servo unit by its connection to the engine inlet manifold and with this condition applying on one side of the diaphragm, atmospheric pressure applied on the other side of the diaphragm is harnessed to assist the foot pressure on the master cylinder. With the brake pedal released, the diaphragm is fully recuperated and held against the rear shell by the return spring. The operating rod assembly is also fully recuperated and a condition of vacuum exists each side of the diaphragm.

When the brake pedal is applied, the valve rod assembly moves forward until the control valve closes the vacuum port. Atmospheric pressure then enters the chamber to the rear of the diaphragm and forces the diaphragm plate forward to actuate the master cylinder pistons through the medium of the servo unit pushrod.

When pressure on the brake pedal is released, the vacuum port is opened and the atmospheric pressure in the rear chamber is extracted through the non-return valve. The atmospheric pressure inlet port remains closed as the operating rod assembly returns to its original position by action of the coil return spring.

The diaphragm then remains in its position with vacuum conditions on both sides until the next depression of the brake pedal, when the cycle is repeated.

26 Vacuum servo unit - removal and refitting

1 Destroy the vacuum effect in the servo unit by repeated applications of the foot pedal.

2 Disconnect the vacuum hose from the servo unit.

3 Disconnect the hydraulic circuit fluid pipes from the master cylinder unions and plug the pipes to prevent ingress of dirt.

4 Disconnect the leads from the master cylinder pressure switches.

5 From inside the vehicle disconnect the operating rod from the brake pedal arm, then unscrew and remove the four servo unit securing nuts from their studs.

6 Remove the vacuum servo unit, complete with master cylinder and regulator valve, from its location on the engine rear bulkhead.

7 Remove the regulator valve securing bolt and the four nuts which hold the master cylinder to the front face of the vacuum servo unit and withdraw the master cylinder from the servo unit.

8 Refitting is the reverse of the removal procedure, but check the pedal height and bleed the hydraulic system (Sections 24 and 17).

27 Vacuum servo unit - dismantling and reassembly

1 If the vacuum servo unit is found to be faulty it is recommended that a factory exchange unit is obtained or the existing unit is repaired by a Toyota dealer. This is particularly so with the Asco servo unit which requires several special tools for dismantling. The JKK unit can be dismantled more readily using two home-made tools if it is really considered worthwhile. The procedure is given in the following paragraphs.

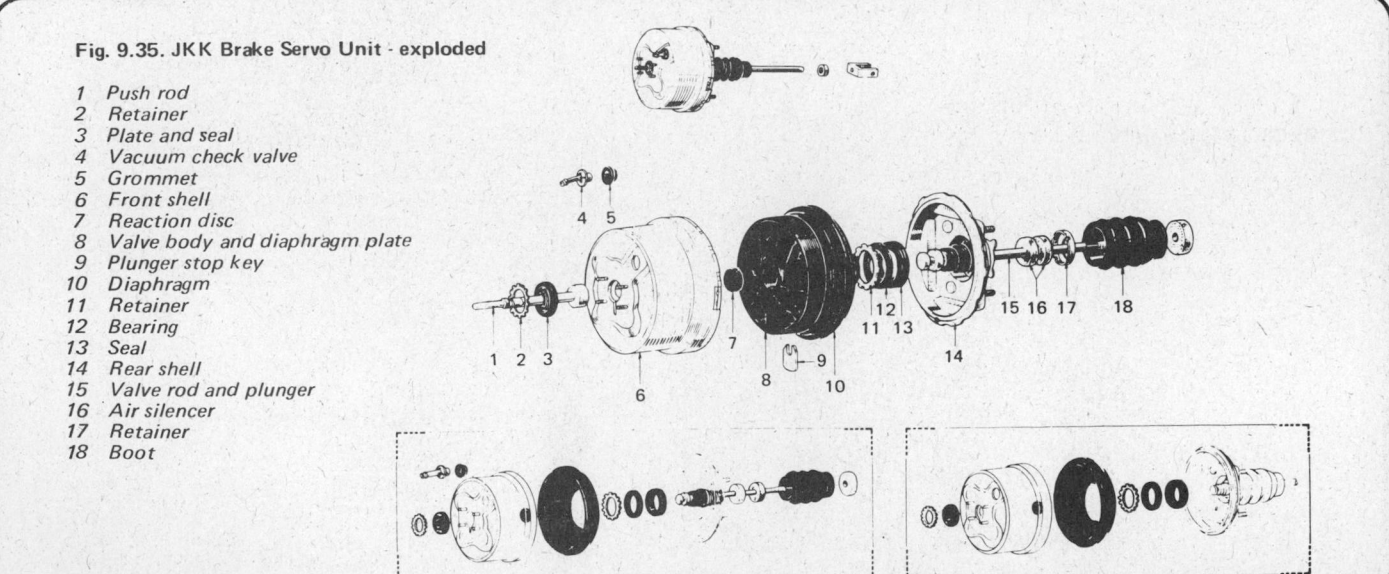

Fig. 9.35. JKK Brake Servo Unit - exploded

1   Push rod
2   Retainer
3   Plate and seal
4   Vacuum check valve
5   Grommet
6   Front shell
7   Reaction disc
8   Valve body and diaphragm plate
9   Plunger stop key
10 Diaphragm
11 Retainer
12 Bearing
13 Seal
14 Rear shell
15 Valve rod and plunger
16 Air silencer
17 Retainer
18 Boot

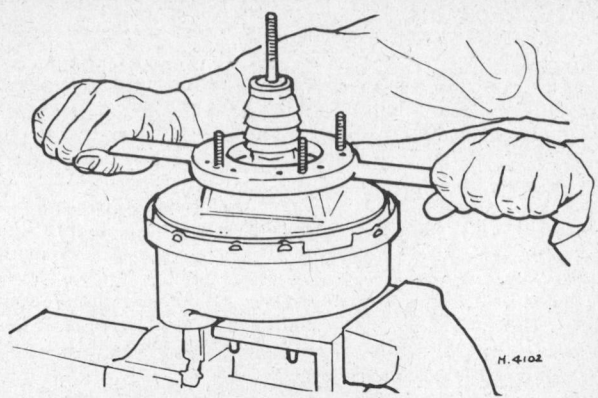

Fig. 9.36. Removing servo unit rear shell

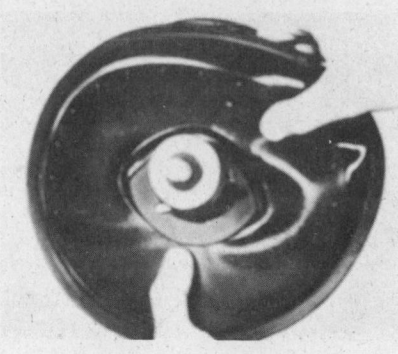

Fig. 9.37. Removing the diaphragm from the diaphragm plate

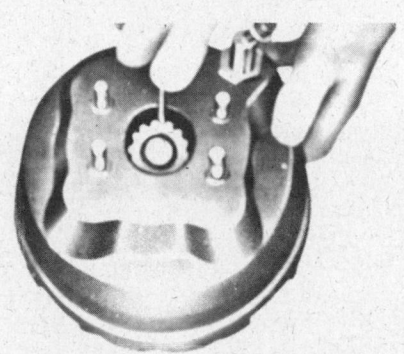

Fig. 9.38. Removing retainer from front shell

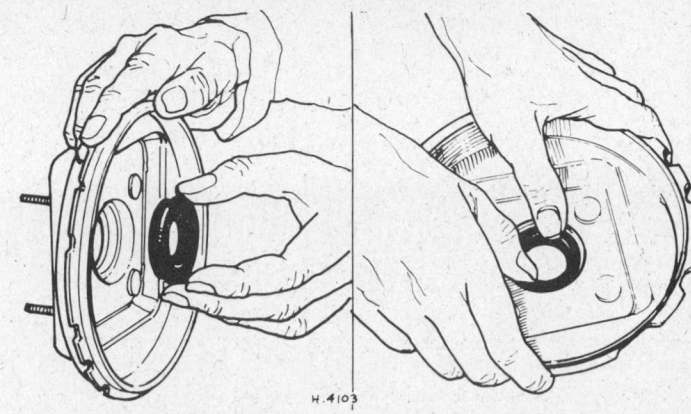

Fig. 9.39. Assembling seal (1) and bearing (2) to rear shell

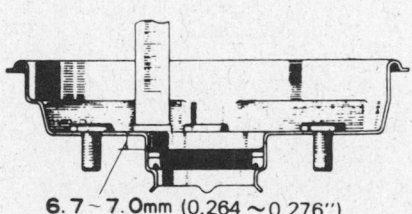

6.7 ~ 7.0mm (0.264 ~ 0.276'')

Fig. 9.40. Rear shell assembly diagram

Filter   Silencer

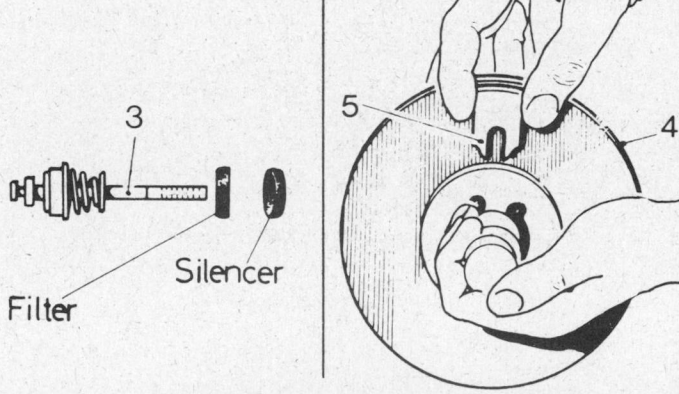

Fig. 9.41. Servo unit plunger assembly

3 Plunger assembly   5 Key
4 Diaphragm plate

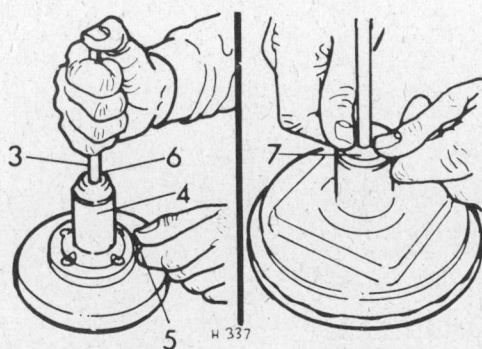

Fig. 9.42. Fitting air filter/silencer

3 Plunger   6 Filter/silencer
4 Diaphragm plate 7 Retainer
5 Key

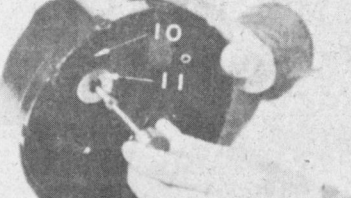

Fig. 9.43. Fitting plate and seal assembly (11) to front shell (10)

2 Scratch mating marks on the front and rear shells.
3 Holding the mounting studs of the front shell in a plate drilled to receive them, rotate the rear shell anti-clockwise to release it using a tool similar to the one shown. Remove the diaphragm return spring (Fig. 9.36).
4 Withdraw the diaphragm plate from the rear shell and remove the retainer, bearing and seal. The diaphragm plate is made of brittle plastic and should be handled carefully.
5 Remove the diaphragm from the diaphragm plate.
6 Remove the filter/silencer retainer, then the key by pointing the keyhole downwards and pressing the valve operating rod. Withdraw the valve plunger assembly.
7 Remove the retainer, plate and seal and push the rod from the front shell.
8 Clean all components in methylated spirit and check for cracks, corrosion and distortion, and the diaphragm and seals for deterioration (these are best renewed in any event).
9 Smear silicone oil of recommended grade to the seal (1) and bearing (2) and fit them into the rear shell then secure them with a retainer (Fig. 9.39).
10 Apply silicone oil to the plunger disc outer edge and assemble.
11 Fit a new air filter/silencer and press the retainer into the diaphragm plate.
12 Fit the diaphragm to the diaphragm plate and the reaction disc, first having smeared it with silicone oil.
13 Smear the outer edge of the diaphragm with silicone oil and then fit the diaphragm plate assembly and the valve body to the rear shell.
14 Fit the plate and seal assembly (11) to the front shell (10) using a smear of silicone oil and then install the pushrod (Fig. 9.43).
15 Secure the front shell in the holding tool and insert the diaphragm

return spring. Align the shell mating marks and engage the front and rear shells with a clockwise twisting motion. If they are difficult to engage, apply a smear of silicone oil to the diaphragm edges.
16 Using the tool which was required for dismantling the front and rear shells, tighten the rear shell until it comes up against the stop on the front shell.
17 Whenever the vacuum servo unit has been dismantled and reassembled check that there will be a clearance of 0.012 in (0.3 mm) between the end of the servo unit pushrod and the end of the master cylinder piston. Check by using the official tool or making up a depth gauge so that the projection of the servo unit pushrod can be compared with the depth of the recess to the end of the master cylinder piston. Carry out any adjustment by loosening the locknut and rotating the front section of the vacuum servo unit pushrod.

28 Pressure regulating valve

1 As previously described, this valve is incorporated in the hydraulic circuit close to the master cylinder. It varies the hydraulic pressure between the front and rear circuits in order to prevent the rear wheels locking during heavy brake applications.
2 The valve cannot be adjusted or repaired, and in the event of the valve leaking or a tendency for the rear wheels to lock, renew the valve complete.
3 Disconnect the fluid pipes from the valve body by unscrewing the unions, then remove the valve securing bolts and lift the valve away.
4 Installation of the new valve is the reverse of the removal procedure, but bleed the hydraulic system as described in Section 17.

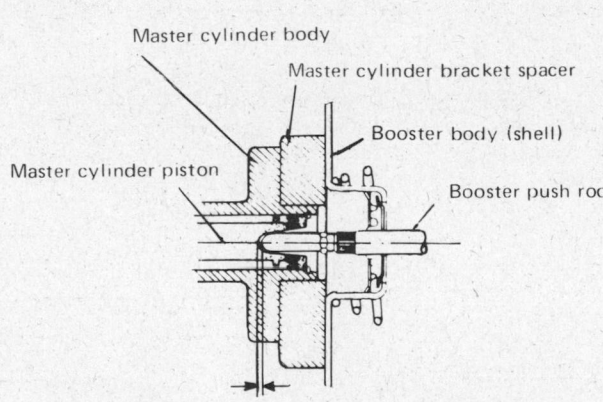

Fig. 9.44. Pushrod to master cylinder clearance diagram

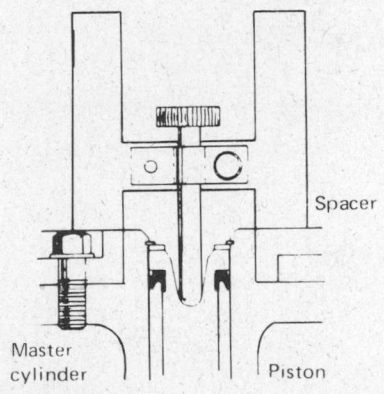

Fig. 9.45. Suitable tool for measuring depth of master cylinder recess during pushrod clearance adjustment

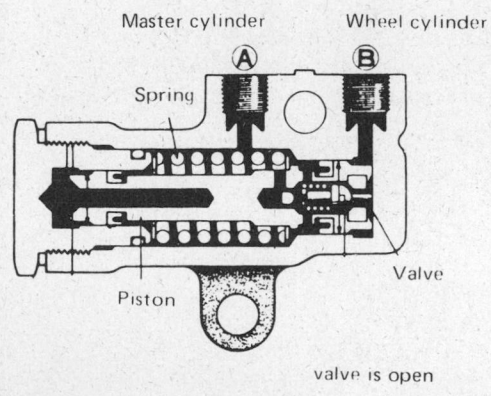

valve is open

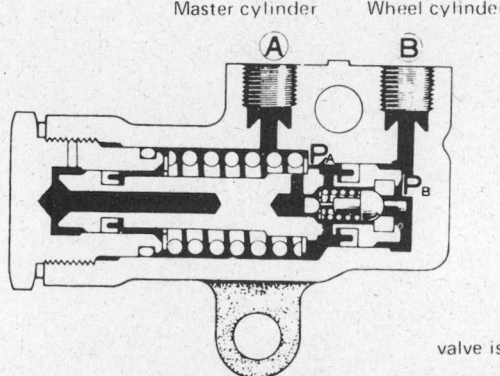

valve is closed

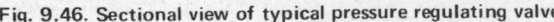

Fig. 9.46. Sectional view of typical pressure regulating valve

29 Fault diagnosis - braking system

Symptom	Cause
Brake grab	Brake shoe linings or pads not bedded-in.
	Contaminated with oil or grease.
	Scored drums or discs.
	Servo unit faulty.
Brake drag	Master cylinder faulty.
	Brake foot pedal return impeded.
	Blocked filler cap vent.
	Master cylinder reservoir or compartments overfilled.
	Seized wheel caliper or cylinder.
	Incorrect adjustment of handbrake.
	Weak or broken shoe return springs.
	Crushed or blocked pipelines.
Brake pedal feels hard	Friction surfaces contaminated with oil or grease.
	Glazed friction material surfaces.
	Rusty disc surfaces.
	Seized caliper or wheel cylinder.
	Faulty servo unit.
Excessive pedal travel	Low fluid level in reservoir.
	Automatic rear shoe adjusters faulty.
	Excessive disc runout.
	Worn front wheel bearings.
	System requires bleeding.
	Worn pads or linings.
Pedal creep during sustained application	Fluid leak.
	Faulty master cylinder.
	Faulty servo.
Pedal 'spongy' or 'springy'	System requires bleeding.
	Perished flexible hose.
	Loose master cylinder.
	Cracked brake drum.
	Linings not bedded-in.
	Faulty master cylinder.
Fall in master cylinder fluid level	Normal disc pad wear.
	Leak.
	Internal fluid leak from servo.

Servo unit fault diagnosis

Symptom	Cause
Hard pedal, lack of assistance when engine running	Lack of vacuum due to:
	Loose connections.
	Restricted hose.
	Blocked air filter/silencer.
	Major fault in unit.
Slow action of servo	Faulty vacuum hose.
	Blocked air filter/silencer.
Lack of assistance during heavy braking	Air leaks in:
	Non-return valve grommet.
	Non-return valve.
	Dust cover.
	Hoses and connections.
Loss of fluid	Major failure in unit.
Brake pedal pushes back against foot pressure	Hydraulic inlet and outlet pipes incorrectly connected at regulator valve.
	Major fault in unit.

Chapter 10 Electrical system

For modifications and information applicable to later USA models, refer to Supplement at end of manual

Contents

Specifications

System type ... ...   12 volt, negative earth (ground)

Battery capacity ... ...   60 amp hr

Alternator
Output ... ...   12 volts, 40 or 45 amp
Minimum exposed brush length ... ...   0.22 in (5.5 mm)

Alternator regulator
Regulating voltage ... ...   13.8 to 14.8 volts
Relay operating voltage ... ...   4.0 to 5.8 volts

Starter motor
Type ... ...   Pre-engaged; standard or reduction type

	Cars with 18R engine	Cars with 20R engine - standard type	Cars with 20R engine - reduction type
Rating	50A max. at 11.5V	50A max. at 11V	80A max. at 11.5V
Armature shaft/bush clearance	0.004 to 0.008 in (0.1 to 0.2 mm)	0.002 to 0.008 in (0.05 to 0.2 mm)	—
Armature shaft thrust clearance (endfloat)	0.032 in (0.8 mm) max.	0.002 to 0.024 in (0.05 to 0.6 mm)	—
Brush length, minimum	0.47 in (12 mm)	0.47 in (12 mm)	0.39 in (10 mm)
Commutator runout, maximum	0.016 in (0.4 mm)	0.012 in (0.3 mm)	0.002 in (0.05 mm)
Commutator diameter, minimum	1.22 in (31 mm)	1.22 in (31 mm)	1.14 in (29 mm)

Insulation depth	...	...	...	...	...	...	...	0.008 to 0.031 in (0.2 to 0.8 mm)	0.008 to 0.031 in (0.2 to 0.8 mm)	0.008 to 0.035 in (0.2 to 0.9 mm)
Pinion end/stop collar clearance		...	...	...	...	...	...	0.041 to 0.16 in (1.0 to 4.0 mm)	0.008 to 0.16 in (0.2 to 4.0 mm)	—

Bulbs

										Wattage USA	Wattage UK
Headlights											
Inner	...	...	...	...	...	...	...	...	...	37.5	37.5
Outer	...	...	...	...	...	...	...	...	...	37.5/50	37.5/50
Front turn signal lights	...	...	...	...	...	...	...	...	...	27	21
Front parking lights	...	...	...	...	...	...	...	...	...	8	5
Side marker lights	...	...	...	...	...	...	...	...	...	8	5
Reverse lights	...	...	...	...	...	...	...	...	...	27	21
Stop and tail lights	...	...	...	...	...	...	...	...	...	27/8	21/5
Rear turn signal lights	...	...	...	...	...	...	...	...	...	27	21
Number plate lights	...	...	...	...	...	...	...	...	...	7.5	10
Interior lights	...	...	...	...	...	...	...	...	...	10	8
Front interior light (Coupe)	...	...	...	...	...	...	...	...	5	—
Back door light (Estate)	...	...	...	...	...	...	...	...	10	8
Courtesy lights (Coupe)	...	...	...	...	...	...	...	...	5	—
Inspection light (Engine room light)	...	...	...	...	...	...	...	7.5	—
Glove box light	...	...	...	...	...	...	...	...	...	3.4	3.4

Fuses

Designation	Rating	Circuits
Radio	5 amp	Radio and tape player
Lighter	10 amp *	Cigarette lighter, clock, door warning light
Tail	15 amp	Light control relay, parking lights, side markers, panel lights, tail lights, number plate lights, seat belt buzzer **
Horn	15 amp	Horn, hazard warning, stop lights, key reminder buzzer, seat belt buzzer **
Room lamp	10 amp	Interior lights, door courtesy lights, seat belt buzzer **
Spare	15 amp	—
Wiper	20 amp ***	Wiper, washer
Ignition coil (engine)	10 amp ****	Ignition coil resistor
Turn	15 amp	Turn signal lights, regulator IG terminal and main relay
Gauge/heater	15 amp *****	Heater, air conditioner, gauges, reverse lights, brake warning lights, ESP warning lights
Defog	15 amp	Rear window defogger

* 15 amp on some SR-5 models; also protects spot light
** Alternatives, according to model year
*** 15 amp after 1975 models
**** 5 amp for 1974 models
***** 20 amp for 1976 USA models

Fusible link and ammeter fuses

    These are connected in the wiring harnesses. The fusible link also protects the headlight circuit as well as the main circuits (except the starting circuit)

Torque wrench setting

									lb f ft	kg f m
Alternator pulley nut	...	...	...	...	...	...	...	...	42	5.8

1 General description

    The electrical system is of the 12 volt negative earth (ground) type. The major components comprise a battery, an alternator and a pre-engaged starter motor.

    The battery supplies a steady current to the ignition system and to the vehicle's electrical equipment. All electrical circuits incorporate fuses and a fusible link is inserted in the battery lead to the fuse block.

2 Battery - removal and refitting

1   The battery is located at the front on the right-hand side of the engine compartment.

2   Disconnect the lead from the negative terminal by unscrewing the clamp bolt.

3   Disconnect the lead from the positive terminal and remove the battery securing bolts and frame.

4   Lift the battery carefully from its tray; avoid spilling electrolyte on the paintwork.

5   Refitting is the reverse of the removal procedure. If any corrosive deposits have been noticed on the terminals, clean them using ammonia then apply a light coating of petroleum jelly before the clamps are refitted. Finally smear the clamps with petroleum jelly after refitting.

3 Battery - maintenance

1   Carry out the regular weekly maintenance described in the Routine

Maintenance Section at the front of this manual.

2   Clean the top of the battery, removing all dirt and moisture.

3   As well as keeping the terminals clean and covered with petroleum jelly, the top of the battery, and especially the top of the cells, should be kept clean and dry. This helps prevent corrosion and ensures that the battery does not become partially discharged by leakage through dampness and dirt.

4   Once every three months, remove the battery and inspect the battery securing bolts, the battery clamp plate, tray and battery leads for corrosion (white fluffy deposits on the metal which are brittle to touch). If any corrosion is found, clean off the deposits with ammonia and paint over the clean metal with an anti-rust/anti-acid paint.

5   At the same time inspect the battery case for cracks. If a crack is found, clean and plug it with one of the proprietary compounds marketed for this purpose. If leakage through the crack has been excessive then it will be necessary to refill the appropriate cell with fresh electrolyte as detailed later. Cracks are frequently caused to the top of the battery cases by pouring in distilled water in the middle of winter *after* instead of *before* a run. This gives the water no chance to mix with the electrolyte and so the former freezes and splits the battery case.

6   If topping-up the battery becomes excessive and the case has been inspected for cracks that could cause leakage, but none are found, the battery is being over-charged and the voltage regulator will have to be checked and reset.

7   With the battery on the bench, at three monthly intervals, measure its specific gravity with a hydrometer to determine the state of charge and condition of the electrolyte. There should be very little variation between the different cells and if a variation in excess of 0.025 is present it will be due to either:

a) *Loss of electrolyte from the battery at some time caused by spillage or a leak, resulting in a drop in the specific gravity of the electrolyte when the deficiency was replaced with distilled water instead of fresh electrolyte.*

b) *An internal short circuit caused by buckling of the plates or a similar malady pointing to the likelihood of total battery failure in the near future.*

8   The specific gravity of the electrolyte for varying conditions of charge at a mean temperature of 68ºF (20ºC) are listed below:

1.260	*fully charged*
1.210	*¾ charged*
1.160	*½ charged*
1.110	*¼ charged*
1.060	*fully discharged*

4   Electrolyte - replenishment

1   If the battery is in a fully charged state and one of the cells maintains a specific gravity reading which is 0.025 or more lower than the others, and a check of each cell has been made with a voltage meter to check for short circuits (a four to seven second test should give a steady reading of between 1.2 to 1.8 volts), then it is likely that electrolyte has been lost from the cell with the low reading at some time.

2   Top-up the cell with a solution of 1 part sulphuric acid to 2.5 parts of water. If the cell is already fully topped-up draw some electrolyte out of it with a hydrometer.

3   When mixing the sulphuric acid and water **never add water to sulphuric acid** - always pour the acid slowly onto the water in a glass container. **If water is added to sulphuric acid it will explode.**

4   Continue to top-up the cell with the freshly made electrolyte and then recharge the battery and check the hydrometer readings.

5   Battery charging

1   Under normal operating conditions there should be no need to charge a battery from an external source, and if it is found to be necessary either the battery or alternator is at fault.

2   When a vehicle has not been used for a period of time (particularly in very cold conditions) and it is found that the battery condition will not allow the engine to start, it is a good idea to charge the battery for about five hours at an initial charging current of around five amps (the amount of charge and charging time will obviously depend on the battery condition, but the charging current will fall as the battery charge builds up). Alternatively a trickle charge at an initial current of about 1.5 amps can safely be used overnight.

3   The use of rapid boost chargers, which are claimed to restore the full charge of a battery in a very short time, should be avoided if at all possible as the battery plates are likely to suffer damage.

6   Alternator - general description, maintenance and precautions

1   The alternator generates three-phase alternating current which is rectified into direct current by three positive and three negative silicone diode rectifiers installed within the end frame of the alternator.

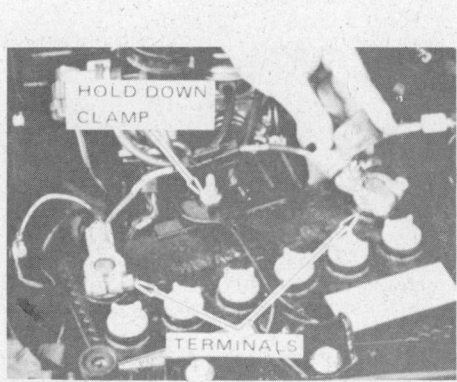

Fig. 10.1. Battery installation

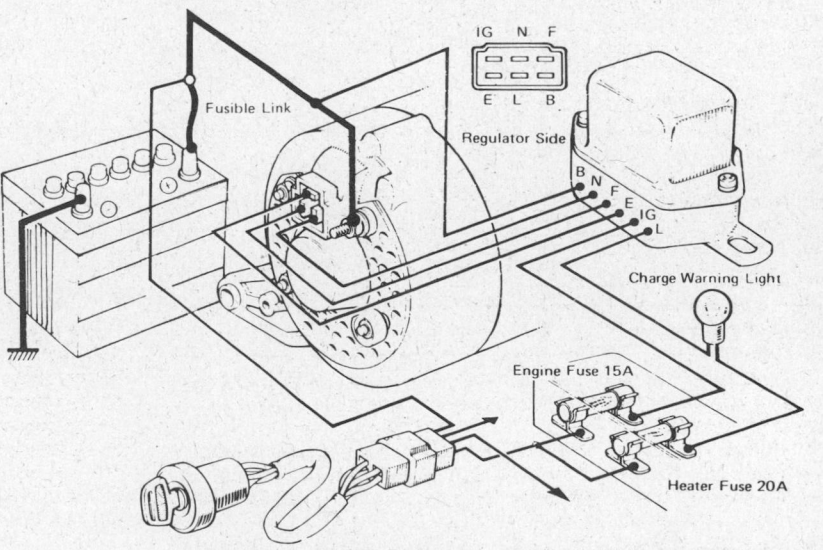

Fig. 10.2. Typical alternator connections

156

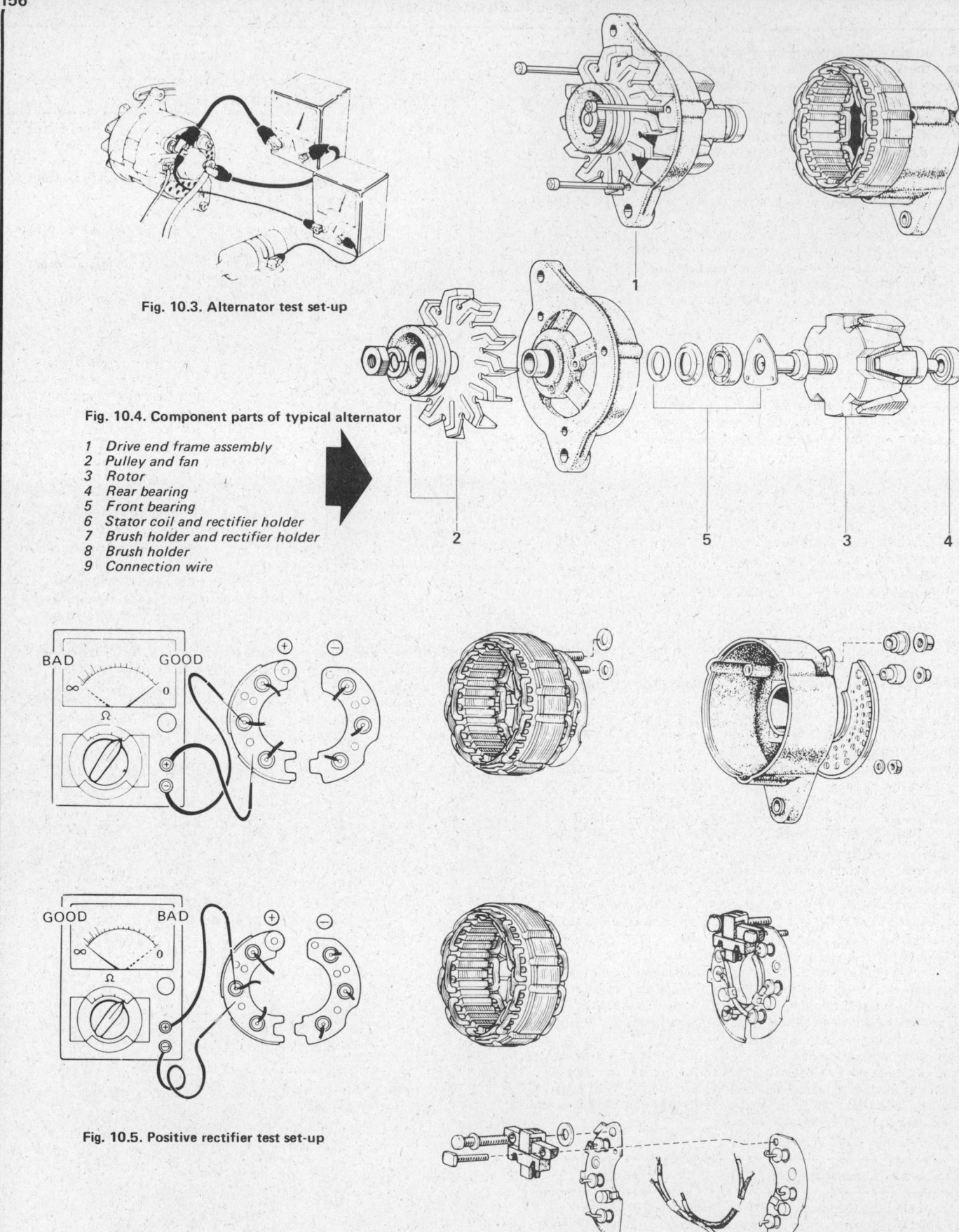

Fig. 10.3. Alternator test set-up

Fig. 10.4. Component parts of typical alternator

1 Drive end frame assembly
2 Pulley and fan
3 Rotor
4 Rear bearing
5 Front bearing
6 Stator coil and rectifier holder
7 Brush holder and rectifier holder
8 Brush holder
9 Connection wire

Fig. 10.5. Positive rectifier test set-up

2   A voltage regulator unit is incorporated in the charging circuit to control the exciting current and the current applied to the voltage coil.
3   Check the drivebelt tension every 6,000 miles (9,600 km) and adjust, as described in Chapter 2, by loosening the mounting bolts. Pull the alternator body away from the engine block; do not use a lever as it will distort the alternator casing.
4   No lubrication is required as the bearings are grease sealed for life.
5   Take extreme care when making circuit connections to a vehicle fitted with an alternator and observe the following.
6   When making connections to the alternator from a battery, always match correct polarity.
7   Before using electric-arc welding equipment to repair any part of the vehicle, disconnect the connector from the alternator and disconnect the earth battery terminal. Never start the car with a battery charger connected. Always disconnect the battery earth lead before using a mains charger. If boosting from another battery, always connect in parallel using heavy cable.

7   Alternator - testing in the car

1   In the event of failure of the normal performance of the alternator, carry out the following test procedure paying particular attention to the possibility of damaging the charging and electrical system unless the notes are observed.

   a) Ensure that the alternator output 'B' terminal is connected to the battery at all times. When the ignition switch is operated, the 'F' terminal is also at battery voltage.
   b) Never connect the battery leads incorrectly or the rectifiers and flasher unit will be damaged.
   c) Never run the engine at high revs with the alternator 'B' terminal disconnected otherwise the voltage at the 'N' terminal will rise abnormally and damage to the voltage relay will result.

2   Check the security of the alternator mountings, the terminal leads and the drivebelt tension (Chapter 2).
3   Check the turn signal and heater fuses, renew them if they are blown.
4   Switch on the vehicle radio and tune into a local transmitter. Start the engine and increase its speed from idling to 2000 rev/min. If a distinct humming sound is heard from the radio speaker then this indicates that the alternator rectifier is shorted or open.
5   Connect a voltmeter and ammeter to the alternator as shown in Fig. 10.3. Start the engine and gradually increase its speed to 2300 rev/min. The voltmeter should read between 13.8 and 14.8 volts and the ammeter under 10 amps. If the amperage is greater than the specified figure, the battery is either discharged or there is an internal short circuit. If the voltmeter needle fluctuates, the regulator contacts may be dirty or arced, or the alternator 'F' terminal may be loose.
6   If the voltage reading is too high then, (i) the regulator contact gaps may be too wide, (ii) there is an open circuit at the regulator and voltage relay coil, (iii) 'N' and 'B' regulator terminals are open and (iv) the regulator has a defective earth connection.
7   Switch off the engine and disconnect the wiring harness connecting plug. Turn on the ignition switch (engine **not** running), and measure the voltage between the 'F' and 'E' sockets of the connecting plug. This should be 12 volts. If the reading is low or zero, check for, (i) faulty fuse connection, (ii) open circuit 'F' and 'IG' terminals, or (iii) the regulator contact points fused together.
8   Repeat the tests described in the preceding paragraphs 5 and 6 but run the engine at only 1100 rev/min with all lights and accessories switched on; the ammeter reading should be in excess of 30 amps. If the reading is less than 30 amps it is indicative of open rectifiers, stator coil circuit or short circuited rectifiers.

8   Alternator - removal and refitting

1   Disconnect the lead from the battery negative terminal.
2   Loosen the alternator mounting bracket bolts and the adjustment link bolts and then push the alternator in towards the engine block so that the driving belt can be removed from the pulley.
3   Disconnect the electrical leads from the alternator terminals, remove the mounting bolts and lift the unit from its location.
4   Refitting is the reverse of the removal procedure; adjust the drive

belt tension as described in Chapter 2.

9   Alternator - dismantling, servicing and reassembly

1   Remove the three tie bolts which secure the two end frames together.
2   Insert screwdrivers in the notches in the drive end frame and separate it from the stator.
3   Hold the front end of the rotor shafts still with an Allen key and remove the securing nut, pulley, fan and spacer.
4   Press the rotor shaft from the drive end frame.
5   Remove the bearing retainer, bearing, cover and felt ring from the drive end frame.
6   Remove the rectifier holder and brush holder securing screws and detach the stator from the rectifier end frame.
7   Remove the brush lead and stator coil 'N' terminals from the brush holder by prising with a small screwdriver.
8   Test the rotor coil for an open circuit by connecting a circuit tester between the two slip rings located at the rear of the rotor. The indicated resistance should be from 4.1 to 4.3 ohms, but if this value is not obtained the coil is open and the rotor must be renewed as an assembly.
9   Now connect the tester between each slip ring in turn and the rotor shaft. If the tester needle moves then the rotor must be renewed as it is earthed.
10   Inspect the rotor bearing for wear and renew if necessary by removing it from the shaft with a two legged puller.
11   Clean the slip rings and rotor surfaces with a solvent moistened cloth.
12   Test the insulation of the stator coil by connecting the tester between the stator coil and the stator core. If the tester needle moves then the coil is earthed through a breakdown in the insulation, and must be renewed.
13   To test the stator coil for open circuit, the coil leads must be disconnected from the rectifier leads. Apply the soldering iron to the joint for the minimum time to prevent any heat travelling to the rectifier which is easily damaged.
14   Check the four stator coil leads for continuity. If the tester needle does not flicker then the coil has an open circuit and it must be renewed.
15   Testing of the rectifiers can be carried out using an ohmmeter as shown in Figs. 10.5 and 10.6. If unsatisfactory readings are obtained, the rectifier assembly must be renewed.

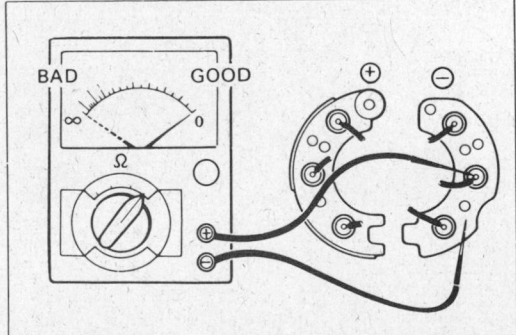

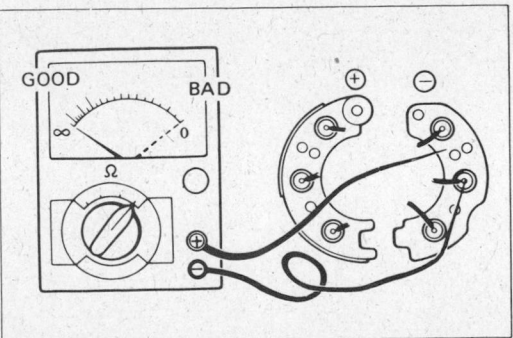

Fig. 10.6. Negative rectifier test set-up

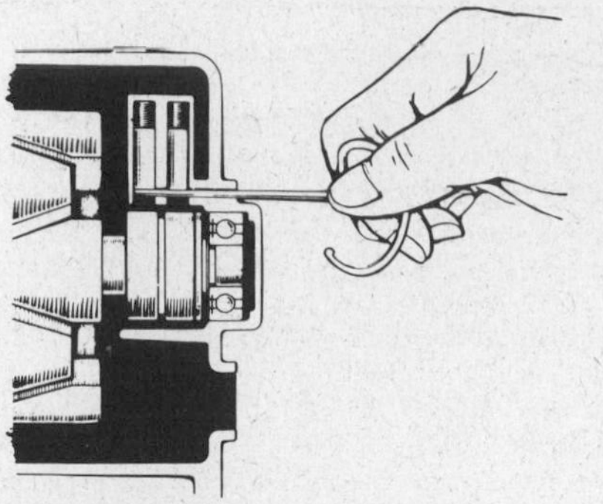

Fig. 10.7. Supporting the brushes during reassembly

Adjusting Arm

Contact Spring Deflection (PO)

Point Holder (P₁)

Point Holder (P₂)

Point Gap

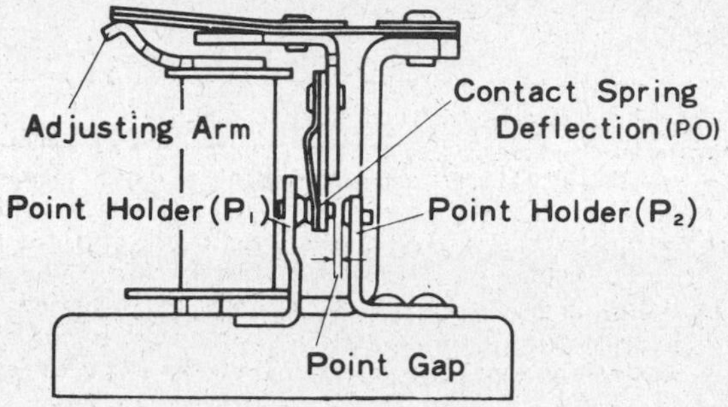

Fig. 10.9. Voltage relay

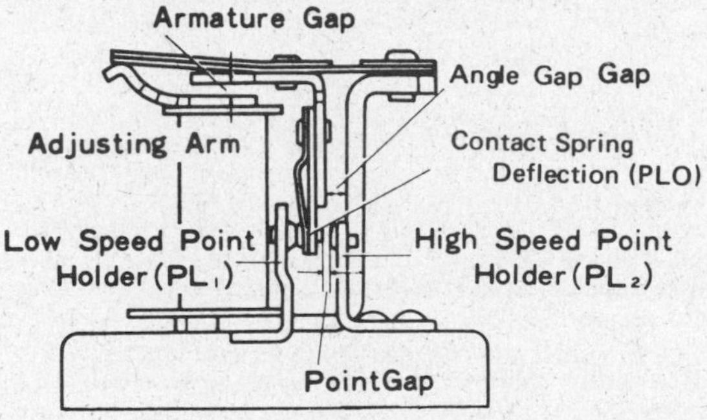

Fig. 10.8. Regulator terminal positions

Armature Gap

Angle Gap Gap

Adjusting Arm

Contact Spring Deflection (PLO)

Low Speed Point Holder (PL₁)

High Speed Point Holder (PL₂)

PointGap

Fig. 10.10. Regulator

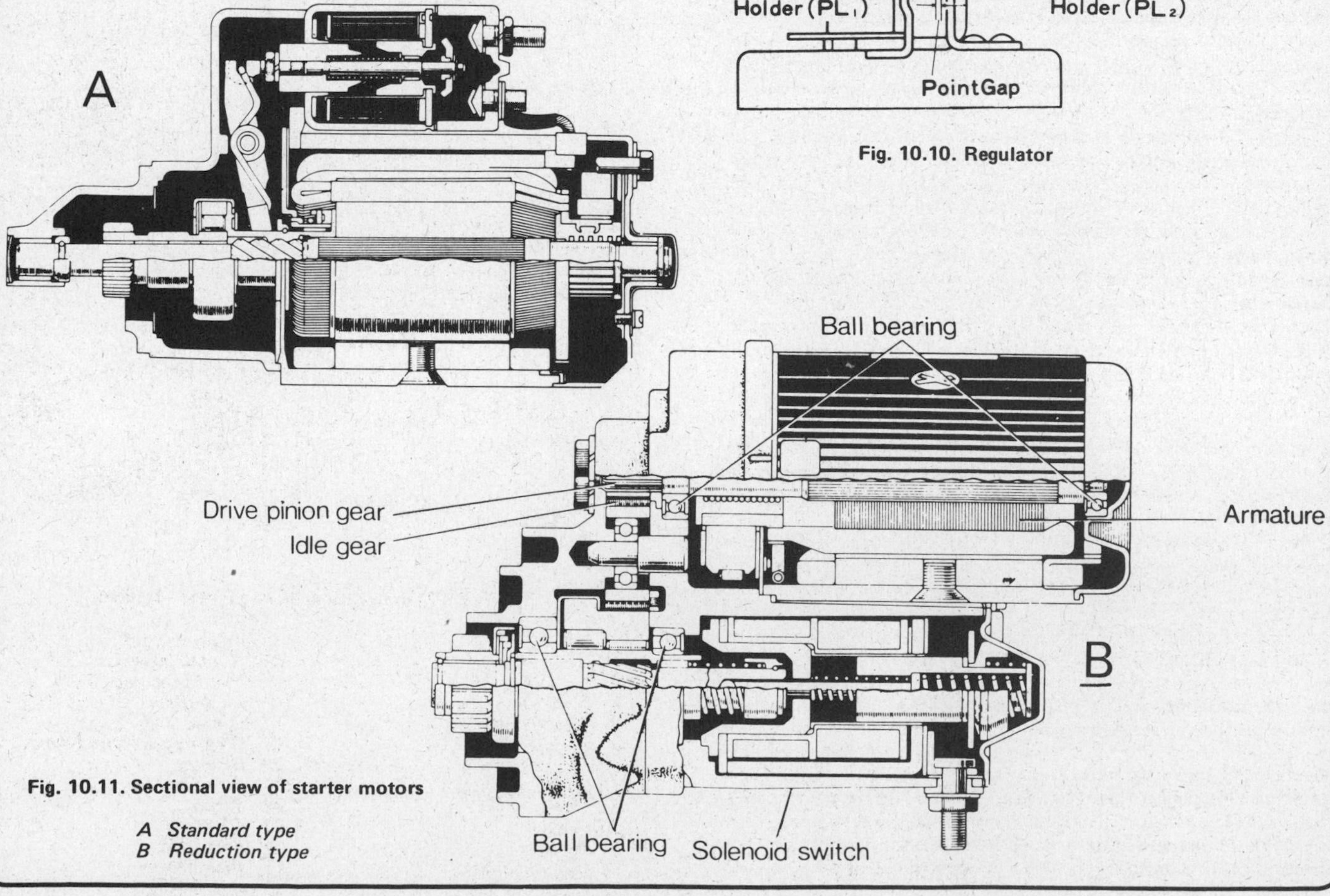

A

Ball bearing

Drive pinion gear

Idle gear

Armature

B

Fig. 10.11. Sectional view of starter motors

A Standard type
B Reduction type

Ball bearing   Solenoid switch

16 If more than one of the preceding tests proves unsatisfactory, it will be economically sound to exchange the alternator complete for a factory reconditioned unit rather than renew more than one individual component.

17 Finally, examine the brushes for wear. If they are less than the minimum specified length, renew them. Remove the old brushes and insert the new ones in their holders, checking to see that they slide freely. Ensure that the brush does not project more than 0.5 in (12.5 mm) from its holder and then solder the brush lead, cutting off any surplus wire.

18 Commence reassembly of the alternator by fitting the stator coil 'N' terminal to the brush holder, then a terminal insulator followed by the brush negative lead.

19 Fit the two insulating washers between the rectifier positive holder and the end frame and install the 'B' terminal and the retaining bolt insulators and secure the holder with its four retaining nuts. Secure the negative rectifier holder with its four nuts.

20 Fit the brush holder with its insulating plate and tighten the securing screws passing them through the terminal insulators. Locate the stator coil in the rectifier end frame.

21 To the drive end frame, fit the felt ring, cover (convex face to pulley) bearing (packed with multi-purpose grease) and bearing retainer (3 screws).

22 Fit the spacer ring to the rotor shaft and then press the drive end frame onto the shaft. Fit the collar, fan and pulley and tighten the securing nut to the specified torque.

23 Connect the drive end frame assembly to the rectifier end frame assembly and secure with the three tie bolts. Use a piece of wire to support the brushes in the raised position during this operation. (Fig. 10. 7).

10 Alternator regulator - testing and adjustment

1 Testing of the relay operating voltage and the regulator out-put voltage and amperage levels should be left to an auto-electrician as special equipment is needed. However, circuit testing and mechanical adjustments may be carried out in the following manner:

2 Disconnect the regulator connector plug. Remove the cover from the regulator unit and inspect the condition of the points. If they are pitted, clean with very fine emery cloth otherwise clean them with methylated spirit.

3 Connect a circuit tester between the 'IG' and 'F' terminals of the connector plug when no resistance should be indicated. If a resistance is shown, then the regulator points PL1 and PLO are making poor contact. Now press down the regulator armature and check the resistance which should be about 11 ohms. If it is much higher, the control resistance is defective and must be renewed.

4 Connect the circuit tester between the connector plug 'L' and 'E' terminals when no resistance should be indicated. If a resistance is shown then the contact points P1 and P0 are making poor contact. Press down the relay armature and check the resistance which should be about 100 ohms. If it is higher, the voltage coil has an open circuit or if lower, the points P1 and P0 are fused together or the coil is shorted.

5 Connect the circuit tester between the 'N' and 'E' terminals when a resistance of 25 ohms should be indicated. If the resistance is much higher, the pressure coil has an open circuit, if lower then it is short circuited.

6 Connect the circuit tester between the 'B' and 'L' terminals and depress the voltage relay armature. There should be no indicated resistance but if there is, this will show that the contact of the points P0 and P2 is poor.

7 Connect the circuit tester between the 'B' and 'E' terminals when the indicated resistance should be infinity. Where this is not so, the points P0 and P2 are fused together. Depress the relay armature and check the resistance which should be about 100 ohms. If the resistance is higher then the voltage coil has an open circuit and if lower it has a short circuit.

8 Connect the circuit tester between the 'F' and 'E' terminals when the indicated resistance should be infinity. Where this is not the case the points PLO and PL2 are fused together. Depress the regulator arm-ature and check the resistance which should be zero. If there is a resistance indicated on the tester then the points PLO and PL2 are making poor contact.

9 **With the connector plug still disconnected** carry out the following mechanical checks.

10 Refer to Fig. 10.9 and depress the voltage relay armature. Using a feeler gauge check the deflection gap between the contact spring and its supporting arm. This should be between 0.008 and 0.024 in (0.20 and 0.60 mm), if not, bend the contact point holder (P2). Release the armature and check the point gap which should be between 0.016 and 0.047 in (0.4 to 1.2 mm) if not, bend the contact point holder (P1).

11 Check the armature gap on the voltage regulator which should be in excess of 0.012 in (0.30 mm) otherwise bend the contact point holder PL2 to adjust (Fig. 10.10). Check the voltage regulator point gap which should be between 0.012 and 0.018 in (0.30 and 0.45 mm) otherwise bend the contact point holder PL2 to adjust. Depress the voltage regulator armature and check the deflection gap between the contact spring and its supporting arm. This should be between 0.008 and 0.024 in (0.2 and 0.6 mm). If not renew the regulator as an assembly. Finally depress the voltage regulator armature and check the angle gap at its narrowest point. This gap should not exceed 0.008 in (0.2 mm) otherwise renew the unit as an assembly.

12 Starter motor - testing in the car

1 If the starter motor fails to operate, check the state of charge of the battery by testing the specific gravity with a hydrometer or switching on the headlamps. If they glow brightly for several seconds and then gradually dim, then the battery is in an uncharged state.

2 If the tests prove the battery to be fully charged, check the security of the battery leads at the battery terminals, scraping away any deposits which are preventing a good contact between the cable clamps and the terminal posts.

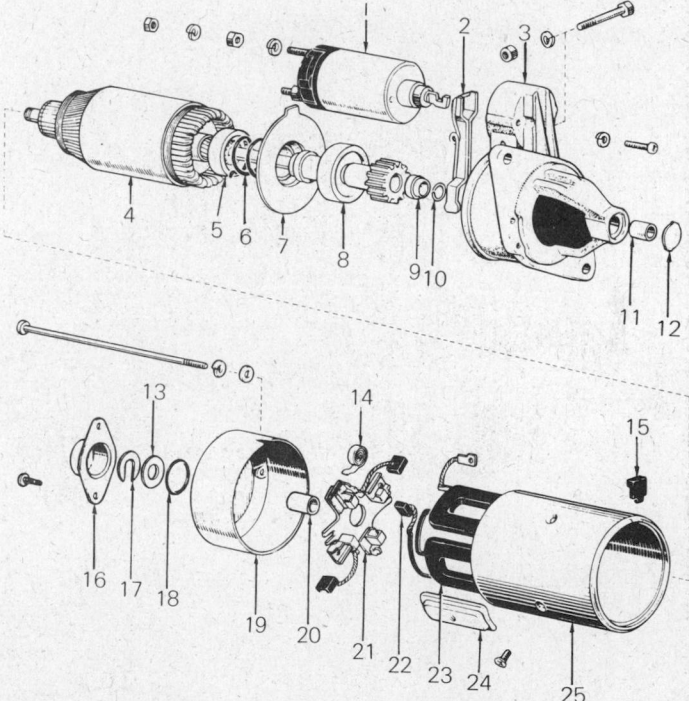

Fig. 10.12. Standard type starter motor - typical

1	Solenoid	14	Brush spring
2	Drive lever	15	Rubber plate
3	Drive housing	16	End frame cap
4	Armature	17	Lock plate
5	Spring holder	18	O-ring
6	Spring	19	Commutator end frame
7	Centre bearing	20	Bushing
8	Clutch assembly	21	Brush holder
9	Collar	22	Brush
10	Circlip	23	Field coil
11	Bushing	24	Pole shoe
12	Bushing cover	25	Field frame
13	Shim		

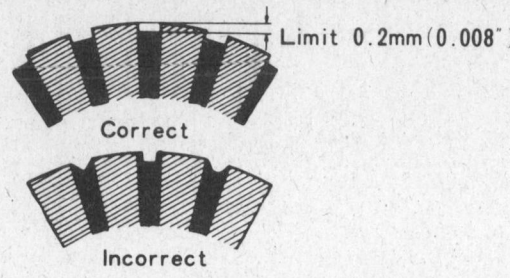

Fig. 10.13. Undercutting diagram for commutator segments

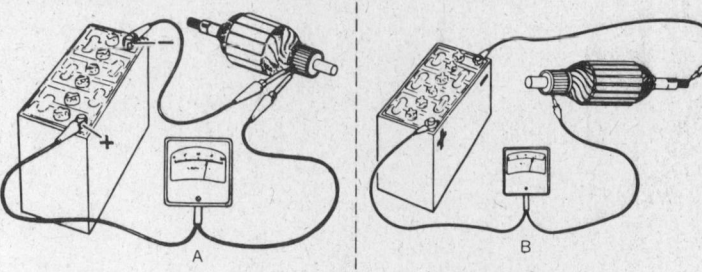

Fig. 10.14. Testing the starter motor armature for open circuit (A) and for insulation breakdown of windings (B)

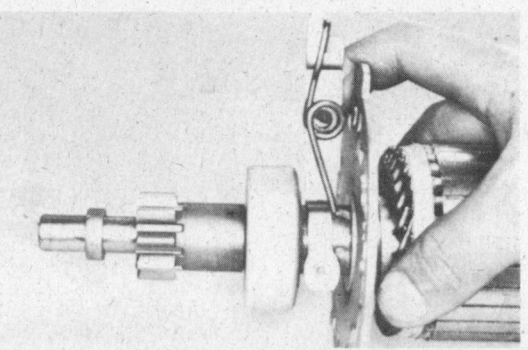

Fig. 10.15. Attaching the drive lever

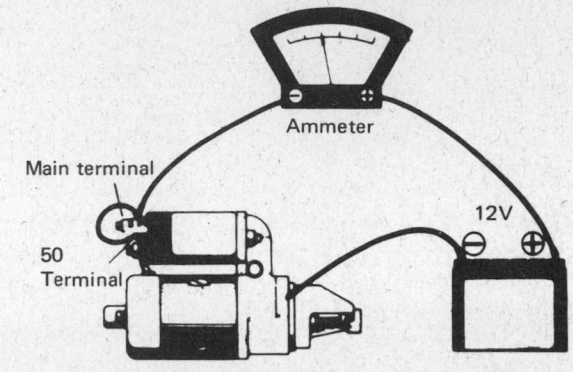

Fig. 10.16. Testing starter motor after reassembly

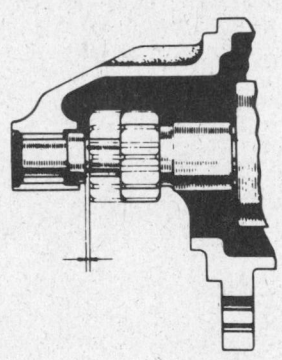

Fig. 10.17. Pinion to end stop clearance measuring point

Fig. 10.18. Exploded view of reduction gear type starter motor

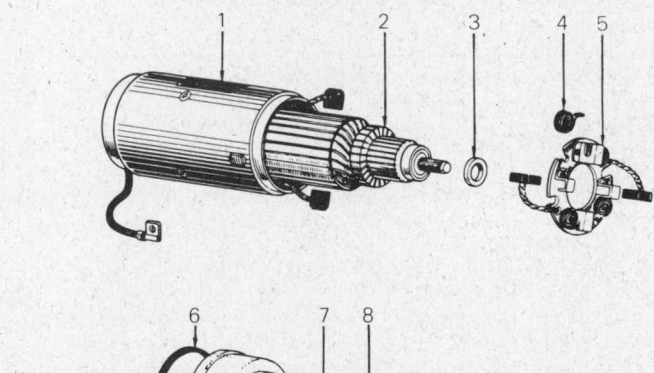

1 Field frame (yoke)	7 Pinion gear
2 Armature	8 Idler gear
3 Felt seal	9 Solenoid assembly
4 Brush spring	10 Steel ball
5 Brush holder	11 Clutch assembly
6 'O' ring	12 Reduction gear housing

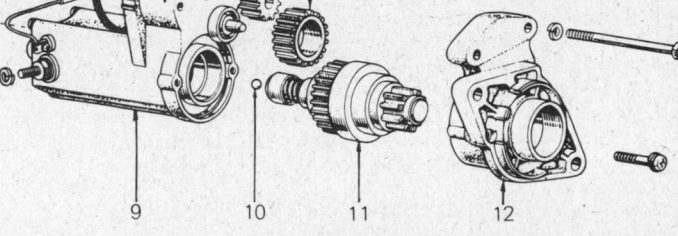

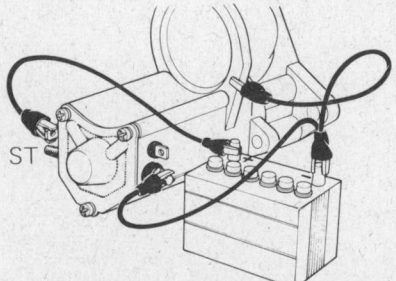

Fig. 10.19. Solenoid check for reduction type starter motor

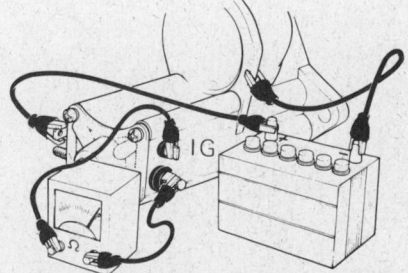

Fig. 10.20. Continuity check for reduction type starter motor

3   Check the battery negative lead at its body frame terminal, scraping the mating faces clean if necessary.
4   Check the security of the cables at the starter motor and solenoid switch terminals.
5   Check the wiring with a voltmeter for breaks or short circuits.
6   Check the wiring connections at the ignition/starter switch terminals.
7   If everything is in order, remove the starter motor as described in the next Section and dismantle, test and service as described later in this Chapter.

13 Starter motor - removal and refitting

1   Disconnect the lead from the battery negative terminal.
2   Disconnect the cables from the starter solenoid terminals.
3   Unscrew and remove the starter motor securing bolts and withdraw the unit from the clutch bellhousing (or torque converter housing - automatic transmission).
4   Refitting is the reverse of the removal procedure.

14 Starter motor (standard type) - dismantling

1   Disconnect the field coil lead from the starter solenoid main terminal.
2   Remove the two securing screws from the solenoid and withdraw the solenoid far enough to enable it to be unhooked from the drive engagement lever fork.
3   Remove the end frame cover, the lockplate, washer, spring and seal.
4   Unscrew and remove the two tie bolts and withdraw the commutator end frame.
5   Pull out the brushes from their holders and remove the brush holder assembly.
6   Pull the yoke from the drive end frame.
7   Remove the engagement lever pivot bolt from the drive end frame and detach the rubber buffer and its backing plate. Remove the armature, complete with drive engagement lever from the drive end frame.
8   With a piece of tubing, drive the pinion stop collar up the armature shaft far enough to enable the circlip to be removed and then pull the stop collar from the shaft together with the pinion and clutch assembly.

15 Starter motor (standard type) - servicing and testing

1   Check the armature end pole shoes for signs of rubbing; if this has occurred the drive housing and end frame bushes must be renewed. This can be done by prising out the bushing cover, pressing out the old bushes and pressing in new ones. These should then be reamed to provide the minimum specified armature shaft/bush clearance. Stake the bush in position.
2   Check the armature runout. if, necessary, this can be shimmed on a lathe to bring it within the specified limit.
3   Check the commutator segments and undercut the insulators if necessary, using a hacksaw blade ground to the correct thickness. If the commutator is burnt or discoloured, clean it with a piece of fine glass paper (not emery or carborundum) and finally wipe it with a solvent moistened cloth.
4   To test the armature is not difficult, but a voltmeter or bulb and 12 volt battery are required. The two tests determine whether there may be a break in any circuit winding or if any wiring insulation is broken down. Fig. 10.14 shows how the battery, voltmeter and probe connectors are used to test whether, (a) any wire in the windings is broken or, (b) whether there is an insulation breakdown. In the first test the probes are placed on adjacent segments of a clean commutator. All voltmeter readings should be similar. If a bulb is used instead, it will glow very dimly or not at all if there is a fault. For the second test, any reading or bulb lighting indicates a fault. Test each segment in turn with one probe and keep the other on the shaft. Should either test indicate a faulty armature the wisest action in the long run is to obtain a new starter. The field coils may be tested if an ohmmeter or ammeter can be obtained. With an ohmmeter the resistance (measured between the terminal and the yoke) should be 6 ohms. With an ammeter, connect it in series with a 12 volt battery, again from the field terminal to the yoke. A reading of 2 amps is normal. Zero (amps) or infinity (ohms) indicate an open circuit. More than 2 amps or less than 6 ohms indicates a breakdown of the insulation (Fig. 10.14). If a fault in the field coils

is diagnosed then a reconditioned starter should be obtained as the coils can only be removed and refitted with special equipment.
5   Check the insulation of the brush holders and the length of the brushes. If these have worn to below the minimum specified, renew them. Before fitting them to their holders, dress them to the correct contour by wrapping a piece of emery cloth round the commutator and rotating the commutator back and forth.
6   Check the starter clutch assembly for wear or sticky action, or chipped pinion teeth; renew the assembly, if necessary.

16 Starter motor (standard type) - reassembly

1   Fit the clutch assembly to the armature shaft followed by a new pinion stop collar and circlip. Pull the stop collar forward and stake the collar rim over the circlip. Grease all sliding surfaces.
2   Locate the drive engagement lever to the armature shaft as shown in Fig. 10.15 with the spring towards the armature and the steel washer up against the clutch.
3   Apply grease to all sliding surfaces and locate the armature assembly in the drive end frame. Insert the drive engagement lever pivot pin, well greased.
4   Fit the rubber buffer together with its backing plate, then align and offer into position the yoke to the drive end frame.
5   Fit the brush holder to the armature and then insert the brushes.
6   Grease the commutator end frame bearing then fit the end frame into position. Insert and tighten the tie bolts.
7   Fit the seal, washer lockplate and end cover (half packed with multi-purpose grease). Check the armature shaft endfloat, if this exceeds that given in the Specifications, remove the end cover and add an additional thrust washer.
8   Install the solenoid switch, making sure that its hook engages **under** the spring of the engagement lever fork.
9   Set up a test circuit similar to the one shown in Fig. 10.16, and check that the motor rotates smoothly at a current loading of less than 50 amps. With the solenoid switch energised, insert a feeler gauge between the end face of the clutch pinion and the pinion stop collar. This should be as given in the Specifications. If the clearance is incorrect, remove the solenoid switch and adjust the length of the adjustable hooked stud by loosening its locknut.
Note: During this test, the starter motor must be adequately supported due to the very high starting torque.

17 Starter motor (reduction type) - dismantling

1   Disconnect the leads from the solenoid.
2   Unscrew the two securing bolts and withdraw the field frame (yoke) complete with armature.
3   Extract the 'O' ring and the felt seal.
4   Remove the two securing screws and withdraw the reduction gear housing.
5   Withdraw the clutch assembly and gears.
6   Extract the ball from the hole in the end of the clutch shaft.
7   Pull out the brushes from the brush holder, remove the brush holder and withdraw the armature from the field frame (yoke).

18 Starter motor (reduction type) - servicing and testing

1   This procedure is similar to that described in Section 15 for the conventional type starter motor, except that ball bearing assemblies are used throughout. Any bearing which is stiff to rotate must be renewed.
2   To check the solenoid, connect up a test circuit as shown in Fig. 10. 19, and check that the plunger extends. Then disconnect the negative lead from the main terminal and check that the plunger remains extended. At this point there should be electrical continuity between the main and IG terminals (see Fig. 10.20).
Note: This test must be completed in less than 5 seconds to avoid overheating the coil.

19 Starter motor (reduction type) - reassembly

1   Apply high melting point grease to the armature rear bearing and then insert the armature into the field frame.

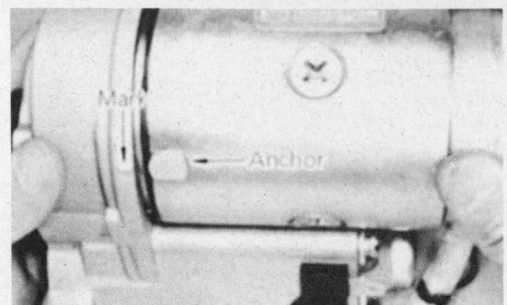

Fig. 10.21. Alignment mark for reassembly

Fig. 10.22. Fitting the clutch assembly

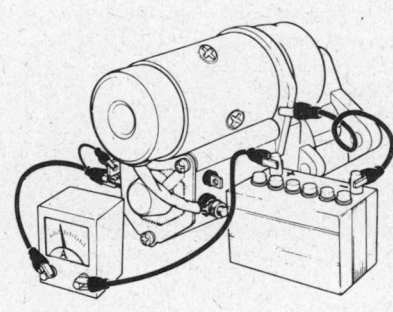

Fig. 10.23. Testing starter motor after reassembly

2 Install the brush holder, aligning its tab with the notch in the field frame.
3 Install the brushes into their holders and make sure that their leads are not earthed.
4 Fit the felt seal to the armature shaft and the 'O' ring to the field frame. Position the field coil leads towards the solenoid and install the field frame with armature to the solenoid housing, making sure that the raised bolt anchors are in alignment with the marks on the solenoid housing.
5 Apply grease and fit the starter pinion and idler gears.
6 Place a dab of grease into the clutch shaft hole and insert the ball.
7 Fit the clutch assembly.
8 Apply grease liberally to the gears, then install the reduction gear housing.
9 Set up a test circuit similar to that shown in Fig. 10.23, and check that the motor rotates smoothly at a current of less than 85 amps.
Note: During this test, the starter motor must be adequately supported due to the very high starting torque.

20 Headlights - removal and refitting

Lens unit
1 Remove the retaining screws and take off the headlight housing (saloon and estate) or radiator grille (coupe).
2 Loosen the three retaining ring screws, turn the retaining ring clockwise and pull out the assembly. Detach the lens unit connector.
3 Refitting is the reverse of the removal procedure.

Headlight assembly
4 Disconnect the battery earth cable, then remove the headlight housing as described in paragraph 1.
5 Remove the two screws and four bolts, and remove the headlight assembly.
6 Refitting is the reverse of the removal procedure.

21 Headlight beam - adjustment

Headlight beam adjustment is by means of the arrowed screws in Fig. 10.25. However, in view of the different regulations in different operating territories, it is impossible to give any specific adjustment procedure. If adjustment is considered to be necessary, either because the light pattern is inadequate or because other drivers 'flash' their headlights at you when driving at night, contact your Toyota dealer who will be able to do the job for you using optical alignment equipment.

22 Light lenses and bulbs - removal and refitting

1 Access to the front turn signal bulbs, sidelight bulbs, front side marker light bulbs and number plate light bulbs is by removal of the lens retaining screws. The bulbs are a bayonet fitting type.
2 The rear combination light bulbs for saloon and coupes are accessible

Fig. 10.24. Headlight removal screws (1)

Fig. 10.25. Headlight beam adjusting screws (arrowed)

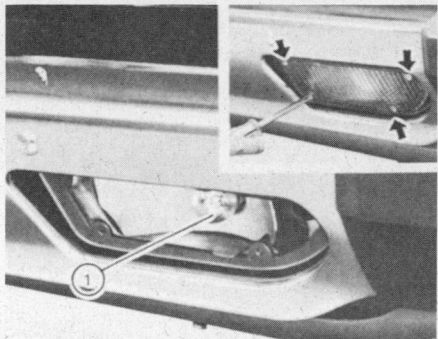

1 Front turn signals

2 Front side lights

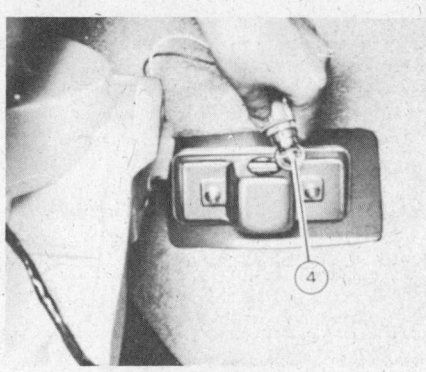

3 Front side marker lights

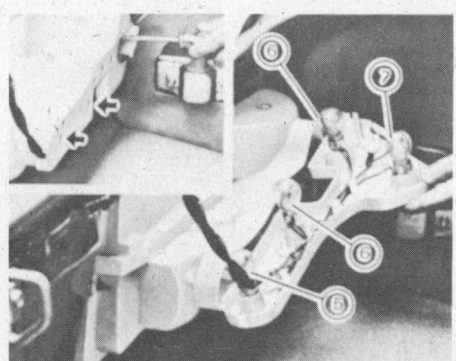

Saloon and Coupe

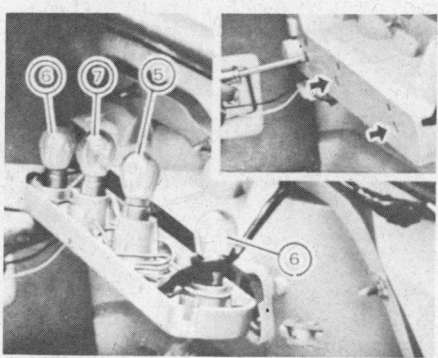

Saloon

4 Rear side marker lights

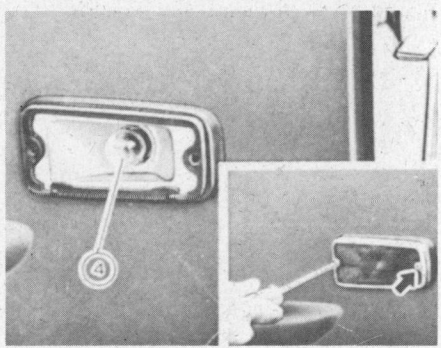

Estate

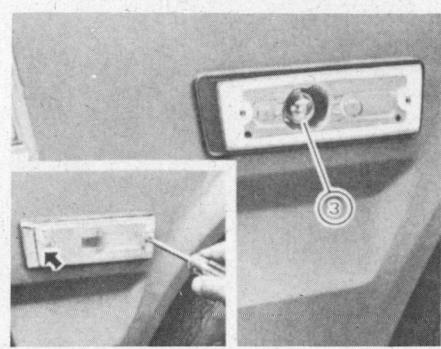

Coupe

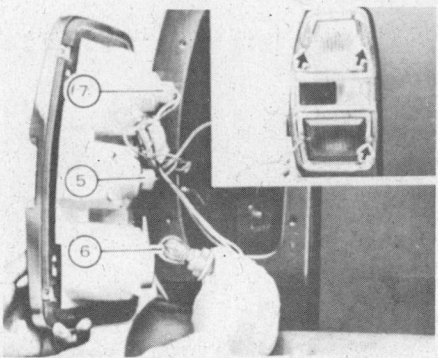

Estate

5, 6, 7 Rear turn signal, tail/stop and reverse lights

Fig. 10.26A. Light bulbs and lenses

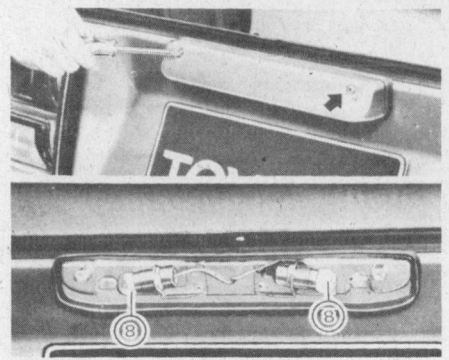

A Saloon and Coupe

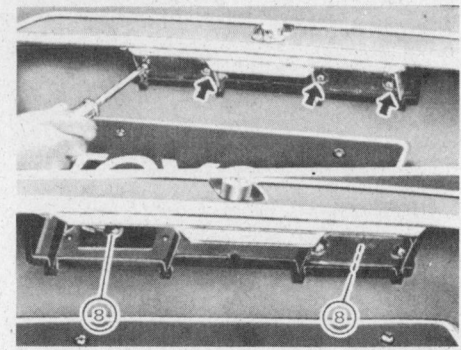

B Estate

8 Number plate lights

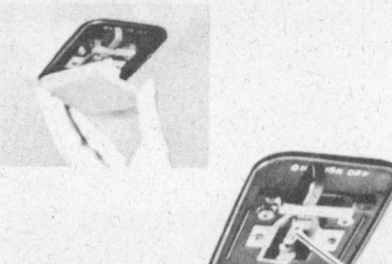

A Saloon and Estate

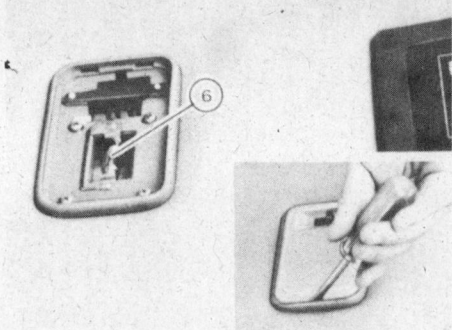

B Coupe

9 Interior light

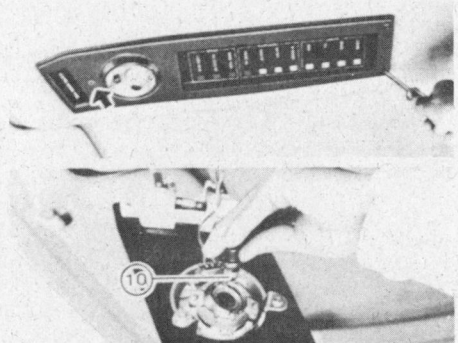

10 Front interior light - SR Coupe

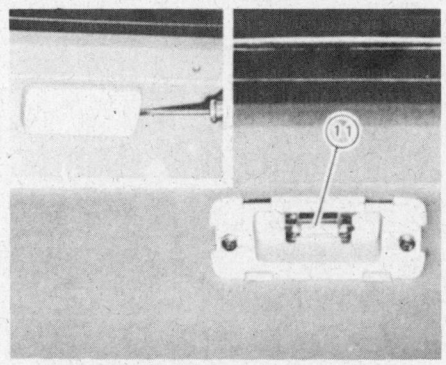

11 Rear interior light - Estate

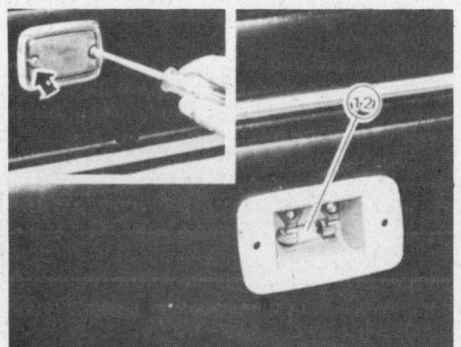

12 Door courtesy light - Coupe

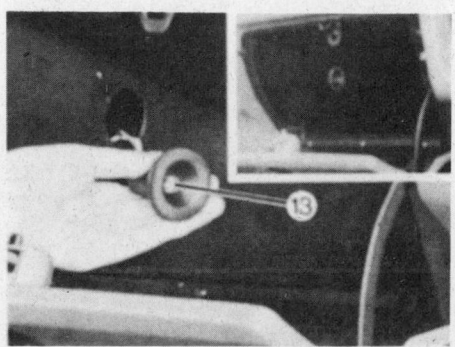

13 Glovebox light

Fig. 10.26B. Light bulbs and lenses

after the luggage boot rear trim panel is removed. They are in a plastic housing which is retained by crosshead screws. The bulbs are a bayonet fitting type.

3 The rear combination light bulbs for estate cars are only accessible after the four light unit retaining screws have been removed, and the assembly pulled out. The bulbs are a bayonet fitting type in separate retainers.

4 Access to the rear side marker light bulbs on estate cars is similar to that described for the front ones. On coupe and saloon models, the bulbs are accessible from inside the luggage compartment.

5 The interior light lenses are either removed by careful levering with a screwdriver, or by squeezing the lamp lens sides; the bulbs are festoon types. On coupe models with ESP, the three panel retaining screws must be removed for access to the miniature bulb.

6 Door courtesy light bulbs on coupes use a festoon type bulb, the lens being retained by two crosshead screws.

7 For access to the cigarette lighter bulb, remove the lighter as described in Section 24. Remove the bulb socket and take out the bulb.

8 To remove the instrument panel bulbs, remove the combination meter as described in Section 23. For non-tachometer models, remove the turn signal and speedometer pilot light bulbs; for tachometer models, remove the main beam indicator bulb and speedometer pilot light bulb. Remove the combination gauge assembly (Section 23) then remove the remaining bulbs as necessary.

23 Instruments and sender units - removal and refitting

Combination meter assembly

1 Disconnect the battery earth lead, then remove the instrument finish panel (refer to Chapter 12 if necessary).

2 Remove the side ventilator knob; on models which have a clock, also remove the clock knob.

3 Remove the five combination meter panel retaining screws.

4 Detach the speedometer cable and unplug the wire harness connector. Draw out the meter assembly.

5 Refitting is the reverse of the removal procedure.

Combination gauge assembly

6 Disconnect the battery earth lead, then remove the instrument finish panel (refer to Chapter 12 if necessary).

7 Remove the heater control indicator lens and the instrument centre panel (see Fig. 10.28). Remove the heater control indicator light.

8 Remove the instrument panel (4 screws), unplug the harness connector and remove the gauge assembly.

9 Refitting is the reverse of the removal procedure.

Speedometer

10 Remove the combination meter as previously described.

11 Remove the meter lens and screws, and take out the speedometer.

12 Refitting is the reverse of the removal procedure.

Fuel and water temperature gauges

13 Remove the combination gauge assembly or meter as previously described.

14 Remove the meter lens and take out the gauge.

15 Refitting is the reverse of the removal procedure.

Testing fuel and water temperature gauges

16 If an ohmmeter is available, check for a resistance of approximately 25 ohms when tested as shown in Fig. 10.33 or 10.34.

17 An alternative test is to connect a 12V, 3W bulb in series with the gauge, and apply 12 volts from a battery to the same terminals as in paragraph 16. The bulb should illuminate dimly and the pointer deflect smoothly.

Note: Do not apply battery voltage directly to the gauges.

Testing voltage stabilizer

18 If an ohmmeter is available, check for a resistance of approximately 120 ohms when tested as shown in Fig. 10.35.

19 An alternative test is to connect a 12V, 3W bulb in series with the voltage stabilizer, and apply 12 volts from a battery to the same terminals as in paragraph 18. The bulb should initially illuminate dimly then, after a short time, should extinguish.

Note: Do not apply battery voltage directly to the voltage stabilizer.

Oil pressure gauge and ammeter

20 Remove the combination gauge as previously described.

21 Remove the meter lens and take out the gauge. Note that the ammeter must be removed first if the oil pressure gauge is to be removed.

22 Refitting is the reverse of the removal procedure.

Testing oil pressure gauge

23 If an ohmmeter is available, check for a resistance of approximately 42 ohms when tested as shown in Fig. 10.36.

24 An alternative test is to connect a 12V, 3W bulb in series with the gauge, and apply 12 volts from a battery to the same terminals as in paragraph 23. The bulb should illuminate dimly and the pointer deflect smoothly.

Note: Do not apply battery voltage directly to the gauge.

Testing ammeter

25 To test the shunt-type ammeter, connect 12 volts from the battery *through* a 12V, 8W bulb. A reading of approximately 8 amps should be obtained.

Note: Do not apply battery voltage directly to the ammeter or use a bulb of a higher rating than 10W.

Tachometer

26 Remove the combination meter as previously described.

27 Remove the meter lens and five retaining screws, and take out the tachometer. Take care that it is not subjected to any vibration or shock loads when removed, or permanent damage may occur.

28 Refitting is the reverse of the removal procedure.

Testing water temperature sender

29 The sender can be checked in situ using an ohmmeter connected between the terminal and earth. At a water temperature of 50°C (122°F) the resistance should be approximately 136 ohms and at 105°C (221°F) should be approximately 23 ohms. Between these

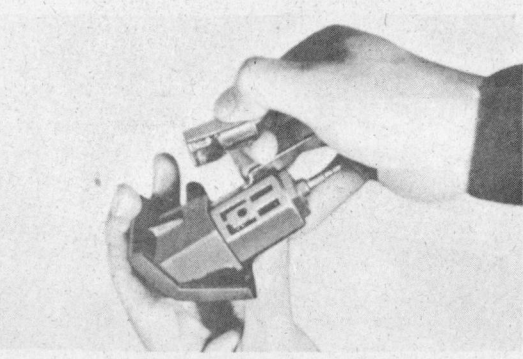

Fig. 10.27. Cigarette lighter light

Fig. 10.28. Heater control indicator light and centre panel screws (arrowed)

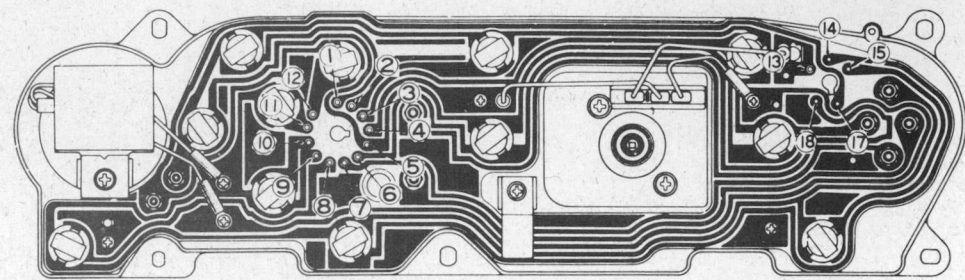

Fig. 10.29. Instrument panel connections

Top - Saloon
Saloon and Coupe
(left-hand drive)

1   Water temperature gauge
2   Right-hand indicator lamp
3   Left-hand indicator lamp
4   Main beam indicator lamp
5   Switch
6   Clock (+) door open indicator lamp
7   Handbrake indicator lamp
8   Spare/parking brake indicator light (Coupe)
9   Combination instrument (−)
10 Instrument lamp (+)
11 Ignition warning lamp
12 Switch
13 Seat belt indicator lamp
14 Seat belt indicator lamp
15 Oil pressure warning lamp
16 Fuel gauge (Saloon) spare (Coupe)
17 Combination instrument (+)
18 Door open indicator lamp

Bottom - Coupe
Saloon and Coupe
(right-hand drive)

1   Right-hand direction indicator lamp
2   Main beam warning lamp
3   Left-hand direction indicator lamp
4   Switch
5   Instrument lamp (+)
6   Combination instrument (−)
7   Fuel gauge
8   Spare (Saloon) handbrake indicator lamp (hardtop)
9   Combination instrument (+)
10 Ignition warning lamp
11 Oil pressure warning lamp
12 Door open indicator lamp (−)
13 Combination instrument (−)
14 Seat belt indicator lamp
15 Fuel contents warning lamp
16 Handbrake indicator lamp (Saloon) spare (Coupe)
17 Clock (+) door open indicator
18 Water temperature gauge

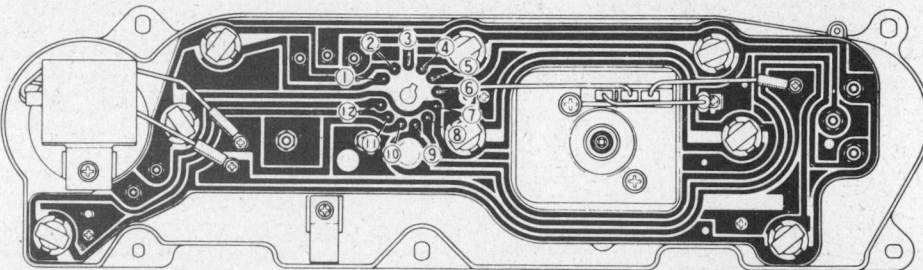

Fig. 10.30. Instrument panel connections - models with tachometer

Saloon and Coupe
(left-hand drive)

1   Right-hand direction indicator lamp
2   Tachometer
3   Left-hand direction indicator lamp
4   Main beam indicator lamp
5   Combination instrument (−)
6   Instrument lamp
7   Clock (+)
8   Switch
9   Handbrake 'ON' warning lamp
10 Combination instrument (+)
11 Spare
12 Fuel gauge

Saloon and Coupe
(right-hand drive)

1   Right-hand direction indicator lamp
2   Tachometer
3   Combination instrument (−)
4   Main beam indicator lamp
5   Left-hand direction indicator lamp
6   Switch
7   Instrument lamp (+)
8   Fuel gauge
9   Fuel warning lamp
10 Combination instrument (+)
11 Handbrake 'ON' warning lamp
12 Clock (+)

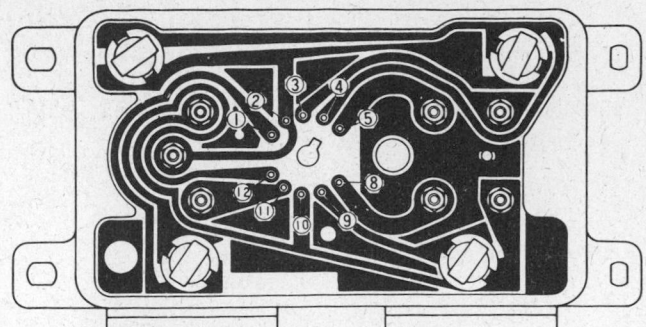

Fig. 10.31. Combination gauge assembly

Top - right-hand drive
RHD Terminal connections

1 Door open indicator lamp (—)
2 Combination instrument (—)
3 Oil pressure gauge
4 Instrument lamp (+)
5 Ammeter (+)
6 Spare
7 Spare
8 Ammeter (—)
9 Seat belt indicator lamp
10 Combination instrument (+)
11 Water temperature gauge
12 Door open indicator lamp (+)

Bottom - left-hand drive
LHD Terminal connections

1 Seat belt indicator lamp
2 Combination instrument (+)
3 Door open indicator lamp
4 Door open indicator lamp
5 Oil pressure warning lamp
6 Ignition warning lamp
7 Spare
8 Instrument lamp
9 Spare
10 Spare
11 Combination instrument (—)
12 Water temperature gauge

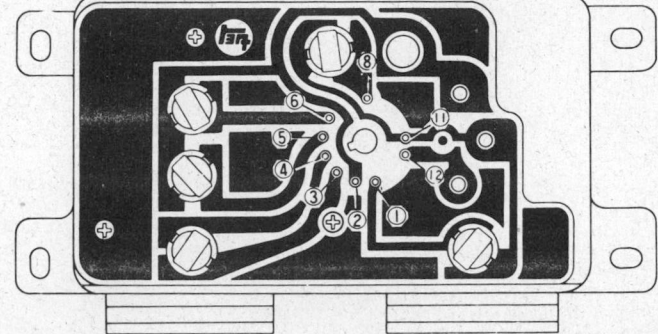

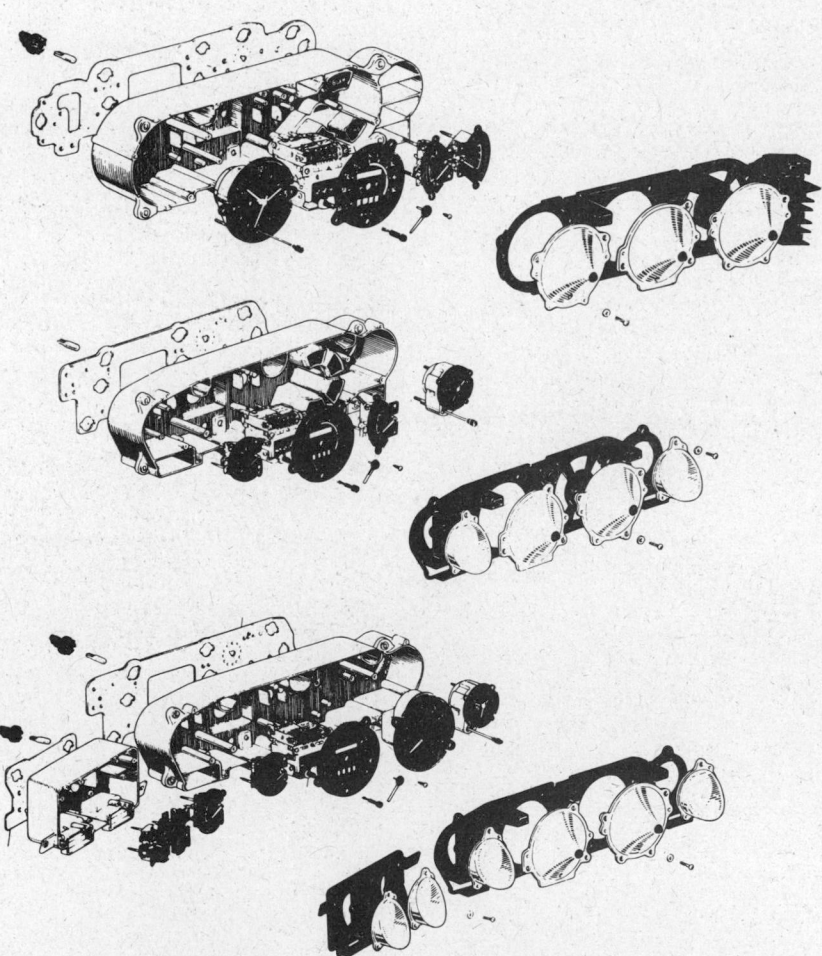

Fig. 10.32. Instruments used on different models

temperatures the resistance will alter accordingly.

Testing fuel tank sender

30 The sender can be checked in situ using an ohmmeter connected between the terminal and earth. With fuel tank empty, a resistance of approximately 120 ohms should be obtained; at half full, the resistance should be approximately 45 ohms; when full, the resistance should be approximately 17 ohms.

Testing fuel level warning switch

31 With the fuel tank empty and the ignition switched on, there should be a voltage of 5 to 6 volts at the level switch terminals. With the fuel tank full, this voltage should be 11 to 12 volts.

Testing oil pressure switch

32 On vehicles with a warning light, a continuity tester should show a closed circuit between the switch terminal and earth when the engine is not running. When the engine is started the switch contacts should open.

33 On vehicles with a pressure gauge, an ohmmeter should indicate an open circuit between the switch terminal and earth when the engine is not running. With the engine idling there should be a high resistance which decreases when the engine speed is increased.

---

24 Switches - removal and refittings

Steering column combination switch assembly

1 This procedure is given in Chapter 11, Section 15.

Heater blower switch

2 Remove the retaining screws and take out the glove compartment (disconnect the harness connector first).

3 Remove the heater blower switch from the base of the heater.

4 Refitting is the reverse of the removal procedure.

Defogger switch

5 With the hand behind the fuse box, push the switch outwards.

6 Refitting is the reverse of the removal procedure.

Automatic transmission neutral safety switch

7 Remove the control shaft lever.

8 Fold back the tab of the lock washer, then remove the nut and bolt (Fig. 10.40).

9 Pull out the switch and turn it through 180° to remove it. Do not remove it from the shaft or damage the shaft.

10 Refitting is the reverse of the removal procedure, but care should be taken over the following points.

    a) Clamp the breather hose to the throttle cable taking care that the hose is not kinked.

    b) Adjust the switch within a 4° range so that the switch groove will be aligned with the neutral basic line (Fig. 10.40).

Courtesy light switch

11 Pull back the rubber switch cover, and remove the switch from the mounting point.

12 When refitting, install the switch then use a Philips-head screwdriver to press in the retaining pegs of the switch cover.

Cigarette lighter

13 Disconnect the battery earth cable.

14 Push up the lighter base and release the two claws so that the base can be removed.

15 Unplug the connector, then remove the locknut and take the lighter out of the case.

16 Refitting is the reverse of the removal procedure, but ensure that the pilot light is diagonally upward from the right (Fig. 10.42).

Fig. 10.33. Testing fuel gauge

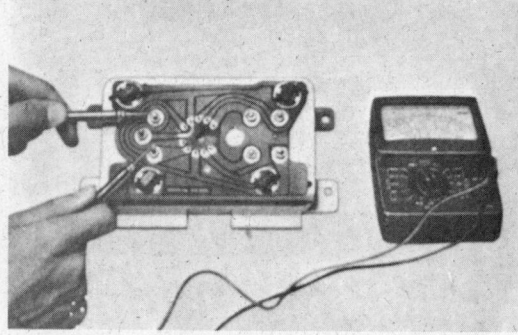

Fig. 10.34. Testing water temperature gauge

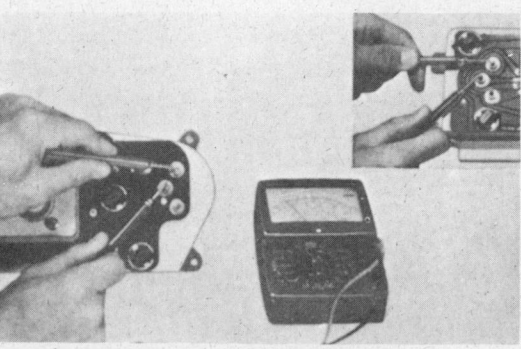

Fig. 10.35. Testing voltage regulator

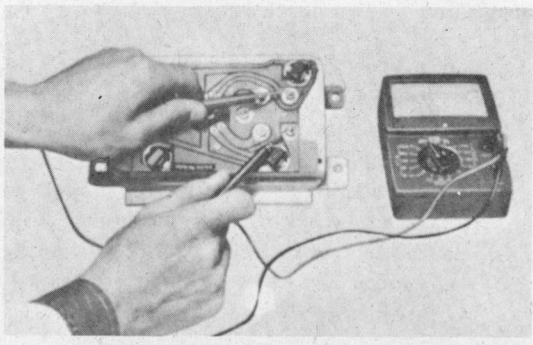

Fig. 10.36. Testing oil pressure gauge

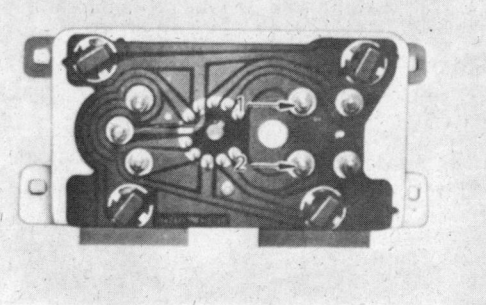

Fig. 10.37. Test terminals (1 and 2) for ammeter

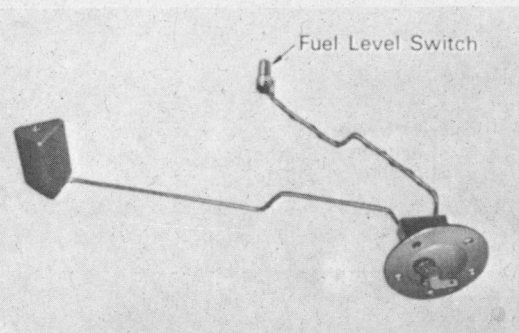

Fuel Level Switch

Fig. 10.38. Fuel tank sender and level switch

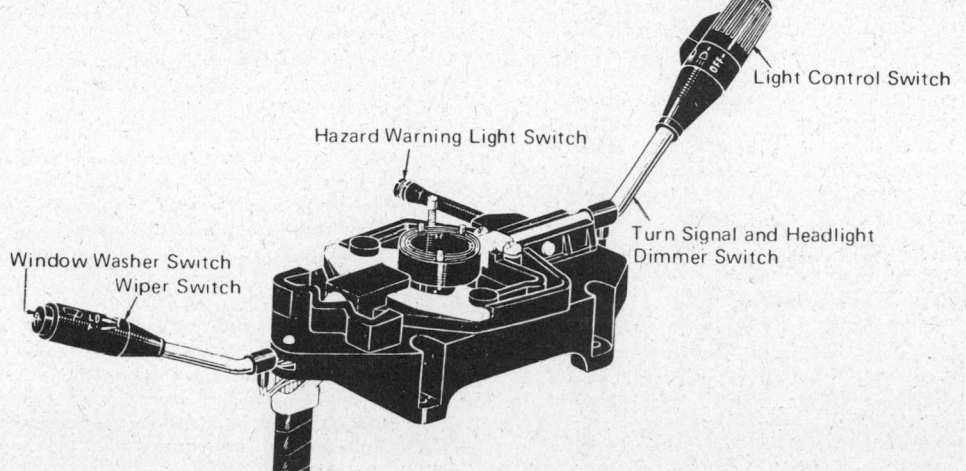

Hazard Warning Light Switch

Light Control Switch

Turn Signal and Headlight Dimmer Switch

Window Washer Switch
Wiper Switch

Fig. 10.39. Steering column combination switch

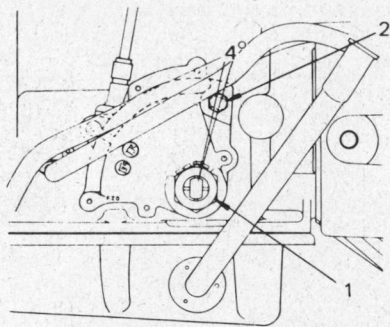

Fig. 10.40. Neutral safety switch

1 Nut   2 Bolt

Fig. 10.41. Removing the cigarette lighter

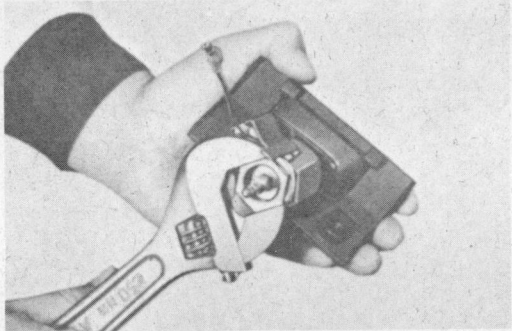

Fig. 10.42. Installing the cigarette lighter

25 Electrical relays - description and testing

1   A number of relays are fitted to the vehicle and their locations
are illustrated. Each relay is of sealed type and cannot be repaired but
must be renewed if, after carrying out the tests described in this
Section, it is proved to be faulty (Fig. 10.43).

Tail light relay

2   With the connector securely plugged into the relay, short circuit the
'Ts' terminal to earth. The relay should be heard to operate and the
tail light illuminate if the unit is in good order.

Headlight relay

3   With the connector securely plugged into the relay, short circuit
tne 'HS' terminal to earth. The relay should be heard to operate and the
headlights should illuminate. If the relay is inoperative, check that
battery voltage is applied across the terminals 'TB' and 'HB'.

Main relay

4   Turn the ignition switch on and listen for the points closing within
the relay.
5   Connect battery voltage to terminal 3 and earth. There should be
continuity between terminals (1) and (2) (Fig. 10.44).

26 Fuses and fusible link

1   The fuse block is located under the facia panel. The fuse ratings
and circuits protected vary according to model and date of manufacture but the fuse block is clearly marked and the cover incorporates
two spare fuses.
2   In the event of a fuse blowing, always find the reason and rectify
the trouble before fitting the new one. Always replace a fuse with one
of the same amperage rating as the original.
3   A double protection is provided for the electrical harness by a
fusible link installed in the lead running from the battery positive
terminal. The fusible link must never be by-passed and, should it
melt, the cause of the circuit overload must be established before
renewing the link with one of similar type and rating. On some
vehicles ammeter fuses are incorporated.

27 Hazard warning and direction indicator lamps

1   If the flashers fail to work properly first check that all the bulbs are
serviceable and of the correct wattage. Then check that the nuts which
hold the lamp bodies to the car are tight and free from corrosion.
These are the means by which the circuit is completed and any
resistance here could affect the proper working of the coils in the
flasher unit.
2   Check the security of all leads after reference to the appropriate
wiring diagram.
3   If everything is in order then the unit must be faulty and as it
cannot be repaired, it must be renewed. The unit is located beneath
the facia panel.

28 Electro sensor panel (ESP) - description

1   This is a system of transmitter switches, a computer and a warning
light panel which indicate to the driver immediately there is a
failure in any component or drop in fluid level, pressure or vacuum
conditions which is likely to affect the safety of the vehicle. It is only
fitted to SR and SR-5 coupe (hardtop) models.
2   The warning lamp panel is mounted in the roof interior lining and
indicates the following conditions:

   i)   Failure of rear licence plate, stop and tail lamps, also headlights.
   ii) Low levels in the radiator, engine, battery, windscreen, washer,
        brake fluid reservoir.
   iii) Low vacuum pressure in the brake servo unit.
   iv) Front disc pads worn below specified limit.
   v)   High engine oil temperature.

3   Whenever one of the indicator bulbs lights up, investigate the reason
and rectify it at once.
4   Any failure of a section of the system should be checked out by
first testing the bulb and the connecting wiring. The transmitter
switches are not repairable, and where tests of the circuit have proved
satisfactory, the transmitter switch must be renewed (see next Section).

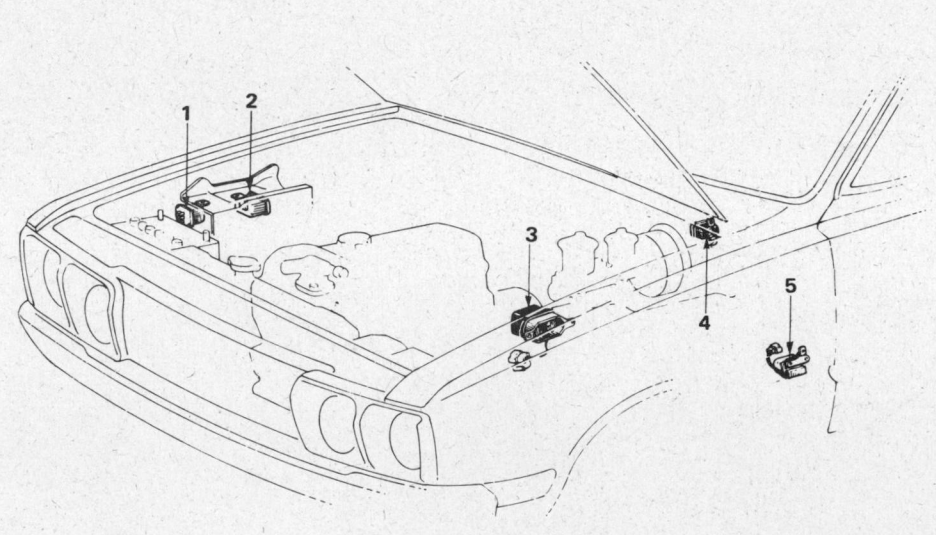

Fig. 10.43. Location of relays

1	Tail light control relay	4 Turn signal flasher
2	Horn relay	5 Main relay
3	Alternator regulator	

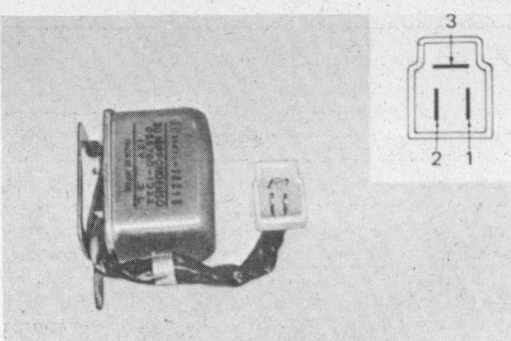

Fig. 10.44. Main relay

Fig. 10.45. Fuse box

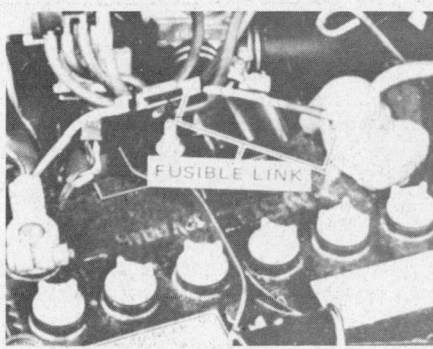

Fig. 10.46. Fusible link

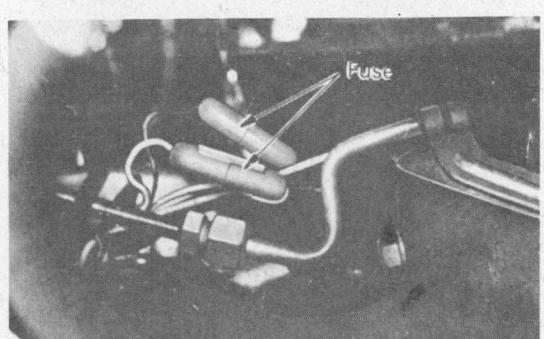

Fig. 10.47. Ammeter fuses

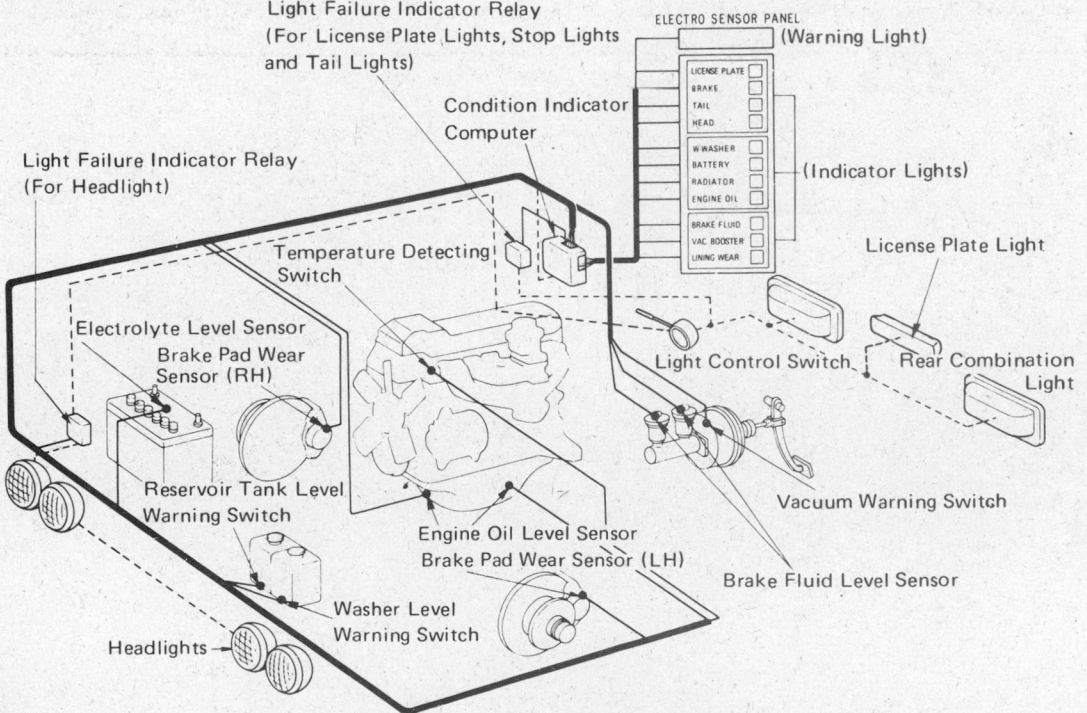

Fig. 10.48. Electro sensor panel components

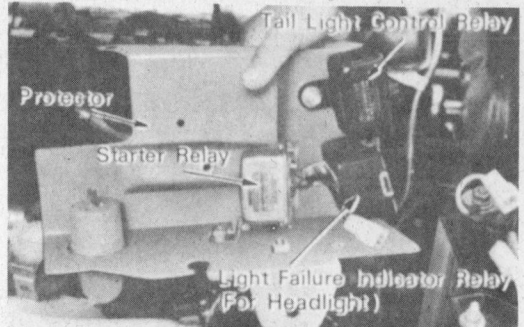

Fig. 10.49. Headlight failure indicator relay

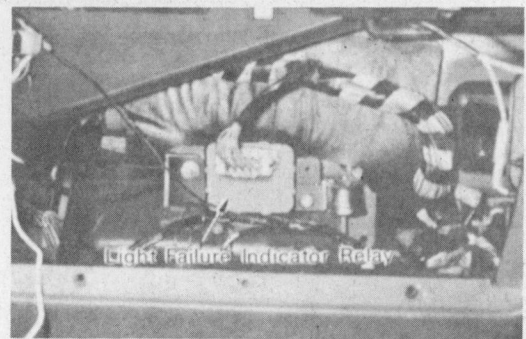

Fig. 10.50. Rear light failure indicator relay

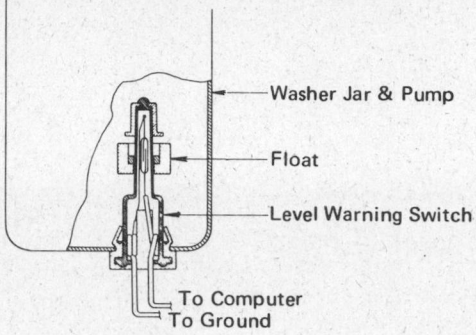

Fig. 10.51. Washer level warning switch

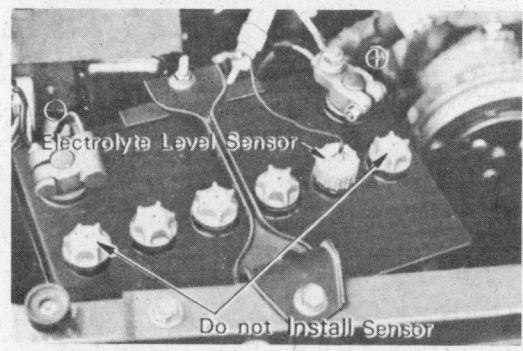

Fig. 10.52. Electrolyte level sensor

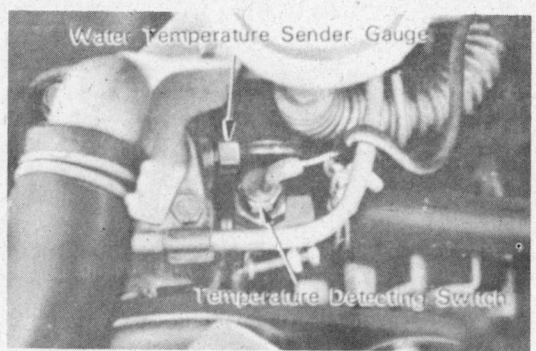

Fig. 10.53. Temperature detecting switch

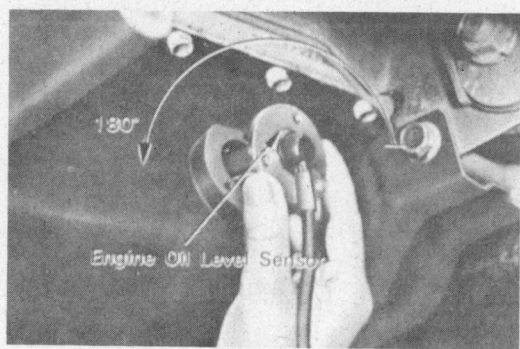

Fig. 10.54. Engine oil level sensor

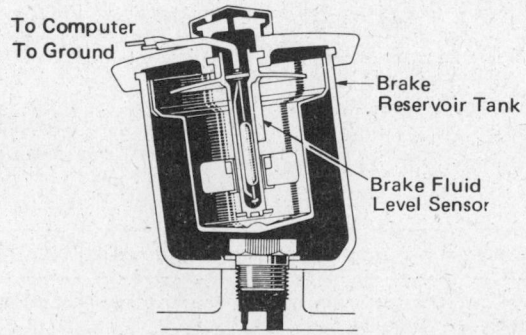

Fig. 10.55. Brake fluid level sensor

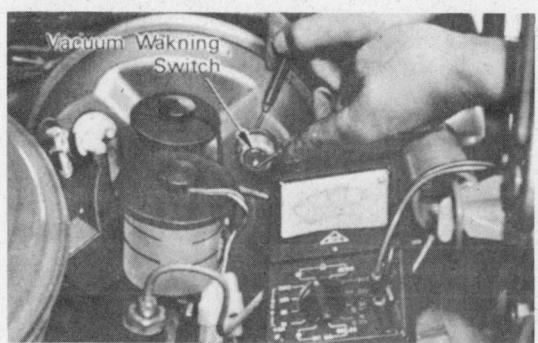

Fig. 10.56. Vacuum warning switch

29 Electro Sensor Panel (ESP) components - removal, refitting and checking

Warning light and condition indicator panel

1 Disconnect the battery earth cable.
2 Take off the overhead console cluster and warning light.
3 Remove the retaining screws to release the condition indicator panel.
4 Refitting is the reverse of the removal procedure.

Condition indicator computer (OK monitor)

5 Disconnect the battery earth cable.
6 Remove the left-hand side cowl-trim, then unplug the harness connector.
7 Remove the retaining screws to release the computer.
8 Refitting is the reverse of the removal procedure.

Headlight failure indicator relay

9 Disconnect the battery earth cable.
10 Remove the fender apron wire harness protector and take out the relay.
11 If a continuity tester is available the relay can be checked by disconnecting the 17-pin harness connector to the computer, and connecting the indicator relay connector. There should be continuity between terminals 5 and 8 with the headlights on, but no continuity with the headlights off. If necessary, with the indicator relay removed, continuity can be checked at the following relay terminals: 1 - 2, 3 - 4, 3 - 7, 5 - 3 (one direction only), 5 - 6 (one direction only), 6 - 7.
12 Refitting is the reverse of the removal procedure.

Rear light failure indicator relay

13 Remove the retaining screws and take out the glove compartment (disconnect the harness connector first).
14 Disconnect, then detach, the indicator relay.
15 If a continuity tester is available the relay can be checked by disconnecting the 17-pin harness connector to the computer, and connecting the indicator relay connector. There should be continuity between terminal 6 and the relay body, and between terminal 7 and 8 and the body when the lights are on, but no continuity with the light off. If necessary with the indicator relay removed, continuity can be checked at the following relay terminals: 1 - 6 (one direction only), 3 - 7 (one direction only), 4 - 8 (one direction only), 1 - 5, 2 - 3, 2 - 4, 5 - relay body, 2 - relay body.
16 Refitting is the reverse of the removal procedure.

Radiator level warning switch

17 The switch, mounted in the radiator reservoir, can be checked for continuity between the terminals when the level is above the switch.

Washer level warning switch

18 The switch, mounted in the washer reservoir, can be checked for continuity between the terminals when the level is above the switch.

Battery electrolyte level sensor

19 Detach the sensor connector, and unscrew the sensor from the battery.
20 With the sensor removed, there should be continuity between the sensor probe and the connector.
21 Refitting is the reverse of the removal procedure. Ensure that the sensor never contacts either of the battery terminals, and that it is only refitted in one of the four middle battery cells.

Temperature detecting switch

22 Detach the sensor connector, and unscrew the switch from the cylinder head.
23 With the switch removed, the phial can be immersed in a heated oil bath and a continuity check made between the terminal and switch body. The switch circuit should be broken between 60 and 105°C (140 and 221°F), made below 60°C (140°F) and made above 105°C (221°F).
24 Refitting is the reverse of the removal procedure, but apply a little non-setting sealant to the screw threads.

Engine oil level sensor

25 Remove the drain plug and drain the oil into a container of suitable size.
26 Remove the wiring clips and unplug the connector.
27 Remove the retaining screws, pull the sensor out a little then raise it a little, turn it 180° anticlockwise and withdraw it.
28 The sensor can be checked with a continuity tester. There should be continuity between the body and the connector when the float is moved to about the mid-travel position.
29 Refitting is the reverse of the removal procedure. Apply a little non-setting sealant to the flange and block faces, after ensuring that they are clean. If the bolts need renewing, only use the correct Toyota part number bolts.

Brake fluid level sensor

30 Detach the sensor connector(s), then check that there is continuity between the sensor leads when there is adequate brake fluid in the reservoir.
31 Gradually pull up the sensor(s) and check that when raised slightly there is still continuity.

Vacuum warning switch

32 With the engine stopped, pump the brake pedal several times to release all the vacuum from the brake servo. Unplug the harness connector to the switch and check that there is continuity between the switch body and connector terminal.
33 Start the engine and allow it to idle, then check again for continuity between the switch body and connector terminal.

Brake pad wear sensor

34 Remove the wire harness clip and unplug the connector.
35 Remove the brake pad as described in Chapter 9, then detach the sensor from the pad.
36 If the sensor is serviceable, there should be continuity between the harness connector terminals.
37 Refitting is the reverse of the removal procedure; refer to Chapter 9 for refitting the brake pad.

---

30 Windscreen wiper arms and blades - removal and refitting

1 The wiper blades can be removed by unscrewing the two small crosshead screws at the ends of the wiper arms.
2 To remove a wiper arm, remove the retaining nut on the spindle, then carefully prise off the splined fitting from the spindle. When refitting, position the arm to give a satisfactory wiping sweep before tightening the nut.

---

31 Windscreen wiper motor and linkage - removal and refitting

1 Unplug the harness connector then remove the service hole cover from the engine compartment bulkhead.
2 Remove the four mounting bolts, then slide back the protective cover and carefully prise off the wiper link.
3 Remove the wiper arms as described in the previous Section, then remove the link assembly.

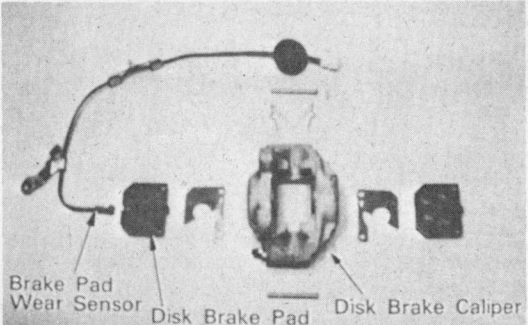

Fig. 10.57. Brake pad wear sensor and associated parts

Brake Pad Wear Sensor   Disk Brake Pad   Disk Brake Caliper

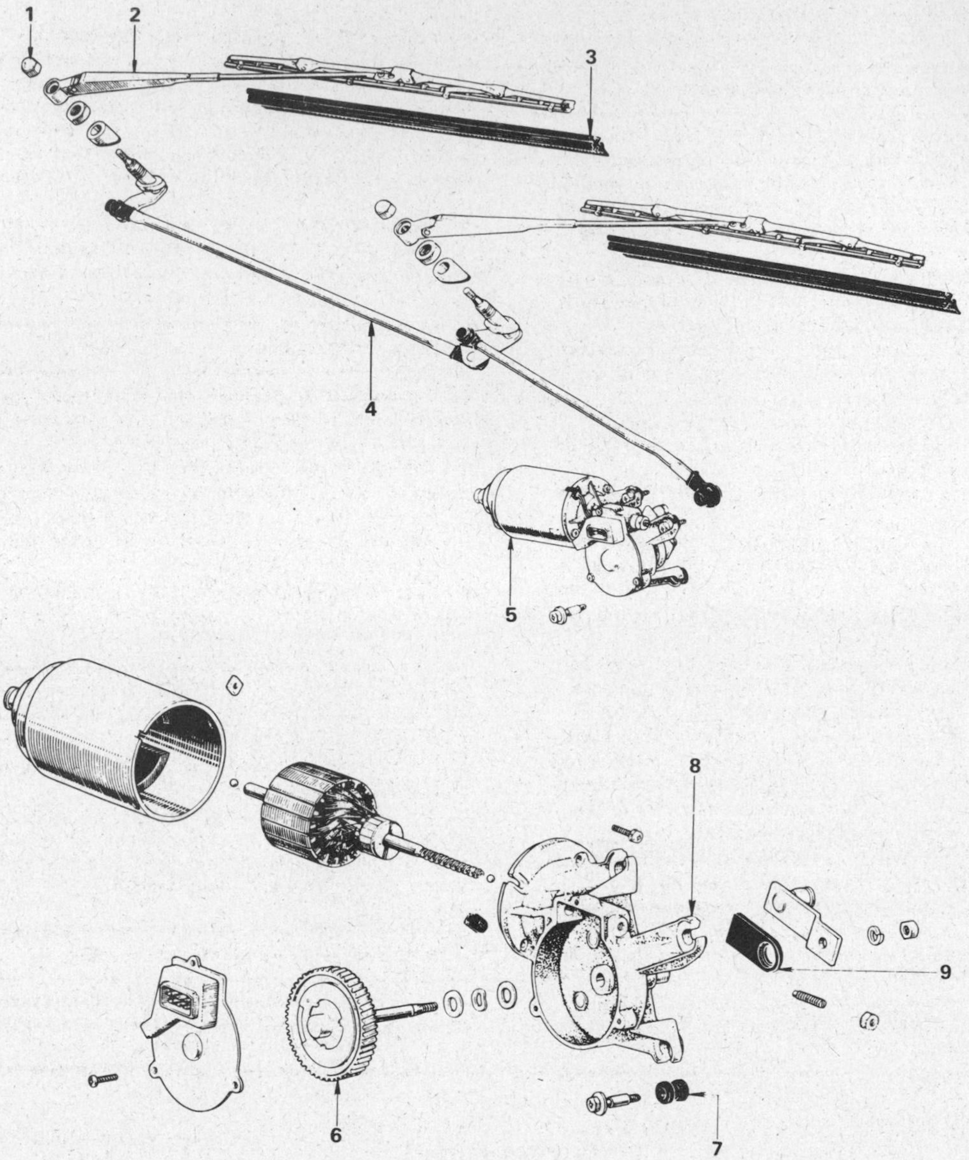
1
2
3
4
5
8
9
6
7

Fig. 10.58. Wiper motor and linkage

1 *Nut*
2 *Wiper arm*
3 *Blade*
4 *Wiper link*
5 *Wiper motor*
6 *Gear*
7 *Housing cover bushing*
8 *Housing*
9 *Cover seat*

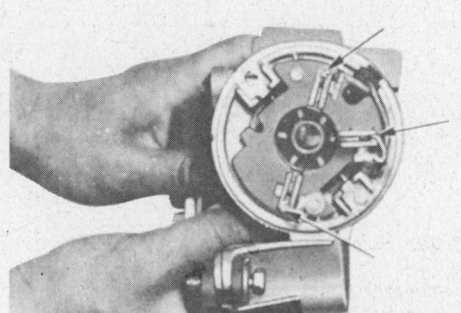

Fig. 10.59. Installing the brushes (see arrows)

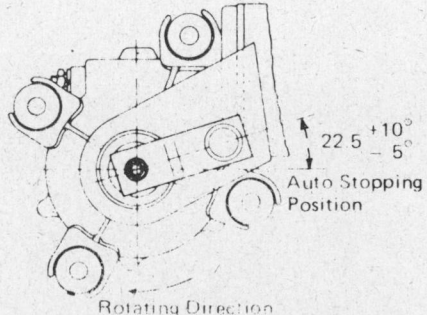

22.5 +10° − 5°
Auto Stopping Position
Rotating Direction

Fig. 10.60. Installed position of crank arm

4   Refitting is the reverse of the removal procedure.

32 Windscreen wiper motor - dismantling and reassembly

1   Remove the gear housing cover plate but do not detach the soldered wires unless the brush holder or gear housing is being renewed.
2   Detach the crank from the wiper motor by removing the retaining nut and pulling the crank arm from the splined tapered shaft of the drive gear. Retain the thrust and wave washers. Detach the rubber seat.
3   Remove the gear housing from the stator by withdrawing the two securing screws. Retain the ball from the end of the armature shaft. Remove the thrust adjuster screw from the gear housing.
4   Pull the armature from the stator using enough force to overcome the magnetic attraction. Retain the ball from the other end of the armature shaft.
5   Clean the grease from all components and inspect for wear or damage. Check the drive shaft endfloat and if it exceeds 0.008 in (0.2 mm) renew the thrust washer.
6   Check the brushes for wear and if they are less than 0.31 in (8.0 mm) in length, renew them.
7   Commence reassembly by fitting the brushes and springs to the brush holders so that the leads pass over the lips of the cut-away portions.
8   Assemble the armature to the gear housing, first packing the shaft bush with grease.
9   Pack the stator rear bearing with grease and insert the thrust ball. Carefully wipe out the interior of the stator to remove any ferrous filings which may be adhering to it due to magnetic attraction.
10 Align the stator and gear housing, and secure them together with the two bolts and nuts inserted through the slots in the stator casing. A piece of adhesive tape attached to the nuts will help to hold them in position while engaging the bolts in them. Seal the stator to gear housing joint and the nut slots with gasket sealant.
11 Grease the drive shaft/gear assembly liberally, also the thrust and wave washers and insert the components into the gear housing.
12 Drop the remaining ball into the thrust adjuster screw hole, insert the adjuster screw and tighten it until all armature endfloat disappears. Secure the screw with the locknut only finger tight at this stage.
13 Check the height of the automatic switch lever from the inside surface of the gear housing cover plate. This should be 0.39 in (10 mm),

adjust if necessary.
14 Connect the wiring plug to the gear housing cover plate connector and turn the wiper motor switch on. Connect an ammeter between the battery and fusible link; with the wiper motor running under no load conditions (minimum current) screw in the adjuster screw until the current just starts to rise and secure it with its locknut. Endfloat adjustment can only be satisfactorily carried out in this manner because of the compressibility of the armature rear bearing rubber thrust pad.
15 Switch the motor off by using the wiper switch so that the motor will come to rest in its normal parked position. Fit the crank to the drive shaft so that it takes up the position shown in Fig. 10.60.

33 Windscreen washer

1   The windscreen washer reservoir is attached to the engine compartment front member, and is integral with the radiator reservoir. It is attached by three bolts.
2   The washer pump is attached to the reservoir, and can readily be removed after removing the electrical connection.
3   Never operate the washer without fluid in the reservoir or keep the washers operating continuously for more than 20 seconds, or the pump motor will overheat.
4   Keep the reservoir clean and the electrical connections secure, and ensure that the connecting pipes are securely attached.

34 Horns

1   A trumpet type horn is normally mounted behind each pair of headlight units. Each horn is mounted on a bracket, and has two push-on electrical connections.
2   The horns are not adjustable; if they fail to operate satisfactorily first check the electrical connections, and ensure that they are securely mounted. If this does not cure the problem, it will almost certainly mean that a replacement item is required.

35 Seat belt warning and interlock systems

1   1974 models produced for the USA market are fitted with an elaborate electrical warning and safety interlock system. Basically

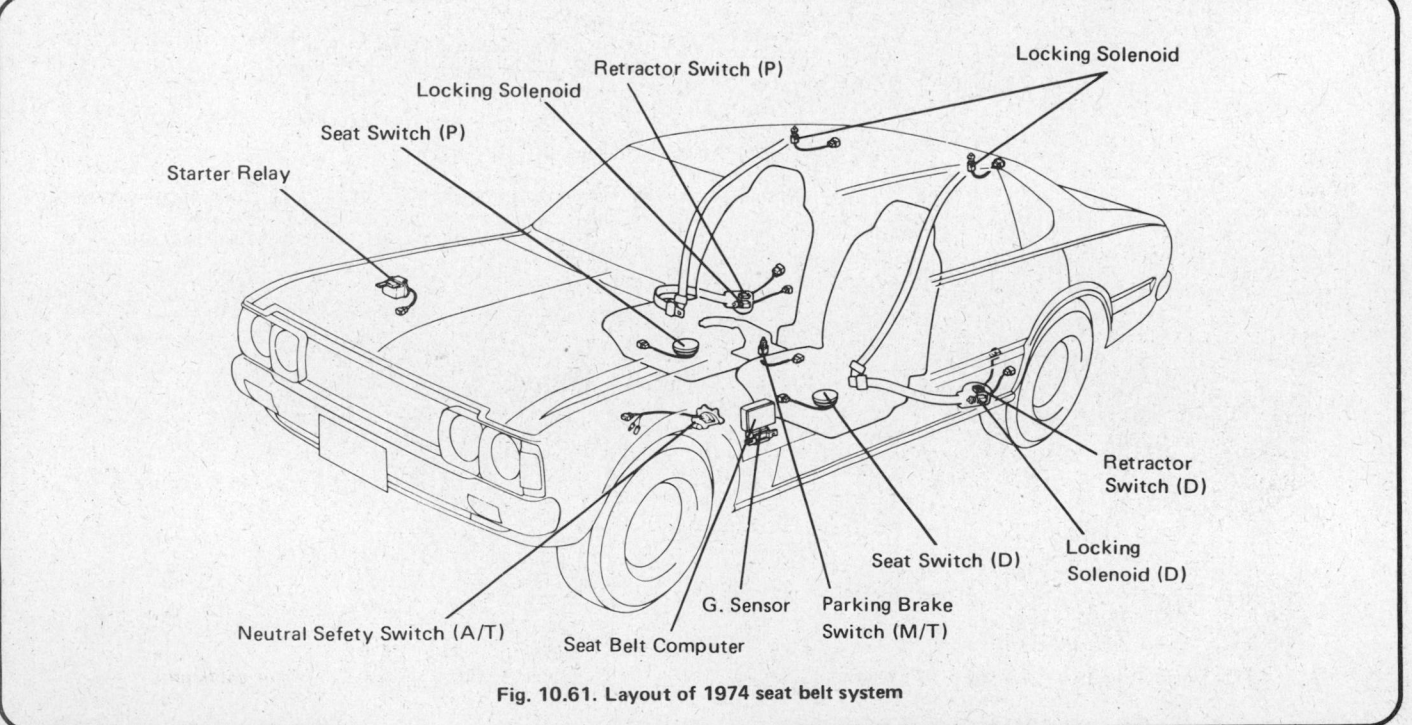

Fig. 10.61. Layout of 1974 seat belt system

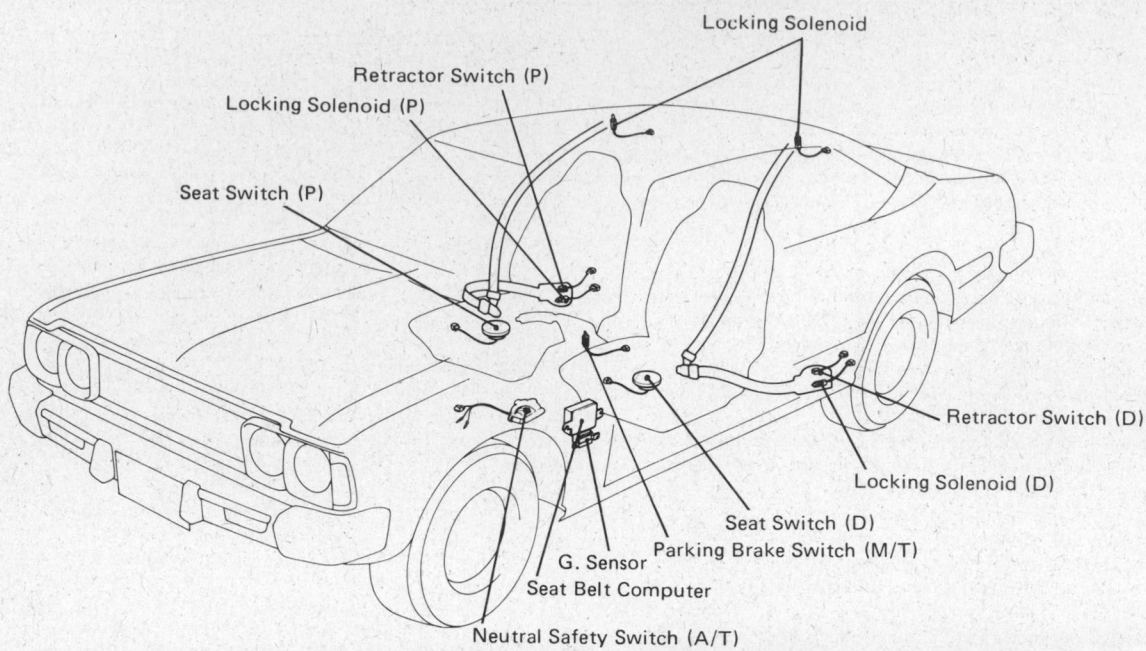

Fig. 10.62. Layout of seat belt system for later models

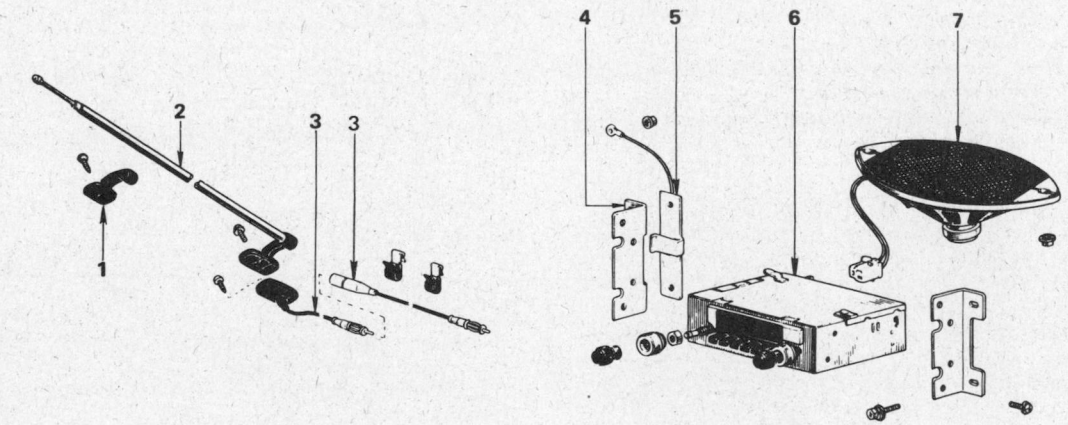

Fig. 10.63. Standard fitment radio and associated parts

| 1 Aerial holder | 3 Cable | 5 Radio bracket nut | 7 Speaker |
| 2 Aerial | 4 Radio bracket | 6 Radio | |

Fig. 10.64. Rear retaining screws for console mounted radio (arrowed)

Fig. 10.65. Removing the aerial

if either of the two front seat belts are not fastened, the following actions occur:

    i) a warning buzzer and lamp actuate if the ignition key is turned to the 'start' position.
    ii) the starter will not operate when the key is turned (it will operate if the driver's belt is connected and there is no weight on the front passenger seat, also the inertia belt not in use is fully retracted).

2 The engine can of course be started for repairs etc. by reaching into the vehicle interior to turn the starter switch. Although the seat belts are not fastened, neither is there any weight on the seats to actuate the interlock switches and so the engine can be started.
3 The system also incorporates a deceleration sensor which locks the inertia type seat belt reels in advance of impact, should a collision occur.
4 Individual components of the system are sealed units and can only be renewed as such. Maintenance should be limited to occasionally checking the security of the connecting wiring, in conjunction with the wiring diagrams provided later in this manual.
5 Later USA models, and models produced for Canada, do not have the interlock system, but still have the buzzer system to remind the front seat passenger and driver to fasten the seat belts.

36 Radio and associated equipment (standard fitment type)

Instrument panel radio - removal and refitting
1 Remove the instrument finish panel and instrument centre panel (Section 23).
2 Remove the radio tuner bracket then unplug the harness and aerial connectors.
3 Remove the radio and tape player together.
4 Refitting is the reverse of the removal procedure.

Console box radio - removal and refitting
5 Remove the console box. On models with a centre arm rest, lower the arm rest rearwards and remove the console box by lifting up the centre panel.
6 Unplug the harness and aerial connectors, then remove the tuner bracket.
7 Remove the radio and tape player together.
8 Refitting is the reverse of the removal procedure.

Stereo tape player - removal and refitting
9 Remove the radio as previously described.
10 Remove the radio tuner bracket, then loosen the retaining band with a screwdriver and slide the tape player off the radio.
11 Refitting is the reverse of the removal procedure.

Aerial - removal and refitting
12 Unplug the wiring connector from the radio then remove the screw (1) Fig. 10.65 and screws (2). Pull out the aerial wire.
13 Refitting is the reverse of the removal procedure; run the aerial wire over the side ventilator duct.

Radio speaker - removal and refitting
14 Remove the instrument finish panel and instrument centre panel (Section 23), then remove the speaker.
15 Refitting is the reverse of the removal procedure.

Stereo speaker - removal and refitting
16 Remove the rear seat (on coupe tilt the seat forward).
17 Remove the package tray trim, then remove the speaker.
18 Refitting is the reverse of the removal procedure.

37 Radios and tape players (after market type) - fitting (general)

A radio or tape player is an expensive item to buy and will only give its best performance if fitted properly. It is useless to expect concert hall performance from a unit that is suspended from the dash panel on string with its speaker resting on the back seat or parcel shelf! If you do not wish to do the installation yourself there are many in-car entertainment specialists who can do the fitting for you.

Make sure the unit purchased is of the same polarity as the car, and ensure that units with adjustable polarity are correctly set before commencing installation.

It is difficult to give specific information with regard to fitting, as final positioning of the radio/tape player, speakers and aerial is entirely a matter of personal preference. However, the following paragraphs give guidelines to follow, which are relevant to all installations.

Radios
Most radios are a standardised size of 7 inches wide, by 2 inches deep - this ensures that they will fit into the radio aperture provided in most cars. If your car does not have such an aperture, then the radio must be fitted in a suitable position either in, or beneath, the dashpanel. Alternatively, a special console can be purchased which will fit between the dashpanel and the floor, or on the transmission tunnel. These consoles can also be used for additional switches and instrumentation if required. Where no radio aperture is provided, the following points should be borne in mind before deciding exactly where to fit the unit:

    a) The unit must be within easy reach of the driver wearing a seat belt.
    b) The unit must not be mounted in close proximity to an electric tachometer, the ignition switch and its wiring, or the flasher unit and associated wiring.
    c) The unit must be mounted within reach of the aerial lead, and in such a place that the aerial lead will not have to be routed near the components detailed in the preceding paragraph 'b'.
    d) The unit should not be positioned in a place where it might cause injury to the car occupants in an accident; for instance, under the dashpanel above the driver's or passengers' legs.
    e) The unit must be fitted really securely.

Some radios will have mounting brackets provided together with instructions: others will need to be fitted using drilled and slotted metal strips, bent to form mounting brackets - these strips are available from most accessory shops. The unit must be properly earthed, by fitting a separate earthing lead between the casing of the radio and the vehicle frame.

Use the radio manufacturers' instructions when wiring the radio into the vehicle's electrical system. If no instructions are available refer to the relevant wiring diagram to find the location of the radio 'feed' connection in the vehicle's wiring circuit. A 1-2 amp 'in-line' fuse must be fitted in the radio's 'feed' wire - a choke may also be necessary (see next Section).

The type of aerial used, and its fitted position is a matter of personal preference. In general the taller the aerial, the better the reception. It is best to fit a fully retractable aerial - especially, if a mechanical car-wash is used or if you live in an area where cars tend to be vandalised. In this respect electric aerials which are raised and lowered automatically when switching the radio on or off are convenient, but are more likely to give trouble than the manual type.

When choosing a site for the aerial the following points should be considered:

    a) The aerial lead should be as short as possible - this means that the aerial should be mounted at the front of the car.
    b) The aerial must be mounted as far away from the distributor and HT leads as possible.
    c) The part of the aerial which protrudes beneath the mounting point must not foul the roadwheels, or anything else.
    d) If possible the aerial should be positioned so that the coaxial lead does not have to be routed through the engine compartment.
    e) The plane of the panel on which the aerial is mounted should not be so steeply angled that the aerial cannot be mounted vertically (in relation to the 'end-on' aspect of the car). Most aerials have a small amount of adjustment available.

Having decided on a mounting position, a relatively large hole will have to be made in the panel. The exact size of the hole will depend upon the specific aerial being fitted, although, generally, the hole required is of ¾ inch (19 mm) diameter. On metal bodied cars, a 'tank-cutter' of the relevant diameter is the best tool to use for making the hole. This tool needs a small diameter pilot hole drilled through the panel, through which, the tool clamping bolt is inserted. On GRP bodied cars, a 'hole-saw' is the best tool to use. Again, this tool will require the drilling of a small pilot hole. When the hole has been made the raw edges should be de-burred with a file and then painted, to prevent corrosion.

Fit the aerial according to the manufacturer's instructions. If the aerial is very tall, or if it protrudes beneath the mounting panel for a considerable distance it is a good idea to fit a stay between the aerial and the vehicle frame. This stay can be manufactured from the slotted and drilled metal strips previously mentioned. The stay should be securely screwed or bolted in place. For best reception it is advisable to fit an earth lead between the aerial and the vehicle frame - this is essential for GRP bodied cars.

It will probably be necessary to drill one or two holes through bodywork panels in order to feed the aerial lead into the interior of the car. Where this is the case ensure that the holes are fitted with rubber grommets to protect the cable, and to stop possible entry of water.

Positioning and fitting of the speaker depends mainly on its type. Generally, the speaker is designed to fit directly into the aperture already provided in the car (usually in the shelf behind the rear seats, or in the top of the dashpanel). Where this is the case, fitting the speaker is just a matter of removing the protective grille from the aperture and screwing or bolting the speaker in place. Take great care not to damage the speaker diaphragm whilst doing this. It is a good idea to fit a 'gasket' between the speaker frame and the mounting panel, in order to prevent vibration - some speakers will already have such a gasket fitted.

If a 'pod' type speaker was supplied with the radio, the best acoustic results will normally be obtained by mounting it on the shelf behind the rear seat. The pod can be secured to the mounting panel with self-tapping screws.

When connecting a rear mounted speaker to the radio, the wires should be routed through the vehicle beneath the carpets or floor mats - preferably the middle, or along the side of the floorpan, where they will not be trodden on by passengers. Make the relevant connections as directed by the radio manufacturer.

By now you will have several yards of additional wiring in the car, use PVC tape to secure this wiring out of harm's way. Do not leave electrical leads dangling. Ensure that all new electrical connections are properly made (wires twisted together will not do) and completely secure.

The radio should now be working, but before you pack away your tools it will be necessary to 'trim' the radio to the aerial. If specific instructions are not provided by the radio manufacturer, proceed as follows. Find a station with a low signal strength on the medium-wave band, slowly, turn the trim screw of the radio in, or out, until the loudest reception of the selected station is obtained - the set is then trimmed to the aerial.

Tape players

Fitting instructions for both cartridge and cassette stereo tape players are the same and in general the same rules apply as when fitting a radio. Tape players are not usually prone to electrical interference like radio - although it can occur - so positioning is not so critical. If possible the player should be mounted on an 'even-keel'. Also, it must be possible for a driver wearing a seat belt to reach the unit in order to change or turn over tapes.

For the best results from speakers designed to be recessed into a panel, mount them so that the back of the speaker protrudes into an enclosed chamber within the car (eg; door interiors or the boot cavity).

To fit recessed type speakers in the front doors first check that there is sufficient room to mount the speakers in each door without it fouling the latch or window winding mechanism. Hold the speaker against the skin of the door, and draw a line around the periphery of the speaker. With the speaker removed draw a second 'cutting' line, within the first, to allow enough room for the entry of the speaker back, but at the same time providing a broad seat for the speaker flange. When you are sure that the 'cutting-line' is correct, drill a series of holes around its periphery. Pass a hacksaw blade through one of the holes and then cut through the metal between the holes until the centre section of the panel falls out.

De-burr the edges of the hole and then paint the raw metal to prevent corrosion. Cut a corresponding hole in the door trim panel - ensuring that it will be completely covered by the speaker grille. Now drill a hole in the door edge and a corresponding hole in the door surround. These holes are to feed the speaker leads through - so fit grommets. Pass the speaker leads through the door trim, door skin and out through the holes in the side of the door and door surround. Refit the door trim panel and then secure the speaker to the door using self-tapping screws. **Note:** If the speaker is fitted with a shield to prevent water dripping on it, ensure that this shield is at the top.

Pod type speakers can be fastened to the shelf behind the rear seat, or anywhere else offering a corresponding mounting point on each side of the car. If the pod speakers are mounted on each side of the shelf

behind the rear seat, it is a good idea to drill several large diameter holes through to the boot cavity beneath each speaker - this will improve the sound reproduction. Pod speakers sometimes offer a better reproduction quality if they face the rear window - which then acts as a reflector - so it is worthwhile to do a little experimenting before finally fixing the speaker.

38 Radios and tape players (after market type) - suppression of interference (general)

To eliminate buzzes and other unwanted noises, costs very little and is not as difficult as sometimes thought. With a modicum of common sense and patience and following the instructions in the following paragraphs, interference can be virtually eliminated.

The first cause for concern is the generator. The noise this makes over the radio is like an electric mixer and the noise speeds up when you rev up (if you wish to prove the point, you can remove the drive-belt and try it). The remedy for this is simple; connect a 1.0 uf − 3.0 uf capacitor between earth, probably the bolt that holds down the generator base, and the *large* terminal on the dynamo or alternator. This is most important for if you connect it to the small terminal, you will probably damage the generator permanently (see Fig. 10.66).

A second common cause of electrical interference is the ignition system. Here a 1.0 ohm capacitor must be connected between earth and the 'SW' or '+' terminal on the coil (see Fig. 10.67). This may stop the tick-tick-tick sound that comes over the speaker. Next comes the spark itself.

There are several ways of curing interference from the ignition HT system. One is to use carbon film HT leads but these have a tendency to 'snap' inside and you don't know then, why you are firing on only half your cylinders. So the second, and more successful method is to use resistive spark plug caps (see Fig. 10.68) of about 10,000 ohm to 15,000 ohm resistance. If, due to lack of room, these cannot be used, an alternative is to use 'in-line' suppressors (Fig. 10.68) - if the interference is not too bad, you may get away with only one suppressor in the coil to distributor line. If the interference does continue (a 'clacking' noise) then doctor all HT leads.

At this stage it is advisable to check that the radio is well earthed, also the aerial, and to see that the aerial plug is pushed well into the set and that the radio is properly trimmed (see preceding Section). In addition, check that the wire which supplies the power to the set is as short as possible and does not wander all over the car. At this stage it is a good idea to check that the fuse is of the correct rating. For most sets this will be about 1 to 2 amps.

At this point the more usual causes of interference have been suppressed. If the problem still exists, a look at the causes of interference may help to pinpoint the component generating the stray electrical discharges.

The radio picks up electromagnetic waves in the air; now some are made by radio stations and other broadcasters and some, not wanted, are made by the car. The home made signals are produced by stray electrical discharges floating around the car. Common producers of these signals are electric motors; ie, the windshield wipers, electric screen washers, electric window winders, heater fan or an electric aerial if fitted. Other sources of interference are electric fuel pumps, flashing turn signals, and instruments. The remedy for these cases is shown in Fig. 10.69 for an electric motor whose interference is not too bad and Fig. 10.70 for instrument suppression. Turn signals are not normally suppressed. In recent years, radio manufacturer's have included in the line (live) of the radio, in addition to the fuse, an 'in-line' choke. If your installation lacks one of these, put one in as shown in Fig. 10.71.

All the foregoing components are available from radio shops or accessory shops. For a transistor radio, a 2A choke should be adequate. If you have an electric clock fitted this should be suppressed by connecting a 0.5 uf capacitor directly across it as shown for a motor in Fig. 10.69.

If after all this, you are still experiencing radio interference, first assess how bad it is, for the human ear can filter out unobtrusive unwanted noises quite easily. But if you are still adamant about eradicating the noise, then continue.

As a first step, a few 'experts' seem to favour a screen between the radio and the engine. This is O.K. as far as it goes, literally! - for the whole set is screened and if interference can get past that then a small piece of aluminium is not going to stop it.

A more sensible way of screening is to discover if interference is

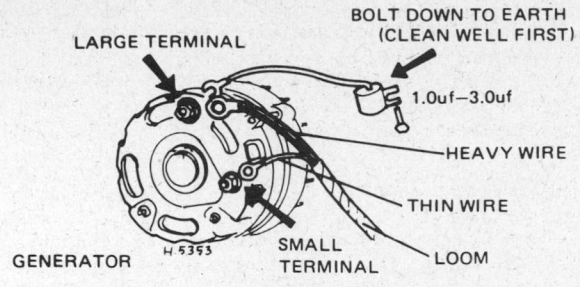

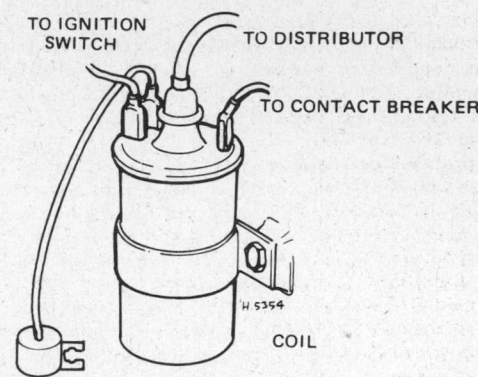

Fig. 10.66. The correct way to connect the capacitor to the generator

Fig. 10.67. The capacitor must be connected to the ignition switch side of the coil

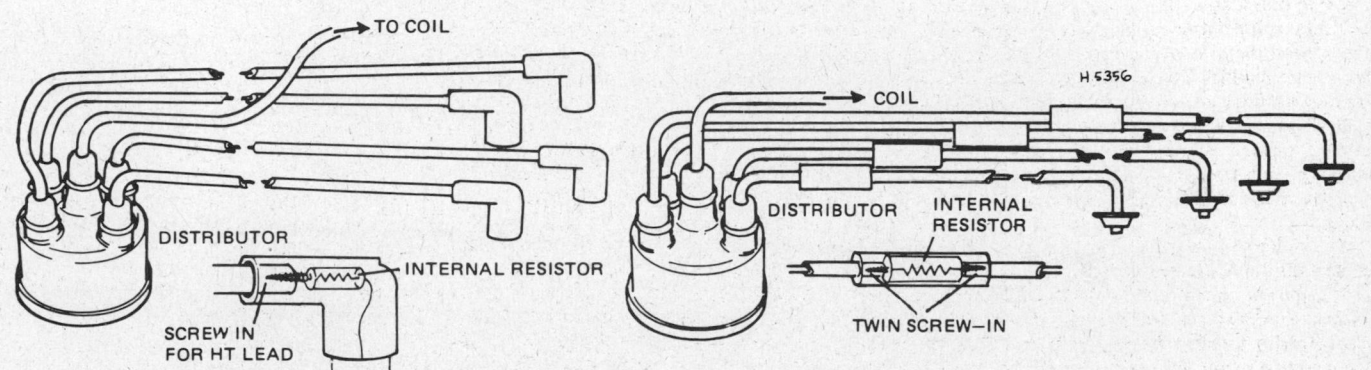

Fig. 10.68. Ignition HT lead suppressors

Fig. 10.69. Correct method of suppressing electric motors

Fig. 10.70. Method of suppressing gauges and their control units

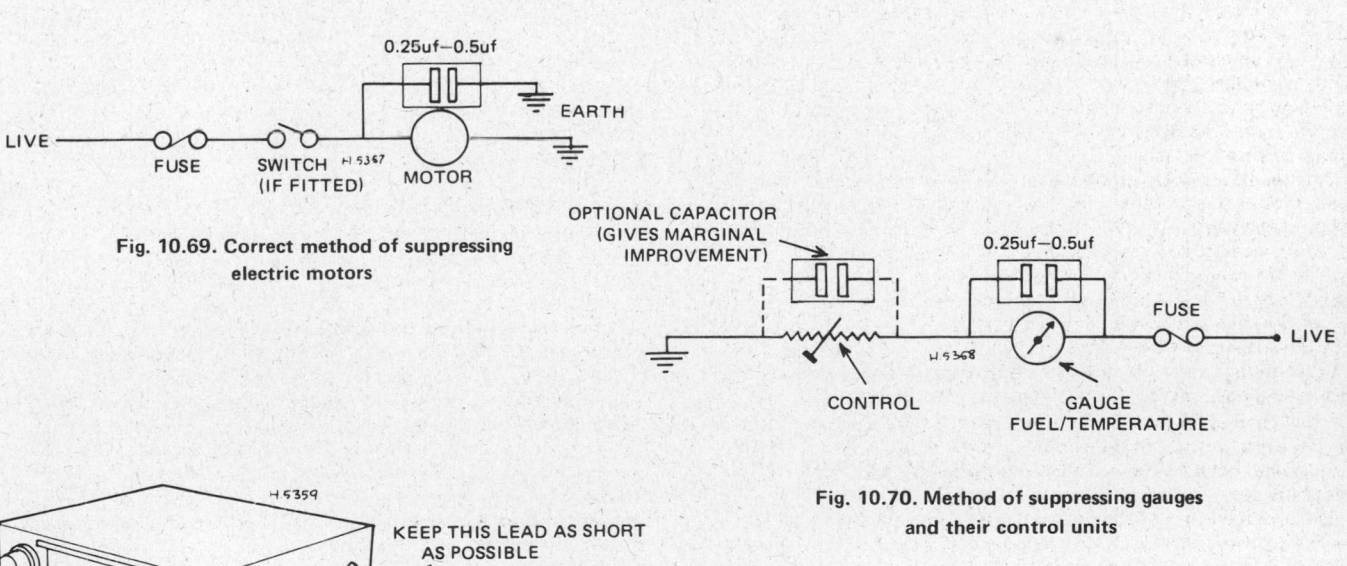

Fig. 10.71. An 'in-line' choke should be fitted into the live supply lead as close to the unit as possible

coming down the wires. First, take the live lead; interference can get between the set and the choke (hence the reason for keeping the wires short). One remedy here is to screen the wire and this is done by buying screened wire and fitting that. The loudspeaker lead could be screened also to prevent 'pick-up' getting back to the radio - although this is unlikely.

Without doubt, the worst source of radio interference comes from the ignition HT leads, even if they have been suppressed. The ideal way of suppressing these is to slide screening tubes over the leads themselves. As this is impractical, we can place an aluminium shield over the majority of the lead areas. In a vee - or twin-cam engine, this is relatively easy but for a straight engine the results are not particularly good.

Now for the really impossible cases, here are a few tips to try out. Where metal comes into contact with metal, an electrical disturbance is caused which is why good clean connections are essential. To remove interference due to overlapping or butting panels you must bridge the joint with a wide braided earth strap (like that from the frame to the engine/transmission). The most common moving parts that could create noise and should be strapped are, in order of importance:

a) Silencer to frame.
b) Exhaust pipe to engine block and frame.
c) Air cleaner to frame.
d) Front and rear bumpers to frame.
e) Steering column to frame.
f) Bonnet and boot lids to frame.
g) Bonnet frame to frame on soft tops.

These faults are most pronounced when (1) the engine is idling, (2) labouring under load. Although the moving parts are already connected with nuts, bolts, etc, these do tend to rust and corrode, thus creating a high resistance interference source.

If you have a 'ragged' sounding pulse when mobile, this could be wheel or tyre static. This can be cured by buying some anti-static powder and sprinkling it liberally inside the tyres.

If the interference takes the shape of a high pitched screeching noise that changes its note when the car is in motion and only comes now and then, this could be related to the aerial, especially if it is of the telescopic or whip type. This source can be cured quite simply by pushing a small rubber ball on top of the aerial (yes, really!) as this breaks the electric field before it can form; but it would be much better to buy yourself a new aerial of a reputable brand. If, on the other hand, you are getting a loud rushing sound every time you brake, then this is brake static. This effect is most prominent on hot dry days and is cured only by fitting a special kit, which is quite expensive.

In conclusion, it is pointed out that it is relatively easy, and therefore cheap to eliminate 95 per cent of all noises, but to eliminate the final 5 per cent is time and money consuming. It is up to the individual to decide if it is worth it. Please remember also, that you will not get concert hall performance from a cheap radio.

Finally at the beginning of this Section are mentioned tape players; these are not usually affected by interference but in a very bad case, the best remedies are the first three suggestions plus using a 3 - 5 amp choke in the 'live' line and in incurable cases screen the live and speaker wires.

Note: If your car is fitted with electronic ignition, then it is not recommended that either the spark plug resistors nor the ignition coil capacitor be fitted as these may damage the system. Most electronic ignition units have built-in suppression and should, therefore, not cause interference.

39 Fault diagnosis - electrical system

Symptom	Cause
Starter motor fails to turn engine	
No voltage at starter motor	Battery discharged.
	Battery defective internally.
	Battery terminal leads loose or earth lead not securely attached to body.
	Loose or broken connections in starter motor circuit.
	Starter motor solenoid faulty.
Voltage at starter motor: faulty motor	Starter brushes badly worn, sticking or brush wires loose.
	Commutator dirty, worn or burnt.
	Starter motor armature faulty.
	Field coils earthed.
Starter motor turns engine very slowly	
Electrical defects	Battery in discharged condition.
	Starter brushes badly worn, sticking or brush wires loose.
	Loose wires in starter motor circuit.
Starter motor operates without turning engine	
Mechanical damage	Pinion or flywheel gear teeth broken or worn.
Starter motor noisy or excessively rough engagement	
Lack of attention or mechanical damage	Pinion or flywheel gear teeth broken or worn.
	Starter motor retaining bolts loose.
Battery will not hold charge for more than a few days	
Wear or damage	Battery defective internally.
	Electrolyte level too low or electrolyte too weak due to leakage.
	Plate separators no longer fully effective.
	Battery plates severely sulphated.
Insufficient current flow to keep battery charged	Battery plates severely sulphated.
	Drive belt slipping.
	Battery terminal connections loose or corroded.
	Alternator not charging.
	Short in lighting circuit causing continual battery drain.
	Regulator unit not working correctly.
Ignition light fails to go out, battery runs flat in a few days	
Alternator not charging	Drive belt loose and slipping or broken.

	Brushes worn, sticking, broken or dirty. Brush springs weak or broken.
Regulator fails to work correctly	Regulator incorrectly set. Open circuit in wiring of regulator unit.

Failure of individual electrical equipment to function correctly is dealt with alphabetically, item-by-item, under the headings listed below:

Horn

Horn operates all the time	Horn push either earthed or stuck down. Horn cable to horn push earthed.
Horn fails to operate	Blown fuse. Cable or cable connection loose, broken or disconnected. Horn has an internal fault.
Horn emits intermittent or unsatisfactory noise	Cable connections loose.

Lights

Lights do not come on	If engine not running, battery discharged. Light bulb filament burnt out or bulbs broken. Wire connections loose, disconnected or broken. Light switch shorting or otherwise faulty.
Lights come on but fade out	If engine not running battery discharged.
Lights give very poor illumination	Lamp glasses dirty. Lamps badly out of adjustment. Incorrect bulb with too low wattage fitted. Existing bulbs old and badly discoloured.
Lights work erratically - flashing on and off, especially over bumps	Battery terminals or earth connection loose. Lights not earthing properly. Contact in light switch faulty.

Wipers

Wiper motor fails to work	Blown fuse. Wire connections loose, disconnected, or broken. Brushes badly worn. Armature worn or faulty. Field coils faulty.
Wiper motor works very slowly and takes excessive current	Commutator dirty, greasy or burnt. Armature bearings dirty or unaligned. Armature badly worn or faulty. Armature thrust adjuster screw overtightened.
Wiper motor works slowly and takes little current	Brushes badly worn. Commutator dirty, greasy or burnt. Armature badly worn or faulty.

Wiring Diagrams - overleaf

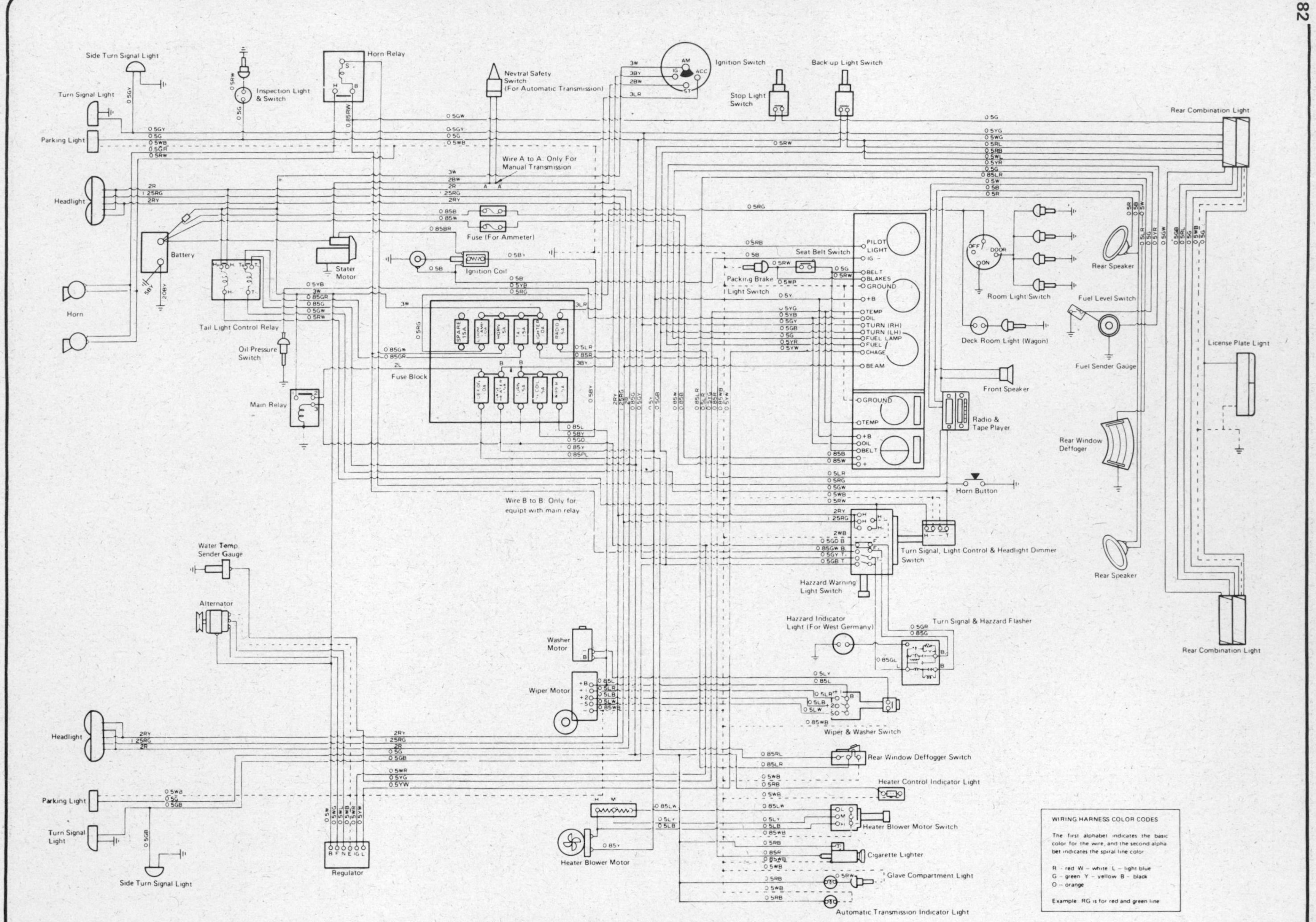

Fig. 10.72. Wiring diagram - general market models

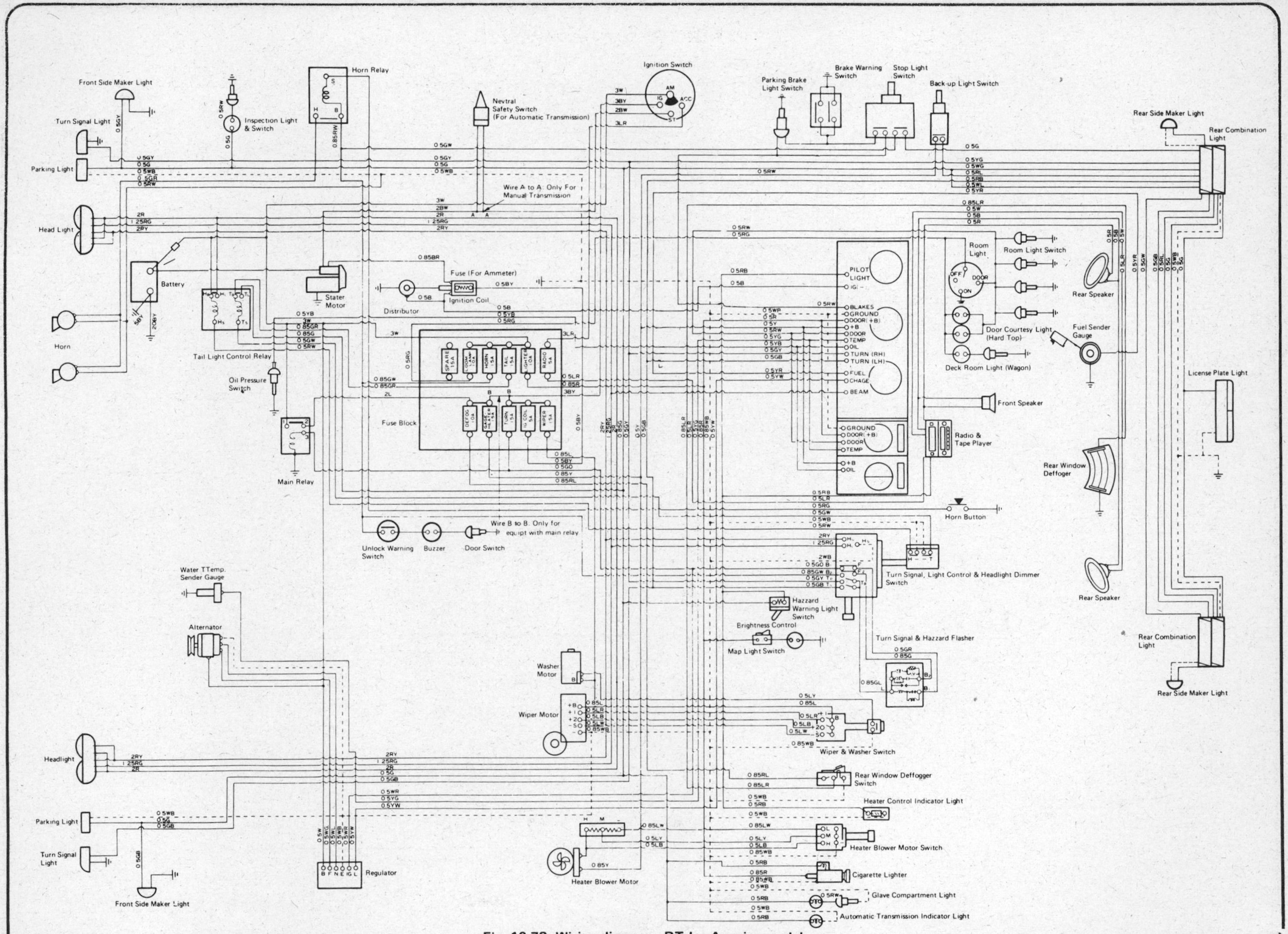

Fig. 10.73. Wiring diagram - RT L - A series models

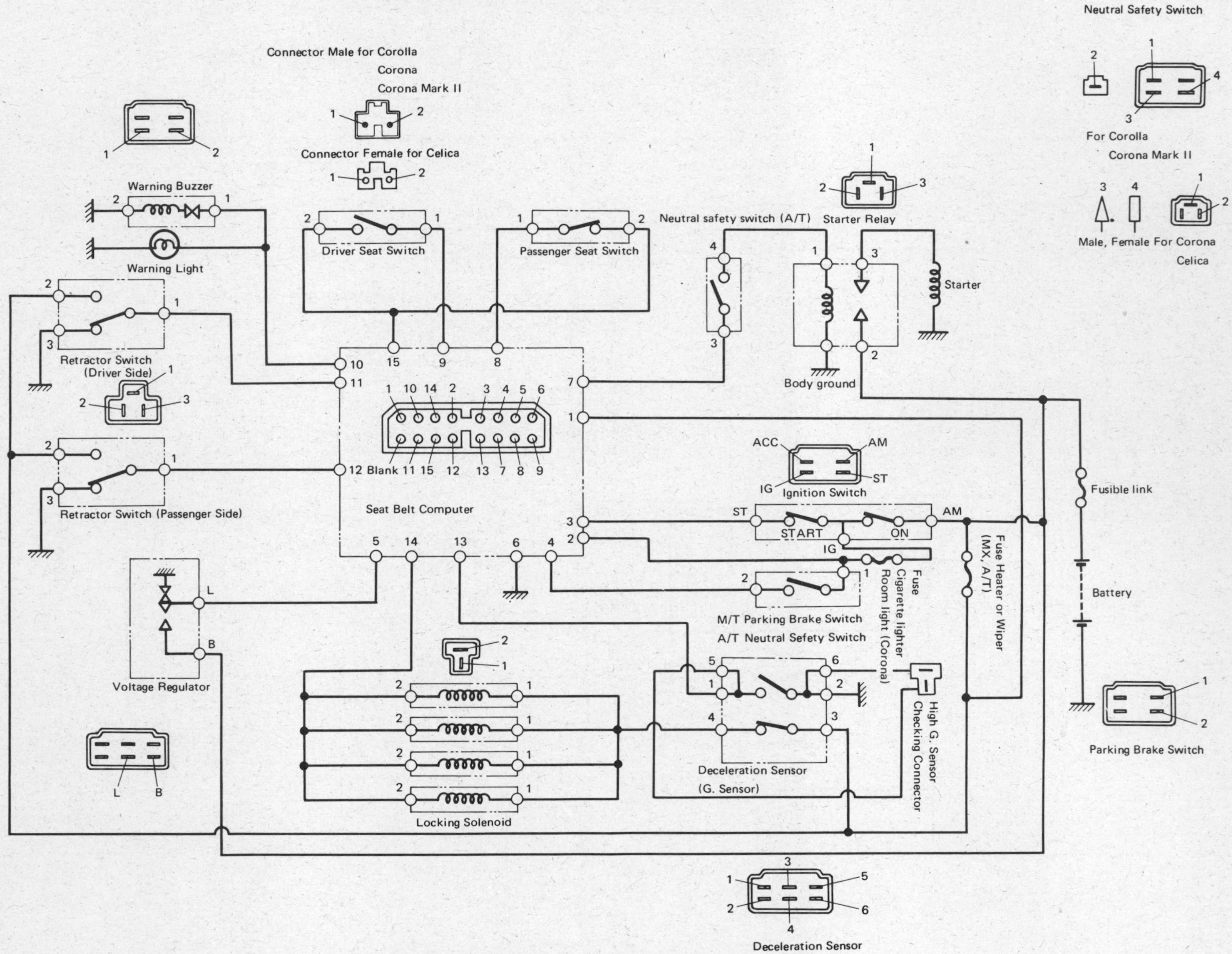

Neutral Safety Switch

For Corolla
Corona Mark II

Male, Female For Corona
Celica

Fusible link

Battery

Parking Brake Switch

Starter

Starter Relay

Neutral safety switch (A/T)

Body ground

Fuse Heater or Wiper
(MX, A/T)

Fuse
Cigarette lighter
Room light (Corona)

High G. Sensor
Checking Connector

Ignition Switch

M/T Parking Brake Switch
A/T Neutral Safety Switch

Deceleration Sensor
(G. Sensor)

Deceleration Sensor

Passenger Seat Switch

Connector Male for Corolla
Corona
Corona Mark II

Connector Female for Celica

Driver Seat Switch

Seat Belt Computer

Locking Solenoid

Warning Buzzer

Warning Light

Retractor Switch
(Driver Side)

Retractor Switch (Passenger Side)

Voltage Regulator

Fig. 10.74. Wiring diagram - USA seat belt system, 1974 models

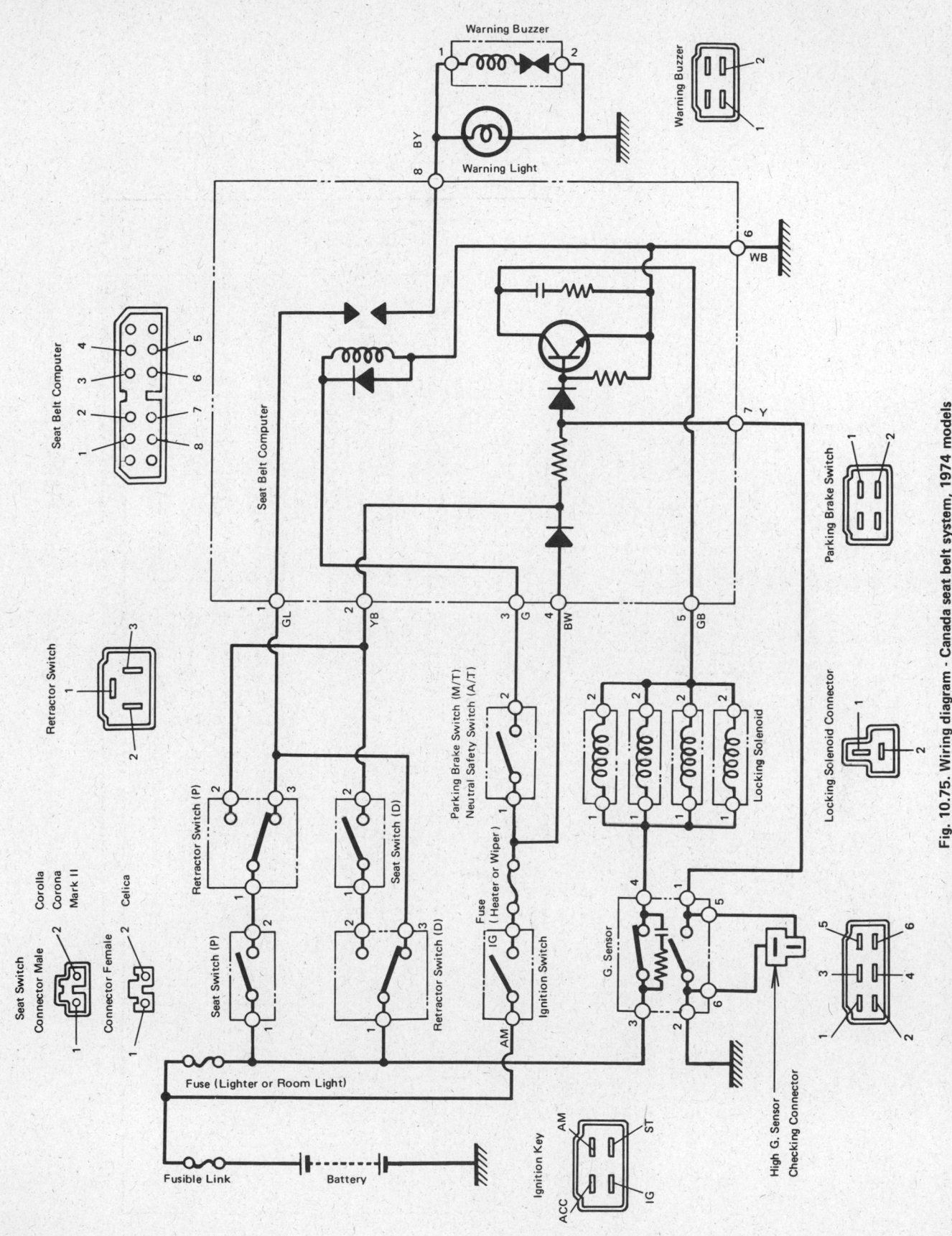

Fig. 10.75. Wiring diagram - Canada seat belt system, 1974 models

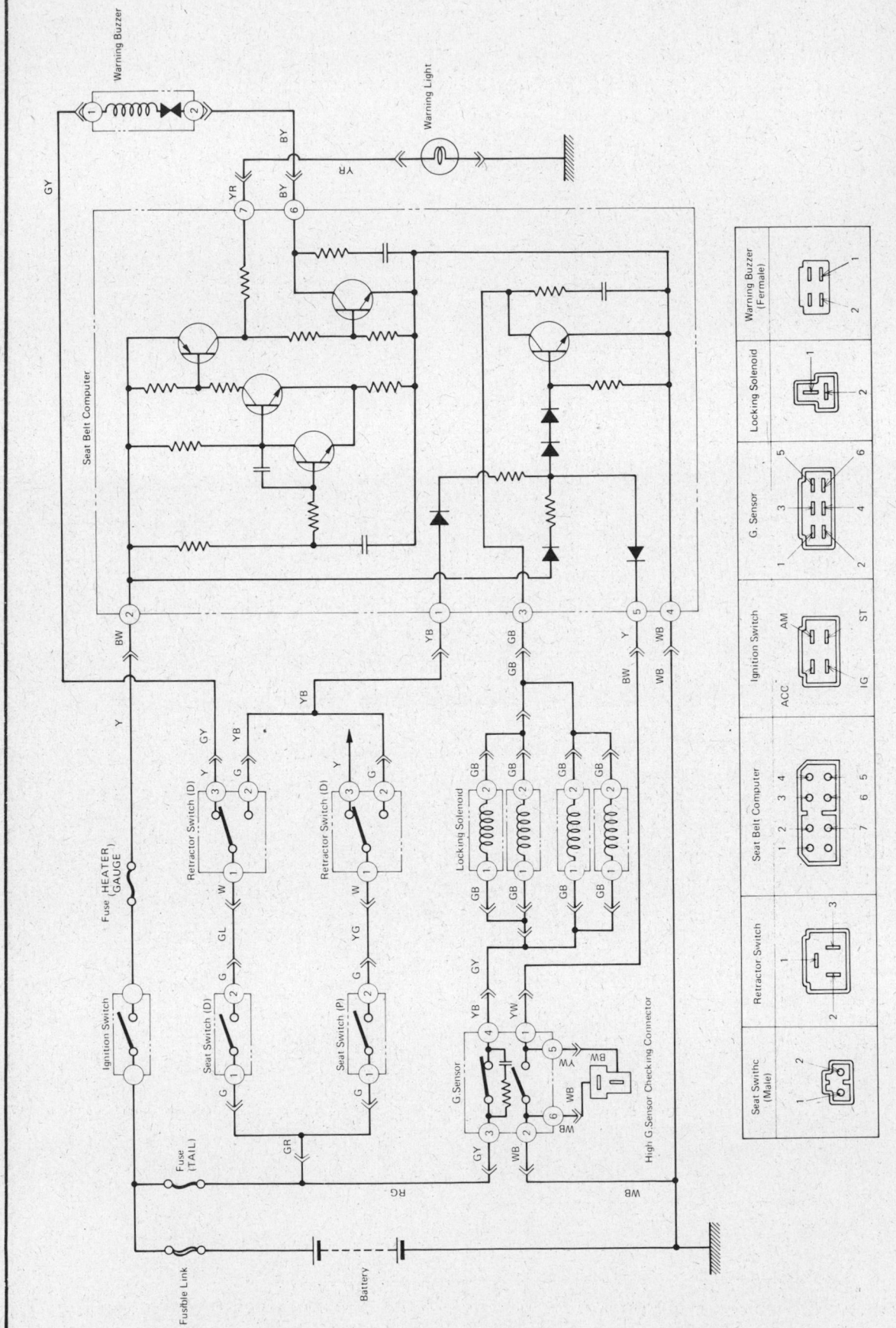

Fig. 10.76. Wiring diagram - USA seat belt system, February 1975 onwards

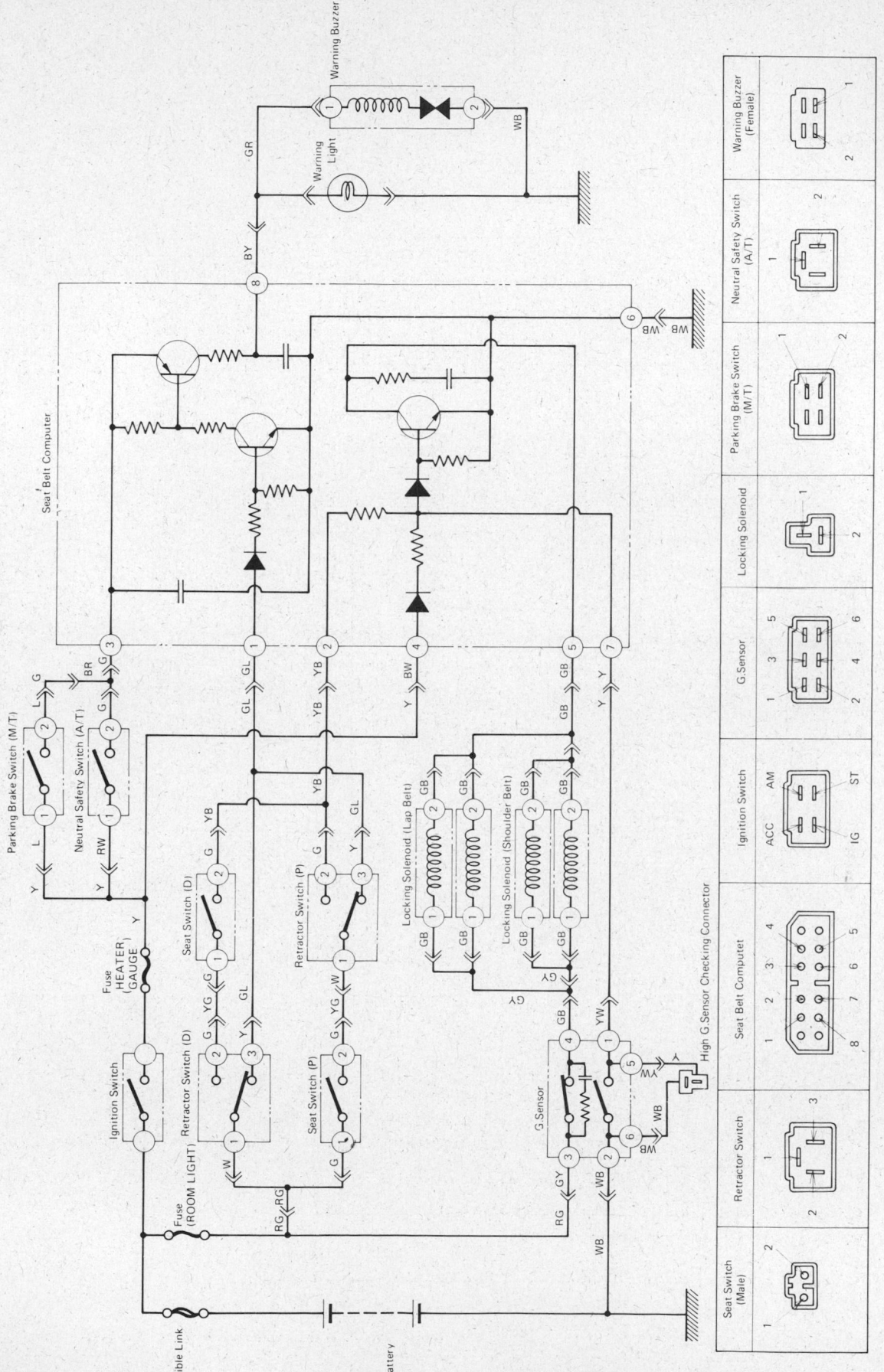

Fig. 10.77. Wiring diagram - Canada seat belt system, 1974 to August 1975

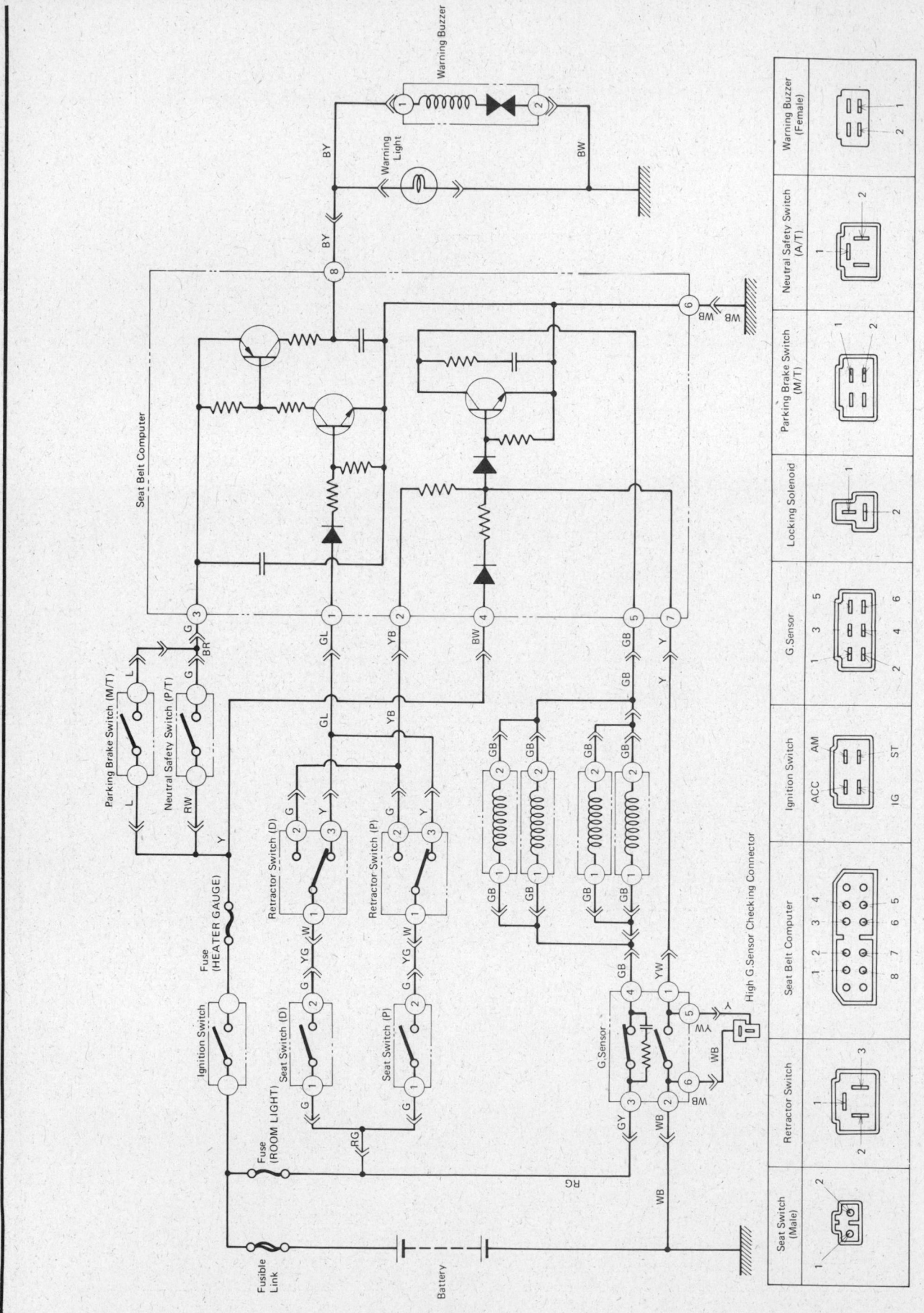

Fig. 10.78. Wiring diagram - Canada seat belt system, September 1975 onwards

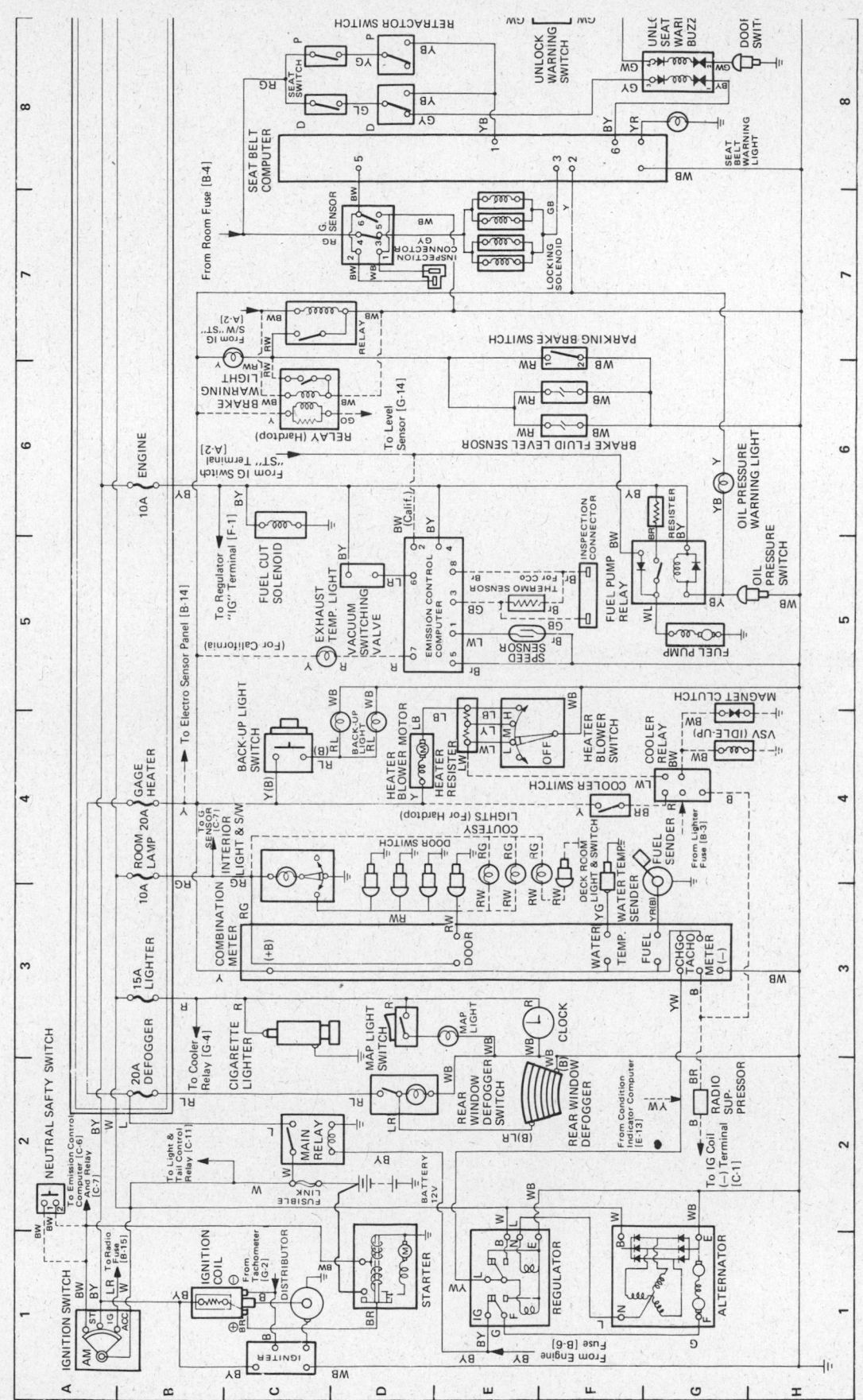

Fig. 10.79. 1A. Wiring diagram (USA and Canada) 1977 model

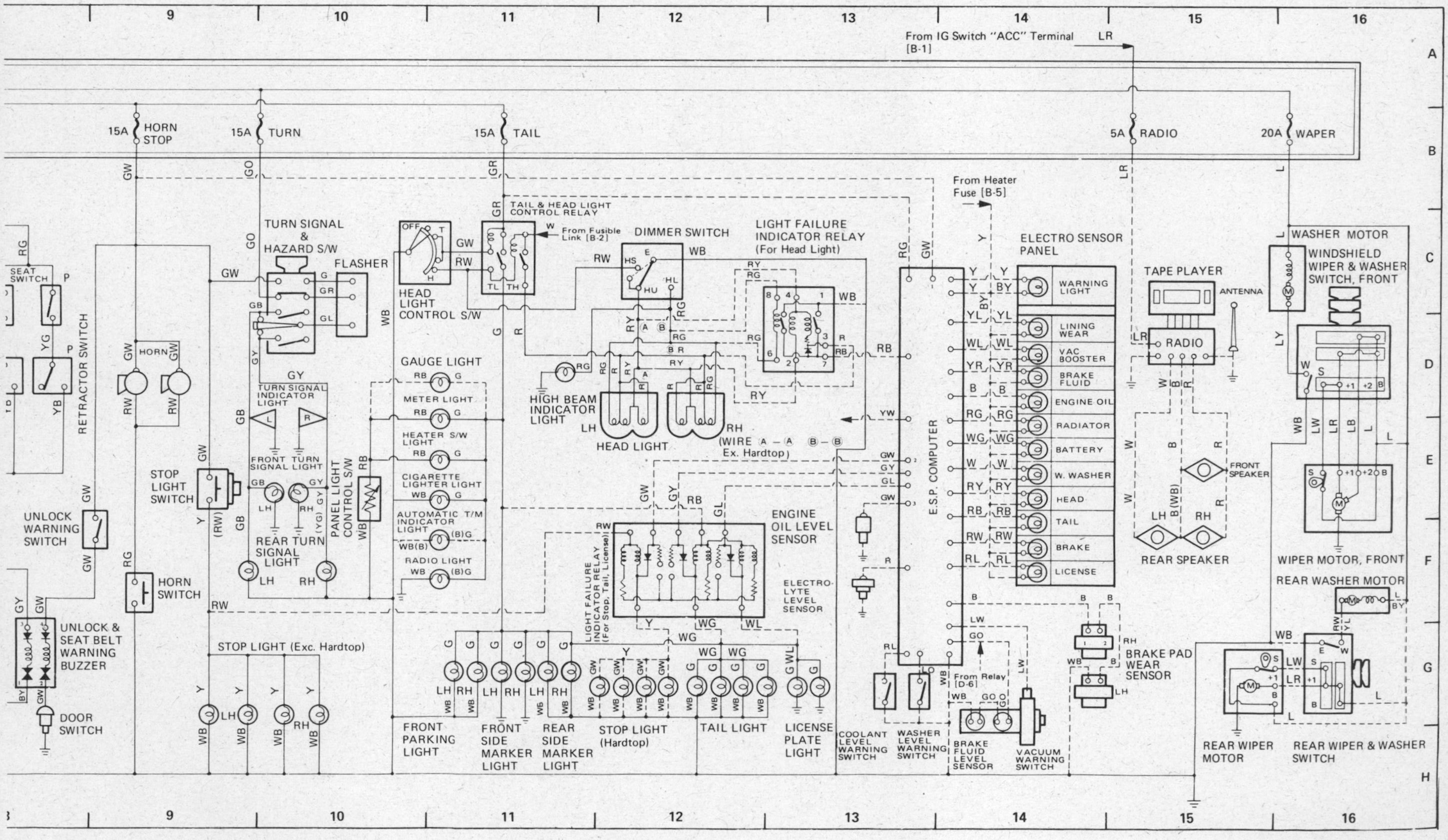

Fig. 10.79. 1B. Wiring diagram (USA and Canada) - 1977 models

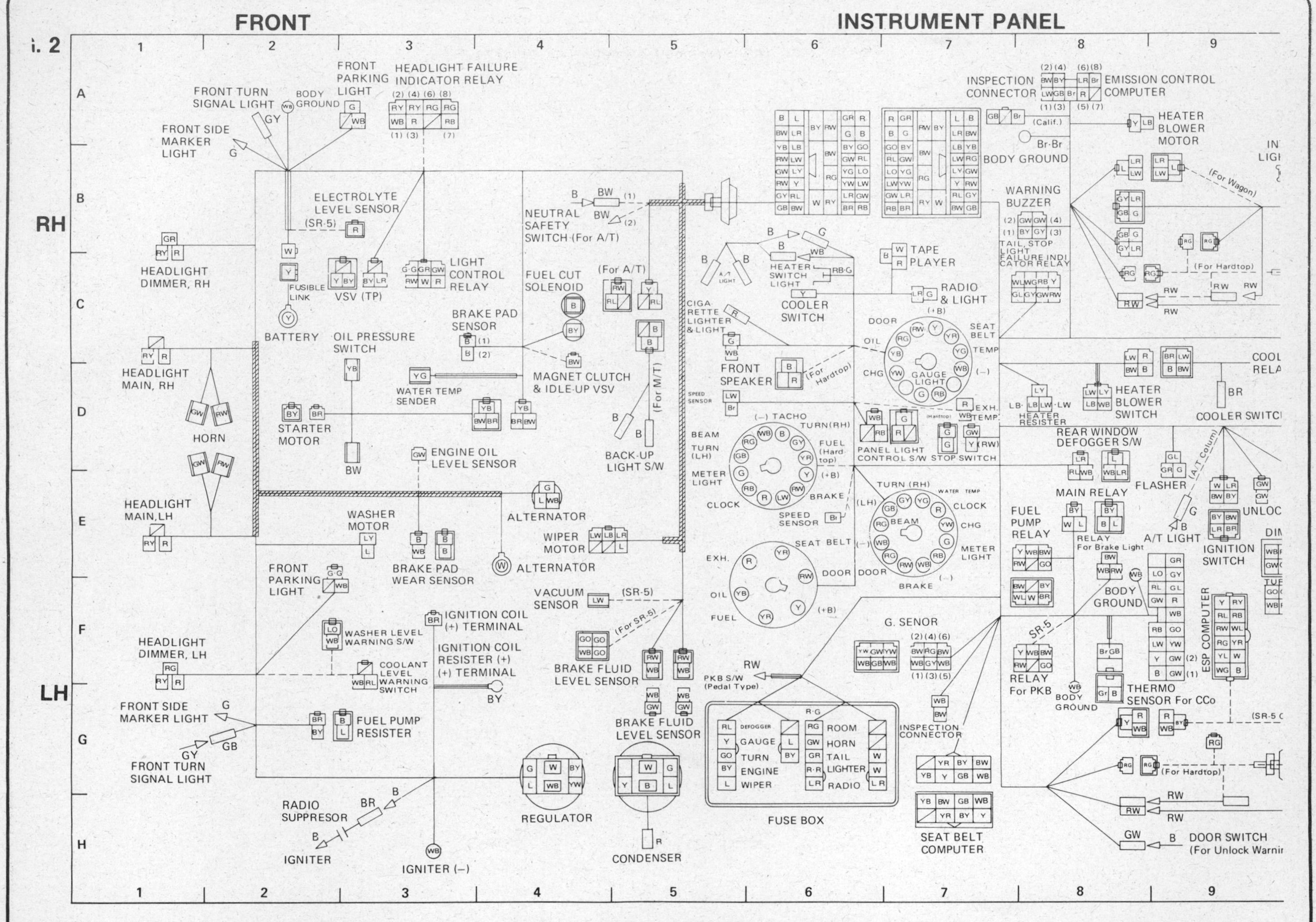

Fig. 10.79. 2A. Wiring diagram - 1977 models

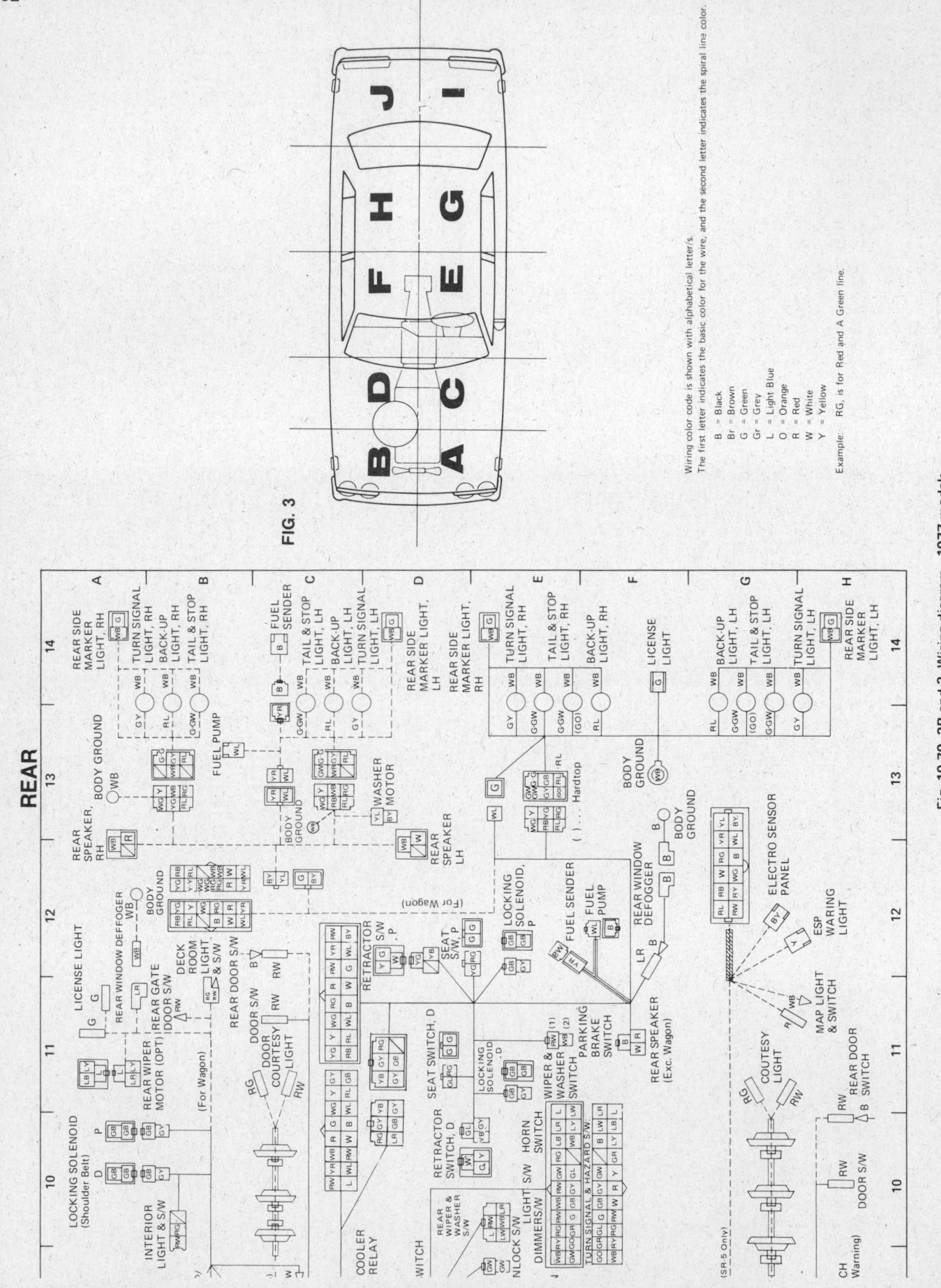

FIG. 3

REAR

Fig. 10.79. 2B and 3. Wiring diagram - 1977 models

Wiring color code is shown with alphabetical letter/s.
The first letter indicates the basic color for the wire, and the second letter indicates the spiral line color.

B = Black
Br = Brown
G = Green
Gr = Grey
L = Light Blue
O = Orange
R = Red
W = White
Y = Yellow

Example: RG, is for Red and A Green line.

Chapter 11 Steering and suspension

For modifications and information applicable to later USA models, refer to Supplement at end of manual

Contents

Specifications

Front suspension ... ... Independent, double wishbone and coil springs, telescopic shock absorbers and stabilizer bar

Rear suspension ... ... Semi-elliptic leaf springs with telescopic shock absorbers (stabilizer bar on some models)

Steering
Type ... ... Variable ratio recirculating ball nut and worm
Ratio ... ... 20 : 1 (approximately)
Steering box lubricant type ... ... SAE 90 gear oil

Steering/suspension angles
Toe in ... ... 0.04 to 0.12 in (1 to 3 mm)
Camber angle ... ... — 25' to 1° 20'
Castor angle ... ... — 40' to 1° 50'

Wheels ... ... Pressed steel

Tyres
UK and general market models

Model	Tyre size	Pressure (Heavy loads)		Pressure (Light loads)	
		Front	Rear	Front	Rear
All saloons and coupes	5.60-13	30 (2.1)	30 (2.1)	26 (1.8)	26 (1.8)
	6.45-13	28 (2.0)	28 (2.0)	24 (1.7)	24 (1.7)
	165 SR13	28 (2.0)	28 (2.0)	24 (1.7)	24 (1.7)
	165 SR14	27 (1.9)	27 (1.9)	24 (1.7)	24 (1.7)
	175 SR14	24 (1.7)	24 (1.7)	—	—
	185/70 HR14	24 (1.7)	24 (1.7)	—	—
Estate cars	5.60-13	30 (2.1)	36 (2.5)	26 (1.8)	31 (2.2)
	6.45-13	28 (2.0)	36 (2.5)	26 (1.8)	26 (1.8)
	165 SR13	28 (2.0)	32 (2.3)	24 (1.7)	28 (2.0)
	165 SR14	24 (1.7)	31 (2.2)	—	—

USA models

Model	Tyre size	Front	Rear
All saloons	6.45-14	26 (1.8)	26 (1.8)
	B78-14	26 (1.8)	26 (1.8)
	165 SR14	24 (1.7)	24 (1.7)
	175 SR14	24 (1.7)	24 (1.7)
All coupes except SR and SR-5			
	B78-14	26 (1.8)	26 (1.8)
	175 SR14	24 (1.7)	24 (1.7)
SR and SR-5	185/70 HR14	24 (1.7)	24 (1.7)
	185/70 SR14	24 (1.7)	24 (1.7)
All estate cars	B78-14	26 (1.8)	26 (1.8)
	175 SR14	24 (1.7)	24 (1.7)

Pressures are in lbf/in^2 and kgf/cm^2; they should always be checked when the tyre is cold. Add 4 lbf/in^2 (0.3 kgf/cm^2) for sustained high speed driving; never exceed the maximum cold tyre inflation pressure marked on the tyre sidewall.

Torque wrench settings

	lbf ft	kgf m
Front suspension		
Hub nut (initial tightening)	20	2.8
Suspension upper arm pivot bolts	100	13.9
Suspension lower arm pivot bolts	100	13.9
Front crossmember bolts	65	9.0
Upper balljoint to stub axle carrier	45	6.2
Lower balljoint to stub axle carrier	60	8.3
Steering arm to stub axle carrier	50	6.9
Shock absorber upper mounting	22	3.0
Shock absorber lower mounting	15	2.1
Strut to suspension lower arm (up to 1973)	50	6.9
Rear suspension		
Shock absorber upper mounting	22	3.0
Shock absorber lower mounting	15	2.1
'U' bolt nuts		
Saloon and Coupe	34	4.7
Estate car	57	8.0
Rear shackle bolt	44	6.1
Front eye bolt		
Saloon and Coupe	70	9.5
Estate car	27	3.8
Stabilizer bar to body	140	19.0
Steering		
Steering wheel nut	25	3.5
Steering column bracket bolts	14	1.9
Cover plate bolts (steering box)	15	2.1
Flexible coupling pinch bolt	20	2.8
Steering box to bodyframe bolts	45	6.2
Drop arm nut	100	13.9
Idler arm nut	85	12.0
Idler arm support bracket to bodyframe	50	7.0
Steering linkage balljoints	45	6.2
Worm adjusting screw locknut	65	9.0

1 General description

All models in the range have independent front suspension which is of upper and lower wishbone type and incorporates coil springs, double acting telescopic type hydraulic shock absorbers and a stabiliser bar.

The rear suspension is a leaf spring type with hydraulic shock absorbers. Some models have a rear stabiliser bar.

The steering gear is of recirculating ball design and most models have a steering column which is of a collapsible type.

2 Maintenance and inspection

1 Regularly inspect the condition of the balljoint rubber covers for splits or deterioration, and renew if necessary. Also check the condition of the rear suspension bushes for wear and renew if there is any movement.

2 Check the security of all suspension nuts and bolts, checking particularly those on the balljoints and on the estate car rear road spring 'U' bolts. Tighten them if necessary to the torques specified.

3 Every 24,000 miles (38,000 km) clean and repack the front wheel hub bearings and adjust them as described in this Chapter. At similar mileage intervals, check the front wheel alignment (Section 18).

4 For other information and maintenance intervals, refer to the Routine Maintenance Section at the beginning of the manual.

3 Shock absorbers - removal, testing and refitting

1 The front shock absorbers are attached at their upper ends by nuts, retainers and bushes which fit over the threaded end of the shock absorber central rod. At the lower end a slotted plate and two bolts are

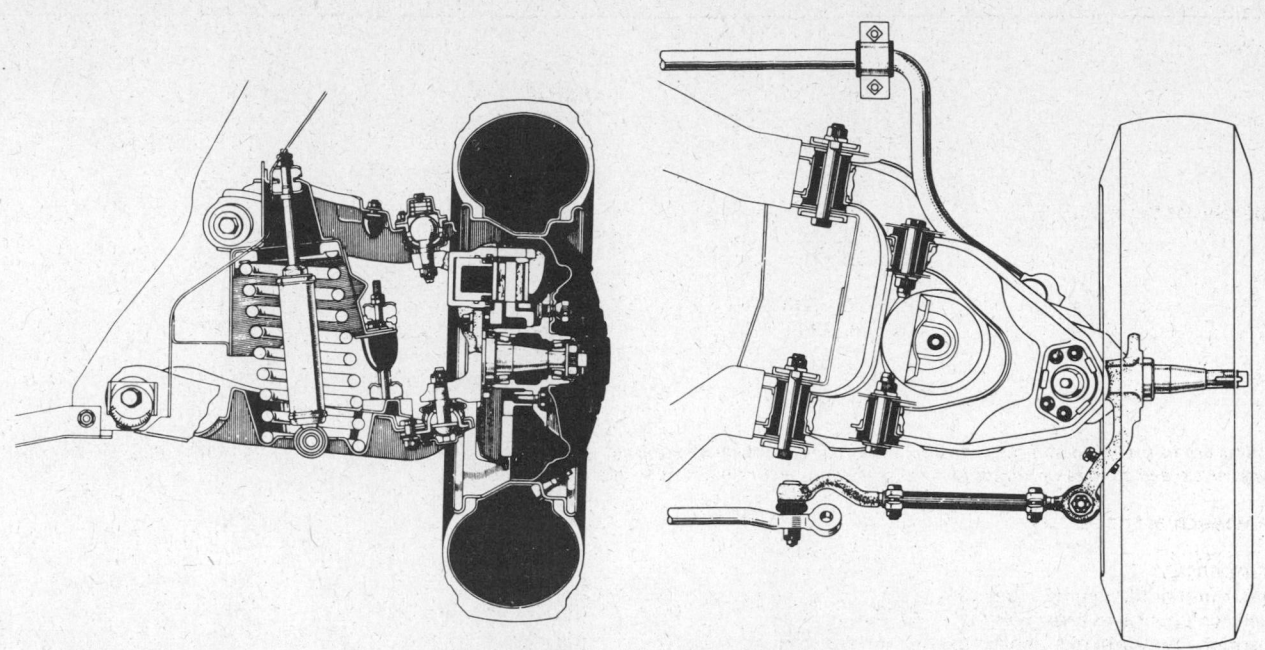

Fig. 11.1. Sectional view of front suspension

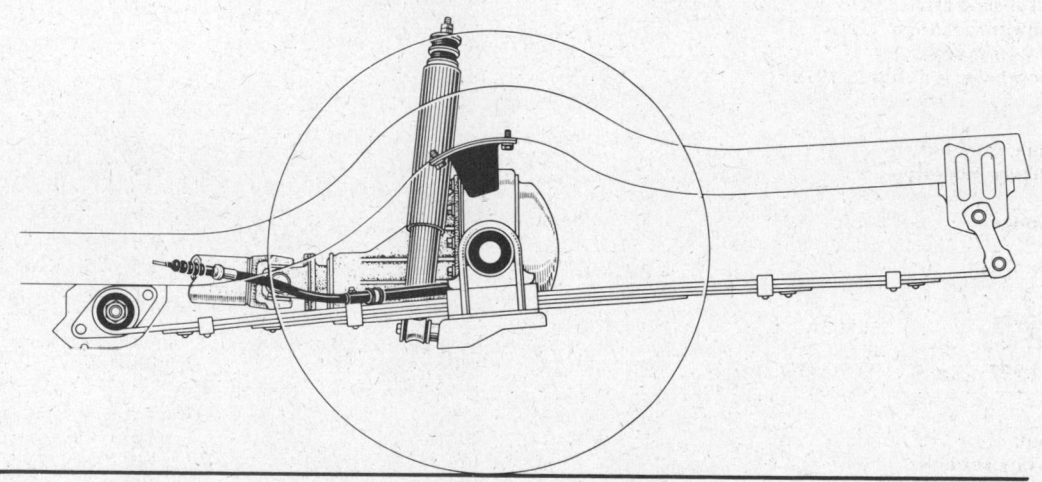

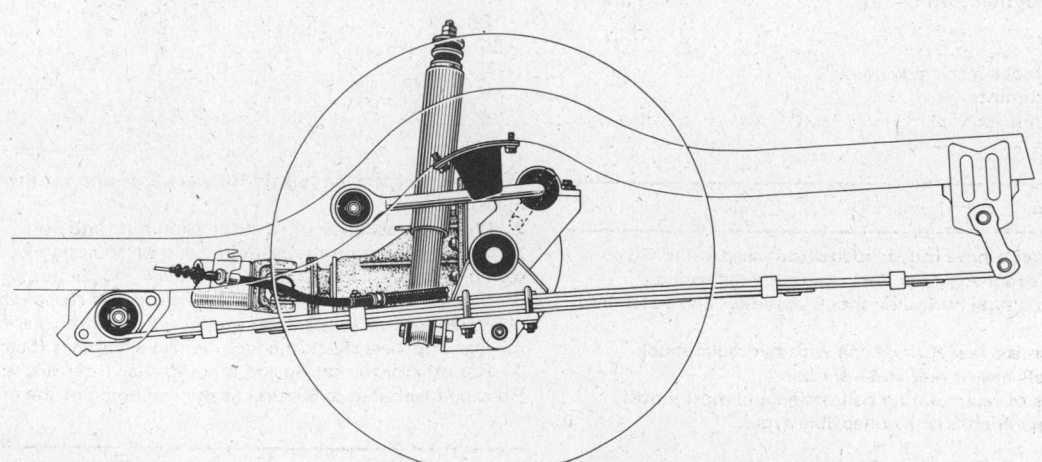

Fig. 11.2. Sectional view of alternative types of rear suspension

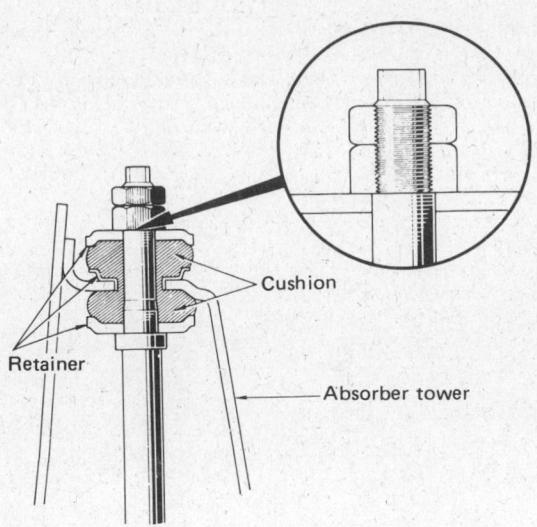

Fig. 11.3. Front shock absorber upper mounting

A Lower

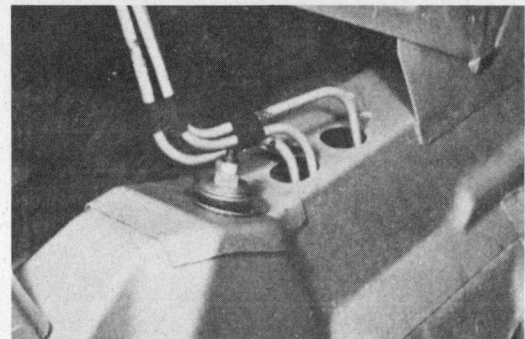

B Upper

Fig. 11.4. Rear shock absorber attachment points

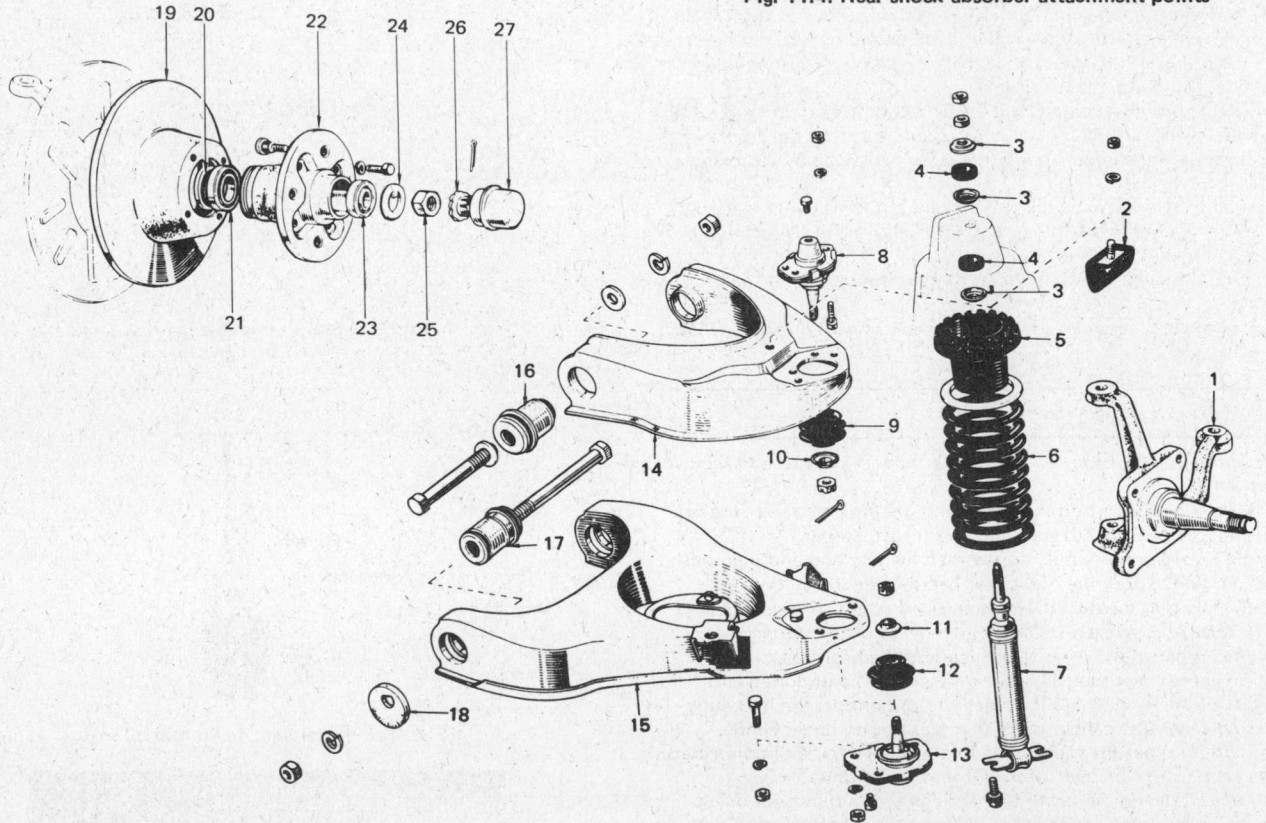

Fig. 11.5. Exploded view of one side of the front suspension (disc brake type shown)

1	Stub axle carrier	8	Upper balljoint	15	Suspension lower arm	22	Hub
2	Bump stop	9	Rubber boot	16	Pivot bush	23	Outer bearing
3	Retainer	10	Retainer	17	Pivot bush	24	Lock washer
4	Rubber bush	11	Collar	18	Eccentric cam plate	25	Nut
5	Insulator	12	Rubber boot	19	Disc	26	Adjusting cap
6	Coil spring	13	Lower balljoint	20	Oil seal	27	Grease cap
7	Shock absorber	14	Suspension	21	Inner bearing		

used for attachment to the lower wishbone.

2   The rear mountings are very similar, except that an eye and bush is used at the lower end for attachment to the spring bracket mounting.

3   Removal of both types of shock absorber is simply a matter of removing the attachment nuts or bolts, and withdrawing the unit. Do not remove a shock absorber with the vehicle jacked up and the road-wheel hanging free. If working clearance is required always jack up the car in the correct place (see Jacking Points in the Introduction), then raise the suspension arm or spring to keep the spring in compression.

4   To test a shock absorber, grip the lower mounting in a vice with the unit in a vertical position. Extend and contract the shock absorber to the full extent of its travel about ten times. There should be a **definite** resistance in both directions, otherwise renew the unit. Any sign of oil leakage around the operating rod seal will also indicate the need for renewal as the units are not repairable.

5   Refitting is the reverse of the removal procedure, but tighten the retaining nuts and bolts to the correct torque.

4   Suspension arm balljoints - testing and renewal

1   To test for wear in these components, jack up the front suspension in the correct place (see Jacking Points in the Introduction) then raise the suspension arm with a jack to compress the spring.

2   Grip the roadwheel and move it vertically up and down and then in and out in a horizontal direction.

3   Assuming that the wheel bearings are correctly adjusted (see Section 5), there should only be movement of up to 0.04 in (1 mm) in the vertical direction and 0.08 in (2 mm) in the horizontal direction.

4   Where excessive wear is found, the balljoints must be renewed as follows:

5   The use of a balljoint separator will now be essential as there is no room to attempt to jar them apart using the wedge or hammer method.

6   On models with ESP, disconnect the wire harness for the brakes, and separate the clamp from the arm.

7   Unscrew and almost remove the lower balljoint stud nut and, using the separator tool, detach the balljoint taper stud from the stud axle carrier. Remove the balljoint from the lower wishbone by removing the three securing bolts.

8   Removal of the upper balljoint is carried out in a similar way, but do not strain the brake flexible hose once it is detached by allowing the weight of the hub to hang upon it.

9   Refitting the upper and lower balljoints is the reverse of the removal procedure.

10   Tighten the balljoint taper stud nuts to the specified torque wrench setting.

5   Front hubs - servicing and adjustment

1   Jack up the front of the vehicle, chock the rear wheels, and remove the roadwheel.

2   *On vehicles with front drum brakes,* tap off the grease cap, extract the split pin, remove the nut, retainer and thrust washer.

3   Pull the hub/drum assembly forward an inch or two and then push it back. This will expose the hub outer bearing which can then be extracted. Now pull the hub/drum assembly straight off the stub axle.

4   *On vehicles with front disc brakes,* removal of the hub/disc assembly is similar to the procedure just described for hub/drum assemblies, except that the caliper must first be unbolted and tied up out of the way. There is no need to disconnect the hydraulic pipe on single cylinder caliper units (F type) but on dual cylinder calipers (Girling type) the rigid brake line will have to be disconnected from the caliper. For further information refer to Chapter 9.

5   Wash out all old grease from the bearings and hub interior using paraffin or petrol, taking care not to damage the oil seal. Check the bearings and tracks for wear, damage or scoring.

6   If they are in good condition, repack the inside of the hub with grease (see Fig. 11.6).

7   If there is evidence of grease seepage onto the discs, drive out the old seal and tap in a new one using a tubular drift.

8   If either the inner or outer bearings require renewal, drive out the tracks with a brass drift and press in the new ones. Where both front hubs are being serviced at the same time, do not mix the bearing components as the race and the track are matched in production.

9   The disc should not be removed from the hub assembly unless it is

to be renewed or re-faced as described in Chapter 9.

10   Reassembly is the reverse of the dismantling procedure, but the bearings must be adjusted in the following way.

11   Tighten the hub nut to the specified initial tightening torque, rotating the hub at the same time. Unscrew the nut and then tighten it using only the socket gripped in the hand.

12   Check the bearing preload by attaching a spring balance to one of the roadwheel studs. The pull required to rotate the hub should be between 12.3 and 30.6 oz (350 and 870 gram).

13   When adjustment is correct, fit the adjuster cap and insert a new split pin.

14   Fill the grease cap 1/3rd full with grease and knock it into position.

15   On vehicles with dual cylinder type calipers, bleed the brake hydraulic system (see Chapter 9).

16   Refit the roadwheel and lower the jack.

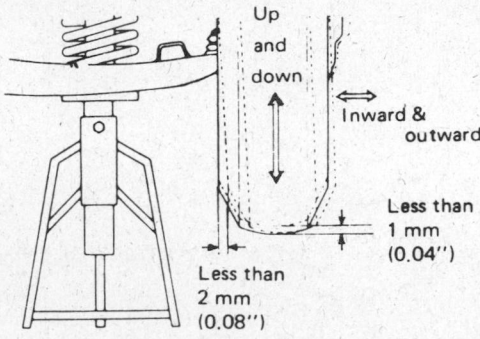

Fig. 11.6. Wear checking diagram for suspension balljoints

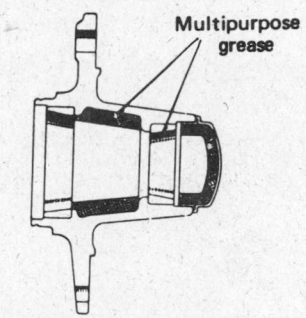

Fig. 11.7. Front hub grease packing areas

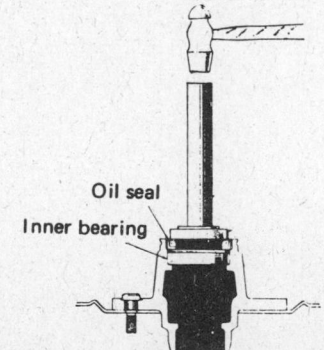

Fig. 11.8. Installing a front hub oil seal

Fig. 11.9. Separating a track rod end balljoint

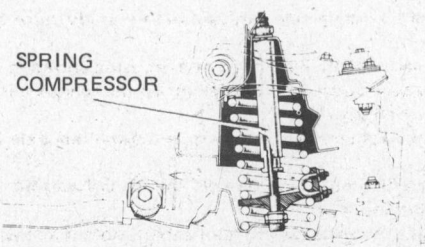

Fig. 11.10. Coil spring compressor in use

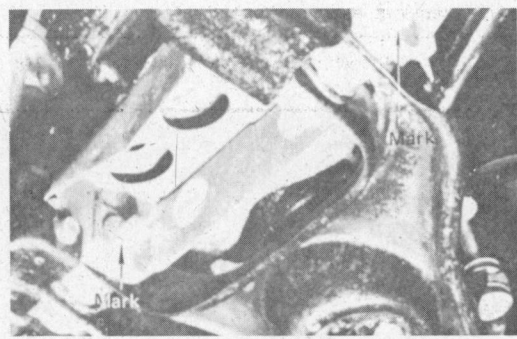

Fig. 11.11. Cam plate index marks

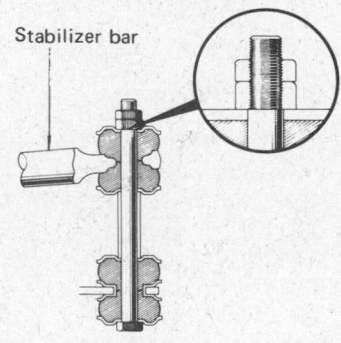

Fig. 11.12. Front stabilizer bar attachments

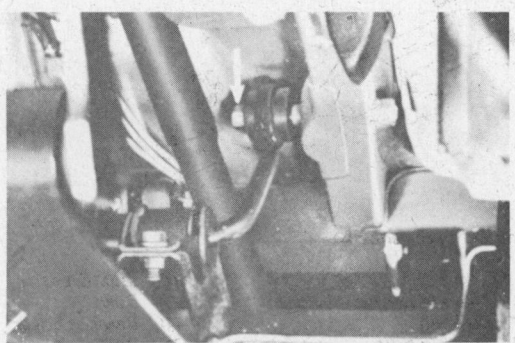

Fig. 11.13. Right-hand rear attachment of stabilizer bar

6 Stub axle carrier - removal and refitting

1   Jack up the front of the vehicle supporting it securely under the main crossmember.

2   Place a second jack under the lower wishbone of the suspension and raise it to compress the spring.

3   Remove the hub/drum or hub/disc assembly as described in the preceding Section.

4   Unbolt the shield (disc brakes) or the backplate (drum brakes). In the case of the latter, tie it up out of the way to avoid straining the hydraulic flexible hose.

5   Using a balljoint separator, disconnect the trackrod-end from the steering arm of the stub axle carrier (for further information also see Section 12).

6   Separate the suspension wishbone upper and lower balljoints and withdraw the stub axle carrier.

7   Refitting is the reverse of the removal procedure.

7 Suspension upper arm - removal and refitting

1   Working from within the engine compartment unscrew and remove the suspension upper arm securing nuts **but do not attempt to knock out the pivot bolts** at this stage.

2   Jack up the front of the vehicle and then place an axle stand under the suspension lower arm so that the coil spring is under compression. Remove the roadwheel.

3   On models with ESP, disconnect the wire harness for the brakes and separate the clamp from the arm.

4   Using a balljoint separator, disconnect the upper balljoint, and support the brake hydraulic hose to prevent it from being strained.

5   Extract the suspension upper arm bolts, and lever the arm from its location.

6   If the suspension arm bushes have deteriorated, they must be renewed by a service station which has the necessary press and guide tools.

7   The suspension upper arms are handed left and right, and are not interchangeable.

8   Refitting is the reverse of the removal procedure, but the arm will have to be tapped into position between the bodyframe mountings.

9   Insert the pivot bolts, but only tighten the nuts finger-tight at this stage.

10 Reconnect the upper balljoint to the stub axle carrier.

11 Refit the roadwheel, lower the vehicle to the ground, then rock it on its suspension several times before tightening the pivot bolts to the specified torque.

12 Check the front wheel alignment as described in Section 18.

8 Suspension lower arm and coil spring - removal and refitting

1   Jack up the front of the vehicle, supporting it securely under the front crossmember.

2   Remove the roadwheel.

3   Remove the shock absorber (see Section 3).

4   Disconnect the stabiliser bar from the suspension lower arm.

5   A coil spring compressor will now be required. One may be made up if necessary from a length of studding, cross plates and nuts. Compress the coil spring so that its bottom coil is no longer in contact with the suspension lower arm spring pan (see Fig. 11.10).

6   Support the suspension lower arm on a jack and then disconnect the lower balljoint from the stub axle carrier (see Section 4).

7   Unscrew the nuts from the pivot bolts, remove the cam plates, noting carefully the setting of each cam plate index mark (see Section 18).

8   Tap out the pivot bolts and withdraw the suspension lower arm.

9   Carefully release the coil spring compressor and remove the coil spring.

10 If the suspension arm bushes have deteriorated, they must be renewed by a service station having the necessary press and guide tools.

11 Commence reassembly by offering up the suspension lower arm to the bodyframe and inserting the pivot bolts.

12 Fit the cam plates and screw on the nuts only finger-tight.

13 Install the coil spring so that it fits correctly in the upper insulator and then compress it using the spring compressor.

14 Jack up the lower arm and using a piece of wood, prise the coil spring (lower coil) into its pan so that the end of its coil is correctly located in the spring seat.

15 Connect the lower balljoint to the stub axle carrier.

16 Connect the stabilizer bar to the lower arm. Do not overtighten the securing nut or locknut.

17 Remove the coil spring compressor and refit the shock absorber.

18 Refit the roadwheel and lower the vehicle to the ground.

19 Rock the vehicle on its suspension several times, then turn the cam plates to their original settings and tighten the pivot bolts to the specified torque setting.

9 Stabilizer bars - removal and refitting

1 The procedure for front and rear bars is similar. Disconnect the end attachments, then the brackets and rubber insulator which secure the stabilizer bar to the bodyframe. At the right-hand end of the rear stabilizer bar take care that the fuel pipe is not damaged when removing the nut (see Fig. 11.13).

2 If the end bushes of the rear stabilizer bar need renewing, they must be pressed out and new ones pressed in so that the slot is in the downwards position when the vehicle is unladen.

3 Refitting is the reverse of the removal procedure, but do not over compress the end fitting nuts or locknuts.

10 Rear spring silencer pad - renewal

1 Jack up the rear of the vehicle and support the bodyframe on stands or blocks.

2 Place a second jack under the differential housing and raise it until any downward pressure caused by the weight of the rear axle is removed from the road springs.

3 Remove the nut, washers and bolt to separate the rear axle from the spring.

4 Remove the retaining nuts and take off the 'U' bolts so that the spring seat can be removed.

5 If the bushes are damaged (where applicable), obtain a new spring seat.

6 Refitting is the reverse of the removal procedure, but ensure that the seat is correctly located before tightening the bolts to the correct torque wrench setting.

11 Rear spring - removal, examination and refitting

1 Jack up the rear of the vehicle by placing the jack under the

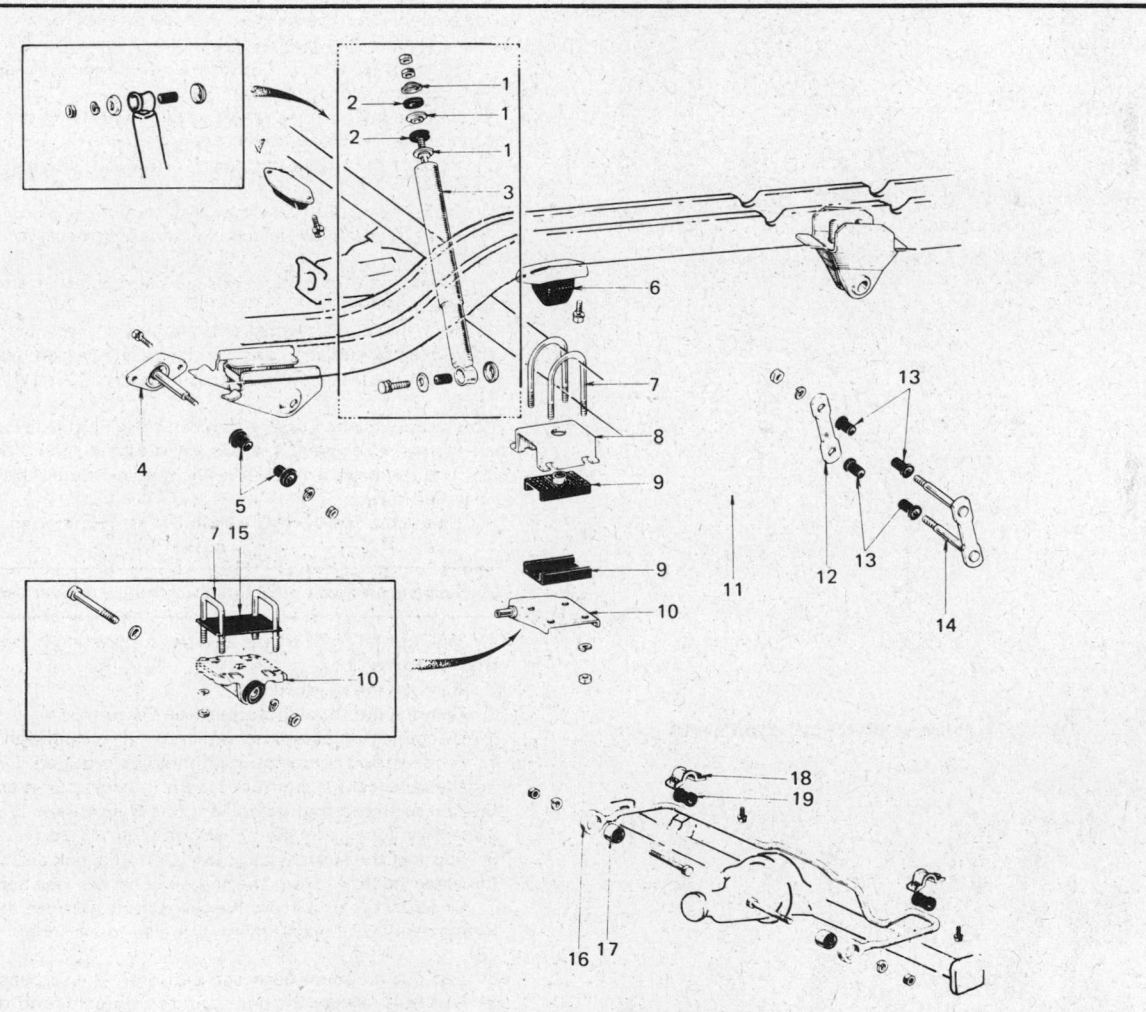

Fig. 11.14. Rear spring attachments (alternative types shown)

1 Cushion retainer	6 Spring bumper	11 Leaf spring	16 Stabilizer bar
2 Cushion	7 U-bolt	12 Shackle plate	17 Bush
3 Shock absorber	8 Pad retainer	13 Bushing	18 Bracket cover
4 Eye bolt	9 Pad	14 Shackle bolt	19 Bush
5 Bushing	10 Spring U-bolt seat (alternative type)	15 U-bolt retainer	

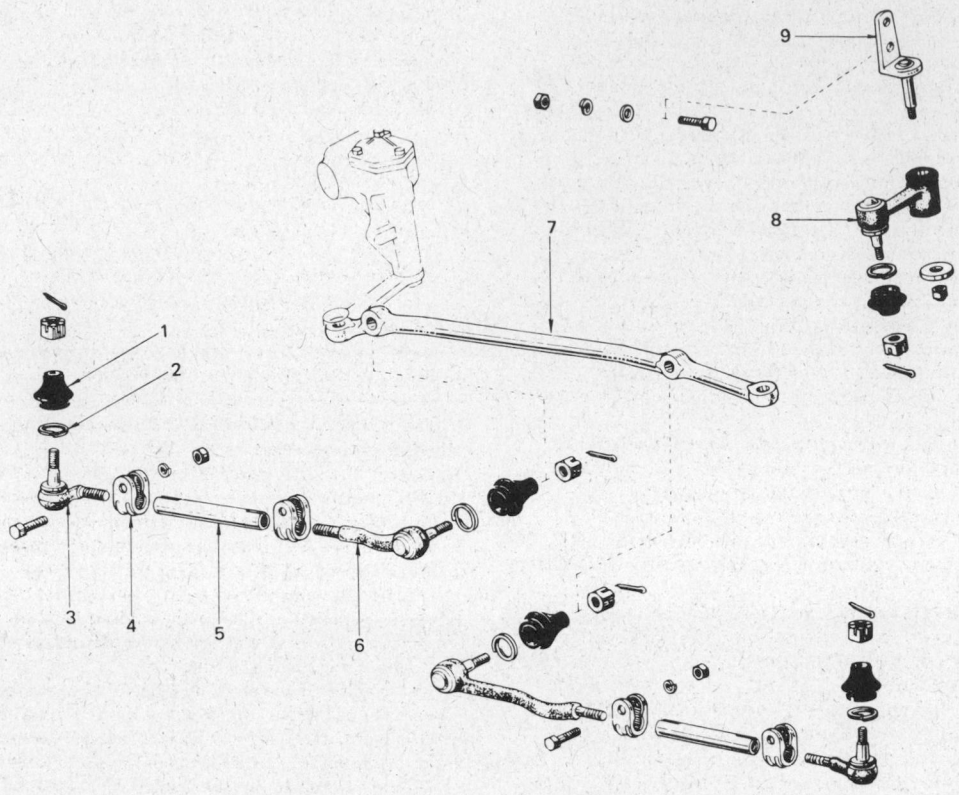

Fig. 11.15. Steering linkage layout

1 Rubber boot	4 Clamp	6 Track rod end	8 Idler arm
2 Retaining ring	5 Track rod	7 Relay rod	9 Idler support
3 Track rod end			

Fig. 11.16. Separating parts of the steering linkage

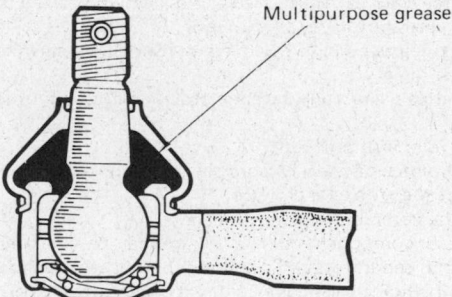

Multipurpose grease

Fig. 11.17. Steering balljoint showing grease

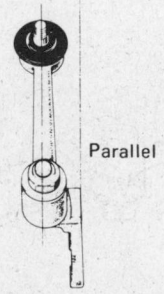

Parallel

Fig. 11.18. Idle arm parallel to frame when installed

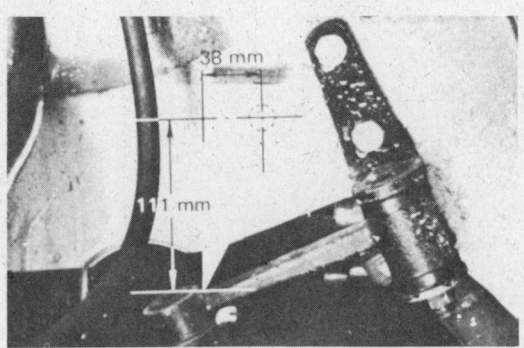

Fig. 11.19. Setting idler arm height

differential housing. Support the body frame with stands and then remove the roadwheels.

2   Remove the road spring 'U' bolt retaining nuts and detach the retaining plate and rubber insulating pad. Detach the handbrake cable clamp from its support plate.

3   Jack up the differential until the leaf springs are relieved of the weight of the rear axle and then remove the 'U' bolts.

4   Remove the shackle bolt from the spring rear eye and the eye bolt from the front eye, and remove the road spring.

5   During the period when the rear road springs are removed from the rear axle, the axle must not be moved rearwards otherwise the sliding sleeve of the propeller shaft may become disconnected and the rear flexible brake hose may be strained and damaged.

6   Scrub the spring clean in a paraffin bath using a wire brush. Examine each leaf edge throughout its length for cracks. If a crack or broken leaf is found, do not attempt to dismantle it, but either exchange it for a new unit or have it professionally repaired by the insertion of a new leaf.

7   The spring eye bushes are of the split rubber type and should be renewed if perished or worn; no press is required but a little hydraulic brake fluid will assist in fitting them into the spring eyes.

8   Refitting should commence by connecting the front eye bolt followed by the rear shackle bolt; tighten the nuts only finger-tight. Note that the shorter length of the spring (eye to centre bolt) is located to the front of the rear axle.

9   Fit the insulating pads and retainers to the spring, then lower the jack under the rear axle ensuring that the spring centre bolt engages in its locating hole in the rear axle mounting plate.

10 Fit the 'U' bolts and their nuts finger-tight.

11 Reconnect the handbrake cable clamps, then fit the roadwheels, remove the support stands and lower the vehicle to the ground.

12 Bounce the vehicle up and down several times to settle the suspension, then tighten the nuts to the specified torque.

12 Steering linkage - removal and refitting

1   Before dismantling the steering linkage it is essential to obtain a balljoint separator. This may be of screw type or consist of a pair of wedges. It is possible to jar the balljoint taper pin free from its eye by striking opposite sides of the eye simultaneously with two club hammers, but the available space to do this is very restricted and the use of a proper extractor is recommended.

2   Unscrew and remove the nut which secures the drop arm to the shaft of the steering gear.

3   Using a suitable extractor, draw the drop arm from the splined shaft.

4   Unbolt the idler arm bracket.

5   Using a balljoint separator, disconnect the trackrod ends from the steering arms of the stub axle carriers.

6   Withdraw the complete steering linkage.

7   The individual components of the linkage may be separated by using the balljoint separator and loosening the trackrod clamps.

8   Check each balljoint for slackness or excessive stiffness, also for split or deteriorated rubber dust excluders, and renew as necessary. Check the idler arm bushes.

9   When fitting a balljoint dust cover, pack the interior with a molybdenum disulphide multi-purpose grease.

10 Reassembly is the reverse of the dismantling procedure, but observe the following points:

  a) *Fit the idler arm to the support so that it conforms to the specified setting angle (see Figs. 11.18, 11.19 and 11.20).*

  b) *Tighten the self-locking nut to the specified torque without altering the setting.*

  c) *Screw the trackrod-ends into their tubes by an equal amount and position the clamp bolts over the adjusting tube slots.*

  d) *Refit the drop arm so that the mating marks are in alignment.*

  e) *When refitting of the linkage is complete, check and adjust the front wheel alignment as described in Section 18.*

13 Steering wheel - removal and refitting

1   From behind the steering wheel spokes, remove the screws so that the steering wheel pad can be taken off.

2   Detach the horn lead then unscrew the steering wheel retaining nut. Make alignment marks on the end of the shaft and the steering wheel so that the wheel can be refitted in exactly the same position.

3   Remove the steering wheel by tapping it gently at the rear with the palms of the hands. If it does not come off, on no account attempt to jar it off or to hammer the end of the shaft as damage to the column will result, particularly if it is of collapsible type. If the wheel is stuck, use an extractor with a centre screw, taking care to protect the surfaces of the steering wheel and hub.

4   Installation of the steering wheel is the reverse of the removal procedure, but make sure that the mating marks made before removal, are in alignment. Make sure that the hole in the steering wheel and the direction indicator switch cancelling cam are in alignment.

5   Tighten the steering wheel securing nut to the specified torque.

14 Steering upper bracket and bush - removal and refitting

1   Remove the steering wheel as described in the previous Section.

2   Remove the steering column garnish and unplug the harness connectors.

3   Remove the retaining screws and take off the steering column upper and lower covers.

4   On column shift automatic transmission models, depress the shift lever pins to allow the shift lever to be pulled out.

5   Remove the combination switch retaining screws (Fig. 11.25) and carefully lift off the switch assembly.

6   Insert the ignition key and turn it to the ACC position. Push in the switch stop key with a stiff wire or small screwdriver, and pull out the key cylinder.

7   Remove the retaining screws to release the steering column shaft bearing retainer and bracket bolts.

8   Using circlip pliers, remove the circlip so that the upper bracket can be withdrawn.

9   Using a suitable diameter drift, carefully drive out the upper bearing (if necessary).

10 When pressing in the new bearing, ensure that the upper surface is

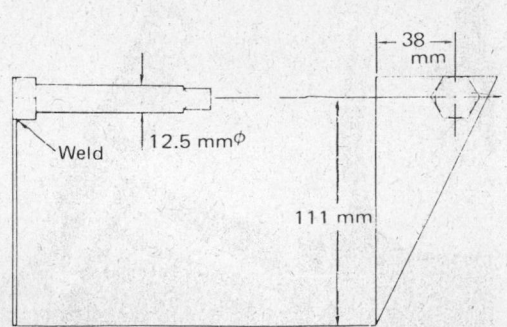

Fig. 11.20. Dimensions for idler arm height setting gauge

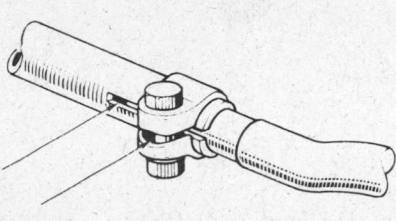

Fig. 11.21. Installed position of trackrod ends

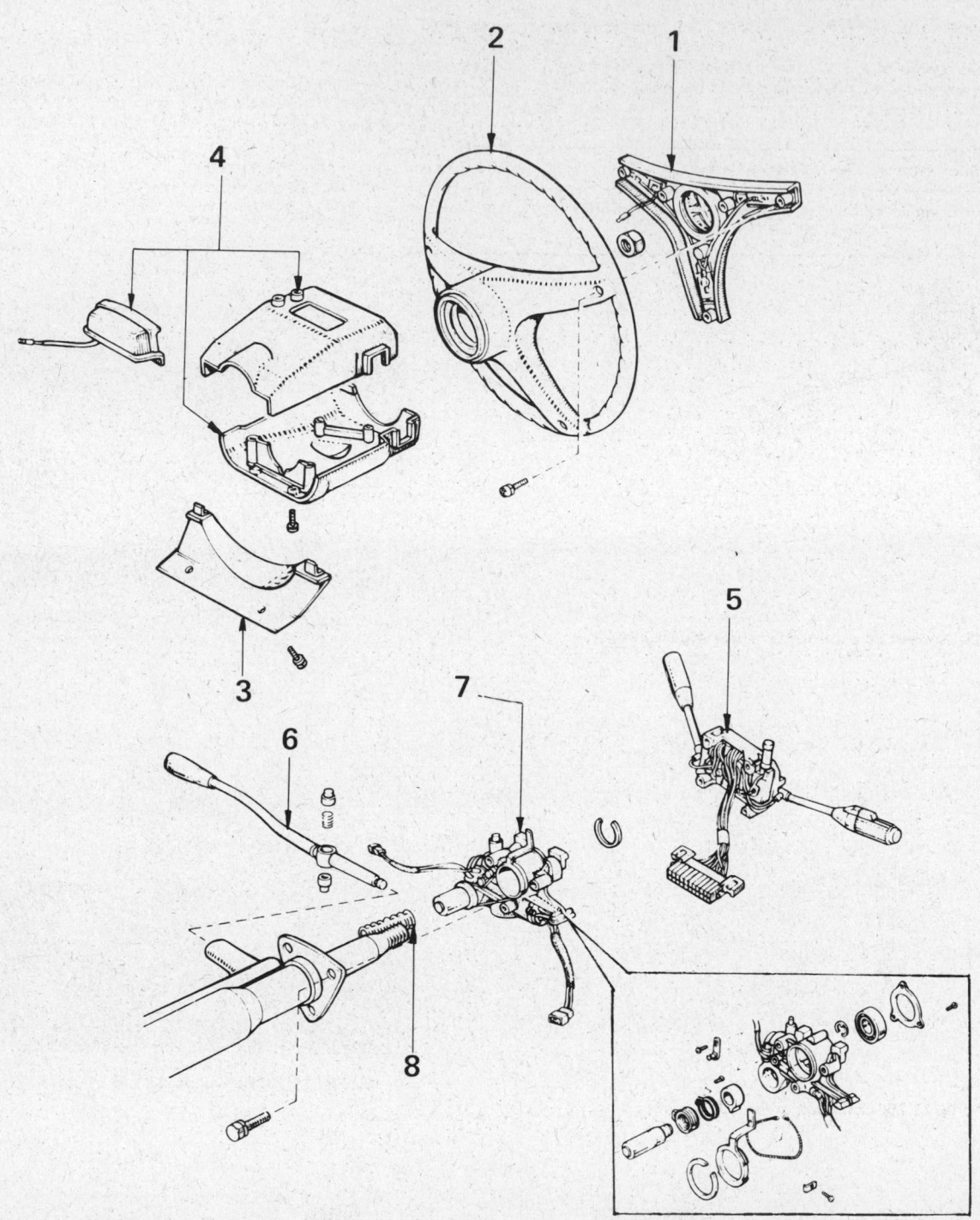

Fig. 11.22. Steering wheel and upper bracket (column shift automatic transmission type shown)

1 Steering wheel pad
2 Steering wheel
3 Steering column garnish

4 Steering column covers and
   position indicator housing

5 Combination switch
6 Shift lever

7 Upper bracket assembly
8 Spring

flush with the upper surface of the bracket, then pack multi-purpose grease into the bearing.

11 Refitting is the reverse of the removal procedure, but don't forget that the ignition key and key cylinder must be in the ACC position when the assembly is inserted into the bracket.

15 Steering column - removal, servicing and refitting

1 Remove the steering upper bracket as described in the previous Section.

2 At the lower end of the steering column, remove the pinch bolt from the coupling.

3 Remove the bolts from the steering column hole cover and from the steering column clamp (breakaway bracket).

4 Withdraw the shaft from the steering column and remove the dust seal.

5 Remove the flexible coupling from the inner shaft.

6 Unbolt the hole cover plate from the column tube.

7 Inspect all components for wear and renew as appropriate. Check

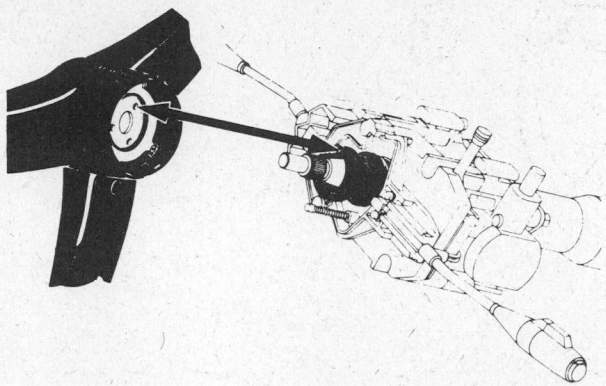

Fig. 11.23. Correct position for installing steering wheel

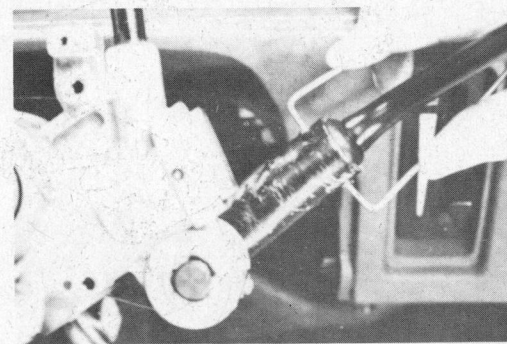

Fig. 11.24. Remove column shift lever

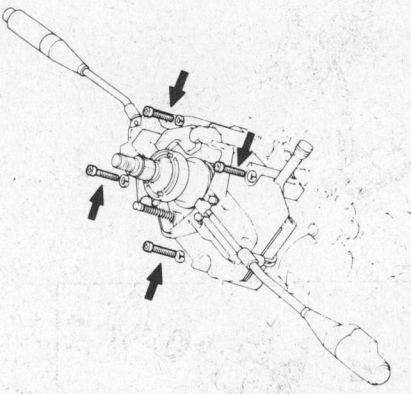

Fig. 11.25. Combination switch screws

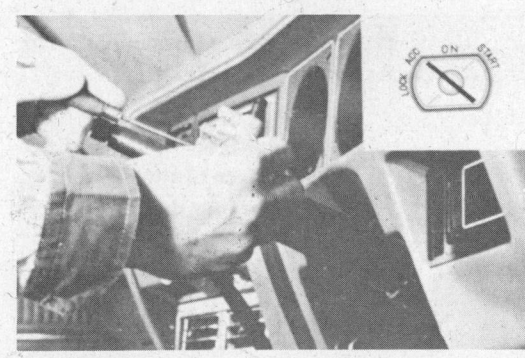

Fig. 11.26. Removing the key cylinder

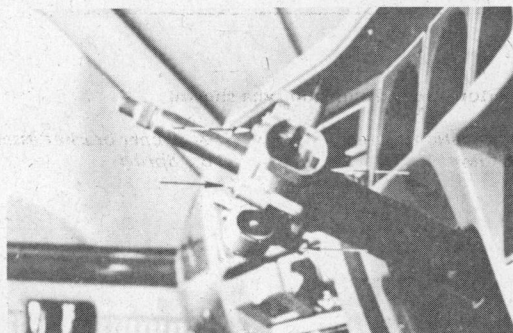

Fig. 11.27. Bearing retainer screws (arrowed)

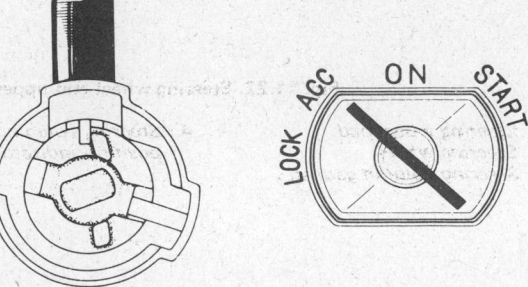

Fig. 11.28. Installing the key cylinder

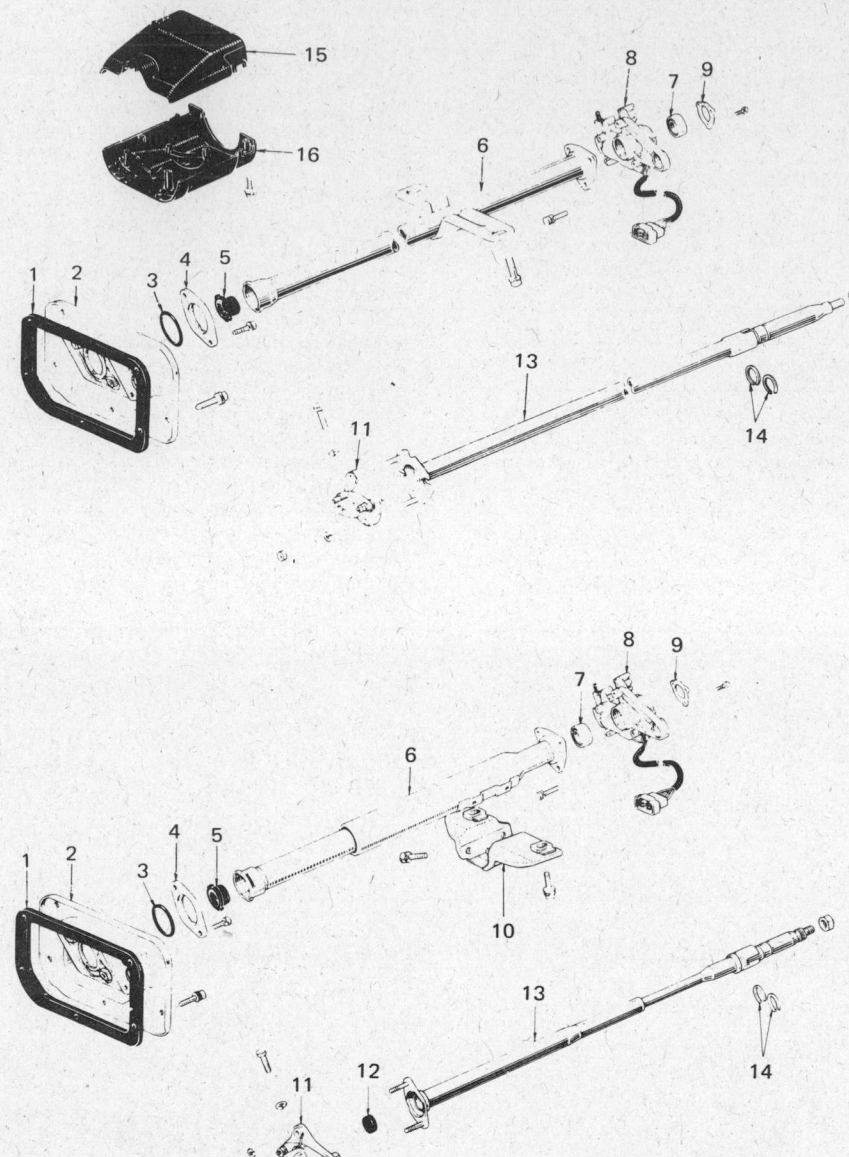

Fig. 11.29. Alternative types of steering column

1	Hole shield	5	Dust seal	9	Bearing retainer	13	Steering shaft
2	Hole cover	6	Steering column	10	Breakaway bracket	14	Snap ring
3	'O' ring	7	Bearing	11	Flexible coupling	15	Upper cover
4	Hole plate	8	Upper bracket	12	Plug	16	Lower cover

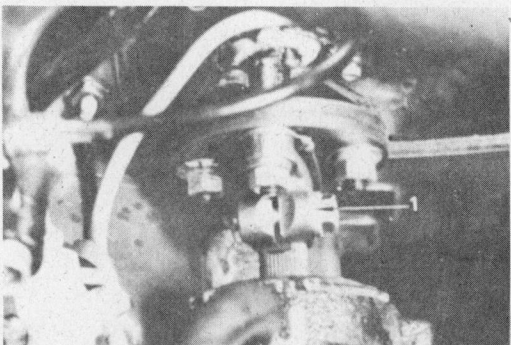

Fig. 11.30. Steering coupling bolt (1)

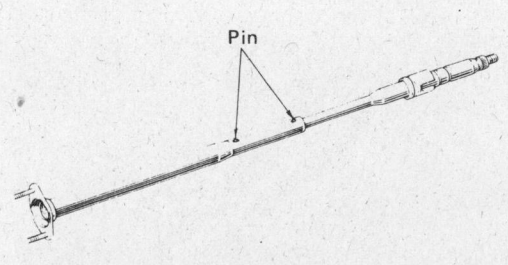

Fig. 11.31. Steering shaft plastic pins

for the loosening of the plastic pins which secure the collapsible sections of the steering shaft.

8 Assembly is the reverse of the dismantling procedure, but apply grease to the upper bearing and to both sides of the dust seal.

9 Install the column assembly, connect the coupling and tighten the pinch bolt.

10 Locate the column bracket but insert the bolts only finger-tight.

11 Tighten the column hole cover bolts.

12 Push the steering column fully downward and then tighten the column bracket bolts to the specified torque. **It is imperative that the pin in the hole cover locates in the cut-out in the outer column (see Fig. 11.33).**

16 Steering box - removal and refitting

1 Remove the drop arm from the shaft.

2 Remove the pinch bolt from the steering shaft coupling. On left-hand drive models the flexible coupling bolts and the air cleaner must also be removed.

3 Unbolt the steering box and remove it from the car.

4 Refitting is the reverse of the removal procedure, but align the mating marks on the drop arm and shaft endface.

5 Check the oil level and top-up with the specified grade.

17 Steering box - dismantling and reassembly

1 Remove the steering box as described in the previous Section.

2 Loosen the rocker shaft adjusting screw locknut, then remove the bolts so that the cover plate and rocker shaft can be removed.

3 Remove the worm adjusting screw locknut then unscrew the adjuster screw from the steering box housing. The adjuster screw requires a special peg spanner, and if a suitable one is not available it will be necessary to purchase Toyota tool No. 09616-30011.

4 Withdraw the worm/nut assembly complete with bearings from the steering box. Do not try to remove the nut.

5 Examine the worm and nut, and bearings, for wear, scoring or damage; run the nut up and down the worm during the checking, but take great care not to contact either end of the worm.

6 If the worm or nut show signs of wear or damage then they must be renewed as an assembly.

7 Remove the oil seal from the adjusting screw and steering box.

8 Remove the needle roller bearings from the steering box, then clean out all the old lubricant.

9 Commence reassembly by greasing the needle roller bearings and positioning them in the steering box (see Fig. 11.37). Fit both oil seals and smear the lips with grease.

10 Lubricate the worm/nut assembly with gear oil then position it in

Fig. 11.32. Installed position of steering shaft

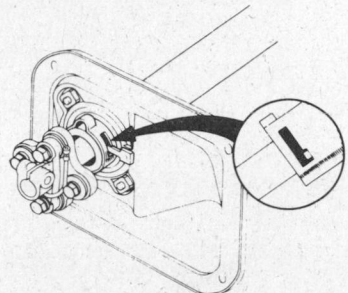

Fig. 11.33. Position the pin in the cut-out in the outer column

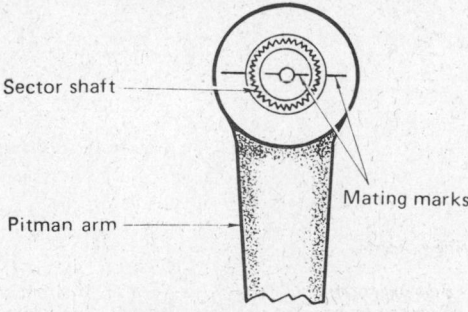

Sector shaft

Mating marks

Pitman arm

Fig. 11.34. Installed position of drop arm

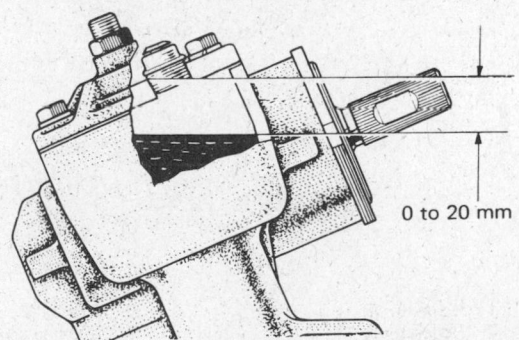

0 to 20 mm

Fig. 11.35. Correct oil level in steering box

09616-30011

Fig. 11.36. Adjusting screw peg spanner in use

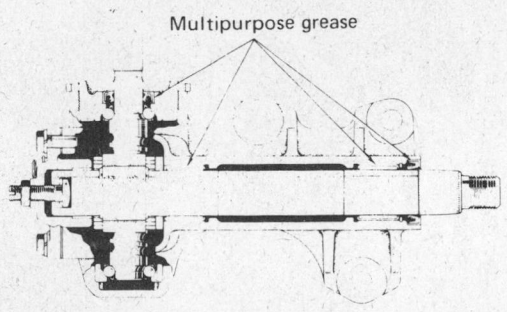

Multipurpose grease

Fig. 11.37. Apply multi-purpose grease to the needle roller bearings and oil seals

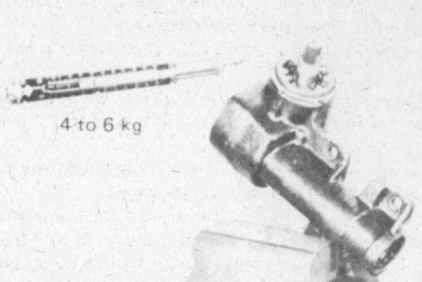

Fig. 11.38. Checking the preload

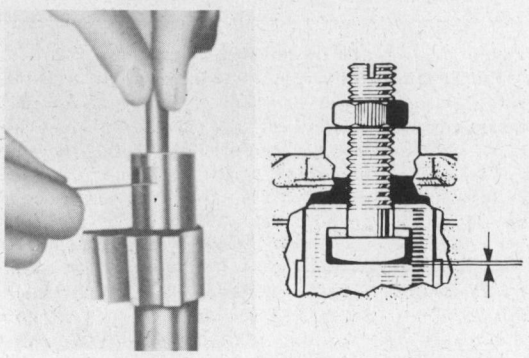

Fig. 11.39. Checking the thrust washer clearance

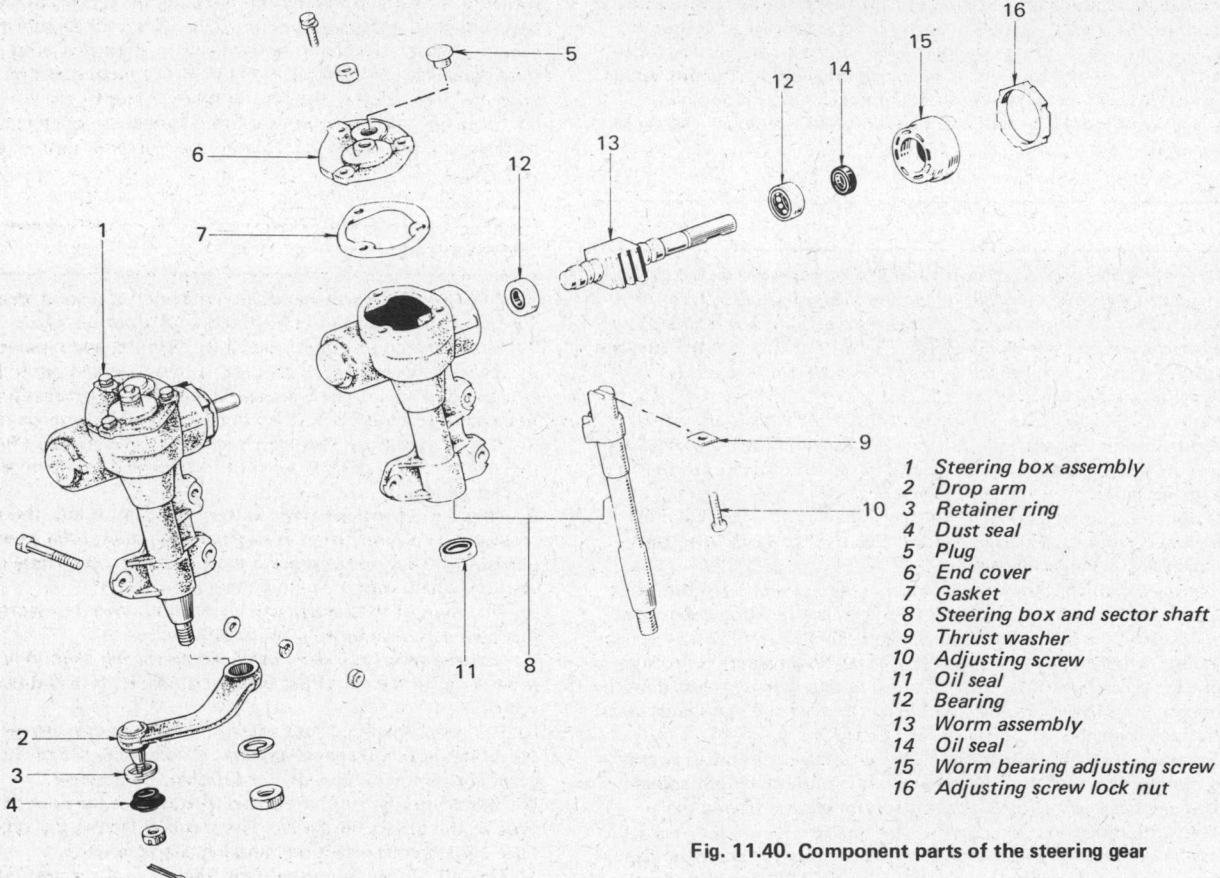

1 Steering box assembly
2 Drop arm
3 Retainer ring
4 Dust seal
5 Plug
6 End cover
7 Gasket
8 Steering box and sector shaft
9 Thrust washer
10 Adjusting screw
11 Oil seal
12 Bearing
13 Worm assembly
14 Oil seal
15 Worm bearing adjusting screw
16 Adjusting screw lock nut

Fig. 11.40. Component parts of the steering gear

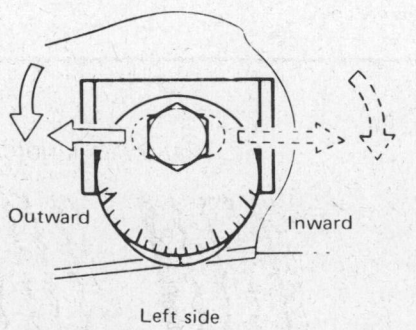

Outward   Inward

Inward   Outward

Left side

Right side

As seen from rear

Fig. 11.41. Effect of suspension lower arm cam adjustment

the steering box followed by the adjuster screw and locknut.

11 Wind a thin cord round the splined pinion of the worm gear and attach a spring balance to it. Adjust the adjuster screw until the spring balance registers between 9 and 13 lb (4.0 and 6.0 kg) when given an even pull; this is the required worm bearing pre-load. Without moving the adjuster nut, tighten the locking ring to the specified torque.

12 Using a feeler gauge, measure the clearance between the convex face of the adjuster screw and its rocker shaft contact face. The clearance should not exceed 0.002 in (0.05 mm). If it does, change the thrust washer. The following thrust washer thicknesses are available:

0.079 in (2.00 mm), 0.080 in (2.04 mm), 0.082 in (2.08 mm),
0.083 in (2.12 mm), 0.085 in (2.16 mm), 0.087 in (2.20 mm).

13 Refit the rocker shaft, ensuring that the nut is positioned in the centre of the steering worm.

14 Loosen the cover plate adjuster screw right off and then fit the cover plate complete with new gasket (smeared both sides with jointing compound). Tighten the cover plate bolts to the specified torque.

15 Rocker shaft adjustment can be carried out if slackness develops when the steering box is in the vehicle by removing the steering wheel and winding the cord round the shaft splines, taking the preload reading as just described. It will be necessary also to detach the drop arm when doing this.

18 Front wheel alignment

1 Accurate front wheel alignment is essential for good steering and even tyre wear. Before considering the steering angles, check that the tyres are correctly inflated, that the front wheels are not buckled, the hub bearings are not worn or incorrectly adjusted and that the steering linkage is in good order, without slackness or wear at the joints.

2 Wheel alignment consists of four factors:

Camber, which is the angle at which the front wheels are set from the vertical when viewed from the front of the car. Positive camber is the amount (in degrees) that the wheels are tilted outwards at the top from the vertical.

Castor, is the angle between the steering axis and a vertical line when viewed from each side of the car. Positive castor is when the steering axis is inclined rearward.

Steering axis inclination, is the angle, when viewed from the front of the car, between the vertical and an imaginary line drawn between the upper and lower suspension swivel balljoints.

Toe-in, is the amount by which the distance between the front inside edges of the roadwheels (measured at hub height) is less than the diametrically opposite distance measured between the rear inside edges of the front roadwheels.

3 Due to the need for precision gauges to measure the small angles set in the steering and suspension layout it is preferable that adjustment of camber and castor is left to a service station having the necessary equipment.

4 Camber and castor angles are varied by turning the eccentric cam adjusters on the suspension lower arm pivot bolts. These angles are normally set for 'life' during production and if the suspension is to be dismantled, always record the cam setting in relation to its reference mark before starting work.

5 Front wheel tracking (toe-in) may be checked and adjusted by carrying out the following operations.

6 Place the car on level ground with the wheels in the straight ahead position.

7 Obtain or make a toe-in gauge. One may be easily made from tubing, cranked to clear the sump and bellhousing, having an adjustable nut and setscrew at one end.

8 With the gauge, measure the distance between the two wheel inner rims (at hub height) at the rear of the wheel.

9 Rotate the wheel through 180º (half a turn) and measure the distance between the wheel inner rims (again at hub height) at the front of the wheel. This measurement should be less by an amount which corresponds with the specified toe-in (see Specifications).

10 Where the toe-in is found to be incorrect, slacken all four trackrod clamp bolts and rotate each track rod equally. It is a good plan to first measure each trackrod between the balljoint centres in case they have been adjusted unevenly by a previous owner. When adjustment is correct, tighten the clamp bolts, ensuring that the clamp openings are in alignment with the slots in the trackrod tubes and that the trackrod ends are positioned in the centres of their arcs of travel.

11 Steering lock stop bolts are fitted to the rear of the stub axle carriers, and are adjustable to limit the full lock travel in each direction (see Fig. 11.42).

19 Wheels and tyres

1 Whenever the roadwheels are removed it is a good idea to clean the insides of the wheels to remove accumulations of mud.

2 Check the condition of the wheel for rust, and repaint if necessary.

3 Examine the wheel stud holes. If these are tending to become elongated, or the dished recesses in which the nuts seat have worn or become overcompressed, then the wheel will have to be renewed.

4 With a roadwheel removed, pick out any embedded flints from the tyre tread, and check for splits in the sidewalls or damage to the tyre carcass generally.

5 Where the depth of tread pattern is 1 mm or less, the tyre must be renewed. The tyres fitted as original equipment have tread wear indicators at six points around the circumference. These markers give warning of 1.6 mm of tread remaining.

6 Rotation of the roadwheels to even out wear is a worthwhile idea if the wheels have been balanced off the car.

7 If the wheels have been balanced on the car then they cannot be moved round the car as the balance of wheel, tyre and hub will be upset.

8 It is recommended that wheels are balanced whenever new tyres are fitted, and re-balanced halfway through the life of the tyre to compensate for the loss of tread rubber due to wear.

9 Whenever rear tyres are fitted, ensure that they are of the same ply type as the others on the car. Never mix different ply types as this can have a dangerous effect on handling characteristics.

10 Finally, always keep the tyres (including the spare) inflated to the recommended pressures, and always fit the dust caps on the valves. Tyre pressures are best checked first thing in the morning when the tyres are cold.

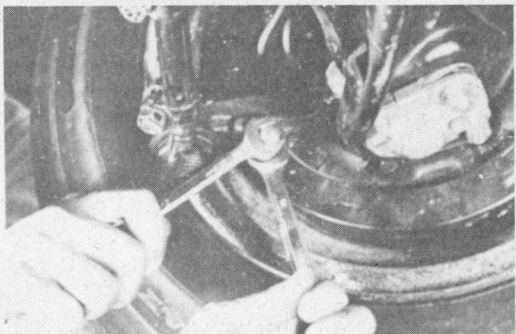

Fig. 11.42. Steering angle adjustment

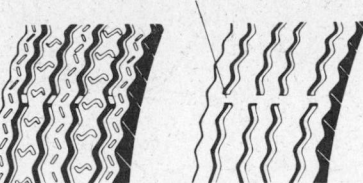

TREAD WEAR INDICATOR

NEW TREAD   WORN TREAD
Tyre should be renewed

Fig. 11.43. Typical tread wear indicators

20 Fault diagnosis - steering and suspension

Before diagnosing faults from the following chart, check that any irregularities are not caused by:

> *1 Binding brakes*
> *2 Incorrect 'mix' of radial and crossply tyres*
> *3 Incorrect tyre pressures*
> *4 Misalignment of the bodyframe*

Symptom	Cause
Steering wheel can be moved considerably before any sign of movement of the wheels is apparent	Wear in the steering linkage, gear and column coupling.
Vehicle difficult to steer in a consistent straight line - wandering	As above. Wheel alignment incorrect (indicated by excessive or uneven tyre wear). Front wheel hub bearings loose or worn. Worn suspension unit swivel joints.
Steering stiff and heavy	Incorrect wheel alignment (indicated by excessive or uneven tyre wear). Excessive wear or seizure in one or more of the joints in the steering linkage or suspension unit balljoints. Excessive wear in the steering gear unit.
Wheel wobble and vibration	Roadwheels out of balance. Roadwheels buckled. Wheel alignment incorrect. Wear in the steering linkage, suspension unit bearings or track control arm bushes. Broken front spring.
Excessive pitching and rolling on corners and during braking	Defective shock absorbers and/or broken spring.

Chapter 12 Bodywork

For modifications and information applicable to later USA models, refer to Supplement at end of manual

Contents

Specifications

Main dimensions - 1974 models, USA

Overall lengths:

Estate: except California	175 in (444.5 cm)
Estate, California	175.8 in (446.5 cm)
Other models, except California	171.9 in (436.6 cm)
Other models, California	172.6 in (438.4 cm)

Width, including side moulding	63.8 in (162 cm)

Height

Saloon	55 in (139.7 cm)
Coupe	54 in (137.2 cm)
Estate	56.3 in (143 cm)

Ground clearance

Estate	6.5 in (16.5 cm)
Coupe SR	6.7 in (17 cm)
Other models	6.9 in (17.5 cm)

Main dimensions, 1975/77 models, USA

Overall length

Estate	176.4 in (448 cm)
Other models	173.2 in (439.9 cm)

Width, including side moulding	63.8 in (162 cm)

Height

Saloon	55.1 in (139.9 cm)
Coupe	54.1 in (137.4 cm)
Estate	56.3 in (143 cm)

Ground clearance

Estate	6.5 in (16 cm)
Other models	6.9 in (17.5 cm)

Main dimensions, UK and general market models

Overall length
Saloon	165.7 in (421 cm)
Coupe	165.9 in (421.5 cm)
Estate	168.5 in (428 cm)

Width
Saloon and Estate	63.4 in (161 cm)
Coupe	63.8 in (162 cm)

Height
Saloon	54.7 in (139 cm)
Coupe	53.7 in (136. 5 cm)
Estate	55.9 in (142 cm)

Ground clearance
Saloon	6.5 in (16.5 cm)
Coupe	6.5 in (16.5 cm)
Estate	6.1 in (15.5 cm)

1 General description

The body and underframe is of a steel, welded, unitary construction with detachable front wings (fenders), It is available as a saloon (sedan), coupe (hardtop) or an estate car (wagon).

All models have a heater/ventilator, but models for some markets may also have an air conditioning system.

2 Maintenance - bodywork and underframe

1   The general condition of a car's bodywork is the one thing that significantly affects its value. Maintenance is easy but needs to be regular. Neglect, particularly after minor damage, can lead quickly to further deterioration and costly repair bills. It is important also to keep watch on those parts of the car not immediately visible, for instance the underside, inside all the wheel arches and the lower part of the engine compartment.

2   The basic maintenance routine for the bodywork is washing - preferably with a lot of water, from a hose. This will remove all the loose solids which may have stuck to the car. It is important to flush these off in such a way as to prevent grit from scratching the finish. The wheel arches and underbody need washing in the same way to remove any accumulated mud which will retain moisture and tend to encourage rust. Paradoxically enough, the best time to clean the underbody and wheel arches is in wet weather when the mud is thoroughly wet and soft. In very wet weather the underbody is usually cleaned of large accumulations automatically and this is a good time for inspection.

3   Periodically it is a good idea to have the whole of the underside of the car steam cleaned, engine compartment included, so that a thorough inspection can be carried out to see what minor repairs and renovations are necessary. Steam cleaning is available at many garages and is necessary for removal of accumulation of oily grime which sometimes is allowed to cake thick in certain areas near the engine, gearbox and back axle. If steam facilities are not available, there are one or two excellent grease solvents available which can be brush applied. The dirt can then be simply hosed off.

4   After washing paintwork, wipe off with a chamois leather to give an unspotted clear finish. A coat of clear protective wax polish will give added protection against chemical pollutants in the air. If the paintwork sheen has dulled or oxidised, use a cleaner/polisher combination to restore the brilliance of the shine. This requires a little effort, but is usually caused because regular washing has been neglected. Always check that the door and ventilator opening drain holes and pipes are completely clear so that water can drain out. Bright work should be treated the same way as paintwork. Windscreens and windows can be kept clear of the smeary film which often appears, if a little ammonia is added to the water. If they are scratched, a good rub with a proprietary metal polish will often clear them. Never use any form of wax or other body or chromium polish on glass.

3 Maintenance - upholstery and carpets

1   Mats and carpets should be brushed or vacuum cleaned regularly to keep them free of grit. If they are badly stained, remove them from the car for scrubbing or sponging and make quite sure they are dry before refitting. Seats and interior trim panels can be kept clean by a wipe over with a damp cloth. If they do become stained (which can be more apparent on light coloured upholstery) use a little liquid detergent and a soft nail brush to scour the grime out of the grain of the material. Do not forget to keep the headlining clean in the same way as the upholstery. When using liquid cleaners inside the car do not overwet the surfaces being cleaned. Excessive damp could get into the seams and padded interior causing stains, offensive odours or even rot. If the inside of the car gets wet accidentally it is worthwhile taking some trouble to dry it out properly, particularly where carpets are involved. **Do not** leave oil or electric heaters inside the car for this purpose.

4 Minor body damage - repair

See photo sequence on pages 214 and 215.

Repair of minor scratches in the car's bodywork
If the scratch is very superficial, and does not penetrate to the metal of the bodywork - repair is very simple. Lightly rub the area of the scratch with a paintwork renovator, or a very fine cutting paste, to remove loose paint from the scratch and to clear the surrounding bodywork of wax polish. Rinse the area with clean water.

Apply touch-up paint to the scratch using a thin paint brush; continue to apply thin layers of paint until the surface of the paint in the scratch is level with the surrounding paintwork. Allow the new paint at least two weeks to harden, then, blend it into the surrounding paintwork by rubbing the paintwork in the scratch area with a paintwork renovator or a very fine cutting paste. Finally apply wax polish.

An alternative to painting over the scratch is to use paint patches. Use the same preparation for the affected area; then simply pick a patch of a suitable size to cover the scratch completely. Hold the patch against the scratch and burnish its backing paper; the patch will adhere to the paintwork, freeing itself from the backing paper at the same time. Polish the affected area to blend the patch into the surrounding paintwork.

Where a scratch has penetrated right through to the metal of the bodywork, causing the metal to rust, a different repair technique is required. Remove any loose rust from the bottom of the scratch with a penknife, then apply rust inhibiting paint to prevent the formation of rust in the future. Using a rubber or nylon applicator fill the scratch with body-stopper paste. If required, this paste can be mixed with cellulose thinners to provide a very thin paste which is ideal for filling narrow scratches. Before the stopper paste in the scratch hardens, wrap a piece of smooth cotton rag around the tip of a finger. Dip the finger in cellulose thinners and then quickly sweep it across the surface of the stopper paste, this will ensure that it is slightly hollowed. The scratch can now be painted over as described earlier in this Section.

Repair of dents in the car's bodywork

When deep denting of the car's bodywork has taken place, the first task is to pull the dent out, until the affected bodywork almost attains its original shape. There is little point in trying to restore the original shape completely, as the metal in the damaged area will have stretched on impact and cannot be reshaped fully to its original contour. It is better to bring the level of the dent up to a point which is about 1/8 in (3 mm) below the level of the surrounding bodywork. In cases where the dent is very shallow anyway, it is not worth trying to pull it out at all.

If the underside of the dent is accessible, it can be hammered out gently from behind, using a mallet with a wooden or plastic head. Whilst doing this, hold a suitable block of wood firmly against the outside of the dent. This block will absorb the impact from the hammer blows and thus prevent large areas of bodywork from being 'belled-out'.

Should the dent be in a section of the bodywork which has a double skin or some other factor making it inaccessible from behind, a different technique is called for. Drill several small holes through the metal inside the dent area - particularly in the deeper sections. Then screw long self-tapping screws into the holes just sufficiently for them to gain a good purchase in the metal. Now the dent can be pulled out by pulling on the protruding heads of the screws with a pair of pliers.

The next stage of the repair is the removal of the paint from the damaged area, and from an inch or so of the surrounding 'sound' bodywork. This is accomplished most easily by using a wire brush or abrasive pad on a power drill, although it can be done just as effectively by hand using sheets of abrasive paper. To complete the preparations for filling, score the surface of the bare metal with a screwdriver or the tang of a file, or alternatively, drill small holes in the affected area. This will provide a really good 'key' for the filler paste.

To complete the repair see the Section on filling and respraying.

Repair of rust holes or gashes in the car's bodywork

Remove all paint from the affected area and from an inch or so of the surrounding 'sound' bodywork, using an abrasive pad or a wire brush on a power drill. If these are not available a few sheets of abrasive paper will do the job just as effectively. With the paint removed you will be able to gauge the severity of the corrosion and therefore decide whether to renew the whole panel (if this is possible) or to repair the affected area. New body panels are not as expensive as most people think and it is often quicker and more satisfactory to fit a new panel than to attempt to repair large areas of corrosion.

Remove all fittings from the affected area except those which will act as a guide to the original shape of the damaged bodywork (eg, headlamp shells etc). Then, using tin snips or a hacksaw blade, remove all loose metal and any other metal badly affected by corrosion. Hammer the edges of the holes inwards in order to create a slight depression for the filler paste.

Wire brush the affected area to remove the powdery rust from the surface of the remaining metal. Paint the affected area with rust inhibiting paint; if the back of the rusted area is accessible treat this also.

Before filling can take place it will be necessary to block the hole in some way. This can be achieved by the use of one of the following materials: Zinc gauze, Aluminium tape or Polyurethane foam.

Zinc gauze is probably the best material to use for a large hole. Cut a piece to the approximate size and shape of the hole to be filled, then position it in the hole so that its edges are below the level of the surrounding bodywork. It can be retained in position by several blobs of filler paste around its periphery.

Aluminium tape should be used for small or very narrow holes. Pull a piece off the roll and trim it to the approximate size and shape required, then pull off the backing paper (if used) and stick the tape over the hole; it can be overlapped if the thickness of one piece is insufficient. Burnish down the edges of the tape with the handle of a screwdriver or similar, to ensure that the tape is securely attached to the metal underneath.

Polyurethane foam is best used where the hole is situated in a section of bodywork of complex shape, backed by a small box section (eg, where the sill panel meets the rear wheel arch - most cars). The mixing procedure for this foam is as follows: Put equal amounts of fluid from each of the two cans provided in the kit, into one container. Stir until the mixture begins to thicken, then quickly pour this mixture into the hole, and hold a piece of cardboard over the larger apertures. Almost immediately the polyurethane will begin to expand, gushing frantically out of any small holes left unblocked. When the foam hardens it can be cut back to just below the level of the surrounding bodywork with a hacksaw blade.

Having blocked off the hole, the affected area must now be filled and sprayed - see Section on bodywork filling and respraying.

Bodywork repairs - filling and re-spraying

Before using this Section, see the Sections on dent, deep scratch, rust hole, and gash repairs.

Many types of bodyfiller are available, but generally speaking those proprietary kits which contain a tin of filler paste and a tube of resin hardener are best for this type of repair. A wide, flexible plastic or nylon applicator will be found invaluable for imparting a smooth and well contoured finish to the surface of the filler.

Mix up a little filler on a clean piece of card or board - use the hardener sparingly (follow the maker's instructions on the pack), otherwise the filler will set very rapidly.

Using the applicator, apply the filler paste to the prepared area; draw the applicator across the surface of the filler to achieve the correct contour and to level the filler surface. As soon as the contour that approximates the correct one is achieved, stop working the paste - if you carry on too long the paste will become sticky and begin to 'pick-up' on the applicator.

Continue to add thin layers of filler paste at twenty-minute intervals until the lever of the filler is just 'proud' of the surrounding bodywork. Once the filler has hardened, excess can be removed using a plane or file. From then on, progressively finer grades of abrasive paper should be used, starting with a 40 grade 'wet-and-dry' paper. Always wrap the abrasive paper around a flat rubber cork, or wooden block - otherwise the surface of the filler will not be completely flat. During the smoothing of the filler surface the 'wet-and-dry' paper should be periodically rinsed in water - this will ensure that a very smooth finish is imparted to the filler at this final stage.

At this stage the 'dent' should be surrounded by a ring of bare metal, which in turn should be encircled by the finely 'feathered' edge of the good paintwork. Rinse the repair area with clean water, until all of the dust produced by the rubbing-down operation is gone.

Spray the whole repair area with a light coat of grey primer - this will show up any imperfections in the surface of the filler. Repair these imperfections with fresh filler paste or body-stopper, and once more smooth the surface with abrasive paper. If body-stopper is used, it can be mixed with cellulose thinners to form a really thin paste which is ideal for filling small holes. Repeat this spray and repair procedure until you are satisfied that the surface of the filler, and the feathered edge of the paintwork are perfect. Clean the repair area with clean water and allow to dry fully.

The repair area is now ready for spraying. Paint spraying must be carried out in a warm dry, windless and dust free atmosphere. This condition can be created artificially if you have access to a large indoor working area, but if you are forced to work in the open, you will have to pick your day carefully. If you are working indoors, dousing the floor in the work area with water will 'lay' the dust which would otherwise be in the atmosphere. If the repair area is confined to one body panel, mask off the surrounding panels; this will help to minimise the effects of a slight mis-match in paint colours. Bodywork fittings (eg, chrome strips, door handles etc) will also need to be masked off. Use genuine masking tape and several thicknesses of newspaper for the masking operation.

Before commencing to spray, agitate the aerosol can thoroughly, then spray a test area (an old tin, or similar) until the technique is mastered. Cover the repair area with a thick coat of primer; the thickness should be built up using several thin layers of paint rather than one thick one. Using 400 grade 'wet-and-dry' paper, rub down the surface of the primer until it is really smooth. While doing this, the work area should be thoroughly doused with water, and the 'wet-and-dry' paper periodically rinsed in water. Allow to dry before spraying on more paint.

Spray on the top coat, again building up the thickness by using several thin layers of paint. Start spraying in the centre of the repair area and then using a circular motion, work outwards until the whole repair area and about 2 inches of the surrounding original paintwork is covered. Remove all masking material 10 to 15 minutes after spraying on the final coat of paint. Allow the new paint at least 2 weeks to harden fully, then using a paintwork renovator or a very fine cutting paste, blend the edges of the new paint into the existing paintwork.

5 Major body damage - repair

Where serious damage has occurred or large areas need renewal due to neglect, it means certainly that completely new sections or panels will need welding in and this is best left to professionals. If the damage is due to impact it will also be necessary to completely check the alignment of the bodyshell structure. Due to the principle of construction the strength and shape of the whole can be affected by damage to a part. In such instances the services of a Toyota Dealer or bodywork repair specialist with checking jigs are essential. If a body is left misaligned it is first of all dangerous as the car will not handle properly, and secondly uneven stresses will be imposed on the steering, engine and transmission causing abnormal wear or complete failure. Tyre wear may also be excessive.

6 Maintenance - hinges and locks

1 Oil the hinges of the bonnet, boot and doors with a drop or two of light oil periodically. A good time is after the car has been washed.
2 Oil the bonnet release catch pivot pin and the safety catch pivot pin periodically.
3 Do not over lubricate door latches and strikers. Normally a little oil on the rotary cam spindle alone is sufficient.

7 Doors - tracing rattles and their rectification

1 Check first that the door is not loose at the hinges and that the latch is holding the door firmly in position. Check also that the door lines up with the aperture in the body.
2 If the hinges are loose or the door is out of alignment it will be necessary to reset the hinge positions, as described in Section 8.

3 If the latch is holding the door properly it should hold the door tightly when fully latched and the door should line up with the body. If it is out of alignment it needs adjustment as described in Section 8. If loose, some part of the lock mechanism must be worn out and require renewal.
4 Other rattles from the door would be caused by wear or looseness in the window winder, the glass channels and sill strips, or the door buttons and interior latch release mechanism.

8 Doors - removal, refitting and adjustment

1 Open the door fully and support it under its lower edge with a jack or blocks.
2 Mark round the hinge plates to provide a guide when refitting.
3 Remove the door trim panel (see Section 9).
4 Unscrew and remove the bolts which secure the hinges to the door frame edge and remove the door. If the hinges are to be removed from the body pillars, again mark their positions before removal.
5 Refit the door by reversing the removal procedure, but do not tighten the hinge bolts fully until the fit of the door in the body aperture has been checked. The front and rear gaps of the door should be equal and parallel, and the top gap parallel. At the same time, the top and bottom edges of the door should be in alignment with the front or rear door on the same side of the body (saloon or estate). If necessary, remove the striker plate when adjusting the door position; finally tighten the hinge bolts.

9 Front door glass and regulator - removal and refitting

Saloon and estate
1 Remove the window regulator handle using a hooked tool to detach its securing clip.
2 Remove the armrest (two screws).
3 Remove the interior door handle bezel by removing the screw and withdrawing the assembly sideways.
4 Pull out the trim panel from its retaining clips then carefully peel

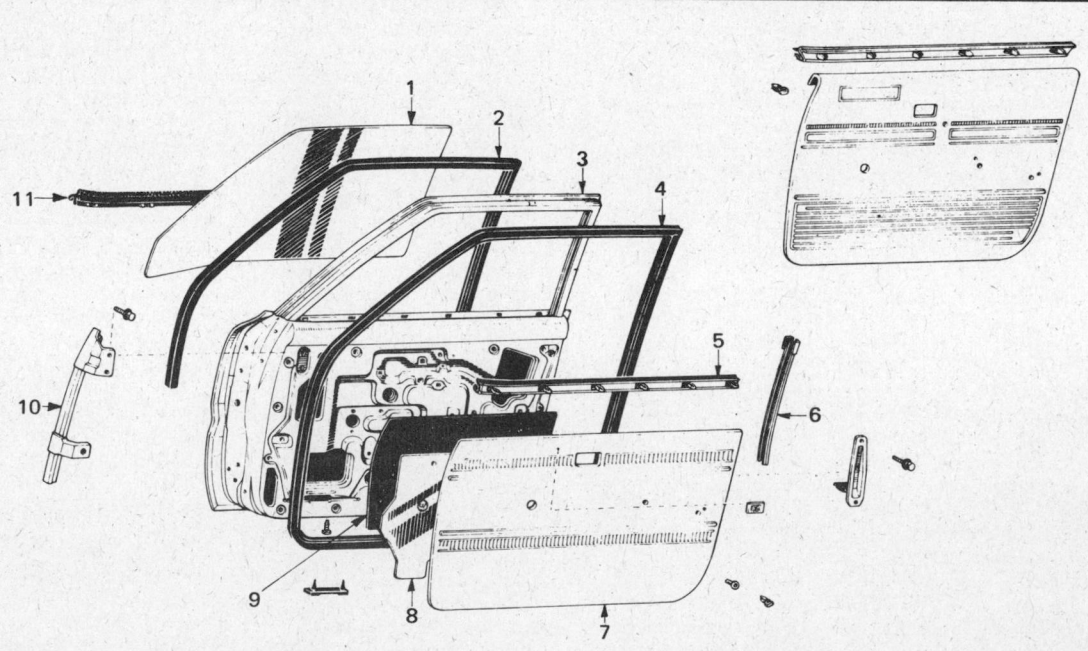

Fig. 12.1. Front door - major parts (Saloon and Estate)

1	Glass	4	Weatherstrip	7	Trim panel	10	Front lower frame
2	Glass run	5	Glass inner weatherstrip	8	Service hole cover	11	Glass outer weatherstrip
3	Door panel	6	Door rear lower frame	9	Silencer pad		

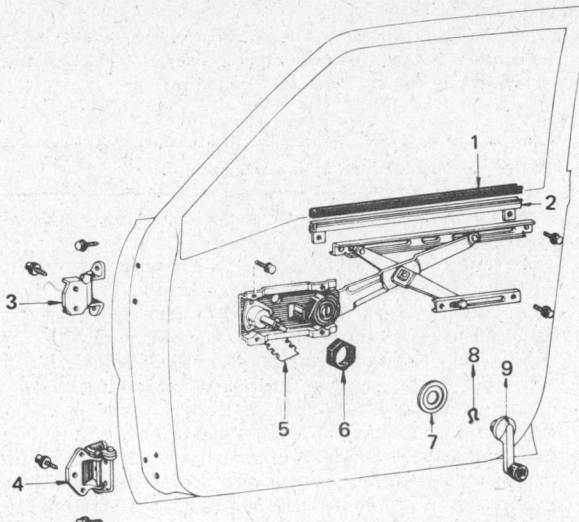

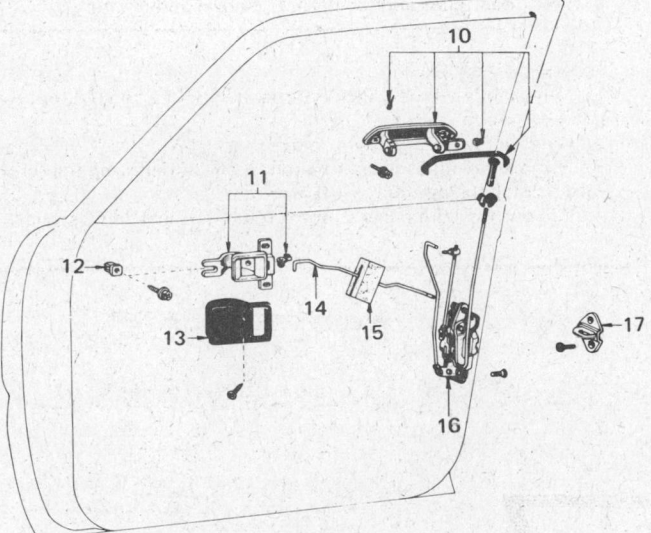

Fig. 12.2. Front door - window and lock mechanism (Saloon and Estate)

1 Glass channel weatherstrip
2 Window glass channel
3 Upper hinge
4 Lower hinge
5 Window regulator
6 Window regulator hole seal
7 Window regulator handle plate
8 Snap ring
9 Window regulator handle
10 Door outside handle
11 Door inside handle
12 Clip
13 Inside handle bezel
14 Door locking control link
15 Door locking silencer
16 Door lock
17 Lock striker plate

Fig. 12.3. Regulator attachment screws (arrowed)

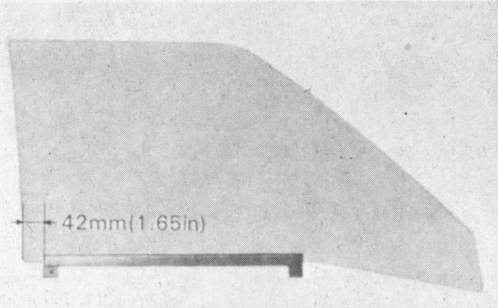

42mm (1.65in)

Fig. 12.4. Position of glass in glass channel - front door

These photos illustrate a method of repairing simple dents. They are intended to supplement *Body repair - minor damage* in this Chapter and should not be used as the sole instructions for body repair on these vehicles.

1   If you can't access the backside of the body panel to hammer out the dent, pull it out with a slide-hammer-type dent puller. In the deepest portion of the dent or along the crease line, drill or punch hole(s) at least one inch apart . . .

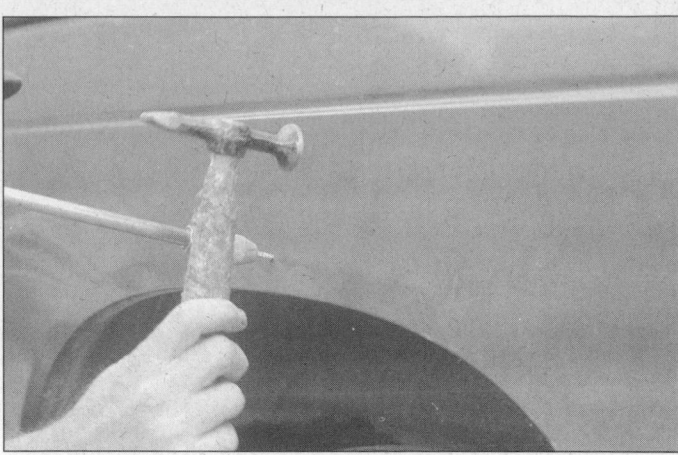

2   . . . then screw the slide-hammer into the hole and operate it. Tap with a hammer near the edge of the dent to help 'pop' the metal back to its original shape. When you're finished, the dent area should be close to its original contour and about 1/8-inch below the surface of the surrounding metal

3   Using coarse-grit sandpaper, remove the paint down to the bare metal. Hand sanding works fine, but the disc sander shown here makes the job faster. Use finer (about 320-grit) sandpaper to feather-edge the paint at least one inch around the dent area

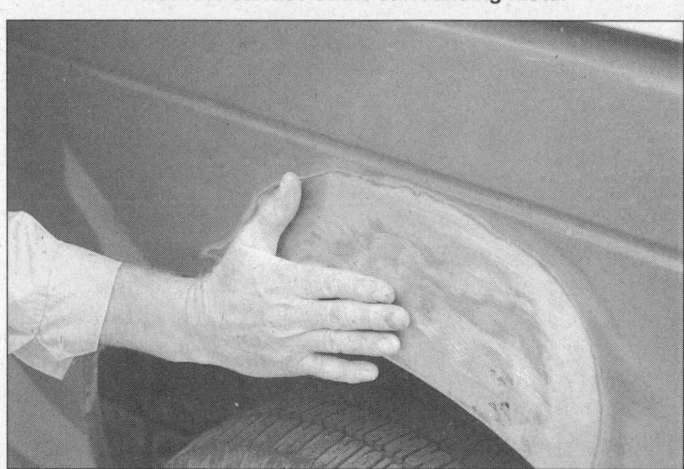

4   When the paint is removed, touch will probably be more helpful than sight for telling if the metal is straight. Hammer down the high spots or raise the low spots as necessary. Clean the repair area with wax/silicone remover

5   Following label instructions, mix up a batch of plastic filler and hardener. The ratio of filler to hardener is critical, and, if you mix it incorrectly, it will either not cure properly or cure too quickly (you won't have time to file and sand it into shape)

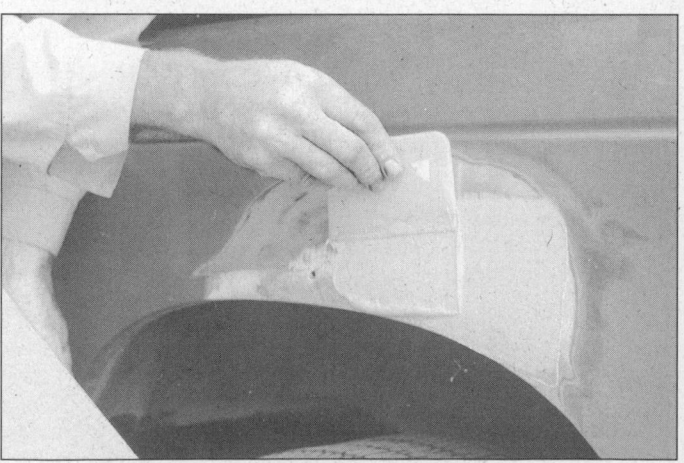

6   Working quickly so the filler doesn't harden, use a plastic applicator to press the body filler firmly into the metal, assuring it bonds completely. Work the filler until it matches the original contour and is slightly above the surrounding metal

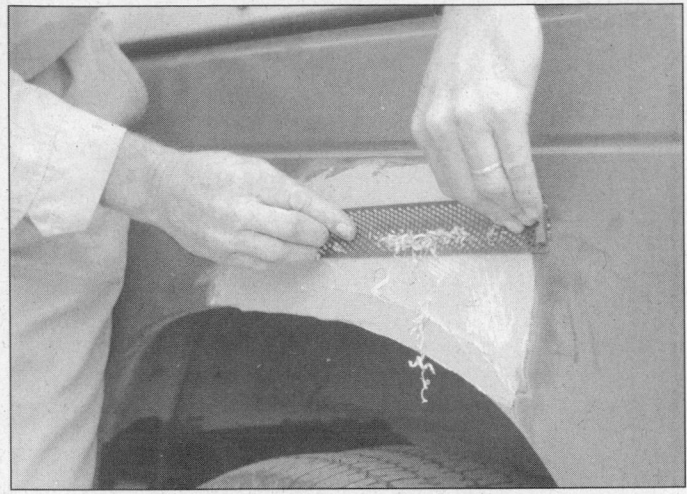

7   Let the filler harden until you can just dent it with your fingernail. Use a body file or Surform tool (shown here) to rough-shape the filler

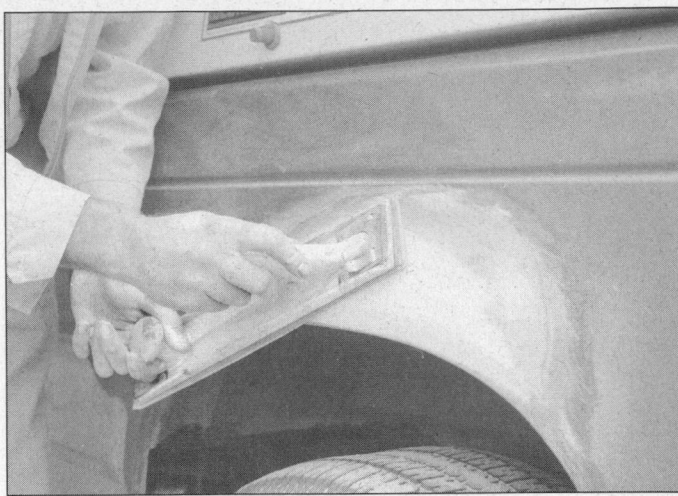

8   Use coarse-grit sandpaper and a sanding board or block to work the filler down until it's smooth and even. Work down to finer grits of sandpaper - always using a board or block - ending up with 360 or 400 grit

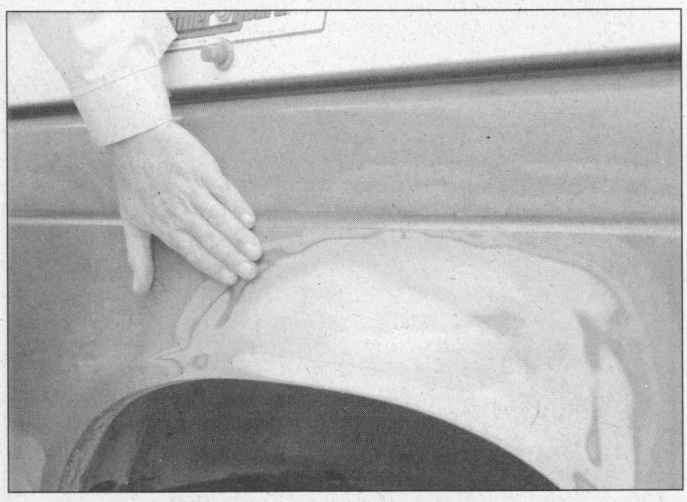

9   You shouldn't be able to feel any ridge at the transition from the filler to the bare metal or from the bare metal to the old paint. As soon as the repair is flat and uniform, remove the dust and mask off the adjacent panels or trim pieces

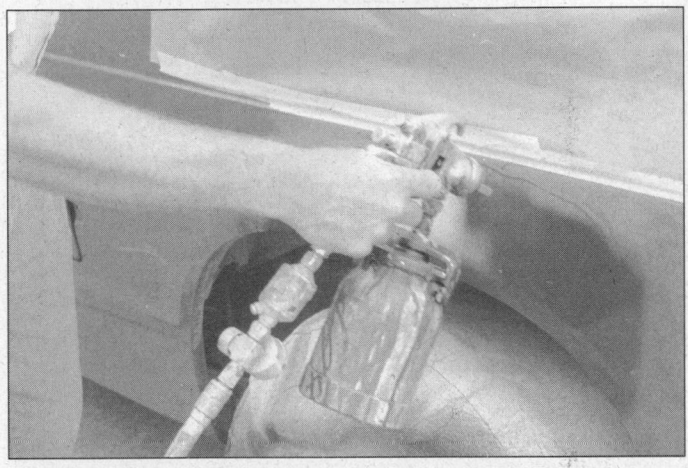

10   Apply several layers of primer to the area. Don't spray the primer on too heavy, so it sags or runs, and make sure each coat is dry before you spray on the next one. A professional-type spray gun is being used here, but aerosol spray primer is available inexpensively from auto parts stores

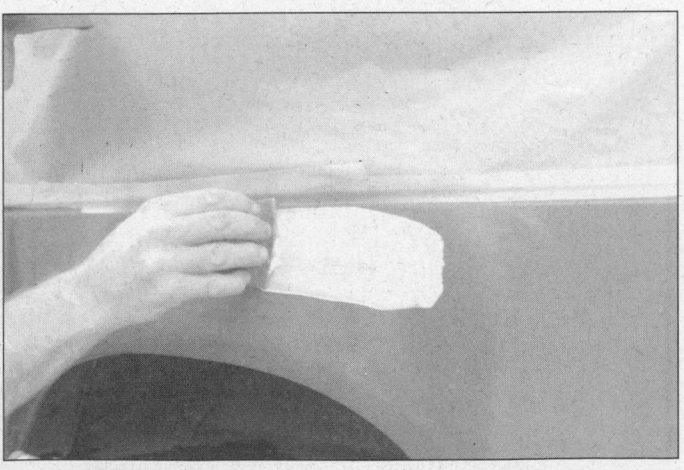

11   The primer will help reveal imperfections or scratches. Fill these with glazing compound. Follow the label instructions and sand it with 360 or 400-grit sandpaper until it's smooth. Repeat the glazing, sanding and respraying until the primer reveals a perfectly smooth surface

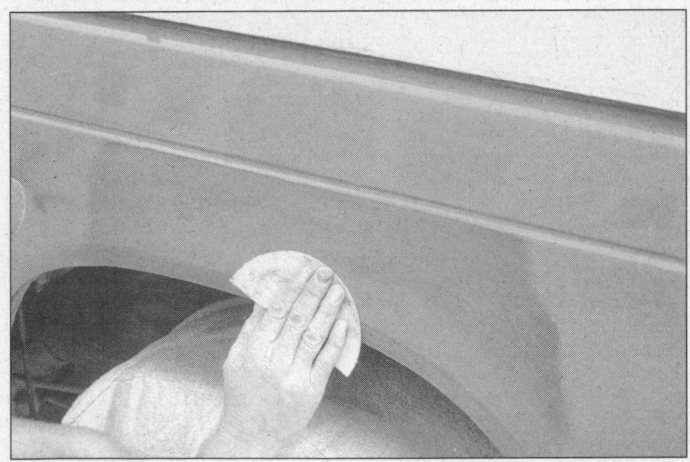

12   Finish sand the primer with very fine sandpaper (400 or 600-grit) to remove the primer overspray. Clean the area with water and allow it to dry. Use a tack rag to remove any dust, then apply the finish coat. Don't attempt to rub out or wax the repair area until the paint has dried completely (at least two weeks)

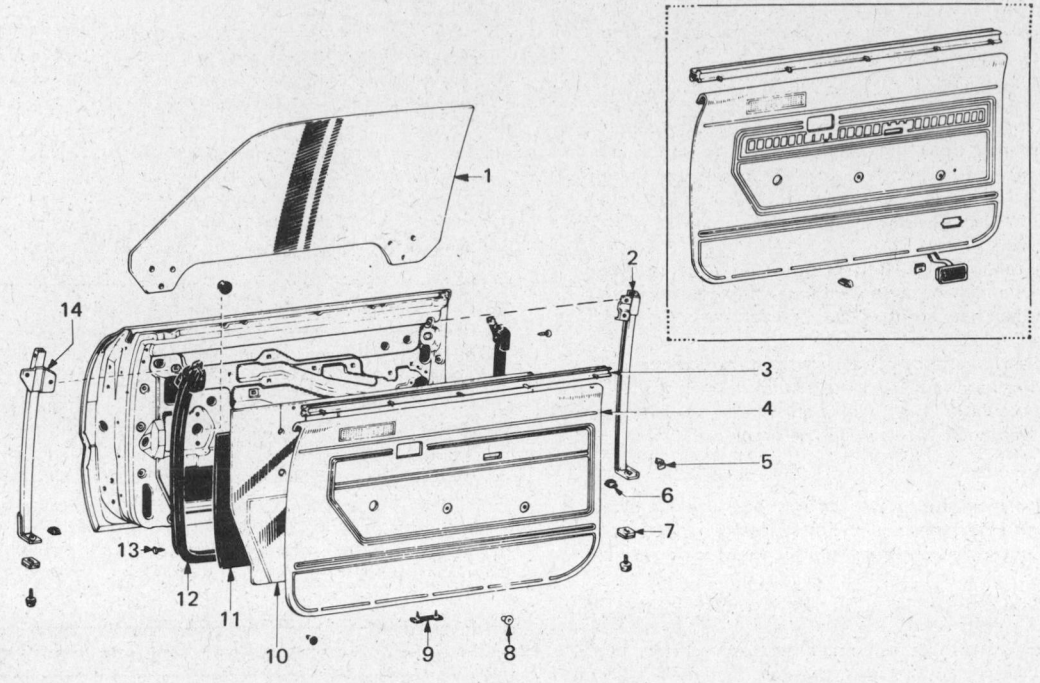

Fig. 12.5. Front door - major parts (Coupe)

1 Glass	4 Trim panel	7 Guide channel bracket gasket	11 Silencer pad
2 Glass rear channel	5 Trim retainer	8 Trim retainer cap	12 Weatherstrip
3 Glass inner weatherstrip	6 Glass lower stopper	9 Drain hole dust shield	13 Weatherstrip clip
		10 Service hole cover	14 Glass run front channel

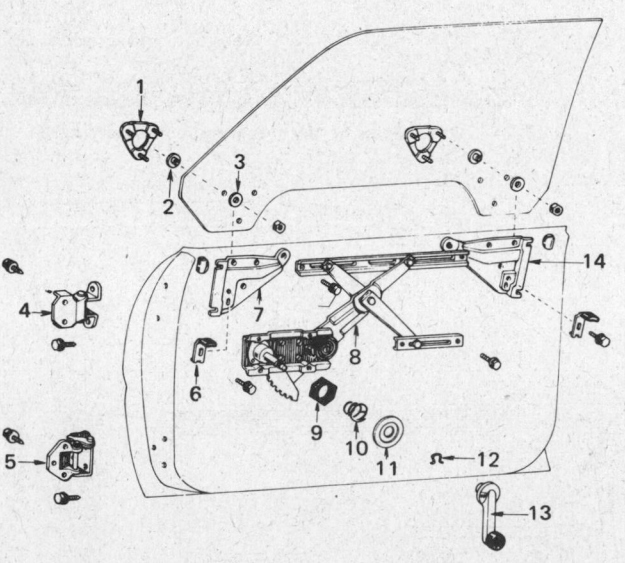

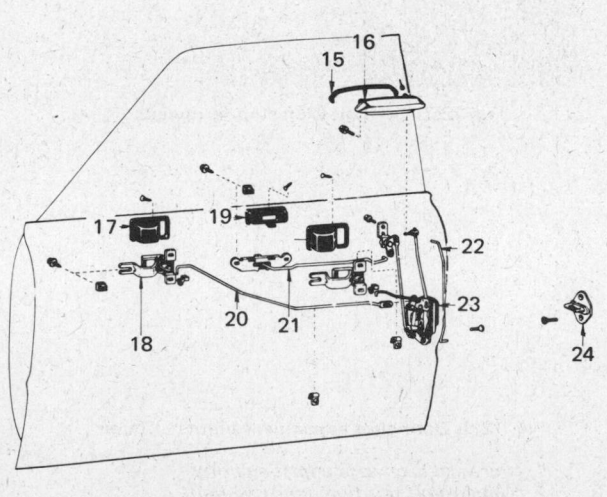

Fig. 12.6. Front door - window and lock mechanisms (Coupe)

1 Glass retainer	7 Glass holder front plate	13 Window regulator handle	19 Locking control bezel
2 Glass holder spacer	8 Window regulator	14 Glass holder rear plate	20 Opening control link
3 Plate washer	9 Window regulator hole seal	15 Outside handle pad	21 Lock control link
4 Upper hinge	10 Conical spring	16 Outside handle	22 Lock control link
5 Lower hinge	11 Window regulator handle plate	17 Inside handle bezel	23 Door lock
6 Glass upper stop	12 Snap ring	18 Inside handle	24 Striker plate

back the service hole cover.

5   Lower the glass right down and unscrew the two bolts attaching the glass channel to the regulator arm.

6   If the regulator only is to be removed, support the glass in the raised position with a piece of wood; alternatively use adhesive tape stuck on the glass, wrapped over the top of the door, then stuck on the other side of the glass to hold it up. The six retaining bolts can now be removed and the regulator taken out through the service hole.

7   If the glass only is to be removed, remove the door belt moulding (Section 19) then carefully prise away the glass inner weatherstrip. The glass can now be removed.

8   If the glass is to be renewed, carefully prise the old glass, or glass pieces, from the glass channel. Apply a soap and water solution to the rubber strip, then tap the channel into place using a wooden mallet in the position shown in Fig. 12.4.

9   Refitting the glass and regulator is the reverse of the removal procedure, but apply a general purpose grease to the pivoting and sliding surfaces of the regulator. If a suitable adhesive is not available for the service hole cover, adhesive tape may be used.

Coupe

10 Remove the window regulator handle, armrest and interior door handle bezel, referring to Paragraphs 1 to 3 as necessary.

11 Remove the retaining screws and take off the door locking control bezel.

12 Remove the courtesy light from the trim panel and disconnect the leads.

13 Pull out the trim panel from its retaining clips then carefully peel back the service hole cover.

14 Remove the two retaining screws and take off the door belt

moulding.

15 Remove the left and right glass up-stops from the glass holders.

16 Remove the bolts securing the glass holder to the regulator, then pull the glass out with the holder attached.

17 Remove the nuts, washers and spacers, and detach the glass from the holder.

18 Refitting is the reverse of the removal procedure, but apply a general purpose grease to the pivoting and sliding surfaces of the regulator. If adjustment is found necessary, refer to Fig. 12.9 which shows the bolts for the various adjustments. If a suitable adhesive is not available for the service hole cover, adhesive tape may be used.

10 Front door lock - removal and refitting

1   Initially remove the door trim panel and service hole cover as described in Section 9.

2   From within the door cavity, detach the retaining clips and the operating rods. On saloon and estate models, unscrew the interior locking button.

3   Remove the retaining screws and withdraw the lock from inside the door cavity.

4   Refitting is the reverse of the removal procedure. If necessary, adjustment may be made by repositioning the striker plate on the pillar for satisfactory closing and opening.

11 Rear door glass and regulator - removal and refitting

1   Remove the window regulator handle using a hooked tool to

Fig. 12.7. Door glass up-stop (arrowed)

Fig. 12.8. Glass holder retaining screws (arrowed)

Fig. 12.9. Door glass adjustment points - Coupe

1   *Forward-backward adjusting bolts*
2   *Upper limit position adjusting bolts*
3   *Width direction adjusting bolts*
4   *Tilt adjusting bolts*

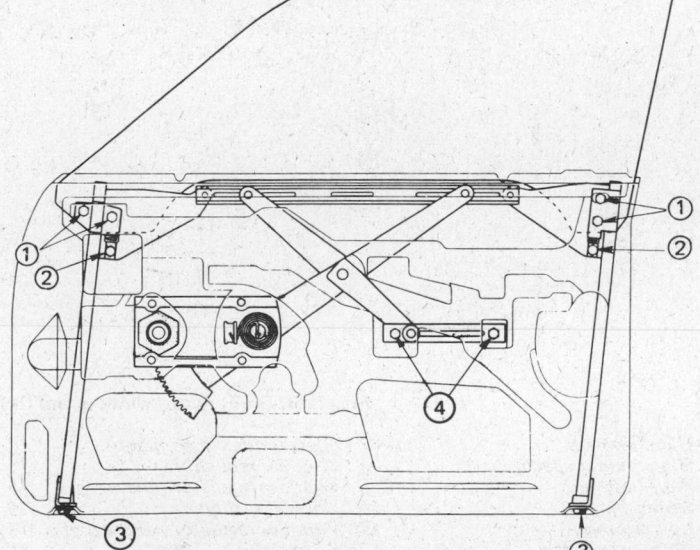

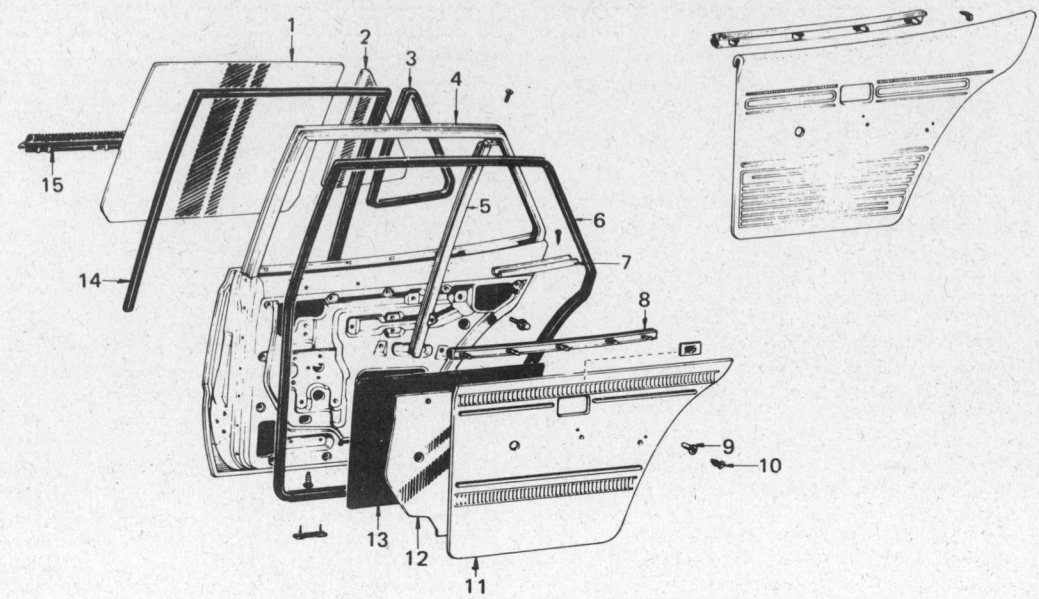

Fig. 12.10. Rear door - major parts (Saloon and Estate)

1 Glass	5 Window division bar	9 Trim retainer cap	13 Silencer pad
2 Quarter window glass	6 Weatherstrip	10 Trim retainer	14 Glass run
3 Quarter window weatherstrip	7 Quarter window lower frame	11 Trim panel	15 Glass outer weatherstrip
4 Door panel	8 Glass inner weatherstrip	12 Service hole cover	

Fig. 12.11. Rear door - window and lock mechanisms (Coupe)

1 Upper hinge
2 Lower hinge
3 Glass channel weatherstrip
4 Glass channel
5 Glass regulator
6 Window regulator hole seal
7 Door window regulator handle plate
8 Shaft snap ring
9 Door window handle
10 Locking button
11 Door inside handle
12 Snap ring
13 Inside handle bezel
14 Locking link silencer
15 Rear door outside handle
16 Door outside handle pad
17 Rear door locking
18 Door strike plate

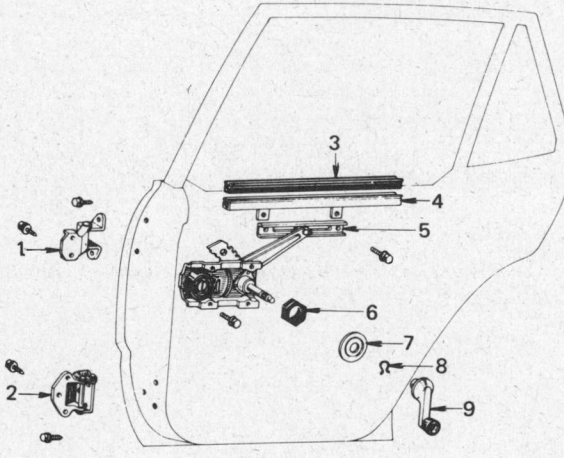

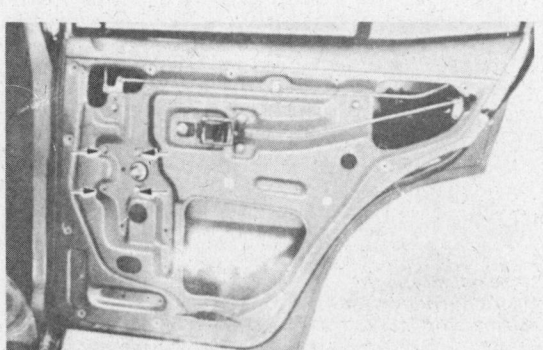

Fig. 12.12. Regulator retaining bolts (arrowed)

detach its securing clip.

2   Remove the armrest.

3   Remove the interior door handle bezel by removing the screw and withdrawing the assembly sideways.

4   Pull out the trim panel from its retaining clips, then carefully peel back the service hole cover.

5   If the regulator only is to be removed, unscrew the two bolts securing the glass channel to the regulator arm. Support the glass in the raised position with a piece of wood; alternatively use adhesive tape stuck on the glass, wrapped over the top of the door, then stuck on the other side of the glass to hold it up. The four retaining bolts can now be removed and the regulator taken out through the service hole.

6   If the glass only is to be removed, remove the division bar and quarter window glass (see Section 19), then unscrew the two bolts securing the glass channel to the regulator arm. The glass can now be lifted out.

7   If the glass is to be renewed, carefully prise the old glass, or glass pieces, from the glass channel. Apply a soap and water solution to the rubber strip, then tap the channel into place using a wooden mallet in the position shown in Fig. 12.13.

8   Refitting the glass and regulator is the reverse of the removal procedure, but apply a general purpose grease to the pivoting and sliding surfaces of the regulator. If a suitable adhesive is not available for the service hole cover, adhesive tape may be used.

12 Rear door lock - removal and refitting

1   Initially remove the door trim panel and service hole cover as described in Section 11.

2   From within the door cavity, detach the retaining clips and the operating rods.

3   Remove the retaining screws and withdraw the lock from inside the door cavity.

4   Refitting is the reverse of the removal procedure. If necessary, adjustment can be made by repositioning the striker plate on the pillar for satisfactory closing and opening.

13 Rear quarter window (coupe) - removal and refitting

1   Remove the rear seat cushion and detach the seat belt retractor from the side member.

2   Remove the screws and take off the rear scuff plate.

3   Remove the window regulator handle using a hook ended tool to detach its securing clip.

4   Remove the four quarter trim retainers and the single screw, and detach the trim panel.

5   Remove the retaining screws and take off the quarter belt moulding, then carefully peel back the service hole cover.

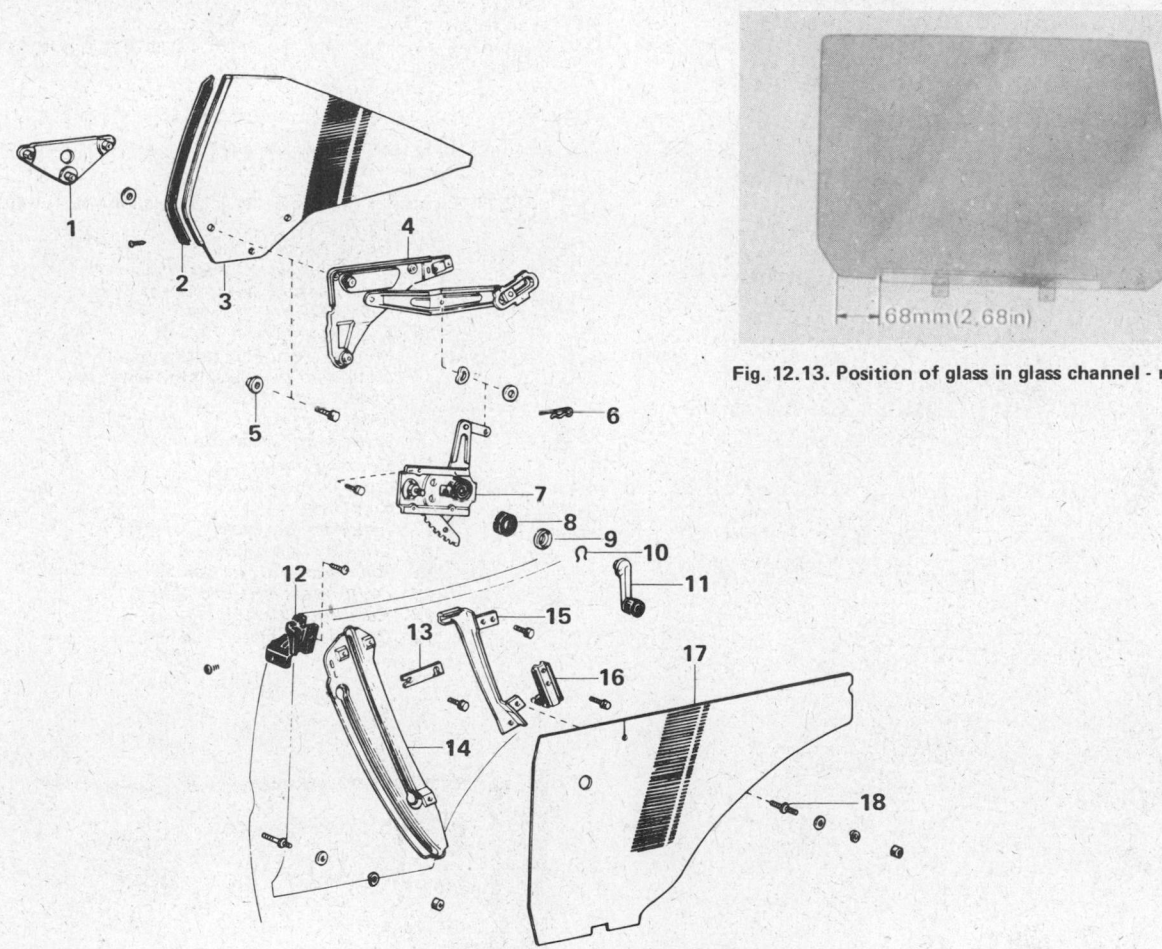

Fig. 12.13. Position of glass in glass channel - rear door

68mm (2.68in)

Fig. 12.14. Rear quarter window parts - Coupe

1 Glass holder spacer	5 Glass holder spacer	9 Regulator handle plate	14 Glass front guide
2 Quarter window front weatherstrip	6 Pin	10 Snap ring	15 Glass rear guide
3 Glass	7 Glass regulator	11 Regulator handle	16 Down stop
4 Regulator bracket	8 Regulator hole seal	12 Corner weatherstrip	17 Service hole cover
		13 Spacer	18 Stud bolt

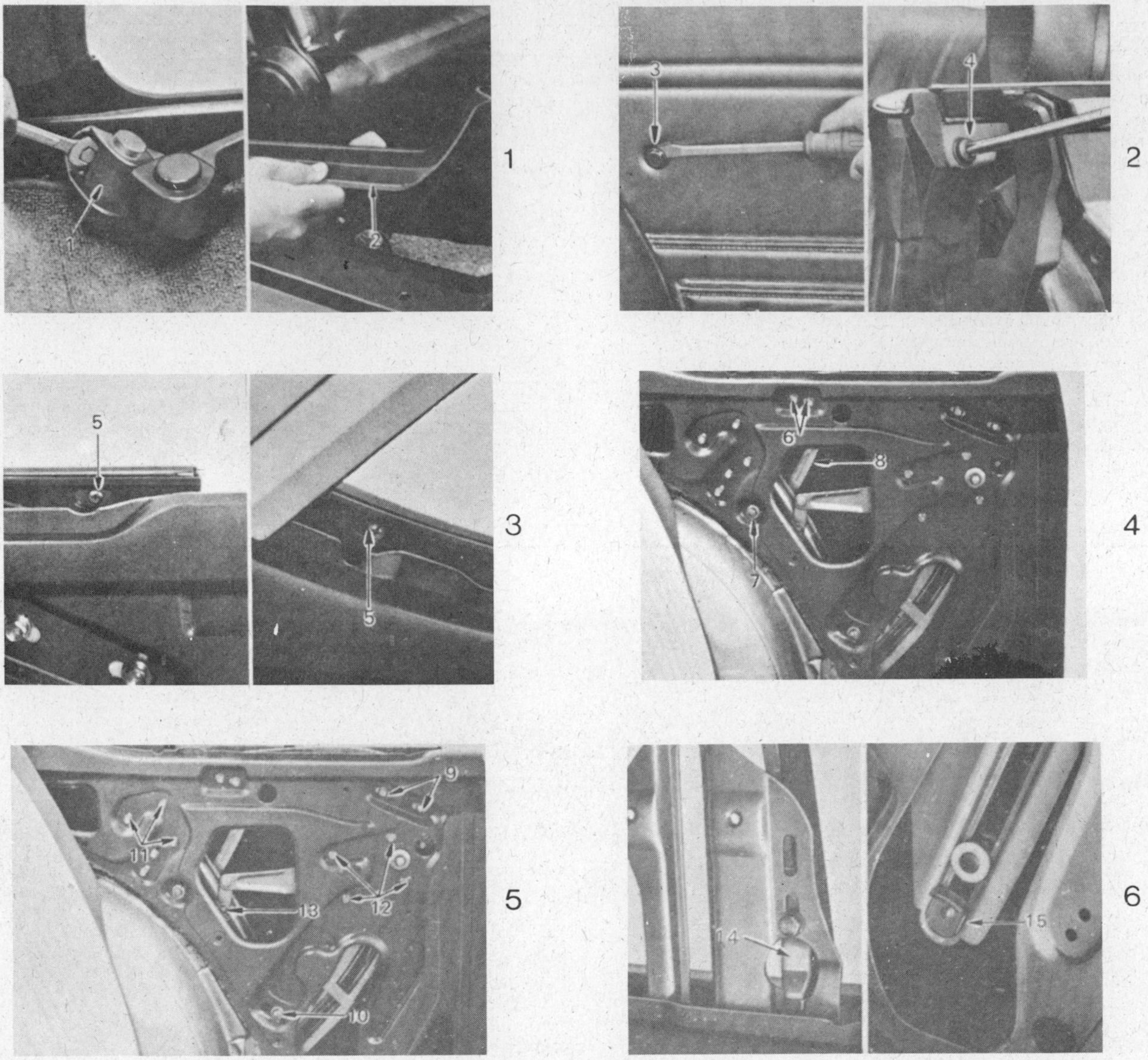

1

2

3

4

5

6

Fig. 12.15. Removal sequence for quarter window glass - Coupe

1 Belt retractor
2 Scuff plate
3 Trim retainers
4 Screw
5 Screws
6 Bolts
7 Stud bolt
8 Rear guide

9 Bolts
10 Stud bolt
11 Bolts
12 Bolts
13 Pin
14 Up-stop
15 Down-stop

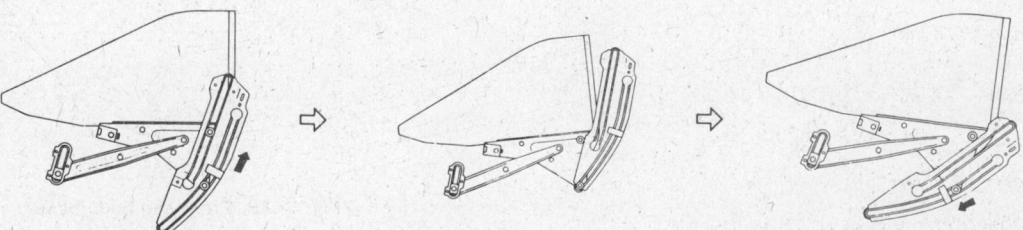

Fig. 12.16. Removing glass holder from front guide - Coupe

6   Remove the two bolts and one stud bolt, and take out the rear guide. **Note:** if the bolt positions are marked before removal, alignment will be easier when refitting.

7   Remove the retaining bolts, stud bolt and pin, take out the regulator. **Note:** When removing bolts (9) - Fig. 12.15 - take care not to drop the spacers which are fitted between the front guide and inner panel.

8   Remove the up-stop and down-stop, then separate the glass holder from the front guide as shown in Fig. 12.16.

9   Take out the glass and front guide from the inner panel.

10 Refitting is the reverse of the removal procedure, but apply a general purpose grease to the pivoting and sliding surfaces of the regulator. If adjustment is found necessary, refer to Fig. 12.17 which shows the various adjustment points. If a suitable adhesive is not available for the service hole cover, adhesive tape may be used.

14 Rear quarter window regulator (coupe) - removal and refitting

1   Remove the quarter trim panel and service hole cover as described in Section 13.

2   Remove the bolts and stud bolt which secure the front guide.

3   Remove the pin connecting the regulator to the equaliser arm; remove the securing bolts then lift the regulator out.

4   Refitting is the reverse of the removal procedure, but apply a general purpose grease to the pivoting and sliding surfaces of the regulator.

15 Bonnet (hood) - removal and refitting

1   Where applicable, disconnect the engine compartment light wiring.

2   Mark around the hinges to simplify alignment when refitting.

3   Remove the bolts which secure the bonnet to the hinges and, with the help of an assistant, lift the bonnet away.

4   Refitting is the reverse of the removal procedure but, if necessary, adjust the mounting bolts to provide an equal gap on both sides.

5   The bonnet should close by gentle pressure, and remain closed without any tendency to rattle when the vehicle is on the road.

6   Adjust the closure action by loosening the locknut on the rubber buffer set screw and turning it, then adjust the lock position by slackening the lock securing screws.

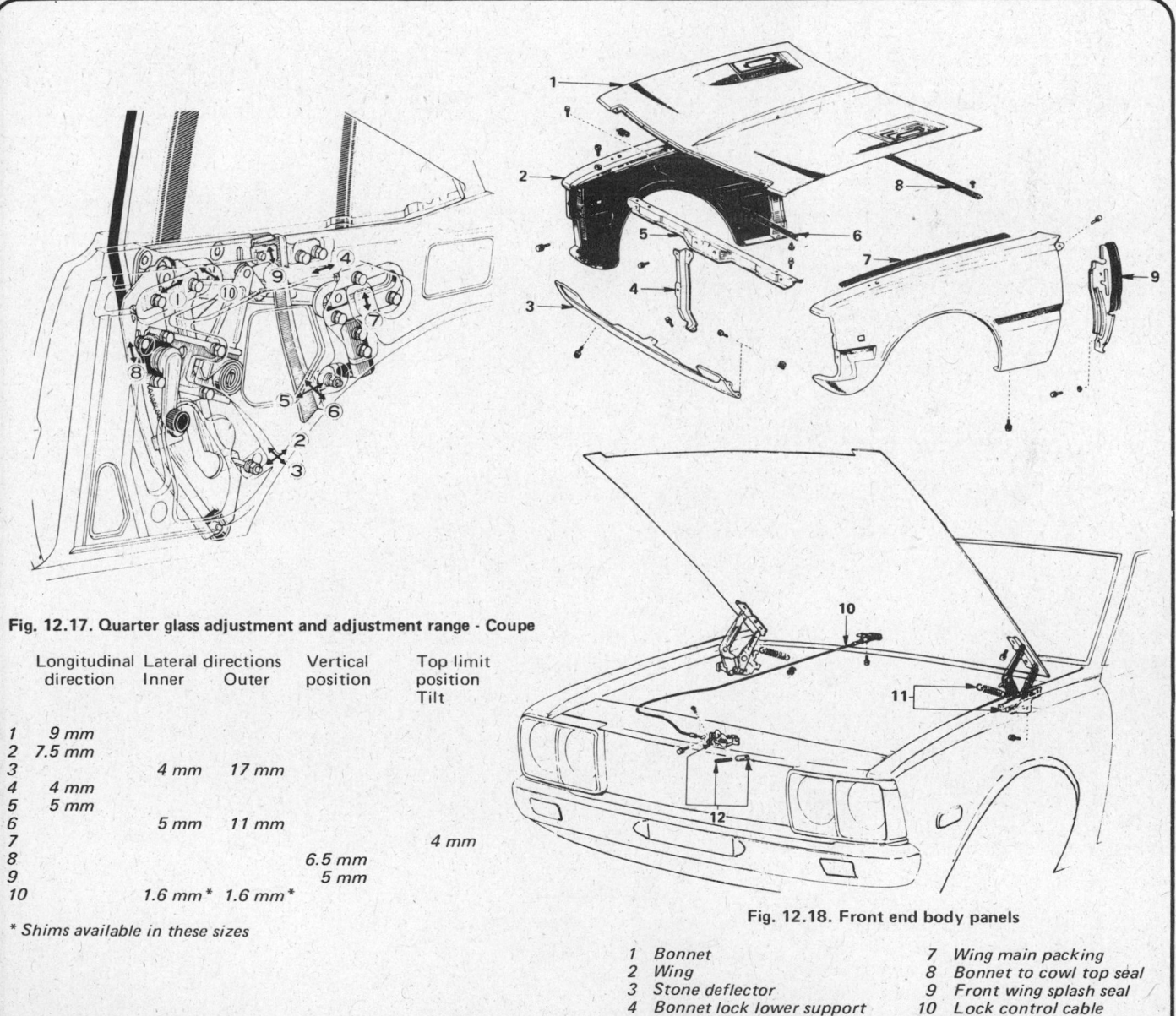

Fig. 12.17. Quarter glass adjustment and adjustment range - Coupe

	Longitudinal direction	Lateral directions Inner	Outer	Vertical position	Top limit position Tilt
1	9 mm				
2	7.5 mm				
3		4 mm	17 mm		
4	4 mm				
5	5 mm				
6		5 mm	11 mm		
7					4 mm
8				6.5 mm	
9				5 mm	
10		1.6 mm*	1.6 mm*		

* Shims available in these sizes

Fig. 12.18. Front end body panels

1	Bonnet	7	Wing main packing
2	Wing	8	Bonnet to cowl top seal
3	Stone deflector	9	Front wing splash seal
4	Bonnet lock lower support	10	Lock control cable
5	Radiator upper support	11	Hinge
6	Bonnet to baffle seal	12	Bonnet lock

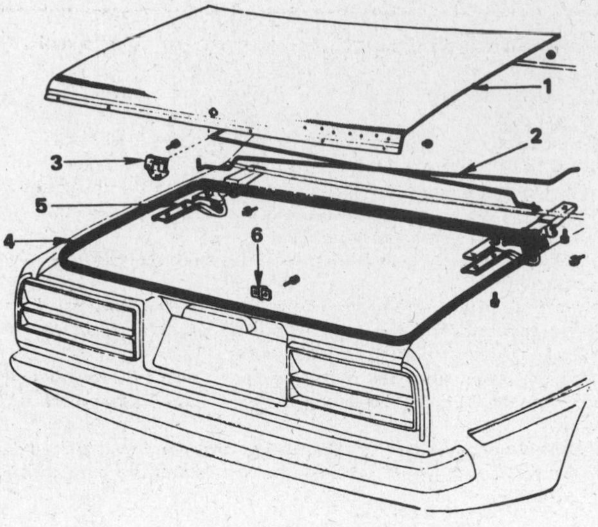

Fig. 12.19. Boot lid components

1	Boot lid	4	Weatherstrip
2	Counter-balance torsion bar	5	Hinge
3	Lock	6	Striker plate

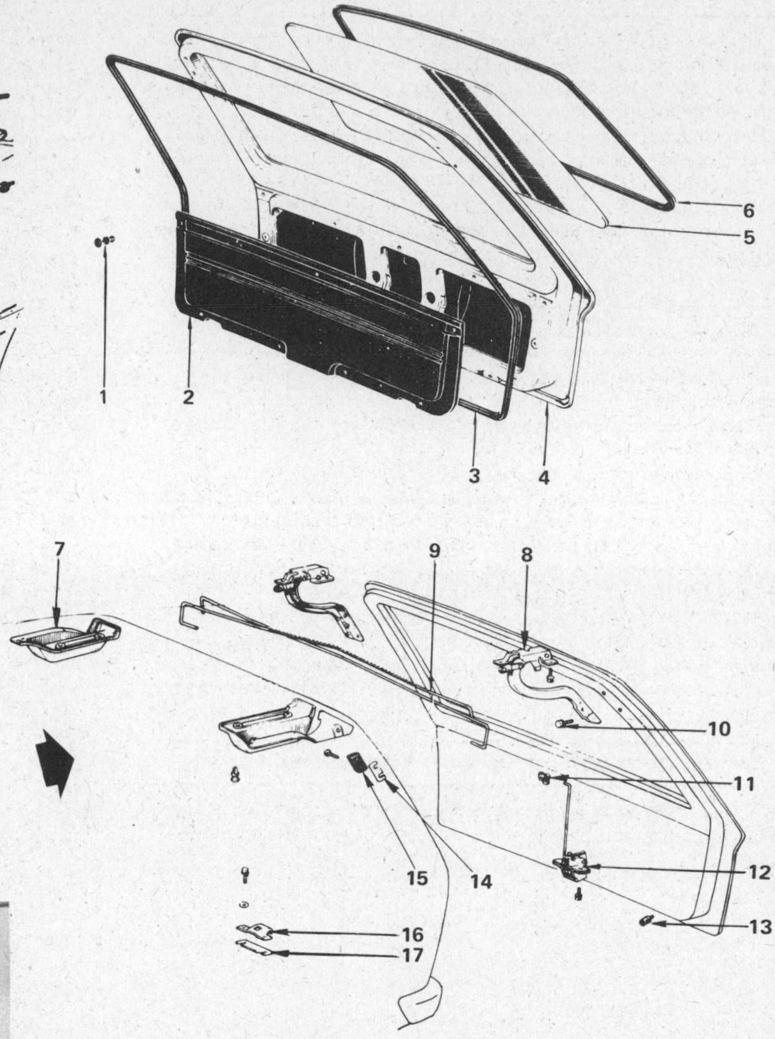

Fig. 12.20. Tailgate parts

1	Clip	10	Bolt
2	Trim board	11	Lock control link adjuster
3	Weatherstrip	12	Door lock
4	Door panel	13	Stopper No. 1
5	Glass	14	Side stopper upper spacer
6	Glass weatherstrip	15	Stopper No. 2
7	Hinge cover	16	Lock striker
8	Hinge	17	Lock striker shim
9	Torsion bar		

Fig. 12.21. Removing hinge cover and hook

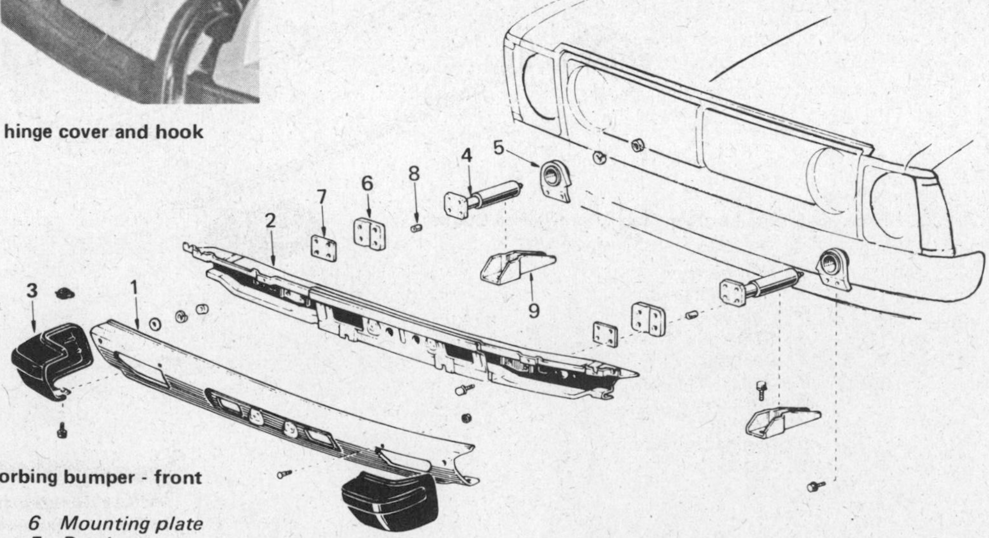

Fig. 12.22. Shock absorbing bumper - front

1	Bumper bar	6	Mounting plate
2	Reinforcement	7	Retainer
3	End guard	8	Spacer
4	Shock absorber	9	Stay
5	Retainer		

16 Boot (luggage compartment) lid - removal and refitting

1   The boot lid is counter-balanced by two torsion bars; these must be removed before the hinge bolts are unscrewed. This can be done by using a large adjustable spanner to disengage the cranked ends of the rods.
2   Mark the location of the hinges before removing them.
3   Refitting is the reverse of the removal procedure. The lock and striker plate may be adjusted to give positive closure by loosening their securing bolts.
4   The torsion bar action may be altered by varying the position of the free end of the bar using the two slots provided. When the torsion bar is engaged in the upper slot, the counter-balance action is increased.

17 Tailgate - removal and refitting

1   Remove the hinge cover by carefully prising out the retaining clips with a screwdriver.
2   Remove the rear interior light, and disconnect the wires for the number plate light.
3   Remove the hooks at the rear end of the roof lining.
4   Support the tailgate in the open position using a length of wood.
5   Using a long screwdriver or steel bar inserted through the 'U' of the torsion bars to depress them, disengage them from their anchorages.
6   Mark the position of the hinge plates, remove the securing bolts, and with the help of an assistant, lift the tailgate away.
7   Refitting is the reverse of the removal procedure; adjust the position of the tailgate and lock mechanism by loosening the securing bolts of the hinges, and lock and striker plates. When the fit is correct, insert the torsion rods, reconnect the wiring harness and refit the trim.

18 Bumpers - removal, dismantling, reassembly and refitting

Note: The procedures given in this Section are for the shock absorbing bumpers installed on USA models. Removal of bumpers on other models is straightforward, but it is necessary to refer to paragraphs 1 and 2.

Front bumper

1   Disconnect the fusible link in the battery positive lead.
2   Detach the harness connector and clamp for the turn signal.
3   Either remove the nut and spring washer securing the shock absorber to each support retainer, or detach the support retainers. Remove the complete bumper assembly from the car.
4   Remove the bumper guards then detach the bumper bar from the reinforcement.
5   Remove the retaining bolts and detach the shock absorbers. Note the mounting retainer, mounting plate and spacer on each unit.
6   If necessary, remove the turn signal lights.
7   Check the shock absorber for damage, and check that its free length is approximately 7.95 in (202 mm). Obtain new shock absorbers as necessary.
8   Reassembly and refitting are the reverse of the removal procedure, but before tightening the mounting bolts ensure that the bumper is aligned squarely.

Rear bumper

9   The procedures for the rear bumpers are similar to those already given for the front bumpers, except for the following:

   a) No turn signal lights are installed on the bumper.
   b) The free length of the rear shock absorbers should be approximately 8.35 in (212 mm).

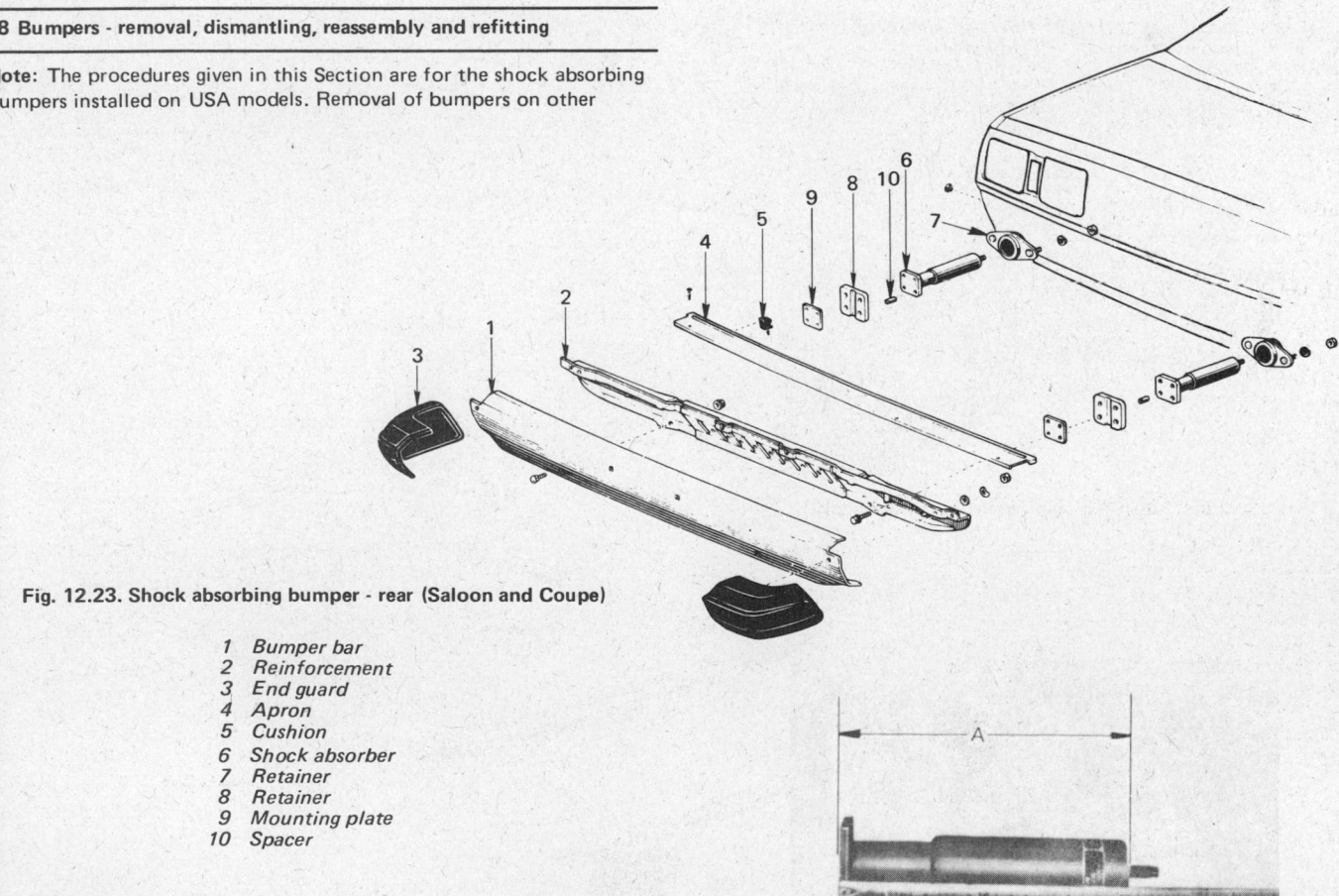

Fig. 12.23. Shock absorbing bumper - rear (Saloon and Coupe)

   1   Bumper bar
   2   Reinforcement
   3   End guard
   4   Apron
   5   Cushion
   6   Shock absorber
   7   Retainer
   8   Retainer
   9   Mounting plate
   10 Spacer

Fig. 12.24. Free length check of shock absorber (A) - for dimension see text

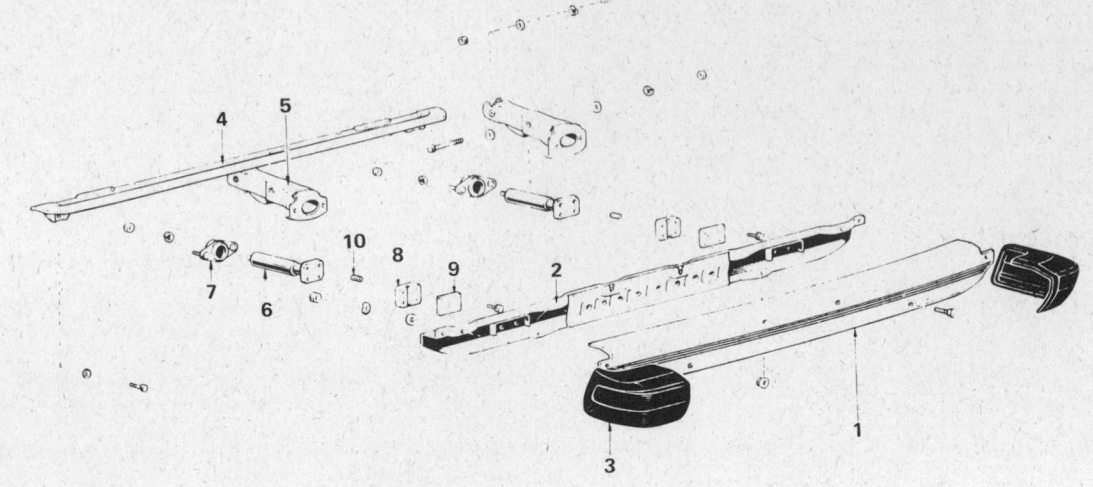

Fig. 12.25. Shock absorbing bumper - rear (Estate)

1	Bumper bar	6	Shock absorber
2	Reinforcement	7	Retainer
3	End guard	8	Mounting plate
4	Apron	9	Retainer
5	Stay	10	Spacer

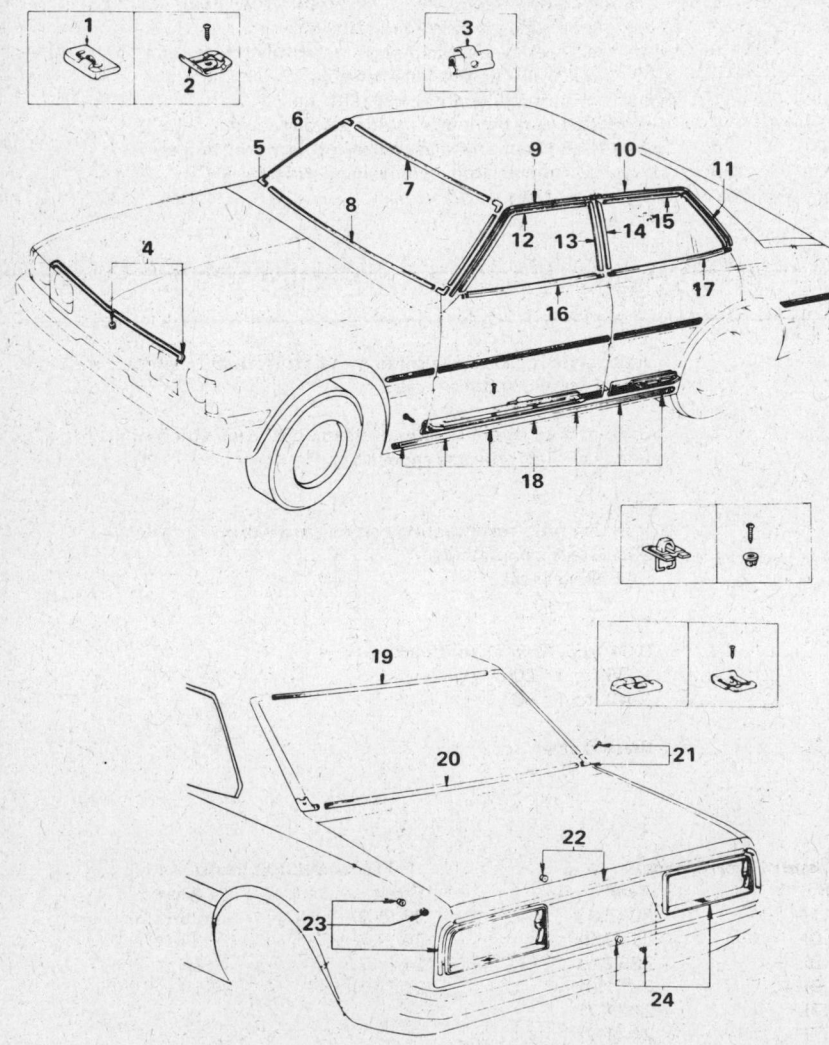

1 Windscreen outside moulding clip (original)
2 Windscreen outside moulding clip (repair item)
3 Roof drip side finish moulding retainer
4 Bonnet front moulding
5 Lower joint cover
6 Outside moulding
7 Outside moulding
8 Outside moulding
9 Roof drip side finish moulding
10 Roof drip side finish moulding
11 Window frame moulding
12 Window frame moulding
13 Window frame moulding
14 Window frame moulding
15 Window frame moulding
16 Door belt moulding
17 Door belt moulding
18 Sill moulding
19 Outside moulding
20 Outside moulding
21 Lower joint cover
22 Door moulding
23 Side moulding
24 Light rim moulding

Fig. 12.26. Exterior trim and mouldings

19 Body mouldings - removal and refitting

Windscreen outside moulding

1   Each of the four moulding joint covers can be removed by carefully prising up with a screwdriver.

2   To remove the upper, lower and side mouldings, Toyota manufacture a special tool (Fig. 12.27); however this should not be difficult to make out of a thin piece of mild steel. It is used to prise up the moulding clip jaws then to twist the mouldings and secure them in the clips, then fit the moulding joint covers.

Roof side vent louvre - saloon and estate

4   Remove the retaining screw, then insert the screwdriver through the hole in the louvre and into the body panel hole. Prise the louvre downwards and away.

5   Refitting is the reverse of the removal procedure.

Roof side vent louvre - coupe

6   Remove the roof side inner garnish at the left-hand side only (Paragraphs 21 to 23).

7   Remove the single screw to detach the quarter belt moulding.

8   Remove the screws, and detach the side finish moulding and louvre.

9   On the left-hand side remove the fuel inlet cover and vent louvre.

10 Remove the retaining nut on the inside of the panel and take off the vent louvre.

11 Refitting is the reverse of the removal procedure.

Front door belt moulding

12 Remove the moulding by carefully prising it upwards with a screwdriver at each of the retaining clips.

13 Refitting is straightforward, pressing the moulding in with the ball of the hand.

Rear door belt moulding

14 Remove the door trim panel and service hole cover (see Section 11).

15 Remove the bolt and screw, and take off the division bar (Fig. 12.29).

16 Remove the quarter window glass and weatherstrip.

17 Remove the single screw attaching the moulding and quarter window lower frame, then carefully prise the moulding upwards with a screwdriver to release it from its retaining clips.

18 Refitting is the reverse of the removal procedure.

Sill panel moulding

19 Remove the two mounting screws then carefully pull the moulding out of the retaining clips.

20 Refitting is the reverse of the removal procedure.

Roof side inner garnish - coupe

21 Remove the quarter trim panel (see Section 13).

22 Remove the four garnish retaining screws.

23 Refitting is the reverse of the removal procedure.

Side finish mouldings - coupe

24 Remove the side inner garnish as previously described.

25 Remove the two screws attaching the quarter belt moulding and take the moulding off.

26 To remove the side finish moulding, remove the single retaining nut from inside the car, and the three bolts from the outside.

27 Refitting is the reverse of the removal procedure.

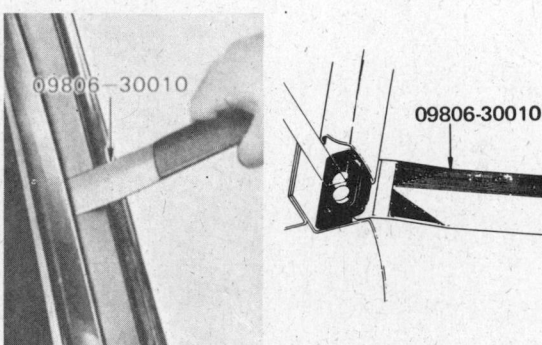

Fig. 12.27. Toyota tool in use on windscreen mouldings

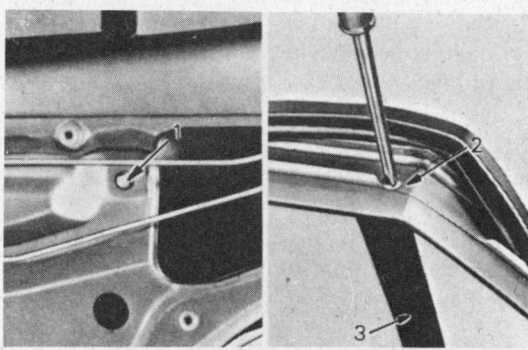

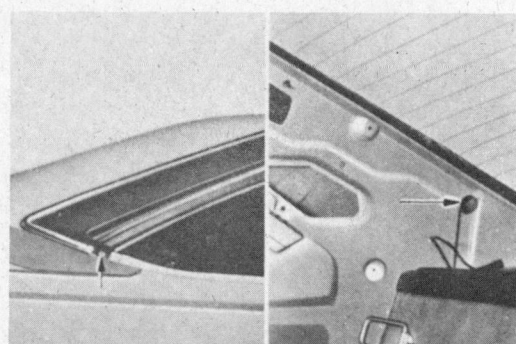

Fig. 12.28. Roof side vent louvre removal - Coupe

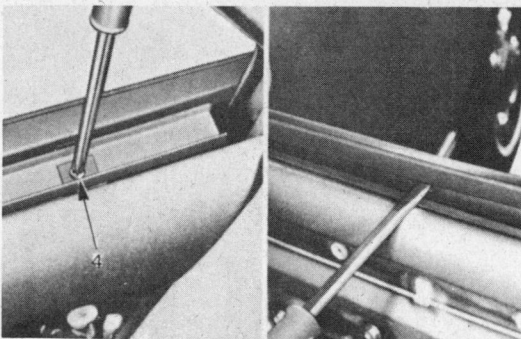

Fig. 12.29. Removing the division bar

1   Bolt   3   Division bar
2   Screw   4   Screw

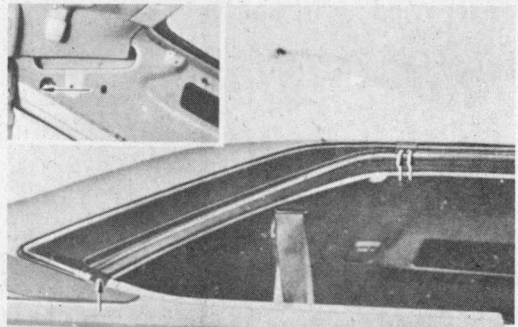

Fig. 12.30. Side finish moulding removal - Coupe
Arrows show attachment points

Fig. 12.31. Using a cord when fitting tailgate glass

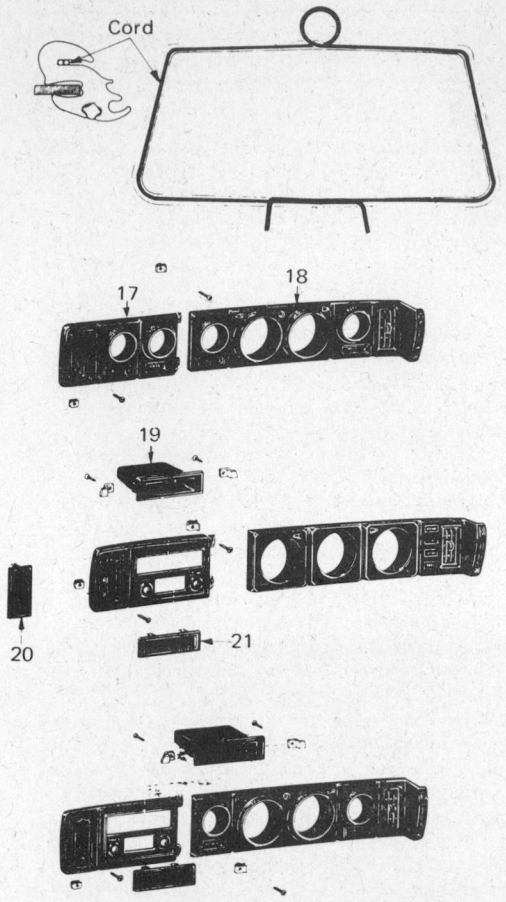

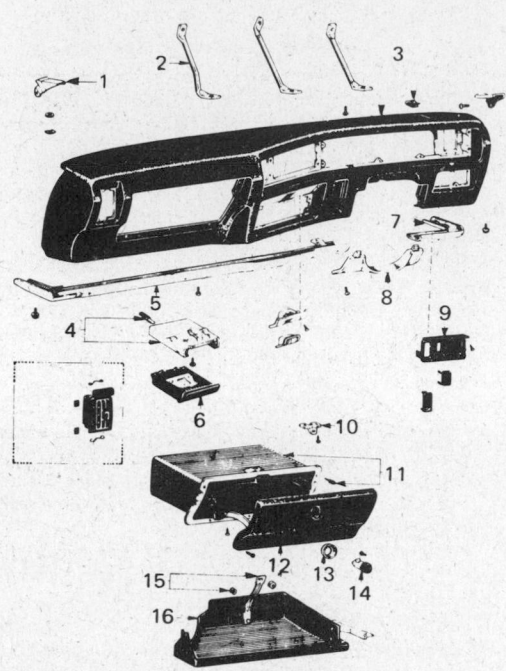

Fig. 12.32. Instrument panel parts

1 Instrument panel side garnish
2 Cowl to instrument panel brace
3 Instrument panel
4 Ashtray retainer
5 Instrument panel reinforcement No. 1
6 Ashtray
7 Instrument panel reinforcement No. 2
8 Steering column garnish
9 Switch base
10 Retainer
11 Glove compartment
12 Glove compartment door
13 Lock bezel
14 Lock cylinder
15 Instrument panel under tray bracket No. 1
16 Instrument panel under tray
17 Instrument finish centre panel
18 Instrument finish panel
19 Tape player opening cover
20 Heater control panel light cover
21 Radio tuner opening cover

Fig. 12.33. Combination meter retaining screws (arrowed)

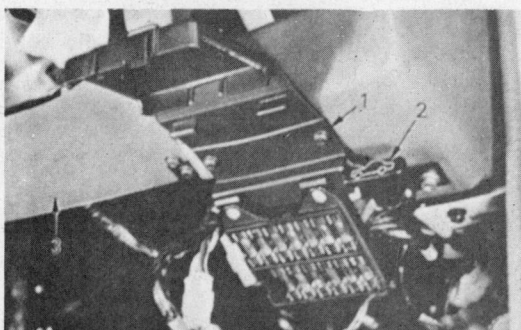

Fig. 12.34. Fuse block (1), bonnet lock control
(2) and steering column garnish (3) retaining screws

Fig. 12.35. Instrument panel screws (arrowed)

1 Blower fan   3 Blower motor resistor
2 Blower motor   4 Radiator (heat exchanger)

20 Windscreen and rear window glass - removal and refitting

Windscreen
1 On models covered by this Manual, fitting a new windscreen glass is definitely not a job for the home mechanic. This is because a special range of adhesives, hardeners and primers is used (according to the ambient temperature) when bonding the glass into the moulding, instead of having a glass which is 'self-retaining' in a rubber moulding as used for most cars.

Rear window
2 The information in the previous paragraph is applicable to rear windows except those on estate cars, where the following is applicable.
3 Using a screwdriver, carefully prise out the lipped part of the weatherstrip from the body flange over approximately half of its length.
4 With the help from an assistant, so that the glass does not drop, carefully press the glass out.
5 Ensure that the tailgate aperture flange is free from corrosion and any sealant which may have been used. If necessary, use a proprietary product for removing any rust, and touch-up the paintwork as necessary.
6 Fit the weatherstrip around the glass; if the old weatherstrip is being used, first ensure that it is not perished, and is clean.
7 Insert a thin, strong card in the aperture flange groove so that the two ends overlap at the bottom centre, leaving a loop at the top (Fig. 12.31).
8 Apply a little soap and water solution to the aperture flange groove of the weather strip, then position the glass against the aperture. With an assistant pressing the glass from the outside, pull the cord ends alternately at the top and bottom from the inside of the tailgate to pull the weatherstrip seal over the aperture flange.
9 Tap the glass firmly with the ball of the hand to ensure that the edges settle into the weatherstrip and the weatherstrip settles onto the flange. If necessary, a non-setting mastic-type glazing compound can be used around the weatherstrip if problems are encountered due to leakage.

21 Instrument panel - removal and refitting

Note: The procedure given in this Section deals with the instrument panel for models with a tachometer, but this is almost identical to the procedure for other models. For removal of the main instruments, refer to Chapter 10.
1 Initially detach the battery earth cable.
2 Remove the retaining screws and take off the instrument finish panel. Note the recessed screws in the instrument nacelles.
3 Pull out the heater control panel light cover, then remove the retaining screws and take off the instrument centre panel.
4 Pull out the speedometer cable from the rear of the instrument.
5 Remove the five retaining screws, then disconnect the harness connector and take out the combination meter.
6 Remove the four retaining screws, then disconnect the harness connector and take out the combination gauges.
7 Remove the mounting screws and separate the heater control from the cluster housing.
8 Remove the three heater control mounting screws from the reverse of the cluster housing, and take out the brightness control.
9 Remove the two mounting screws and draw out the switch base. Disconnect the wire harness and pilot bulb, then pull out the switch base.
10 Remove the glove compartment mounting screws then pull out the compartment, detaching the harness connector.
11 Detach the fuse block, bonnet lock control and steering column garnish.
12 Detach the remaining harness connectors from the rear of the meters.
13 Remove the instrument panel screws (Fig. 12.35) and withdraw the instrument panel.
14 Refitting the panel is the reverse of the removal procedure. To avoid damage, take care and do not tighten any of the mounting screws until all the screws have been fitted to avoid distorting any parts.

22 Heater blower motor - removal and refitting
1 Remove the retaining screws and take off the under tray and trim board.
2 Unplug the heater motor connector.
3 Remove the three mounting bolts and remove the blower motor complete with fan.
4 Refitting is the reverse of the removal procedure.

23 Heater assembly - removal and refitting
1 Initially detach the battery earth cable.
2 Drain the engine coolant (refer to Chapter 2 if necessary).
3 Remove the hoses from the heater unit (in the engine compartment).
4 Remove the console box (for models with a radio in the console, see Chapter 10).
5 Remove the under tray and the heater air front duct.
6 Remove the glove compartment mounting screws then pull out the compartment, detaching the harness connector.
7 Remove the heater air rear ducts and centre ventilator ducts.
8 Remove the combination meter, radio, tape player and combination gauge, as applicable (see Chapter 10).
9 Remove the heater control assembly (see Section 24).
10 Remove the retaining screws and take off the defroster nozzle.
11 Place some old flat newspapers on the floor below the heater, then remove the retaining screws, tilt the heater towards the left and draw it out from the under tray side. Be prepared for some spillage of the coolant as the heater is drawn out.
12 If necessary, the heater radiator unit (heat exchanger) can be removed by taking off the water valve and outlet hose connection, then removing the clip band and bolt.
13 Reassembly and refitting is the reverse of the removal procedure. Do not forget to fill the cooling system on completion (refer to Chapter 2 if necessary).

24 Heater control assembly - removal and refitting
1 Remove the instrument finish panel and centre panel (refer to Chapter 10 if necessary).
2 Detach the heater control cable, air inlet valve cable and the defroster cable at the ends remote from the contact levers.
3 Pull out the heater control.
4 Refitting is the reverse of the removal procedure.

25 Air conditioning system - general description and maintenance
1 The optionally specified system comprises a heater and cooling unit, a belt driven compressor, a condenser and a receiver, together with the necessary temperature controls.
2 The oil filled compressor is driven from the crankshaft pulley and incorporates a magnetic type clutch.
3 Servicing of the system is outside the scope of the home mechanic as special equipment is needed to purge or recharge the system with refrigerant gas, and dismantling of any part of the system must not be undertaken, in the interest of safety, without first having discharged the system pressure.
4 To maintain optimum performance of the system, the owner should limit his operations to the following:

a) Checking the tension of the compressor driving belt. (See Chapter 2).
b) Checking the security of all hoses and unions.
c) Always keeping the ignition timing correctly set.
d) Checking the security of the electrical connections.
e) Regularly cleaning the air intake filter.

5 Use a soft brush to remove accumulations of dust and flies from the condenser fins.
6 During the winter months, operate the air conditioning system for a few minutes each week to lubricate the interior of the compressor pump, as lack of use may cause deterioration in the moving parts.

Fig. 12.36. Heater assembly and associated parts

1 Fan
2 Blower motor
3 Resistor
4 Radiator unit
5 Water pipe
6 Water valve
7 Defroster duct
8 Water hose (outlet)
9 Water hose (inlet)
10 Air front duct
11 Blower
12 Air inlet control cable
13 Heater control cable

14 Defroster control cable
15 Heater control
16 Blower switch
17 Heater control indicator light lens
18 Ventilator duct No. 1
19 Ventilator duct No. 2
20 Ventilator louvre
21 Heater radiator
22 Air rear duct
23 Air rear duct No. 1
24 Air rear duct No. 2
25 Air duct guide

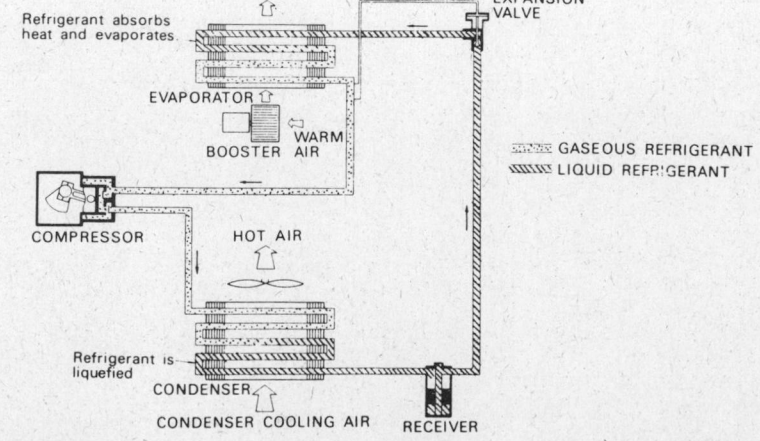

Fig. 12.37. Schematic diagram of air conditioning system

COOL AIR

Refrigerant absorbs heat and evaporates.

EVAPORATOR

EXPANSION VALVE

BOOSTER

WARM AIR

COMPRESSOR

HOT AIR

Refrigerant is liquefied

CONDENSER

CONDENSER COOLING AIR

RECEIVER

▨▨ GASEOUS REFRIGERANT
▧▧ LIQUID REFRIGERANT

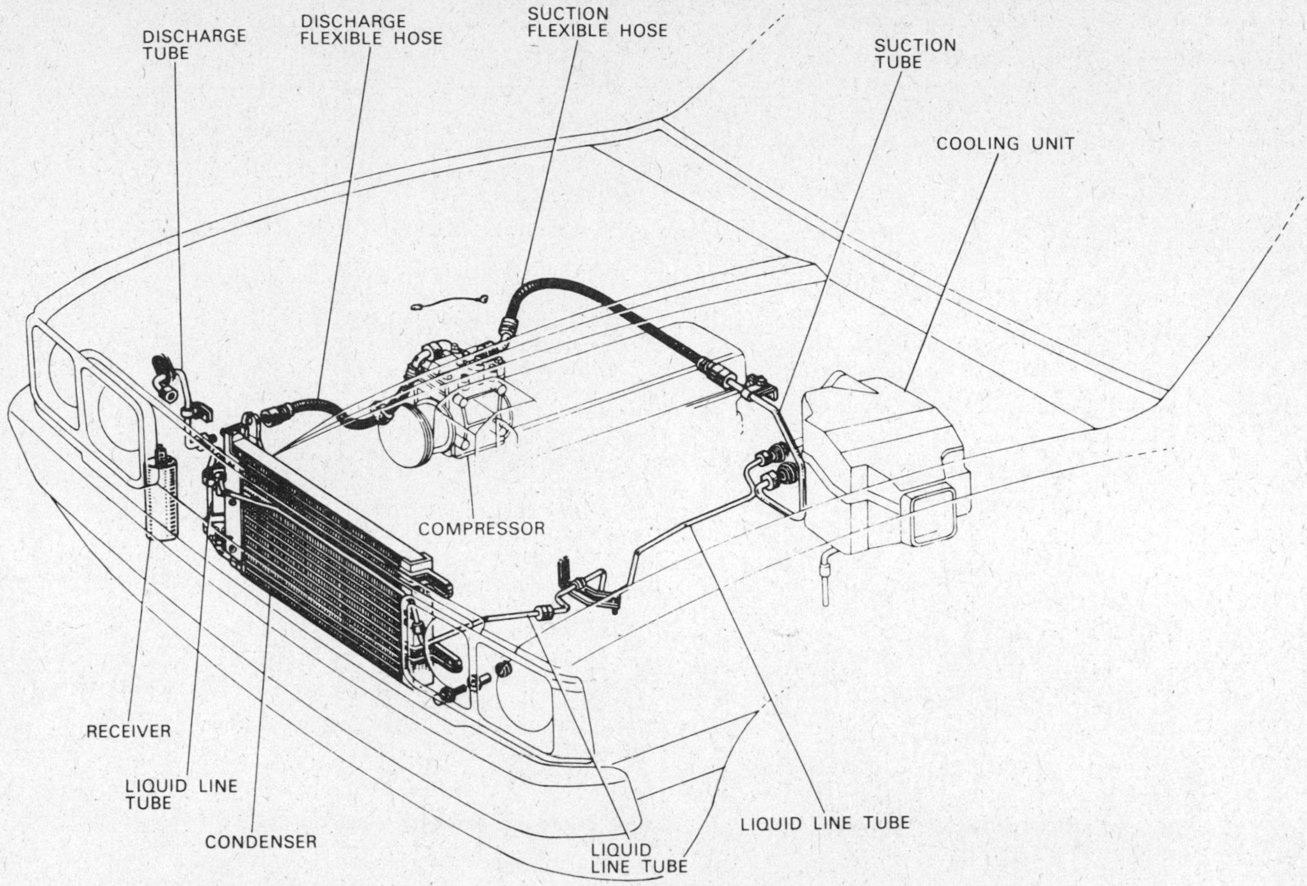

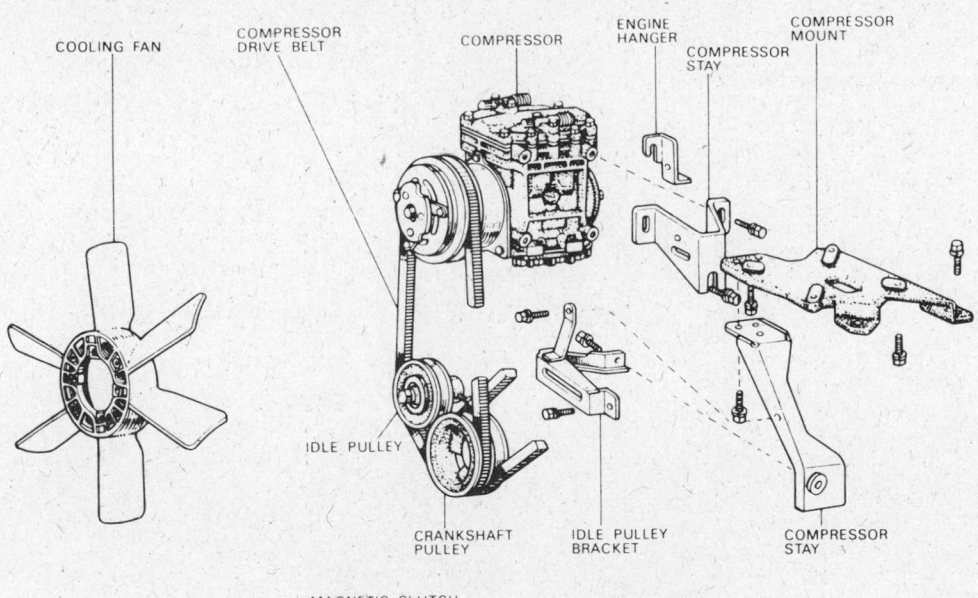

DISCHARGE TUBE

DISCHARGE FLEXIBLE HOSE

SUCTION FLEXIBLE HOSE

SUCTION TUBE

COOLING UNIT

COMPRESSOR

RECEIVER

LIQUID LINE TUBE

CONDENSER

LIQUID LINE TUBE

LIQUID LINE TUBE

Fig. 12.38. Air conditioning system layout

COOLING FAN

COMPRESSOR DRIVE BELT

COMPRESSOR

ENGINE HANGER

COMPRESSOR STAY

COMPRESSOR MOUNT

IDLE PULLEY

CRANKSHAFT PULLEY

IDLE PULLEY BRACKET

COMPRESSOR STAY

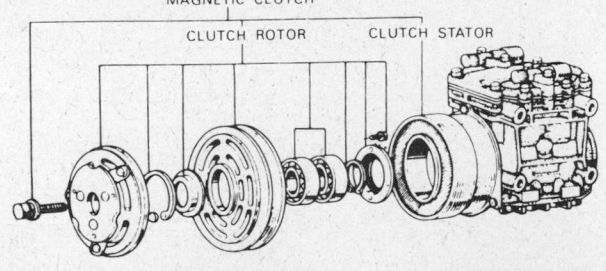

MAGNETIC CLUTCH

CLUTCH ROTOR

CLUTCH STATOR

Fig. 12.39. Air conditioning system compressor details

26 Fault diagnosis - air conditioning system

Symptom	Cause
Little or no cooling effect	Magnetic clutch not engaging due to:
	blown fuse.
	defective microswitch
	defective resistor
	defective thermistor
	broken electrical lead
	Loose compressor drive belt.
	Defective compressor pump.
	Insufficient refrigerant.
	Defective expansion valve.
	Choked receiver.
	Clogged air filter.
	Control dampers inoperative.
Restricted air ejection	Blower fuse blown.
	Blower motor defective.
	Blower switch or resistor defective.
	Clogged air filter.
Noisy operation	Dry or worn blower motor bearing.
	Worn compressor.
	Compressor mountings loose.
	Low oil level in compressor.
	Magnetic clutch bearings worn.
	Slack drive belt.
	Worn idler pulley bearing.
Overheating of engine (see also Fault diagnosis, Chapter 2)	Condenser fins clogged.

Chapter 13 Supplement:
Revisions and information on later USA models

Contents

1 Introduction

The purpose of this supplement is to cover all modifications and new service procedures introduced to the Corona line since 1977. The original material in this manual still applies unless any amendments are given in this Chapter. Owners of vehicles manufactured in 1978 or later should refer to this supplement *before* implementing the instructions shown in the original Chapters of this manual.

Many changes have come to the Corona since 1977. Most of them are minor design modifications to existing components and systems. Other changes required entirely new components, such as the larger 144.4 cu in (2366 cc) engine introduced in 1981 and the newer version of the 5-speed transmission (W55) introduced that same year.

It should be noted that some changes, though still very important, are so small they are not included in the text of the supplement. Changes in bearing tolerances and torque settings are examples of such alterations. Be sure to check the Specifications in this Chapter before assuming a component or procedure has gone unchanged.

2 Routine maintenance

1978 thru 1980 models

The recommended maintenance schedule for vehicles built in 1978 through 1980 follows. Note that these recommendations are from the manufacturer. In the interest of vehicle longevity, we recommend shorter intervals on certain operations such as fluid and filter replacements.

Every 7500 miles (12 000 km) or six months

Engine
Replace the engine oil and oil filter

Chassis and body
Inspect the brake pedal, clutch pedal and parking brake
Inspect the front brake pads and discs. Replace as necessary
Inspect the brake lines and hoses
Inspect the brake fluid level
Check the power steering fluid level
Check the balljoints and dust covers
Check the manual transmission and differential oil

Check the automatic transmission fluid level
Check all fasteners on the chassis and body. Tighten if necessary

Every 15 000 miles (24 000 km) or 12 months

Engine
Check and adjust the valve clearances
Inspect drive belt tension
Check the cooling system hoses and connections
Check all vacuum fittings, hoses and connections
Inspect the exhaust system

Fuel system
Adjust carburetor idle speed and mixture
Check the choke system and adjust if necessary
Inspect the air filter and clean if necessary
Check the throttle positioner system
Check the auxiliary fuel pump
Check and adjust the deceleration control system

Ignition system
Change the spark plugs
Inspect the ignition wiring and replace as necessary
Check the spark control valve and replace if necessary

Emission control systems
Inspect the PCV system
Inspect the carbon storage canister of the fuel vapor storage system
Inspect the fuel vapor storage system, hoses and connections

Electrical system
Inspect all wiring harnesses and connections

Chassis and body
Check the rear brake linings and drums
Check the steering wheel, linkage and gearbox oil
Check the seatbelt warning system

Every 30 000 miles (48 000 km) or two years

Engine
Replace the drivebelts
Replace the engine coolant

Fuel system
Replace the fuel filter
Replace the air filter
Replace the fuel tank cap gasket

Emission control systems
Replace the PCV valve
Inspect the air injection system

Chassis and body
Replace the manual transmission and differential oil
Replace the automatic transmission fluid
Replace the grease in the wheel bearings and balljoints

1981 and 1982 models

The following is the manufacturer's recommended maintenance schedule for 1981 and 1982 models. In the interest of vehicle longevity, we recommend shorter intervals on certain operations such as fluid and filter replacements.

Every 15 000 miles (24 000 km) or 12 months

Engine
Check and adjust the valve clearances
Check the exhaust pipes and mountings

Fuel system
Adjust the idle speed and fast idle speed
Check the choke system and adjust if necessary

Ignition system
Replace the spark plugs

Chassis and body
Check the brake pads and discs
Check the brake linings and drums
Check the brake lines and hoses
Check the balljoints and dust covers
Check the steering linkage and steering gearbox
Check the manual transmission and differential oil levels
Check all fasteners on the chassis and body and tighten if necessary

Every 30 000 miles (48 000 km) or two years

Engine
Replace all drivebelts
Replace the engine coolant
Replace the air filter

Fuel system
Inspect the fuel lines and connections
Inspect the fuel tank cap

Ignition system
Inspect the ignition wiring

Emission control systems
Inspect the PCV system
Replace the PCV valve
Inspect the emissions system charcoal canister
Check the fuel vapor storage system (fuel tank) hoses and
   connections

Chassis
Replace the grease in the wheel bearings and balljoints

---

3 Specifications

Note: *The information given in this section is supplementary to the Specifications in the twelve main Chapters of the manual. Owners of vehicles built in 1978 or later should refer to these Specifications before looking elsewhere in the book.*

Engine (22R)

General

Type	4 Cylinder, inline, single OHC
Displacement	2366 cc (144.4 cu in)
Compression pressure	171 psi (12.0 Kg/cm^2)
Compression limit	142 psi (10.0 Kg/cm^2)
Permissible difference between cylinders	14 psi (1.0 Kg/cm^2)
Compression ratio	9.0 : 1
Bore	3.62 in (92.0 mm)
Ignition timing	8° BTDC at 950 rpm max (vacuum advance disconnected)
Oil capacity	
With oil filter change	4.9 quarts (4.6 liters)
Without filter change	4.0 quarts (3.8 liters)
Firing order	1 - 3 - 4 - 2

Cylinder head

	in	mm
Surface warpage limit	0.0059	0.15
Manifold mounting surface warpage limit	0.0079	0.20
Valve seat		
Contacting surface angle	45°	
Contacting width	0.047 to 0.063	1.2 to 1.6
Refacing angle		
Intake	30°, 45°, 60°	
Exhaust	30°, 45°, 65°	

Valves & guide bushings

	in	mm
Valves		
Head edge thickness limit		
Intake & Exhaust	0.024	0.60
Face angle		
Intake & Exhaust	44.5°	

	in	mm
Overall length		
Intake	4.468	113.5
Exhaust	4.425	112.4
Stem end refacing limit		
Intake & Exhaust	0.020	0.50
Stem diameter (standard)		
Intake	0.3145 to 0.3188	7.970 to 7.985
Exhaust	0.3136 to 0.3142	7.965 to 7.980
Stem oil clearance limit		
Intake	0.0031	0.08
Exhaust	0.0039	0.10
Guide bushing		
Inner diameter		
Intake	0.3150 to 0.3161	8.0 to 8.03
Exhaust	0.3154 to 0.3161	8.01 to 8.03
Outer diameter (standard)	0.5134 to 0.5138	13.040 to 13.051

Valve springs

	in	mm
Free length	1.795	45.6
Installed length	1.594	40.5
Installed tension		
Standard	60 lb	27.2 Kg
Limit	54 lb	24.5 Kg

Camshaft

	in	mm
Circle runout (limit)	0.008	0.20
Thrust clearance		
Standard	0.0031 to 0.0071	0.08 to 0.18
Limit	0.0098	0.25
Oil clearance		
Standard	0.0004 to 0.0020	0.01 to 0.05
Limit	0.004	0.10
Journal diameter (standard)	1.2984 to 1.2992	32.98 to 33.00
Cam height		
Standard		
Intake	1.6783 to 1.6819	42.63 to 42.72
Exhaust	1.6807 to 1.6842	42.69 to 42.78
Limit		
Intake	1.6705	42.43
Exhaust	1.6728	42.49

Timing chain, tensioner & damper

	in	mm
Tensioner head thickness limit	0.433	11.0
Damper No. 1 thickness limit	0.197	5.0
Damper No. 2 thickness limit	0.177	4.5
Chain elongation limit at 17 links	5.787	147.0
Crankshaft sprocket wear limit	2.339	59.4
Camshaft timing sprocket wear limit	4.480	113.8

Piston & piston rings

	in	mm
Piston diameter (standard)	3.6196 to 3.6208	91.938 to 91.968
Oversizes available		0.50, 1.00
Cylinder-to-piston clearance	0.0020 to 0.0028	0.052 to 0.072
Piston ring end gap		
No. 1	0.0110 to 0.0157	0.28 to 0.40
No. 2	0.0110 to 0.0157	0.28 to 0.40
Oil	0.0118 to 0.0315	0.30 to 0.80
Ring-to-groove clearance (all rings)	0.008	0.20

Connecting rod & bearing

	in	mm
Thrust clearance		
Standard	0.0063 to 0.0102	0.16 to 0.26
Limit	0.0118	0.30
Bearing oil clearance		
Standard	0.0010 to 0.0022	0.025 to 0.055
Limit	0.004	0.10
Bend per 100 mm (3.94 in) limit	0.0020	0.05
Twist per 100 mm (3.94 in) limit	0.0059	0.15

Crankshaft

	in	mm
Runout limit	0.004	0.10
Thrust clearance		
Standard	0.0008 to 0.0087	0.02 to 0.22
Limit	0.012	0.3

Crankshaft (continued)

	in	mm
Main journal		
Diameter (standard)	2.3614 to 2.3622	59.98 to 60.00
Taper and out-of-round (limit)	0.0004	0.01
Oil clearance		
Standard	0.0010 to 0.0022	0.025 to 0.055
Limit	0.0031	0.08
Crank pin journal		
Diameter (standard)	2.0862 to 2.0866	52.99 to 53.00
Taper and out-of-round (limit)	0.0004	0.01
Oil clearance		
Standard	0.0010 to 0.0022	0.025 to 0.055
Limit	0.004	0.10
Thrust washer thickness (standard)	0.0787	2.00

Cylinder block

	in	mm
Warpage (limit)	0.0020	0.05
Cylinder bore (standard)	3.6220 to 3.6232	92.00 to 92.03
Wear (limit)	0.008	0.20
Taper and out-of-round (limit)	0.0004	0.01

Oil pump

	in	mm
Body clearance		
Standard	0.0035 to 0.0059	0.09 to 0.15
Limit	0.008	0.20
Tip clearance		
Driven gear-to-crescent		
Standard	0.0059 to 0.0083	0.15 to 0.21
Limit	0.012	0.30
Drive gear-to-crescent		
Standard	0.0087 to 0.0098	0.22 to 0.25
Limit	0.012	0.30
Side clearance		
Standard	0.0012 to 0.0035	0.03 to 0.09
Limit	0.0059	0.15
Relief valve operating pressure	64 psi	4.5 Kg/cm^2)

Torque wrench settings (22R engine)

	Ft-lb	Kg-m
Timing chain cover-to-head	11	1.6
Intake manifold	15	2.0
Exhaust manifold	36	5.0
Crankshaft bearing cap	80	11.0
Connecting rod cap	45	6.5
Crankshaft pulley	130	18.0
Flywheel	86	12.0
Camshaft timing sprocket	65	9.0
Camshaft bearing cap	15	2.1
Camshaft chain tensioner	15	2.1
Camshaft chain damper	11	1.6
Spark plug	15	2.1

Cooling system

Water pump

Bearing installing temperature	185°F	85°C

Radiator (1979 through 1982)

Radiator cap relief valve opening pressure		
Standard	10.7 to 14.9 psi	0.75 to 1.05 Kg/cm^2
Limit	8.5 psi	0.6 Kg/cm^2

Thermostat (22R engine only)

	Low temp. type	High temp. type
Valve opening temperature		
Starts to open at	176 to 183°F (80 to 84°C)	186 to 194°F (86 to 90°C)
Fully opens at	203°F (95°C)	212°F (100°C)
Valve opening travel	0.31 in (8 mm)	0.31 in (8 mm)

Fuel, exhaust and emission control systems

Carburetor (1978 models)

	in	mm
Float level, raised	0.276	7.0
Float level, lowered	0.040	1.0
Throttle positioner	0.009	0.22
Accelerator pump stroke	0.177	4.5
Kick-up	0.008	0.20

	in	mm
Fast idle	0.031	0.79
Throttle valve full open angle		
Primary	90° from horizontal	
Secondary	75° from horizontal	
Unloader angle	50° from horizontal	
Choke breaker angle (1st stage)	38° from horizontal	
Choke breaker angle (2nd stage)	50° from horizontal	
Idle mixture adjusting screw presetting	Screw out 1 3/4 turns	

Carburetor (1979 models)

Same as 1978 except for the following:

	in	mm
Float level, raised	0.200	5.0
Float level, lowered	0.040	1.0
Accelerator pump stroke	0.150	3.9
Idle mixture adjusting screw presetting	Screw out 2 turns	

Carburetor (1980 models)

Same as 1978 except for the following:

Fast idle angle	24° from horizontal
Throttle positioner angle	16.5° from horizontal
Idle mixture screw presetting	
Carburetor numbers 21100 to 38331	Screw out 1 1/3 turns
All others	Screw out 1 1/2 turns
Choke breaker angle (second stage)	60° from horizontal

Carburetor (1981 models)

	in	mm
Float level		
Raised position (float top to air horn)	0.413	10.5
Lowered position (float bottom to air horn)	1.890	48.0
Accelerator pump stroke	0.161	4.1
Throttle valve full open angle		
Primary	90° from horizontal	
Secondary	90° from horizontal	
Throttle valve closed angle		
Primary	9° from horizontal	
Secondary	20° from horizontal	
Fast idle angle	24° from horizontal	
Unloader angle	45° from horizontal	
Idle mixture screw presetting	Screw out 2 1/2 turns	
Idle mixture speed		
Manual transmission	740 rpm	
Automatic transmission	790 rpm	
Throttle positioner angle	16° from horizontal	

Carburetor (1982 models)

Same as 1981 except for the following:

	in	mm
Float level (raised position)	0.386	9.8
Unloader angle	45° from horizontal	
Idle speed		
Manual transmission	700 rpm	
Automatic transmission	750 rpm	

Ignition system

General

	in	mm
System type	Transistorized	
Ignition timing	8° BTDC with vacuum advance disconnected	
Distributor air gap	0.008 to 0.016	0.2 to 0.4

Ignition coil

1978 through 1980 models	
Primary coil resistance	1.3 to 1.7 ohms
Secondary coil resistance	12000 to 16000 ohms
Resistor wire resistance	1.1 to 1.3 ohms
1981 and 1982 models	
Primary coil resistance	0.8 to 1.0 ohms
Secondary coil resistance	11500 to 15500 ohms

Clutch and transmission

Clutch

	in	mm
1978 models		
Pedal height	6.34 to 6.73	161 to 171
1981 and 1982 models		
Pedal height	6.5 to 6.9	166 to 176
Pedal free play	0.2 to 0.6	5 to 15
Maximum friction plate runout	0.03	0.8

Transmission

	in	mm
Transmission identification number (1981 and 1982)	W55	
Transmission tolerances		
Output shaft		
2nd gear journal diameter limit	1.6870	42.85
3rd gear journal diameter limit...	1.4882	37.80
Flange thickness limit	0.2205	5.60
Runout limit	0.0024	0.06
1st gear inner race flange thickness limit	0.1850	4.70
1st gear inner race outer diameter limit	1.6870	42.85
1st & 2nd gear inner diameter limit	1.9350	49.15
3rd gear inner diameter limit	1.5020	38.15
Counter 5th gear inner diameter limit	1.3051	33.15
Reverse idler gear inner diameter limit	0.795	20.20
Counter gear		
Center bearing journal outer diameter limit	1.1772	29.90
5th gear journal outer diameter limit	1.0571	26.85
Reverse idler gear shaft outer diameter limit	0.783	19.90
Reverse shift arm shoe-to-idler gear groove clearance limit ...	0.035	0.90
Gear thrust clearance		
1st, 2nd & 3rd		
Standard	0.0039 to 0.0098	0.10 to 0.25
Limit	0.30	
Counter 5th		
Standard	0.0039 to 0.0161	0.10 to 0.41
Limit	0.46	
Gear oil clearance		
1st & 2nd		
Standard	0.0004 to 0.0023	0.009 to 0.060
Limit	0.15	
3rd		
Standard	0.0024 to 0.0041	0.060 to 0.103
Limit	0.20	
Counter 5th		
Standard	0.0004 to 0.0024	0.009 to 0.062
Limit	0.15	
Shift fork-to-hub sleeve clearance limit	0.039	1.00
Synchronizer ring-to-gear clearance		
Standard	0.028 to 0.067	0.7 to 1.7
Limit	0.020	0.50

Available input shaft snap-ring thicknesses	Mark	in	mm
	1	0.0807 to 0.0827	2.05 to 2.10
	2	0.0827 to 0.0846	2.10 to 2.15
	3	0.0846 to 0.0866	2.15 to 2.20
	4	0.0866 to 0.0886	2.20 to 2.25
	5	0.0886 to 0.0906	2.25 to 2.30
	11	0.0906 to 0.0925	2.30 to 2.35
	12	0.0925 to 0.0945	2.35 to 2.40

Available output shaft snap-ring thicknesses	Mark	in	mm
for Front			
	D	0.0709 to 0.0728	1.80 to 1.85
	11	0.0732 to 0.0752	1.86 to 1.91
	12	0.0756 to 0.0776	1.92 to 1.97
	13	0.0780 to 0.0799	1.98 to 2.03
	14	0.0803 to 0.0823	2.04 to 2.09
	15	0.0827 to 0.0846	2.10 to 2.15
for Rear			
	8	0.0906 to 0.0925	2.30 to 2.35
	9	0.0933 to 0.0953	2.37 to 2.42
	10	0.0957 to 0.0976	2.43 to 2.48
	11	0.0980 to 0.1000	2.49 to 2.54
	12	0.1004 to 0.1024	2.55 to 2.60
	13	0.1028 to 0.1047	2.61 to 2.66
	14	0.1055 to 0.1075	2.68 to 2.73
	15	0.1079 to 0.1098	2.74 to 2.79
for Reverse gear			
	5	0.0886 to 0.0906	2.25 to 2.30
	11	0.0906 to 0.0925	2.30 to 2.35
	12	0.0925 to 0.0945	2.35 to 2.40
	13	0.0945 to 0.0965	2.40 to 2.45
	14	0.0965 to 0.0984	2.45 to 2.50
	15	0.0984 to 0.1004	2.50 to 2.55
	16	0.1004 to 0.1024	2.55 to 2.60
	17	0.1028 to 0.1047	2.61 to 2.66
	18	0.1051 to 0.1071	2.67 to 2.72

		in	mm
	19	0.1075 to 0.1094	2.73 to 2.78
	20	0.1098 to 0.1118	2.79 to 2.84
	21	0.1122 to 0.1142	2.85 to 2.90
	22	0.1146 to 0.1165	2.91 to 2.96
	23	0.1169 to 0.1189	2.97 to 3.02

Available countershaft snap-ring thicknesses

for Front	Mark		
	1	0.0807 to 0.0827	2.05 to 2.10
	2	0.0827 to 0.0846	2.10 to 2.15
	3	0.0846 to 0.0866	2.15 to 2.20
	4	0.0866 to 0.0886	2.20 to 2.25
	5	0.0886 to 0.0906	2.25 to 2.30
	6	0.0906 to 0.0925	2.30 to 2.35
	7	0.0925 to 0.0945	2.35 to 2.40

for Rear	Mark		
	1	0.0748 to 0.0768	1.90 to 1.95
	2	0.0772 to 0.0791	1.96 to 2.01
	3	0.0795 to 0.0815	2.02 to 2.07
	4	0.0819 to 0.0839	2.08 to 2.13
	5	0.0843 to 0.0862	2.14 to 2.19
	6	0.0866 to 0.0886	2.20 to 2.25
	7	0.0890 to 0.0909	2.26 to 2.31

for Clutch hub no. 3	Mark		
	2	0.0811 to 0.0831	2.06 to 2.11
	3	0.0835 to 0.0854	2.12 to 2.17
	4	0.0858 to 0.0878	2.18 to 2.23
	5	0.0882 to 0.0902	2.24 to 2.29

Propeller shaft (1979 through 1982 models)

	in	mm
Spider axial play	0.002	0.05 maximum
Flexible coupling seat axial play	0.002	0.05 maximum
Propeller shaft runout	0.010	0.25 maximum
Available flexible coupling snap-ring thicknesses	0.056	1.42
	0.057	1.45
	0.058	1.48
	0.059	1.51
	0.061	1.54
Flexible coupling sleeve runout limit	0.040	1.10
Hole snap-ring thicknesses available	0.0935 to 0.0955	2.375 to 2.425
	0.0955 to 0.0974	2.425 to 2.475
	0.0974 to 0.0994	2.475 to 2.525
	0.0994 to 0.1014	2.525 to 2.575

Rear axle

	in	mm
Rear axle shaft runout		
Flange limit	0.010	0.20
Shaft limit	0.080	2.00

Braking system

Brake booster

	in	mm
Pushrod-to-piston clearance		
At idling vacuum	0.004 to 0.020	0.1 to 0.5
With no vacuum	0.024 to 0.026	0.60 to 0.65
Parking brake lever travel		
Center type	3 to 7 notches	
Pedal type	4 to 8 notches	

Brake Pedal

	in	mm
Height (1979 through 1982)	6.5 to 6.9	166 to 176
Free play (1979 through 1982)	0.1 to 0.2	3 to 6

Electrical system

Alternator (1981 and 1982)

	in	mm
Output		
With IC regulator	40A, 55A, 60A	
Without IC regulator	40A, 45A, 50A, 55A	
Brush exposed length	0.217	5.5 minimum
Rotor coil resistance		
With IC regulator	2.8 to 3.0 ohms	
Without IC regulator	3.9 to 4.1 ohms	

Starter (1978 through 1980 models)	Conventional type	Reduction type
Rating	50A max. at 11V	80A max. at 11.5V
Armature shaft-to-bush clearance	0.002 in (0.05 mm)	0.002 in (0.05 mm)
Commutator runout (maximum)	0.002 in (0.05 mm)	0.002 in (0.05 mm)

Starter (1981 and 1982 models)

Standard type	0.8 kw model	1.0 kw model
Armature shaft thrust clearance	0.039 in (1.0 mm)	0.039 in (1.0 mm)
Commutator		
Outer diameter (minimum)	1.06 in (27 mm)	1.22 in (31 mm)
Runout (maximum)	0.012 in (0.3 mm)	0.012 in (0.3 mm)
Brush length (minimum)	0.39 in (10 mm)	0.39 in (10 mm)
Pinion end-to-stop collar clearance	0.004 to 0.157 in (0.1 to 4.0 mm)	0.004 to 0.157 in (0.1 to 4.0 mm)

Reduction type	1.0 kw model	1.4 kw model
Commutator		
Outer diameter (minimum)	1.14 in (29 mm)	1.14 in (29 mm)
Runout (maximum)	0.008 in (0.2 mm)	0.008 in (0.2 mm)
Insulation depth (minimum)	0.008 in (0.2 mm)	0.008 in (0.2 mm)
Brush		
Length (minimum)	0.39 in (10 mm)	0.39 in (10 mm)
Spring tension (minimum)	2.6 lbs (1200 g)	2.6 lbs (1200 g)

Steering and suspension

1979 through 1982	in	mm
Steering wheel free play	0 to 1.2	0 to 30
Sector shaft thrust clearance	0.002	0.05
Power steering		
V-belt tension	0.3 to 0.4	7 to 9
Slipper thickness (minimum)	0.055	1.40
Slipper length (minimum)	1.572	39.92
Shaft-to-bushing clearance (maximum)	0.001	0.03
Flow control valve spring length (minimum)	1.85	47.0
Cross shaft thrust clearance (maximum)	0.006	0.15
Steering/suspension angles		
Toe-in		
Bias tire	0.12 ± 0.04 in (3 ± 1 mm)	
Radial tire	0.04 ± 0.04 in (1 ± 1 mm)	
Camber	1° ± 30'	
Caster	1° 30' ± 30'	
Steering angle		
Inside	38° 10'	
Outside	31° 15'	

Torque wrench settings	Ft-lb	Kg-m
Strut bar-to-lower arm	29 to 39	4.0 to 5.5
Strut bar-to-bracket	55 to 79	7.5 to 11.0
Stabilizer bar	11 to 15	1.4 to 2.2
Crossmember-to-body	55 to 75	7.5 to 10.5
Steering pitman arm	80 to 101	11.0 to 14.0

4 Engine (Model 22R — 1981 and 1982)

Engine/transmission — removal
Use the same procedure given in Chapter 1, Section 5 with these additions before paragraph 24.

1 Remove the power steering drivebelt and pump if so equipped. Tie the pump out of the way with mechanic's wire or string twine. Do not disconnect the hoses.

2 On cars equipped with air conditioning, have the system discharged of freon gas before disconnecting the air conditioner compressor and pipes. This job is best left to a professional. Have the system recharged after reassembly. Be sure to disconnect the air conditioner condenser before removing the radiator.

3 Remove the engine shock absorber from the left motor mount.

4 Remove the motor mount bolts from each side of the engine.

5 From beneath the car, remove the two engine shock absorber mount bolts and the two bolts securing the engine shock absorber cover. Remove these components.

6 Disconnect the reverse light switch wire from the transmission.

7 Disconnect the electrical connectors from the Neutral start switch and the overdrive solenoid on vehicles equipped with automatic transmissions.

Continue removing the engine/transmission, beginning with paragraph 24 of Section 5 in Chapter 1.

Sump and timing gear — removal
8 If the sump is to be removed with the engine still in the car, it will be necessary to remove the engine undercover, engine shock absorber cover, engine shock absorber, motor mounts and jack up the engine about an inch (25 mm) before the sump can be removed.

Timing Components — examination and renovation
9 Refer to Section 22, of Chapter 1.

10 In addition, measure 17 links pulled tight. This measurement should be no more than 5.787 in (147.0 mm). Measure at random, in at least three different places, and replace the chain if over the limit anywhere along its length.

11 Wrap the chain around the sprocket and measure the outer sides of the chain rollers using a vernier caliper. Measure the camshaft sprocket to be at least 4.480 in. (113.8 mm) and the crankshaft sprocket to be at least 2.339 in. (59.4 mm). Replace if necessary.

12 Inspect the chain tensioner for wear. Measure the tensioner with a vernier caliper. Minimum thickness is 0.43 in. (11 mm).

13 Check the chain dampeners for wear and measure them with a micrometer. The No. 1 dampener has a minimum of 0.197 in. (5.0 mm) and

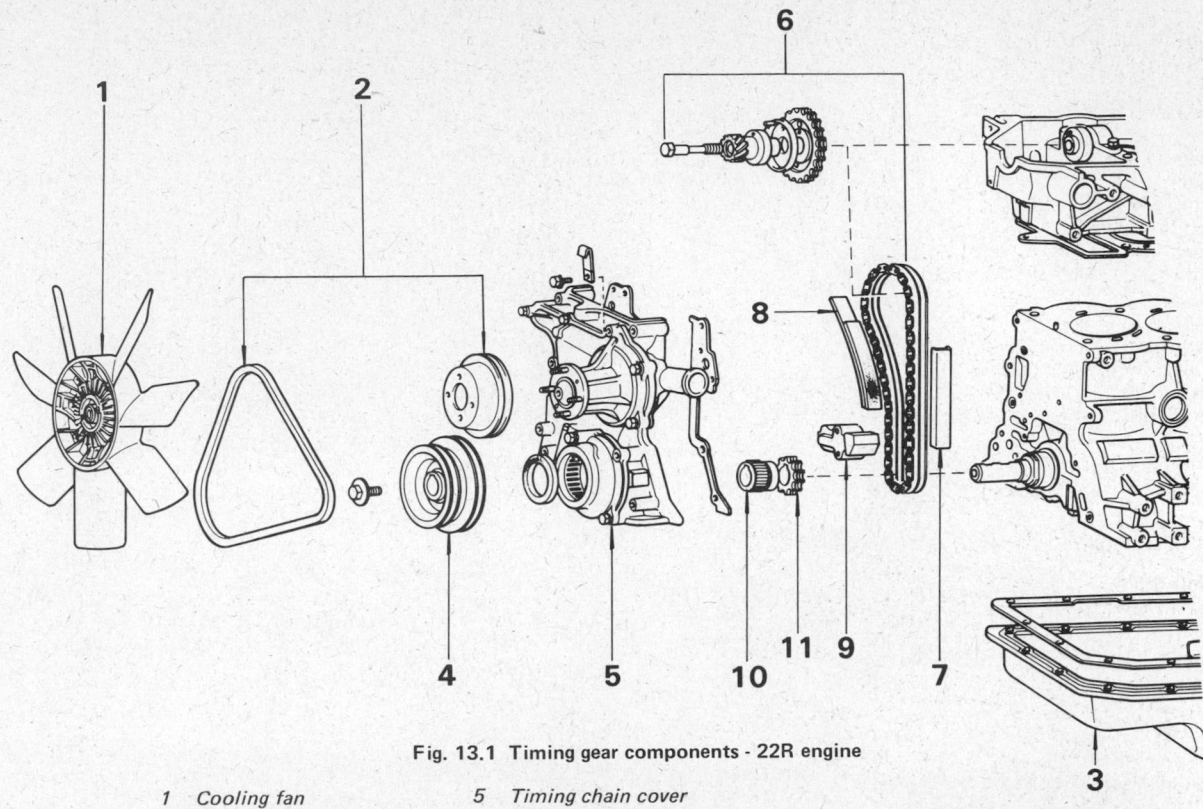

Fig. 13.1 Timing gear components - 22R engine

1 Cooling fan	5 Timing chain cover
2 Drivebelt & fan pulley	6 Timing chain & camshaft sprocket
3 Oil pan	7 Chain damper No. 1
4 Crankshaft pulley	8 Chain damper No. 2

9 Chain tensioner
10 Oil pump drive spline
11 Crankshaft sprocket

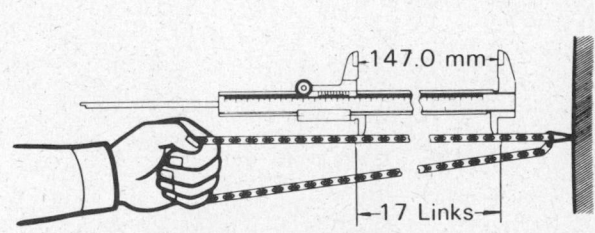

Fig. 13.2 Measure timing chain wear by stretching the chain and measuring the length of 17 links (22R engine)

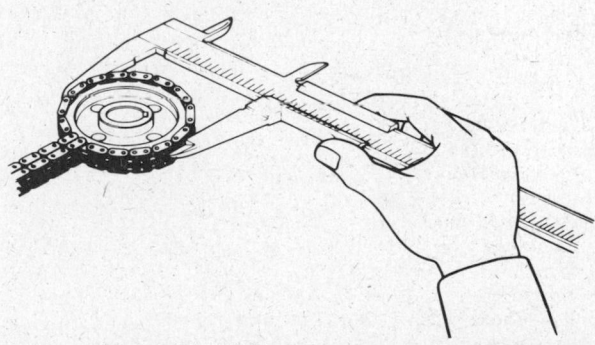

Fig. 13.3 Measuring timing gear wear (22R engine)

the No. 2 has a minimum of 0.177 in. (4.5 mm). Replace if the part is worn or less than the minimum.

5 Fuel, exhaust and emission control systems

Carburetor (1978 thru 1982) — removal
1   Remove the carburetor from the vehicle as described in Chapter 3.
2   The carburetor should not be unnecessarily dismantled. If the carburetor has had prolonged use and is likely to be badly worn, it is better to purchase a new or exchange unit which has been tested and calibrated rather than to try to obtain a lot of replacement parts.
3   Before starting to disassemble the carburetor, it is vital to have a clean work space, the correct tools and several clean containers in which to put the parts of each assembly and sub-assembly.
4   Clean the outside of the carburetor with solvent or carburetor

cleaner before beginning the disassembly process.

Carburetor (1978 thru 1980) — rebuild
Disassembly
Air horn
5   Remove the pump arm pivot screw and pump arm with the connecting rod.
6   Remove the connecting links and air horn screws.
7   Remove the choke opener and lift the air horn and the gasket out away from the body.
8   Remove the float pivot pin while holding the float in place and remove the float.
9   Remove the needle valve, spring, plunger and seat from beneath where the float arm tang was.
10 Pull out the pump plunger. Remove the power piston retainer, the power piston and the spring.

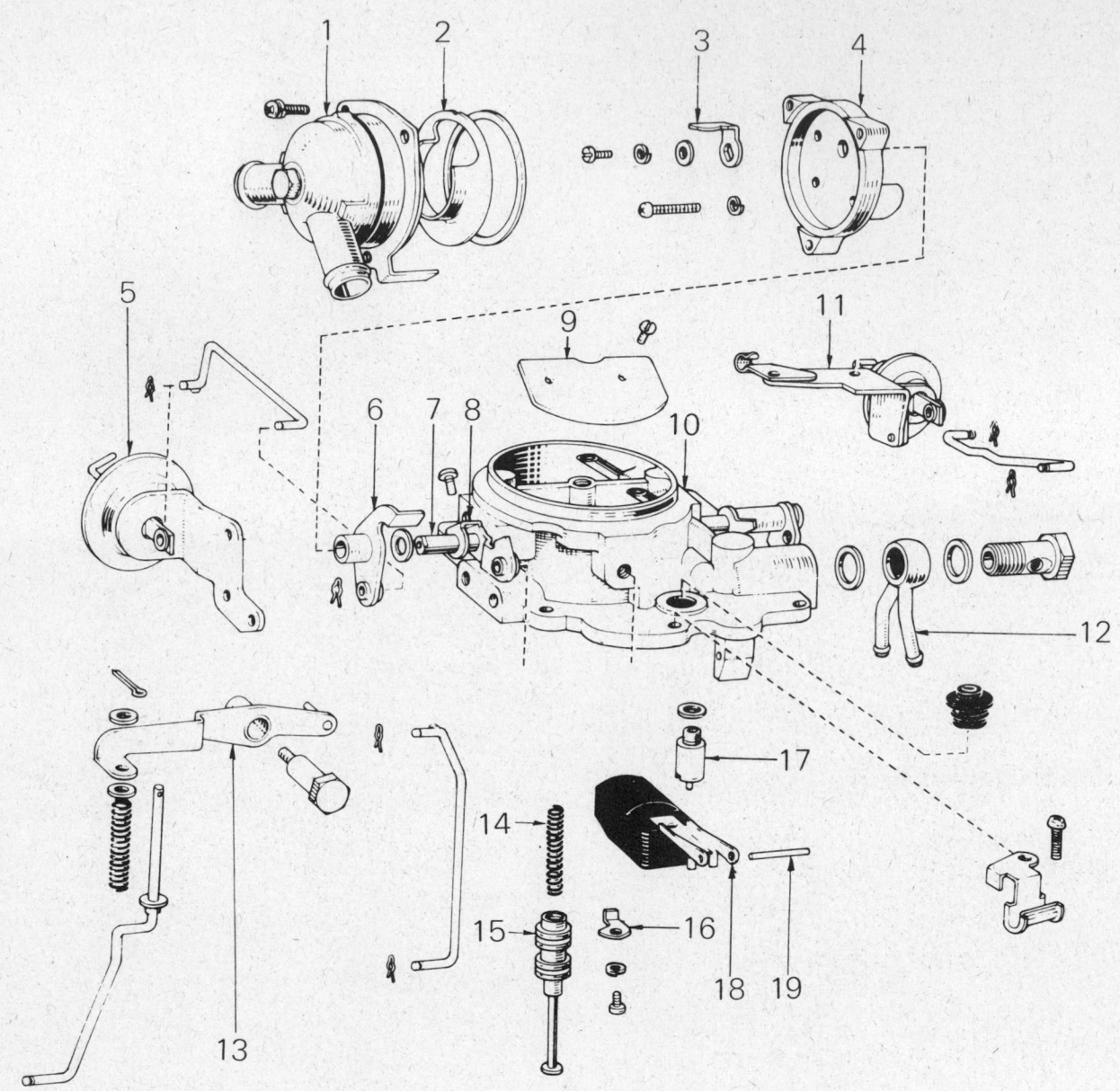

Fig. 13.4 Air horn component parts (1978 thru 1980 models)

1	Water and coil housing	8	Connecting lever	13	Pump arm
2	Coil housing plate	9	Choke valve	14	Spring
3	Choke lever	10	Air horn	15	Power piston
4	Coil housing body	11	Choke opener	16	Piston retainer
5	Choke breaker	12	Union	17	Needle valve set
6	Relief lever			18	Float
7	Choke shaft			19	Float pivot pin

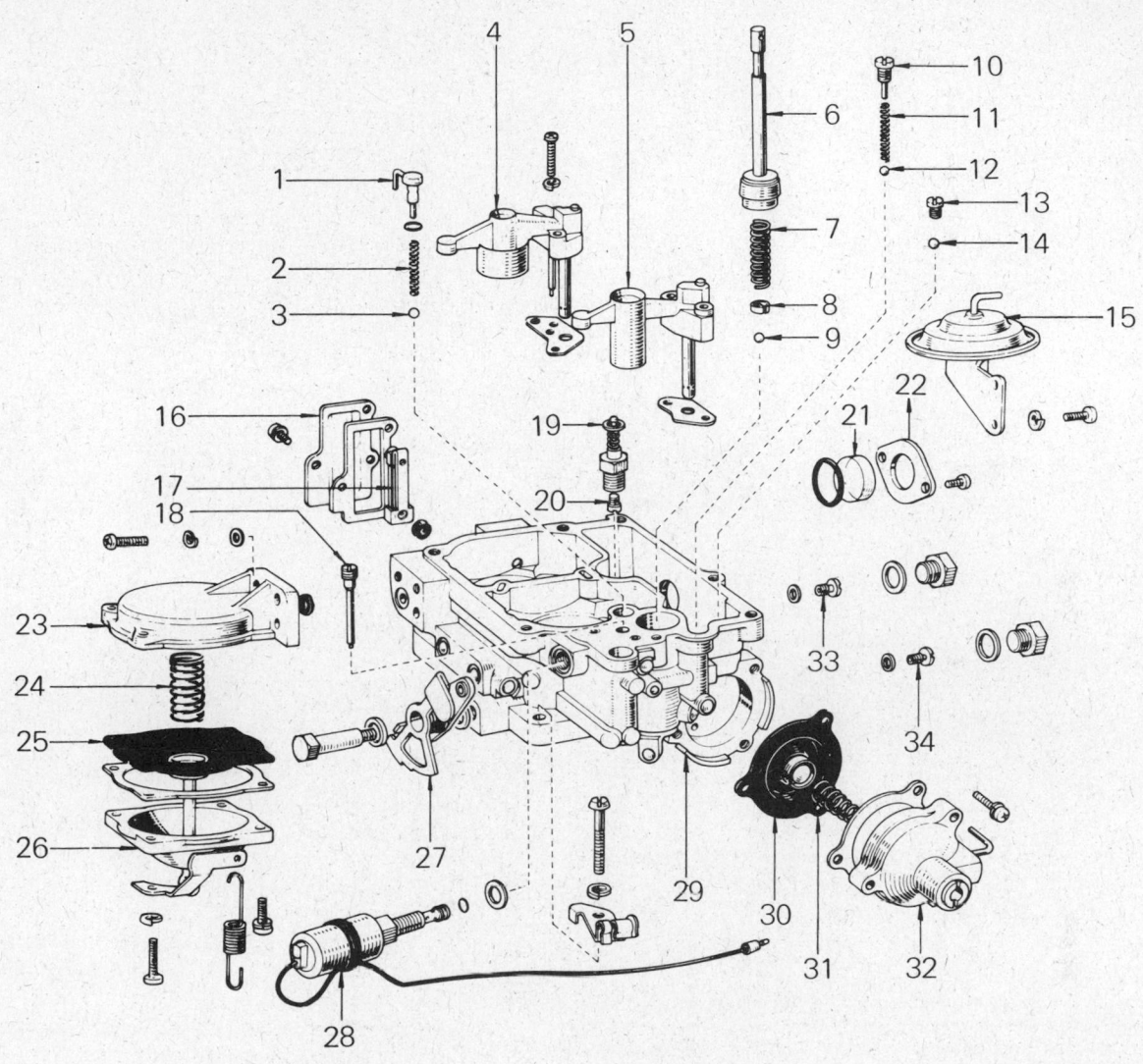

Fig. 13.5 Carburetor body component parts (1978 thru 1980 models)

1 Pump jet	10 Plug	18 Primary slow jet	26 Housing
2 Spring	11 Spring	19 Power valve	27 Fast idle cam
3 Outlet check ball	12 AAP outlet check ball	20 Power jet	28 Solenoid valve
4 Secondary small venturi	13 Plug	21 Sight glass	29 Carburetor body
5 Primary small venturi	14 AAP inlet check ball	22 Glass retainer	30 Diaphragm
6 Pump plunger	15 Throttle positioner	23 Diaphragm housing cap	31 Spring
7 Spring	16 Thermostatic valve cover	24 Spring	32 AAP housing
8 Ball retainer	17 Thermostatic valve	25 Diaphragm	33 Secondary main jet
9 Inlet check ball			34 Primary main jet

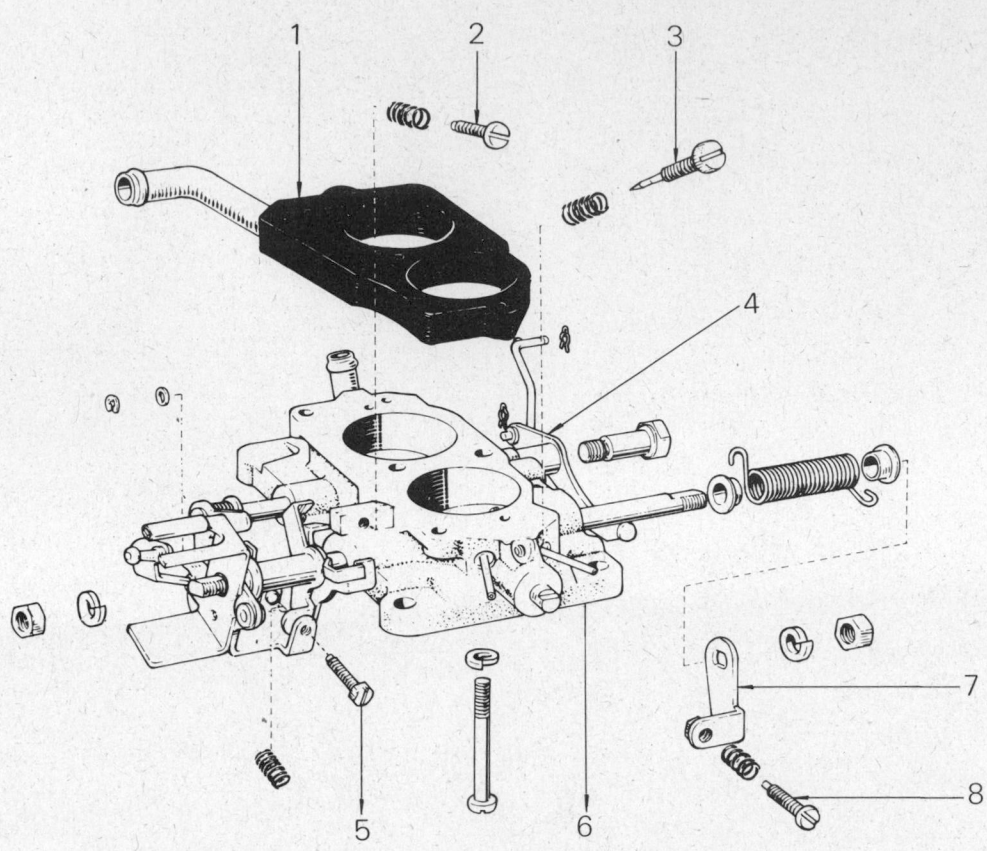

Fig. 13.6 Flange component parts (1978 thru 1980 models)

1	Insulator	5	Fast idle adjusting screw
2	Idle speed adjusting screw	6	Carburetor flange
3	Idle mixture adjusting screw	7	Throttle lever
4	Positioner lever	8	Throttle positioner adjusting screw

Automatic choke

11 Loosen the housing set screws from the water housing and remove the water and coil housing, housing plate and gasket.

12 Loosen the shaft and body screws and take off the choke lever and coil housing body.

13 Remove the choke breaker with the relief lever and link.

Carburetor body

14 Remove the two venturis and take out the pump jet O-ring spring and ball. Take out the pump damping spring and, using tweezers, take out the retainer and ball below the damping spring.

15 Remove the slow jet and power valve.

16 Remove the two plugs with the appropriate size wrench and remove the main jets with a small screwdriver.

17 Remove the cover and take out the thermostatic valve and O-ring.

Note: *Do not disassemble the thermostatic valve.*

18 Remove the sight glass retainer screws, the sight glass and the O-ring.

19 Remove the throttle positioner and link.

20 Remove the auxiliary acceleration pump inlet plug and ball.

21 Remove the outlet plug, spring and ball.

22 Remove the auxiliary acceleration pump housing, diaphragm, spring and gasket.

23 Remove the large spring from its position on the diaphragm. Remove the small spring clip from the diaphragm plunger and disconnect the link. Remove the diaphragm assembly and O-ring.

24 Remove the solenoid valve and fast idle cam.

25 Loosen the three body screws and remove the carburetor body and insulator from the flange.

Flange

26 Remove the idle mixture adjusting screw.

27 Remove the throttle lever, throttle lever spring and the collars.

28 Remove the throttle positioner lever.

Inspection

29 Before inspecting the carburetor parts, wash them thoroughly in carburetor cleaner. Blow all dirt and foreign matter from the jets and similar parts with compressed air. Also clear the fuel passages and any restrictions in the body. Wash and clean the cast parts with a soft brush. Do not use a brush with metal bristles.

30 If there are any carbon deposits or varnish around the throttle valve, clean these off with solvent and a small brush.

31 Never clean any orifice or jet in the carburetor with metal objects or a drill bit. Either of these methods could inlarge the openings and have adverse effects on fuel metering.

32 Inspect the following parts and replace any part found defective.

Air horn

33 Check the entire air horn for cracks, damaged threads and wear on the choke shaft bores.

34 Check the floats for cracks, damage or the presence of fuel in the float body.

35 Check for wear in the float pivot pin holes. Check the needle valve surface which contacts the valve seat. If there is a ridge, replace the needle valve.

36 Check the strainer for rust and breakage.

37 Check the power piston for scratches and excessive wear. If the

Fig. 13.7 Remove the following parts in order

1 Pump arm pivot screw	4 Connecting link
2 Pump arm	5 Connecting link
3 Connecting rod	

Fig. 13.8 Remove the pump components

1 Plunger	3 Power piston
2 Power piston retainer	

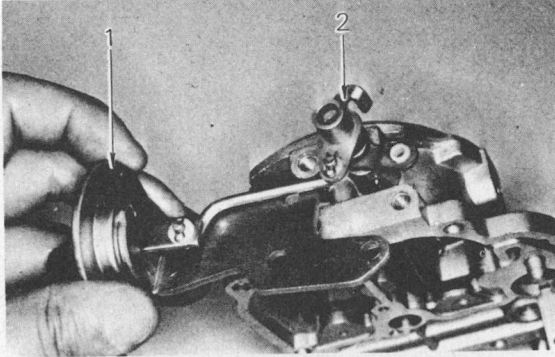

Fig. 13.9 Removing the choke breaker (1) and relief lever (2)

Fig. 13.10 Remove the plugs (1), mainjets (2) and the thermostatic valve cover (3)

Fig. 13.11 Remove the AAP inlet plug and ball (1), the outlet plug (2), and the AAP housing (3)

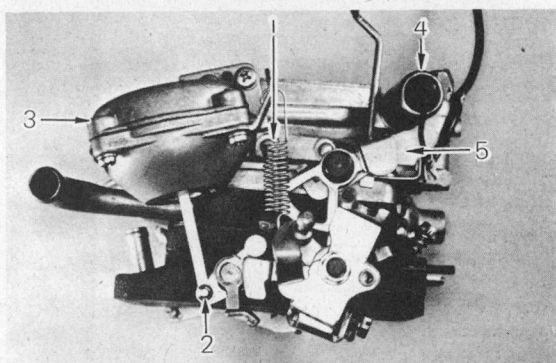

Fig. 13.12 Remove the spring (1), link (2), diaghragm assembly (3), solenoid valve (4), and fast idle cam (5)

power piston is broken or deformed, replace it.
38 Check the choke valve and the choke shaft for wear or damage, bending or improper fit in the housing.
39 Check the coil housing for cracks. Check the thermostatic bi-metal coil for rust and deformation.

Carburetor body
40 Check the body for cracking and scoring on the mounted surfaces and check the threads for damage.
41 Check the jets for damaged contacting surfaces, damaged threads or screwdriver slots.
42 Check the power valve for faulty opening and closing action, damage on the contacting surface and damaged threads.
43 Check the venturis for damage and wear.
44 Check the pump damping spring for rust and breakage.
45 Check the pump check ball for rust and damage and check the pump

plunger for wear at the sliding surface or damaged seal.
46 Check the thermostatic valve and solenoid valve for damage.

Flange
47 Check the flange body for cracks, damaged mounting surfaces and threads and wear at the throttle shaft bearings.
48 Check the throttle valves for wear and damage.
49 Check the idle mixture adjusting screw for damage at the tip or threads.

Reassembly
Note: *Be sure to use all new gaskets and O-rings when reassembling and be sure that all metal parts have been thoroughly cleaned in carburetor cleaner. Do not apply solvent or cleaner to the gaskets or rubber parts. Do not use gasoline for a solvent.*

Flange
50 Install the idle mixture adjusting screw into the spring and install the screw and spring.

Fig. 13.13 During reassembly of the choke coil housing, align the tang on the bimetal spring with the choke lever

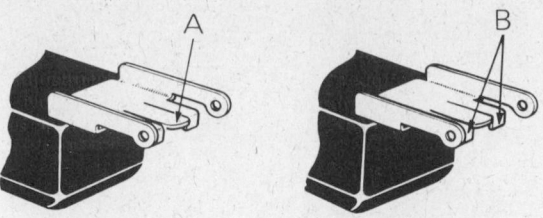

Fig. 13.14 Float height adjustment points

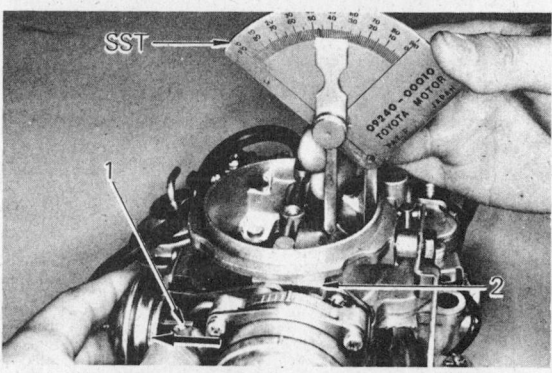

Fig. 13.16 Adjusting the choke breaker by pushing in on the breaker rod (1), and making adjustments at the relief lever (2)

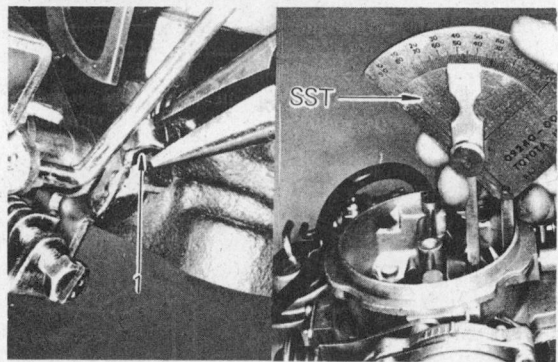

Fig. 13.15 Adjusting the unloader with the Toyota special service tool (SST)

Fig. 13.17 Remove the solenoid valve by turning the body as indicated

51 Install the throttle positioner lever to the flange. Assemble the collar spring onto the throttle shaft and install the throttle lever.
52 Install the insulator and body onto the flange and secure it with the three screws.
53 Insert the automatic choke shaft into the air horn and install the choke with two screws.
54 Install the choke breaker and relief valve, the coil housing body and choke lever.
55 Install the choke housing plate over the gasket being sure to align its hole with the pin in the choke housing body.
56 Align the bi-metal spring flange with the choke lever and install the coil housing.

Air horn
57 Install the power piston spring and piston into the bore.
58 Install the retainer with the screw.
59 Install the needle valve seat over the gasket into the fuel inlet.
60 Install the needle valve, spring, plunger and float. Secure the float with the pivot pin.
61 Adjust the float level by turning the carburetor body so that the float hangs vertically by its own weight. Check the clearance between the float tip and the air horn with calipers or an accurate rule. Adjust the float height by bending the A tang on the flat lip.
62 Adjust the float in the lower position by lifting up the float and checking the clearance between the needle valve plunger and the float lip. Make this adjustment by bending the B part of the float lip.

Carburetor body
63 Install the primary main jet (brass) and secondary main jet (chrome).
64 Install the float bowl plugs over the new gaskets. Install the sight glass O-ring, glass and retainer.
65 Install the slow jet auxiliary acceleration pump outer ball, spring and plug, the auxiliary accelerator pump inlet ball and plug, the pump inlet ball and retainer and the power valve.
66 Install new gaskets on the primary and secondary venturis and install the venturis.

67 Install the thermostatic valve.
68 Install the throttle positioner.
69 Assemble and install the auxiliary accelerator pump.
70 If the choke diaphragm was disassembled, assemble it and position a new O-ring at its mount and install the diaphragm assembly.
71 Reconnect the diaphragm rod with the small washer and spring clip and install the return spring.
72 Install the fast idle cam and screw in the solenoid valve over a new gasket.
73 Install the new pump jet spring and jet with a new O-ring.
74 Install the pump plunger.
75 Install the air horn assembly being sure to use a new gasket.
76 Install the choke opener.
77 Connect the pump connecting link to the throttle lever and install the pump arm.
78 Connect the fast idle and choke opener links.

Carburetor (1978 thru 1980) — adjustments
79 Adjustments of these carburetors require a special Toyota service tool No. 09240-00011, which measures the angles of the butterfly valves on the carburetor.

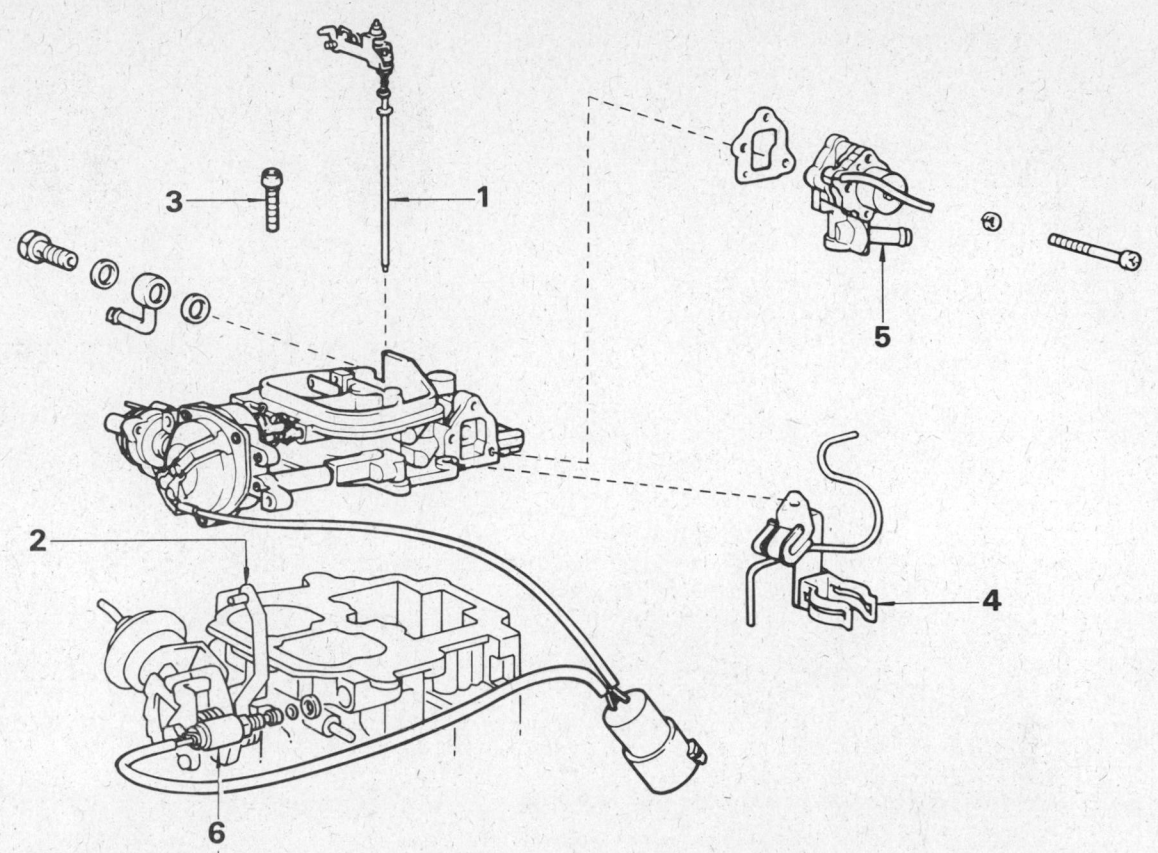

Fig. 13.18 Air horn component parts (1981 and 1982 models)

1	Metering needle	4	MCV support
2	Fast idle link	5	Outer vent control valve
3	Air horn screw	6	Solenoid valve

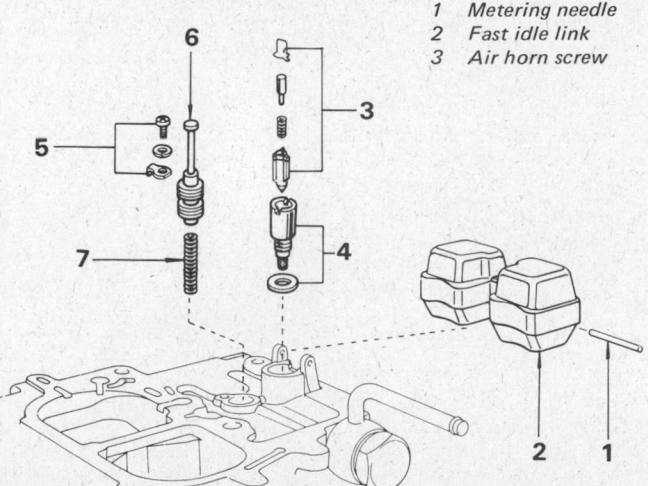

Fig. 13.19 Float assembly exploded view (1981 and 1982 models)

1	Pivot pin	5	Power piston retainer
2	Float	6	Power piston
3	Needle valve	7	Spring
4	Needle valve seat		

Kick-up

80 With the primary throttle valve fully opened, check the secondary throttle valve opening. Adjust the kick-up by bending the secondary throttle lever.

Unloader

81 With the primary throttle valve fully opened, check the choke valve angle. Adjust by bending the fast idle lever.

Choke breaker

82 Push in the choke breaker rod to open the choke valve and check the choke valve angle. Adjust the choke breaker by bending the relief lever.

Carburetor (1981 and 1982) — rebuild

Disassembly

Air horn

83 Loosen the screw and remove the metering needle.

84 Disconnect the fast idle link from the throttle shaft lever.

85 Remove the five screws retaining the air horn to the carburetor body and lift away the air horn and gasket.

86 Loosen the solenoid valve and remove it by rotating the body counterclockwise.

87 If the air horn is to be dismantled, remove the float pivot pin and float. Remove the needle valve spring, plunger and seat.

88 Pull out the pump plunger, remove the power piston retainer, the power piston and the spring.

89 Remove the outer vent control valve.

Carburetor body

90 On US vehicles equipped with automatic transmissions, remove the dashpot.

91 Remove the slow jet, power valve, metering needle guide, secondary main jet, plug and primary main jet.

92 Remove the accelerator pump housing, the diaphragm and the spring.

93 Remove the auxiliary accelerator pump housing, diaphragm and spring.

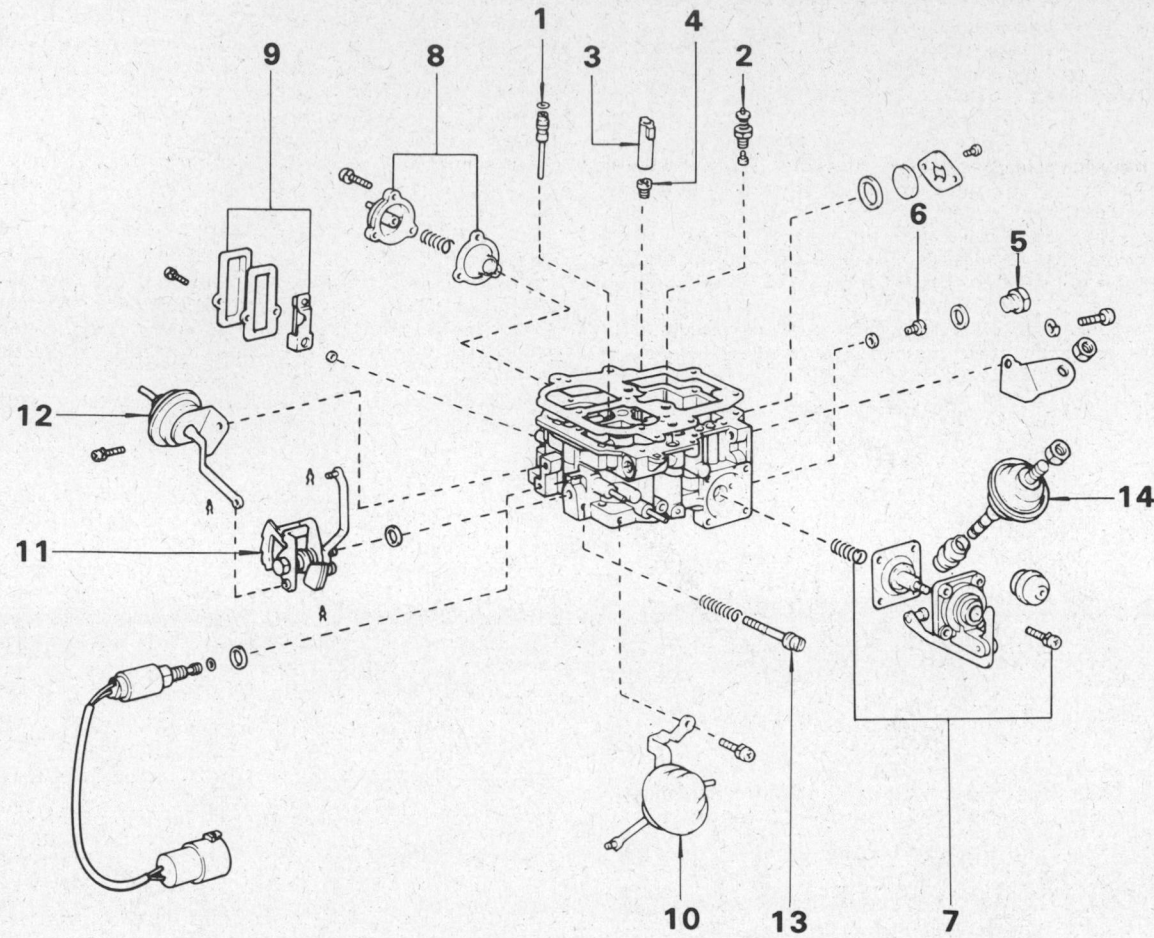

Fig. 13.20 Carburetor body components (1981 and 1982 models)

1	Slow jet	6	Primary main jet	10	Throttle positioner
2	Power valve with jet	7	Acceleration pump	11	Fast idle cam
3	Metering needle guide	8	AAP	12	Choke opener
4	Secondary main jet	9	Thermostatic valve	13	Idle speed adjusting screw
5	Plug			14	Dash pot

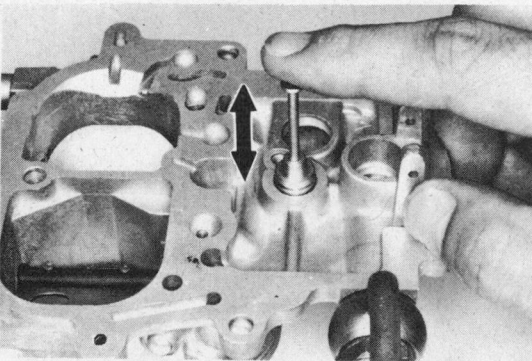

Fig. 13.21 Check the power piston for smooth operation as shown

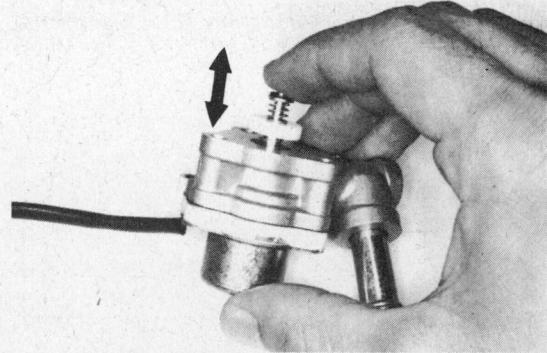

Fig. 13.22 Checking the operation of the outer vent control valve rod

94 Remove the hot idle compensation (HIC) valve cover, the thermostatic valve and the rubber valve seat.

95 Disconnect the idle up diaphragm link and remove the diaphragm.

96 Disconnect the choke opener link and remove the choke opener. Separate the flange from the body.

Inspection

97 Check all parts for damage and wear. Blow out the jets and the air passages to clear them but do not attempt to use wire or drill bit to clean the jets and orifices.

98 Inspect the vent control valve and valve seats for damage. Check that the rod moves slowly. Measure resistances between the terminal and solenoid body to be 63 to 73 ohms at 68°F (20°C) with an ohmmeter.

99 Inspect the choke breaker diaphragm by applying vacuum. The choke valve should slightly open and should not loose vacuum pressure immediately.

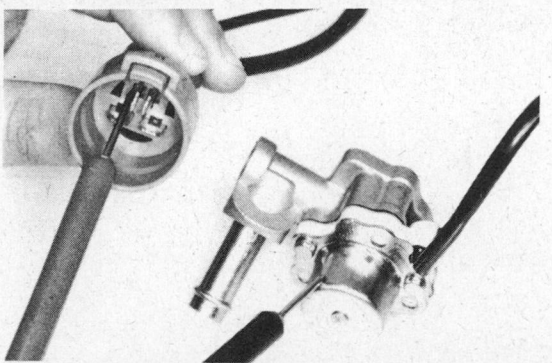

Fig.13.23 Measuring the resistance between the terminal and solenoid valve body with an ohmmeter

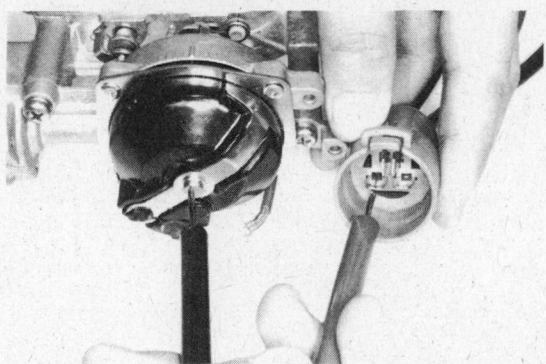

Fig. 13.24 Measuring the resistance at the choke heater housing with an ohmmeter

100 Measure the resistance between the terminal and choke heater housing to be 16 to 20 ohms at 68°F (20°C).

101 Connect the jumper lead from the negative terminal of the battery to the negative side of the fuel cut-out solenoid. When the positive side is connected with another jumper wire to the positive terminal of the battery, a clicking sound should be heard.

102 Apply vacuum to the choke opener diaphragm. The vacuum should not drop immediately and the link should move.

103 Apply vacuum to the idle-up diaphragm. Check that the vacuum does not drop immediately and that the link moves.

Reassembly

104 Wash all parts with carburetor cleaner before reassembly. Use new gaskets and as each unit is reassembled check that any sliding or rotating parts move smoothly. If screws have been peened and filed to remove the painting they should be discarded and new screws fitted. The new screws should be peened after tightening.

105 Temporarily install the idle mixture screw if it has been removed.

106 Attach the body to the flange using a new gasket.

Carburetor body

107 Install the primary main jet and plug over a new gasket.

108 Install the metering needle guide, secondary main jet, power valve with jet and slow jet with new O-ring.

109 Install the HIC valve, valve seat and cover over a new gasket.

110 Install the auxilliary accelerator pump components in order; diaphragm (with outer gasket), spring, cover and screws.

111 Install the accelerator pump components in order; spring, diaphragm, (with outer gasket), cover, boot and screws.

112 Install the choke opener, idle up diaphragm and dash pot (where equipped).

Air horn

113 Install outer vent control valve on the air horn with a new gasket.

114 Install the power piston spring and piston in the bore. While push-

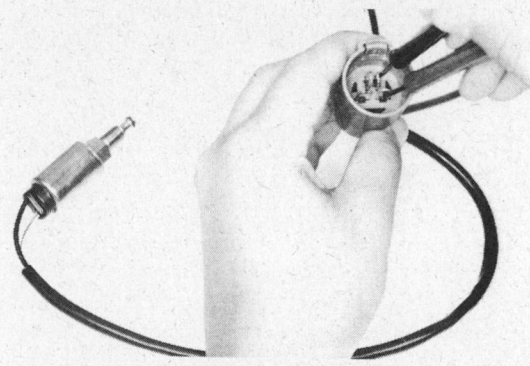

Fig. 13.25 Checking the solenoid valve by applying voltage from the battery

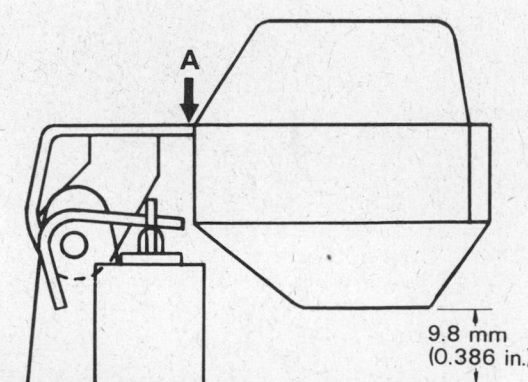

Fig. 13.26 Checking the float height in the lowered position (adjust the height by bending the float arm at point A)

9.8 mm (0.386 in.)

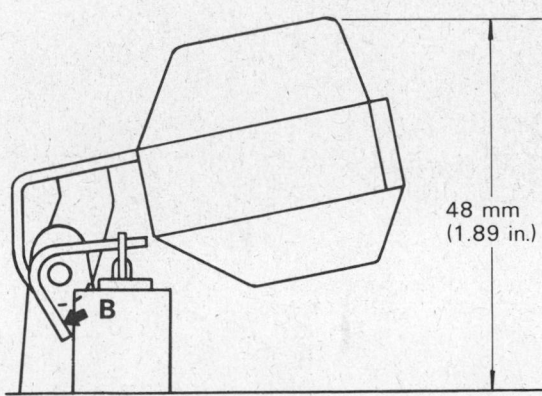

Fig. 13.27 Checking the float height in the raised position (adjust the height by bending the tang at point B)

48 mm (1.89 in.)

ing on the piston, rotate the retainer over the piston and tighten the retainer screw.

115 Install the needle valve and seat.

116 Place the lip of the float under the wire of the needle valve and secure the float with the pivot pin.

117 Let the float hang down by its own weight. Measure and adjust the clearance between the float top and air horn (without gasket) with a float gauge. Lift the float and measure the distance from the float bottom to the air horn using a vernier caliper. Adjust as necessary. Install the solenoid valve with a new O-ring into the carburetor body by rotating the body clockwise.

118 Carefully join the air horn to the body using a new gasket.

119 Install the fuel inlet bracket, number plate, fast idle link, wire clamp and the four screws.

120 Install the metering needle. Hook the spring end into the hole and tighten the screw with two washers.

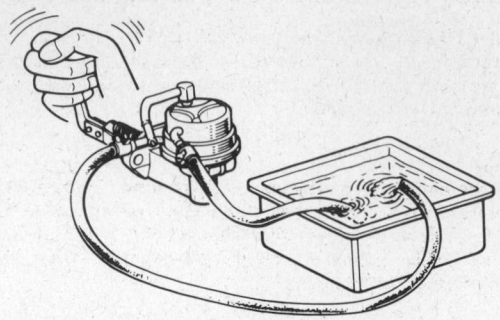

Fig. 13.28 Checking the operation of the fuel pump

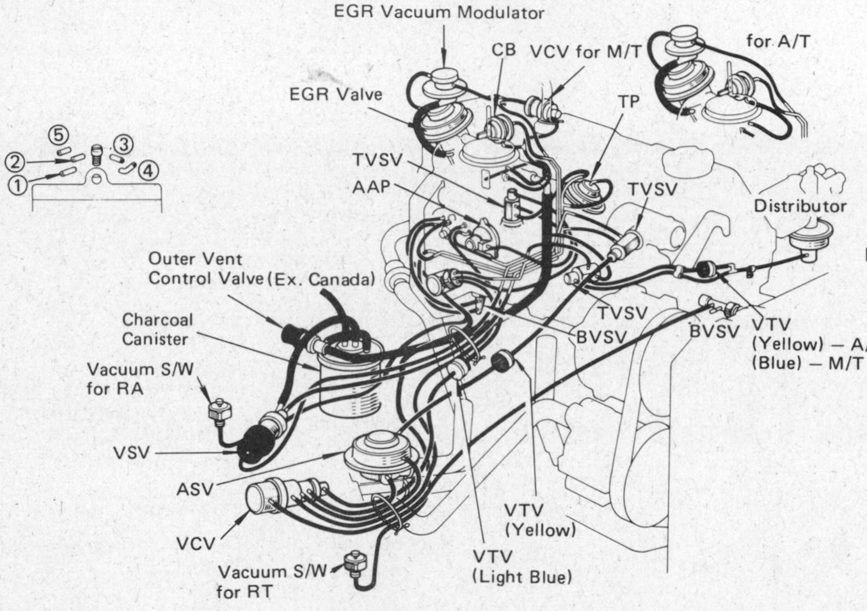

Fig. 13.29 Emission control devices used on 1978 California vehicles

1   EGR port
2   Spark control port
3   AI control port
4   Advancer port
5   Fuel cut port

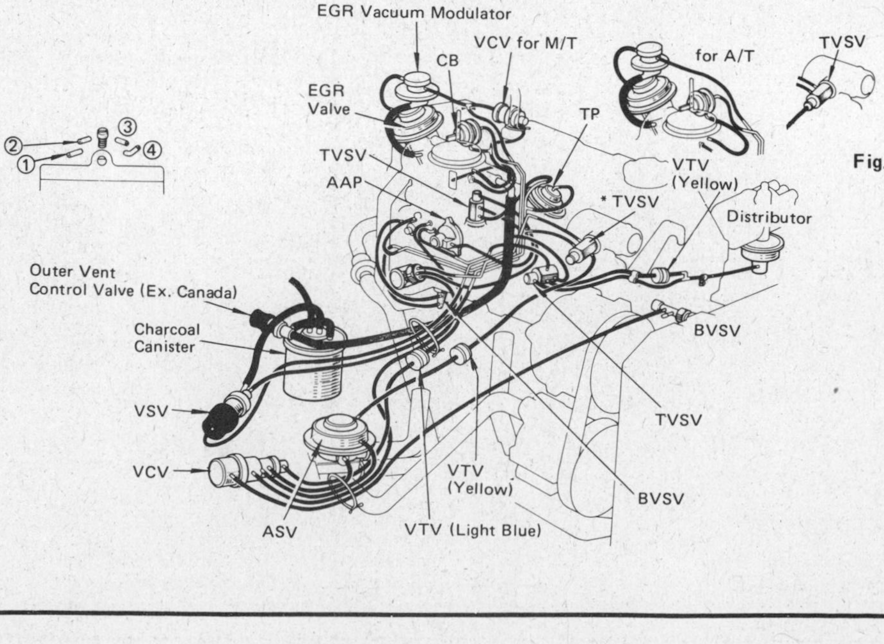

Fig. 13.30 Emission control devices used on 1978 non-California vehicles

1   EGR port
2   Spark control port
3   AI control port
4   Advancer port

Carburetor (1981 and 1982) — adjustments

121 The procedures given in Chapter 3 for adjusting the 20R engine carburetor are accurate for this engine also with the exception of the Specifications and the following:

Choke opener

122 Adjust the choke opener by applying vacuum. Check that the fast idle cam is on the fourth step then bend the choke opener lever as necessary. Release the vacuum, set the fast idle lever to the first step and close the choke valve. Now check for clearance between the choke opener lever and the fast idle cam.

Kick-up diaphragm

123 Apply vacuum to the throttle positioner diaphragm. Check the throttle valve opening angle and adjust it by turning the adjusting screw.

Choke breaker

124 Apply vacuum to the choke breaker diaphragm and close the choke valve by hand. Measure the choke valve opening angle.

125 Install the carburetor. Connect the throttle linkage, PCV hose, fuel line and emission control hoses. Put the air cleaner on and connect the remaining hoses.

Fuel pump — removal, checking and installation

The later model fuel pump can be removed and replaced as described in Chapter 3. A simple test can be performed as shown in the accompanying figure. Remove the pump, insert both the inlet and outlet fuel lines into a container of gasoline and operate the pump lever. If the pump does not operate properly, replace it with a new one.

Emission controls — general information

126 Many of the emission control devices used prior to 1978 are used

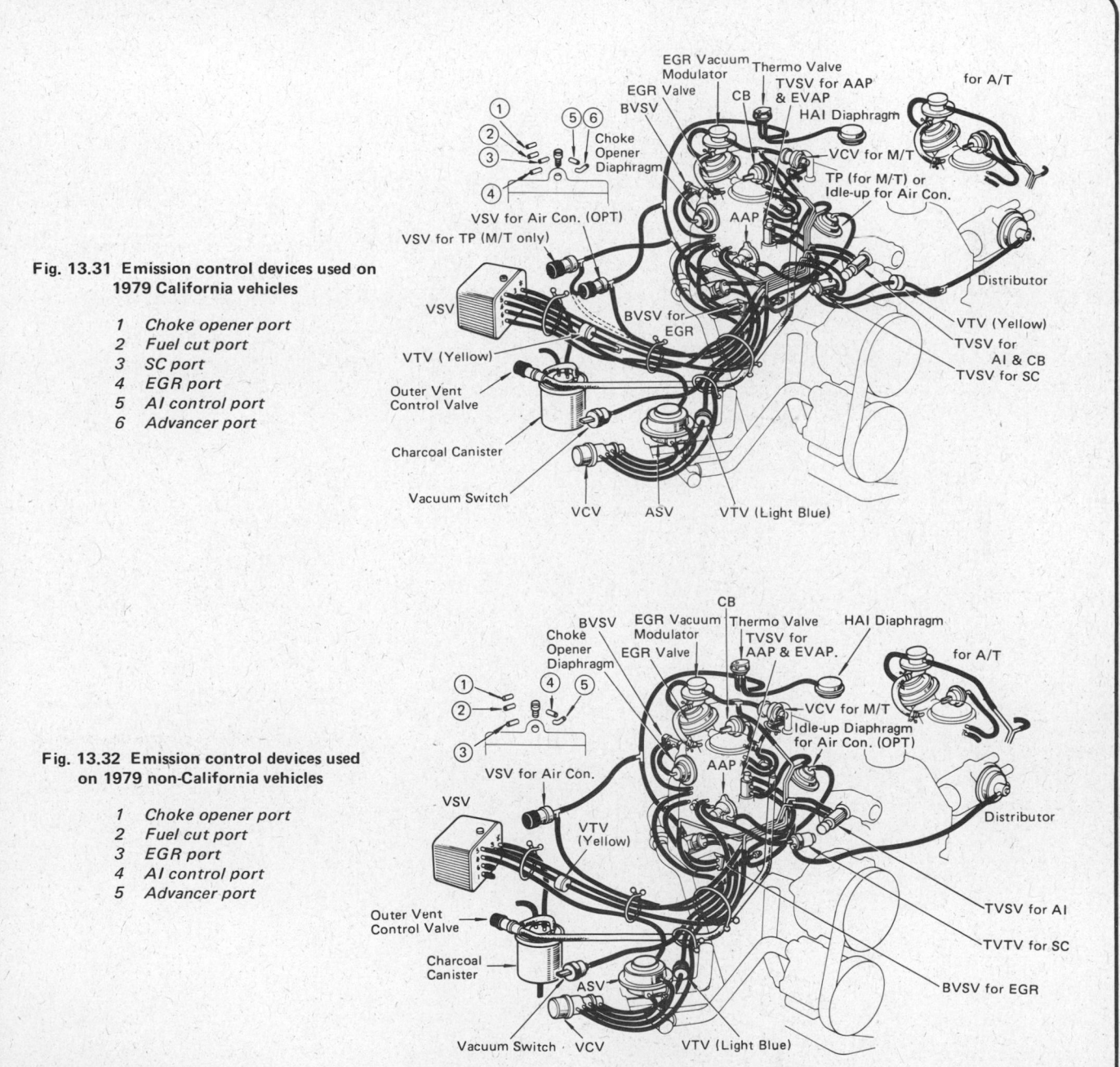

Fig. 13.31 Emission control devices used on 1979 California vehicles

1   Choke opener port
2   Fuel cut port
3   SC port
4   EGR port
5   AI control port
6   Advancer port

Fig. 13.32 Emission control devices used on 1979 non-California vehicles

1   Choke opener port
2   Fuel cut port
3   EGR port
4   AI control port
5   Advancer port

in later years. These devices and their testing procedures have gone virtually unchanged. The following devices have been added since 1977.

System	Year added
Deceleration fuel cut system	1978
Secondary slow circuit fuel cut system	1979
Mixture control (MC) system	1980
Fast idle cam breaker system (FICB)	1980
Air suction system (AS)	1981
Three-way catalyst system (TWC)	1981
Oxidation catalyst system (OC)	1981
Idle advance system	1981
Air bleed system	1981

127 1982 models use all of the systems used in 1981 except for the air bleed system.

Deceleration fuel cut system (California and high altitude vehicles only)

128 This system cuts off part of the fuel in the slow circuit of the carburetor to prevent overheating and afterburning in the exhaust system.
129 To inspect the operation of this system, connect the vacuum switch to the intake manifold with a piece of vacuum hose. Start the engine and check to see that the engine runs normally.
130 Gradually increase the engine speed to 2800 rpm. Check to see that the engine misfires slightly between 2400 and 2800 rpm. **Note:** *Perform this inspection quickly to avoid overheating the catalytic converter.*
131 Unplug the wiring connector to the solenoid valve with the engine idling. The engine should idle roughly.
132 If the above tests are positive, the inspection is finished. If the inspections were negative, perform the following inspections.

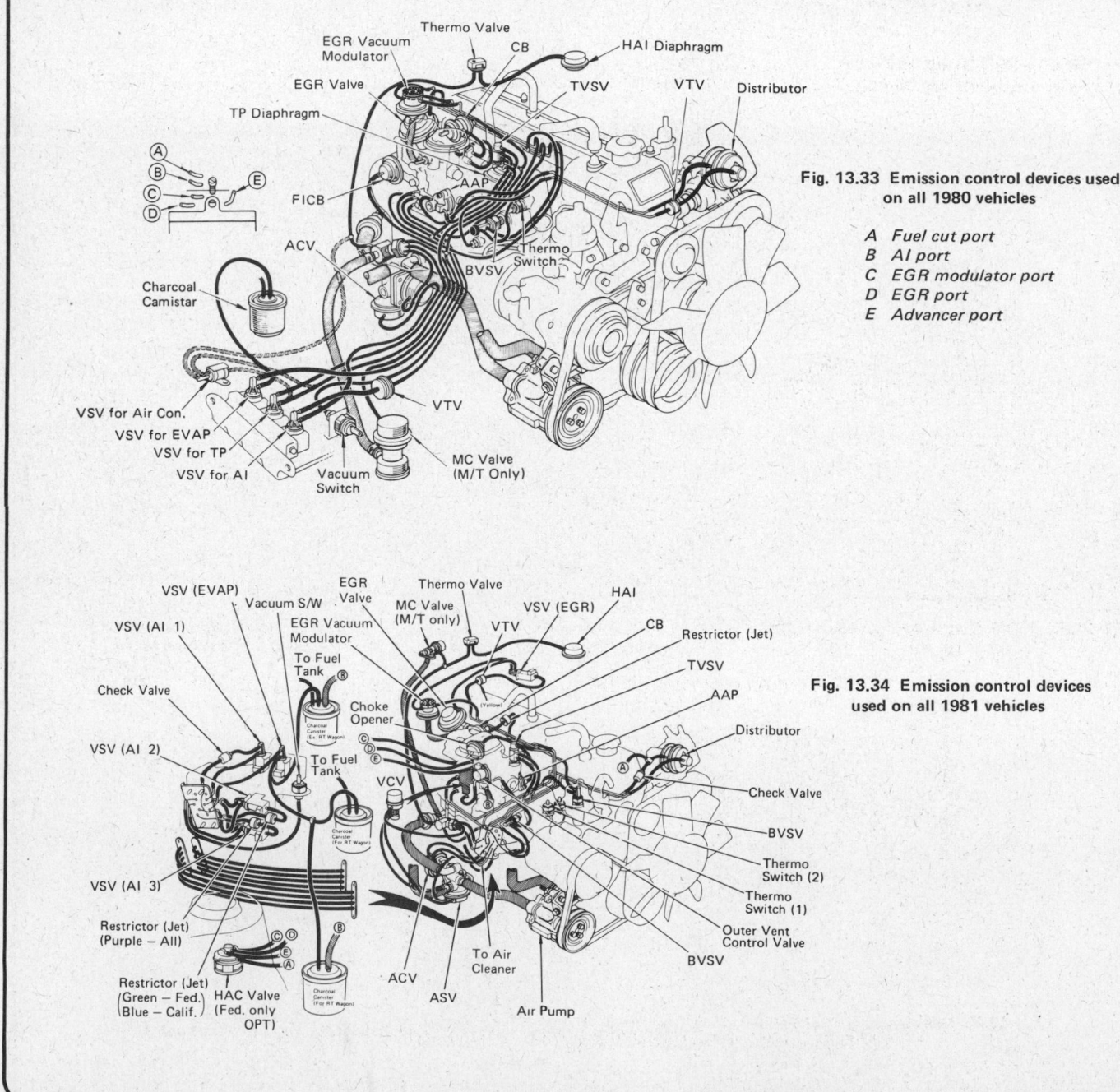

Fig. 13.33 Emission control devices used on all 1980 vehicles

A   *Fuel cut port*
B   *AI port*
C   *EGR modulator port*
D   *EGR port*
E   *Advancer port*

Fig. 13.34 Emission control devices used on all 1981 vehicles

133 Inspect the fuel cut solenoid valve by removing the solenoid valve and connecting the two terminals to the battery terminals. Listen for a clicking sound in the solenoid valve when current is applied. If there is no sound, replace the solenoid valve.

134 Inspect the vacuum switch by checking to see that current flows between the switch terminal and the switch body using an ohmmeter.

135 Start the engine and check for continuity (current flow) in the same locations on the vacuum switch. There should not be any current flowing. If either of these tests proves negative, replace the vacuum switch.

Secondary slow circuit fuel cut system

136 This system prevents 'dieseling' by cutting off part of the fuel in the secondary slow circuit of the carburetor.

137 Measure the stroke of the fuel cut valve by fully opening and closing the throttle valve. This measurement should be between 0.059 and 0.079 in (1.5 to 2.0 mm).

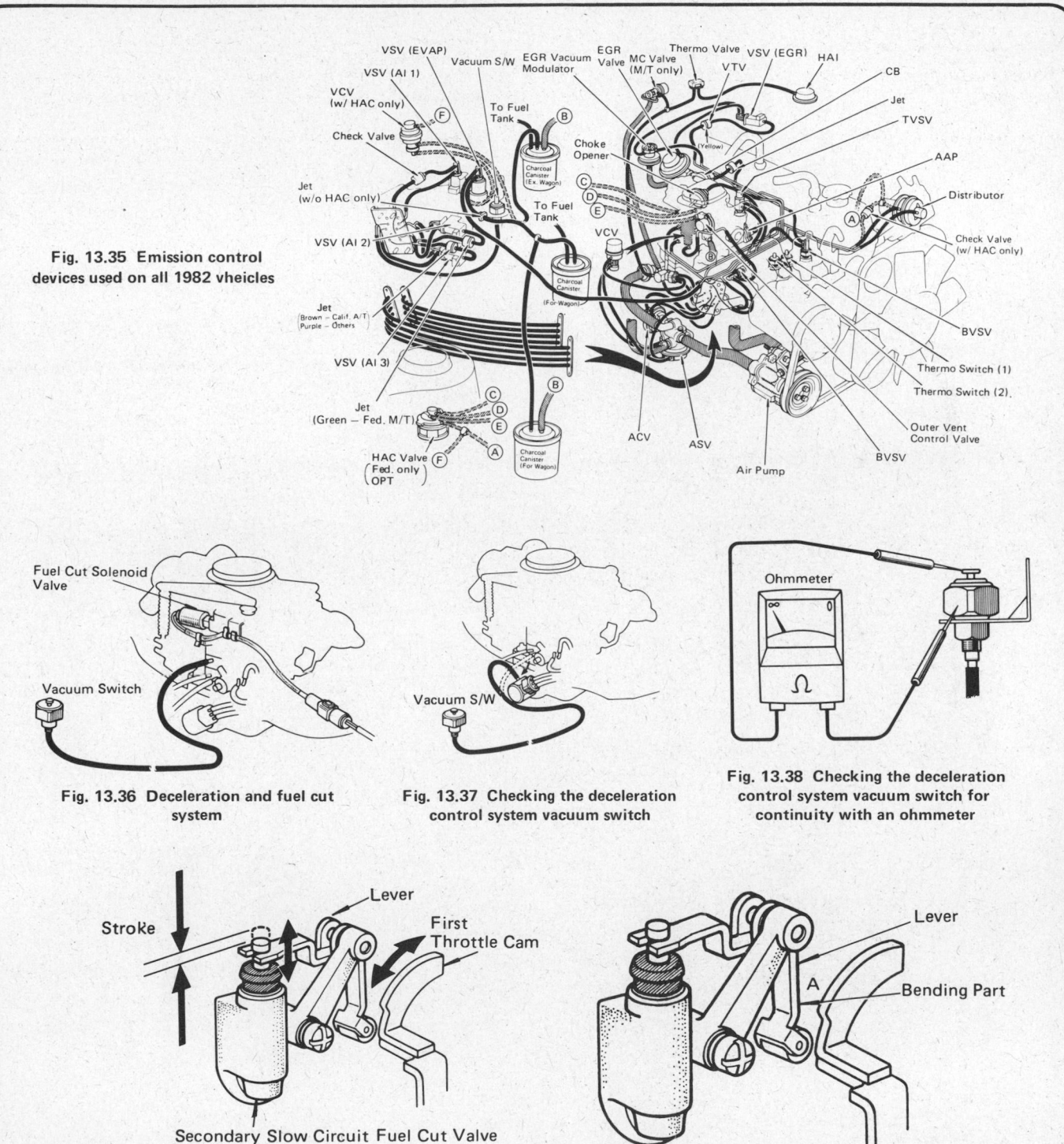

Fig. 13.35 Emission control devices used on all 1982 vheicles

Fig. 13.36 Deceleration and fuel cut system

Fig. 13.37 Checking the deceleration control system vacuum switch

Fig. 13.38 Checking the deceleration control system vacuum switch for continuity with an ohmmeter

Fig. 13.39 Measuring the stroke of the secondary slow circuit fuel cut valve

Fig. 13.40 Adjust the valve stroke at point A

138 The stroke can be adjusted by bending the lever. This should be adjusted before the secondary throttle valve opens.

Mixture control (MC) system

139 The mixture control system allows fresh air to enter the intake manifold during sudden deceleration to reduce carbon monoxide and hydrocarbon emissions.

140 With the engine running, put your hand over the inlet of the MC valve and disconnect the vacuum hose. You should not feel any vacuum until the hose is reconnected. It is normal at this time for the car to idle rough or die.

Fast idle cam breaker (FICB) system

141 The fast idle cam breaker system lowers the engine speed after warm-up by forcibly releasing the fast idle cam to the third step.

142 Stop the engine after warm-up and disconnect the hose from the FICB. Hold the throttle valve slightly open and set the fast idle cam by pulling up on the FICB linkage and releasing the throttle.

143 Start the engine without touching the accelerator pedal.

144 Reconnect the hose. The fast idle cam should be released to the third step. If not, check the linkage hoses and the TVSV. Also, apply vacuum to the FICB diaphragm and check that the linkage moves.

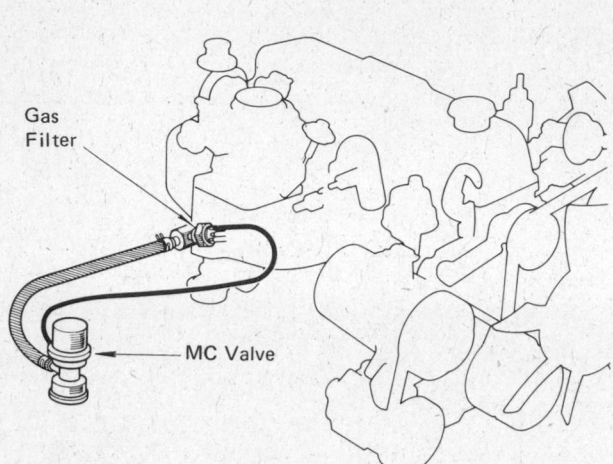

Fig. 13.41 Location of the mixture control (MC) system components

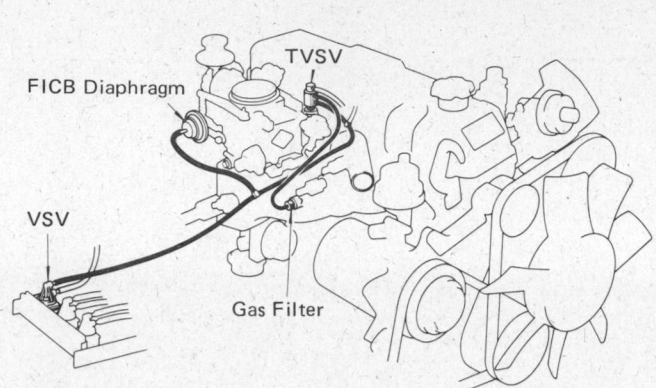

Fig. 13.42 Location of the fast idle cam breaker (FICB) system components

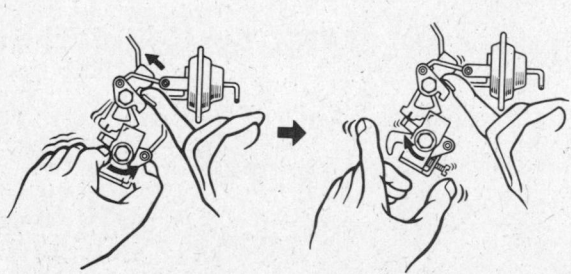

Fig. 13.43 Setting the fast idle cam by pulling up on the FICB linkage and releasing the throttle

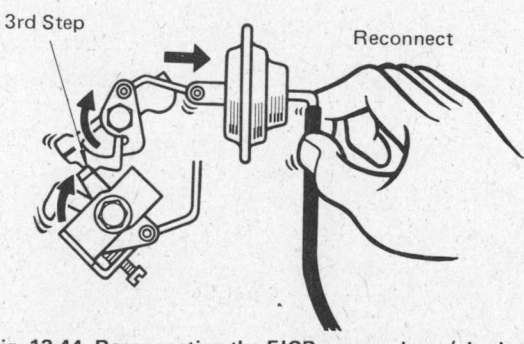

Fig. 13.44 Reconnecting the FICB vacuum hose (check to see that the fast idle cam returns to the third step)

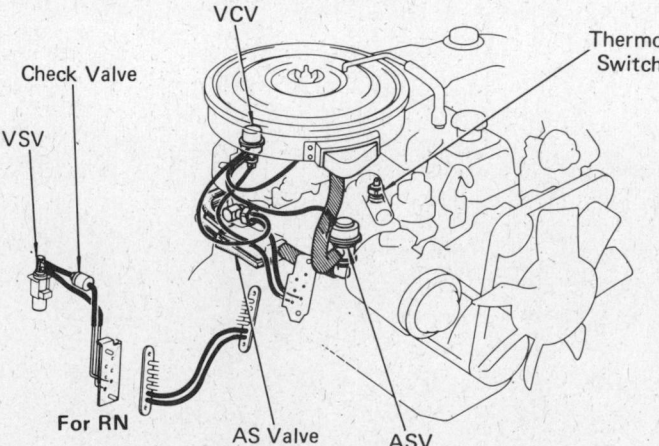

Fig. 13.45 Location of air suction system components

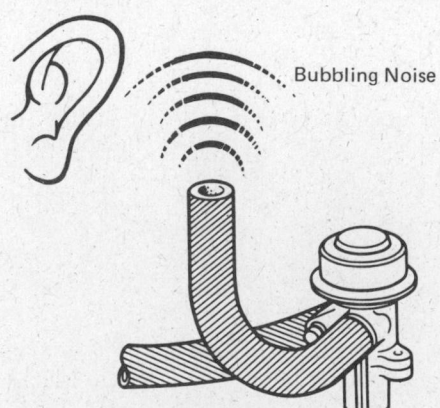

Fig. 13.46 Check the ASV by disconnecting the suction hose and listening for a bubbling noise

Air suction system

145 This system draws air into all exhaust ports to accelerate fuel burning using vacuum generated by the exhaust pulsation in the exhaust manifold.

146 Warm up the engine. Disconnect the air suction hose from the air cleaner and check that a bubbling noise is heard from the AS hose at idle.

147 Check the check valve by disconnecting the vacuum hose between the check valve and vacuum pipe bracket at the check valve side and plug the hose end. Check that the bubbling noise is still heard from the AS hose at idle.

148 Check the air suction valve by blowing air into each pipe. Check that air flows from the air cleaner side to the outlet pipe side. Also check that air does *not* flow from the outlet pipe side to the air cleaner side.

149 Check ASV by blowing air into the pipe. Apply vacuum to the ASV diaphragm, blow air into the pipe and check that the ASV opens. Release the vacuum and check that the ASV closes.

Three-way catalyst system (TWC) and oxidation catalyst (OC) system

150 Both of these systems are incorporated into what was formally known as the catalytic converter system. These systems reduce hydrocarbon, carbon monoxide and nitrogen monoxide emissions. When the catalyst and either the three-way or oxidation catalyst system is overheated (above 785°C or 1445°F) the thermo sensor in the catalyst turns the system off.

151 Check all exhaust pipe connections for looseness or damage. Check the clamps for weakness, cracks or damage.

152 Check the outer surface of the catalyst container for dents or damage. There should be no dents deeper than .79 in (20 mm). Shake the catalyst and check for rattling. Replace it if the rattling noise is excessive.

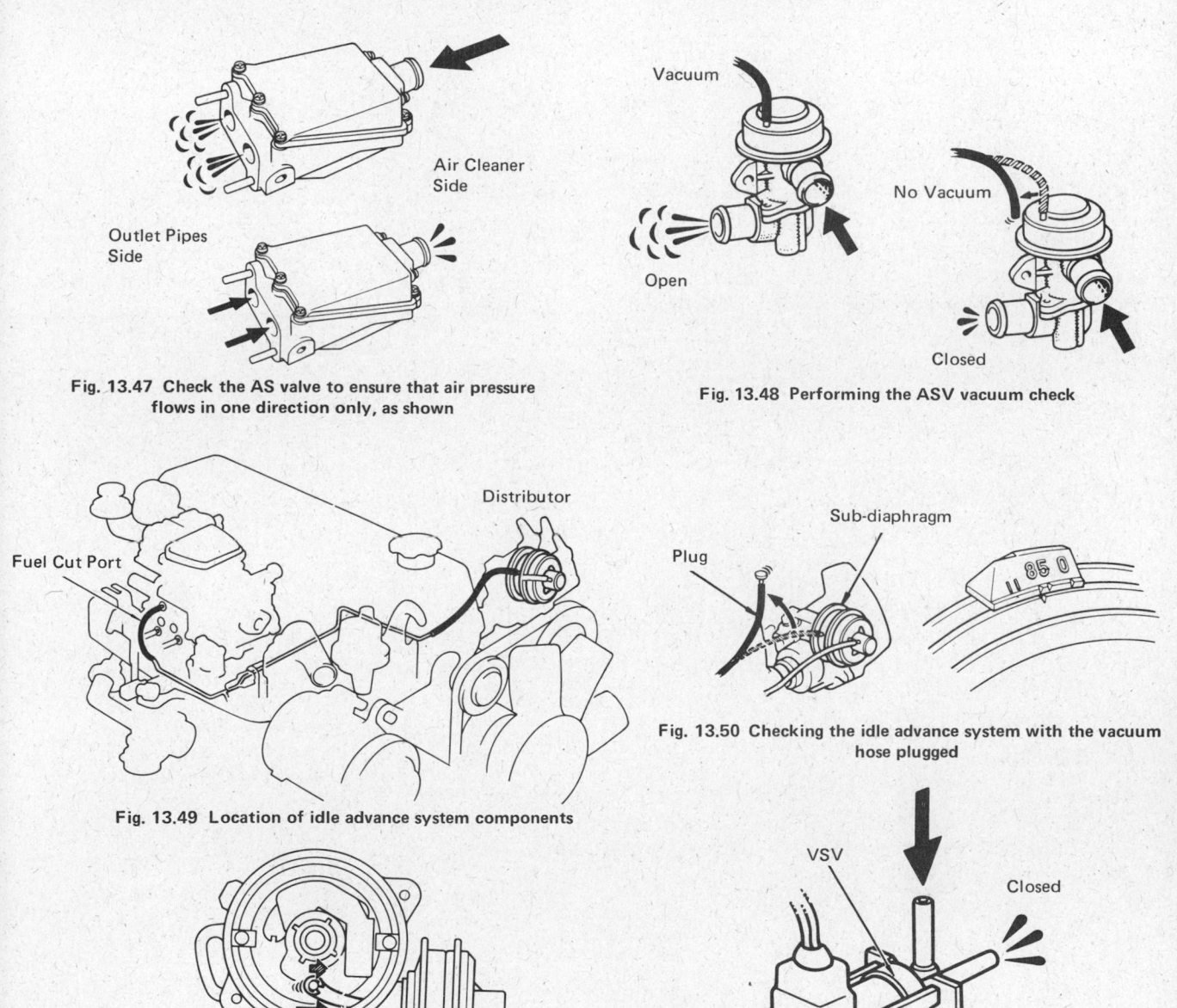

Fig. 13.47 Check the AS valve to ensure that air pressure flows in one direction only, as shown

Fig. 13.48 Performing the ASV vacuum check

Fig. 13.49 Location of idle advance system components

Fig. 13.50 Checking the idle advance system with the vacuum hose plugged

Fig. 13.51 Check that the distributor vacuum advancer moves (arrows) when engine vacuum is applied

Fig. 13.52 Check the VSV valve at idle by blowing air into the pipe (arrow) - no air should pass through

254

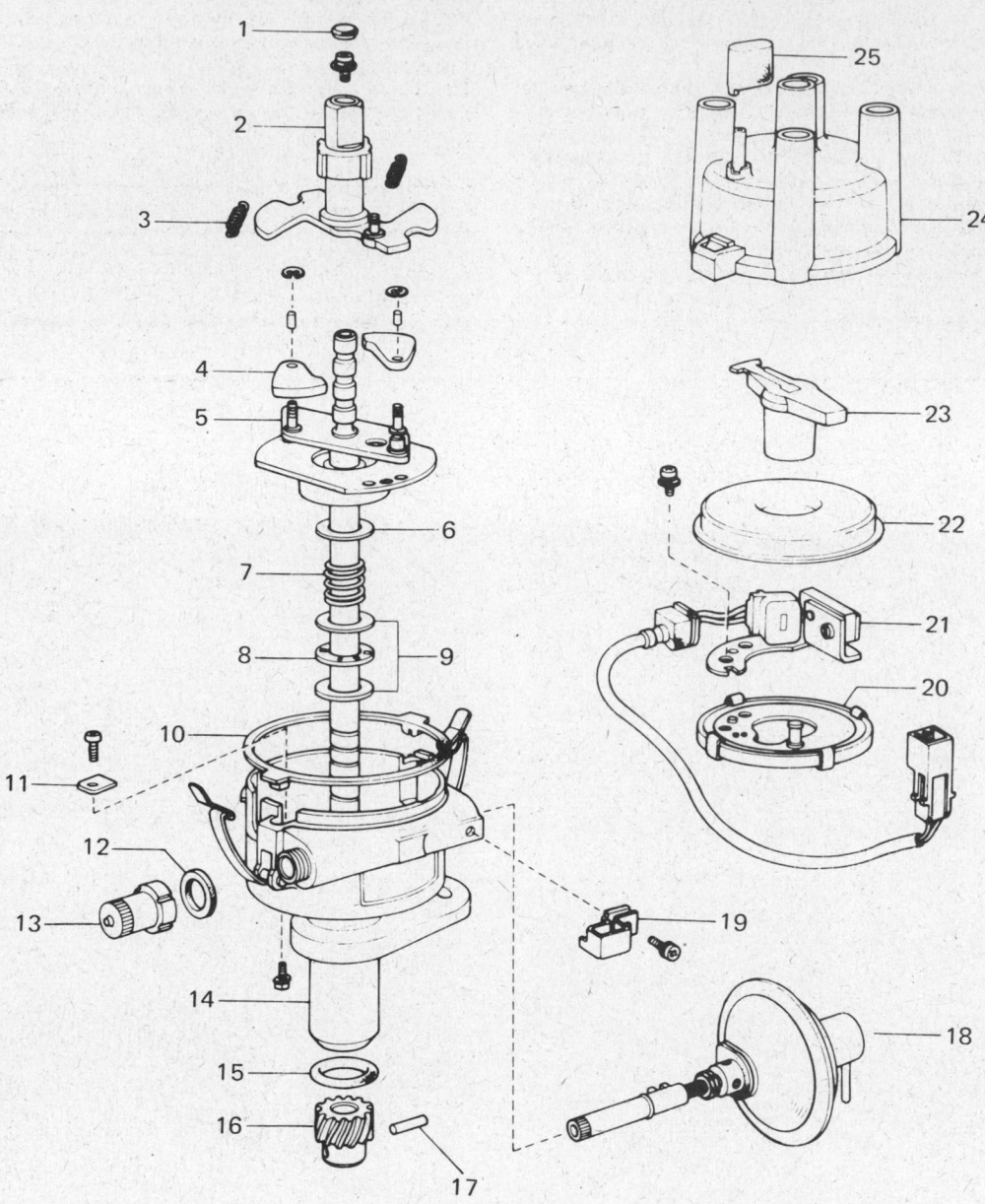

Fig. 13.53 Distributor exploded view — 1978 thru 1980 models

1	Cam grease stopper	10	Dustproof packing	18	Vacuum advancer
2	Signal rotor	11	Steel plate washer	19	Cord clamp
3	Governor spring	12	Rubber washer	20	Breaker plate
4	Governor weight	13	Octane selector cap	21	Signal generator
5	Governor shaft	14	Housing	22	Dustproof cover
6	Plate washer	15	O-ring	23	Distributor rotor
7	Compression coil spring	16	Spiral gear	24	Distributor cap
8	Thrust bearing	17	Pin	25	Rubber cap
9	Washer				

153 Check the thermo sensor by measuring the resistance between both terminals of the thermo sensor with the engine idling. Resistance should be 2 to 200 K ohms.

Idle advance system

154 This system causes the ignition timing to advance at idle to improve fuel economy.

155 Warm the engine to normal operating temperature and check the ignition timing as described in Chapter 4. At idle it should be 15° before top dead center (BTDC).

156 Disconnect the vacuum hose from the distributor sub-diaphragm and plug the hose as shown.

157 Check that the ignition timing has retarded to 8° BTDC at idle.

158 Reconnect the vacuum hose and remove the timing light. If the timing does not change, remove the distributor cap and the rotor. Check that the advancer moves when vacuum is applied and repair or replace it if necessary.

159 Install the distributor cap and rotor.

Air bleed system

160 This system prevents the air-fuel ratio from becoming too rich by introducing air into the primary high-speed circuit of the carburetor when the engine is running at high speed.

161 Disconnect the vacuum hoses from the VSV and, with the engine idling, blow air into the VSV pipe as shown. Check that the VSV is closed.

162 Now increase the engine speed to above 3300 rpm. Blow air into the pipe of the VSV and check that the VSV is open.

6 Ignition system

General information

1 The ignition systems used on 1978 thru 1982 models are transistorized. A transistorized system uses a signal generating mechanism on

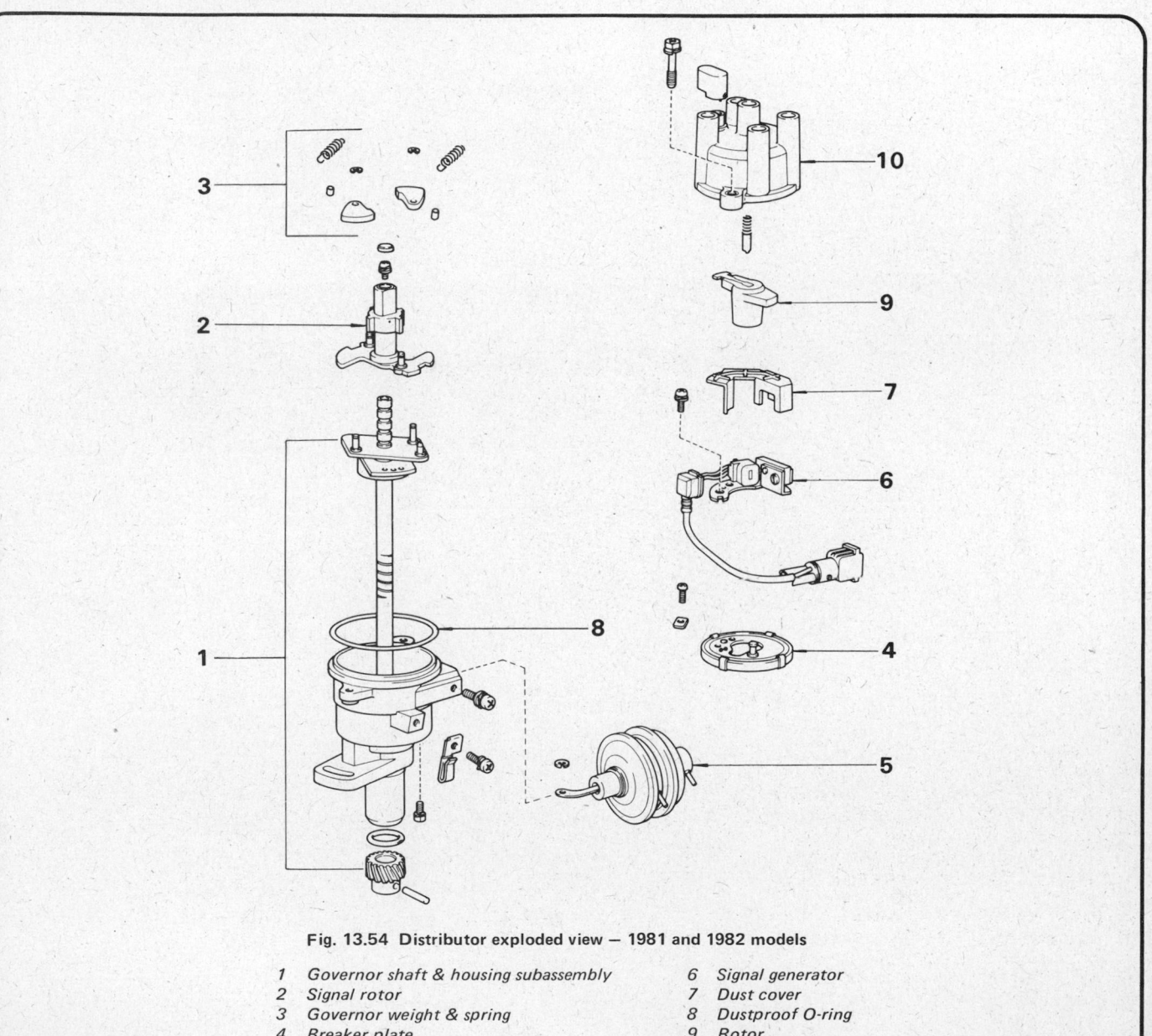

Fig. 13.54 Distributor exploded view — 1981 and 1982 models

1 Governor shaft & housing subassembly	6 Signal generator
2 Signal rotor	7 Dust cover
3 Governor weight & spring	8 Dustproof O-ring
4 Breaker plate	9 Rotor
5 Vacuum advancer diaphragm	10 Distributor cap

the coil instead of distributor contact points. The removal and disassembly procedures are covered in Chapter 4. The only difference is on the 1981 and 1982 distributors where the thrust bearing, spring and washers were left off the shaft. Adjust ignition timing in the same way you would with a conventional distributor.

Air gap — checking

2   On the transistorized system the equivalent of checking the contact breaker point gap is checking the air gap. Check the air gap according to the accompanying figure with the proper size feeler gauge. Adjust as necessary.

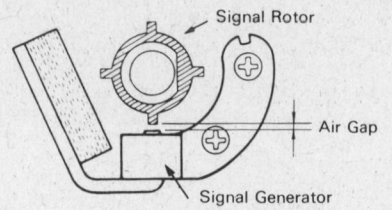

Fig. 13.55 Check the distributor air gap (adjust the gap by loosening the two screws and shifting the signal generator plate)

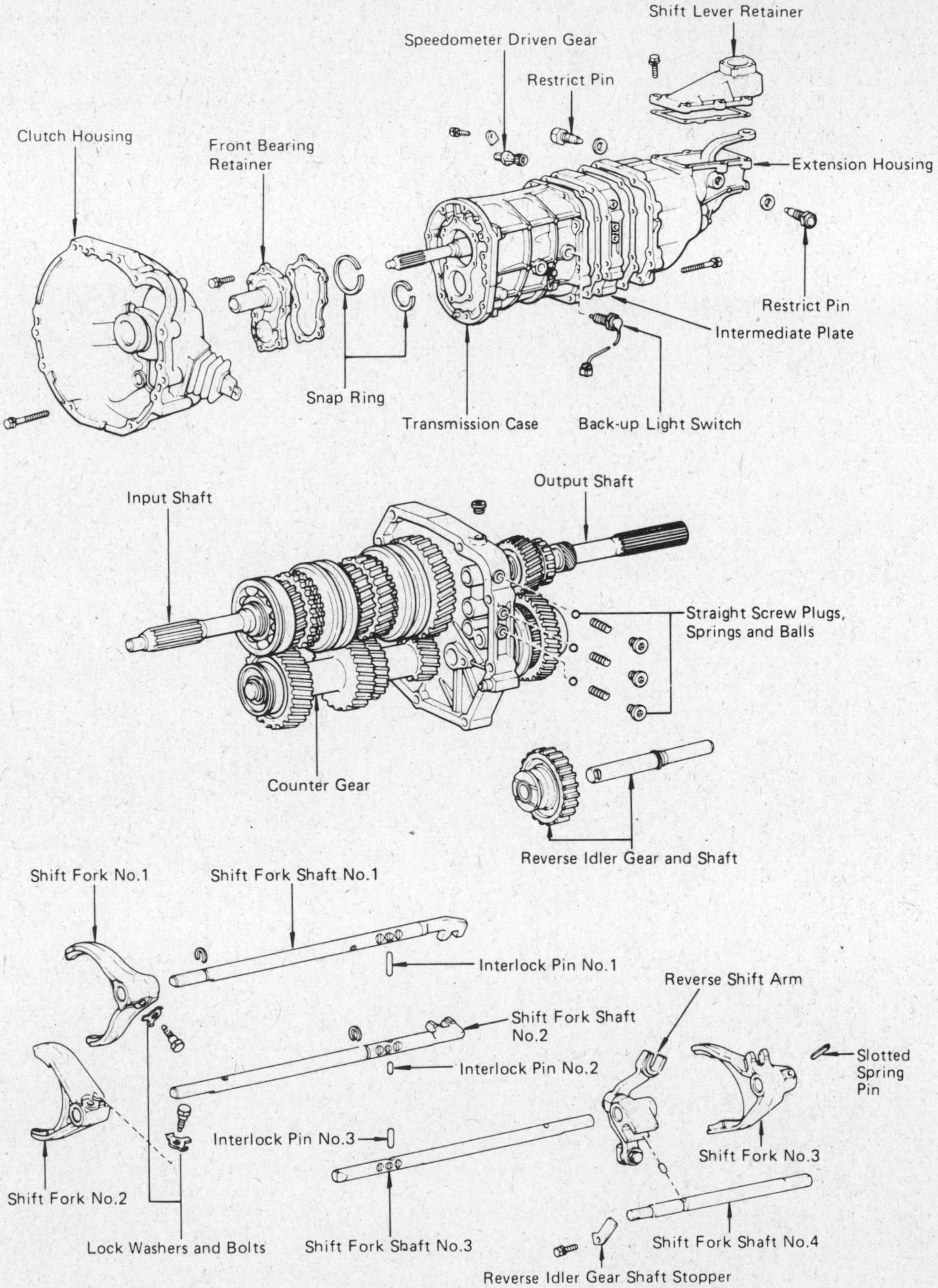

Fig. 13.56 5-speed (W55) manual transmission — exploded view

7   Transmission

Manual transmission (W55) — disassembly

1   With the transmission removed from the car as described in Chapter 6, clean off all external dirt.
2   Remove the clutch release mechanism from inside the bellhousing.
3   Unbolt and remove the bellhousing.
4   Unscrew and remove the reverse lamp switch and the restrictor pins, springs and plugs.

5   Unbolt and remove the shift lever retainer, the extension housing and the front bearing retainer.
6   Extract the clips from the input shaft and countershaft front bearings.
7   Remove the transmission case from the intermediate plate by tapping the intermediate plate away with a soft metal drift.
8   Using a socket wrench, unscrew and remove the plugs from the edge of the intermediate plate and extract the springs and detent balls.
9   Remove the set bolts from the No.1 and No.2 fork shaft and drive out the pin from the No.3 shaft.

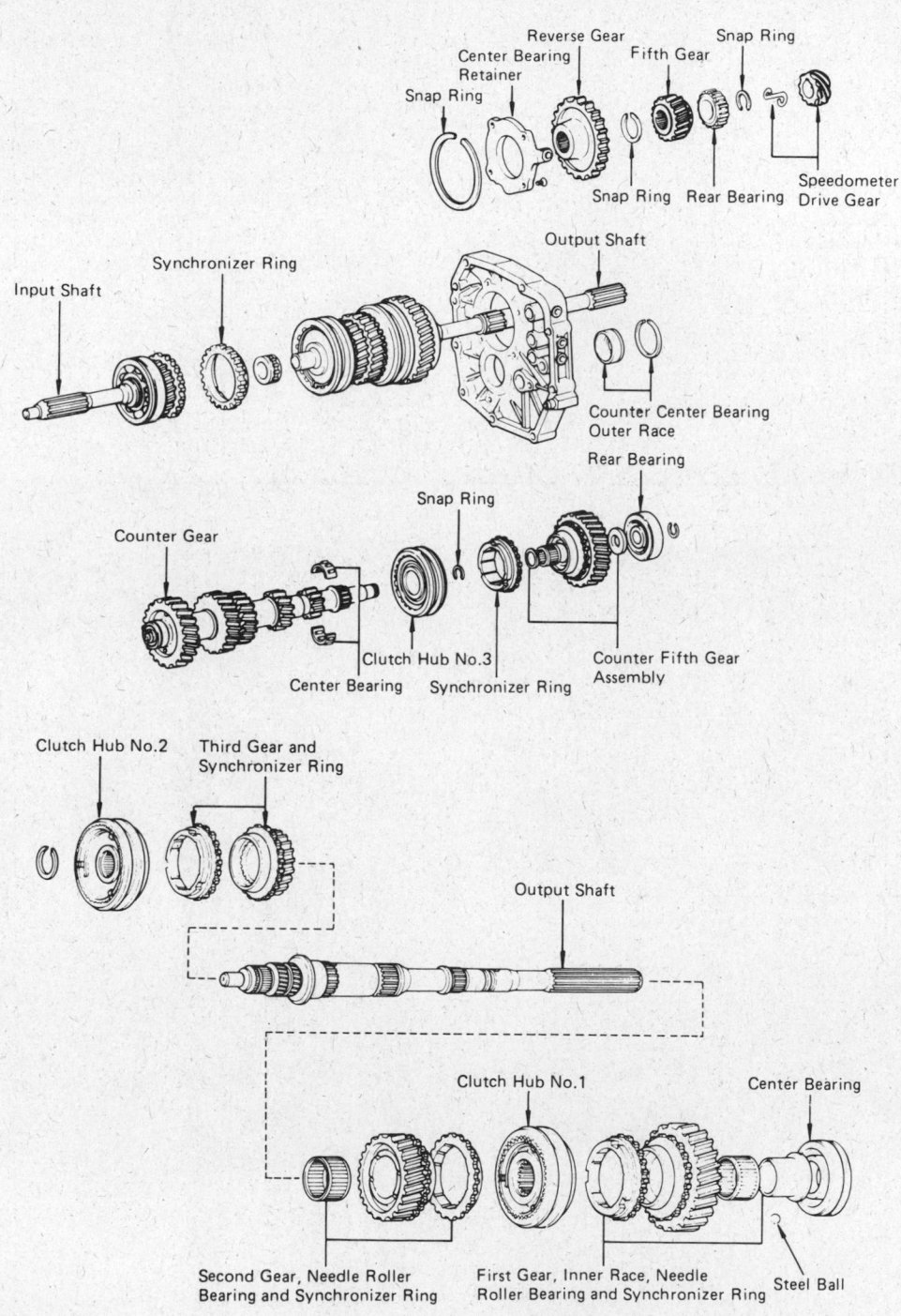

Fig. 13.57 5-speed (W55) manual transmission gear train components — exploded view

10 Remove the snap-rings from No.1 and No.2 shafts and the Reverse idle gear shaft stopper.

11 Remove the shift fork shaft No.1 and interlock pins No.1 and No.2.

12 Remove the shift fork shaft No.2 and interlock pin No.3.

13 Pull out the shift fork shaft No.4. Remove the shift fork No.3 and Reverse shift arm with pin.

14 Remove the Reverse idler gear and shaft.

15 Remove the speedometer drive gear and snap-ring from the output shaft.

16 Remove the countershaft rear bearing, spacer, counter 5th gear and the needle roller bearing using a two-legged puller.

17 Remove the snap-ring and clutch hub No.3 with a two-legged puller.

18 Remove the snap-ring from the mainshaft, then using a puller, remove the rear bearing and 5th gear.

19 Remove the snap-ring and remove Reverse gear from the mainshaft with a puller.

20 Remove the center bearing retainer using a TORX socket wrench.

21 Remove the snap-ring and, while tapping the intermediate plate with a mallet, remove the input shaft, mainshaft and counter gear as a unit.

22 Remove the input shaft from the output shaft.

23 From the rear end of the mainshaft, draw off the bearing. A press will be required for this operation.

24 Remove 1st gear, the needle roller bearing, bearing inner track and synchronizer ring. Take care not to lose the inner track locking ball.

25 Press off 2nd gear complete with synchronizer ring, Reverse gear and 1st/2nd gear synchro unit.

26 Remove the snap-ring from the front of the shaft.

27 Remove the clutch hub sleeve No.2, 3rd gear and the synchronizer ring.

28 Clean all components thoroughly and examine for worn or chipped teeth and grooving or scoring of the shaft. The gears should have a running clearance between their internal bores and the shaft of between 0.0004 to 0.0024 in. for 1st, 2nd and counter 5th gear and between 0.0024 to 0.40 in for 3rd gear.

29 Check the synchronizer units as described in Section 4, Chapter 6 paragraph 10. Reassemble the units in accordance with the diagrams.

30 Begin reassembly of the mainshaft by installing the 3rd/4th gear synchronizer ring to 3rd gear and then fitting them to the shaft.

31 Fit the 3rd/4th gear synchronizer unit, positioning it tightly against the mainshaft shoulder. Secure it with a snap-ring to give a minimum clearance between snap-ring and synchro unit yet will still fit fully into the groove.

32 Snap-rings are available in many different thicknesses from a Toyota dealership. Use the snap-ring that allows the minimum axial play.

Manual transmission (W55) — reassembly

33 Grip the intermediate plate in a soft-jawed vise and check that the dowel pin projects between 0.24 and 0.32 in (6.0 and 8.0 mm) from the front face of the plate.

34 Apply grease to the needle bearing in the recess at the end of the input shaft and fit the input shaft to the front end of the mainshaft.

35 Mesh the teeth of the mainshaft and countergear assemblies and install them simultaneously to the intermediate plate.

36 Fit the retaining snap-ring to the mainshaft bearing.

37 Fit the bearing retainer to the intermediate plate.

38 Install Reverse gear and the correct snap-ring.

39 Install 5th gear, the output shaft rear bearing and the correct snap-ring.

40 Install the clutch hub No.3 and shifting key to the hub sleeve.

41 Install the shifting key springs, positioned so their end gaps will not be in line, under the shifting keys.

42 Install the shifting key retainer using a socket wrench or piece of pipe as a drift.

43 Install the clutch hub No.3 and the correct snap-ring.

44 Install the counter 5th gear assembly, aligning the synchronizer ring

Fig. 13.58 Measuring the countershaft 5th gear thrust clearance with a feeler gauge

Fig. 13.59 Remove the output shaft, input shaft and counter gear as a unit from the intermediate plate

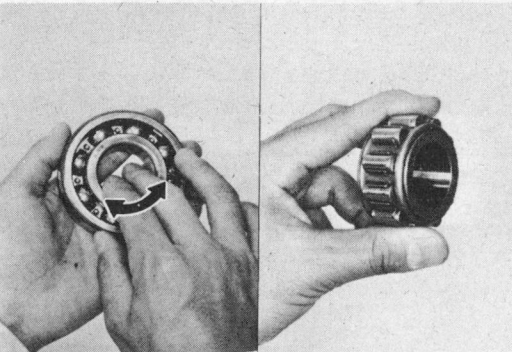

Fig. 13.60 Check to see that there is no drag on the bearings when they are turned with force (check the rollers and the inside diameter for scoring, galling and other signs of wear)

Fig. 13.61 Select a snap-ring that will allow minimum axial play and install it on the shaft

slots with the shifting keys.

45 Install the spacer and bearing with a hammer and socket.

46 Install the correct snap-ring.

47 Install the speedometer drive gear and clip onto the output shaft.

48 Install the Reverse idler gear and shaft.

49 Insert shift fork shaft No.3 through the Reverse shift arm and shift fork No.3, aligning the shift fork to the hub sleeve No.3 groove.

50 Put the Reverse shift arm into the pivot of the bearing retainer and slip the shift fork shaft into the intermediate plate.

51 Push the pin in the Reverse shift arm hole into the groove of shift fork shaft No.3 and slip shift fork shaft No.4 into the intermediate plate.

52 Drive the slotted spring pin through the pin hole in the fork into the hole in the shaft until it is flush with the fork.

53 Install interlock pin No.3 into the intermediate plate hole.

54 Install shift fork No.2 onto the shift fork shaft No.2 and into the groove of hub sleeve No.2.

55 Install shift fork shaft No.2 to the intermediate plate.

56 Install the fork shaft snap-ring No:2 and the interlock pin No.1.

57 Install shift fork No.1 onto the shift fork shaft No.1 and into the groove of hub sleeve No.2.

58 Install shift fork shaft No.1 to the intermediate plate and attach the No.1 shaft snap-ring.

59 Install the shift fork set bolts.

60 Insert the detent balls and springs into their holes in the edge of the intermediate plate. Coat the threads of the socket screws with jointing compound and torque them accordingly.

61 Install the Reverse idler gear shaft stopper.

62 Attach the transmission case to the intermediate plate.

63 Install the two bearing snap-rings and the front bearing retainer.

64 Fit the extension housing using a new gasket. Turn the remote control rod during the operation so that the rod dog connects with the selector rods.

65 Tighten the extension housing bolts to the specified torque.

66 Install the restrictor pins with a new gasket.

67 Install the shift lever retainer.

68 Install the reverse light switch and wire clamp.

69 Install the speedometer drive gear, clutch housing, release fork and bearing.

70 Fill the transmission with the correct fluid after it has been installed in the car.

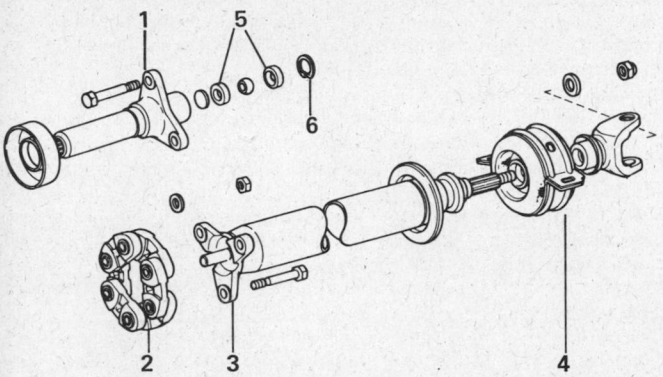

Fig. 13.62 Driveshaft with flexible coupling — exploded view

1	Forward flange	4	Center bearing
2	Flexible coupling	5	Seals
3	Rear flange	6	Snap-ring

8 Driveshaft (1979 thru 1982)

1 A two or three joint driveshaft may be fitted according to the model. In 1979 the forward universal joint was replaced with a flexible coupling. After extended use this coupling, being made of rubber, will wear out and should be replaced.

2 Remove the driveshaft from the car according to the procedure in Chapter 7. The flexible coupling is mounted between two triangular flanges. Each flange is fastened to the coupling by three bolts for a total of six bolts.

3 Remove the forward flange from the coupling by removing the three bolts.

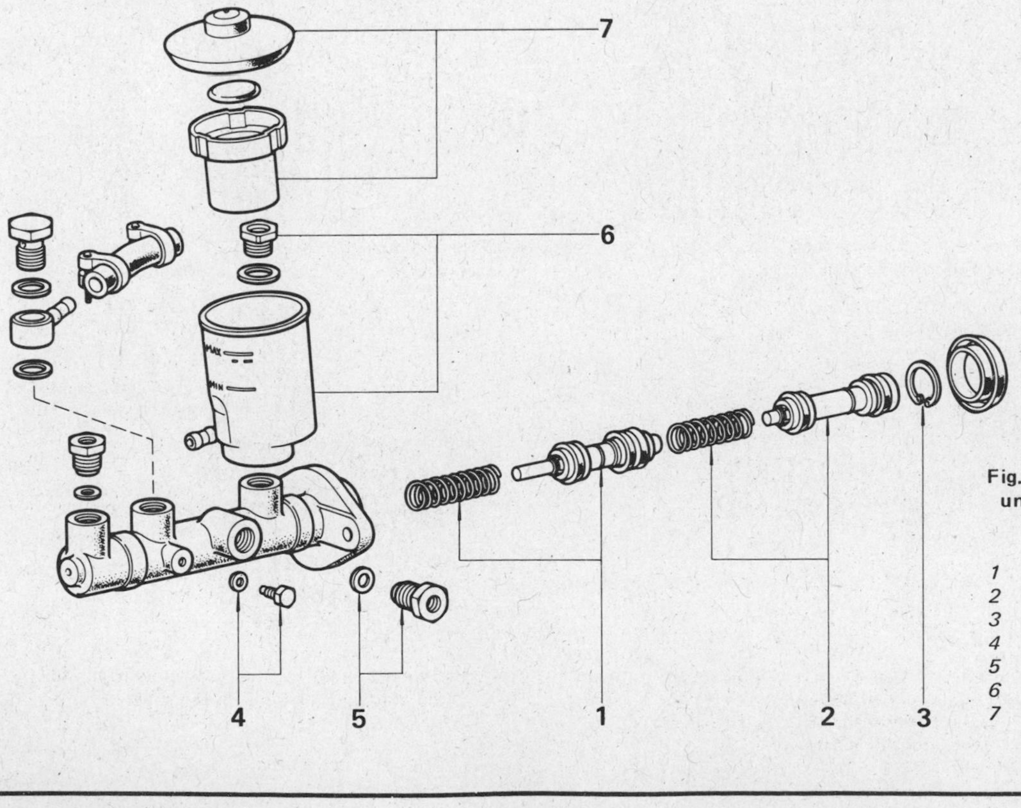

Fig. 13.63 Master cylinder unit (1979 thru 1982) — exploded view

1 Piston No.2 and spring
2 Piston No. 1 and spring
3 Snap-ring
4 Piston stopper bolt
5 Outlet check valve
6 Reservoir
7 Cap and strainer

4   Remove the coupling from the rear flange by removing the three rear bolts.

5   The forward flange and shaft is equipped with two seals and a snap-ring. To gain access to the seals, remove the snap-ring, replace the seals and a new snap-ring having a thickness that will provide minimum clearance (see Specifications).

6   While the driveshaft is out of the car, check the center bearing and the universal joints for damage and wear. Replace them if necessary. Procedures for these operations can be found in Chapter 7.

7   Reassemble the flexible joint in the reverse of disassembly, being sure the bolts are properly tightened.

9   Braking system

Master cylinder/brake booster

In 1979 the tandem master cylinder/brake booster was replaced by the single master cylinder type similar to that found in earlier years. Servicing and rebuilding of this unit can be carried out according to the procedures for the single cylinder master cylinder in Chapter 9. Note the design differences in the accompanying figure.

10 Electrical system

Alternator (1979 thru 1982) — testing and repair

1   1979 through 1982 vehicles are equipped with IC regulators built into the alternator.

In-vehicle testing

2   Disconnect the alternator B terminal wire. Connect the voltmeter positive terminal to the alternator B terminal and connect the negative terminal of the voltmeter to a ground. Check the reading on the voltmeter. If the voltage reading is less tham 13.5 volts, check the alternator and IC regulator as follows: Turn the starter switch to the On position and check the voltage reading at the alternator IG terminal. If there is no voltage, check the engine fuse and/or starter switch.

3   Remove the end cover from the IC regulator and check the voltage reading at the regulator L terminal. If the voltage reading is 0 to 2 volts, check the alternator.

4   If the voltage reading at the L terminal is the same as the battery voltage, turn the starter switch to the Off position and check that there is continuity (current flowing) between the regulator terminals L and F. If there is no continuity, check the alternator. If there is continuity, replace the IC regulator.

5   Run the engine at 2000 rpm. Turn on the headlights and all accessories, then check the readings on the ammeter and voltmeter. The current should be more than 30 amps and the voltage should be between 14.0 and 14.7 volts.

Alternator — disassembly

6   Disassembly of the alternator is the same as described in Chapter 10 except that the IC regulator must be removed.

7   Remove the regulator end cover. Inside the regulator remove the three screws on the terminals.

8   Remove the two screws from the top and remove the regulator.

9   Remove the plastic regulator housing and the rubber seal around the terminals by prying with a small screwdriver.

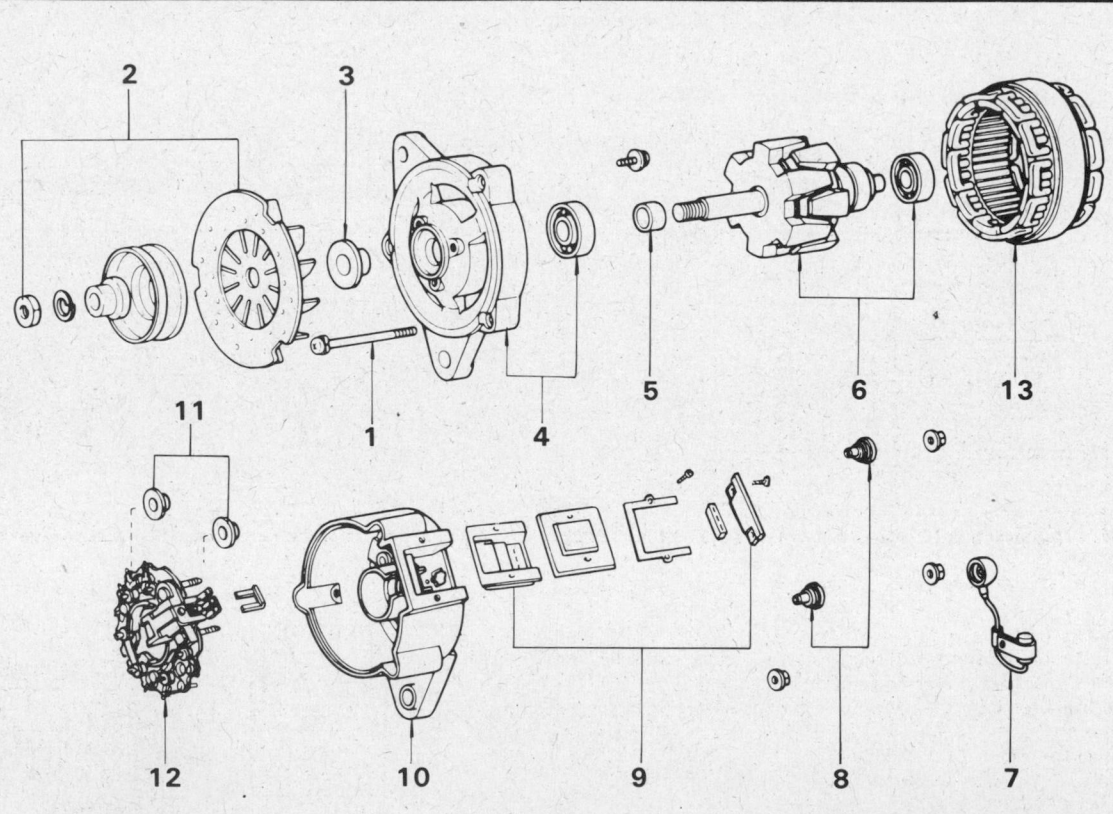

Fig. 13.64 Alternator with built-in IC regulator (1979 thru 1982) — exploded view

1 Through bolt	6 Rotor & rear bearing	10 Rear end frame
2 Space collar, pulley & fan	7 Noise suspression condenser	11 Insulator
3 Space collar	8 Insulator	12 Brush holder & rectifier holder
4 Drive end frame & front bearing	9 IC regulator	13 Stator coil
5 Space collar		

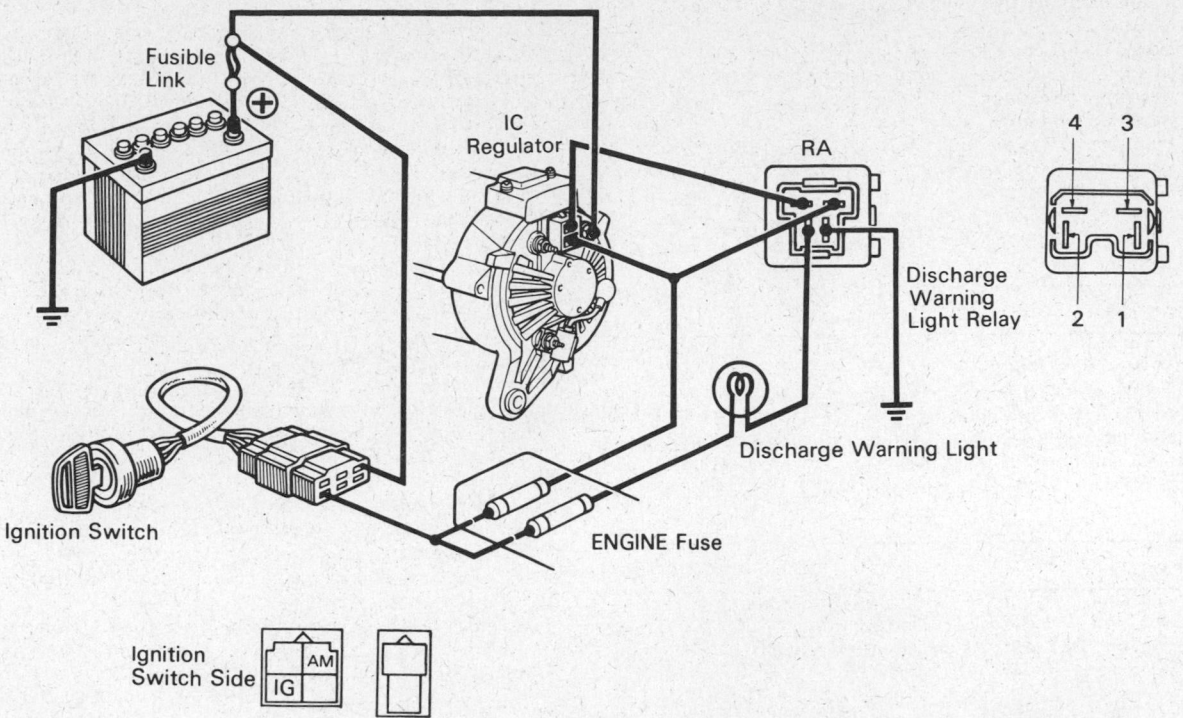

Fig. 13.65 Charging system circuit (1979 thru 1982)

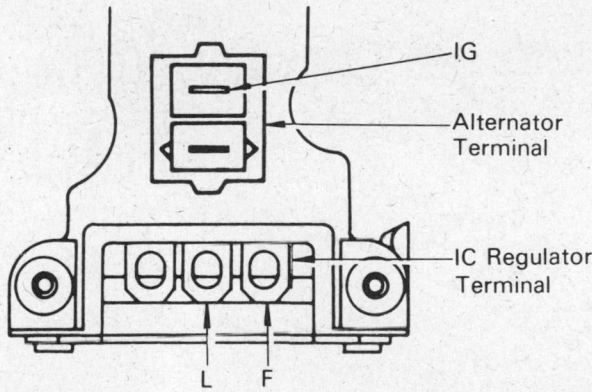

Fig. 13.66 Alternator and IC regulator terminals (1979 thru 1982)

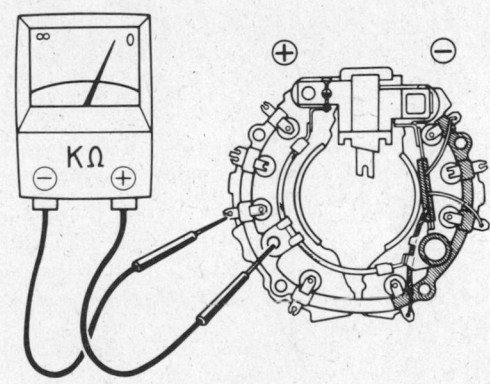

Fig. 13.67 Checking the rectifier holder positive side with an ohmmeter

Alternator — reassembly
10 Install the plastic regulator housing and the rubber seal over the terminals. Check the seal for cracking and other damage.
11 Install the regulator with the two screws and install the three screws on the terminals.
12 Install the end cover.

Alternator — bench testing
13 Disassemble the alternator. Connect an ohmmeter positive lead to the rectifier holder (positive side as shown) and the negative lead to the rectifier terminal. If there is no continuity, the rectifier assembly must be replaced.
14 Reverse the test leads and check again. If there is continuity, the rectifier assembly must be replaced.
15 Connect an ohmmeter positive lead to the rectifier terminal shown and the negative lead of the meter to the rectifier holder. If there is no continuity, the rectifier assembly must be replaced.
16 Reverse the test leads and check again. If there is continuity, replace the rectifier assembly.

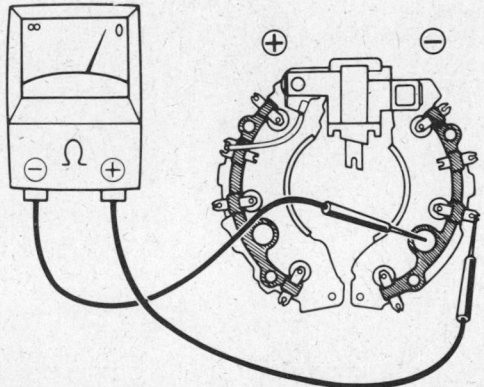

Fig. 13.68 Checking the rectifier holder negative side with an ohmmeter

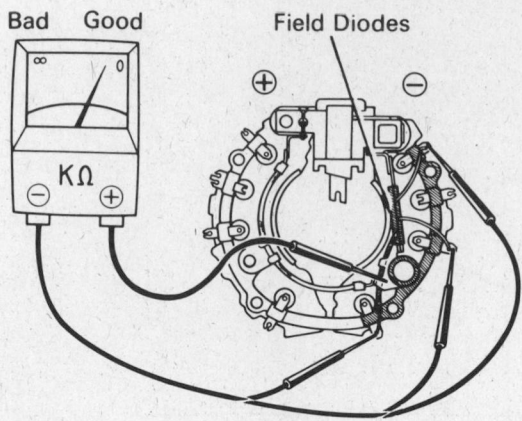

Fig. 13.69 Checking the alternator field diodes with an ohmmeter

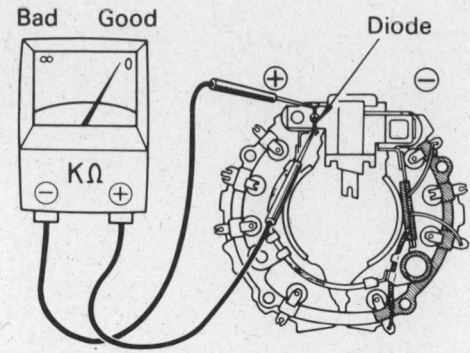

Fig. 13.70 Checking the alternator diode with an ohmmeter

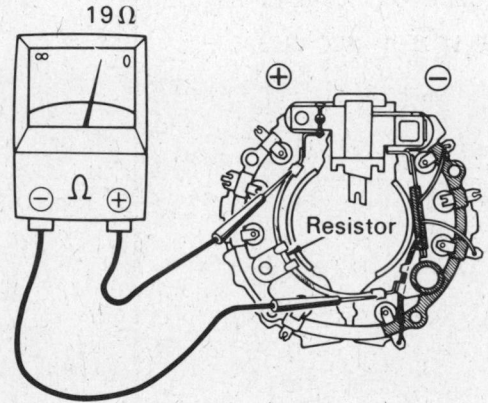

Fig. 13.71 Checking the alternator resistor (it is not necessary to reverse the ohmmeter test leads in this check)

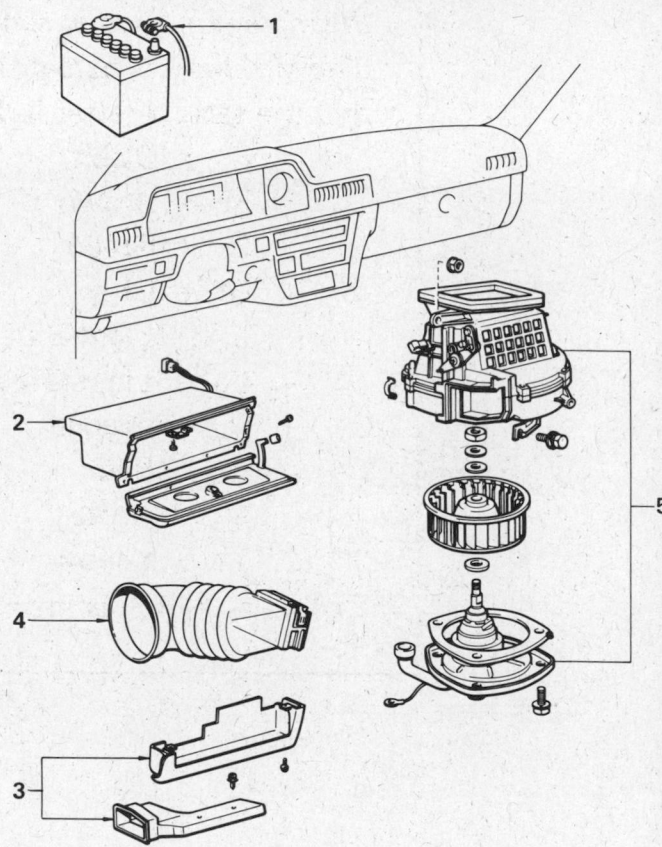

Fig. 13.72 Heater blower motor component removal sequence (1979 thru 1982)

1	Battery terminal (ground)	4	Blower duct
2	Glove compartment	5	Blower motor assembly
3	Under tray & air duct		

Alternator field diodes — testing

17 Connect the ohmmeter positive lead to the rectifier holder and the negative lead to the field diode terminal shown. If there is no continuity, replace the rectifier assembly.
18 Reverse the test leads and check again. If there is continuity, replace the rectifier assembly.

Diode

19 Connect the ohmmeter positive lead to the resister side shown and the negative lead to the diode other side. If there is no continuity, replace the rectifier assembly.
20 Reverse the test leads and check again. If there is continuity, replace the rectifier assembly.

Resistor

21 Measure the resistance of the resistor as shown with an ohmmeter. The resistance should be 19 ohms.

Starter (1979 thru 1982)

22 Starters on later models may be 0.8 kilowatt or 1.0 type. All procedures for these starters are the same as in Chapter 10, Sections 10 through 19 except for the Specifications at the beginning of this Supplement.

Heater blower motor — removal and installation

23 Remove the negative terminal on the battery.
24 Remove the four screws retaining the glove compartment box.
25 Detach the glove compartment light connector and pull the glove compartment free of the dash panel.
26 Remove the screws retaining the under tray and air duct and remove the tray and duct.

27 Remove the blower duct by first sliding the round end off of the duct mouth piece and then removing the duct from the blower motor.
28 Remove the three retaining bolts from the underside of the blower motor and remove the blower motor complete with fan.
29 Installation is the reverse of removal.

Light lenses and bulbs — servicing

Since 1978, the sidelamp, taillight and turn signal lenses have undergone various changes of design. Most of these changes have occurred for the sake of appearance and have not altered disassembly, maintenance and reassembly procedures. See Chapter 10, Sections 20 to 23 for servicing information.

Wiring color code is shown with alphabetical letter/s.
The first letter indicates the basic color for the wire,
and the second letter indicates the spiral line color.

B = Black
Br = Brown
G = Green
Gr = Grey
L = Light Blue
Lg = Light Green
O = Orange
R = Red
W = White
Y = Yellow

Example: RG, is for Red and a Green line.

1978 body electrical wiring diagram (1 of 2)

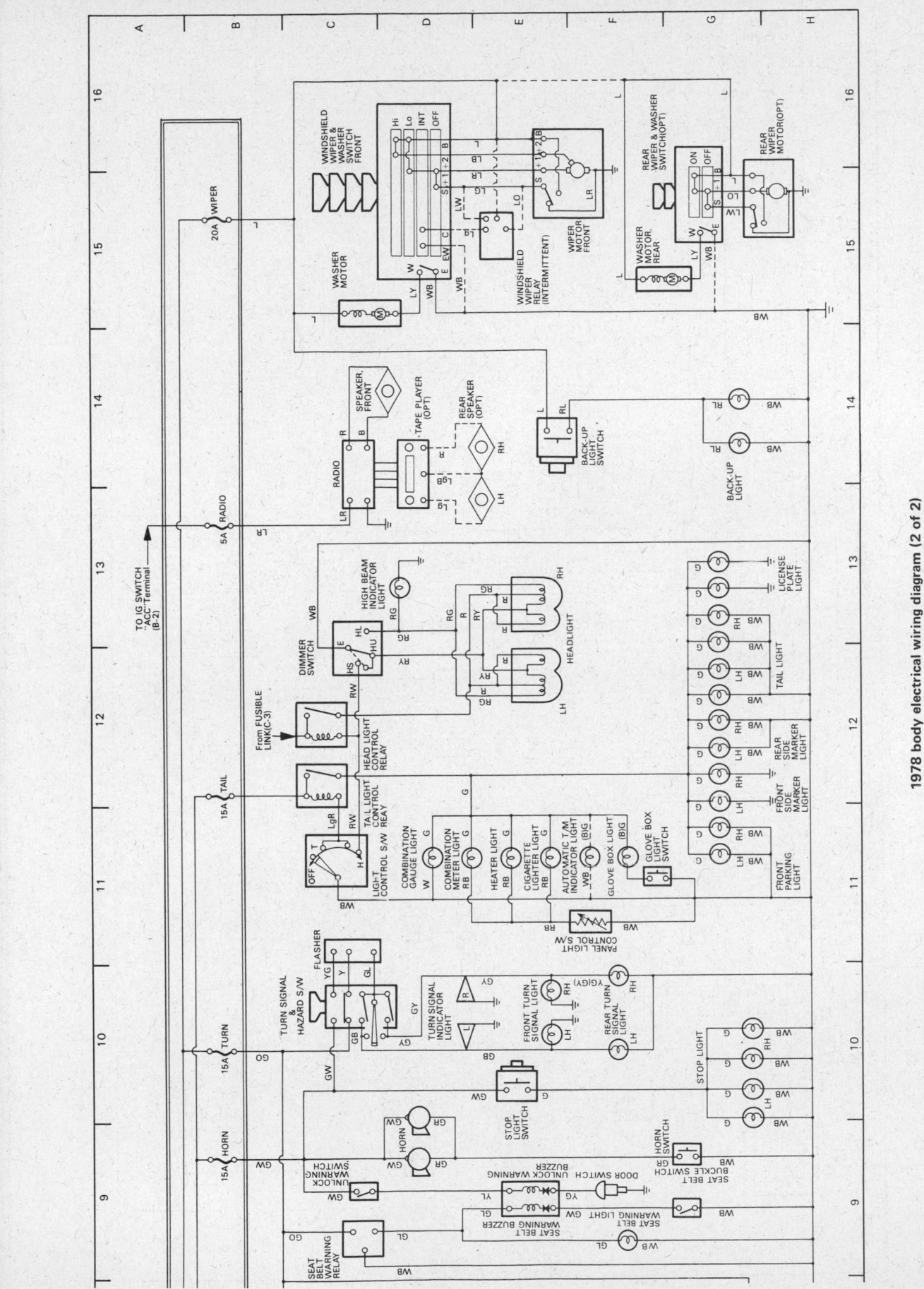

1978 body electrical wiring diagram (2 of 2)

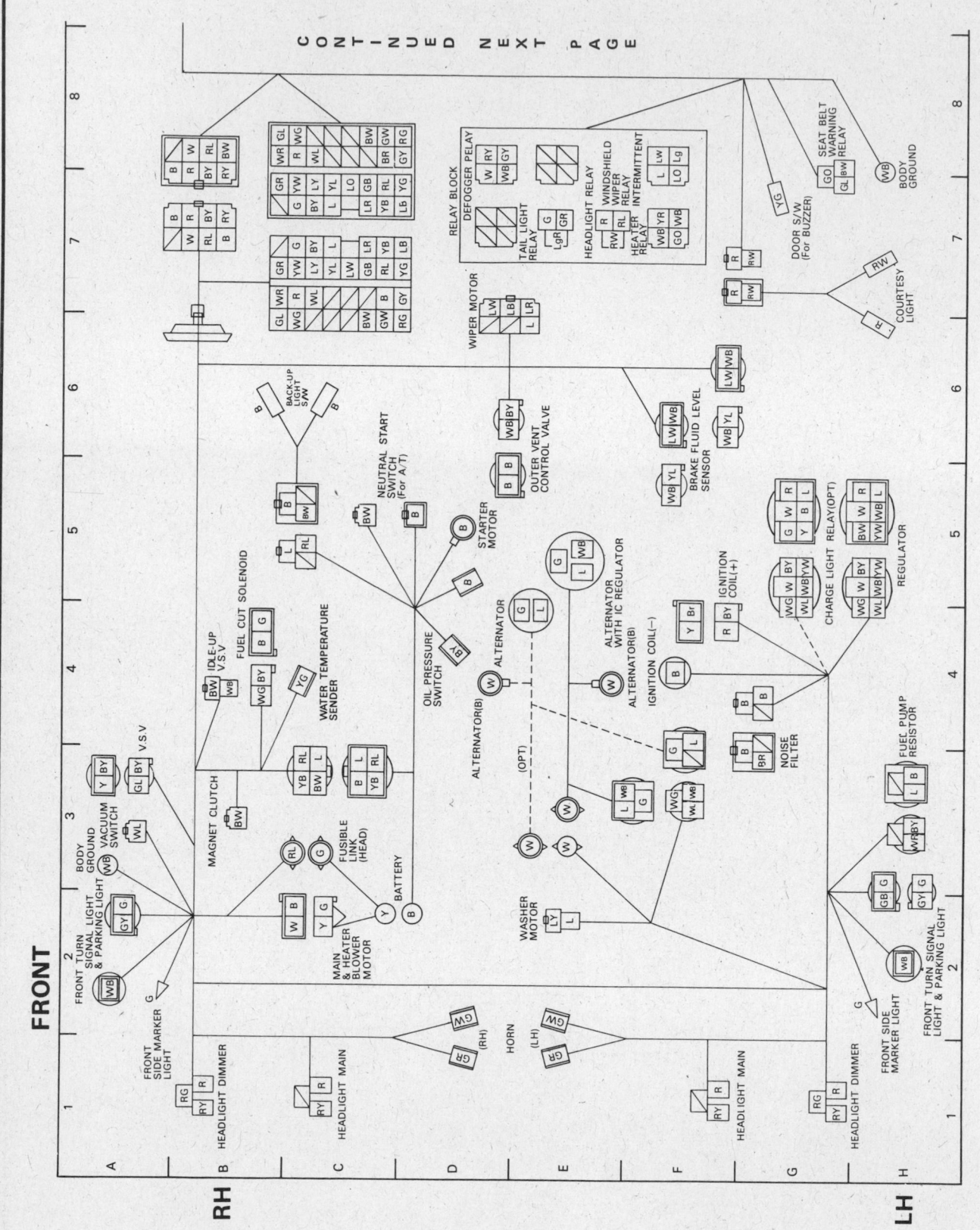

CONTINUED NEXT PAGE

1978 dash panel wiring diagram (1 of 2)

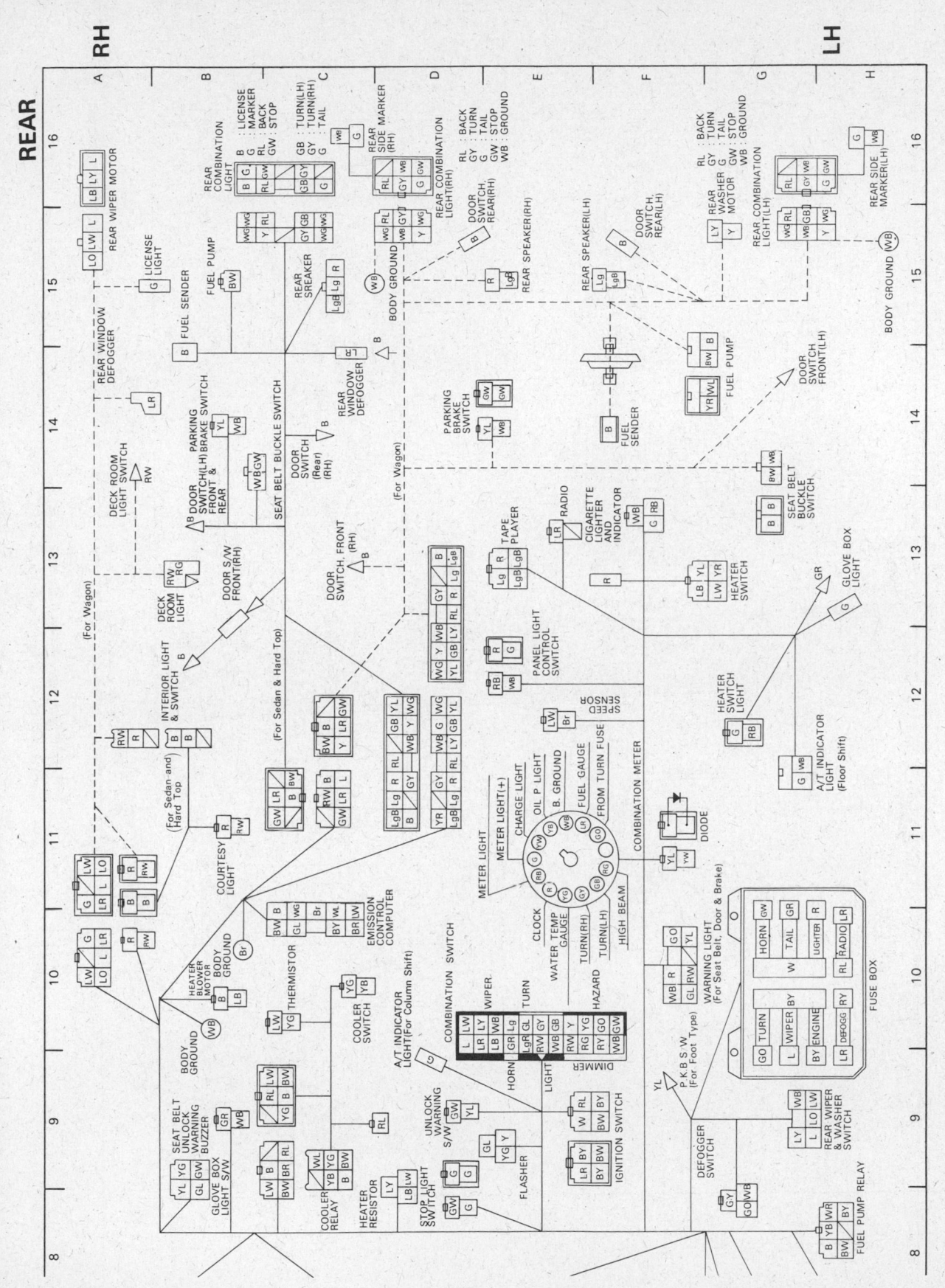

1978 dash panel wiring diagram (2 of 2).

1979 body electrical wiring diagram (1 of 2)

1979 body electrical wiring diagram (2 of 2)

FRONT

RH

LH

1979 dash panel wiring diagram (1 of 2)

ROOM LIGHT & S/W
LIGHT
GLOVE BOX SWITCH
LOW CUT PRESSURE SWITCH
UNLOCK WARNING S/W
WIPER & WASHER S/W REAR
PKB S/W
IGNITION SWITCH

LIGHTER
TURN
METER
DEFOGGER
PANEL
TAIL (R)
TAIL (L)
STOP
FUSE BOX

LIGHT REMINDER
FUEL PUMP RELAY
HEATER BLOWER MOTOR
HEATER RELAY(-)
ANTENNA S/W MOTOR
FLASHER

RELAY BLOCK
MAIN
DEFOGGER
TAIL LIGHT
WINDSHIELD WIPER RELAY
INTERMITTENT
HEATER

SPEAKER (RH) FRONT
SEAT BELT BUCKLE S/W
BODY GROUND
DOOR S/W (FR. LH)
DOOR S/W (RR.LH)
DOOR S/W (For Buzzer)
SEAT BELT RELAY & BUZZER
SPEAKER (LH) FRONT
BODY GROUND

A/T INDICATOR LIGHT (For Floor Shift)
PKB S/W (Floor)
THERMO SENSOR

EMISSON CONTROL COMPUTER
WIPER MOTOR
VACUUM SWITCH
IDLE-UP V.S.V
OUTER VENT CONTROL VALVE
FUEL PUMP RESISTER
V.S.V

ENGINE
WIPER
HEAD (R)
HEAD
HORN
CHARGELIGHT RELAY
MAIN RELAY
HEADLIGHT RELAY

BRAKE OIL SENSOR

BODY GROUND
FUSIBLELINK
MAGNET CLUTCH
BACK-UP LIGHT S/W
NEUTRAL START SWITCH (For A/T)
FUEL CUT SOLENOID
WATER TEMP SENDER
OIL PRESSURE SWITCH
STARTER MOTOR
IGNITION COIL & IGNITER
ALTERNATER (With IC Regulator)
WASHER MOTOR
BODY GROUND

SIDE MARKER LIGHT
SIDE MARKERLIGHT

FRONT TURN (RH)
HEADLIGHT MAIN
HEADLIGHT
HORN (RH)
HORN (LH)
HEADLIGHT
HEADLGT MAIN
FRONT TURN (LH)

CLEARANCE LIGHT (RH)
CLEARANCE LIGHT (LH)

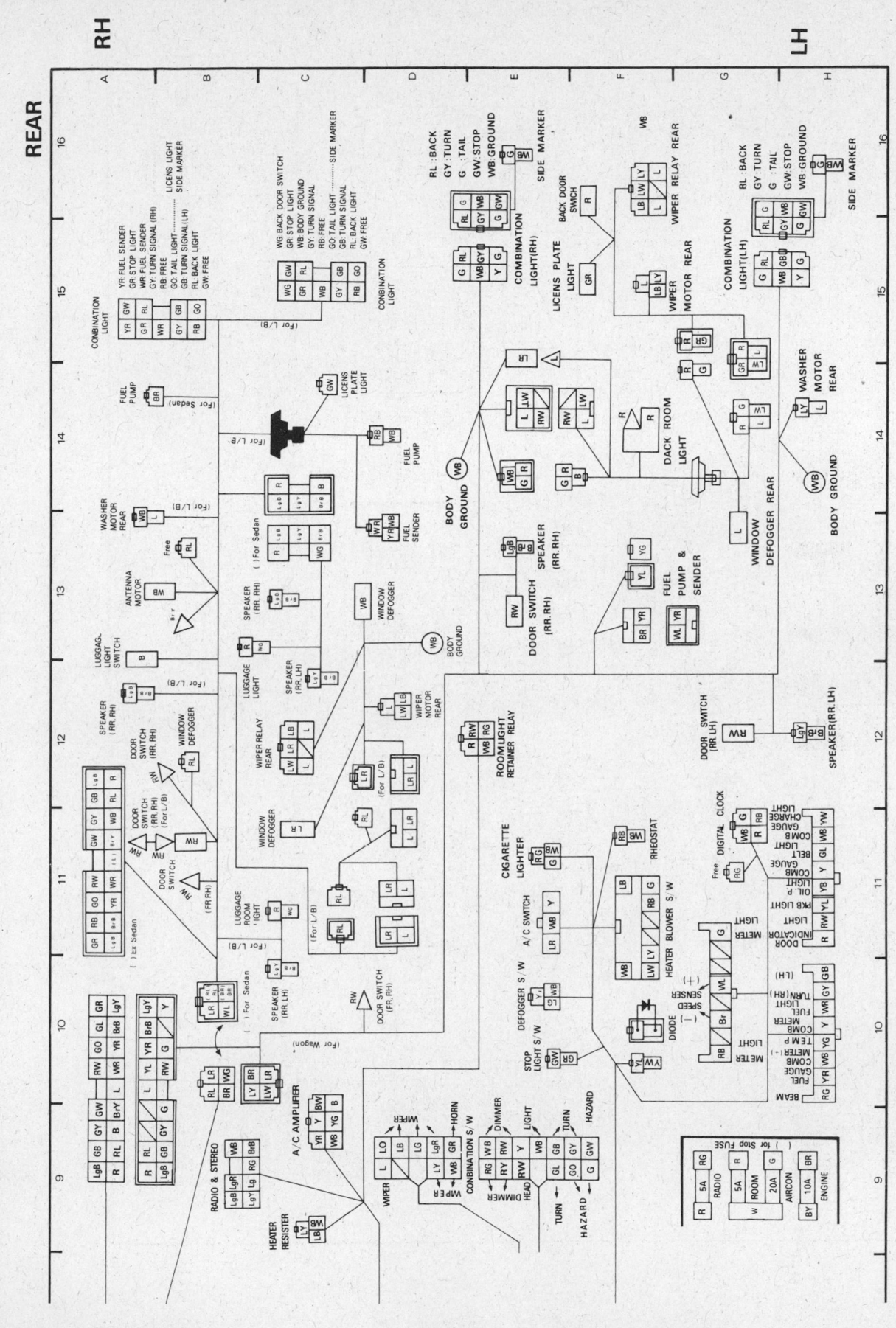

1979 dash panel wiring diagram (2 of 2)

1980 body electrical wiring diagram (1 of 2)

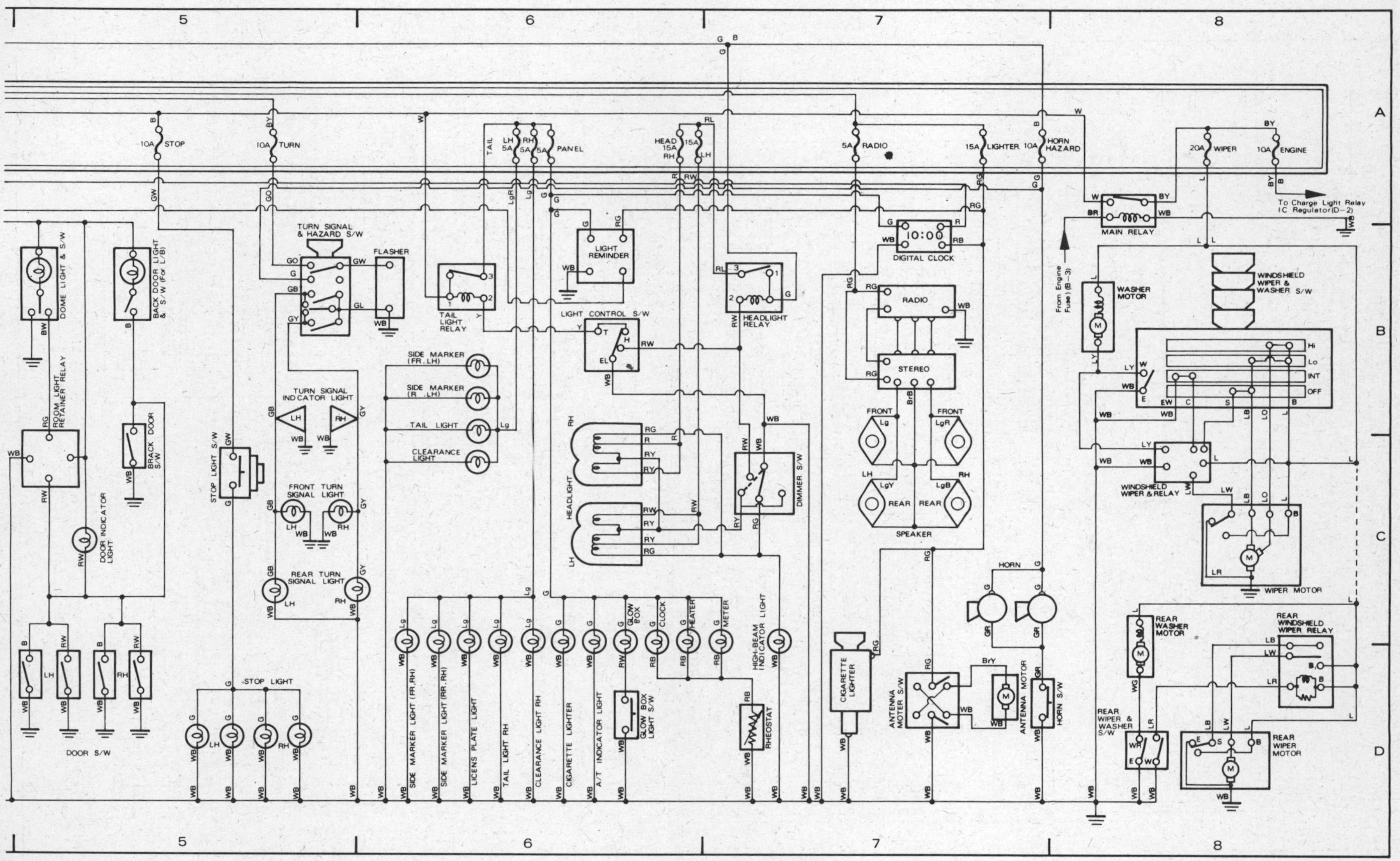

1980 body electrical wiring diagram (2 of 2)

CONTINUED NEXT PAGE

1980 dash panel wiring diagram (1 of 2)

FRONT

RH

LH

FUSE BOX

PANEL — TAIL(R) — TAIL(L) — STOP

DOME LIGHT S/W
GLOVE BOX S/W
LOW CUT PRESSURE S/W
(For Wagon)
LIGHT REMINDER
HEATER BLOWER MOTOR
P.K.B S/W
HEATER REAR GROUND
MOTOR ANTENNA S/W
FLASHER

RELAY BLOCK
MAIN — DEFOGGER — TAIL — HEATER
WINDSHIELD WIPER RELAY INTERMITTENT
SEAT BELT RELAY & BUZZER

FRONT SPEAKER (R)
FRONT SPEAKER (L)
BUCKLE S/W
BODY GROUND
DOOR S/W FR (LH)
DOOR S/W RR (LH)
DOOR S/W
CIRCUIT BREAKER
BODY GROUND

A/T INDICATOR LIGHT
P.K.B S/W (Floor)
CCo SENSOR

WIPER MOTOR
VACUUM S/W
THERMOSTAT
WATER TEMPERATURE SENDER
DOOR LOCK VALVE
FUEL CUT SOLENOID VALVE
V.S.V (EGR)
COOLER IDLE-UP
V.S.V (Ai)(TP)
EMISSION CONTROL COMPUTER

WIPER 20A — ENGINE 20A
CHARGE LIGHT RELAY
HEAD(R) 15A — HEAD(L) 15A
MAIN RELAY
HORN 10A
HEADLIGHT RELAY

BRAKE OIL SENSOR
IG COIL & IGNITER
CONDENSER
SIDE MARKER LIGHT

SIDE MARKER LIGHT
COOLER COMPRESSOR
OIL PRESSURE S/W
BACK UP S/W
STARTER MOTOR
FUSIBLE LINK
NEUTRAL START S/W
A/T BACK-UP S/W
BATTERY
ALTERNATOR
WASHER MOTOR
BODY GROUND

CLEARANCE LIGHT (RH)
HEADLIGHT MAIN
HEADLIGHT
FRONT TURN (RH)
FRONT TURN (LH)
HORN (R)
(L) HORN
HEADLIGHT
HEADLIGHT MAIN
CLEARANCE LIGHT (LH)

A B C D

1 2 3 4

REAR

RH   LH

1980 dash panel wiring diagram (2 of 2)

1981 and 1982 body electrical wiring diagram (1 of 2)

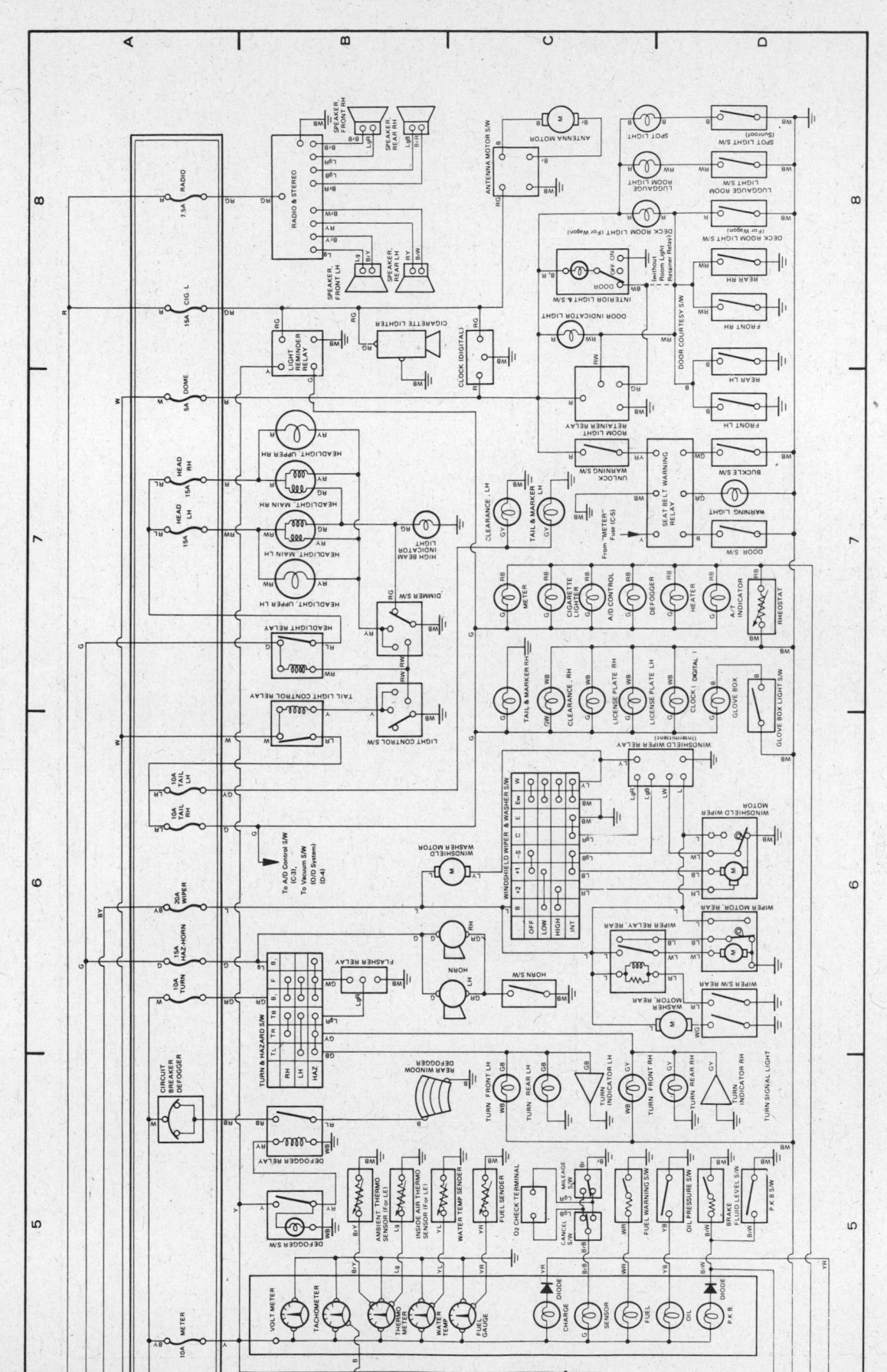

1981 and 1982 body electrical wiring diagram (2 of 2)

FRONT

1981 and 1982 dash panel wiring diagram (1 of 2)

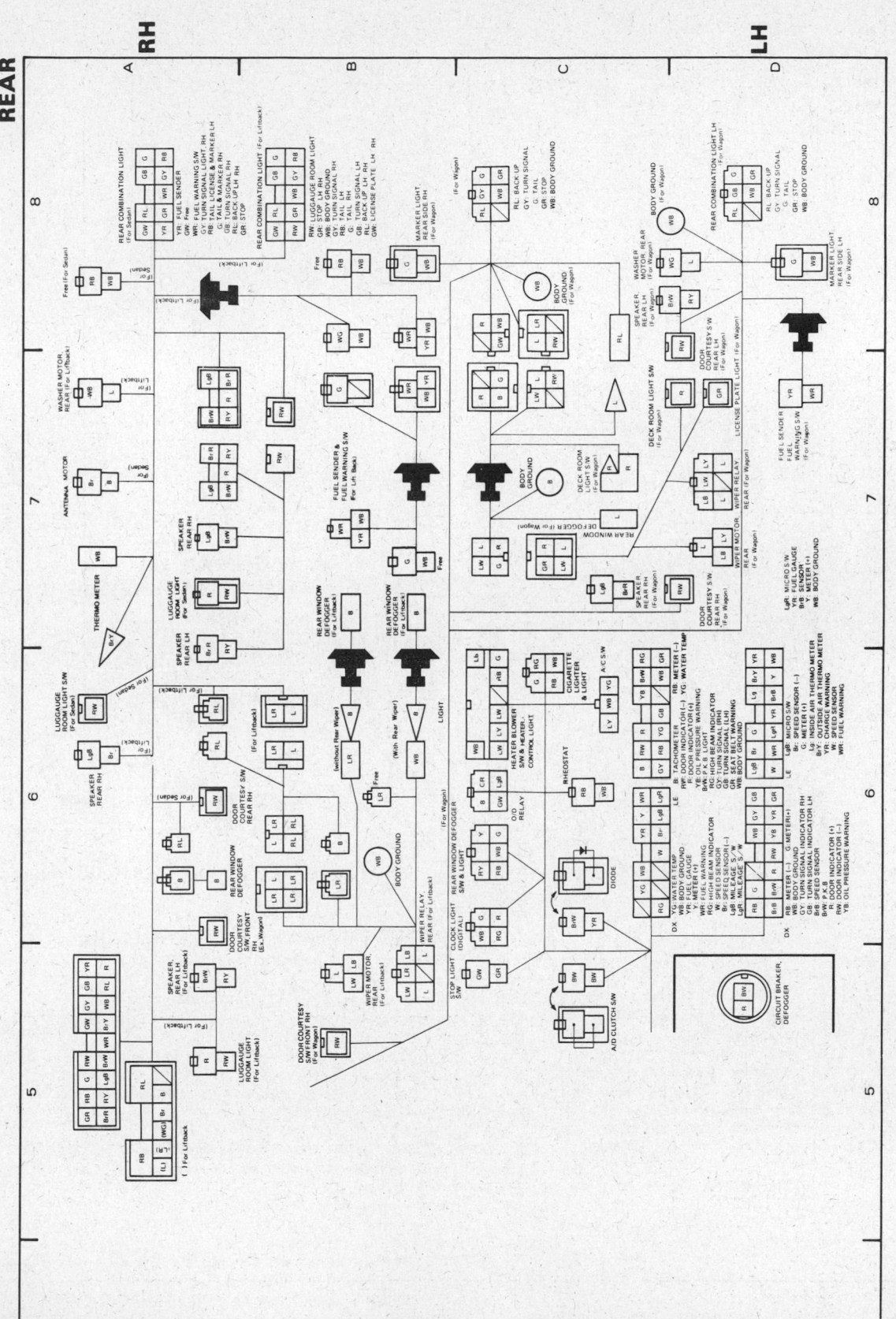

1981 and 1982 dash panel wiring diagram (2 of 2)

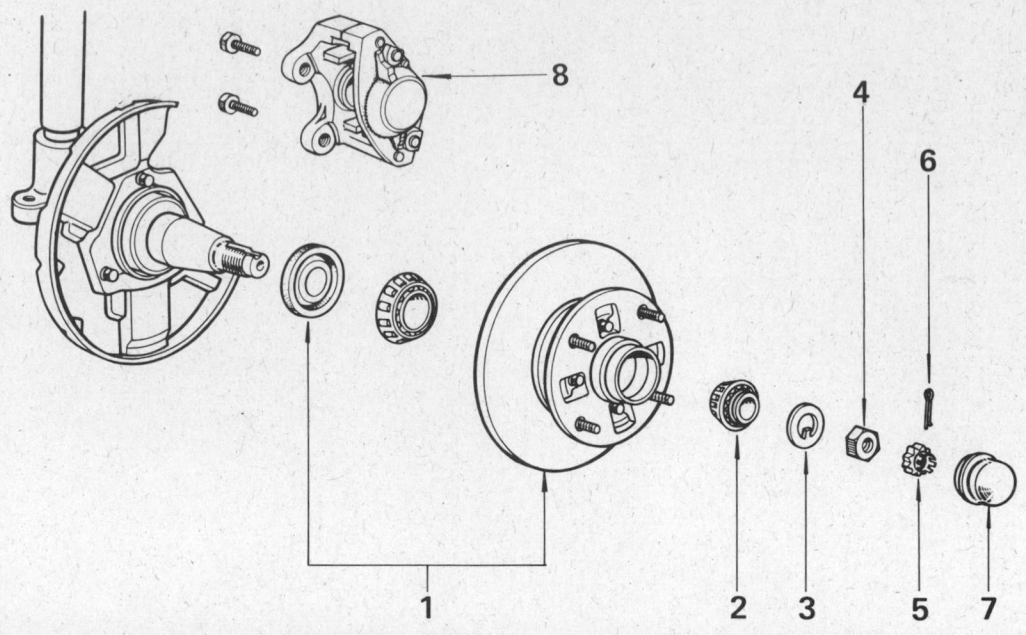

Fig. 13.73 Front hub assembly (1979 and later models) — exploded view

1 Axle hub with disc	4 Claw nut	6 Cotter pin
2 Bearing	5 Adjusting cap	7 Grease cap
3 Claw washer		8 Disc brake caliper

11 Steering and suspension

Front suspension (1979 thru 1982) — general information

In 1979, the conventional double wishbone type front suspension was replaced with an independent MacPherson strut with coil springs and stabilizer bar.

Front hubs — servicing and adjustment

1 Raise the front of the vehicle, support it on jack stands and remove the wheel. Remove the disc pads and then detach the caliper and tie it up out of the way without straining the flexible hose.
2 Tap off the grease cap, remove the cotter pin and nut retainer.
3 Unscrew the retaining nut and remove the thrust washer. Pull the hub forward an inch or two and then push back. This will expose the hub outer bearing which may then be removed.
4 Pull the hub assembly straight off the hub spindle.
5 Wipe out all old grease from the bearings and hub interior, taking care not to damage the oil seal. Check the bearings and tracks for wear, damage or scoring.
6 If they are in good condition, repack the inside of the hub as shown.
7 If there is evidence of grease seepage onto the discs, drift out the old seal and tap in a new one using a tubular drift.
8 If either the inner or outer bearings require renewal, drift out the tracks with a brass drift and press in the new ones. Where both front hubs are being serviced at the same time, do not mix the bearing components as the race and the track are matched in production.
9 The disc should not be removed from the hub assembly unless it is to be replaced/or refaced.
10 Reassembly is a reversal of dismantling, but the bearings must be adjusted *before* the disc pads are fitted.
11 Tighten the hub nut to 22 lbf ft (30 Nm) rotating the hub at the same time. Unscrew the nut and then tighten it again using finger pressure only.
12 All endplay should have now been eliminated and the nut retainer and a new cotter pin can be installed.
13 Tap the grease cap into position, install the caliper and wheel.
14 Repeat the operations on the opposite front hub and then lower the car to the ground.

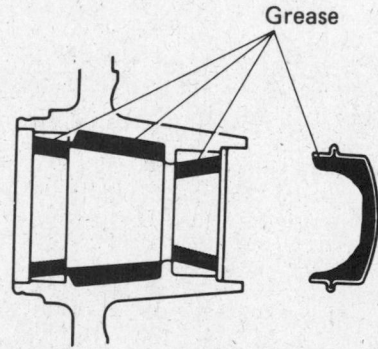

Fig. 13.74 Apply grease to these areas of the hub during reassembly

Front stabilizer bar — removal and installation

15 Raise the front of the car and support it securely under the cross-member.
16 Remove the splash shield from under the engine.
17 At each end of the stabilizer bar, disconnect the drop link from the lower control arms.
18 Remove the stabilizer bar brackets and withdraw the stabilizer bar.
19 Installation is the reversal of removal but tighten the nuts and bolts to the specified torque and ensure that the drop link mountings are correctly assembled.

Front suspension strut rod — removal and installation

20 Raise the front of the car and support it under the front cross-member.
21 Disconnect the strut rod from the frame.
22 Unbolt the opposite end of the strut rod from the lower control arm and remove the rod.
23 Installation is a reversal of removal. The inner nut on the threaded end of the rod is normally staked in position to facilitate reassembly. If it has been moved for any reason or new components fitted, set the connection of the rod to the frame as shown in the diagram. Make sure that the mountings are correctly assembled and tighten nuts and bolts to the specified torque.

281

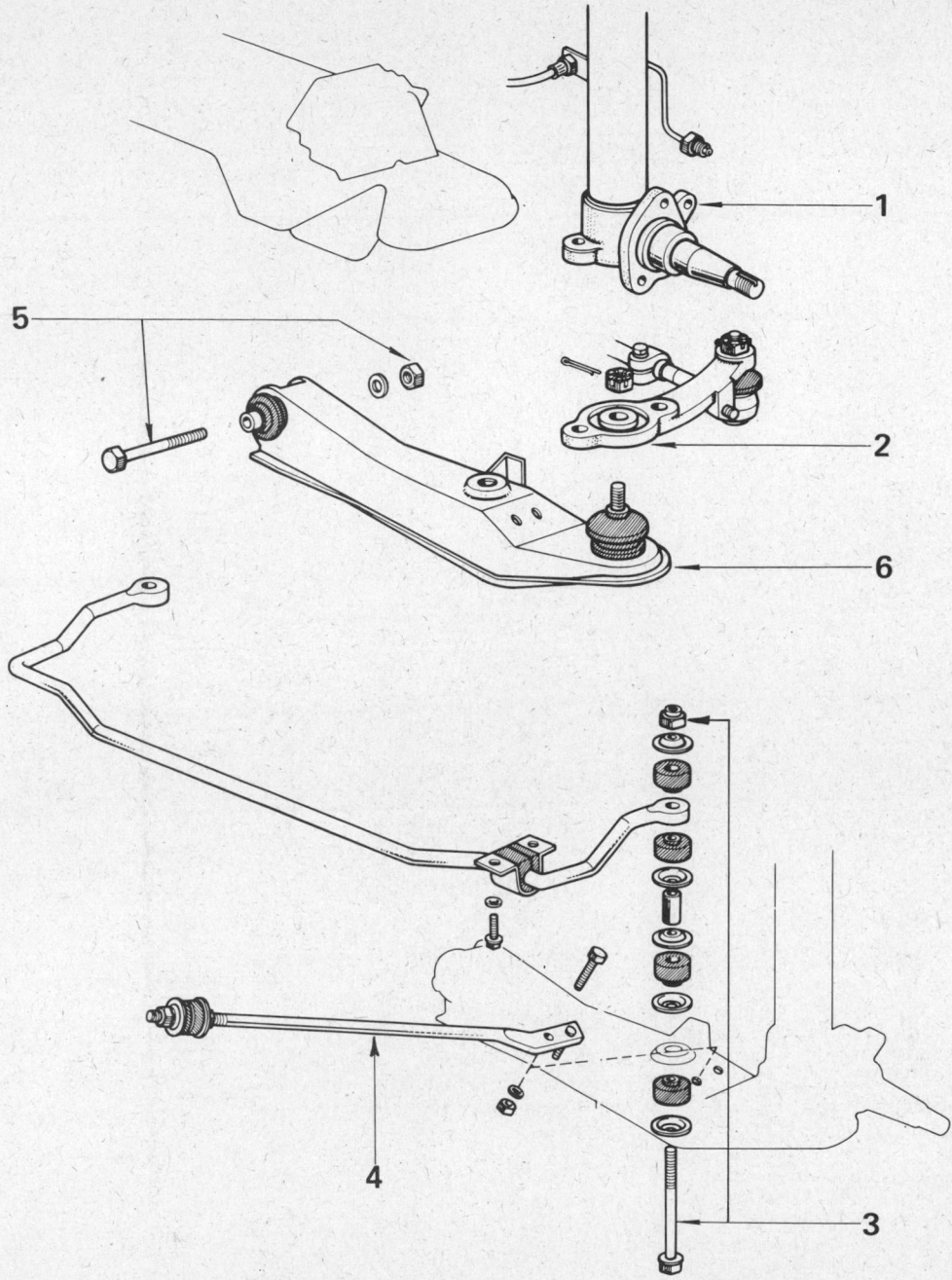

Fig. 13.75 Front suspension components (1979 and later models) — exploded view

1 Shock absorber shell   4 Strut bar
2 Knuckle arm   5 Lower arm pivot bolt
3 Stabilizer bar cushion bolt & nut   6 Lower arm

Lower arm — removal and installation

24 Raise the car and support it securely under the crossmember.
25 Remove the wheel.
26 Disconnect the stabilizer bar drop link from the control arm.
27 Unbolt the strut rod from the control arm.
28 Remove the pivot and release the control arm from the suspension crossmember.
29 Using a suitable balljoint separator, disconnect the tie-rod end from the steering knuckle arm.
30 Unscrew and remove the two bolts which secure the steering knuckle arm to the base of the suspension leg.

31 If required, the control arm can be disconnected from the steering knuckle arm using a suitable extractor.
32 If the control arm balljoint is worn then the control arm will have to be renewed complete.
33 If the control arm inner bush is worn, this can be renewed by pressing out the bush towards the front of the car (control arm in its normally installed position). Install the new bush from the front of the car. A vise and suitable distance pieces are required for this work.
34 Installation is a reversal of removal but tighten the control arm pivot bolt finger-tight only until the car is lowered to the ground. Bounce the car up and down several times to settle the suspension and then tighten the pivot bolt to the specified torque.

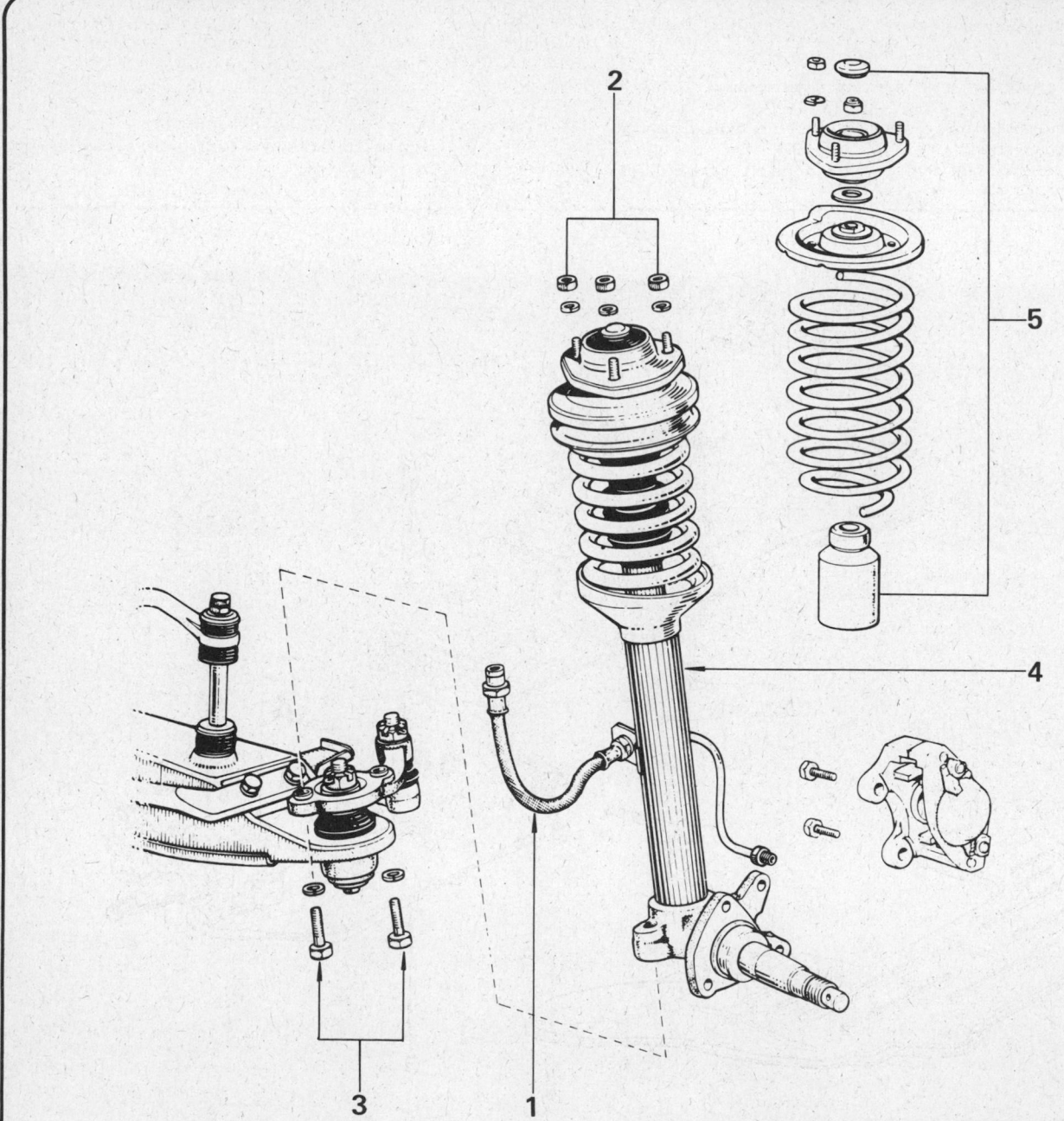

Fig. 13.76 Front shock absorber and related components (1979 and later models) — exploded view

1	Brake tube	4	Shock absorber with front brake
2	Nut	5	Suspension support, spring seat, spring & dust cover
3	Bolt		

Front shock absorber — removal and installation

35 Raise the front of the car and support it under the crossmember.
36 Remove the wheel.
37 Disconnect the rigid and flexible brake hoses from the support bracket on the suspension strut. Plug the open hydraulic lines to prevent loss of fluid and entry of dirt.
38 Within the engine compartment disconnect the suspension shock absorber top mounting by unscrewing and removing the three nuts.
39 Unscrew and remove the two bolts which retain the steering knuckle arm to the base of the shock absorber.
40 Withdraw the shock absorber complete with hub assembly from under the fender. The shock will have to be lifted slightly to separate it from the knuckle arm due to the use of positioning collars installed between the two components.
41 Using spring compressors, compress the spring until it is loose within the spring pans.
42 Pry out the bearing dust cover.
43 Holding the seat still with a suitable tool, unscrew the nut from the top of the piston rod.
44 Remove the suspension support plate and then withdraw the coil spring (still in its compressed state).
45 Remove the hub and brake components and unbolt the disc shield

from the stub axle carrier.
46 When a shock absorber has become damaged or faulty in operation it is recommended that it should be replaced on a reconditioned exchange basis. Alternatively, replacement cartridges can be obtained and the old internal components removed and the new cartridge installed in accordance with its manufacturer's instructions. It is emphasized that any exchange or replacement unit will not include the coil spring or brake or hub components and these must be removed from the old unit as previously described.
47 Installation is a reversal of removal but note the following points.
48 Make sure that the suspension support plate locates properly on the end of the piston rod.
49 Always use a new self-locking nut for securing the support plate to the piston rod and tighten all the nuts and bolts to the specified torque.
50 Pack the space around the piston rod above the support plate with multi-purpose grease.
51 Adjust the front hub bearings (Section 4).
52 Bleed the front brake circuit.

Front crossmember — removal and installation

53 Raise the front of the car and support it securely under the body sideframe members.

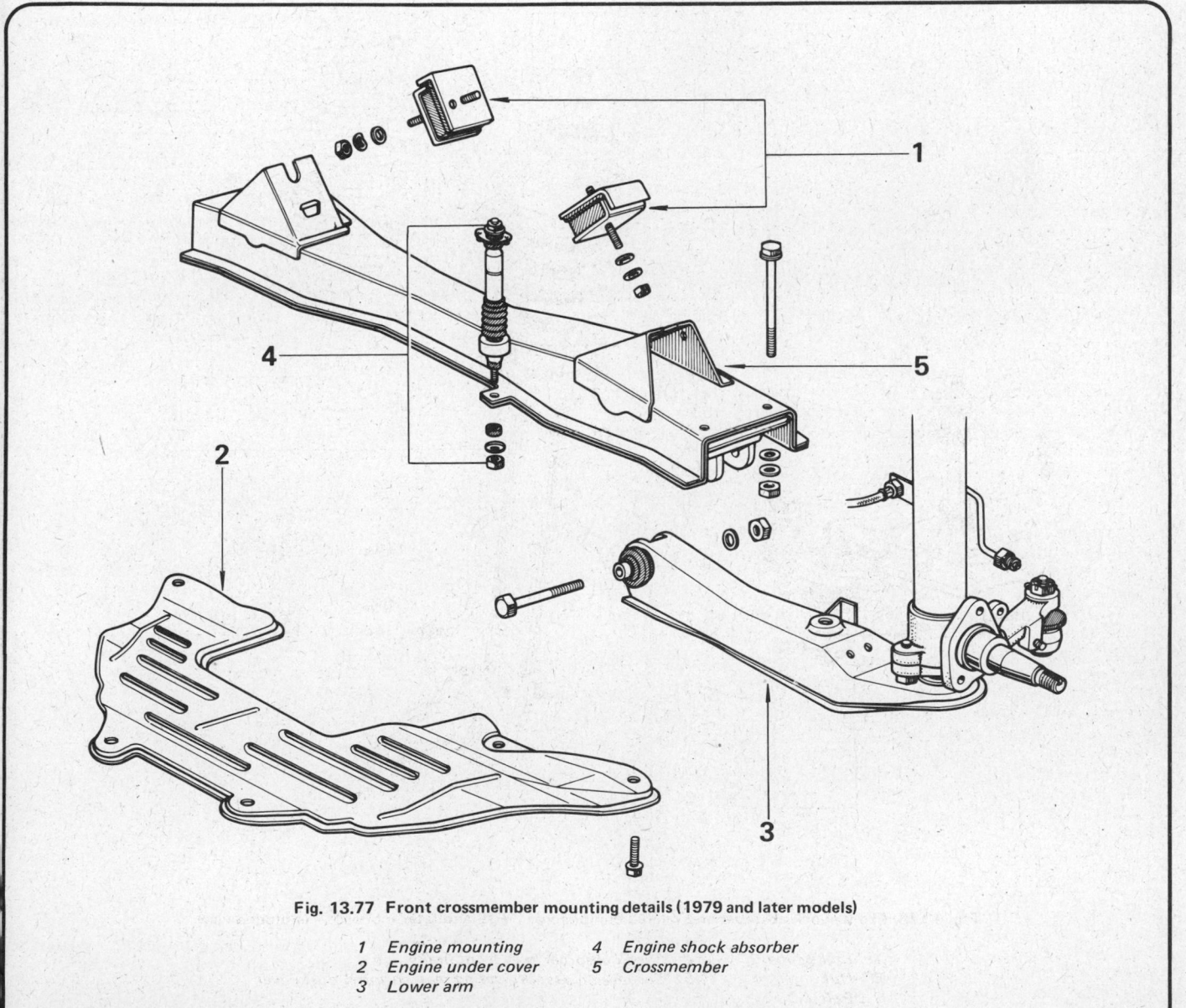

Fig. 13.77 Front crossmember mounting details (1979 and later models)

1 Engine mounting	4 Engine shock absorber
2 Engine under cover	5 Crossmember
3 Lower arm	

54 Remove the two front wheels.

55 Using a jack and wooden block as an insulator, support the weight of the engine under the sump.

56 Disconnect the engine mountings from the crossmember.

57 Disconnect the stabilizer bar drop links from the lower control arms.

58 Disconnect the strut bars from the lower control arms.

59 Unscrew and remove the lower control arm pivot bolts from the crossmember.

60 Depress both suspension lower control arms to release them from the crossmember and then remove the four crossmember securing bolts and lift it from the car.

61 Installation is a reversal of removal. Tighten all bolts and nuts to the specified torque.

Power steering system (1979 thru 1982) — servicing

62 Vehicles manufactured in 1979 and later come with an option of power steering.

Power steering — maintenance

63 Check that the drivebelt to the pump is in good condition and that when the mid point of the top run is pressed with the thumb, it will deflect by 0.3 to 0.5 in (8 to 12 mm).

64 With the engine warm and idling at 1000 rpm or less, turn the steering from lock-to-lock several times to raise the oil temperature to at least 100°F (40°C). Check the fluid level in the reservoir with the built-in dipstick and also look for emulsification or foaming of the fluid. Any sign of emulsification or foaming is an indication of air in the system or of insufficient fluid.

65 Top up with approved fluid after checking the system for leaks.

Power steering — bleeding

66 Check that the fluid reservoir is at the correct level and add approved fluid if necessary.

67 Raise the front of the vehicle so that the wheels are clear of the ground and support the body with jackstands.

68 Turn the steering from lock-to-lock two or three times, then check the fluid level.

69 Start the engine and with it idling, again turn the steering from lock-to-lock two or three times.

70 Stop the engine and lower the front wheels to the ground.

71 Start the engine again and with it idling turn the steering wheel from lock-to-lock several times, center the steering wheel and stop the engine.

72 Bleeding is complete if the level of fluid in the reservoir has not risen more than 0.2 in (5 mm) and there is no sign of foaming when the engine has stopped.

73 If there is foaming or an excessive rise in oil level, repeat the procedure.

Power steering — fluid replacement

74 Raise the front wheels of the vehicle clear of the ground and support the body on jackstands.

75 Remove the fluid return hose from the oil reservoir, drain the fluid from the reservoir into a suitable container and put the end of the hose into a container to collect the fluid expelled.

76 Turn the steering wheel from lock-to-lock until no more fluid is expelled.

77 Reconnect the return hose to the fluid reservoir, add fresh fluid and bleed the system.

Power steering pump — removal and replacement

78 Push down hard on the drivebelt to prevent the pump from rotating and loosen the nut securing the pulley to the pump, then remove the pulley and drivebelt.

79 Loosen the clamp on the return hose, prepare to catch the fluid running out and then pull off the return hose.

80 Prepare to catch the fluid running out, then unscrew the pump pressure line connection.

81 Remove the pump fixing bolts and lift the pump clear.

82 Discard the fluid drained from the system.

83 Installation is the reverse of removal. After fitting the drivebelt and tightening the pulley, tension the belt. Add fluid to the system as necessary and bleed the system.

84 It is not recommended that a faulty pump is overhauled. Replace it with a new or factory reconditioned assembly.

Steering gear (power assisted) — dismantling and reassembly

85 With the steering gear removed as described in Chapter 11, clean away external dirt and grease.

86 Extract the end cover bolts and then screw in the adjuster screw which will push off the cover.

87 Using a plastic-faced hammer, tap out the sector shaft.

88 Unscrew the power piston/valve housing bolts and remove them. Now hold the piston nut from turning and rotate the wormshaft in a clockwise direction. Withdraw the valve body and power piston assem-

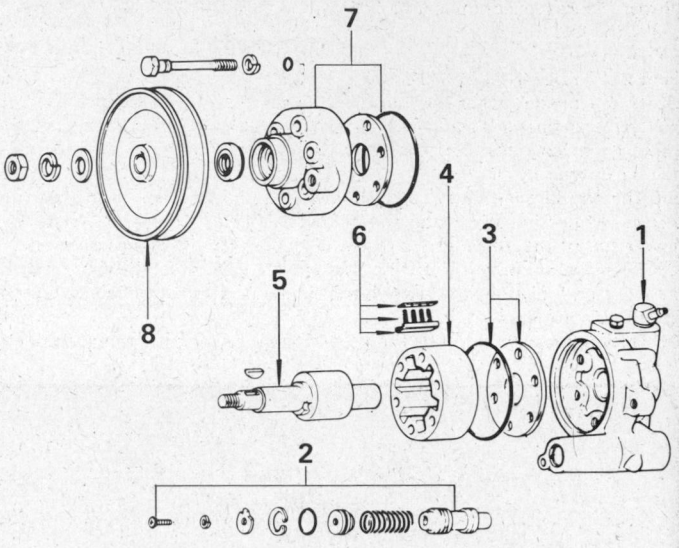

Fig. 13.78 Power steering pump — exploded view

1	Rear housing	5	Rotor shaft
2	Flow control valve	6	Slipper, spring seat & spring
3	Side plate & O-ring	7	Front housing & side plate
4	Fixed Ring	8	Drive pulley

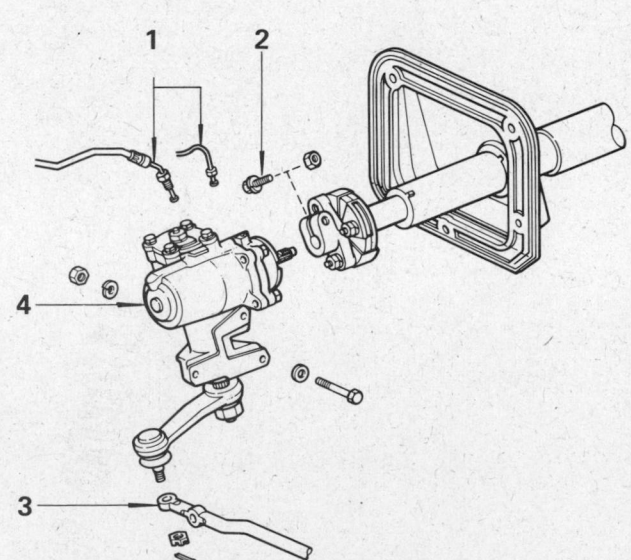

Fig. 13.79 Steering gear and related components (1979 and later models with power steering)

1	Pipe & hose	3	Relay rod
2	Coupling bolt	4	Gear housing

bly. Do not allow the piston nut to run off the wormshaft. **Note:** *Do not dismantle the valve body or remove the power piston from the wormshaft.*

89 If the valve body assembly exhibits more than an almost imperceptible shake on the wormshaft, then the assembly must be replaced.

90 Replace the O-ring in the end cover and check the shaft and tooth surfaces for damage or wear.

91 Check the adjusting screw for thrust (axial) clearance. If it exceeds 0.002 in (0.05 mm) then the staking of the lock nut must be relieved and the screw turned while the lock nut is held stationary. When the thrust clearance is between 0.001 and 0.002 in (0.03 and 0.05 mm) stake the lock nut.

92 Remove the worm bearing plug with a pin wrench, replace the O-ring seal and bearings if necessary.

93 If the needle roller bearings in the main housing are worn, extract the oil and dust seals and withdraw the bearings. When installing the new bearings, make sure that the longer rims of their outer races are facing outward.

94 The top bearing must be flush with the end of the housing bearing recess, while the lower one should be 0.076 in (19.4 mm) from the lower end of the housing. Fit a new O-ring, Teflon ring and spacer.

95 Begin reassembly by fitting the power piston/valve body with a new O-ring. Tighten the cover bolts evenly in diagonal sequence to the specified torque.

96 Now adjust the worm bearing pre-load by turning the threaded plug.

The turning torque of the splined wormshaft should be between 3.5 and 5.6 lbf in (40 and 65 Ncm) in both directions. Ideally, a torque meter should be used but a cord and spring balance will give a reasonably accurate alternative provided the cord is wound around the shaft a sufficient number of times so that it leaves the spring balance 1 in (25 mm) from the center point of the shaft. Tighten the locking ring with a wrench.

97 Tape over the splines on the sector shaft to prevent damage to the oil seal.

98 Align the center spline and groove of the sector shaft and power piston nut gears. Push the shaft into the housing without rotating it. Tighten the cover bolts evenly in diagonal sequence to the specified torque.

99 Center the steering gear. To do this, turn the sector shaft from lock-to-lock and count the number of turns. Now turn the shaft back by half this number of turns. Mark the relative position of the wormshaft to the adjuster plug.

100 With the gear centralized, turn the slotted adjusting screw in the end cover until the starting torque at the wormshaft, measured with a torque meter or using a cord and spring balance, is between 2.6 and 3.5 lbf in (30 and 40 Ncm).

101 Use a new sealing washer and fit the lock nut without disturbing the setting of the adjuster screw. Re-check the pre-load (starting torque) in both directions of travel.

102 Stake the worm plug locking ring nut in three places.

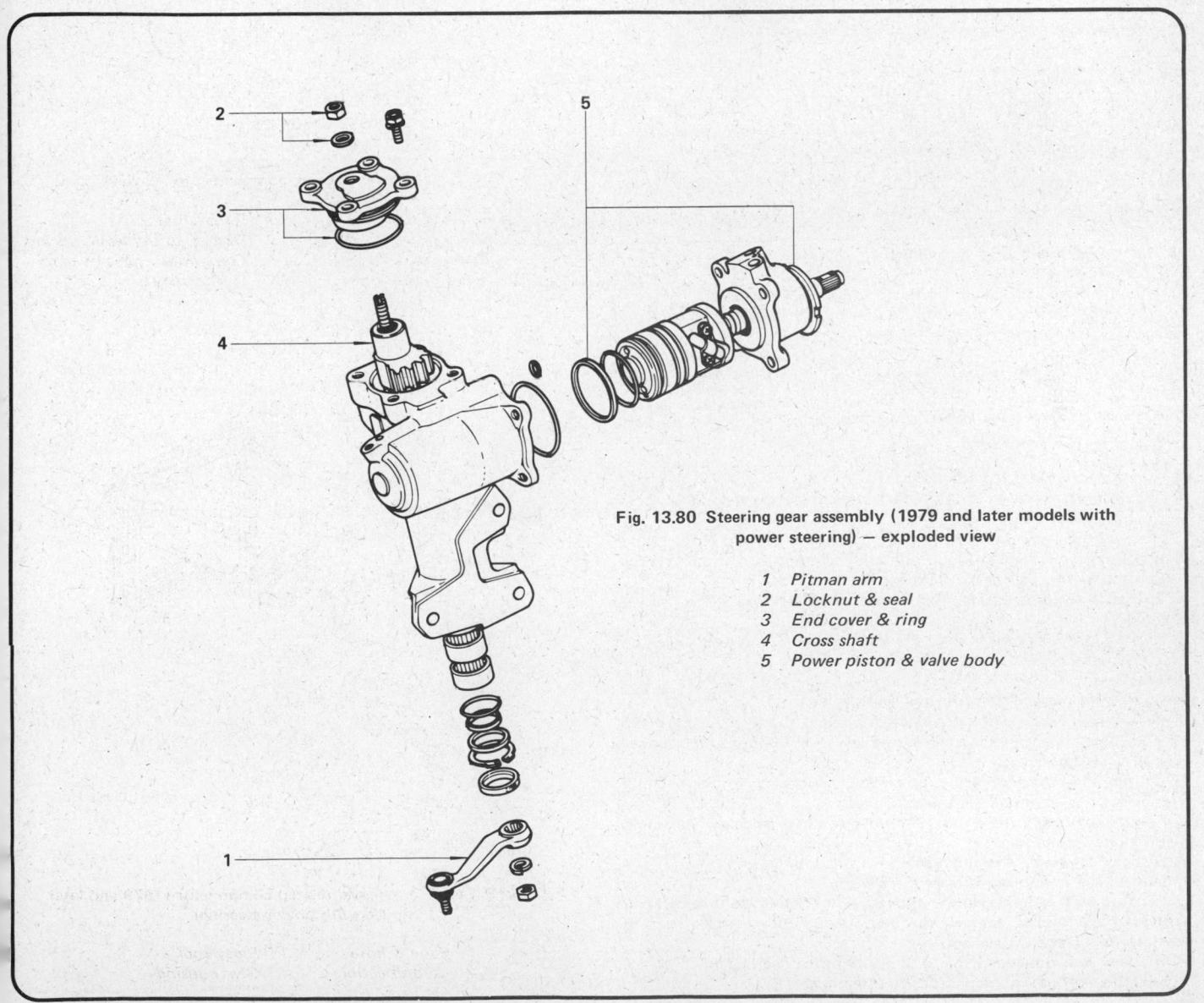

Fig. 13.80 Steering gear assembly (1979 and later models with power steering) — exploded view

1 Pitman arm
2 Locknut & seal
3 End cover & ring
4 Cross shaft
5 Power piston & valve body

Conversion factors

Length (distance)
Inches (in)	X 25.4	= Millimetres (mm)	X 0.0394	= Inches (in)
Feet (ft)	X 0.305	= Metres (m)	X 3.281	= Feet (ft)
Miles	X 1.609	= Kilometres (km)	X 0.621	= Miles

Volume (capacity)
Cubic inches (cu in; in³)	X 16.387	= Cubic centimetres (cc; cm³)	X 0.061	= Cubic inches (cu in; in³)
Imperial pints (Imp pt)	X 0.568	= Litres (l)	X 1.76	= Imperial pints (Imp pt)
Imperial quarts (Imp qt)	X 1.137	= Litres (l)	X 0.88	= Imperial quarts (Imp qt)
Imperial quarts (Imp qt)	X 1.201	= US quarts (US qt)	X 0.833	= Imperial quarts (Imp qt)
US quarts (US qt)	X 0.946	= Litres (l)	X 1.057	= US quarts (US qt)
Imperial gallons (Imp gal)	X 4.546	= Litres (l)	X 0.22	= Imperial gallons (Imp gal)
Imperial gallons (Imp gal)	X 1.201	= US gallons (US gal)	X 0.833	= Imperial gallons (Imp gal)
US gallons (US gal)	X 3.785	= Litres (l)	X 0.264	= US gallons (US gal)

Mass (weight)
Ounces (oz)	X 28.35	= Grams (g)	X 0.035	= Ounces (oz)
Pounds (lb)	X 0.454	= Kilograms (kg)	X 2.205	= Pounds (lb)

Force
Ounces-force (ozf; oz)	X 0.278	= Newtons (N)	X 3.6	= Ounces-force (ozf; oz)
Pounds-force (lbf; lb)	X 4.448	= Newtons (N)	X 0.225	= Pounds-force (lbf; lb)
Newtons (N)	X 0.1	= Kilograms-force (kgf; kg)	X 9.81	= Newtons (N)

Pressure
Pounds-force per square inch (psi; lbf/in²; lb/in²)	X 0.070	= Kilograms-force per square centimetre (kgf/cm²; kg/cm²)	X 14.223	= Pounds-force per square inch (psi; lbf/in²; lb/in²)
Pounds-force per square inch (psi; lbf/in²; lb/in²)	X 0.068	= Atmospheres (atm)	X 14.696	= Pounds-force per square inch (psi; lbf/in²; lb/in²)
Pounds-force per square inch (psi; lbf/in²; lb/in²)	X 0.069	= Bars	X 14.5	= Pounds-force per square inch (psi; lbf/in²; lb/in²)
Pounds-force per square inch (psi; lbf/in²; lb/in²)	X 6.895	= Kilopascals (kPa)	X 0.145	= Pounds-force per square inch (psi; lbf/in²; lb/in²)
Kilopascals (kPa)	X 0.01	= Kilograms-force per square centimetre (kgf/cm²; kg/cm²)	X 98.1	= Kilopascals (kPa)
Millibar (mbar)	X 100	= Pascals (Pa)	X 0.01	= Millibar (mbar)
Millibar (mbar)	X 0.0145	= Pounds-force per square inch (psi; lbf/in²; lb/in²)	X 68.947	= Millibar (mbar)
Millibar (mbar)	X 0.75	= Millimetres of mercury (mmHg)	X 1.333	= Millibar (mbar)
Millibar (mbar)	X 0.401	= Inches of water (inH$_2$O)	X 2.491	= Millibar (mbar)
Millimetres of mercury (mmHg)	X 0.535	= Inches of water (inH$_2$O)	X 1.868	= Millimetres of mercury (mmHg)
Inches of water (inH$_2$O)	X 0.036	= Pounds-force per square inch (psi; lbf/in²; lb/in²)	X 27.68	= Inches of water (inH$_2$O)

Torque (moment of force)
Pounds-force inches (lbf in; lb in)	X 1.152	= Kilograms-force centimetre (kgf cm; kg cm)	X 0.868	= Pounds-force inches (lbf in; lb in)
Pounds-force inches (lbf in; lb in)	X 0.113	= Newton metres (Nm)	X 8.85	= Pounds-force inches (lbf in; lb in)
Pounds-force inches (lbf in; lb in)	X 0.083	= Pounds-force feet (lbf ft; lb ft)	X 12	= Pounds-force inches (lbf in; lb in)
Pounds-force feet (lbf ft; lb ft)	X 0.138	= Kilograms-force metres (kgf m; kg m)	X 7.233	= Pounds-force feet (lbf ft; lb ft)
Pounds-force feet (lbf ft; lb ft)	X 1.356	= Newton metres (Nm)	X 0.738	= Pounds-force feet (lbf ft; lb ft)
Newton metres (Nm)	X 0.102	= Kilograms-force metres (kgf m; kg m)	X 9.804	= Newton metres (Nm)

Power
Horsepower (hp)	X 745.7	= Watts (W)	X 0.0013	= Horsepower (hp)

Velocity (speed)
Miles per hour (miles/hr; mph)	X 1.609	= Kilometres per hour (km/hr; kph)	X 0.621	= Miles per hour (miles/hr; mph)

Fuel consumption*
Miles per gallon, Imperial (mpg)	X 0.354	= Kilometres per litre (km/l)	X 2.825	= Miles per gallon, Imperial (mpg)
Miles per gallon, US (mpg)	X 0.425	= Kilometres per litre (km/l)	X 2.352	= Miles per gallon, US (mpg)

Temperature

Degrees Fahrenheit = (°C x 1.8) + 32   Degrees Celsius (Degrees Centigrade; °C) = (°F - 32) x 0.56

*It is common practice to convert from miles per gallon (mpg) to litres/100 kilometres (l/100km), where mpg (Imperial) x l/100 km = 282 and mpg (US) x l/100 km = 235

Index

Haynes Automotive Manuals

NOTE: New manuals are added to this list on a periodic basis. If you do not see a listing for your vehicle, consult your local Haynes dealer for the latest product information.

ACURA
*1776 Integra & Legend all models '86 thru '90

AMC
Jeep CJ - see JEEP (412)
694 Mid-size models, Concord, Hornet, Gremlin & Spirit '70 thru '83
934 (Renault) Alliance & Encore all models '83 thru '87

AUDI
615 4000 all models '80 thru '87
428 5000 all models '77 thru '83
1117 5000 all models '84 thru '88

AUSTIN
Healey Sprite - see MG Midget Roadster (265)

BMW
*2020 3/5 Series not including diesel or all-wheel drive models '82 thru '92
276 320i all 4 cyl models '75 thru '83
632 528i & 530i all models '75 thru '80
240 1500 thru 2002 all models except Turbo '59 thru '77
348 2500, 2800, 3.0 & Bavaria all models '69 thru '76

BUICK
Century (front wheel drive) - see GENERAL MOTORS (829)
*1627 Buick, Oldsmobile & Pontiac Full-size (Front wheel drive) all models '85 thru '95
Buick Electra, LeSabre and Park Avenue; **Oldsmobile** Delta 88 Royale, Ninety Eight and Regency; **Pontiac** Bonneville
1551 Buick Oldsmobile & Pontiac Full-size (Rear wheel drive)
Buick Estate '70 thru '90, Electra'70 thru '84, LeSabre '70 thru '85, Limited '74 thru '79
Oldsmobile Custom Cruiser '70 thru '90, Delta 88 '70 thru '85,Ninety-eight '70 thru '84
Pontiac Bonneville '70 thru '81, Catalina '70 thru '81, Grandville '70 thru '75, Parisienne '83 thru '86
627 Mid-size Regal & Century all rear-drive models with V6, V8 and Turbo '74 thru '87
Regal - see GENERAL MOTORS (1671)
Skyhawk - see GENERAL MOTORS (766)
Skylark '80 thru '85 - see GENERAL MOTORS (38020)
Skylark '86 on - see GENERAL MOTORS (1420)
Somerset - see GENERAL MOTORS (1420)

CADILLAC
*751 Cadillac Rear Wheel Drive all gasoline models '70 thru '93
Cimarron - see GENERAL MOTORS (766)

CHEVROLET
*1477 Astro & GMC Safari Mini-vans '85 thru '93
554 Camaro V8 all models '70 thru '81
866 Camaro all models '82 thru '92
Cavalier - see GENERAL MOTORS (766)
Celebrity - see GENERAL MOTORS (829)
625 Chevelle, Malibu & El Camino all V6 & V8 models '69 thru '87
449 Chevette & Pontiac T1000 '76 thru '87
550 Citation all models '80 thru '85
*1628 Corsica/Beretta all models '87 thru '95
274 Corvette all V8 models '68 thru '82
*1336 Corvette all models '84 thru '91
1762 Chevrolet Engine Overhaul Manual
704 Full-size Sedans Caprice, Impala, Biscayne, Bel Air & Wagons '69 thru '90

Lumina - see GENERAL MOTORS (1671)
Lumina APV - see GENERAL MOTORS (2035)
319 Luv Pick-up all 2WD & 4WD '72 thru '82
626 Monte Carlo all models '70 thru '88
241 Nova all V8 models '69 thru '79
*1642 Nova and Geo Prizm all front wheel drive models, '85 thru '92
420 Pick-ups '67 thru '87 - Chevrolet & GMC, all V8 & in-line 6 cyl, 2WD & 4WD '67 thru '87; Suburbans, Blazers & Jimmys '67 thru '91
*1664 Pick-ups '88 thru '95 - Chevrolet & GMC, all full-size pick-ups, '88 thru '95; Blazer & Jimmy '92 thru '94; Suburban '92 thru '95; Tahoe & Yukon '95
*831 S-10 & GMC S-15 Pick-ups all models '82 thru '93
*1727 Sprint & Geo Metro '85 thru '94
*345 Vans - Chevrolet & GMC, V8 & in-line 6 cylinder models '68 thru '95

CHRYSLER
2114 Chrysler Engine Overhaul Manual
*2058 Full-size Front-Wheel Drive '88 thru '93
K-Cars - see DODGE Aries (723)
Laser - see DODGE Daytona (1140)
*1337 Chrysler & Plymouth Mid-size front wheel drive '82 thru '93
Rear-wheel Drive - see Dodge Rear-wheel Drive (2098)

DATSUN
402 200SX all models '77 thru '79
647 200SX all models '80 thru '83
228 B - 210 all models '73 thru '78
525 210 all models '78 thru '82
206 240Z, 260Z & 280Z Coupe '70 thru '78
563 280ZX Coupe & 2+2 '79 thru '83
300ZX - see NISSAN (1137)
679 310 all models '78 thru '82
123 510 & PL521 Pick-up '68 thru '73
430 510 all models '78 thru '81
372 610 all models '72 thru '76
277 620 Series Pick-up all models '73 thru '79
720 Series Pick-up - see NISSAN (771)
376 810/Maxima all gasoline models, '77 thru '84
Pulsar - see NISSAN (876)
Sentra - see NISSAN (982)
Stanza - see NISSAN (981)

DODGE
400 & 600 - see CHRYSLER Mid-size (1337)
*723 Aries & Plymouth Reliant '81 thru '89
1231 Caravan & Plymouth Voyager Mini-Vans all models '84 thru '95
699 Challenger & Plymouth Saporro all models '78 thru '83
Challenger '67-'76 - see DODGE Dart (234)
236 Colt all models '71 thru '77
610 Colt & Plymouth Champ (front wheel drive) all models '78 thru '87
*1668 Dakota Pick-ups all models '87 thru '93
234 Dart, Challenger/Plymouth Barracuda & Valiant 6 cyl models '67 thru '76
*1140 Daytona & Chrysler Laser '84 thru '89
*545 Omni & Plymouth Horizon '78 thru '90
*912 Pick-ups all full-size models '74 thru '91
*556 Ram 50/D50 Pick-ups & Raider and Plymouth Arrow Pick-ups '79 thru '93
2098 Dodge/Plymouth/Chrysler rear wheel drive '71 thru '89
*1726 Shadow & Plymouth Sundance '87 thru '93
*1779 Spirit & Plymouth Acclaim '89 thru '95
*349 Vans - Dodge & Plymouth V8 & 6 cyl models '71 thru '91

EAGLE
Talon - see Mitsubishi Eclipse (2097)

FIAT
094 124 Sport Coupe & Spider '68 thru '78
273 X1/9 all models '74 thru '80

FORD
*1476 Aerostar Mini-vans all models '86 thru '94
788 Bronco and Pick-ups '73 thru '79
*880 Bronco and Pick-ups '80 thru '95
268 Courier Pick-up all models '72 thru '82
2105 Crown Victoria & Mercury Grand Marquis '88 thru '94
1763 Ford Engine Overhaul Manual
789 Escort/Mercury Lynx all models '81 thru '90
*2046 Escort/Mercury Tracer '91 thru '95
*2021 Explorer & Mazda Navajo '91 thru '95
560 Fairmont & Mercury Zephyr '78 thru '83
334 Fiesta all models '77 thru '80
754 Ford & Mercury Full-size,
Ford LTD & Mercury Marquis ('75 thru '82); Ford Custom 500,Country Squire, Crown Victoria & Mercury Colony Park ('75 thru '87); Ford LTD Crown Victoria & Mercury Gran Marquis ('83 thru '87)
359 Granada & Mercury Monarch all in-line, 6 cyl & V8 models '75 thru '80
773 Ford & Mercury Mid-size,
Ford Thunderbird & Mercury Cougar ('75 thru '82);
Ford LTD & Mercury Marquis ('83 thru '86); Ford Torino,Gran Torino, Elite, Ranchero pick-up, LTD II, Mercury Montego, Comet, XR-7 & Lincoln Versailles ('75 thru '86)
*654 Mustang & Mercury Capri all models including Turbo. Mustang, '79 thru '93; Capri, '79 thru '86
357 Mustang V8 all models '64-1/2 thru '73
231 Mustang II 4 cyl, V6 & V8 models '74 thru '78
649 Pinto & Mercury Bobcat '75 thru '80
1670 Probe all models '89 thru '92
*1026 Ranger/Bronco II gasoline models '83 thru '93
*1421 Taurus & Mercury Sable '86 thru '94
*1418 Tempo & Mercury Topaz all gasoline models '84 thru '94
1338 Thunderbird/Mercury Cougar '83 thru '88
*1725 Thunderbird/Mercury Cougar '89 and '93
344 Vans all V8 Econoline models '69 thru '91
*2119 Vans full size '92-'95

GENERAL MOTORS
*829 Buick Century, Chevrolet Celebrity, Oldsmobile Cutlass Ciera & Pontiac 6000 all models '82 thru '93
*1671 Buick Regal, Chevrolet Lumina, Oldsmobile Cutlass Supreme & Pontiac Grand Prix all front wheel drive models '88 thru '95
*766 Buick Skyhawk, Cadillac Cimarron, Chevrolet Cavalier, Oldsmobile Firenza & Pontiac J-2000 & Sunbird all models '82 thru '94
38020 Buick Skylark, Chevrolet Citation, Olds Omega, Pontiac Phoenix '80 thru '85
1420 Buick Skylark & Somerset, Oldsmobile Achieva & Calais and Pontiac Grand Am all models '85 thru '95
*2035 Chevrolet Lumina APV, Oldsmobile Silhouette & Pontiac Trans Sport all models '90 thru '94
General Motors Full-size Rear-wheel Drive - see BUICK (1551)

GEO
Metro - see CHEVROLET Sprint (1727)
Prizm - see CHEVROLET Nova (1642)
*2039 Storm all models '90 thru '93
Tracker - see SUZUKI Samurai (1626)

GMC
Safari - see CHEVROLET ASTRO (1477)
Vans & Pick-ups - see CHEVROLET (420, 831, 345, 1664)

(Continued on other side)

---

* Listings shown with an asterisk (*) indicate model coverage as of this printing. These titles will be periodically updated to include later model years - consult your Haynes dealer for more information.

Haynes North America, Inc., 861 Lawrence Drive, Newbury Park, CA 91320 • (805) 498-6703

Haynes Automotive Manuals (continued)

NOTE: New manuals are added to this list on a periodic basis. If you do not see a listing for your vehicle, consult your local Haynes dealer for the latest product information.

HONDA

351	**Accord CVCC** all models '76 thru '83
1221	**Accord** all models '84 thru '89
2067	**Accord** all models '90 thru '93
42013	**Accord** all models '94 thru '95
160	**Civic 1200** all models '73 thru '79
633	**Civic 1300 & 1500 CVCC** '80 thru '83
297	**Civic 1500 CVCC** all models '75 thru '79
1227	**Civic** all models '84 thru '91
*2118	**Civic & del Sol** '92 thru '95
*601	**Prelude CVCC** all models '79 thru '89

HYUNDAI

*1552	**Excel** all models '86 thru '94

ISUZU

*1641	**Trooper & Pick-up,** all gasoline models Pick-up, '81 thru '93; Trooper, '84 thru '91

JAGUAR

*242	**XJ6** all 6 cyl models '68 thru '86
*478	**XJ12 & XJS** all 12 cyl models '72 thru '85

JEEP

*1553	**Cherokee, Comanche & Wagoneer Limited** all models '84 thru '93
412	**CJ** all models '49 thru '86
50025	**Grand Cherokee** all models '93 thru '95
*1777	**Wrangler** all models '87 thru '94

LINCOLN

2117	**Rear Wheel Drive** all models '70 thru '95

MAZDA

648	**626** Sedan & Coupe (rear wheel drive) all models '79 thru '82
*1082	**626 & MX-6** (front wheel drive) all models '83 thru '91
267	**B Series Pick-ups** '72 thru '93
370	**GLC Hatchback** (rear wheel drive) all models '77 thru '83
757	**GLC** (front wheel drive) '81 thru '85
*2047	**MPV** all models '89 thru '94
	Navajo-see Ford Explorer (2021)
460	**RX-7** all models '79 thru '85
*1419	**RX-7** all models '86 thru '91

MERCEDES-BENZ

*1643	**190 Series** all four-cylinder gasoline models, '84 thru '88
346	**230, 250 & 280** Sedan, Coupe & Roadster all 6 cyl sohc models '68 thru '72
983	**280 123 Series** gasoline models '77 thru '81
698	**350 & 450** Sedan, Coupe & Roadster all models '71 thru '80
697	**Diesel 123 Series** 200D, 220D, 240D, 240TD, 300D, 300CD, 300TD, 4- & 5-cyl incl. Turbo '76 thru '85

MERCURY

See FORD Listing

MG

111	**MGB** Roadster & GT Coupe all models '62 thru '80
265	**MG Midget & Austin Healey Sprite** Roadster '58 thru '80

MITSUBISHI

*1669	**Cordia, Tredia, Galant, Precis & Mirage** '83 thru '93
*2097	**Eclipse, Eagle Talon & Plymouth Laser** '90 thru '94
*2022	**Pick-up & Montero** '83 thru '95

NISSAN

1137	**300ZX** all models including Turbo '84 thru '89
*1341	**Maxima** all models '85 thru '91
*771	**Pick-ups/Pathfinder** gas models '80 thru '95
876	**Pulsar** all models '83 thru '86

*982	**Sentra** all models '82 thru '94
*981	**Stanza** all models '82 thru '90

OLDSMOBILE

	Bravada - see CHEVROLET S-10 (831)
	Calais - see GENERAL MOTORS (1420)
	Custom Cruiser - see BUICK Full-size RWD (1551)
*658	**Cutlass** all standard gasoline V6 & V8 models '74 thru '88
	Cutlass Ciera - see GENERAL MOTORS (829)
	Cutlass Supreme - see GM (1671)
	Delta 88 - see BUICK Full-size RWD (1551)
	Delta 88 Brougham - see BUICK Full-size FWD (1551), RWD (1627)
	Delta 88 Royale - see BUICK Full-size RWD (1551)
	Firenza - see GENERAL MOTORS (766)
	Ninety-eight Regency - see BUICK Full-size RWD (1551), FWD (1627)
	Ninety-eight Regency Brougham - see BUICK Full-size RWD (1551)
	Omega - see GENERAL MOTORS (38020)
	Silhouette - see GENERAL MOTORS (2035)

PEUGEOT

663	**504** all diesel models '74 thru '83

PLYMOUTH

Laser - see MITSUBISHI Eclipse (2097)
For other PLYMOUTH titles, see DODGE listing.

PONTIAC

	T1000 - see CHEVROLET Chevette (449)
	J-2000 - see GENERAL MOTORS (766)
	6000 - see GENERAL MOTORS (829)
	Bonneville - see Buick Full-size FWD (1627), RWD (1551)
	Bonneville Brougham - see Buick (1551)
	Catalina - see Buick Full-size (1551)
1232	**Fiero** all models '84 thru '88
555	**Firebird** V8 models except Turbo '70 thru '81
867	**Firebird** all models '82 thru '92
	Full-size Front Wheel Drive - see BUICK Oldsmobile, Pontiac Full-size FWD (1627)
	Full-size Rear Wheel Drive - see BUICK Oldsmobile, Pontiac Full-size RWD (1551)
	Grand Am - see GENERAL MOTORS (1420)
	Grand Prix - see GENERAL MOTORS (1671)
	Grandville - see BUICK Full-size (1551)
	Parisienne - see BUICK Full-size (1551)
	Phoenix - see GENERAL MOTORS (38020)
	Sunbird - see GENERAL MOTORS (766)
	Trans Sport - see GENERAL MOTORS (2035)

PORSCHE

*264	**911** all Coupe & Targa models except Turbo & Carrera 4 '65 thru '89
239	**914** all 4 cyl models '69 thru '76
397	**924** all models including Turbo '76 thru '82
*1027	**944** all models including Turbo '83 thru '89

RENAULT

141	**5 Le Car** all models '76 thru '83
	Alliance & Encore - see AMC (934)

SAAB

247	**99** all models including Turbo '69 thru '80
*980	**900** all models including Turbo '79 thru '88

SATURN

2083	**Saturn** all models '91 thru '94

SUBARU

237	**1100, 1300, 1400 & 1600** '71 thru '79
*681	**1600 & 1800** 2WD & 4WD '80 thru '89

SUZUKI

*1626	**Samurai/Sidekick and Geo Tracker** all models '86 thru '95

TOYOTA

1023	**Camry** all models '83 thru '91
92006	**Camry** all models '92 thru '95
935	**Celica Rear Wheel Drive** '71 thru '85
*2038	**Celica Front Wheel Drive** '86 thru '92
1139	**Celica Supra** all models '79 thru '92
361	**Corolla** all models '75 thru '79
961	**Corolla** all rear wheel drive models '80 thru '87
*1025	**Corolla** all front wheel drive models '84 thru '92
636	**Corolla Tercel** all models '80 thru '82
360	**Corona** all models '74 thru '82
532	**Cressida** all models '78 thru '82
313	**Land Cruiser** all models '68 thru '82
*1339	**MR2** all models '85 thru '87
304	**Pick-up** all models '69 thru '78
*656	**Pick-up** all models '79 thru '95
*2048	**Previa** all models '91 thru '93
2106	**Tercel** all models '87 thru '94

TRIUMPH

113	**Spitfire** all models '62 thru '81
322	**TR7** all models '75 thru '81

VW

159	**Beetle & Karmann Ghia** all models '54 thru '79
238	**Dasher** all gasoline models '74 thru '81
*884	**Rabbit, Jetta, Scirocco, & Pick-up** gas models '74 thru '91 & Convertible '80 thru '92
451	**Rabbit, Jetta & Pick-up** all diesel models '77 thru '84
082	**Transporter 1600** all models '68 thru '79
226	**Transporter 1700, 1800 & 2000** all models '72 thru '79
084	**Type 3 1500 & 1600** all models '63 thru '73
1029	**Vanagon** all air-cooled models '80 thru '83

VOLVO

203	**120, 130 Series & 1800 Sports** '61 thru '73
129	**140 Series** all models '66 thru '74
*270	**240 Series** all models '76 thru '93
400	**260 Series** all models '75 thru '82
*1550	**740 & 760 Series** all models '82 thru '88

TECHBOOK MANUALS

2108	**Automotive Computer Codes**
1667	**Automotive Emissions Control Manual**
482	**Fuel Injection Manual, 1978 thru 1985**
2111	**Fuel Injection Manual, 1986 thru 1994**
2069	**Holley Carburetor Manual**
2068	**Rochester Carburetor Manual**
10240	**Weber/Zenith/Stromberg/SU Carburetors**
1762	**Chevrolet Engine Overhaul Manual**
2114	**Chrysler Engine Overhaul Manual**
1763	**Ford Engine Overhaul Manual**
1736	**GM and Ford Diesel Engine Repair Manual**
1666	**Small Engine Repair Manual**
10355	**Ford Automatic Transmission Overhaul**
10360	**GM Automatic Transmission Overhaul**
1479	**Automotive Body Repair & Painting**
2112	**Automotive Brake Manual**
2113	**Automotive Detailing Manual**
1654	**Automotive Eelectrical Manual**
1480	**Automotive Heating & Air Conditioning**
2109	**Automotive Reference Manual & Illustrated Dictionary**
2107	**Automotive Tools Manual**
10440	**Used Car Buying Guide**
2110	**Welding Manual**

SPANISH MANUALS

98905	**Códigos Automotrices de la Computadora**
98915	**Inyección de Combustible 1986 al 1994**
99040	**Chevrolet & GMC Camionetas** '67 al '87 Incluye Suburban, Blazer & Jimmy '67 al '91
99041	**Chevrolet & GMC Camionetas** '88 al '95 Incluye Suburban '92 al '95, Blazer & Jimmy '92 al '94, Tahoe & Yukon '95
99075	**Ford Camionetas y Bronco** '80 al '94
99125	**Toyota Camionetas y 4-Runner** '79 al '95

---

* Listings shown with an asterisk (*) indicate model coverage as of this printing. These titles will be periodically updated to include later model years - consult your Haynes dealer for more information.

Over 100 Haynes motorcycle manuals also available

2-96

Haynes North America, Inc., 861 Lawrence Drive, Newbury Park, CA 91320 • (805) 498-6703